The Rest Is Silence

The Rest Is Silence

Death as Annihilation
in the English Renaissance

ROBERT N. WATSON

UNIVERSITY OF CALIFORNIA PRESS

BERKELEY / LOS ANGELES / LONDON

University of California Press
Berkeley and Los Angeles, California

University of California Press, Ltd.
London, England

1994 by
The Regents of the University of California

Watson, Robert N.
  The Rest is Silence: death as annihilation in the English Renaissance / Robert N.
Watson.
    p. cm.
  Includes bibliographical references and index.
  ISBN 0-520-08494-2 (alk. paper)
  1. English literature—Early modern, 1500–1700—History and criticism. 2. Death
in literature. 3. Annihilationism in literature. 4. Shakespeare, William, 1564–1616—
Criticism and interpretation. 5. Donne, John, 1572–1631—Criticism and interpreta-
tion. 6. Kyd, Thomas, 1558–1594. Spanish Tragedy. 7. Herbert, George, 1593–
1633. Temple. 8. Renaissance—England. I. Title.
PR428.D4W38 1994
820.9'354—dc20   93-45004
                                                                                  CIP

Printed in the United States of America
9 8 7 6 5 4 3 2 1

The paper used in this publication meets the minimum requirements of American
National Standard for Information Sciences—Permanence of Paper for Printed Library
Materials, ANSI Z39.48-1984.

To
Dana Cairns Watson

... in what eternal, unstirring paralysis, and deadly, hopeless trance, yet lies antique Adam who died sixty round centuries ago; how it is that we still refuse to be comforted for those who we nevertheless maintain are dwelling in unspeakable bliss; why all the living so strive to hush all the dead; wherefore but the rumor of a knocking in a tomb will terrify a whole city. All these things are not without their meanings.

But Faith, like a jackal, feeds among the tombs, and even from these dead doubts she gathers her most vital hope.

—Herman Melville,
"The Chapel," *Moby-Dick*

Contents

Acknowledgments

This project has been generously supported by annual U.C.L.A. Faculty Senate Research Grants and a University of California President's Research Fellowship in the Humanities. The British Library, the Huntington Library, the Folger Library, the Clark Library, and the Warburg Institute all granted me full access to their collections, which proved indispensable. An earlier version of my chapter on *Hamlet* appeared in *Renaissance Drama*, new series, 21 (1990); an earlier version of my chapter on *Measure for Measure* appeared in *Shakespeare Quarterly* 41 (1990); both journals have kindly granted me permission to reprint those articles, and I owe particular thanks to their editors, Mary Beth Rose and Barbara Mowat.

Many other colleagues have offered extremely helpful advice on the manuscript: A. R. Braunmuller, Reg Foakes, Chris Grose, Carol Ann Johnston, Walter Kaiser, Gillian M. Kendall, Ron Levao, Jayne Lewis, Claire McEachern, Jonathan Post, David Riggs, Michael Schoenfeldt, Debora Shuger, Margaret Sullivan, and Barbara Bellow Watson. The project has benefitted greatly from excellent research assistance provided by Sybil Brabner, Lisa Hernandez, Sarah McNamer, Ilana Nash, Erin Quinn, Owen Staley, and Linda Weitzman. My greatest debt is to my wife, Dana, who radiates so much joy that she deserves the dedication of a more cheerful book as well as a better one.

A Note on Texts

I have silently modernized the "u," "v," and "s" forms into modern orthography, but have not otherwise altered spellings, nor have I added or removed italics. Quotations and citations noted parenthetically in the text are based on the following works and editions:

Becker, Ernest. *The Denial of Death*. New York: Free Press, 1973.

Browne, Sir Thomas. *The Major Works*. Edited by C. A. Patrides. Harmondsworth: Penguin, 1977.

Donne, John. *The Complete Poetry of John Donne*. Edited by John T. Shawcross. New York: Anchor Books, 1967. I have slightly altered Shawcross's titles for some poems for the sake of clarity and consistency.

——— *Devotions upon Emergent Occasions*. Edited by Anthony Raspa. New York: Oxford University Press, 1987.

——— *Letters to Severall Persons of Honour*. Edited by Charles E. Merrill, Jr. New York: Sturgis and Walton, 1910.

———— *The Sermons of John Donne.* Edited by Evelyn M. Simpson and George R. Potter. 10 vols. Berkeley and Los Angeles: University of California Press, 1953–62.

Drummond, William. *A Cypress Grove.* 1623. Reprint. Edinburgh: Hawthornden Press, 1919.

Herbert, George. *The English Poems of George Herbert.* Edited by C.A. Patrides. London: J.M. Dent, 1974.

Kyd, Thomas. *The Spanish Tragedy.* Edited by Philip Edwards. *The Revels Plays.* London: Methuen, 1959.

Shakespeare, William. *Hamlet.* Edited by Harold Jenkins. *The Arden Shakespeare.* London: Methuen, 1982.

———— *Macbeth.* Edited by A.R. Braunmuller. *The New Cambridge Shakespeare.* Cambridge: Cambridge University Press, 1994.

———— *Measure for Measure.* Edited by J.W. Lever. *The Arden Shakespeare.* London: Methuen, 1965.

———— All other works. *The Riverside Shakespeare.* Edited by G.B. Evans et al. Boston: Houghton Mifflin, 1974.

Introduction

      This book will argue that the fear of death as annihilation produced a crisis in English Renaissance culture, a crisis discernible in both Shakespearean drama, which criticizes and parodies traditional promises of immortality, and Metaphysical poetry, which experiments with new versions of those promises. By placing the brutalities and banalities of death within heroic stories and artistic forms, literature helps to disguise the conflict between the psychological necessity known as narcissism and the physical necessity known as mortality. English Renaissance literature fiercely questions the validity of this function, even while dutifully performing it.

      To the familiar idea that art gives order to a chaotic universe, I would add that art allows a society to consider which order that should be. Because they make no affirmative claim to mirroring reality, the imaginative arts allow a human group to re-examine its definitions of morality and even of reality, without acknowledging the nature of the task. Otherwise the group would be obliged to acknowledge its morality and reality as arbitrary choices—which would destroy precisely the illusion it strives (at some collective preconscious level) to preserve. Like the evolution of species, the process of change in cultures therefore proceeds by punctuated equilibrium; by periods of rapid change—marked by revolutions in artistic method—and long intervals that are relatively static.[1] The changes are not essentially progressive, any more than evolution is. They are mutations and adaptations in changing environments, and they cannot be objectively moralized.

One may therefore posit a causal model for the creation of art without accepting an often mechanistic Marxist model that treats art as a sub-function of economic organization. Whatever its contributions to the concealment or exposure of class conflict, art also creates and reflects the cognitive organization by which we assimilate the infinitely various phenomenal universe. The production of cognitive order requires a perpetual negotiation between the idiosyncracies of individual experience and the need to communicate and cooperate with other members of society. Government censorship, which has proven such a fruitful topic in recent studies of Renaissance literature, is only the most explicit manifestation of that comprehensive negotiation. The need to regulate thought exists independent of any specific thought that a government might wish to regulate, and psychology should not be subordinated to politics in the study of cultures.

Death provokes this need for thought-control in an extreme form, because it opens a window out of the self and into the infinite. The regulation of thoughts about death, particularly as imprinted on English literature during the half century centered around the reign of King James I, is my primary topic. As Ernest Becker has shown so brilliantly in *The Denial of Death*[2]—a fundamental inspiration for this book—human beings need culture to numb these thoughts, presumably because mortality has become a fixture of our consciousness, rather than an intermittent and unarticulated incentive to obey our survival instincts. Modern Western cultures, like most others, have found it necessary to decorate, contextualize, and mythologize death, presumably to prevent a devastating loss of orientation and morale. Death is a kind of Medusa we can watch only as a reflection in our defensive shields, only in the secondary distortions it produces in the cultural field around it. Like many other crises, the mortality-crisis of Jacobean England was evidently produced by the familiar laws of supply and demand: assurance about personal salvation was declining while attachment to both the external properties and the internal subjectivities of the human individual were increasing. The resulting demands on the promise of afterlife became so great that the Christian denial of death threatened to become visible as a mere ideology, a manipulative illusion rather than an absolute truth.

Could some aspects of traditional Christian belief be shored up by propping them against the recoveries of classical philosophy and the discoveries of new science that had helped undermine such beliefs? The appealing commonplace that poets are always a century ahead of philosophers would predict that the flirtations with atheism pervading Enlightenment culture explicate notions already present in Jacobean literature. But to imagine Jacobean annihilationism as a sort of preparatory deism is to read cultural history in the wrong direction. More likely, deism arose from an effort to provide a soft landing for the human individual plunging into the abyss of a universe that now seemed indifferent; to dispel the resentments underlying satiric Renaissance attacks on traditional beliefs by conjuring a new, diffuse, and rationalistic version of providence; and to make the resulting evacuation of individuality, both human and divine, seem a thing of beauty and a joy forever.

THESIS

> When death shall part us from these kids,
> And shut up our divided lids,
> Tell me, Thyrsis, prithee do,
> Whither thou and I must go.[3]

In early seventeenth-century England, that was indeed the question, and not only in the minds of rustic materialists like Marvell's Dorinda. Despite its ferocious displays of Christian conviction, Jacobean culture struggled with the suspicion that death was a complete and permanent annihilation of the self, not merely some latency of the body awaiting Last Judgment. The balanced forms and predictable images of most sixteenth-century funeral writing in England reflect a complacency that gives way to more complex cultural pressures—and therefore richer art—in the senescence of the Tudor period. By a kind of Freudian slip, Jacobean literature often reverts from its surface narrative to repressed anxieties about death as eternal annihilation, especially during moments of silence, eclipses of light, collapses of identity, unspoolings of time, and approaches of closure. These dark constellations generate a sinister gravity which constantly threatens to topple the confident Christian stance.

My claim is not that the Jacobeans were all covert atheists, a vast School of Night conspiring to conceal its real beliefs in code. The religious passions of the period were authentically engaged in doctrinal disputes within Christianity. But shrewd observers (such as Donne, Bacon, and Hooker) could already see that the multiplying cross-accusations of heresy within Christianity inevitably bred skepticism toward the belief as a whole, that (as Heywood put it) "many from Schisme grow into Atheisme."[4] The multivocal aspects of literary art could easily have amplified all these conflicts and dubieties, even while striving to endorse Christian orthodoxy.

Though it is certainly risky to project Existentialist anxieties back onto a Renaissance culture that had a very different way of understanding its universe, only a facile and even patronizing reading of human psychology, as well as an incomplete reading of the historical record, can insist that Renaissance minds were incapable of registering the fear of personal annihilation. Neither human individuality nor human responses to common and fundamental events are likely to change as abruptly as Michel Foucault has encouraged contemporary cultural analysts to imagine.[5] I am more sympathetic to Freud's assertion that "the attitude of our unconscious towards the problem of death [remains] almost exactly the same as that of primaeval man," and that mythological evasions of the notion of annihilation were probably conjoined with the very first human recognition of death.[6] As the human womb has retained the same fluid salinity as the ocean from which the species evolved, so the human confrontation with mortality retains its primitive profile.

Clearly, not even these primal events are wholly immune to the refractions of local culture. Both birth and death were evidently placed later in the biological cycle during the Renaissance than they are now. The abortion debate leads us to speculate how long before birth human life actually begins, whereas many people in the Renaissance believed that full human existence did not begin before baptism.[7] The debate about medical technology and euthanasia leads us to speculate how long before complete lifelessness death actually occurs, whereas people in the Renaissance were not exactly dead until burial, since corpses were sometimes arrested for worldly debts on the way to the churchyard. Indeed, for those who believed in soul-sleeping, the book was not closed on a life until Last Judgment, so corpses could be disinterred for posthumous honors or (as in the case of Cromwell) punishments.[8]

But the primary changes in English Renaissance culture would only have accentuated the primal fear of annihilation. The extraordinarily punitive attitudes toward suicide in sixteenth and early seventeenth century England suggest a terrible anxiety about the surrender of the self.[9] Social historians such as Phillipe Ariès have plausibly associated heightened anxiety about death in Renaissance Europe with the heightened sense of personal identity generated by new social configurations (which emphasized domestic privacy) and reflected in the emergence of autobiography as a literary genre as well as in the increasing use of names and personal histories on tombstones.[10] Interpretations of High Renaissance art and philosophy have (following Jacob Burckhardt) traditionally emphasized the liberation of individual consciousness.

The Protestant Reformation played a major role in this change, shifting the locus of redemption from group ritual to personal conscience. That shift, moreover, is only a small part of the role the Reformation played in heightening the psychological burdens of mortality. Both the inscrutable determinism and the systematic iconoclasm of Calvinist theology created a blank wall between the living and the dead, encouraging the ominous inference that all might be blankness or darkness beyond it. Since (*pace* Max Weber and R. H. Tawney) worldly conduct was no longer a reliable guide to otherworldly destiny, the illusion of continuity was lost; the resulting uncertainties were aggravated by the erasure of other aids for visualizing the hereafter. By eliminating the doctrine of purgatory, Reformation theology precluded efficacious prayers for parted souls, putting the fate of the dead beyond the control of the living.[11] Even ordinary funeral rituals came under attack by Calvinists and, more rigorously, by Anabaptists.[12] And the fate of the living was beyond the control of the dead, since saints were deprived of any intercessory power.

To a significant degree, the Reformation arose directly from a recognition that the fear of death was being manipulated by churchmen for material advantage—specifically, through the selling of indulgences. Other less obvious consolatory devices disappeared alongside that one. For example, by forbidding belief in the miraculously preserved reliquary remains of saints, Protestantism forbade the hope that piety might somehow exempt the body from physical decay. In this sense, the Reformers had a difficult package to sell; what made sense theologically made trouble psychologically. The vacillations of Luther and Calvin on the question of soul-sleeping may reflect a delicate negotiation in which the Reformers sought to posit a form of oblivion prior to the Last Judgment without rousing the annihilationist model latent in anxious Renaissance minds. The vivid blankness of a common Jacobean notion that "the bodie lyeth in the grave senseles, and without motion even as a blocke or stone"[13] would have roused a considerable need for reassurance about the experience of the soul.

A challenge to traditional ideas of afterlife would have followed logically from other Reformation challenges to the manipulative institutions that had accreted around the original Word of God. The fresh and close reading of the Bible recommended by Protestantism threatened (as Isaac Casaubon discovered) to destabilize and disunify that principal cultural text, and specifically to undermine its supposed promises concerning personal afterlife. Though modern histories have mostly effaced it, the most explicitly annihilationist theology in this period arises from the radical wing of the Reformation: Familists, Ranters, and Quakers.[14] In 1545, England received a group of theological refugees who "would teach out of scripture, that there is neither place of rest ne pain after death; that hell is nothing else but a tormenting and desperate conscience."[15] Even mainstream Protestant theology, by its particular emphasis on individual interiority, on the sinfulness of that interiority, and on the lack of any purgatorial process that could winnow out that sinfulness, must have made it virtually impossible to imagine satisfactorily the survival of a full selfhood in heaven. Indeed, as Giles Firmin noted bitterly in 1670, anyone who "useth diligently all means whereby he may be saved" is admonished by Calvinists that "this is but a way of self-love, and a way to Hell; *self* must be hated."[16] No wonder poets such as Donne and Herbert—and radical Protestant mystics such as Boehme—find themselves uneasily begging God for the erasure and the salvation of the self simultaneously.[17] Calvin's *Institutes* depict a God who sometimes allows people destined to damnation to feel an inward conviction of salvation; so it became futile to project even the positive aspects of the self into the next world. The annihilationist fear—losing the interior affective self into an infinity that does not care for it—was a Calvinist fact.

Under Catholicism, the choice of lifelong virginity projected an absolute confidence in the afterlife, a certainty that the Christian devotee would be abundantly compensated for abjuring worldly pleasures and failing in the category of genetic survival. In this sense, vows of celibacy were the counterpart of duelling (as *Measure for Measure*, I will argue, is the counterpart of *Hamlet*). The declaration that honor is an all-important good serves to refute the supposition that death is an all-consuming evil, and "Whole plays were built around the belief that virginity accompanied by death is preferable to the loss of it accompanied by life."[18] The Protestant effort to valorize fruitful marriage (an effort that arguably culminates in *Paradise Lost*) certainly makes sense as an effort to justify the Reformation rejection of monasticism, but a supplementary motive may have been the desire to reconstruct the Catholic promise of immortality in a doctrinally acceptable form. Procreation became, in part, a displacement of sacramentalism and transubstantiation: a tangible and communal form of immortality tied to the cycle of human life, a consuming of the body in the hope of rendering life eternal.

Yet the moment of conception only reinscribed both parent and child in the entropic economy of Original Sin; and while procreation might have offered Protestants at least a biological simulacrum of immortality, it could offer little promise of preserving their precious interiority. Sir Thomas Browne remarked that the "conceit and counterfeit subsisting in our progenies seemes to mee a meere fallacy,"[19] and many Renaissance thinkers seized on the models offered by the survival of classical culture, and advocated living for art (with its peculiar ability to preserve precisely what procreation does not), or for honor (through the Christian stoicism that makes interiority a stay against the mutability of a fallen world). If one's entire being can be channeled into an idea, then that being can outlast the mortal body. But as Browne suggests in *Hydriotaphia* (pp. 308–9), unearthing the classical past was not an entirely reassuring experience for those hoping to project their identities into an infinite future: "to subsist in bones, and be but Pyramidally extant, is a fallacy in duration. Vain ashes, which in the oblivion of names, persons, times, and sexes, have found unto themselves, a fruitlesse continuation, and only arise unto late posterity, as Emblemes of mortall vanities." The more of the past that was found, the more that was known to be lost, and the scope of human enterprises was belittled by deep time as well as by Christian eschatology.

Nearly all the famous transforming achievements of the Renaissance had side-effects that must have magnified the terrors of mortality. In revealing the size and variety of the world, imperialistic and mercantile exploration aggravated the threat already presented by the rediscovery of classical cultures: the threat to reveal the arbitrariness of local consolatory formulas, leaving commentators such as Browne to save the appearances by positing "a Geography of Religions as well as Lands."[20] The navigational technology developed for those explorations led to an astronomy that revealed the scope, the heliocentric shape, and the unlimited mutability of the universe. As a result, the soul was becoming disastrously devalued against its material context.[21] All these discoveries—which Western culture is still struggling to assimilate—put extraordinary pressure on traditional consolations and denials. All these developments heightened the fear that human beings might actually be meaningless little entities lost in the dizzyingly vast, varied, and powerful universe.

In his efforts to prove that fideism renders him immune to the psychic dangers of scientific thinking, Browne boldly anatomizes and historicizes the denial of death: "To be ignorant of evils to come" allows us to "digest the mixture of our few and evil dayes," like the ancients who,

rather then be lost in the uncomfortable night of nothing, were content to recede into the common being, and make one particle of the publick soul of all things, which was no more then to return into their unknown and divine Originall again. Aegyptian ingenuity was more unsatisfied, contriving their bodies in sweet consistences, to attend the return of their souls. But all was vanity, feeding the winde, and folly. The Aegyptian Mummies, which *Cambyses* or time hath spared, avarice now consumeth. Mummie is become Merchandise, *Mizraim* cures wounds, and *Pharaoh* is sold for balsoms. In vain do individuals hope for Immortality, or any patent from oblivion, in preservations below the Moon: Men have been deceived even in their flatteries above the Sun, and studied conceits to perpetuate their names in heaven. The various Cosmography of that part hath already varied the names of contrived constellations; *Nimrod* is lost in *Orion*, and *Osyris* in the Dogge-starre. While we look for incorruption in the heavens, we finde they are but like the Earth; Durable in their main bodies, alterable in their parts: whereof besides Comets and new Stars, perspectives begin to tell tales. (pp. 311–12)

Condensed into this single continuous passage are skeptical "perspectives" on virtually every quest for immortality except the Christian one. Fame, generational succession, social role, preservation in body or in name—none of these can withstand the corrosive effects of scientific inquiry (or, in the case of the mummies, of capitalist commodification). Moreover, if "conceits to perpetuate their names in heaven" were delusions, and if the superlunary "heavens" prove, on closer inspection, no less corruptible than the earth, then the Christian sphere of salvation is hardly safe either, though Browne would not consciously attack it. To describe the constellations as "contrived" is very nearly to acknowledge that all the systems by which we reduce the phenomenal universe to a human scale and form are arbitrary (Juliet's plea that Romeo should be posthumously cut out "in little stars / And he will make the face of heaven so fine / That all the world will be in love with night" identifies constellation-making as a tactic against the inhumane infinitude of death). To say that such myths are constructed against the fear of becoming "lost in the uncomfortable night of nothing" is surely to raise the threat of annihilationism, and to suggest that all visions of immortality might be projections of psychological expediency.

The pressures of annihilationism intensified under the surface of Jacobean culture, testing (like volcanic magma) any weakness in the protective barrier. Predictably, they found expression primarily in the mythmaking functions of literature. Prominently in Marlowe's *Doctor Faustus*, and more subtly throughout later Renaissance tragedy, waves of ambition crested and crashed, as aspiring minds found they could not overcome the limits of their mortal bodies. On the Jacobean stage, a fundamental narcissistic resentment of mortality expressed itself through the introverted courtier's frustration that his individual worth was cruelly ignored by an all-powerful lord; whatever its other sociological bases, the black-clad malcontent was also a doomed Everyman. In the motivating ghosts of revenge-tragedy, the Nietzschean resentment we imagine in the dead storms back into the realm of the living, a community that must be punished for carrying on without them. Dramatic portrayals of rebellion against divine law may sometimes have been tendentious displacements, designed to underscore the inherent evils of rebellion against an earthly sovereign; yet they also contained displaced expressions of rebellion against natural law on behalf of human immortality.

The rise of Elizabethan and Jacobean tragedy coincides with the emergent scientific view of the universe—a view which necessarily contradicts our narcissism, both as individuals and as a species: "in both ancient Greece and Renaissance Europe, the major developments in tragedy coincide with the rise of science. . . . during this process of change, 'a sense of injustice appears, compounded of ignorance, fear, unfulfilled desire, and suffering, the mark of an "absence" which of necessity escapes organization'—that is, meaninglessness."[22] The primary story-line of tragedy is the one-way street that leads a human being from the triumphs of life to defeat in death. If there was a growing suspicion that this was also a dead-end street, the tensions invested in tragedy would have become increasingly complex and powerful. If the English Church no longer permitted Christ to play so explicit a physical-sacrificial role in the tragic ritual known as Mass, then some new form of tragic hero would have to become our advance scout into the unknown country of death.[23] If prayers for the dead were discouraged in churches, then revenge on behalf of a ghost would be performed in theaters; diplomacy with God would give way to war on a demonized fellow-human.

It has become a critical commonplace that, except in a few tragically diseased minds such as John Webster's, Christian afterlife was an unquestioned premise of English Renaissance culture, and atheism would have been "too arduous an intellectual effort to contemplate."[24]

The ingenious New Historicist reading of the history of mentalities—
the claim that, when Renaissance theologians complain about atheists,
they are inventing and demonizing an Otherness that did not yet exist—
thus echoes the conclusion of old-fashioned campaigns to identify
Shakespeare as a Christian propagandist. These campaigns have marked
educational uses of Shakespeare for a century, and the accompanying
scholarly tradition is evident from S. L. Bethell's Christianizing studies
in the 1940s to Roy Battenhouse's revealing complaint that efforts to
associate the ideas in the plays with secular Renaissance culture necessarily "imply a Shakespeare whose ultimate values were sub-Christian."[25]
Since then, critics heavily educated in Christian religion have naturally
looked for a Christian Shakespeare, and critics lacking that education
have deferred to them on religious questions. The resulting distortion
has been reinforced, from the other end of the political spectrum, by
overzealous efforts to deny authors any autonomy from the self-perpetuating projects of their cultural milieux.

Nostalgia for a posited age of piety is understandable, but the English
Renaissance was not such an age. The Introduction to an Elizabethan
translation of Calvin's treatise on the immortality of the soul asserts that

at that tyme that Maister Calvin wrote this booke, it should seeme by his
preface ensuing, that there were many grevously infected with this monstrous
opinion, that the Soules of men dyed together with the bodies. Which foule
and hellish error, I feare, hath possessed and poysoned at this day, the hartes
and mindes of a great number, here at home, within this lande. . . . Wherefore,
seeing this pamflet, was at that tyme necessary to be published, for the
confuting of all such Atheists, Epicures, and belly Gods, as then lyved, I think
it in my poore opinion, at this present most necessary and needefull. But here,
me thinketh I heare some men say, that it is impossible for any, in so great
light of the Gospell to be of this minde: whom I feare, I may with griefe of
hart justly answere: that there are too too many such.[26]

Admittedly Calvin was more concerned with mortalism than
annihilationism, but Stocker's remarks raise the stakes by invoking
atheists and Epicures, who respect no God and fear no reprisal for their
earthly indulgences. So the efforts of historicizing modern scholars to
describe English Renaissance culture as an epistemically closed system of
Christian belief overlook the way contemporary commentators such as
Stocker tried and failed to make the same claim. This "great light of the
Gospell" did not completely fail, but surely it flickered, whatever people
protested to the contrary: "The greatest wondre is, to se such nombre of

heresyes so nygh home, so manye infected with them within this Ile of England: Within Englande I saye, where everye man, every woman pretendeth to be a gospeller. . . . "[27]

Admittedly, too, spiritual uneasiness and fear of death are not the same as confirmed and radical atheism. As Calvin himself demanded, "If all fear is branded as unbelief, how shall we account for the dread with which we read, He was heavily stricken?"[28] Renaissance Christianity generally made some allowances for doubt and worldly sorrow. A fear of pain or damnation, however, is far more compatible with Christian faith than a fear of annihilation, which contradicts a fundamental incentive to Christian belief; and the level of annihilationist anxiety manifest in Jacobean culture is incompatible with the Christian hegemony commonly depicted. Browne opens *Religio Medici* by conceding that atheism is "the generall scandall of my profession" (p. 61). In 1608 a funeral sermon was published "as a remedie against the horrible prophaneness, Atheisme and contempt of GOD, which (as some great floud) doth at this time, overflow the bancks of this whole Land."[29] One pious first-hand commentator on the fear of death in Jacobean culture felt compelled to offer a chapter on "Why this disease was not so Epidemicall in ancient as in latter times;" another reports that "there are now more then ever there were, (thogh they professe not in words) who think in their hearts there is no God."[30] Ultimately, then, for all its universalizing impulses, my argument remains markedly historical. Jacobean literature was demonstrably working on problems peculiar to an egoistic culture, which tries to defend the individual against the erosions of form and fame by time and mortality, and to patch the resulting gaps in our self-esteem.[31] These plays and poems show deformations from the first impact of the disastrous collision between modern Western narcissism and modern Western skepticism.

DEATH, POLITICS, AND ART

A few years ago, one of my teaching assistants convinced her husband, an evolutionary biologist, to lend her the human skull from his lab collection so that she could confront her discussion section on *Hamlet* with the shock of the thing itself, unaccommodated death, a little touch of Yorick in the late afternoon. The class passed the skull around with all due reverence, until one amazed student managed to ask the teaching assistant where she could possibly have acquired it. She, not thinking of course about how it would sound, replied cheerfully, "Oh, it's my husband's."

At that moment the physical fact of the skull surely became less shocking than the social malfunction this reply seemed to represent. The teaching assistant seemed to be displaying what psychologists call "inappropriate affect" (a term implying the need for consensus on our styles of emotional behavior) to a degree that would mark her as a sociopath (a term implying the dangers of falling outside that consensus). She had overachieved her goal of pulling the skull, and the play, free from their safe cultural context.

This is surely too ponderous an analysis for an accidental occasion of laughter, but laughter (in a Freudian model) arises from the release of forbidden thoughts,[32] and the story therefore makes a fitting epigraph for an argument about the forbiddenness of unaccommodated death. Like those students, like Hamlet himself in the graveyard, my reader will be asked to make the disorienting leap from a blithe analytic distance to an almost unthinkable horror—and to recognize that horror may be a more rational response than detachment.

Contemporary Western societies generally contrive to hide the corpse behind institutional screens such as hospitals and funeral parlors, but out of sight is not quite out of mind. The systematic distortions practiced by our public media show how badly we still need the help of culture to control the terror of mortality and the prospect of oblivion. The people of Jacobean London, so lacking in privacy and reliable medical care, were under far more persistent pressure to reconcile the sight of corpses with the heroic and salvational narratives by which their society sustained its morale. Indeed, a traditional Christian's chief joy and discipline consisted of gazing at a slumped and bloody corpse on a cross, and believing it a god capable of achieving and bestowing immortality. Even if the Scriptures "were silent, yet experience doth speake out the matter so plainly, that the greatest dullard and rude person may understand. For to what ende serve so many Funeralls of all sorts, olde, young, rich, poore, noble, and base? so many drie bones cast out of the Graves? . . . but to set forth visiblie before our eyes, the mortall estate of mankinde."[33]

That is not merely a rhetorical question, and art is not merely decorative, any more than religion is merely a Sunday pastime: a culture exists because it has necessary work to do, and art is one of the workers, a specialist (according to the Platonic formula) in the construction of lies capable of reconfiguring our interiority. Those lies may be insidious or soothing or (according to the Cultural Materialist formula) insidious *because* soothing. Yet, as Sidney's *Apology for Poetry* argues, poets are not exactly liars: they keep a safe distance from affirmations of fact so that they can approach a higher reality and present it coherently, undamaged by local or temporary confusions. From a less idealistic perspective, poets have superior access to truth precisely because they are backstage at the creation of mass illusions. To the extent that human groups actively construct their reality, artists are more honest about their work than ostensibly more objective observers. To the extent that artists are aware that interpreting death is an urgent but arbitrary cultural task, they can devise more effective consolations—or provide a more corrosive analysis of that artificial consolatory process.

By emphasizing the competition for power, much recent New Historicist and Cultural Materialist criticism has underestimated the importance of these functions. Cultural analysis based in economics, with a superstructure of political science, inevitably overlooks powerful motives based in biology, with a superstructure in psychology. The conspiracy of political authorities to forestall rebellion is no more primary than the organization of consciousness to forestall insanity, and the fact that either form of repression can become excessive does not mean that it is entirely dispensable or inherently sinister.

The pressures toward political realignment and economic redistribution are not the only ones that threaten the stability of a culture. Against the pressure of life's desires—for this man's crown or that man's food—there is also a pressure of mortal terror; and stories must be invented to help regulate both kinds of pressure. Certain genres of imaginative literature are primarily a form of armor that our species has invented to protect the places where our self-consciousness makes us vulnerable to the bewildering variety of the universe and the crushing scale of universal space and time.[34] A culture deprived of its consensual view of that universe—that is, a culture whose blinders to alternative views have worn through to transparency—faces a cognitive crisis potentially as devastating as any political rebellion. Imagine the psychological condition of a person incapable of what Otto Rank calls "partialization," receiving all the noumenal world's broadcasts simultaneously and indiscriminately, like a radio with a broken tuner; then imagine the condition of a society made up of such multiphrenics. If religion is indeed "the mother of peace" (as a 1605 attack on atheists claimed) it may be on this level of mental organization.[35]

Pico della Mirandola's fifteenth-century "Oration on the Dignity of Man" interprets our lack of the bodily defenses given other animals as a parable of our obligation to choose and construct our moral selves. As Becker's work suggests (pp. 50–52), a similar burden arises from our lack of the peremptory instinctive programming that allows other animals to function efficiently. The systems of cognitive selectivity are the inward institutions of human existence, and everyone has a psychological interest in stabilizing them by mutual affirmation.[36] Otherwise the society would suffer some macrocosmic version of the hyper-receptivity of the schizophrenic. It is not surprising that creative artists, perpetually recognizing possible new configurations for reality, and dangerously aware of the artificiality of the old ones, are so often threatened with both social ostracism and mental illness.

Scientists also risked ostracism in the Renaissance, and for similar reasons. In *Novum Organum* (1620), Francis Bacon exposed the false "idols" that stabilize cognitive patterns for the individual and the society alike.[37] Though based on the belief that an objective reality awaits human discovery, this exposition both reflected and threatened to amplify an emerging suspicion that the perceived universe is an arbitrary selection and translation from an utterly unstable and indeterminate text, where once had stood a Book of Life immune to deconstruction. As Ronald Levao has eloquently demonstrated, "Renaissance thought and letters . . . brought increased attention to bear on both the power and contingency of constructions—literary and extraliterary—and came ultimately to contribute to a vision of culture, not as structured by eternal categories, but as a distinctly human artifact."[38] This vision—evident also in Fulke Greville's "Treatie of Humane Learning," which begins, "The mind of man is this world's true dimension"—would have magnified exponentially the fear of death as an erasure of consciousness. If God cannot be relied on to make sense of the universe, then the human mind must remain perpetually, categorically vigilant; but if God cannot be relied on to save that mind from extinction with the body, then the project is hopeless. This helps to explain why cultures such as the Renaissance that face a radical challenge to their assurances about afterlife display psychotic tendencies.[39]

For the Jacobeans, the Christian God was therefore a necessary anchor in a troublesome sea of mutability: "He onely is stable in his being, it is he onely, that borders and limits the stormes and tempests of the world."[40] But if God began to lose His unity and stability through doctrinal schism, then the culture as a whole would become vulnerable again to unbounded thinking, vulnerable in particular to the dizzying idea that the organizing consciousness might utterly and eternally disappear. This cultural crisis parallels the psychological crisis of the schizoid individual: according to contemporary psychological theorists such as Heinz Kohut and D. W. Winnicott, patients experience a terror of death in direct proportion to the threat of character disintegration in their psychic lives.[41] Indeed, in the aftermath of their Civil War—political violence provoked by a religious schism that divided the national identity—the English became sharply sensitive to the social necessity of stable belief-systems. This sensitivity manifests itself in several ways—for instance, the weird disjunctions and kaleidoscopic perspectives of time and space in Marvell's "Upon Appleton House" seem inseparable from anxieties about the unresolved Civil War—but most forcefully in arguments against atheism. If it is true (as one Enlightenment attack on deism asserted) that "No community ever was or can be begun or maintained, but upon the Basis of Religion,"[42] it may be because political order depends on a shared cognitive organization. According to another attack, "Atheism offers such violence to all our faculties, that it seems scarce credible it should ever really find any footing in human understanding."[43]

One legible subtext of these dismissive remarks is an anxiety that social order can find no footing without shared systems of understanding, and that such understanding can find no real footing without positing an organizing deity:

> if every man . . . should follow his owne private humour, what manner of Church or Commonwealth should wee have amongst us? Would not all grow into confusion and disorder, and returne into that stupidity of ignorance which swayed in the World before the true Religion was first propagated and . . . at the last it must necessarily come to mutiny, if not massacre.[44]

Later in the seventeenth century, Richard Bentley would similarly warn atheists that their desire to reject religion as an instrument of social control would quickly "reduce all once again to thy imaginary State of Nature of Original Confusion"; in a subsequent lecture he argues that God has given us limited senses because excessively rich sight "would be very little better than blindness," and excessively rich hearing would forbid us to "retire from perpetual buzzing and humming."[45] Clearly the Christian story of creation out of chaos has foundations in the formative stages of each human psyche that must tame the infinite variations of sense-experience into a coherent universe governed by a perpetual benign intelligence.

The control-hungry Utopia that Thomas More envisioned was cozy enough in its communism, but it could not tolerate doubts about afterlife.[46] Renaissance England shared with this Utopia the assumption that annihilationism necessarily implied libertinism. The standard accusation that atheists are susceptible to every kind of lawlessness and debauchery may be a way of placing anxieties about this loss of boundaries back into a conventional moral framework.[47] Remember death, and you will never sin, said the preachers; but to remember death too well may be to lose all ethical bearings. It must have required a very precise calibration for Renaissance Christians, especially Protestants, to sustain a recognition of death without entertaining a suspicion of mere oblivion; yet on the distinction they had rested the entire moral order of their society.

As Shakespeare's Richard II ruefully acknowledges, even the most absolute earthly monarch exercises very marginal power; eternity and mutability can make even the vaunted "material base" seem virtually immaterial (Richard's experience came to mind when my dentist recently offered me "a temporary crown" to "hold off decay"). The complaint that historical criticism tends to fetishize power may be true in a specific psychoanalytic sense, to the extent that the exalted successive monarchy and its control over human destiny serves (as does the artificial fetish-object) to eclipse the vulnerability of the mortal body. Contrary to the assumption of some political critics, the cult of monarchy may have served a need of the subjects no less than of the monarch. Queen Elizabeth and King James doubtless used the common people for many kinds of material advantage, but the people also used their sovereigns as immortality-surrogates, investing them with bodies-politic co-eternal and co-extensive with their nations, and granting them the power to impose death partly because that function implies an obverse power to preserve life (as in the curative force of the royal touch).[48] Furthermore, mourning for celebrities (royal or otherwise) allows people to stage observances that answer to the grandiose needs of their own narcissism, wounded by a recognition of mortality. In any case, there must certainly have been a great many people in England, especially outside London, who did not know or care much about Elizabeth's portraits or James's masques, but had a close and compelling view of the face of death and the drama of the deathbed.

So while this book attempts to practice "cultural poetics"—the reading of literature as part of other ideological constructions—it resists the New Historicist tendency to emphasize political power in a way that excludes personal psychology, and to emphasize anthropological distance in a way that precludes personal sympathy. And where the modal New Historicist analysis might begin with a slide of a specific Renaissance map or a detailed anecdote from a Renaissance diary—something that would have been seen by very few, however neatly it may be generalized into a cultural signature—what I have chosen to poise for interrogation at the top of my document is that anonymous skull, the like of which spoke in eloquent silences to so many Renaissance thinkers. On behalf of mortality and its moral lessons, "The chief *Speaker* and *Orator* is he who hath now forgotten to *speak*; for the *locking up* of his *Senses*, the silence of his *Tongue* . . . have more force . . . than the most *Eloquent Strains* of the best *Rhetorician*."[49]

This critique of New Historicism does not of course apply to all the practitioners of a movement that is nearly impossible to define, except perhaps as a variety of adaptations of cultural anthropology and Marxist ideology designed to refresh literary criticism and restore its social relevancy without oversimplifying historical causation. Supremely admirable as that project is in the abstract, it is often limited in practice by a determination to identify literature as largely an effort to disguise the merely arbitrary and fictional aspects of government authority. My point is that *all* the mythologies by which we define ourselves and attribute meaning to our lives exist under the same constant threat of exposure. As religious schism and scientific discovery put Medieval beliefs increasingly at risk, literature begins uneasily testing the wound in the culture, trying sometimes to patch it up with new consolations, sometimes to articulate its pain and fear. And, just as (New Historicists have shown) authors find equivocal ways to subvert the very power-structures their fictions legitimize, Jacobean literature sometimes exposes as wishful thinking the very figurations of immortality it helped construct.

Another limiting aspect of common New Historicist practice has proven harder for me to avoid than the reduction of cultural order to political order: the assumption that literature is valuable primarily as the record of successive epidemics of social pathology. In this, the harshest critics of the humanist tradition reinforce its central legacy, namely, a socially utilitarian view of the arts. The project of excavating the secret ironic meaning of literary texts, which has come to seem tired and even dishonest over the last twenty years, has largely given way to another, more openly adversarial kind of excavation; but making literature a series of sociological symptoms seems finally no more satisfactory than making it a series of aesthetic symmetries. Many conference papers consist largely of reading, to a snickering audience, passages in which some canonical author violates our current consensus on issues of race, class, or gender, as if these passages were wiretap transcripts that might finally bring an arrogant career-criminal to justice, or Freudian slips on behalf of an entire culture that disclose its dysfunctions. Obviously this book reflects a conviction that the repressions of a culture can be productively excavated and abreacted, but not strictly for the sake of accusing the past of lacking the enlightenment of my ideal future.

Of course we should not cover all the faults of the past with a mystifying aura of canonicity; but we overlook a central value of story-telling and art-making if we assume that it profits a critic to gain a sociological document and lose a work of imagination that (perhaps because it bridges alternative systems of coherence) defies paraphrase of any sort. Autopsy has a purpose, but it is not the only real transaction between human beings, and far from the most appealing. Of course we should lament the aspects of past cultures that encouraged cruelty, injustice, and closed-mindedness; but perhaps we should also recognize whatever virtues and beauties those cultural arrangements enabled, however poor a compensation the wonders of any world order must seem for the ignorance and suffering of its creatures.

Every pedagogical and critical stance—aestheticist, humanist, Marxist, deconstructionist—has political implications, but that is not the same as saying they are ultimately nothing but politics. Every meal we eat and every kiss we bestow carries strong political implications as well, and yet surely those experiences cannot be summarized as merely assertions of (say) our vegetarianism or heterosexuality without sacrificing much of the richness of human experience. A literary scholar who (fleeing the instability of language) becomes entirely an analyst and advocate of political positions abandons a site of tradition, sympathy, and uncertainty that serves as a buffer zone between a society's temporary notions of justice and propriety, and the series of totalitarian states those notions would otherwise generate.

Yet if that scholar entirely abandons the role of ethicist, the study of literature tends to become either an evanescent dance of verbal wit or a laborious expedition into linguistic theory.[50] If literature lacks anything like a soul, legible at least in palimpsest, then it is finally only a collection of ABCs conspiring to simulate meaning, as a soulless human race would be a collection of DNA conspiring their own preservation and replication. Surely the prestige and affection bestowed on poets across so many centuries and cultures has not all come from the top down, as an endorsement of their role in mystifying and legitimizing the political status quo; nor would the poets evoke that prestige and affection if they were primarily cynical philosophers of language who mocked the meat they fed on. The appetite of New Historicism for both symbolic indeterminacy and political relevancy offers a promising middle ground, but its practitioners have tended to subordinate the three necessary premises of ethics—love, free will, and imagination—to their virtual opposites, by concentrating on the repression of sexual deviation, on illusory subversion that subserves containment, and on subliminally determined conspiracies in defense of the established material order. The implication is that tough-minded historicism forbids ascribing freedom of love, will, or imagination to English Renaissance minds; but I believe that the literature displays a fierce struggle to defend all three categories from the impingements of mortality.

DOUBTFUL BELIEFS

My grandmother recently tried to explain to me how exasperatingly attached my late grandfather had been to the pleasures of food, drink, and good fellowship. "Why, if he knew he was dead," she snapped, "it would *kill* him." Such are the paradoxes of annihilationist terror. As Montaigne argued, if we did not mind our non-being prior to birth, it makes little sense to fear non-being after death.[51] Shakespeare's Prospero implies the same thing in consoling Ferdinand: "our little life / Is rounded with a sleep," not merely ended with one (*The Tempest*, 4.1.157–58).

Yet there is something in the human mind—perhaps a survival instinct channeled through a modern Western notion of sacred selfhood[52]—that is terrified to imagine itself extinguished in the vasts of time and space. Perhaps the comparison of death to birth, so common in Renaissance consolation literature, reflects a deep truth about the fear of annihilation. The primary psychic tasks of infancy—to defend the fragile unity of the self in separation from the world of objects, and to make that infinitely large and various phenomenal world comprehensible and predictable—seem analogous to and connected to the primary anxieties of annihilationism. The same narcissistic illusions deployed against vulnerability and cognitive chaos at the beginning of human life make it virtually unbearable to accept an utter dissolution at the end of it, when the objective world reabsorbs the passive self into a limitless and meaningless mutability. Moreover, what is needed for healthy psychic development resembles what is needed for Christian complacency toward death: trust in the benevolence and omnipotence of a creator who recognizes and responds to the self so tentatively and laboriously carved out of the world.

Applying this contemporary psychological theory to Jacobean minds presumes a substantial continuity in human sensibilities over nearly four centuries—which seems to me a defensible presumption. Foucault's influential idea that cultures perceive radically different realities from century to century has bred an epidemic of exaggeration in cultural criticism, often at a real cost to what Clifford Geertz calls the precious "power of the scientific imagination to bring us in touch with the lives of strangers."[53] Surely it is possible to recognize kinship, across space or time, without brutally imposing sameness. (Indeed, many Foucauldian critics could themselves be accused of imposing sameness; replicating the maneuver they so effectively expose in Renaissance culture, they construct the complicated human past as a conveniently absolute Other.) Illusory empathy is a corrupt sentiment, but an illusory estrangement, by implying that the Other does not feel as we feel, induces a tolerance of injustice and cruelty. In her generally excellent summary and advocacy of New Historicism, Jean Howard echoes Tzvetan Todorov's lament that Central American Indians were "denied inclusion within the category of the human" by Renaissance Spaniards, who could therefore torture them remorselessly. Yet she also echoes—and endorses as the first precept of New Historicist criticism—Jonathan Dollimore's claim that political virtue can arise only from a belief "that there is no shared human essence . . . no traits not the product of social forces at a particular historical juncture."[54] By denying that "humanity" is a legitimate experiential category apart from local cultural configurations, these theories authorize the notorious tendency to identify members of sub-cultures as sub-human, and to treat them as such. This political danger remains virulent today: repressive Asian governments have begun telling the United Nations "that Western definitions of human rights are culture-bound and thus inappropriate," creating "one of the most serious threats ever mounted against the 45-year old Universal Declaration on Human Rights."[55]

The essentialist overtones of my argument derive not only from this political concern, but also from a personal investment in empathy and in the validity of a psychoanalytic reading of human behavior. By asserting that the Jacobeans shared our modern sense of a personal identity threatened by mortality, this book posits some meaningful continuities: both synchronically in the self, and diachronically in the species. It also assumes some meaningful (if coded) continuity between the interior self of these authors and the personae through whom they speak, and a continuity between my "modern self" and yours as we confront these questions and these texts. Naturally these similarities are not absolute, but neither are the differences. Though the acceptance of imperfect similarities has become disreputable in elite scholarship—dismissed as naively sentimental or politically regressive by scholars interested in hermeneutic gaps or historical fractures and the otherness thereby produced—I hope to revive one side of a dialogue that is as vital for historical scholarship as the dialogue between the recognition of difference and the recognition of similarity is for any cognitive process.

Particularly relevant to my argument is the widespread assumption that the demoralizing materialist reading of death was simply unavailable in the Christian culture of Renaissance England. In the most cited and anthologized essay of this generation in Renaissance studies, "Invisible Bullets," Stephen Greenblatt argues that, while charges of atheism were frequent, "Few if any of these investigations turned up what we would call atheists, even muddled or shallow ones; the stance that seems to come naturally to the greenest college freshman in late 20th-century America seems to have been almost unthinkable to the most daring philosophical minds of late sixteenth-century England."[56] Much virtue in "almost." The status of the atheistical hypothesis has clearly changed over the centuries, at some level more pervasive than official doctrine, from forbidden to commonplace. But as Greenblatt himself concedes, to say that it is unsafe to write about a particular idea, and imperative to disavow it in official interrogations, is hardly the same as to say that it was unthinkable. And, clearly, it was thinkable to the accusers, whose zealous campaigns were presumably fueled by a projection of unmanageable inward doubts. This book will argue that annihilationist terror affects far more than the occasional "extravagant, zany exception" Greenblatt acknowledges.[57] Even in the hands of one of its most brilliant and fair-minded practitioners, New Historicism characteristically risks overrating the ability of a centralized cultural consensus to manipulate not only the consciousness, but also the subconsciousness, of an entire population. In this it oddly mimics the tendency of old historicists to identify certain ideas as universally held in a society—a tendency New Historicists generally revile (in the work of Tillyard, for example) as a naive or complicit misreading of a campaign of ideological repression.

Granted, it was difficult for most Renaissance minds to relinquish the Christian premises of their world-views. This led to some ludicrously circular arguments which cite as proof of God's existence the fact that the Bible—which is after all the God-given truth—asserts that He exists.[58] A slightly more subtle circularity often marks attacks on annihilationism. Told that "there is a secte that teacheth that there is neither hell nor heaven, nor god, nor devill; and that the soule is mortall and dyeth with the bodye," an Elizabethan minister replies that "if there should not be such a secte the worde of god were faulce which did teach that towardes the latter end there should be such that shoulde fall awaye."[59] The Jacobean version is more psychological: "Yea aske but the Conscience of the vilest Atheist, it will be a thousand witnesses of this truth; how often are they filled with unspeakable horrours especially in death? wherefore? but because they know there is a judgement that followes it."[60] Donne argues that "no man dares think upon the last Judgement, but he that can thinke upon it with comfort"—implying that people suppose themselves annihilationists only because they know they are damned— and demands that atheists "answer their own terrors, and horrors alone at midnight, and tell themselves whence that proceeds, if there be no God" (Sermons, VI, 277; III, 257). Yet some Elizabethans recognized such strenuous misreadings of atheism as evasions: when one figure in a dialogue claims that professed atheists would, on close examination, "confesse, that they think there is a God," his interlocutor sympathizes with the effort to "make the best of their Atheisme . . . but I can assure you that there are such, that denie not onely the providence, but even the very nature and existence of God."[61]

By denying the existence, even the possibility, of meaningful Renaissance atheism, modern commentators such as Lucien Febvre[62] replicate what was actually the defensive reflex of a truly endangered Christian hegemony. Martin Fotherby's *Atheomastix* offers the standard Renaissance version of the modern dictum that there are no atheists in foxholes: "No dreame, no vision, no thunder, no lightening, doth so affright the *Atheist*, as the thought of death doth; and what will follow after death . . . the cogitation of a state of death, doth strike him, with a feare of an eternall death."[63] By this Fotherby means, or says he means, the fear of God's punishment; he never mentions the possibility that the fear of eternal death might arise from a fear of eternal death. Atheism stands refuted by the evidence that no one can sustain it on a deathbed, or that "no one can dye in their wits, that die not in the faith of our Lord Christ";[64] yet this evidence is potentially far less subversive to atheism than to Christianity, which becomes vulnerable to Voltaire's skeptical observation that, if God did not exist, it would be necessary to invent Him. Furthermore, to argue (as Donne does, for example)[65] that there are no atheists because the human mind could not function without a belief in God not only provokes this skepticism about origins, it is also self-contradictory, since it involves positing and entering an atheistical mentality for the purpose of deeming it unachievable. This is precisely the kind of paradox that Greenblatt's "Invisible Bullets" sets out to explore: the way invaders of alien cultures find themselves hoist with their own petard, exposing the arbitrary character of their own belief-systems by exploiting (cynically, improvisationally) the beliefs of others. Attacks on annihilationism may have had the same kind of ramifications for orthodox Christianity.

A subliminal recognition of this danger may lie behind the Renaissance tendency to accuse overt attackers of atheism of covertly endorsing atheism, since they disseminate the forbidden ideas in the course of refuting them.[66] The other fundamental paradox at the heart of nearly all seventeenth-century attacks on atheism and annihilationism is that authors felt obliged to refute rationally what they claimed no rational person could assert, to mount vigorous rescue operations into theological territory they claimed was uninhabited. These tracts describe a fundamental hegemony of religious belief, like that implied by Febvre and Greenblatt, but their description is clearly tendentious. Thomas Browne's *Pseudodoxia Epidemica* (p. 183) dismisses disbelievers as either too stupid or too clever to see the most obvious truths, yet disputes at length with these phantoms. In a breathtaking display of revisionist appropriation, Browne's *Religio Medici* analyzes the forces that "have perverted the devotion of many unto Atheisme," yet a few paragraphs later declares that actually

there was never any. Those that held Religion was the difference of man from beasts, have spoken probably, and proceed upon a principle as inductive as the other: That doctrine of *Epicurus*, that denied the providence of God, was no Atheism, but a magnificent and high-strained conceit of his Majesty, which

hee deemed too sublime to minde the triviall actions of those inferiour creatures: That fatall necessitie of the Stoickes, is nothing but the immutable Law
of his will. (pp. 84–86)

Christian anagogy thus inoculates itself against comparative anthropology. Ancient pagan belief in the immortality of souls, which could be
used to argue that such belief is a human psychological need rather than
a truth of revelation or natural reason, is read as a verifying premonition
of Christianity. Browne (pp. 86–87) goes on to claim that even the
author of the notorious (and probably apocryphal) *De tribus
impostoribus*, "though divided from all Religions, and was neither Jew,
Turk, nor Christian, was not a positive Atheist." All Browne will
concede is that "the Rhetorick of Satan . . . may pervext a loose or
prejudicate beleefe," particularly in befuddled classicists: "I remember a
Doctor in Physick of Italy, who could not perfectly believe the immortality of the soule, because *Galen* seemed to make a doubt therof."
Perhaps, he adds, there was also once a Frenchman similarly misled by
Seneca.

When the printed record does acknowledge atheistical views, the
acknowledgments always disarm the threat by ad hominem attacks on
the disbelievers. Sometimes, as in Browne, the disbelievers are tainted by
association with lower animals or the pagan past, if not by sheer mental
incapacity. All these guilty associations conjoin into a kind of Circe
motif, visible in Hooker's astonishment "that base desires should so
extinguish in men the sense of their own excellency, as to make them
willing that their souls should be like the souls of beasts, mortal and
corruptible with their bodies?"[67] Disbelief is thus commonly portrayed
as a rationalization for hedonism, as the disbeliever himself would
miserably confess on his deathbed: by "experience of all ages it hath been
proved that *Atheists* themselves, that is, such as in their health and
prosperitie for more libertie of sinning, would strive against the being of
a God, when they come to die or fall into any great miserie, they of all
other would shew themselves most fearfull of this God."[68]

These logical, rhetorical, and theological mazes were constructed to
entrap Jacobean annihilationism and channel it back into Christian
affirmation. In 1608 Robert Pricke observed that

Atheists (whereof we have too many examples) puffe out a little warme breath
in scorne and derision, saying, there goeth my soule: he being therein fowlie
deceived, and sheweth himselfe utterlie impudent and shamelesse. It were a
blessed thing for thee, oh thou *Atheist*, if thou wert in the estate of a bruit

beast. But alas, thou art indued with an immortal soule, which can never die: whereof thou art even convinced in thy selfe; but that the divell hath blinded thine eyes, and strongly possessed thy heart. For what is the reason that thou doest so tremble at death, and art so loth to die? . . . the cause is the guilt and accusation of an evill conscience: from which thou doest conclude, that immediately after death, thou shalt suffer everlasting torments and confusion in hel fire: which doth plainely prove to thy shamelesse face, that a principall part of thee doth still remaine after death; and that is thy soule.[69]

The atheistical fear of annihilation supposedly proves valid and universal the Christian belief in afterlife. To deny the Christian model of the universe is to prove that the Biblical devil has made you a liar. This device is clearly at work in the deathbed crises discussed in my Epilogue, and it looks ahead to the tricks of denial by which Enlightenment Christians continued to claim that atheism was impossible even when someone openly asserted it, on the grounds that such a person could not vow his or her atheistic convictions by God, and therefore earned no credence— a sort of theological Catch-22.

These efforts to make the Christian belief-system self-verifying prove that it was not inherently so. If no one was in a position to assault it from outside, why were there such frantic efforts to pull the wagons into a circle? Naturally it was a long time before anyone could actually advocate atheistic beliefs in print, but that hardly proves there were no real atheists. After encountering so many examples, Renaissance and modern, of the tendency to disallow the evidence of atheism, to make conventional intellectual history a barrier against unconventional thought, to claim that no one could think that way because no one had yet thought that way, one can appreciate the exasperated effort of William Hammon to establish a *terminus ad quem* of unbroken belief: "Be it therefore for the future remembered, that in London in the kingdom of England, in the year of our Lord one thousand seven hundred and eighty-one, a man publickly declared himself to be an atheist."[70]

In Jacobean usage "atheist" did not always mean a person who refused to believe in any form of deity. It was often a term of anathema applied to anyone who deviated from the writer's preferred form of Christianity rather than a specific term for those denying the existence of God.[71] Yet one may still wonder why "atheist" (to the extent that the term was part of a rhetorical strategy) served as the darkest condemnation, and (to the extent that the term expressed a sincere horror) why people felt that the only alternative to their particular doctrine of personal salvation was the terrifying abyss of unbelief.[72] Vague and factional uses of the term have sometimes been cited to sustain the claim that atheism in the pure form was not possible in the Renaissance, but in many Jacobean instances "atheism" carries its specific modern sense. John Dove's *Confutation of Atheism* concedes that "Sometimes under the name of Atheists are comprehended Pagans, Infidels and Idolators," but he attacks the thing itself, which he considers far worse.[73] William Perkins's *Treatise of Mans Imaginations* asserts that some men "avouch, hould, & maintain that there is no God at all; this is the highest degree of Atheisme," which he calls "the most notorious, and vile damnable thought that can be in a naturall man." Indeed, Perkins offers a Christian essentialist refutation of theories about insular Renaissance belief: "we must not thinke that this wicked thought is onely in some notorious and hainous sinners; but it is in the corrupt minde and Imagination of every man that commeth of *Adam* naturally, not one excepted, save Christ alone. . . . by nature his corrupt heart is prone to think *there is no God*."[74] Martin Fotherby's *Atheomastix* draws fairly sophisticated distinctions among unbelievers, whom he divides into Atheists, Epicures, and Naturalists.[75] Donne studies various types of atheists, concluding that "we have all, all these . . . in our owne bosomes" (*Sermons*, IX, 171). Thomas Adams, another very prominent Jacobean preacher, identifies atheism as "the highest theft against God, because it would steal from him not *sua, sed se,* his goods, but himself." In another sermon, Adams identifies a bad congregation as "semi-atheistical cosmopolites"; in a third, he describes Judas as worse than "absolute atheists."[76] Robert Welcome's Jacobean funeral sermon contrasts the woman he is eulogizing to "many lukewarm *Politicians* that either are *Atheists,* of no religion at al; or els *Chameleon*-like turne with the time."[77] At mid-century, the author of *Atheismus Vapulans* announces as his target those who deny God, and claims there is one such in his own circle;[78] and toward the end of the century, the "Methodizer of the Second Spira" sets out to refute "those that either own no God; or at least deny the *Separate Existence and Immortality of the Soul,* I think there are but few of the first. But upon my personal Knowledge there's too many of the *last Opinion*."[79]

As this last quotation indicates, annihilationism does not necessarily connote atheism, even for Christians. Averroes and Pompanazzi led influential Medieval and Renaissance revivals of Origen's notion that human souls might be reabsorbed into a sort of world-soul at death; while nominally Christian, this theology can hardly have satisfied the increasingly common desire to have one's unique interiority preserved eternally. In the early seventeenth century, William Birnie's *Blame of Kirk-Buriall* remarks that the "Saducean herisie denied the resurrection" without calling that heresy atheism,[80] and Socinians were regularly accused of disbelieving in the eternity of hell, without being accused of disbelieving in God.[81]

Still, atheism and annihilationism were intimately connected in the common discourse (and marked together as capital crimes in the Blasphemy Bill of 1648–50), if only because the chief anxiety expressed about atheism—that without the fear of eternal punishment people would behave immorally—applies to annihilationism as well. There are indications that Jacobean culture felt annihilationism to be the greatest threat of all: "it is Epicurisme, Atheisme, and the greatest Apostacie from faith that may be" to suppose that "we shal bee heareafter as though wee had never been," that "the Spirit vanisheth as the soft ayre."[82] Browne cannot understand how Epicurus and Seneca managed "to be honest without a thought of Heaven or Hell" to reward or punish at resurrection, and concludes that "without this, all Religion is a Fallacy, and those impieties of *Lucian, Euripides,* and *Julian* are no blasphemies, but subtile verities, and Atheists have beene the onely Philosophers" (pp. 119–20). Later in the seventeenth century, Bayle argued that hell was useless as a moral deterrent,[83] but—as with similar evidence about the death-penalty in our own society—people still felt a psychological need for that absolute stay against the prospect of moral chaos.

In Adams's analysis, "There are some feare to die, others not so much to die as to bee dead. The former are cowardly, the other unbelieving soules . . . But when the last extremitie comes, *mori cupiant*, they desire to die."[84] His point is a familiar one, that unbelievers will be surprised by hell, but he acknowledges that they were already frightened of mere oblivion. Doubtless hellfire was a more compelling threat, but it was also far more widely acknowledged and far better contextualized. The fear of non-being was therefore more likely to build up pressure in the psychic economy and to find indirect means of expression: in poetry, for example, rather than in laws or sermons, and therefore in a form more accessible to literary critics than to historians. Even if annihilationism tends to be the discourse of an Other, it may find an outlet in drama, where authors and actors never quite speak as themselves. And even if subversion tends to mirror official doctrine, annihilationist resentment against the universe may manifest itself in the form of parodies of the sacred system.

The shortage of more explicit annihilationist assertions in the written record can hardly be considered conclusive, since it would have been dangerous in Renaissance society to write such things, worse to save them, and virtually suicidal to publish them. Under such circumstances, heterodoxies can be recuperated from the responses of the orthodox authorities, as the dark shape with whom those authorities appear to be shadow-boxing; they reach us by indirect discourse, and through the indirections of art. Perhaps (as Kyd and Marlowe learned the hard way) it was far too risky to propose a Machiavellian explanation for official religion outside of dramatic personae, but if no one had such suspicions in late Elizabethan England, why would Henrie Smith bother writing that "a religious devotion of feare toward God is bred and borne with every man, and therefore there cannot be any pollicie of humane invention."[85] Roger Ascham's *Scholemaster* ends up inscribing this suspicion in his curriculum by attempting to attack it.[86] A Jacobean preacher opens the same Machiavellian perspective in his very effort to extol Christianity: "It is Religion, that holdeth us at a bay, and keepeth the heart of the Subject in awe, that it swelleth not against the Soveraigne."[87] At least one Jacobean woman proved capable of believing "That the Scriptures are not his Word, but a Pollicie," and holding to that belief for six years; but we would never have known it, if another preacher had not chosen to celebrate her progress from indoctrinated Catholicism through miserable atheism to triumphant Protestantism.[88] Thus schism not only encouraged atheism, it helped plant it in the explicit historical record.

Lengthy though it is, this introduction has quoted only a fraction of the annihilationist instances I found, which are surely only a fraction of those existing, which are in turn only a fraction of those originally published, which would have represented only a fraction of the cases actively suspected. So the traditional assumption that Jacobeans would automatically have believed in afterlife is at best an exaggeration. To such overreadings of the history of mentalities, one may reply with an updating of Carlyle's dictum: close thy Foucault, open thy Ecclesiastes. There is no new thing under the sun, and the biological-materialist reading of death is probably one of the oldest. Browne suggests that heresies are cyclically recurrent, and his discussion evolves into reincarnationist metaphors and mortalist apologetics that, in their defensiveness, suggest an unresolved struggle with annihilationism:

Heresies perish not with their Authors, but like the River *Arethusa*, though they lose their currents in one place, they rise up againe in another . . . for as though there were a *Metempsuchosis*, and the soule of one man passed into another, opinions doe finde after certaine revolutions, men and mindes like those that first begat them. . . . there was none then, but there hath been some one since that parallels him, and is as it were his revived selfe. Now the first of [Browne's heresies] was that of the Arabians, that the soules of men perished with their bodies, but should yet bee raised againe at the last day; not that I did absolutely conceive a mortality of the soule; but if that were, which faith, not Philosophy hath yet throughly disproved . . . yet I held the same conceit thereof that wee all doe of the body, that it should rise againe. Surely it is but the merits of our unworthy natures, if wee sleepe in darkenesse, untill the last alarum: . . . so I might enjoy my Saviour at the last, I could with patience be nothing almost unto eternity. (pp. 66–67)

This crucial word "almost"—semantically, a limiting function against the absolute—performs a similar service in the dedicatory epistle to *Hydriotaphia*, which claims that the remains of the ancients "lay, almost in silence among us" (p. 264). The prospect of personal annihilation was always asserting itself—staring up from plaguy corpses, rising in the inscrutable remains of classical antiquity, threatening to become legible even in the Bible itself. Jacobean culture was obliged to find ways to unthink that thought, to talk itself out of fear, to quarantine a potentially catastrophic cultural epidemic.

THE RHETORIC OF DENIAL

For all the pious and rational warnings that death is universal, human beings are notoriously ready to disbelieve in their own mortality. This was apparently as characteristic of the Jacobeans as it is of us. *Memento mori* stands in the foreground of nearly every Jacobean funeral sermon; yet at the same time the preachers appear to offer, as an incentive to orthodoxy, the hope that annihilation can be isolated in an Other. Recently much has been made of the invention and oppression of aliens for the purposes of political advantage, but a comparable transaction necessarily occurs in the formation of the individual psyche,[89] and in the evasions of mortality a culture offers its constituents. Just as (according to Freud) it is impossible to believe in one's own mortality, so cultures systematically project their annihilationist anxieties onto an Other consciousness.

William Worship's *The Christians Mourning Garment* (1603) claims that the worst heretics are those who

hold that their soules in death vanish away like a dogges. This Satanicall paradore possest the hart of that great Physitian Galen. A man might have cast his water and found filthy sediments of Athisme. But he is dead long ago, & I would this sin had died with him. Good Christian, never come thou nere those Carrions that maintaine the soule to be a vapour, unlesse thou have the winde of them.[90]

This is a quip, but it contains several characteristic signatures of anti-annihilationist rhetoric. Worship isolates annihilation as the fate of lower animals, enables himself to talk about annihilationism by locating it in a disastrously misguided classical authority, and associates that authority (and any Renaissance followers) with contagion and bodily decay, as if those who resisted the spiritual disease would somehow be spared such decay. The fact that such heterodox notions—that the corpses of the virtuous might avoid vermiculation, that the souls of the wicked might be simply annihilated—permeate these pious presentations suggests they were powerful hopes and fears that the preachers could hope only to channel, not wholly to suppress.

Jacobean culture bristles with these projections: human beings are encouraged to project their unacceptable mortality onto other animals, men to project theirs onto women, Christians onto pagans, Catholics and Protestants onto each other. The distinction between all other animals, in whom people witnessed the simple and decisive work of mortality, and human beings, who were supposedly made for immortality, was the easiest of these binarisms to assert, because the categories were stable and the theology orthodox. Even the usually generous and inclusive Browne joins in this theological version of kicking the dog: "I beleeve that the whole frame of a beaste doth perish, and is left in the same state after death, as before it was materialled unto life; that the soules of men know neither contrary nor corruption, that they subsist beyond the body, and outlive death by the priviledge of their proper natures" (p. 108). Henrie Smith's *Gods Arrowe against Atheists* begins with the assertion that "Atheisme and Irreligion was ever odious even amonge the Heathen themselves . . . as being more like rude beastes than reasonable men."[91] The implication is that those who live like dogs (that is, without religion) will die like dogs (that is, unredeemed from mere physical decay). "Certainly," one Jacobean preacher assured his audience, "though sinful man be like unto the beasts that perish, yet he doth not perish like the beasts, whose bodies are turned into ashes, and their spirits vanish. . . . "[92] Another preacher pushes the same allusion a step further, suggesting that those who do not recognize the Christian God "shall be like the beast which perisheth," before (inconsistently) reverting to a warning about hellfire.[93]

Often a syntactical parallelism serves to secure and neaten this arguably tenuous distinction: "To dye is the course of Nature, to dye well, of Christian Art: that is common to men with beasts; this proper unto Gods servants alone."[94] Clearly these structures serve to restrain a suspicion that becomes momentarily audible in the testimony that one Jacobean gentleman believed "there was noe god & noe resurrection, & that men died a death like beasts."[95] When the annihilationist side acquires its own voice (though, typically, as the straw-man in a pious argument), it attacks precisely this consoling distinction: "you and I are nothing else but *Brutes*, and if we have any priviledge above *Lions* and *Foxes*, 'tis from a more Exquisite Fabric; our clockwork is something finer than theirs; and our Organs are more apposite and proper for abstracted perception."[96] The current controversy over animal rights, particularly as it affects medical care for human beings, suggests that the struggle on this point is far from over.

A more elusive but perhaps more pervasive version of this pattern allowed men to isolate the condition of annihilation in women. The behavioral traits that Renaissance manuals repeatedly suggest were prized in wives—silence, coldness, containment, and passivity—bear a striking resemblance to the traits of the dead as conceived by annihilationism. Though sexually frustrated, Shakespeare's Bertram adores the maiden who strikes him as

> a monument.
> When you are dead, you should be such a one
> As you are now; for you are cold and stern. . . .
>
> (*All's Well*, 4.2.6–8)

This pattern did not, I think, reflect an outbreak of necrophilia—though references to women as "painted Sepulchres,"[97] a devotion to pallid complexions, and sporadic black humor about corpse-kissing in Jacobean tragedy, might seem to support that hypothesis. An alternative explanation for this correspondence is that Jacobean men used women as subjects in an elaborate experiment on the condition of oblivion. This experiment would have yielded the comforting datum that one can endure a great deal of personal erasure and still retain some form of existence. The choice of women as experimental subjects is hardly surprising, since men have often projected their unwanted inner traits onto the opposite sex, and since an extensive misogynist tradition going back at least as far as the Genesis story clearly blames women—their heat, their appetite, their persuasion—for the onset of mortality in the species.

This theological view likely received reinforcement through the biological, psychological, and sociological functions that encourage men to perceive women as mates provoking decadent sexuality and as mothers issuing the fallible flesh in which our consciousness is so precariously sustained.[98] So the projective explanation edges toward another explanation, this one vengeful, talionic. The scapegoats for mortality become the guinea-pigs for annihilation. Women must be made to endure in life what they have betrayed men into enduring in death. If this is not a homeopathic cure for the disease of mortality, it is at least a punishment of the guilty party, which—as revenge-tragedy clearly shows—is considered the next best thing.

Inevitably, Catholics and Protestants turned against each other the theological weaponry developed to justify the oppression of other species and of women. Two predominant strains of recusant propaganda make sense only as efforts to associate the Reformation with annihilation, presumably on the assumption that people would avoid any faction tainted by the extinction of consciousness and the decay of the body. The first strain exploits Protestant asceticism and iconoclasm in order to identify the Reformation with pure negation. Thus, the anonymous author of the 1633 tract *The Non-Entity of Protestantism* wittily informs the Reformers that, since their principal project is undoing the worldly accretions of Roman practice, "your Religion is in it selfe a meere *Non-Entity; Its Being* consisting in a *Not-being*, and Essence, in *want of Essence.*"[99] The second strain is visible later in the same tract, in the description of Calvin's death: "being in despayre, and calling upon the Divell, he gave up his wicked soule, swearing, cursing, and blaspheming: he died of the disease of lice & wormes, increasing in a most loathsome ulcer, about his privy parts, so as none could endure the stench."[100] This is of course a rather comprehensive smear, but once again the primary threat is vermiculation rather than hellfire: Calvin is tainted by association with the horror of mere bodily decay, as Judas, Herod, and Arius had been before him, and in implied contrast to reliquary saints, who were distinguished by bodily preservation. Why should a man's susceptibility to posthumous decay be taken as a divine condemnation of his views, unless one were clinging to the idea that a particular orthodoxy forestalled it? By offering a kind of time-lapse image of a Protestant hero's rotting corpse, this propagandist vividly links Calvinist theology to materialist death.

The theological arguments against the Reformation thus blend into emotional ones. Catholics repeatedly implied that Protestantism untamed death—which may explain why Puritan preachers were so desperate (as my Epilogue shows) to deny that a notable parishioner had died in wild desperation. A 1615 recusant document addressed "*to some particular friends in England,*" chronicling "*the miserable ends of such as have impugned the Catholike Church,*" lists first among the "foure sorts of Christians in the world out of the Catholike Church," those who "doe not beleeve either hell or heaven."[101] By mid-century the tendentious association between extinction of the soul and deterioration of the flesh becomes fairly explicit, and can be used against atheists and schismatics alike. Instead of threatening unbelievers with hellfire, Towers warns that such badly sowed seed of the soul "does not only not multiply, but it perishes, it does not only not laugh and sing, but it weeps, and dyes, and comes to nothing, to nothing but that, which is most like to nothing, to putrefaction."[102]

Perhaps the greatest threat to the integrity of Renaissance Christian culture was the rediscovery of ancient pagan culture. Elizabethan scholars made a commodity of this potential disease, converting the misguided Other into an outlet for their own forbidden anxieties. Noting a heavy "reliance on examples from classical antiquity" in English Renaissance discussions of atheism, historians have concluded that there must not have been any native atheistic impulse to be confronted;[103] but perhaps the classical emphasis reflects an evasion rather than an invention of more local disbelief. Speculative atheism may come and go, but the 1597 commentator who isolates it safely back in Diagoras simultaneously tries to isolate in Epicurus a tendency that is surely transhistorical: the hedonistic neglect of high morality.[104] Even Lyly's warning about rampant atheism at Oxford reflects this displacement: "Be there not many at Athens which think there is no God, no redemption, no resurrection?"[105]

Jacobean commentaries on classical authors repeatedly employ them in this defensive maneuver. Thomas Tuke's *Discourse of Death*, for example, locates in the ancients both annihilationism ("Amongst the heathen some there were, that held the death a dissolution of the soule, as *Democritus, Epicurus* . . . ") and the Machiavellian interpretation of religion ("the Emperour *Theodosius* . . . thought it better to binde his Subjects to him by Religion, then by terror").[106] The Roman legacy thus provides both a rationale for exploring taboo topics, and a conveniently distant screen on which to project current doubts about Christian providence and statecraft. Casaubon's preface to Marcus Aurelius's *Meditations* warns that many scholastics typify the tendency of unaided reason toward atheism, and therefore "incurre both the just suspicion of being Atheists themselves, and the certaine guilt and crime of having made many others so."[107] Humphreys's commentary on Athenagoras argues that Ecclesiastes (a favorite text of the annihilationist Sadducees) must be read as a dialogue between Solomon and an atheist.[108] In distinguishing themselves from the obviously non-Christian material they were editing, Casaubon and Humphreys can perform a kind of curative amputation on the decaying body of Renaissance Christianity.

Occasionally, however, the containment of annihilationism within classical paganism sprang a leak. Robert Welcome's *State of the godly, both in this life, and in the life to come* (1606) virtually explodes with energy when it discovers this expedient for speaking (by a kind of *praeteritio*) what it is usually obliged to silence:

This stops the beastly and blasphemous mouth of the *Sadduces*, and fully puts them to silence; who affirmed, that there is no resurrection, nor *Angell*, nor spirit: and of *Epicurus* the belligod Philosopher, who was a most detestable defender of pleasure, and thought that Man was onely borne to enjoy pleasure, and sayd that the Soule dyeth after the death of the body: and of *Plinie*, who was not ashamed to write, *that it fares with all men after the last day as it did before the first day: and that there is no more sense and feeling, eyther of body, or minde, after we are dead, then there was before we were borne; and of Lucretius* a fat swine of *Epicurus* stie, who impudently opens his uncleane mouth against heaven. . . . [109]

Many of the ancients believed that death was simply the end of everything, according to Samuel Gardiner's *Doomes-day Book*, and something about their assumptions seemed uncomfortably familiar: "In these darkenesse lay almost all the rabblement of the Orators, Philosophers, and Poets of the Gentiles. And if we shall ransacke the militant Church, we shall find many monstrous minded men in this matter."[110] The Jacobeans conjured an enemy out of classical culture, and sometimes discovered that the enemy was themselves.

Another interesting feature of Jacobean attacks on annihilationism is their peculiarly consistent recourse to rhetorical questions. The need to dismiss the fear of death without denying its existence regularly evokes this quirk of style in authors who rarely employ it elsewhere:

For why should he feare death whom death doth *helpe*, not hurt, and *ease* rather than end? . . . For where should the soules of men be after Death, but either in Heaven with Christ, or in Hell with the Divell?[111]

Damnable are all the assertions, that maintaine the mortality of the soule: for if shee did perishe with the body, and had no sense & feeling after death: how can the godly after death bee in Gods presence . . . ?[112]

. . . shall wee, certaine that there is a Life hereafter full of unspeakable felicitie, bee affraid of the way which GOD hath ordained as a passage to it?[113]

Why weep we any more, seeing all teares are wiped from their eyes?[114]

. . . for what is death to the people of God? what is it to them to die?[115]

I have a greater [inheritance] after the death of this body, and shall I be loath to come to that?[116]

. . . why then should the living sorow for the ded, as men which have no hope?[117]

. . . who in the sea of this tempestuous world, would not give this world to arrive at the haven of eternall happinesse?[118]

In Drummond's 1623 *Cypress Grove* this device is not an exception, but so tyrannical a rule that it resembles a neurotic compulsion:

They which forewent us did leave a room for us, and should we grieve to do the same to those which should come after us? Who, being admitted to see the exquisite rarities of some antiquary's cabinet, is grieved, all viewed, to have the curtain drawn, and give place to new pilgrims? And when the Lord of this universe hath showed us the various wonders of his amazing frame, should we take it to heart, when he thinketh time to dislodge? (pp. 26–27)

Two pages later Drummond intensifies his questioning:

But is this life so great a good that the loss of it should be so dear unto man? If it be, the meanest creatures of nature thus be happy, for they live no less than he. If it be so great a felicity, how is it esteemed of man himself at so small a rate, that for so poor gains, nay, one disgraceful word, he will not stand to lose it? What excellency is there in it, for the which he should desire it perpetual, and repine to be at rest, and return to his old Grandmother Dust? Of what moment are the labours and actions of it, that the interruption and leaving-off of them should be to him so distasteful, and with such grudging lamentations received? Is not the entering into life weakness? the continuing sorrow? (pp. 28–29)

And over the next twenty-five short pages, some forty more such questions are shored against our mortal ruin.

Perhaps there is an echo of "O, Death where is thy sting?" in some of these questions,[119] but I suspect they also reflect a kind of rhetorical brinkmanship, an expedient generated by a double bind that increasingly skeptical Jacobean audiences imposed on their preachers. On the one hand, to pretend that death was not immensely mysterious and terrifying would be to forfeit all relevance to the fears of skeptics. Straightforward assertions that death is a blessing sound very hollow to modern readers, and in this the Jacobeans were evidently our contemporaries, because such assertions diminish rapidly in the literature of consolation around the beginning of the seventeenth century. On the other hand, to admit that death is mysterious and terrifying would contradict a consolation fundamental to the appeal of Christianity. As Donne notes in the *Devotions* (p. 30), "I should belie *Nature*, if I should deny that I feard this, & if I should say that I feared *death*, I should belye *God*." In other words, this rhetorical quirk reflects the same contradiction as the logical quirk whereby strenuous rational refutations of the atheistical position were accompanied by denials that any rational person could hold that position. Both quirks indicate declining confidence in divine providence.

Jacobean mourners faced an agonizing ambivalence, parallel to the double bind imposed on preachers. Faced with the apparent failure of Christianity to cure mortality, they needed to express their bewilderment without quite accusing God of dereliction; so, through rhetorical questions, they half-heartedly accused themselves. When Jonson's epitaph "On My First Son" asks "why / Will man lament the state he should envy?" (5–6) the huge ambivalence of the poem comes into focus. Donne's Holy Sonnet on the death of his wife asks God, "why should I begg more Love, when as thou / Dost woe my soul, for hers" (9–10); yet clearly he cannot quite satisfy himself with the bargain. Preachers could demand of a widow, "Is not God to you in stead of ten husbands?"[120] But the implied answer does not erase what provoked the question.

The rhetorical question was a device for entrapping and disguising mortality-anxiety, and shaming it into silence. It resembles a psychoanalytic reaction-formation, coping with an unacceptable idea or impulse by representing it as its opposite. But death remained an unanswered question in many minds, and if we break the rhetorical spell that kept these anxieties suspended, we are left with a real question: why should death (the cessation of life, not death-throes or damnation) have been so terrifying in a culture supposedly saturated with Christian belief?[121]

Many Renaissance attempts to reconcile the fear of death and mourn-ing for the dead with the Christian idea of heaven have an air of rationalization. The promise of afterlife provided a way of moderating the otherwise uncontainable grief of the bereaved: "Egyptians mourne unmeasureably, as thinking death to be a destruction of all things; *Joseph* as a Christian, hopefully expecting the promise of Resurrection."[122] A primary function of religion is to restore measure to the infinite, which threatens to destroy the sanity of the living world; but, again, the necessity of a consolation does not prove the validity of that consolation. The quest for *The Meane in Mourning* (the title of a Jacobean funeral sermon by Thomas Playfere) seems to constitute an illogical compro-mise in the choice between an infinitely blessed or an infinitely meaning-less universe—as if the preachers were not quite sure they had the votes to push through an absolute affirmation of Christianity, and sought instead a compromise resolution.

The familiar association of Christianity with light becomes, through-out the seventeenth century, a rhetorical resource for extorting ortho-dox Christian belief from those who fear that death will impose an immeasurable darkness. Citing Augustine's belief that in hell, "flame shall burne them, without affording light at all," Jean Pierre Camus warns that unredeemed death enforces "so deepe a blindnes, and so deadly a numnesse" that no man could stand the thought of it. For those who have eyes but will not see the Christian revelation in life, this kind of death is poetic justice.[123] Timothy Oldmayne warns that "godlesse persons . . . have no reason at all to looke for the Resurrection day . . . sith to them it will bee a day of Darknesse, and not light."[124] Thomas Adams uses the same associations to condemn "Atheists such as have voluntarily, violently extinguished to themselves the Sun-light of the Scripture" out of a shortsighted desire to "act the workes of darkenesse."[125] The "Pastour" in Zacharie Boyd's *Last Battle of the Soul in Death* (1629) tells a fearful man, "This heere is your griefe, that death will strik you with a blindness"—a grief suiting only a pagan, because "though both his eyes should sinke downe into his head, or droppe out like blobbes or droppes of water," the Christian shall still "see his Redeemer." "Once I sat in *darkenesse*," Boyd later proclaims; "hee is now my *Light*. Once I was in *death*, hee is now my *Life*." Again the association is conventional enough, but it is worth noticing what the analogy assumes about death, and about the human fear of death as "a place of silence" and a "dungeon of darknesse."[126] A decade later the same manipulative metaphors persist: for true Christians, death is actually an escape from "a darke dungeon . . . to the light"; the fear of death is only "for those who are blinded with the Mist Atheisme and Impiety."[127] By making light a figuration of Christian morality, then letting the metaphor collapse to a literal level, such commentators can subliminally exploit our instinctive fear of the dark, which annihilationism infinitely intensifies.

As the seventeenth century progresses, the annihilationist notion of sensory deprivation becomes increasingly explicit. Jean Paget describes the decay of sight and hearing in human senescence as a warning of what is to follow, leaving the visionary soul as the only consolation "when the eyes of the body . . . beginne to be darke."[128] *A Mourning-Ring* asserts that "The Grave, into which we are all going, is a place of silence," that the fear of death is augmented by "a natural fear of darkness," and that "*by shutting their Eyes and Mouth,* we do intimate, that the dead are no more to take delight in the Objects of this visible World."[129] According to Thomas Fuller, "our Atheist hath a dead palsey, is past all sense, and cannot perceive God who is everywhere presented unto him,"[130] as if the disbeliever's life were infected by the oblivion he must envision beyond it. Clearly these writings evince anxiety in seventeenth-century England about the oblivion of death, whether one chooses to interpret them as efforts to cure that anxiety or to exploit it. Furthermore, this fear is not the product of some bizarre antique *episteme*; the same anxieties are still visible in stories of near-death experiences, which commonly feature an intense white light summoning from the beyond, a light generally read as a manifestation—indeed, a verification—of Christian afterlife.

Royal deaths provide a special instance of this pattern; perhaps the notion that the monarch embodied the nation allowed a release of annihilationist anxieties through a suggestion that subjects are rendered senseless by the royal demise. Arthur Gorges's poem on the death of Prince Henry claims that

> My Muse did want her selfe, my sence was nume,
> My heart grew faint, my quicker power grew slow,
> Myne eyes weare dimme, my tongue was taken dumbe,
> My inke no longer from my penn would flowe,
>   For inke, tongue, eyes, power, hart, sence, muse, apawled,
>   Became thick dumbe dymme, slow, faint nume, and stald.[131]

Thomas Newton's funeral poem for Queen Elizabeth persistently associates death with blindness, which the mourners acquire as a sort of hysterical sympathetic symptom.[132] An elegy written in the last year of King James's life similarly describes how all five senses are emptied by the process of mourning, characterizing death as "deafe, and blind," and the grave as "eternall night"; the poet later warns that "our passions must not for ever transport us into obscurity and darknesse" which "will in a moment change our dazling into starke blindnes"; and urges therefore, "let not our eies take any rest" until they have seen "the true path" to heaven.[133]

REPRESENTING DEATH

> Art eyther perfits nature, or doth imitate it. This for imitation hath nothing, because death is nothing but the corruption of Nature, the defect and privation of life, the divorce and dissolution of our essentiall parts. . . . Art therfore must perfit this deformity more truly in the maske wherewith it come covered then in the thing it selfe which is without horrour, unles it be of such as our selves cast upon it.[134]

If the Jacobeans were "much possessed by death" (as T. S. Eliot suggested in "Whispers of Immortality"), that fascination with mortality does not finally acquit them of denying it. In fact, many of the macabre gestures associated with this culture are ultimately legible as evasions of the full implications of death. The grotesquely redundant practice of Renaissance executions, in which a man might be hanged, disembowelled, beheaded, drawn and quartered, and burnt at the stake, implies that the punitive power of the state is not circumscribed by the boundary between life and death, as it would be if death were absolute oblivion.[135] A more avowedly dramatic version of this over-kill, in which a single character is murdered more than once (as in *The Jew of Malta* and *The Revenger's Tragedy*), similarly resists the idea that death is a single and absolute event; at the same time, these depictions invite our uneasy laughter at a denial we commonly practice, the unarticulated belief that the corpse cares how gently it is treated. Nor—considering Jonson's epitaph on his first daughter and Laertes' farewell to his sister— can this dissonance be explained away by claiming that Jacobeans were somehow unable to project tenderness toward corpses as we do. Another common stage practice of the period—bringing heroines such as Desdemona and the Duchess of Malfi briefly back from a breathless demise—also encourages spectators to deny the simple finality of death.[136] Presumably that is why Shakespeare hints at such a moment at the end of *King Lear*, and why his stubborn refusal to fulfill that hint has proved so devastating to the morale of audiences. A later chapter will argue that George Herbert attempts to console his readers by systematically differentiating death from closural silence.

Epidemics, especially bubonic plague, pressed death to the forefront of Renaissance consciousness, but largely as a problem of public health and an occasion for conventional moral admonition. If "Th'all-conquering Pox" is a "forraine guest / The Divell-instructed *Indies* to us sold / To recompense the filching of their Gold," and if the plague is "a dreary Punishment, Heaven's curse,"[137] then at least death is part of a political and providential narrative. As in public executions and Augustinian theology, construing death as punishment returns it to the realm of human meaning. Contagion without guilt would come too close to demonstrating that death is an ordinary unpleasant fact of our bodies that no retribution can correct: "By one another (strange!) so many di'de / And yet no murder here, no Homocide."[138]

The macabre imagery that the plague helped to provoke is generally assumed to reflect an unmediated confrontation with death; but illustrating and moralizing the stages of decay is only a conditional surrender of denial, since it allowed people to focus on a gradual process rather than on the absurdly binary shift from a unity to a nullity of consciousness. Along with the *danse macabre* and the morality play, morbid illustrations helped capture death within the arena of ritual and representation. If it is true that, in sixteenth-century England, "We rarely find the word 'death' used alone; it is qualified by some descriptive phrase which at once brings it sharply before our eyes,"[139] perhaps that is because Elizabethans needed to contextualize and visualize death, in order to forestall the terrors of an infinite darkness. Making death a voice rather than a silence, a visible agency rather than a Black Hole, removes its nihilistic sting.[140] Portraying the deceased in the *transi* mode of tomb statuary, which showed the corpse in putrefaction, placed kinetic decay back in the containment of static art; placing such statuary inside a church was a further act of containment (and bravado). Even the ferocious Renaissance disputes about the proper path to the afterlife could have been consoling, if they distracted people from the idea that there might be no destination.

One could hardly call consoling the terrifying depictions of hellfire in sermons and paintings; but they did powerfully preclude any supposition that the senses would merely expire. Perhaps this is why "it was detailed vividness which seemed the essence" of Medieval visions of purgatory.[141] People were drawn to such depictions even while professing themselves horrified, as we are to scenes of violent death in action movies and news reports, and partly for the same reason: because their contingency and vividness helps us repress the suspicion that death consists of a banal extinction. This fear of erasure informs Abraham Holland's complaint, on the brink of his death in 1625, about "The dolefull silence of the standers by / As if they were all speechlesse, and from me / Did draw one generall stupid sympathy."[142] In 1613, Lewes Bayly's popular *The Practise of Pietie* similarly warned that "They who come to visit the sicke must have a speciall care not to stand *dumbe* and *staring* in the sicke persons face to disquiet him," as if to avoid mirroring back to the sufferer the conditions of silence and blindness that he must fear await him. Earlier in the book, Bayly notes the onset of deafness and blindness as final symptoms of the moribund.[143] If these are the fears and symptoms, then Bayly's hell is almost a relief and a cure: "There thy *lascivious Eyes* shall be afflicted with sights of *ghastly Spirits:* thy *curious Eares* shall be affrighted with hydeous noyse of *howling divels. . . .*"[144] Whatever the costs, the show must go on.

Ambivalences similarly generate contradictions in Jean Pierre Camus's 1632 *A Draught of Eternitie*, which warns "that the damned shall be in thicker obscurities than those of Egipt, and that the tempest of darknes shall possesse them for ever. . . . the eyes of the damned, though otherwise capable of sight, see nothing but that which may trouble and torment them."[145] Indeed, Camus does cite St. Thomas's argument "that the *non-esse* being considered purely in it selfe, is the evil of evils, and the most miserable condition imaginable," before going on to insist that hell must somehow be worse.[146] When Camus defines hell as "the accursed denne, where DEATH doth eternally inhabite," it sounds almost indistinguishable from the annihilationist grave. More-over, when he attempts to conjure up that hell, it looks suspiciously like a displacement of fears about the mere decay of the corpse, as he himself seems uneasily aware: "Thence that *immortall worme*, which incessantly shall gnaw them, mentioned by ISAY, a worme which S. THOMAS, and all the Doctors hold to be spirituall, not corporall. . . ."[147]

Evidence of this kind of slippage is crucial to my argument that the pious terror of damnation increasingly served as a disguise for the blasphemous terror of annihilation. Though the conventional wisdom expressed in one of Thomas Adams's sermons—"Yes, rather had they bee dead with out sense, then alive in torment"[148]—reflects a sincere and widespread belief, it does not reflect all facets of the Renaissance psyche. It was true for Milton's Moloch, but not for his Satan, and perhaps not for his Adam either. At the 1601 Rakow Colloquy, the Socinian idea that the damned would eventually be utterly annihilated was defended on the grounds that "it should be considered much more absurd if the wicked were given immortality, which is a most special gift and blessing of God."[149] Thomas Tuke thinks it worth asserting that "forso much as the soule doth survive the bodie, and live, when it is dead, it should comfort men against the dread, that death brings with it. For they shall not be *Nothing*, nor *Nowhere*."[150] It is suggestive in this regard that, as tomb sculpture was explicitly exempted from Parliamentary attacks on superstitious monuments, so images of the Last Judgment enjoyed a surprising immunity from Protestant iconoclasm in general.[151] Perhaps the annihilationist fear of perpetual blindness, already exacerbated by Reformation theology, was too disturbing to be left unrelieved by visual treatment of the scene where the dead are restored to their senses.

Protestant theology made it difficult to describe the experience of heaven as anything other than a negation of earthly experience: "The state of the bodie shall bee such as no labours or sorrowes shall seaze any more uppon it . . . the slaverie of sinne shall no more take holde of it, the flesh . . . shal no more overcrowe it, it being then at quietnesse with the spirit."[152] In Marvell's "Dialogue," the shepherd Thyrsis answers Dorinda's request for a description of life in Elysium with another series of negations and obliviations:

> Oh, there's neither hope nor fear,
> There's no wolf, no fox, no bear.
> No need of dog to fetch our stray,
> Our Lightfoot we may give away;
> No oat-pipe's needful; there thy ears
> May sleep with music of the spheres. (lines 21–26)

When another notable Puritan poet attempts to depict Death frighteningly in *Paradise Lost*, he speaks of

> The other shape,
> If shape it might be call'd that shape had none
> Distinguishable in member, joint or limb,
> Or substance might be call'd, that shadow seem'd,
> For each seem'd either; black it stood as Night. . . . [153]

Having foresworn ritual and idolatry, Puritans must have found death a difficult idea to contain.

As "The variety of Monuments hath often obscured true graves" (Browne, p. 290), so a variety of rituals have served to obscure true death. The familiar Renaissance *ars moriendi* was part of an elaborate cultural construction designed to block our view of nothingness. Voluminous meditations focused on the moment of dying as artful performance, thus putting the emphasis on technique rather than implications, on the doorway rather than the house of eternity. Most recent studies of death in Renaissance culture accept a basic Renaissance strategy of denial when they accept the rituals surrounding death as if they were death itself, and as if the moment of death could therefore subsume the eternity that follows.[154] Royal figures from Mary to Charles I, and cultural celebrities from More to Essex to Ralegh, rehearsed stage business and scripted one-liners to impress the crowds at their executions; ordinary people studied how to stage edifying death-bed dramas for their families; all as if the right kind of death could somehow defeat mortality itself. Precisely because of their theatrical and manipulative aspects, these performances must not be taken as simply the outward expressions of an inward Christian assurance. Indeed, they invite us to examine other scripts composed in the same culture, to see whether they were staged as part of, or as critique of, the same urgent task: to sustain a distinction between death and annihilation.

OUTLINE

Having introduced the skull, I now present the skeleton. This book turns first to canonical English Renaissance drama, seeking to transcribe a half-stifled cry of protest by the increasingly valued human individual against personal extinction at death. The plays suggest considerable uncertainty about the prospects of Christian afterlife, if only by searching so earnestly for alternative models of salvation and permanence. The plays then interrogate those alternative models, exposing their contradictions and insufficiencies. In the absence of a salvational theology, there are two usual ways of participating in the ancient human quest for immortality. One is to die for the ancestors' cause, renewing a heroic tribal tradition by refusing to compromise for mere survival; this symbolic defiance of death is proposed and challenged in *The Spanish Tragedy* and *Hamlet*. The other way is to renew the ancestors' likeness through procreation, in a compromise with death; this solution is proposed by the genre of comedy, with its emphasis on types and procreation, challenged in *Measure for Measure*, and bitterly abandoned in *Macbeth*.

Beneath the surface horror of Renaissance revenge-tragedy lies the reassuring implication that death is a contingent event, and that even if death occurs, it can be cured by destroying its immediate agent. Efficient cause masks first cause; mourning becomes effectual. The villain of revenge-tragedy, like the Vice of morality drama, provides a satisfyingly localized and assailable scapegoat for our inward mortal frailties. *The Spanish Tragedy* plays to these fantasies, but also raises some troubling questions about the validity of the metonymic scheme by which we imagine rescuing the people we love from death, and thereby about the entire scheme by which Christ supposedly rescues us from death by taking our place in its clutches.

In *Hamlet*, Shakespeare further excavates and examines this submerged premise of blood-revenge. As mortality progressively enforces its sovereignty, the only sanctuary is a stoic notion of honor which manifests itself variously as the father within (the superego), the father without (the ghost), or the father above (the Christian God). These paternal mandates provide the only alternative to despair, yet to obey them is to submit to an "illusion" that finally renews only death. By inviting a skeptical examination of this social function of denial, *Hamlet* challenges our common willingness to let the ghosts of our fathers tell us to kill and die defending fantasies of immortality.

Measure for Measure, like many Renaissance marriage-comedies, offers the figurative immortality offered by procreation as an alternative to literal Christian immortality. Shakespeare, however, seems intent on exposing procreation as a means of perpetuating, not the individual, but a group and a genotype that exploit the illusion of personal immortality. What are happy demographic solutions for the society as a whole never quite eclipse the psychologically terrible redundancy they imply for the individual caught in the cycles of nature. *Macbeth* reprises this argument in a more imagistic mode, converting its surface concern with royal succession into a parable about the ways time exposes the futility of our aspirations toward individual importance. In both plays, beneath the seeming benevolence of divine justice, natural order, and political legitimacy looms an uncaring machine allied with mere biological process.

The tendency to seek immortality through the physical legacy of progeny (conventionally construed as a female project) thus receives no more convincing an endorsement in Shakespearean drama than the tendency to seek immortality through the legacies of name and power (conventionally male concerns). Healthy and orderly reproduction, the ideal so relentlessly pursued in *Measure for Measure* and *Macbeth*, proves no less illusory than the motivating ghost in *Hamlet*, no less dependent on pietistic deception and denial. A radically communal solution to death is no more satisfactory than a radically individualist one.

Unless we stage a quixotic rebellion against material reality, we remain subject to the relentless, mindless logic of biological nature. Believing in ghosts is arguably a destructive pathology, yet accepting our status as material and mortal beings hardly assures happiness and ethical progress. According to Freud, the undoing of neurotic repression through psychotherapy could promise only to turn "hysterical misery into common unhappiness";[155] similarly, undoing the denial of death may only replace the haunted world of *Hamlet* with the pain and sorrow of *King Lear*, at once extraordinary and all too common. A world of cyclical violence gives way to an entropic universe in which nothing will come of something. The final scene of this most final of tragedies systematically undoes the mythologies that represent death as curable, tolerable, or in any legitimate way consolable. All we are left with is the bare necessity of our denial. Nahum Tate—the playwright whose happy-ending revision of *King Lear* held the stage exclusively, by popular demand, for over 150 years—was English culture's equivalent of the individual's protective superego, the agency of denial. That superego imposes a lie, as Tate imposes a corrupted text; yet to read the world any other way is to risk losing our moral bearings completely. Though considerations of space and morale have dissuaded me from treating *King Lear* extensively in this book, it should be acknowledged here as the brooding absent presence of my argument.

The story of King Lear would certainly seem a period to such as love not sorrow. But always to make Shakespeare the end of the story, the moral of the story, and the bridge to modern skepticism is much too facile. Most of the "alternative Shakespeares" critics have recently generated seem designed to prove that, in our modern academic enlightenment, we all understand what only *he* knew then, a newly decodable message about semiotic indeterminacy, women's disempowerment, or the material base. Shakespeare is handy for revisionist cultural historians, since his multivocal genius can be made to speak against itself and to speak across all the apparent gaps of cultural history. To make my argument proof of anything more than the elusive and illusionist qualities of Shakespeare's art, as they empower the ironizing critic, I thought it important to look also at canonical authors who were more closely associated with the orthodox Christian thought of the period, and were working in a genre inherently more univocal than drama.

The second half of the book therefore studies another literary form characteristic of Jacobean culture: the Metaphysical lyric, as practiced by John Donne and George Herbert, which provides further evidence of literature's uneasy complicity in a conspiracy to obstruct mortal terror. By combining these studies of drama and poetry into a single book, I hope to demonstrate cultural patterns that extend beyond a single author or genre. The pursuit of immortality through symbolic abstraction links the revenge tragedies to Donne; the acceptance of cyclical renewal and bodily destiny links the plays of progeny to Herbert.

Many of Donne's trademark gestures—his conceited valedictory departures, his pursuit of an abstract mutuality with his beloved, his misogyny when that mutuality falters—can be productively read as displacements of his anxieties about his mortal body. His egoism would have made him especially susceptible to the annihilationist fears of his culture, and his secular lyrics reveal a desperate and elaborate mythmaking in which erotic love compulsively undertakes the salvational work ordinarily performed by Christianity.

Herbert, by contrast, seems ostentatiously unanxious about death, yet that very ostentation suggests an effort to answer an unspeakable terror—if not for himself, then for his troubled compatriots. In *The Temple*, this country parson repeatedly constructs his lyrics as models of salvation, surrogates of immortality. As linear sequence consumes these fragile, beautiful entities, they fall not into an endless silence but into the saving eternal word of God; the white space is heaven and not oblivion. In this way the formal structures of the poetry abet its explicit Christian argument by insisting on the distinction between physical closure and spiritual termination.

Since the current critical climate encourages reading Renaissance literature in relation to monarchs, it seems worth noting that the works I have identified with radical symbolic solutions to the problem of mortality—*The Spanish Tragedy*, *Hamlet*, and most of Donne's erotic lyrics—were written in the second half of Queen Elizabeth's reign; at a time, in other words, when the idea of perpetuity at the center of the society had to be invested in ingenious and sometimes violent assertions of the Virgin Queen's inviolability. Perhaps English culture was preparing the society for a metaphysical succession. The works I have identified with a contrastingly simple idea of filial renewal, and the biological mode of immortality—*Measure for Measure*, *Macbeth*, and Herbert's *The*

Temple—were instead written under Stuart monarchs who had sons ready to sustain the royal identity indefinitely into the future.

Clearly this book could have gone on indefinitely as well, but unredeemed death is hardly a topic to live with. Some obvious examples, such as Webster and Burton, remain untouched; but obvious examples are not the best ones if the goal is to demonstrate the way annihilationism manifests itself through evasive resistances. The fact that the fears become more explicit in Caroline authors helps verify my suspicion that it was nascent in Jacobean ones; but explicit statements, by definition, need no explication, and I will leave them to speak for themselves. The only others I try to speak for are the two women discussed in my Epilogue, whose deathbed crises not only confirm that Christian faith was far from stable in Tudor-Stuart England, but also suggest that it sometimes exacerbated rather than alleviated the pain of mortality.

If the book has any ethical thrust, it arises from the suspicion that the dogs of war are still being loosed, and the knots of repression are still being tied, in order to sustain and conceal the conspiracy of faith. This occurs not only through explicit religious inquisitions, but also through compulsive efforts to verify the fantasy that mortal erasure is the fate of an unworthy Other, a fantasy that societies regularly enforce by attacking competing societies and alternative cultures, that men enforce by silencing women, that humans enforce by casually enslaving other animals—and that we at times enforce against ourselves, by repressing our bodily existence. Popular drama, a public and collaborative form, primarily explores the ethical and political diseases produced by the need to disbelieve in mortality. Lyric poetry, generally a more private and individual expression, primarily explores the psychological diseases produced by the same need. Together they allow an investigation of the causes and costs of the denial of death.

CRITICISM AND CHRISTIANITY

If I were to say that I had devoted myself to the study of the Christian religion because nothing else can so effectually rescue the lives and minds of men from those two detestable curses, slavery and superstition. . . . If I communicate the result of my inquiries to the world at large . . . with a friendly and benignant feeling towards mankind . . . I hope to meet with a candid reception from all parties, and that none at least

> will take unjust offence, even though many things should be
> brought to light which will at once be seen to differ from
> certain received opinions.[156]

> To fill up the Measure of their Iniquities, as *Menasse Ben
> Israel* informs us, the Hereticks endeavored to draw the
> inspired Authors also into a Society and Partnership of their
> Atheism and Infidelity.[157]

Is it possible to suggest that Christianity has controlled academic discourse concerning canonical Renaissance literature, or to question more generally the validity of religiosity in critical practices, without courting sharp animosity and charges of reductionism? The question may seem odd, since the proportion of evangelical Christians among American university professors is doubtless far below the national average, and fundamentalist students have often found their perspective unwelcome in elite classrooms. Yet Christianity, as Jonathan Culler observes, has enjoyed a peculiar exemption from the kinds of critique now commonly visited on other cultural institutions.[158] Seeing little tact or profit in stirring this hornets' nest, and fearful perhaps of aggravating the anti-intellectualism of the American mainstream, even non-Christian historicists have located the agencies of reaction and repression in adjacent practices, rather than in religion itself. When they enumerate the crimes of a cultural colonialism that travelled under the banner of Christianity, for example, or argue that the Christianized Chain of Being model protected an unjust political status quo, critics still tend to imply that Christianity has been distorted and abused by secular forces; that despite its emphasis on punishment and submission, authority and hierarchy, Christianity should be presumed innocent of the crimes committed in its name; that the problem lies in the materialist exploitation of religion, rather than in the tendencies religion empowers within the human psyche.

Nothing as complex in its history and implications as Christianity could be proven basically destructive—or basically anything else. In fact, in their search for a repressive hegemony to condemn, New Historicists have generally ignored the progressive aspects of the church's influence.[159] Citing occasions when institutional Christianity has seemingly betrayed its own principles—Crusades, Inquisitions, affiliation with genocidal campaigns of various sorts—is considered acceptable, if a little trite. After all, the Reformation itself implied that institutional Christianity is a paradox if not an oxymoron, that the church tends to betray the original principles of the Gospel. But publicly questioning the intellectual validity of religiosity itself is commonly viewed as a violation of privacy, perhaps even as an incitement to holy war.

When different beliefs collide, they are bound to compete. Even when they make no explicit attempt to conquer each other, their very juxtaposition does violence to a deep human need to understand one's own belief-system as something more than an arbitrary choice. The controversial campaigns for multicultural sensitivity on campuses often overlook the contrary priorities of universities and cultures: universities exist largely to encourage the testing of ideas against other ideas (by a common standard of rationalism), whereas cultures exist largely for the sake of providing the human mind with stable and coherent explanations.[160] The benign tone of contemporary mainstream Christianity, and the popular consensus supporting it, often conceal the fundamental aggressiveness it shares with other belief-systems. This produces a double standard whereby audible assertions of atheism strike most observers as a tasteless and even malicious affront to Christian believers, whereas ordinary assertions of Christian belief are considered nothing other than the practice of spiritual freedom. The pietism of most studies of Donne and Herbert is no more dangerous than a crèche in front of City Hall at Christmastime, but perhaps no less dangerous, either. The fact that such gestures are not generally seen as sectarian and exclusionary is precisely what proves they are part of a drift toward spiritual coercion.

The study of religion seems to be emerging from its strange eclipse in Renaissance cultural studies. Some critics have surely been deterred from this topic by the massive reading in classical languages that it has always demanded, as well as by the recognition that scholarly glory is now usually won by trumping the past, not by following its strong suits. New Historicists may have had further cause to avoid the topic of religion, since they seek to expose the conspiracies and mythographic disguises of established power, and Christian religion was explicitly a conspiracy that felt no need to disguise its reliance on pure belief. Furthermore, New Historicism commonly seeks to expose the way hegemonies of power in a society secretly construct the moral interiority of individuals, and again Christianity was unabashedly explicit about that project.

But surely the interrogation of the way official power redefined extreme punishment as a manifestation of its own benevolence would apply corrosively to the very heart of Christianity, which can function as a religion of forgiveness only because it is founded on a religion of punishment. Like the other controlling agencies, Christianity generates the subversion it calls sin to enable the containment it calls grace; it demands our grateful submission because it forgives the inward crimes it has invented and authorized itself to discipline. What if the formulaic New Historicist essay that begins with a stunningly gruesome narrative of execution were to begin instead with one of the no less horrible descriptions of Crucifixion, or gloating descriptions of damnation, from the period? Why do critics who freely make English Renaissance writers into sophisticated Marxists, deconstructionists, and French feminist Freudians, suppose those same writers utterly incapable of questioning the premises, purposes, and moral validity of these holy terrors, which imprinted themselves on the bodies as well as the minds of so many people? That sort of questioning would have been a logical outgrowth, not only of Protestant accusations against the Roman church, but also of the special miseries the resulting schism imposed on Elizabethans. Yet with few exceptions,[161] New Historicists have proven reluctant to inquire into the dynamics of that cultural negotiation, where materialist philosophy rather than material competition becomes the engine of potential subversion. Considering the extensive skepticism of the Jacobeans and the extraordinary religiosity of most Americans,[162] one may wonder whether the argument that our secular culture must not presume to interpret the Renaissance in our own terms is itself partly an act of denial, an effort by intellectuals to project aspects of contemporary America that do not fit our image of a secular state into an Other culture where they can be safely contained.

Moreover, other methodologies arguably better suited to criticize religion have swerved carefully around it. The tacit agreement to do so becomes most evident in the public gauntlet imposed on those who violate it. Jonathan Culler cites the example of William Empson, whose resistance to the pietism of English criticism was dismissed by Denis Donoghue in the *T.L.S.* as "the most tedious part of [Empson's] mind," and "not the work of a gentleman."[163] Robert Adams's review of Culler's book in the U.S. equivalent of the powerful *T.L.S.*, the *New York Review of Books*, calls the chapter defending Empson "a youthfully harsh assault on religion, primarily Christian religion."[164] The similarity of Donoghue's response and Adams's is revealing. Both seem to say, there is of course something undeveloped about these non-religious sensibilities; we all know it, and hardly need to say a further word about it.

In a widely anthologized essay, C. S. Lewis dismisses atheism and related skepticisms as "boys' philosophies," a phrase he likes so well he says it again, contrasting these "boys' philosophies" to the obvious "manliness" of Manichaean and (especially) Anglican belief.[165] To call such *ad puerum* arguments logically weak is only half the story; the other half is the presumption of a cultural dominance that will protect the weaknesses from serious challenge. Even these leading intellectuals seem to prefer the intimidating power of popular consensus to free debate; even in the secular academy, the atheistical hypothesis must struggle for a fair hearing. This is probably an unexamined legacy from the first half of this century, when literary criticism (particularly of the earlier periods) was dominated by two groups: devout Christians, and Jews wary of losing their tiny crevices of entry into the traditional academy. Particularly in English departments, secular American critics still often feel obligated to try to pass for erudite Edwardian vicars.[166] The time has come to re-examine that legacy, and perhaps to repair the historically conditioned imbalance. The tone struck by Denis Donoghue and C.S. Lewis—somewhere between snide and regretful—is reminiscent of the anti-Semitism pervasive in British aristocratic culture, which associates Judaism with vulgarity, or at best with an undeveloped Christianity. The fist is rather more velvet than most of those by which entrenched belief-systems have historically attacked dissenters, but it is still a fist; and it seems prudent to confront the problem before the next time the gloves come off.

Such a confrontation may seem small-minded and mean-spirited when Christianity is understood as a faith preciously and privately held by one's neighbors; yet, when it is understood as a dominant idea and practice of society, not to question it seems irresponsible. In another prominent review, Donoghue concludes his attack on several recent studies of the Bible as literature by wondering wistfully why such critics would want "to offend people who choose to live their lives in religious terms, in community and prayer. Why not leave them alone?"[167] The few critics who offer a dissenting view of the most powerful book in our culture suddenly appear as an arrogant and brutish horde battering down the walls of the last monastery and torturing the mild charitable monks.

The intention of this book is certainly not to insult Christian believers by despoiling their relics, nor even to pretend that Christianity is irrelevant in the study of Jacobean literature. I have assumed, however, that religious responses to death can be analyzed as psychological responses, in a particular historical matrix, to hard facts that are largely beyond history. This argument depends on a Freudian model of the divided psyche to this extent: it supposes that a mind devoted on one level to Christian faith could find itself in frequent subliminal skirmishes against the demurrals of another, more skeptical part of that mind. This hardly strikes me as a radical proposition; in fact, it seems fundamental to Renaissance Christianity, from Calvin to Hooker.[168] One Jacobean cleric wrote an entire book using the precedent of Doubting Thomas to legitimize the doubts his fellows were evidently reluctant to admit, doubts particularly about resurrection, a doctrine he admitted ran against all reason: "unbelief possesseth men every manner of way, and there is no man in the world altogether free from it, though it be a great deal more in some than other."[169] Another reminds us, "We must know that these two thoughts, *There is a God*, and *there is no God*, may be, and are both in one and the same heart. . . ."[170] Burton's discussion of atheistic despair in *The Anatomy of Melancholy* similarly concedes "that no living man is free from such thoughts in part."[171] Yet several colleagues have already felt compelled to remind me that these authors were, after all, Christians in a Christian land, and so any traces of annihilationism I detect in their writings must result from my anachronistic misreadings.

Implicit endorsements from canonical authors are precious commodities, claimed (through explication or biography) by interpreters working on behalf of many competing belief-systems—including several, such as psychoanalysis, not ordinarily considered religious. Presumably my mistrust of institutional religion partly impels me to retrieve these Renaissance authors from their supposedly uncompromised allegiance to Christian doctrine.[172] As I believe that literature should be more than a mystified symptom of social illness, an artifact dispensed and manipulated by critics, so I believe that spiritual life should be more than an evasive maneuver provoked by the threat of personal annihilation, a consolation dispensed and manipulated by an institutional church.

Finally, I believe that a scholar's duty toward the cultural consensus is in large part the duty of an opposition party—even if that only means keeping power honest, keeping the social incentives to any consensus from exaggerating the factual basis of that consensus. There is as much enlightenment to be gained in the undoing of denial as in the filling of ignorance; the ideas and truths lost in the daily process of collective cultural repression are probably as many and as precious as in the imperfect process of cultural transmission over centuries. Since the fear of personal annihilation has generated a large part of that repression, I have tried to use my grasp of English Renaissance literature to lift up (with all the discomfort this metaphor implies) a corner of the vault in which the fact of death still lies hidden.

ENVOY

> Assure thy selfe, whosoever readeth this booke, that ere many yeares, or decades of months be past, Death (mounted on his pale horse) will rap at thy doore, and alight, & carry thee away (bound head and foote) to a land darke as darknesse it selfe.[173]

> . . . how many physitians who once looked so grimme, and so tetrically shrunk their browes upon their patients, are dead and gone themselves. How many Astrologers, after that in great ostentation they had foretold the death of some others; how many Philosophers after so many elaborate tracts and volumes concerning either mortalitie, or immortalitie. . . . [174]

If I were to say I am dying, and in this I am not any different from you, it might sound sensationalistic; yet anyone could justly make that pronouncement. Three important premises of this book follow from that fact. The first is that, particularly in relation to mortality, human beings have a great deal in common. The second is that language can capture some of those connections, meaning that my experience can bear on yours, and those of Jacobean authors can bear on ours. The third is that, in speaking about mortality, submission will always appear to carry a subtext of bravado, and bravado of submission.

To hold a psychoanalytic view of the self and an annihilationist view of the universe is to suspect that most stable forms of human happiness depend on skillful self-deception, and that most stubborn forms of mental illness arise from self-deceptions so awkward that they must be defended fanatically. But is there any heroic middle ground to be claimed by staring into the face of a God who is not there? A *New Yorker* cartoon by Edward Koren shows a huge toothy monster hovering ominously over a cozy suburban couple, who are telling friends seated on the opposite sofa, "We deal with it by talking about it." Writing this book has been that kind of ludicrously inadequate gesture toward mastery. Perhaps (in the tradition of *Everyman* as well as Montaigne) I am maintaining an unpleasant vigil on the grounds that death comes when least anticipated, as in childhood I forestalled nightmares by deliberately going to sleep with the most frightening possible images in my conscious mind, a concession which dissuaded them from attacking in the subconscious realm of dreams.[175]

In retrospect, my ostensibly objective research has been shaped by personal concerns. The son of a psychologist and a literary critic, I wrote an ambitious book of psychoanalytic criticism claiming that Shakespeare's ambitious young men always submit to their heritage in the effort to transcend it. As a tenure decision approached, I wrote a book of practical criticism about the strategies of professional literary competition; in arguing that Ben Jonson outpositioned rival playwrights by placing their characters belittlingly in his own satiric context, I repeatedly positioned rival Jonson critics belittlingly in the context of my own overarching theory. This is not to imply that nothing is now left for me but death; only that I decided to approach this pattern more honestly this time, or at least more actively, and to see whether Renaissance literature could help me confront fears that have weighed on me since childhood.

Surely I am not alone in this, and I could probably have spared the Jacobeans by seeking a support group in my own social world, but embarrassment forbade me to confess such sophomoric concerns. That same embarrassment, however, helped me recognize the taboos by which my own culture keeps this unspeakable topic unspoken, and to recognize that Renaissance writers might have been circumventing an earlier and fiercer version of that taboo. In the past few years, when asked what I was working on, I have been able to answer with a single conversation-staggering syllable: "death." After an instant of blinking silence, most people react with concern for my health; scholars often follow that with warnings about anachronism. Both those reactions bespeak denial, the belief that we have "no need to trouble [ourselves] with any such thoughts yet" (as Mistress Quickly told the dying Falstaff about God), or that we have no need to trouble ourselves about them any more (as the modern technological approach to the body often seems to suggest).

But I have always loathed the macabre, and now that the book is nearly finished, I am relieved to see that it is less about death itself than about "the feare of death, which presseth us all our life,"[176] and less about the fear of death than about what that fear allows us to examine: the ways culture helps us place our circumscribed individual experience satisfactorily in a seemingly infinite and indifferent universe. The ways a culture handles, not the material problems of death, but the psychological problems of mortality, is a window into the way human beings construct a world they can travel in, whatever their actual destination.

1

Religio Vindicis

Substitution and Immortality
in *The Spanish Tragedy*

> *'Tis not onely the mischiefe of diseases, and the villanie of
> poysons that make an end of us, we vainly accuse the fury
> of Gunnes, and the new inventions of death. . . . There is
> therefore but one comfort left, that though it be in the
> power of the weakest arme to take away life, it is not in
> the strongest to deprive us of death: God would not
> exempt himselfe from that. . . .*
>
> —Sir Thomas Browne,
> *Religio Medici* (p. 115)

As a reliable end to mortal suffering, death may sometimes be a "comfort," but not even Browne can confront its inevitability
without a hint of vengefulness against its "villanie." As Renaissance
Christians called their own mortality God's benign justice rather than
His brutal retaliation, so they interpreted Christ's mortality as voluntary.
Like Shakespeare's Othello preparing to throw away a pearl richer than
all his tribe, they could not bear to call a murder what they had thought
a sacrifice (5.2.247–48, 64–65). But revenge against the God who
imposed death would have been a natural impulse; killing His son would

have been an apt expression of it; and guilt-ridden worship of that son would have been the predictable aftermath. Construing Christ's death as our redemption into eternal life performs the classic delusional function of revenge. Revenge commonly proposes to repeal a loss by imposing an equivalent loss on the entity that caused it, and blood-revenge implies that life can be restored like stolen property.

By displacing it into an earthly political crisis, Thomas Kyd can expose the retaliatory feud between humanity and God. And by displacing the pious rituals of his culture into pagan analogues, he can threaten to expose the emptiness of the consolations they offer, the lack of any ultimate stable referent behind the signifiers of immortality. As the Renaissance church divides and falters in its assurances concerning personal immortality, and as personal identity acquires its own kind of sacredness, English literature struggles to provide a system of compensation for the loss of each human life. Famous as a kind of prop-room for later Renaissance tragedy, *The Spanish Tragedy* is a similarly compendious collection of these anxious experiments in substitution, partly consoling the audience by enacting the compensatory formulas, and partly exposing the delusive aspects of those formulas.

All the permutations that will prove crucial in sustaining the morale of English Renaissance culture are here prominently displayed: parents (such as Hieronimo) whose immortality is precariously located in a child, whose death they can only mimic to sustain the identification; mourning symbols (such as the bloody scarf) that conjure the dead into a synecdochic presence; lovers whose exchanges boast of a timeless transcendence; art that can erect and resurrect representations of life; above all, revengers who convert the villain into a scapegoat for mortality itself, and imagine that relegating the villain into death will somehow liberate his victim back into life. Kyd pioneers, on the English stage, this absurd version of homeopathic medicine—death curing death—which I believe lies near the heart of the drama of blood-revenge.[1]

Revenge-tragedy has in common with marriage-comedy—and with orthodox Christianity—the function of figuratively curing mortality. As marriage promises to replace us with our progeny in the realm of life, so blood-revenge promises to replace us with our killers in the realm of death. No wonder blood-revenge often becomes black-comically hyperbolic in Jacobean tragedy, as revengers seek a dosage adequate to achieve the desired cure; and no wonder audiences tend to sympathize with even these sadistic excesses. A spectator need not have a murdered relative, only a dead one, to share the sense of betrayal and futility that generates dramatic avengers.

The Spanish Tragedy invites us to join an embittered ghost in watching a series of plays-within-plays, staged by personifications of revenge, that tell the ultimate villain, "Death, thou shalt die." Mortality becomes a game of tag, played with swords, in which only one person is "it" at a time; and the loser is the person who dies with no one left alive on whom his death can be avenged. This agon becomes particularly urgent when the procreative alternative has failed. Indeed, the ultimate punishment of the King and Viceroy seems to be precisely that they are left without the means to resist mortality: not only without progeny, but also with no one living on whom they can enact the sort of revenge that gives Hieronimo such satisfaction. The afterlife of lovers and the afterlife of soldiers—the two heavens of *The Spanish Tragedy*—are equally lost to them.

In both the play and the plays within it, death seems only too prominent. But exaggeration can be a tool of denial, and death here is systematically unwritten—or overwritten, so that it remains legible only in palimpsest, only in its living legacies. Revenge promises Don Andrea that in subsequent scenes "thou shalt see the author of thy death, / Don Balthazar, the prince of Portingale, / Depriv'd of life by Bel-imperia" (1.1.87–89). When Isabella finds her husband lamenting over their murdered son's body, she exclaims, "What world of grief—My son Horatio! / O where's the author of this endless woe?" Hieronimo replies in the vocabulary of Revenge: "To know the author were some ease of grief, / For in revenge my heart would find relief" (2.5.38–41).[2] Nothing could be a clearer ad hominem fallacy than the claim that death can be corrected by eliminating its "author." What is written in blood can hardly be erased. But more blood can perhaps render it comfortably illegible: the blood of an enemy, or the blood of the dying Christ effacing our mortal sins, including the Original Sin by which the first "author of our woe" made this "world of grief"—this world of death.

If the trespass that initiates the fatal cycle can be isolated in a villain, rather than universally transmitted like Adam's sin, then the human tragedy ceases to look like divine justice. If Helen Gardner is correct that the Renaissance revenger is characteristically placed "in a situation which is horrible, and felt by him and the audience to be intolerable, but for which he has no responsibility," and if the typical revenge-tragedy "does not display the hero taking a fatal step, but the hero confronted with appalling facts,"[3] then the genre was always a potential medium for a theologically subversive analysis of the problem of mortality. If J. R. Mulryne is correct that each character in *The Spanish Tragedy* "attempts to clear a little space for himself, to impose his will a little, without being able to escape the pattern of consequence established by Revenge,"[4] then the action of this play (as of *Macbeth*) is a potential allegory for the futility of all mortal strivings, an allegory that the verbal details repeatedly evoke and enrich.

THE VENGEFUL GHOST: A SYMPTOM OF ANXIETY

Revenge-tragedy commonly suggests that death is preventable as well as curable; it helps us regulate mortality-anxiety as well as mourning. By its long litanies of universally unnatural perishings, Kyd's play—like modern newscasts—implies that death is an avoidable accident of violence, not an inevitable result of decay. Mortality appears as the contingent history of Cain and Abel, not the universal legacy of Adam and Eve.[5] In the closing Chorus, Don Andrea summarizes the action:

> Horatio murder'd in his father's bower,
> Vild Serberine by Pedringano slain,
> False Pedringano hang'd by quaint device,
> Fair Isabella by herself misdone,
> Prince Balthazar by Bel-imperia stabb'd,
> The Duke of Castile and his wicked son
> Both done to death by old Hieronimo,
> My Bel-imperia fall'n as Dido fell,
> And good Hieronimo slain by himself:
> Ay, these were spectacles to please my soul.
>
> (4.5.3–12)

Didn't anyone die of age or disease in those days? Perhaps it pleased the universally doomed souls in the audience to believe not.[6]

By making death the work of murderous brothers, Kyd spares us from recognizing it as the work of Mother Nature and Father Time, who together impose the consequences of Original Sin. In the opening speech of the play, the Ghost of Don Andrea reminds us of the process of biological decay that carries us all from spring toward winter, yet describes his own death as an abrogation of that system: "But in the harvest of my summer joys / Death's winter nipp'd the blossoms of my bliss" (1.1.12–13). This could perhaps be dismissed as a random rhetorical gesture, except that Hieronimo invokes exactly the same model to lament the death of Horatio:

Had Proserpine no pity on thy youth?
But suffer'd thy fair crimson-colour'd spring
With wither'd winter to be blasted thus?
Horatio, thou art older than thy father:
Ah ruthless fate, that favour thus transforms!

(3.13.147–51)

Violence thus repeatedly—perhaps, in an odd way, consolingly—appropriates the sovereignty of mortality. For mortal beings, in other words, violence is time compressed. Tragedy abets denial by disguising time as violence.

This is Hieronimo's second explicit reference to Proserpine in less than thirty lines, and the previous act implicitly invoked her several times more. In fact, the entire play is framed as Proserpine's plot—an odd choice, unless it derives from her identity, in Renaissance mythography, as a figure of the cyclical replacement of life on earth, and hence of compromise with mortality.[7] The death of Horatio, repeatedly compared to an unseasonable destruction of spring vegetation, stands for mortality in general, and condemns it as a violation. Carried off to Hades, under-age and under protest, Proserpine, like revenge, marks death as both temporary and permanent, both a narrative contingency and a physical inevitability. As Kyd removes his story as a whole from a Christian to a pagan culture, so he specifically translates the Eden myth into the Demeter myth, further developing—and further disguising—his blasphemous critique of the orthodox interpretation of Original Sin.[8] In Kyd's garden, the ordinary person is more sinned against than sinning.

Even violent, premature deaths must be marked as aberrations, if they are as threateningly commonplace as a fatal wound in battle.[9] The murder of Horatio systematically re-enacts the death of Don Andrea, in order to reconceive it as a crime. Don Andrea appears to have died within the ordinary rules of combat, yet we find him in a vengeful rage, and his reasons are not so hard to fathom. The opening conversations among the living reflect our worst fears about how little our deaths will affect the world. The General reports a "Victory . . . with little loss" that left "All well . . . except some few / That are deceas'd by fortune of the war." But, oh, the difference to me, the Ghost of Andrea might comment. The "cheerful countenance" of this messenger would surely have bruised his ego, a fact that could have been staged quite effectively (1.2.1–7; cf. the parenthetical containment of the dead at 1.2.108). No wonder Don Andrea is so determined to have a destructive impact from beyond, and no wonder audiences have responded to him so powerfully. Our guilt about the dead we have forgotten, and our anger at those who will forget us after we die, might easily be projected together into a vengeful ghost. If it is true that in early modern Europe "The dead were widely conceived of as anxious about the neglect of the living, and on occasion menacing towards those they feared would neglect them," and if it is true that the Elizabethans as a group "dreaded nothing so much as the possibility that future generations might not know they had lived,"[10] then it is not surprising that their literature features ghosts so prominently and so ambivalently.

The Ghost of Don Andrea and the figure of Revenge conspire to punish the world of the living and thereby redeem the world of the dead. The story-frame thus indulges two fantasies common in tribal belief-systems: it portrays every death as a crime susceptible to talionic punishment among the living, and it portrays the envious dead as more volitional and more fully conscious than the living, who become merely actors in a play the dead can frame. Death hardly appears a desirable alternative to life—the pagan Club Dead, with its "slimy strond" and "ugly waves," is no threat to put Club Med out of business—yet through revenge the will of Don Andrea continues to thrive beyond his death (much as Castiza's skull in *The Revenger's Tragedy* applies the kiss of death to her murderer). Don Andrea becomes a visible agent in the drama of denial the living act out on his behalf—that is, on their own behalf, prospectively. We kill others to combat our own mortality, and war—like most other forms of hunting—is partly a ritual enabling us to disguise this symbolic project as practical competition. By highlighting the psychological underpinnings of blood-revenge, *The Spanish Tragedy* removes that disguise.

In *The Spanish Tragedy*, metonymy is the master-trope of immortality; but perhaps it makes the merely figurative status of that trope dangerously visible. In a sense the play is itself a metonymic substitution, replacing the rituals of death erased by the Reformation. The essential passivity of the Protestant soul in its own salvation, the doctrine of soul-sleeping maintained for a time by Calvin and other reformers, and the colorlessness of many Protestant burials, all threaten to associate death with mere oblivion. Kyd responds to that threat by offering the spectacle of Don Andrea struggling toward a vividly drawn afterworld, and (in the Chorus following act 3) by overcoming Don Andrea's horror at the inert figure of Revenge with an assurance that revenge can surmount mortality, despite appearances to the contrary: "Nor dies Revenge although he sleep awhile." Don Andrea can then relax: "Rest thee, for I will sit to see the rest." The play on the two meanings of rest—one associated with an ending, the other with a remainder—serves here (as it does in George Herbert's lyrics) to redeem the notion of death as restful sleep from the fear that the rest will be silence, that this sleep will never yield to a restored volitional consciousness.

Don Andrea's posthumous journey is full of Dantesque sound and fury, but subsumed by significant nothings:

> Through dreadful shades of ever-glooming night,
> I saw more sights than thousand tongues can tell,
> Or pens can write, or mortal hearts can think.
>
> (1.1.56–58)

This *praeteritio* is an anxiety-producing device, and it mimics in the audience Don Andrea's own experience of delay and uncertainty:

> When I was slain, my soul descended straight
> To pass the flowing stream of Acheron:
> But churlish Charon, only boatman there,
> Said that my rites of burial not perform'd,
> I might not sit amongst his passengers.
> Ere Sol had slept three nights in Thetis' lap,
> And slak'd his smoking chariot in her flood,
> By Don Horatio, our Knight Marshal's son,
> My funerals and obsequies were done.
> Then was the ferryman of hell content
> To pass me over to the slimy strond
> That leads to fell Avernus' ugly waves.
>
> (1.1.18–29)

The three-day wait associates Don Andrea's obstructed journey into the pagan afterlife with an Elizabethan anxiety that the path to Christian resurrection might prove similarly impassable, and an answering hope that this can occur only when a religious ceremony has been neglected. The two rituals Horatio performs for Don Andrea, funeral and vendetta, reflect the same need: the need to convert mourning into an active and efficacious condition, and to conceal the indifference and powerlessness of the dead. Burial thus serves very much the same purpose as prayers for the dead in purgatory, which the Reformation had suppressed in Kyd's audience; so does revenge, which provided an alternate outlet for the compulsion to redeem the beloved into eternal life.

The Spanish Tragedy puts revenge very much in the place of purgatory: a third course between heaven and hell that appeals to our need for models of retribution that carry over from life to death. The spirit of Don Andrea "trod a middle path" between the heavens of lovers and soldiers on his right, and "deepest hell" on his left. The only other road leads him directly to Proserpine and Revenge (1.1.59–85), whose stories, however violent or tragic, provide a navigable narrative track through the deserts of a vast annihilationist eternity.

Life learns from art the trick of making closure a triumph rather than a defeat. Hieronimo's life is done when his play is, his play when his task is, his task when revenge has symbolically reversed the death that deprived him of immortality by killing his only offspring. Hieronimo then violently seeks his own quietus by biting off his tongue, and by refusing to write anything but his own death scene, to assure that the rest will indeed be silence. The burden of closure thus passes to the audience—specifically, to the fathers of the new victims, who desperately seek a new revenge plot. The playing out of poetic justice is Hieronimo's equivalent of Jonson's epitaph "On My First Son," a "best piece of poetrie" that serves as a metonymic surrogate for the lost life it seeks forlornly to reconstruct.[11] Hieronimo is quite willing to die for his art, even without the proper burial craved by Don Andrea:

> If destiny deny thee life, Hieronimo,
> Yet shalt thou be assured of a tomb:
> If neither, yet let this thy comfort be,
> Heaven covereth him that hath no burial.
> And to conclude, I will revenge his death!
>
> (3.13.16–20)

Revenge, and the model of justice it artfully proposes, is a satisfactory alternative to the other rituals by which death and mourning—not merely the corpse—are safely contained.

Where revenge proves impossible, however, it becomes dangerously difficult to disguise mortality in the black robes of justice. That way madness lies, roused by the pain of futility in its most extreme form:

HIERONIMO: Justice, O justice! O my son, my son,
My son, whom naught can ransom or redeem!

LORENZO: Hieronimo, you are not well-advis'd.

HIERONIMO: Away Lorenzo, hinder me no more,
For thou hast made me bankrupt of my bliss.

Give me my son! You shall not ransom him.
Away! I'll rip the bowels of the earth
[*He diggeth with his dagger*]
And ferry over to th'Elysian plains,
And bring my son to show his deadly wounds.

(3.12.65–73)

It is simply too far to dig; Hieronimo can try to retrieve Horatio with that dagger, but only symbolically, through the wounds of Lorenzo, who thus must ransom Horatio after all. Hieronimo will eventually enact precisely this deadly substitution in the masque, by making Lorenzo take Horatio's role in the displaced re-enactment of Horatio's murder.

Horatio's parents make gestures of desperate protest comparable to the devastation Tamburlaine visits on the landscape for the death of Zenocrate, and to King Lear's anguished questioning over the body of Cordelia: "Why should a dog, a horse, a rat, have life, / And thou no breath at all?" (5.3.307–8). Kyd momentarily allows Isabella a consoling vision of her son in bliss—"To heaven, ay, there sits my Horatio, / Back'd with a troop of fiery cherubins" (3.8.17–18)—but this vision is surrounded with outbursts of evasive madness, as if perhaps the Christian response to death were just one more. She chops down the tree where her son was hanged, as if in symbolic retribution against "that Forbidden Tree, whose mortal taste / Brought death into the world" (*Paradise Lost*, I, 2–3). Hieronimo exclaims that

The blust'ring winds, conspiring with my words,
At my lament have mov'd the leafless trees,
Disrob'd the meadows of their flower'd green,
Made mountains marsh with spring-tides of my tears,
And broken through the brazen gates of hell.

(3.7.5–9)

Such self-conscious enforcement of the pathetic fallacy encourages us to recognize the way we insist on, even hallucinate, the importance of our individual lives, clinging to a Ptolemaic astronomy of the domestic sphere. Like Don Andrea (and like John Donne, I will argue), we would far rather be at war with our universe than ignored by it. If the supposition that Elizabethans all complacently assumed a benevolently ordered universe needs any further refutation, here are characters of considerable appeal who plainly—and vengefully—recognize Mother Nature as an indiscriminate killer. To accuse indifferent biology of complicity in murder is (as Starbuck warns Ahab in *Moby-Dick*) at once an utter absurdity and a dangerous insight. Such an accusation could be framed only by a mind that—having lost the life it cares about most— needs death to seem explicable even more desperately than it needs death to seem contingent.

After struggling vainly to revive his murdered son with accusatory and consolatory mythologies, Hieronimo contemplates suicide (2.5.17–23– 67). In the next act, he tosses aside the dagger and halter as instruments of self-destruction, only to take them immediately up again as weapons against Horatio's killers (3.12.19–21). Here as in *Hamlet*, suicide seems a plausible alternative to revenge because each offers reunion, either by joining the deceased in death or by incorporating his death as a living cause. In one of his final speeches, Hieronimo insists that, by his bloody actions, he has "offered to my son . . . my life" (4.4.159–60), as if somehow by being willing to die in this revenge, he could invest his vitality in his son's body as well as his son's cause.[12]

Amid all the windings of the plot and the whirling words, Hieronimo's speeches always return us to the simple recognitions at the core of tragedy through many of its historical phases: the brutal fact of death that awaits men and women, for all their love and imagination; and the futility of hoping to alter or transcend it through love, honor, progeny, justice, art, or even religion. This thematic focus, more deeply than the shared points of plot, is what *The Spanish Tragedy* bequeaths to Shakespeare's *Hamlet*. It is also a signature concern of Renaissance culture in general, as the relentlessness of physical mortality (and its avatars in error, mutability, and betrayal) erased each dreamer of glory, each aspiringly fashioned self.

THE BLOODY SCARF:
A FLAG OF IMMORTALITY

From the opening lines, *The Spanish Tragedy* defines its story as a struggle between mortality and personal identity:

> When this eternal substance of my soul
> Did live imprison'd in my wanton flesh,
> Each in their function serving other's need,
> I was a courtier in the Spanish Court.
> My name was Don Andrea. . . .

(1.1.1–5)

The principal action of the play that follows is violent murder, and its leading motive is revenge, but its primary psychological condition is mourning. The Viceroy mourns once for Bel-imperia and twice (once prematurely, later correctly) for Balthazar. Bel-imperia, Horatio, and Don Andrea himself mourn for Don Andrea; Don Andrea, Bel-imperia, Isabella, and Hieronimo mourn for Horatio; the Painter and the Senex mourn for their sons; the King mourns for his son, Lorenzo, and his brother, Castile. The resulting violence offers the audience an equivocal lesson about resisting the idea of annihilation—instructions for writing on that blankness. Hieronimo's final revenge allows the audience to participate in powerful action on behalf of the deceased; it also reminds the audience that such actions must be performed on the level of fantasy, whether by viewing a play like *The Spanish Tragedy*, or by performing some other metonymous act, some other act of substitution, upon one's own psychic stage.

After discovering and recovering Andrea's corpse, Horatio

> dew'd him with my tears,
> And sigh'd and sorrow'd as became a friend.
> But neither friendly sorrow, sighs nor tears,
> Could win pale death from his usurped right.
> Yet this I did, and less I could not do,
> I saw him honour'd with due funeral:
> This scarf I pluck'd from off his liveless arm,
> And wear it in remembrance of my friend.
>
> (1.4.36–43)

When Horatio determines to save something about Don Andrea, he settles on this bloody scarf; when Hieronimo memorializes Horatio, he seizes on the same artifact. The exchanges of this token—a sort of flag of the Human Immortality Party—reflect the way we pass along the painful legacy of love for mortal beings, the way each human life becomes devoted to the preservation of another, in an essentially circular argument of life-justification. "Our lives we borrow from each other," writes the atheistical Lucretius in a passage quoted by Montaigne, "And men like runners pass along the torch of life."[13]

By wearing this bright scarf in defiance of "pale death," Horatio becomes the reincarnation as well as the savior of Don Andrea—so thoroughly, in fact, that Bel-imperia becomes his lover, as she was Don Andrea's, to whom she originally gave the scarf. It is the visible legacy of their original erotic sin, re-enacted when her allure again brings death into the garden in 2.4. Her efforts to seize immortality by an infinite regress of substitutions (falling in love with Horatio in recompense for his love for her previous love) necessarily lead to a replication of death as well:

> how can love find harbour in my breast,
> Till I revenge the death of my beloved?
> Yes, second love shall further my revenge.
> I'll love Horatio, my Andrea's friend. . . .
>
> (1.4.64–67)

Bel-imperia is instinctively devoted to the power of metonymy. In both love and battle—a pairing prominent throughout the play—she can undo Don Andrea's deadly defeat by construing Horatio as his resurrected alter ego. Her assertion that she "So lov'd his life, as still I wish their deaths" betrays an assumption that the killing of his killers will somehow revive Don Andrea (4.1.22).

If substitution can promise a kind of immortality, if metonymy as a trope promises that there is something beyond the immediate identity to be signified, these symbolic tactics (like Derridean signifiers) also threaten to reveal the abysmal absences they serve to fill. Social replacements and generational replications are the only hope for sustaining human life, yet they are also the plainest reminders of human death. Each saving substitution in *The Spanish Tragedy* has a dark side. In resurrecting Don Andrea, whom Balthazar killed, Horatio necessarily undertakes the killing of Balthazar. Long before Balthazar actually dies, he perceives Horatio as his "destin'd plague," a mortal enemy threatening not only his immediate survival, but also his hopes for transcending death through honor or dynastic procreation:[14]

> by those wounds he forced me to yield,
> And by my yielding I became his slave.
> Now in his mouth he carries pleasing words,
> Which. . .
>
> in her heart set him where I should stand.
> Thus hath he ta'en my body by his force,
> And now by sleight would captivate my soul
>
> (2.1.118–31)

Bel-imperia's "favor must be won by [Horatio's] remove," Lorenzo tells Balthazar, and therefore Balthazar must seek "revenge." The markers change, but the transaction remains remarkably similar: "revenge" incorporates all the ways of retrieving one's immortality from whoever seems to have stolen it. This is particularly true in a scarcity economy such as *The Spanish Tragedy* depicts, where there is only one royal Balthazar to be claimed as a prisoner and only one royal Bel-imperia to be married, where parents have only a single son to carry their legacies into the future—and where each person has only one life to lose, a life that can often be saved only by taking someone else's.

This zero-sum game—something like musical chairs—connects the Portuguese subplot to the main plot. Like aristocrats in time of war, characters who wish to survive in revenge-tragedy must commonly induce someone to die in their place. Revenge stands in for salvation: an enemy's death becomes a miraculous escape from one's own mortality. "If Balthazar be dead, [Alexandro] shall not live," declares the Viceroy (1.3.91). Once Balthazar is revealed to be alive after all, the very ropes that were to hold Alexandro for execution are unwrapped and put around Villuppo, who had plotted Alexandro's death.

THE EMPTY BOX:
A TERMINAL BETRAYAL

The master version of this pattern of substitution in Renaissance culture is Christ's willingness to die in order to redeem humanity from its mortal failings. In Pedringano's execution, even this transcendent instance of surrogacy comes under cynical interrogation. Lorenzo invokes the basic principles of immortality-by-metonymy to provoke Pedringano to murder Serberine: "For die he must, if we do mean to live."[15] When Pedringano is condemned for this murder, Lorenzo falsely promises a last-minute pardon to guarantee that his own complicity will not be revealed. Like Horatio's martyrdom on a special tree (after harrowing hell to redeem Don Andrea), this execution awkwardly recalls Christ mounted and mocked on the cross. Indeed, Pedringano dies wondering why his lord has forsaken him, haunted by that lord's false promise that faith will disarm mortality. The stratagem by which Lorenzo keeps Pedringano silent about their conspiracy right up to the instant of that hanging bears disquieting resemblances to the entire Christian strategy of consolation. Like an Elizabethan clergyman, Lorenzo's messenger-boy is not exactly required to lie about these glad tidings, only to take their substance and truth on pure faith, and to urge Pedringano to do the same:

Bid him not doubt of his delivery.
Tell him his pardon is already sign'd,
And thereon bid him boldly be resolv'd:
For were he ready to be turned off
(As 'tis my will the uttermost be tried),
Thou with his pardon shalt attend him still:
Show him this box, tell him his pardon's in't,
But open't not, and if thou lov'st thy life.

(3.4.66–73)

The boy—like a Shakespearean clown, assigned to carry the grimmest message in the lightest character, the better to ambush the audience and protect the playwright—cannot resist knowledge of this "forbidden" treasure. What he discovers is that the officially proffered hopes of salvation lack any real basis: "By my bare honesty, here's nothing but the bare empty box" (3.5.6–7). In a twist on St. Paul's formula, the absent letter kills, but by the time a man realizes he has been betrayed, his voice has been strangled and can never warn others of the treachery in high places. As the boy observes, it is a cruel if practical joke to give a condemned man such absurd encouragement. The last laugh is on Pedringano—unless it is on us. "Forgive, O Lord, my little jokes on Thee," writes Robert Frost, "And I'll forgive Thy great big one on me."[16]

Lorenzo's message to Pedringano is particularly suggestive in view of the common Elizabethan characterizations of Christ's sacrifice as a pardon already written that will deliver us from the devil at the uttermost. John Donne concludes a Holy Sonnet with the assurance that an inner faith in the Lord's forgiveness is "as good / As if thou'hadst sealed my pardon, with thy blood"; but in the world of *The Spanish Tragedy* what is written in blood is instead the provocation to revenge, as in Bel-imperia's desperate letter. Pedringano's pardon—and perhaps Christ's—is writ in water. As mortal beings, we all stand on a gallows—"The whole world is but a Cart of condemned persons," as a 1630 tract put it[17]—but (lest we complain) we are told that the magic box to which the hierophant points (with a reassuring smile) holds the imminent pardon promised by our all-powerful intercessor. Like the Lord in the twenty-third Psalm, Lorenzo assures Pedringano that, even in the shadow of death, "He shall not want" (3.4.75).

Kyd seems to highlight the theological parallel by having the hangman warn Pedringano to "hearken to your soul's health," and having Pedringano reply that what "is good for the body is likewise good for the soul: and it may be, in that box is balm for both" (3.6.75–78). Pedringano's jeering from the gallows at his tormentors may be cynical villainy, but it is disquietingly similar to the bravado of the real-life heroes of *The Book of Martyrs,* vaunting their trust in their providential Lord as they faced their own executioners, often clinging to a Bible supposed to hold the ultimate saving Word. At the notorious execution of Bishop Hooper, "When he came to the place appointed where he should die, he smilingly beheld the stake. . . . a box was brought and laid before him upon a stool, with his pardon from the queen, if he would turn."[18] In this context, a merely empty box can be more terrifying than Pandora's overflowing one, as annihilation can be more terrifying than damnation.

It is ominous that Lorenzo (and Kyd) can elide the two levels so easily: that a ruthless death-sentence can sound so much like a promise of perfect redemption, and that a bizarre Machiavellian scene at the gallows can sound so much like the standard Christian deathbed scene. This would of course have been an unusual and dangerous perspective for a playwright to express, even in such indirect terms, and even after artificially displacing his story into a pagan society. Remember, however, that "vile hereticall Conceiptes denyinge the deity of Jhesus Christe our Saviour" were "fownd emongst the papers of Thos Kydd prisoner" in 1593;[19] and that doubting the divinity of the Son could easily lead to doubts about the promises of salvation and resurrection that depend so heavily on the New Testament. Though ownership of these papers is commonly attributed to Christopher Marlowe, remember also that it was Kyd himself who, facing torture, initiated that attribution. The passing of the blame onto a recently deceased associate was predictable whether or not it was true. The two men wrote in the same room, and perhaps they wrote in the same skeptical spirit as well.[20]

THE STATE OF NATURE: A TYRANNY IN PALIMPSEST

Lorenzo's ploy can be read as a local political reference rather than as a grand theological allegory: editors commonly cite its resemblance to a trick played by the Earl of Leicester on an underling. Perhaps we can swallow the topical reference and still have our theological cake by recognizing that, in *The Spanish Tragedy* as in several other compelling Renaissance tragedies, the depredations of social hierarchy partly symbolize the equally unjust depredations of an uncaring material universe, where again the promise of a providential lord proves a hollow fiction. Only in the realm of fantasy—Hieronimo's masque, Kyd's play—can personal will reassert any control, and register any meaningful protest against either kind of tyranny.

Current critical orthodoxies make sexual and political subtexts the heart and soul of Renaissance drama; but for all its cynical politics, sexual and otherwise, *The Spanish Tragedy* seems as deeply concerned with the construal of death as with the constructions of social hierarchy. Political control proves hollow: a false witness named Villuppo can easily damage royal honor and royal hopes, and an old madman named Hieronimo can erase two dynasties in a moment. Renaissance societies commonly generated a decorous notion that mortality is at the service of political authority, but the fictionality of that notion is all too clearly on display in *The Spanish Tragedy*—as it is in *The Revenger's Tragedy*, where the corrupt sovereign brushes aside all those who wish him extremely long life, favoring only the ultimate sycophant who wishes he may never die at all. In the opening act of *The Spanish Tragedy*, Hieronimo says of his newly lionized son, "Long may he live to serve my sovereign liege, / And soon decay unless he serve my liege"; the King replies, "Nor thou nor he shall die without reward" (1.2.98–100), as if (by the politically useful formula) divine redemption were virtually indistinguishable from royal approval. Death again appears to be under official command when the Viceroy declares he is "Procrastinating Alexandro's death" by not executing him more promptly (3.1.28). Really, of course, it is only a question of how much he will *accelerate* that death; delaying it even a day was proverbially beyond the power even of kings. Monarchs are finally only human, and in lamenting the "Infortunate condition of kings" that led to his son's death, the Viceroy closely echoes countless commentaries on the mortal human condition in general: "ever subject to the wheel of chance: / And at our highest never joy we so, / As we both doubt and dread our overthrow" (3.1.1–7). Again the play's political commentary lapses into a meditation on mortality.

Perhaps, then, the corrupt power of the state, concerned with its own hierarchies and their maintenance through dynastic marriage, symbolizes the tyranny of natural mutability that imposes death on behalf of the same generational principle. The dynamic equilibrium of the social system, as it coldly overrules personal desire, proves as dismissive of humane concerns as the dynamic equilibrium of generational biology; the same system that forces Bel-imperia to marry according to the patriarchal suffix of her name also necessitates the murder of Horatio. Death is a decree of the seasonal cycle: Hieronimo predicts that his powerful enemies, "as a wintry storm upon a plain, / Will bear me down with their nobility" (3.13.37–38). From this perspective, natural order is a bureaucracy that regularly performs villainies lacking even the perverse appeal of radical selfishness or sadism—as if the princes in *Richard III* had died from a common typhus instead of an extraordinary tyrant.

If the deceits and oppressions of civil government represent metonymically the failures of divine providence, then there is little point waiting around for either kind of authority to provide satisfactory justice. Presumably that is why the protagonists of Renaissance blood-revenge defy the secular government (by appropriating its juridical functions) at the same time that they abrogate (by appropriating) God's *vindicta mihi*. Hieronimo complains that his

> restless passions,
> That winged mount, and, hovering in the air,
> Beat at the windows of the brightest heavens,
> Soliciting for justice and revenge:
> But they are plac'd in those empyreal heights
> Where, countermur'd with walls of diamond,
> I find the place impregnable, and they
> Resist my woes, and give my words no way.
>
> (3.7.11–18)

His restlessness cannot overcome the silence that stands between us and heaven. To get there he must create his Tower of Babel out of the multilingual revenge-masque—and even if he succeeds, heaven seems likely to prove yet another empty box, a mystification of the silent grave.

Hieronimo's play-within-the-play-within-the-play represents both the triumph and the failure of the revenge genre. Its enactment of justice combines and explicates the consolatory and vengeful functions of substitution, but the body-strewn stage starkly refutes any supposition that life has truly been redeemed. Death may still be isolated as the product of aberrant violence, but it has begun escaping from the metadramatic frame into Hieronimo's audience, and therefore warns Kyd's audience that drama is no longer a safe container for their mortal fears or for the aggressions those fears commonly produce:

> Marry, this follows for Hieronimo:
> Here break we off our sundry languages

And thus conclude I in our vulgar tongue.
Haply you think, but bootless are your thoughts,
That this is fabulously counterfeit,
And that we do as all tragedians do:
To die today, for fashioning our scene,
The death of Ajax or some Roman peer,
And in a minute starting up again,
Revive to please tomorrow's audience.
No, princes, know I am Hieronimo,
The hopeless father of a hapless son,
Whose tongue is tun'd to tell his latest tale,
Not to excuse gross errors in the play.
I see your looks urge instance of these words,
Behold the reason urging me to this: [*Shows his dead son*]
See here my show, look on this spectacle:
Here lay my hope, and here my hope hath end.

(4.4.73–90)

As the elaborate multilingual distancing of the innermost play falls away into the "bare honesty" of plain English, the mechanisms of cultural denial collapse under the weight of corpses. As Renaissance *memento mori* tracts sometimes warned, death comes speaking in the plainest vernacular, for all the courtier's flourishes of exotic language.

The box holding the secrets of life and death, horribly empty at Pedringano's execution, is now horribly full; and it looks more like a tomb than a stage. Hieronimo explicitly refuses the role of epilogue as dramatic apologist, insisting instead that he is a real man, and a dying one. But he thereby assumes the other standard role of an epilogue, obliterating the boundary between the characters and the audience. His son has been sent, "In black dark night, to pale dim cruel death" (4.4.107), and no one in the audience can hope to escape that sort of erasure. The literary conventions only masked temporarily the actual deaths occurring all around us. Our dismaying position resembles that of Balthazar when Bel-imperia literalizes the Petrarchan metaphor of their courtship in this masque by killing him in earnest. The invasion of reality into Hieronimo's fiction attacks our mythology of denial. Kyd exploits our willing suspension of disbelief in the drama in order to compromise our resolute suspension of belief in mortality. The demystification, the collapse of the metadrama, is itself a danger, because it revives the recognition of our mortal destiny that had been systematically repressed through drama, role-playing, metonymy, substitution. Hieronimo suggests that the royal families should not have mocked his apparent madness before they realized that they, too, would go mad if forced to confront the death of their own kind, of their own immortalizing hopes. Clearly we are next—next for the madhouse, if we fully absorb the implication that we are next for the tomb and oblivion.

Though Revenge does seem to revive the specter of Don Andrea, all it can promise, in the play's final words, is an "endless tragedy." There seems to be no higher level, no divine comedy, to which this resolution releases him;[21] only by a kind of destructive repetition-compulsion can he keep from disappearing. In this Don Andrea suffers the annihilation-anxiety common to many dramatic characters, who must relive their story endlessly in order to exist at all;[22] his position here as a sort of *epi*-epilogue reinforces that impression. The story of Hamlet will suggest that this metatheatrical terror has a parallel in the world outside the theater, a world that composes endless cycles of tragic violence to avoid facing unaccommodated death. By the time Hamlet rests in silence (1601) the ghost has become a skull, and by the beginning of *The Revenger's Tragedy* (1607) the genre has begun to grin jeeringly at its own quest for metonymic consolations, for figurative transformations of the plain facts of death.

The performance of revenge as a play-within-the-play in *The Spanish Tragedy* (as in *Hamlet* and *The Revenger's Tragedy*) may constitute an acknowledgment that such satisfactions are possible only at the level of fantasy, where actors stand in for real people and geopolitical treachery stands in for the frustrations of ordinary life. At an aesthetic distance, Hieronimo's final massacre becomes an elaborate sacrifice that exorcises demons of helplessness and perceived injustice, demons so common in the human animal, so heightened in the aspiring minds of the Renaissance, and so focused in the fierce economies of Elizabethan England and Elizabeth's court.

Hieronimo finally dispels the aesthetic distance to complain of the forces that have truly killed his son, and justify his revenge. Countless Elizabethans, bereaved by war, poverty, or religious persecution, could have conceived a similar complaint against their monarch; *The Spanish Tragedy* allows them to witness and approve an extreme act of treason that follows naturally, by the logic of revenge, from that complaint. It allows them an extreme blasphemy, too: disguised as a complaint about violence, developing into a complaint about injustice, it is ultimately a complaint about death itself, in all its forms. If the monarch fails to respond, then we may find ourselves dreaming of killing his only begotten son in compensation.[23]

2

Giving Up the Ghost
Hamlet, Revenge, and Denial

> *Behind what we think of as the Russian menace lies what*
> *we do not wish to face, and what white Americans do not*
> *face when they regard a Negro reality—the fact that life*
> *is tragic. . . . Perhaps the whole root of our trouble, the*
> *human trouble, is that we will sacrifice all the beauty of*
> *our lives, will imprison ourselves in totems, taboos, crosses,*
> *blood sacrifices, steeples, mosques, races, armies, flags,*
> *nations, in order to deny the fact of death, which is the*
> *only fact we have.*
>
> —James Baldwin, *The Fire Next Time*[1]

Countless processions of black letters have reminded us that we must each give up the ghost sooner or later. What dresses me in more than the customary suits of solemn black—perhaps even in the black hat of the villain—is my polemical suggestion that we ought to give up the ghost in a more literal sense, and that *Hamlet* deeply condemns the illusions of afterlife it superficially encourages. The vexed status of King Hamlet's ghost, in the play and its critical history alike, reflects uncertainties about personal immortality. Should that apparition be read as a true spirit or a destructive illusion, a cultural convention or a pathological projection? Obviously its widely witnessed appearance seems to promote a Catholic view rather than a mortalist one. But instead of spurring Hamlet to some pious resolution to ease or avoid his father's suffering, the ghost makes Hamlet resolve to remember and avenge. The visitation renews the young man's hope, not of otherworldly salvation, but of lasting worldly identity, inspiring him to defend his father's memory against the ravages of time, and to attack the proximate cause of his father's death.

The two complaints of this dead ancestor—about his purgatorial agonies and about his unrequited murder—can be condensed into a single, historically based manifestation of survivor anxiety. If I am correct that revenge-tragedy serves partly as a displacement of prayers for the dead forbidden by the Reformation, then Hamlet's guilt-ridden compulsion to help his tormented father may draw on Shakespeare's own guilt toward his recently deceased and reputedly Catholic father. "The motif of the child whose prayers, good works, and penances secure release for the soul of the unshriven parent was a potent one in late medieval thinking," demanding "an elaborate sequence of Masses, fasts, and other mortuary observances."[2] Perhaps Shakespeare peaked like John o' Geneva, and could pray nothing—at least until (like his Wittenberg-trained protagonist) he found an indirect theatrical way to assail the conscience of the King who had taken his father's life (2.2.562–64, 600–601).

Ghosts are the standard-equipment starters of Senecan revenge-tragedies; my point is that this convention reflects a deep motive for stories of blood-revenge, which sustain two precious beliefs: first, that our rights and even our desires exert some force beyond our deaths; and second, that revenge can symbolically restore us to life by defeating the agency of our death, conveniently localized in a villain.[3] We continue to need our versions of these ghostly visitations for much the same reasons Renaissance playwrights needed theirs: to shape life into meaningful plots that motivate action and allow the performance of something complete and significant in the short time allotted. We demand that the culture haunt the theaters of our minds and our worlds—our distracted globes (1.5.97)—with compelling illusions that divert us from the recognition of meaninglessness. A society lacking consensus on the ulterior purpose of human life—lacking a univocal ghost—faces a crisis of morale even more stubborn and painful than Hamlet's. Without the introjected specter of the father—the superego Freud identifies with the socialized individual conscience, the *nom du père* Lacan identifies with

the entire patriarchal and logocentric structure of Western culture—
chaos seems inevitable.[4] So there are powerful protective forces, sociological as well as philological and theological, arrayed to resist my
exorcism. And perhaps I am like Gertrude, the sole observer to whom
the ghost, holy or otherwise, chooses to be transparent. But, in my
skeptical reading, *Hamlet* teaches us to see through this possessive
apparition.

Hamlet and Hamlet and *Hamlet*—the father, the son, and the
ghostly play—creep from death to dusty death, for all their sound and
fury. How we die finally matters less than that we die. In the first act,
Horatio warns Hamlet not to follow the ghost; in the fifth act, he warns
Hamlet instead not to focus "too curiously" on the inglorious indifference of corpses.[5] The spectral "illusion" (1.1.13) represents a threat, but
so does disillusionment. What if the lost father proves to be not a ghost,
but instead a skull; not the victim of extraordinary villainy, but of
ordinary decay? When Hamlet encounters the remains of Yorick, the
man who—kissing and carrying the boy "a thousand times"—was
evidently no less a loving paternal figure than the biological father, the
only tribute young Hamlet can pay him is a rising gorge (5.1.180–89).
Yorick is death demystified; he does not appear in the Dramatis Personae, but he wears the mask of everyone we have ever loved who has died.
Revenge may be "a remedy for grief,"[6] but it is also a remedy for terror;
it presents a bloody horror, but it blocks another, paler kind of horror,
one less susceptible to consolation. Pursuing the specter of a murdered
father—or, in *The Spanish Tragedy*, the specter of a murdered son—
allows one to flee the specters of inevitable decay and unaccommodated
death. An obsession with murder on earth and consequent punishment
forestalls an obsession with meaningless life and subsequent annihilation.

My suggestion is not that we should dismiss the ghost as a mere
hallucination of Hamlet's,[7] but rather that we exorcise it from our own
globe lest it poison or "blast" us (1.1.130)—that we follow the play in
turning away from haunted battlements and accepting in their place a
common graveyard. If the vengeful ghost cannot be exorcised entirely
(and this chapter's subtitle suggests an effort to go Eleanor Prosser[8] one
better), it can at least be isolated as a fiction within a fiction within a
fiction, an "illusion" within a drama within a cultural mythology of
denial. The ghost is a design our psyches read into the threateningly
blank Rorschach page called death. If it appears to be "a composite of
what Catholics, Protestants, and skeptics thought about spirits,"[9] rather

than a consistent entity, that may be because Shakespeare intended it to stand for all projective beliefs about afterlife. What this chapter offers is less a strictly critical analysis than a series of meditations on that point.

The social purpose of these meditations is to extricate from the play something like a psychoanalysis of the culture as a whole, intended to help cure the pathological compulsion to avenge threats against our fantasies of immortality by stabbing blindly through a curtain with no real hope of killing our real enemy. Such a cure would require a shift in our attitudes toward death—and hence in our analyses of revenge-tragedy—resembling a recent shift in approaches to mental illness, which now emphasize less the parents' culpability than "the tragedy of the patients' lives—tragedy which is so much of a piece with the tragedy of life for all of us that the presentation is often a profoundly grief-laden experience for both the presenter and the listeners . . . a picture which is much more deeply shaking than was the blame-colored picture previously often seen."[10] In this sense, Hamlet's fixation on punishing the bad father Claudius in defense of the lost good father not only resembles the classic psychological splitting of a parental figure in response to unmanageable ambivalence. It also exemplifies the neurotic tendency to isolate all threats into a phobic object, where they can be kept under surveillance; and the mechanism of transference, whereby all goodness can be located in a single figure—a therapist, a god, a lover, a parent, a child—and there worshiped and guarded in a strategic displacement of narcissism.

Defending a ghost and eliciting its suppressed voice is a projective defense of the mortal self:

For medieval people, as for us, to die meant to enter a great silence, and the fear of being forgotten in that silence was as real to them as to any of the generations that followed. But for them that silence was not absolute and could be breached. To find ways and means of doing so was one of their central religious preoccupations. For what late medieval English men and women at the point of death seem most to have wanted was that their names should be kept constantly in the memory and thus in the prayers of the living.[11]

This is what Hamlet asks of Ophelia—"Nymph, in thy orisons, / Be all my sins remembered" (3.1.89–90)—but many of the fame-hungry Elizabethans surely wanted prayers in order to be remembered, rather than remembrance in order to receive prayers. In announcing, "This is I, Hamlet the Dane" (5.1.250–51), then promptly leaping into a grave,

Hamlet obeys the familiar Renaissance burial inscriptions that urge us to sympathize with the dead because they were once as we are, and we will someday be as they are. And what Hamlet announces in the graveyard, identifying with his dead father, centuries of audiences have imagined in the theater, identifying elaborately with this protagonist: "It is we who are Hamlet," declares Hazlitt.[12] The danger is that sympathetic identification with a past life—fictional or otherwise—can become a demonic possession of the present, violating a boundary between death and life that should be respected, for all our impulses to cross it.

The sentries in the opening scene stand on guard against some undefined threat to their world, an enemy that (for all its disguises) proves to be mortality itself, the foe against whom our weapons are futile: "For it is as the air, invulnerable, / And our vain blows malicious mockery" (1.1.150–51). This ghost is less "the devil of the knowledge of death"[13] than the tempter toward the denial of death. The motives projected onto the ghost in the opening scene reflect all the conventional fantasies of overcoming mortality. The dead return to this world, often in righteous anger, to oversee their familial, financial, and political legacies (1.1.63–138). At the center of Horatio's speculation stands the vengeful quest of young Fortinbras, which suggests not only (as young Hamlet observes) that life and death alike can be justified by honor, but also that the living child can repair the losses of the dead parent. If Fortinbras can undo one consequence of his father's defeat, the loss of territory, why not another, the loss of life? The procreative remedy for death transmutes into a more obviously symbolic one.

Hopes of resurrection—whether by sons, symbols, or saviors—are timeless functions of human culture; but they are terrifying when they threaten to malfunction. Both the timelessness and the terror are evident when Horatio turns to contemplating a previous eruption of politically ominous ghosts: "A little ere the mightiest Julius fell, / The graves stood tenantless and the sheeted dead / Did squeak and gibber in the Roman streets . . . and the moist star . . . Was sick almost to doomsday with eclipse" (1.1.117–23). The doomsday comparison is more than casual, because Horatio's diction generates a vision of the Last Judgment gone bad. The dead awaken to a nightmare. Though Rome was then a pagan world, the mightiest Julius fell just a little ere the meekest Jesus fell, and the passage evokes Matthew 27:50–53 (in which Jesus dies amid earthquakes, and the saints rise from their graves to wander the city) only to distort horribly its image of resurrection.

Only a dozen short lines beyond this Caesarean mock-Doomsday, Horatio attributes to the ghost a conventional motive that comes too close for comfort to the problems of bodily resurrection:

> if thou hast uphoarded in thy life
> Extorted treasure in the womb of earth,
> For which they say your spirits oft walk in death . . .
>
> (1.1.139–41)

Perhaps the lost treasure for which the ghost mourns, which he wishes his audience would extort in a Caesarean rebirth from the tomb of earth, is nothing other than his own remains; mortal bodies were commonly described as matter temporarily appropriated from the earth. But at this moment the cock crows, cutting off the speech. This "trumpet to the morn," as Horatio calls it, resumes the parodic echoes of the Day of Judgment. The Last Trumpet that resounds here is merely an animal voice that sends the dead back to their graves instead of up into salvation.

Marcellus's rhapsodic response makes the Christian associations explicit, but again this Savior, instead of liberating the dead, remands them to their graves:

> It faded on the crowing of the cock.
> Some say that ever 'gainst that season comes
> Wherein our Saviour's birth is celebrated,
> This bird of dawning singeth all night long;
> And then, they say, no spirit dare stir abroad. . . .
>
> (1.1.162–66)

So the cheer of the morning that now rises in its "russet mantle" is an equivocal cheer. For all Hamlet's eager hyperbole, his father is no Hyperion who resurrects with each sunrise (1.2.140, 3.4.56). The stage action reflects a psychological truth: that rising to the business of a new dawn means leaving behind the awareness of death and the memories of the dead. The mourning of the dead and the morning of the day are incompatible. That may partly explain why Hamlet complains of being "too much in the sun" and clings stubbornly to his midnight-black mantle of protracted sorrow.

This stubbornness is the problem Claudius confronts at the start of the second scene. He tries to bury the fact of death rhetorically in a subordinate clause—a syntactical analogue to the death-denying strategies of the culture as a whole—and tries to bury the same fact practically in the role-based systems of marriage and royalty that subordinate the mortal body-natural to a successively immortal body-politic. It enrages

Hamlet when Claudius identifies himself as Hamlet's father and Denmark's king. Hamlet is determined to resist this ordinary obliteration of the dead and of the facts of death, even before he learns that this particular death demands a particular commemoration. So he attacks the neglect of mourning with black clothing, attacks the impersonal rhetoric of kingship with ironic wit, attacks the usurped roles on the throne and in the royal bed with outright diatribes.

Hamlet attempts to sustain his father's existence by identifying with him, even if that means joining him in death. He wishes not to be himself, not to be alive, even (in the famous soliloquy at 3.1.56) "not to be" at all. In his gloom, passivity, and silence, in the black of his mourning wear, in his closed or staring eyes, and his wish to move out of the sun and into his grave, young Hamlet tries to be a sort of medium at a seance, conjuring the dead man into presence, with all his absentness intact. His mother Gertrude is trapped in a community of denial: she is no more willing to see the dead than to see the mad Ophelia (4.5.1) or the "black and grained spots" of her own mortal frailty (3.4.90). She accuses her son of blindness—as she will later accuse him of madness—for seeing things in death that she cannot bear to confront:

> Good Hamlet, cast thy nighted colour off,
> And let thine eye look like a friend on Denmark.
> Do not for ever with thy vailed lids
> Seek for thy noble father in the dust.
> Thou know'st 'tis common: all that lives must die,
> Passing through nature to eternity.
>
> (1.2.68–73)

Hamlet's edged reply—"Ay, madam, it is common"—suggests that it is precisely the commonness of death that horrifies him, the way it erases distinctions.

Claudius then undertakes the same line of argument, insisting that heaven, the dead, nature, and reason all make up one voice that

> still hath cried
> From the first corse till he that died today,
> 'This must be so'. We pray you throw to earth
> This unprevailing woe, and think of us
> As of a father; for let the world take note
> You are the most immediate to our throne. . . .
>
> (1.2.104–9)

To escape perpetual futile mourning, one must accept the figurations and distractions the culture offers: stepfathers in place of fathers, the deferred promise of glory and material reward. No wonder Claudius is the villain of the piece, when he so perfectly embodies the standard cultural explanation of why we should accept death, expressed (for example) by Drummond: "since it is a necessity, from the which never an age by-past hath been exempted . . . (no consequent of life being more common and familiar), why shouldst thou, with unprofitable and nothing availing stubbornness, oppose to so unevitable and necessary a condition" (p. 24).

But Claudius's rhetorical reference to "the first corse" is a Freudian slip that reveals his special share in the universal guilt that bequeathed mortality. He seems to have forgotten, at least on the conscious level, that (according to his Bible) the first corpse was Abel, killed by his brother: Cain, "that did the first murder" (5.1.76). This unwitting but revealing allusion not only provides a first squeak of the guilt that will eventually be caught in "The Mousetrap"; it also compromises the larger cover story of natural decay by which Claudius's depredations— and perhaps those of all Creation—seek to disguise themselves as something orderly and acceptable, something controllable by a finite commemoration ("for some term / To do obsequious sorrow," as Claudius puts it at 1.2.91–92). As in *The Spanish Tragedy*, the first cause of death—the "author of this woe"—can hide from prosecution behind the efficient causes. "*Cain* was not therefore the first murtherer, but *Adam*, who brought in death" (Browne, p. 141).

From another perspective, the Cain allusions point to the deeper things that this revenge story shares with the Genesis story. Both narratives play to the profound need to perceive death as a contingency, and a correctable one at that. That is the fallacy at the pathetic heart of blood-revenge, the fallacy that inspired the "prophetic soul" of Hamlet himself to suspect his uncle of murdering as well as replacing his father (1.5.41). Just as the play vindicates the disgusted cynicism of adolescence by giving it objective correlatives, so too it vindicates—like many (other) detective stories—the perversely satisfying suspicion that every ordinary death can be exposed as a murder. Every death is both banal and outrageous; nature becomes murder's alibi in Claudius's speech, in a way that reminds us how murder becomes nature's alibi in several popular genres of fiction.[14]

A few lines before he learns that his father's ghost has appeared, Hamlet is already groping for a mythology that will allow him to imagine death as reversible, capping his complaint about his mother's hasty remarriage with the assertion that Claudius is "no more like my father / Than I to Hercules" (1.2.152–53). Given the themes of the soliloquy, this allusion recalls Hercules' expedition into the underworld to return the conjugally loyal Alcestis to her noble husband: if Hamlet were indeed like Hercules, then he could have his real father again in place of his step-father.

Like Milton in "Methought I Saw My Late Espoused Saint," however, Hamlet must eventually awaken from the Alcestis fantasy to the dark, stubborn facts of natural death. The wish this dream fulfills is the wish to evade the ordinary consumption of the body:

> O that this too too sullied flesh would melt,
> Thaw and resolve itself into a dew,
> Or that the Everlasting had not fix'd
> His canon 'gainst self-slaughter.
>
> (1.2.129–32)

This is not merely (as he is commonly characterized) a man so disgusted and weary-spirited that he wishes to surrender to death. On the contrary, he is trying to find an alternative to death, or if he must die, to do so as a willed act, a conquest rather than a surrender. (Intriguingly, the other great voice of morbid intellect in this period, John Donne, was similarly inclined to turn death into a pure melting, as in the "Valediction: Forbidding Mourning," or into a decisively violent suicide, as in *Biathanatos*.)

The alternative to such lovely or sudden endings was much less attractive, as the vivid heritage of macabre medieval art would have reminded Hamlet, Donne, and their audiences. As so often in Renaissance literature (and 5.1.29–31 makes it explicit), gardens become a subconscious euphemistic metaphor for graveyards:

> 'tis an unweeded garden
> That grows to seed; things rank and gross in nature
> Possess it merely. That it should come to this!
> But two months dead.
>
> (1.2.135–38)

At two months dead, the problem is not only faded memories above ground, but also decaying flesh below ground that nature grossly repossesses. Hamlet will talk explicitly about the "convocation of politic worms" that feast on Polonius's corpse (4.3.19–31), but the macabre *transi* image seems already to be on Hamlet's mind in this first soliloquy. When he recalls bitterly that Gertrude used to hang on King Hamlet "As if increase of appetite had grown / By what it fed on"

(1.2.144–45), it sounds as if she were a coffin-worm, and their marriage had been the beginning of King Hamlet's vermiculation. Indeed, early in the bedroom confrontation, Hamlet construes Gertrude's marriages as a mindless feeding on her husbands (3.4.66–67), and he warns Polonius to sequester Ophelia from kissing and conception, lest "the sun breed maggots in a dead dog" (2.2.181–86). Until he fully under-stands the murder as such, Hamlet finds a scapegoat through the familiar misogynist suspicion that women (in the decadent sexuality they evoke, or in the fallible bodies they issue) are the source of men's mortality. "Frailty, thy name is woman" (1.2.146).

The suggestion of vermiculation recurs more disturbingly in Hamlet's complaint that

> The funeral bak'd meats
> Did coldly furnish forth the marriage tables.
> Would I had met my dearest foe in heaven
> Or ever I had seen that day, Horatio.
> My father—methinks I see my father.

(1.2.180–84)

Seeing him is one thing; eating him is another. Hamlet's father, already regurgitated by his tomb (1.4.50–51), becomes all too model a Host at this mixed sacrament, serving as a locus for the communion of his kin. Nor is this so peculiar a transaction as we are provisionally encouraged to imagine: all the bodies in Denmark, Guildenstern tells Claudius, "feed upon your Majesty" (3.3.10). A king "may go a progress through the guts of a beggar," as Hamlet argues (4.3.30–31); he may also go a progress through the guts of his son. The wildest horrors of *Titus Andronicus* lie waiting to be recognized in every meal of our ordinary lives, as we repress the knowledge of the deaths our lives are built on.[15]

Hamlet's reluctance to partake of this feast of renewal is understand-able. He is much more willing to incorporate his father's returning spirit than his father's bodily remains; he prefers communication to commun-ion. Yet, at least in body-language, the ghost communicates nothing but death. Horatio shifts the topic from the funeral meats to the apparition, which he describes as "very pale," its eyes "fix'd" (1.2.233).[16] It came "In the dead waste and middle of the night" and left the sentries "distill'd / Almost to jelly with the act of fear," so that they "Stand dumb and speak not to him" (1.2.198, 204–6). The blank staring, the collapse into silence, even the distillment into jelly (cf. Donne's *Sermons,*

III, 105), suggest that this ghost infects those he encounters with a version of his own unredeemed deadness. Marcellus turns for consolation to the idea of Christ as a bearer of Eternal Life (1.1.163–69), but this ghost offers a parodic inversion of precisely that notion.[17] Its insistent "Remember me" translates into "*memento mori*," not an extension of life, but an invitation into death.

Why, then, is Hamlet so jolly by the end of a visitation that hints at purgatorial torments, reveals earthly horrors, and assigns him a brutal and predictably fatal task? Perhaps he exults because the idea of death as ultimate closure and permanent stillness has been so strikingly refuted. For a creature of faith such as Sir Thomas Browne (p. 115), the pain at the end of life is much more frightening than the prospect of what may follow. But, as C. S. Lewis suggests, this play is haunted, not by "a physical fear of dying, but a fear of being dead."[18] What Hamlet emphasizes repeatedly in greeting the ghost is its bodily escape from the tomb, as if that physical resurrection were more valuable, or at least more plausible, than spiritual salvation:

>   tell
> Why thy canoniz'd bones, hearsed in death,
> Have burst their cerements, why the sepulchre
> Wherein we saw thee quietly inurn'd
> Hath op'd his ponderous and marble jaws
> To cast thee up again. What may this mean,
> That thou, dead corse, again in complete steel
> Revisits thus the glimpses of the moon. . . .
>
>   (1.4.47–53)

The ghost provides simultaneously an explanation and a disproof of simple mortality. The gross decay of this old man's flesh resulted from an evil aberration, and the rest of his spirit is not yet silent.

Better a murdered king on earth than a dead one at peace, if Hamlet's response is any guide. If his father still has a purpose in death, then Hamlet's life, rendered aimless by a confrontation with mortality, can recover purpose also: "Say why is this? Wherefore? What should we do?" (1.4.57). Again the ghost and the project of revenge he advocates serve the same purpose as neurotic symptoms. Like both Hieronimo and Hamlet, any person forced to confront the human situation must become a bit insane in order to continue functioning normally:

the despair and anguish of which the patient complains is not the result of such symptoms but rather are the reasons for their existence. It is in fact these

very symptoms that shield him from the torment of the profound contradictions that lie at the heart of human existence . . . neurotic symptoms serve to
reduce and narrow—to magically transform the world so that he may be
distracted from his concerns of death, guilt, and meaninglessness. The neurotic preoccupied with his symptom is led to believe that his central task is one
of confrontation with his particular obsession or phobia. In a sense his neurosis allows him to take control of his destiny.[19]

"My fate cries out," Hamlet insists over Horatio's warnings, "Still am I
call'd" (1.4.81, 84). "Fate" and "calling" are the words by which
countless Renaissance self-fashioners deemed valid the readings of their
lives that gave them shape and therefore value. An inauthentic madness
helps hold off a true madness, and that internally generated function
may be helpfully masked as compulsion from a meaningful beyond.

Shakespeare thus exposes the inner workings of narrative forms that
rose rapidly to prominence during his lifetime: the call of a conversion
experience, the spiritual autobiography, the revenge story. Without such
provocative mythologies, we might not know what, why, even how to
desire, beyond the sleeping and feeding Hamlet dismisses as merely
bestial (4.4.35). Without such "revelations" to dispel the banality of
death, without them to shape for us a meaningful task of defending good
against evil, we could easily sink into the poisonous *accidie* that grips
Hamlet in the opening scenes. He has to find murder for the same
reason most people have to find God, and the ghost functions as religion
does in general, providing "a system of symbols which acts to establish
powerful, pervasive and long-lasting moods and motivations" and
"clothing these conceptions with . . . an aura of factuality."[20]

Hamlet's responses to the visiting ghost, and even to the visiting
players, provoke us to evaluate our own appetites for stories of murder
and retribution, whether in the Book of Genesis, the story of Pyrrhus, or
the play of *Hamlet*. Revenge drama is, I believe, overdetermined in its
appeal to Renaissance audiences. The revenge-instinct is not unique to
that cultural moment, nor even to the human species; but instances like
The Spanish Tragedy and *Hamlet* offer the supplemental pleasure of
characterizing death as "most foul, strange and unnatural" (*Hamlet*,
1.5.28). If the Biblical question, "Death, where is thy sting?" is no
longer merely rhetorical, at least it now has an answer: "The serpent that
did sting thy father's life / Now wears his crown" (1.5.39–40). In
making death the work of an evil serpent in the garden (or at least the
orchard), to be avenged by a devout son, Shakespeare at once taps and
anatomizes the appeal of Christian mythology. Our desire for Hamlet to

kill Claudius, for the heir to defeat death on the father's behalf, is really another version of a standard dream of immortality regained.

Shakespeare refuses to stabilize this traditional system of denial: even this consolingly specific criminal accusation comports a more general and troubling oedipal riddle about the normal succession to the crown of life, generations guilty of feeding on the bodies of their ancestors. Ernest Jones's classic Freudian interpretation, which argues that Hamlet is paralyzed by the fact that Claudius has merely enacted Hamlet's own oedipal desires, may be expanded into something less purely psychosexual.[21] Perhaps young Hamlet's tendency to think of suicide as an alternative to revenge reflects a recognition that he is precisely what he must attack Claudius for being: the replacement of his father, the symbolic embodiment and direct beneficiary of the process that necessitated the father's death.

Claudius assigns Rosencrantz and Guildenstern to elicit from Hamlet "What it should be, / More than his father's death, that thus hath put him / So much from th'understanding of himself" (2.2.7–9). But (even without oedipal guilt) might not that clearest early warning of death most people encounter—the demise of the same-sex parent, a loss Shakespeare suffered at about the time he was writing *Hamlet*—make it unbearable for us to recognize ourselves sanely, to understand ourselves as the heirs of graves no less than thrones? Thomas Adams—whose Jacobean sermons show a surprising imprint of Shakespeare's works, including *Hamlet*—preached that "common Funerals tell us all men are mortal, but that of a Father speaketh not only plainly, but particularly, thou art so. Where the Father's dead, there can be no pretence or thought of immortality."[22] How should one sanely, self-knowingly, reconcile (as Hamlet attempts to do later in the scene, at 2.2.303–8) the magnificence of humanity with its destiny in dust? Gertrude diagnoses for Claudius the cause of Hamlet's madness as "His father's death and our o'er-hasty marriage" (2.2.57). From Hamlet's perspective, those two events are two stages of the same crime, the commonplace and outrageous obliteration of King Hamlet by time and mortal frailty. The Player Queen makes the idea explicit: "A second time I kill my husband dead, / When second husband kisses me in bed" (3.2.179–80).

On one level, the revelation of Claudius as a murderer is merely the literal fulfillment of a fact that is already true psychologically, symbolically. By replacing the perfect father with a mortal man, by showing that love and memory are ephemeral, and that roles such as husband and king are fungible, the transition from old Hamlet's reign to that of Claudius entails the invention of mortality in young Hamlet's psychic world. No wonder Hamlet calls him "this canker of our nature" (5.2.69); no wonder the comparison of Claudius to that first corpse-maker, Cain, keeps recurring; and no wonder his standard speeches of consolation become indices of his extraordinary guilt, as the spectators are invited to project onto this villain all their own resentment at the unsatisfactory explanations and consolations they have received for the deaths of the people they love. Again—to adapt Voltaire's aphorism about God—if there had been no murder, Hamlet would have been compelled to invent one. And in a work of fictional art, in the work of mythmaking, there can hardly be any absolute distinction between empirical reality and psychological invention. The need to make a hero of the father and a villain of the stepfather not only suggests a familiar psychological syndrome in Hamlet the man. It also reminds us that our pleasure in watching *Hamlet* the play, other stories of blood-revenge, and perhaps even the Christian story, arises from a similar syndrome: a need to cast the world in polarities that give it meaning, to isolate a master truth that can finally be vindicated against the interim victories of mortality.

Claudius proves susceptible to the same convenient allegorization of his own mortality, pleading for England to eradicate Hamlet, "For like the hectic in my blood he rages, / And thou must cure me" (4.3.69–70). Hamlet is indirectly flesh of his flesh, more than kin and less than kind, the outward agency of Claudius's inherent susceptibility to death—as the plot proves him to be. He brings Claudius's poison into Claudius's bloodstream, gives him a taste of his own mortality. The assurance God will not give him in the prayer scene, Claudius begs from the English executioners, by asserting his royal prerogative over life and death. His plots to assassinate Hamlet thus derive from the same projective mythology that shapes Hamlet's plots against him.

Campaigns against death are ostensibly waged in service to the dead (as in the common practice of raising funds for gun control or medical research in the name of victims of crime or disease),[23] but they are primarily functions of denial on the part of the living. Laertes' determination to aid and comfort his dead father and sister—indeed, his illusion that that is his motive—provides a vivid example of the culture's standard mechanisms of denial. Since Polonius has been interred "but greenly / In hugger-mugger" (4.5.83–84), and since Ophelia receives only "maimed rites" (5.1.212), Laertes feels compelled to supplement them with the ritual of revenge. Again the play taps emergent tensions in the surrounding culture, where Puritans would insist—unsuccessfully—that corpses "be immediately interred, without any Ceremony," because "praying, reading, and singing" in funerals "have been grossly abused, are no way beneficial to the dead, and have proved many wayes hurtfull to the living."[24] For Laertes as for Hamlet, the road to blood-revenge is paved by the Reformation.

Even at his most violently rebellious, Laertes is thus as conventional a thinker as his father; he embodies precisely the destructive and delusional determination to wound the living for the sake of the dead that the play as a whole condemns. The point is not that Laertes overreacts—Shakespeare could surely have given him slimmer grounds for outrage, as other Renaissance playwrights gave their honor-mad killers—but that his solution proves so badly misguided. He seems unselfconsciously delighted to rehearse the juicy role of avenger, first on his father's behalf and then on his sister's. Playing this role requires a villain from whom to retake their lives, and Claudius is shrewd enough to cast Hamlet convincingly in that role. Claudius promises Laertes that Ophelia's "grave shall have a living monument" (5.1.292) in the killing of Hamlet, who supposedly caused her death. So the act of revenge is to serve the same purpose as funeral statuary, to give the deceased some representative immortality.

Even shrewder, perhaps, is Claudius's evocation of the Norman horseman's name—Lamord—as a provocation for Laertes to undertake the duel (4.7.91). Claudius's diction then emphasizes that any reticence in revenge constitutes a surrender to death: a submission to time, disease, and mutability (4.7.110–18). By raising for Laertes the same disturbing possibility that events have raised for Hamlet—that loving memory, the last hope of the dead father, decays like a body—Claudius compels Laertes to assert the contrary with bloodshed. By accepting the conventional formula of consolatory vengeance, Laertes will show himself indeed his complacent "father's son / More than in words." But his vow "To cut [Hamlet's] throat i'th' church" sets the immortality-fantasies based in memory, progeny, and vengeance directly against the central immortalizing promise of Christianity (4.7.124–25). We are left uncertain whether revenge should be construed as the correction of murder, as revenge-tragedies generally suggested, or merely as further murder, as Elizabethan orthodoxies insisted. By these contradictions *Hamlet* deconstructs its own genre, forcing us to recognize the arbitrary designations by which we locate absolute eternal values in a mutable world. In distancing himself from Laertes' stock vengefulness, Hamlet offers us a glimpse of a morality undistorted by the denial of death, a way out of the bad faith prompted by existential dread: "In the prison of one's character one can pretend and feel that he *is somebody*, that the world is manageable, that there is a reason for one's life, a ready justification for one's action. To live automatically and uncritically is to be assured of at least a minimum share of the programmed cultural heroics" (Becker, p. 87). Hamlet fails to rescue Laertes from precisely this prison, and it means they will both die in the prison here called Denmark.

When Claudius is given what he earlier called "superfluous death" (4.5.96), the multiple sword-thrusts and poisonings replicate all the killings he has caused, revealing the absurdly systematic way revenge seeks to undo death. This sort of redundant murder also helps conceal the binary nature and fundamental causes of death. As a mortal man, Hamlet must die within a few decades by course of nature; but we hardly notice that tragic fact in its own guise while we are watching him parry more vivid and specific threats: suicidal impulses, marauding pirates, mandated executions, poisoned swords and cups. Laertes claims his poison is so powerful that

> Where it draws blood, no cataplasm so rare,
> Collected from all simples that have virtue
> Under the moon, can save the thing from death
> That is but scratch'd withal.
>
> (4.7.142–145)

But what balm can save anyone from death, even in the absence of a poison-tipped rapier? They should have died hereafter, unless the poison were the eternally redemptive blood of Christ. From this perspective, the duel is a kind of Black Mass that, under Claudius's satanic guidance, undoes all the promises of immortality. Like the guests at Claudius's implicitly cannibalistic wedding-feast, these Danes are feeding on a deadly rather than a redemptive Host.[25]

The black humor of the gravedigger performs the same kind of subversion as that Black Mass. Like the crowing of the cock and the recollection of Julius Caesar in the first act, the scene suggests a parody of the Last Judgment: skulls rise from their graves to endure Hamlet's sentences, and the gravedigger, Hamlet, and Laertes all climb from graves under their own power.[26] This is a place of skulls—"another Golgotha," to borrow a crucifixion reference from *Macbeth* (1.2.40)— but the only resurrection it can offer is exhumation. The clowns analyze the causes and implications of Ophelia's death so badly that they expose the underlying absurdity of allocating burial spots according to the state of mind that once inhabited the decaying corpse. No less absurd is their indignation that the rich and powerful have more right than the poor to hang and drown themselves (5.1.26–29). Much of the graveyard humor arises precisely from the way the decorous official metaphors collapse to a crudely physical level: "The crowner hath sat on her and finds it Christian burial" (5.1.4). But that collapse is as frightening as it is funny. Incoherent theology is not only a poor cover for implacable biology, it suggests that better theology is merely a better cover. Certainly, after seeing the attitude of the gravedigger toward the bodily remains—the way the props are treated by the stagehand after the funeral show is over—we can hardly overlook the empty pomposity of the priest's concern that a full Christian ceremony would "profane the service of the dead" (5.1.229). They are already being served profanely enough, and served in fact to worms.

Laertes tries to answer the priest's chilly arguments with natural facts and feelings, but cannot help inventing his own death-defying miracles (and hence his own supernatural cruelties) in the process:

> Lay her i'th' earth,
> And from her fair and unpolluted flesh
> May violets spring. I tell thee, churlish priest,
> A minist'ring angel shall my sister be
> When thou liest howling.
>
> (5.1.231–35)

Laertes' dramatic leap into the grave, Gertrude's strewing of flowers—how much of this can survive as convincing high sentiment after the gravedigger has sounded the low-comic keynotes? Hamlet accuses Laertes of "rant," then grandly demands to be buried with Ophelia too. He seems to be torn between a need to express his own passionate mourning, and his need to acknowledge sarcastically the hollowness of such gestures. If brother and lover intend to keep raising the verbal dosage until their patient revives, the hyperbole will inevitably, and revealingly, become ridiculous—as the violence does in other revenge-tragedies. Gertrude attributes Hamlet's reactions to "mere madness," but Ophelia's stark indifference to the debates and rivalries over her worldly love and her eternal soul exposes all these competitors and commentators as victims of a typically human madness, a delusive need to replace the indifference of death with the differentiations by which we define and preserve our sanity.

While it is valid for a *Hamlet* scholar to inquire, say, whether aristocratic Renaissance widows were expected to mourn two months or twelve,[27] it is also valid to ask why it should matter. Hamlet exclaims sarcastically to Ophelia, "O heavens, die two months ago and not forgotten yet! Then there's hope a great man's memory may outlive his life half a year. But by'r lady a must build churches then . . . " (3.2.128–31). Patent as it may seem, this tirade still strikes a devastatingly direct blow to a familiar tendency to answer mortal annihilation with the memories of those who loved us, with the legacies of our good deeds and grand monuments, and with the prayers such things elicit for us from those we leave behind.[28] Hamlet's anger reflects a special exasperation with the human tendency—irrationally, but under the name of reasonableness—to measure responses to the infiniteness of death with finite numbers, to suppose that a month's mourning is the right amount for a permanent loss, even that a tanner's body will rot after nine years rather than eight. The popular aphorism about lies needs little revision to apply to attitudes toward death: there are denials, damned denials, and statistics.

The persistence of the facts of deadness against all human constructions comes through clearly in the gravedigger's riddle that makes his profession the best builders, since "The houses he makes lasts till doomsday" (5.1.59). It comes through more subversively in his argument that Adam was the first gravedigger, which not only re-awakens the Cain reference, but also suggests that all mankind has ever really done is tirelessly dig its own graves. This may sound like a prophecy of the nuclear arms race—a logical culmination of that process—but it was already evident to Shakespeare's contemporaries: "Assoon as God set us on work, our very occupation was an Embleme of death; It was to digge the earth; not to digge pitfals for other men, but graves for our selves" (*Sermons*, IV, 52).

The play focuses on this disturbing idea with increasing magnification. First we are told that the gravedigger began his job on "that day that our last king Hamlet overcame Fortinbras," suggesting that the earliest death mentioned in the play was in fact the start of the world's mortality. Moreover, the fact that young Fortinbras takes over young Hamlet's royal legacy at the end of the play demonstrates that time obliterates human achievements, that the things people fought and died for slip, by forfeit or random permutation, back to their opposites or starting-places. Which man won that archetypal single combat between old Hamlet and old Fortinbras finally makes no more difference than whether Ophelia went to the water or the water to Ophelia. The Old

Testament keynote for *Hamlet* may thus be less the vengeful splendors of Genesis and Exodus than the clear-eyed weariness of Ecclesiastes.

The next step is the indirect revelation that this gravedigger's first day on the job was also "that very day that young Hamlet was born" (5.1.143), as if this resting-place had been prepared for him from the beginning of his existence as a physical individual. What was he "born to set . . . right"? Again the specific mission of revenge serves as a metaphor, or perhaps merely as a disguise, for the mysterious assignment implicit in being born a human being. Have we been summoned to perform justice, to defend honor, to protect our families and our nations; or merely to chase illusions and to die? Words, laws, and beauty here lose their meaning; as the surface is scraped off the graveyard, the play exposes the shallowness of its society's fabric of denial (however richly brocaded) beneath which it hides its dark obvious secrets. Culture is a shroud. Hamlet expresses surprise that this worker "sings in grave-making," and Horatio replies that "Custom hath made it in him a property of easiness" (5.1.65–67). This exchange builds on the preceding suggestions of universality, reminding us that, from one perspective, all our works and days constitute singing at grave-making, enabled by habit and by cultural customs that insulate us from the overwhelming facts of death that are always around and ahead of us.

Events forbid Hamlet to keep these observations at the comfortable distance of *contemptus mundi* and *memento mori* commonplaces, a process which serves to remind us that we too may not have truly confronted mortality merely by speaking about it sententiously in the abstract. He begins to identify achingly with the abused disinterred bones, then learns that one skull belonged to his old playmate Yorick—a demystified ghost and a demythologized father. Finally Hamlet stumbles across the funeral of his beloved Ophelia. He asserts his identity almost hysterically as the anonymity of the grave closes in on him, yet in doing so he again allows his father's identity to absorb his own: "This is I, / Hamlet the Dane" (5.1.250–51). The accompanying impulse to descend into the grave—as if the only way to honor a life that has ended were to join it in the functions of death—marks Hamlet's subservience to the scenarios of blood-revenge. That impulse that must be resisted to allow a comic affirmation like that of *The Winter's Tale*, where Leontes finally overcomes his guilt-ridden desire to become as dead as Hermione, and instead ushers her back into the functions of life.

At the brink of death, with all his own *sententiae* about futility and anonymity still fresh in his ears, Hamlet undergoes a sort of deathbed conversion, seeking a final serenity within the Christian formula. This change has often been interpreted as Hamlet's saving revelation, and as the central truth the play serves to inculcate. But Hamlet's attitude toward heaven consistently proves to be an index of how badly he needs faith at any moment; and the graveyard scene expands that pattern to the entire culture, positioning religion as one of the antic dispositions provoked by mortality. Though Hamlet is clearly ineligible for the benefits of the "happy fraud" Thomas Browne (p. 300) attributes to ancient cultures, which believed that ghosts were pained by too much grieving, it is not clear that the Christian happiness about death is any less fraudulent. Hamlet's final "the rest is silence" (5.2.363) seems potentially disturbing for his religious followers in much the way Jesus's "Why hast thou forsaken me" might have been for his.[29]

Furthermore, it is hard to discern much divine care rewarding Hamlet's conversion, or much Christian benevolence in his own actions; the Denmark of act 5 is hardly a kinder, gentler nation.[30] It is also hard to see Hamlet's new version of passivity as especially Christian. Stoicism is the last refuge of many a Renaissance hero, but Hamlet's acceptance of his role as a born avenger and a falling sparrow looks less like a happy declaration of faith than like an agnostic yielding to fate, as best one can read it. What Hamlet seems to posit is less a deity to save his soul than a co-author to advance his heroic scenario over the competing scripts that crowd the stages of Elsinore, and thereby to give his life the narrative shape that makes closure a triumph rather than a surrender.[31] God the Father in act 5 proves to be merely an extension of the father's ghost in act 1—as Freud's theories of religion from the early *Totem and Taboo* to the late *Future of an Illusion* would predict. If my resistance to the Christian references places me in the critical pitfall Richard Levin calls "refuting the ending,"[32] my defense is a kind of *tu quoque*: to accept the conventional consolations as sufficient is to refute the ending of human life, to misrepresent as comic (however cleverly and appealingly) a plot of rise and fall.

The "augury" Hamlet finally declines to defy (5.2.215) is the mysterious but reliable prophecy of death that sits so ill about our hearts, and lies latent in the uncannily inescapable prophecies of so many other tales of tragic irony, where the protagonist finally arrives at the fatal spot that has awaited him since birth. Hamlet justifies his passivity with a parsing that—in its very absurdity and circularity—may be finally all the human mind can "reasonably" conclude about death:

There is special providence in the fall of a sparrow. If it be now, 'tis not to come; if it be not to come, it will be now; if it be not now, yet it will come. The readiness is all. (5.2.215–18)

All one can do is blankly declare that each individual life is significant. All one can choose about death is to be ready—to mythologize the things that happen into a satisfactory story, to prepare a plausible reading of mortality as wholeness rather than emptiness. Hamlet hopes for a benevolent paternal deity behind this inscrutable omnipotence, but we see the duel arising instead from the feigned paternal benevolence of Claudius, a virtual personification of death itself. Shakespeare uses Horatio to encourage our exasperation with Hamlet for submitting to the scheme—thereby compelling us to challenge our own fatal attractions to schemes called honor and religion and revenge, things we choose to die for so that dying can have a "for."

What is there to fight for, what even to live for, in the world of Denmark? That is the question posed so memorably by Hamlet's early soliloquies, and we should not dismiss it as merely the conventional symptomology of the melancholic, or forget its fundamental power when Hamlet conveniently receives an assignment that (in either sense) "distracts" him. Christian religion appears as empty words chewed in the mouth of Claudius and a prayer-book placed for show in the hands of Ophelia. Rosencrantz and Guildenstern expose common friendship as vulnerable to the brief passing of time and the least pressure of realpolitik. To a cynical male eye, romantic love would have been similarly compromised by Gertrude and Ophelia. Claudius poses as a Donne-like lover whose very existence depends on mutual attraction with Gertrude: "She is so conjunctive to my life and soul / That, as the star moves not but in his sphere, / I could not but by her." This, in turn, explains why he does not dispose of Hamlet promptly, since "The Queen his mother / Lives almost by his looks" (4.7.14–16, 11–12). The entire Danish society—and it may not be extraordinary in this—becomes a kind of house of cards, people making the needy lives around them the justification for their own, in an endlessly circular argument of life-motivation.

Hamlet's survey of Fortinbras's "twenty thousand men / That, for a fantasy and trick of fame, / Go to their graves like beds" (4.4.60–62) defines honor as a thin, destructive invention to which one must nonetheless subscribe if one is to posit and preserve any transcendence of our status as physical animals. To avoid perceiving death as an ultimate defeat, one must declare something else more important, and validate that assertion by action. That is why the armies march, and even while acknowledging it as absurd and arbitrary, Hamlet seems to consider it as good a reason as any. Honor is further exposed as the hollow commodity of Polonius's advice, the cipher at the abysmal center of Ophelia's madness, and the heartless heart of Laertes' duelling. The declared stakes of that duel—horses, decorations, reputations (5.2.144–61)—plausibly represent all the fripperies of worldly wealth and ostentation which generally serve, as they do in this specific instance, to distract us from the real situation until we are safely in the clutches of death. As on the level of plot, so too on the level of moral symbolism, these designated objects of rivalrous desire are merely toys designed to keep our minds on the game. As a popular Elizabethan treatise on death warned about the rewards of courtiership, "all these liberalities which the Devill casteth us as out at a windowe, are but baites: all these pleasures but embushes: and that he doth but make his sport of us, who strive one with another for such things."[33] Acquisitive materialism and the competition it breeds keep us from recognizing our common grievance—and perhaps somehow making common cause—against mortality.

That recognition seems to underlie Hamlet's impulses to reconcile himself with Laertes, first in his mourning, then in his dying. Shortly before the fencing match, Hamlet declares that he feels "very sorry, good Horatio, / That to Laertes I forgot myself; / For by the image of my cause I see / The portraiture of his" (5.2.75–78). The specific cause they share is the outrageous death of a father, but as Claudius pointed out in the play's second scene, the whole history of nature is "death of fathers," and it should not seem so particular with Hamlet and Laertes. We all share the simple doom that the revenge story buries and the gravedigger brutally unearths. To continue spilling each other's blood to cover up that fact—to perform vengeful human sacrifices in the service of an illusion—seems a terrible if widespread mistake. It makes us each into Claudius, a "limed soul, that struggling to be free / Art more engag'd" in the business of death (3.3.68–69). Hamlet is right to call it a possessive "madness," not an authentic self, that attacked Laertes' family, foolishly stabbing a foolish man in blind anger, and lashing out at a loving young woman for all the betrayals men have felt in their love of women. In the paranoid management of our missiles, we share the madness whereby Hamlet "shot my arrow o'er the house / And hurt my brother" (5.2.239–40), and risk sharing his fatal guilt.[34]

When Hamlet says that his imagination can "trace the noble dust of Alexander till 'a find it stopping a bung-hole," Horatio warns him that "'Twere to consider too curiously to consider so" (5.1.197–99). It is not merely "the dread of something after death" that robs "enterprises of great pitch and moment" of "the name of action" (3.1.78, 86, 88); the dread of nothingness threatens similar consequences.[35] To be and then not to be puzzles the will. What haunts Hamlet most deeply is not exactly the ghost, and what he finally fears about the sleep of death is not exactly the nightmare of damnation. When Rosencrantz tries to attribute Hamlet's distraction to his worldly ambitions, Hamlet replies, "I could be bounded in a nutshell and count myself a king of infinite space—were it not that I have bad dreams" (2.2.254–56). The prospect of a little grave juxtaposed with the prospect of a limitless universe would disable human ambitions and destroy the human psyche, if that recognition were not tamed by rituals, fictions, and selective perceptions. Better a king of a nutshell than a slave of the infinite. Hamlet's too curious dreams may have shown him that his worldly reign (like Alexander's) is nightmarishly lost in a vastness beyond measure.

If Hamlet has nothing to live for, at least he finds something to live *by*—something like dramatic art. By the time Hamlet completes his revenge, he seems no longer to be working at the behest of the ghost, but on behalf of a compulsion to achieve shape and purpose in his own foreshortened lifetime. He was demonstrably right to mistrust the histrionics of revenge involved in playing "Priam," and even in playing "Hamlet"; yet like the rest of us, he desperately needs a role. His metatheatrical consolation is that he dies as part of a meaningful and repeatable story. It is really the audience, onstage and off, that is in danger of resting in silence, pallor, and oblivion:

> You that look pale and tremble at this chance,
> That are but mutes or audience to this act,
> Had I but time—as this fell sergeant, Death,
> Is strict in his arrest—O, I could tell you—
> But let it be. Horatio, I am dead,
> Thou livest. Report me and my cause aright
> To the unsatisfied.
>
> (5.2.339–45)

Anticipating his arrest to a new kind of prison, Hamlet again resurrects his father's spirit in the process of avenging it: like the ghost, he turns his audience fearfully pale, withholds his secrets, but asks that he be remembered and thereby justified. This time Horatio will have to perform the moralizing and immortalizing work that Shakespeare himself performs, and in a similar way.

But all this telling will be lost to Hamlet, who concentrates on the completion of his earthly story, no longer on any prospect of a judgment beyond:

> Fortinbras . . . has my dying voice.
> So tell him, with th'occurrents more and less
> Which have solicited—the rest is silence.
>
> HORATIO: Now cracks a noble heart. Good night, sweet prince,
> And flights of angels sing thee to thy rest.
>
> (5.2.361–65)

Under the immediate pressure of mourning, the stoic skeptic tries to supply the transcendent music that seems to have forsaken his friend at the moment of death, tries at least to reinterpret that silence as a musical "rest" preparatory to an immortal song.[36] But the music that immediately answers Horatio's plea is a drum, a sound—whether it proclaims victory or death—of determined destruction. Like the heartbeats of Henry King's "Exequy" (1624) that propel him inexorably closer to their silencing and his death, they speak of a forced march through time to timelessness. But they also suggest a kind of heroic measure (to borrow a medical term) in the desperate struggle to replace that lost heartbeat, as war is often a heroic measure in the desperate struggle to efface mortality.

Fortinbras's commentary on this corpse-strewn stage must sound, to an exorcised audience, almost as ironically irrelevant as the English ambassadors' grand announcement of Rosencrantz and Guildenstern's execution (5.2.373–77). That we now perceive Fortinbras's retributive campaign as a misguided response to the emotional needs of mourning is an index of Shakespeare's success as an ethical teacher. Fortinbras becomes a spokesman for a conventional view of heroic death that the play itself has rendered obsolete:

> This quarry cries on havoc. O proud Death,
> What feast is toward in thine eternal cell,
> That thou so many princes at a shot
> So bloodily hast struck?
>
> (5.2.369–72)

The anthropomorphizing of death—even where it is disguised as a grim surrender, as it is here—is actually a consoling fiction. Death (*pace* John

Donne) is not proud; nor is it ashamed. The terror lies in its indifference, which steals away the differences by which and for which we live. The princes who fall bloodily at once would all soon enough have descended in age and sickness to their tombs, no more or less dead than paupers. At death's Lasting Supper, "your fat king and your lean beggar is but variable service," and Shakespeare has disabled the mechanism of denial required to perceive this "feast" as ritual and metaphor, systematically reducing the promises of the supper of the Lamb in heaven to the banquet of the worms underground (4.3.16–37). As in the gravedigger's riddles, the high drama of a gallows must yield place to the sheer duration of a grave (5.1.41–59). A story of royal murder has become a story of human decay, death has become less a ghost than a skull, and the efforts to conceal it by hasty burial (of King Hamlet, Polonius, Ophelia) now yield to the stark deliberate staging of all available corpses (5.2.382–401).

Shakespeare does not give his ghost the last word, as many revenge-tragedians do. The final music of the play is not even that ominous drum, but the numbing, death-bearing sound of the soldiers' memorial shooting. Fortinbras's closing suggestion that all this bloodshed would have been acceptable if it had occurred on the battlefield (5.2.406–7) reflects his psychological need to keep death safely contained within the ancient ritual known as war. It may also alert modern readers to our opposing need, in a century of holocaust and potential holocaust, to eliminate the justifying, distancing category of war and instead to focus on the many individual deaths war entails, which are each inherently tragic. Nor is this only a modern problem: religion, war, vengeance, and sacrifice have together been manufacturing violent suffering from the earliest re-corded incidents of Western civilization, with Agamemnon "making his child a sacrificial beast / To give the ships auspicious winds for Troy / Such are the crimes to which religion leads."[37]

All that these patriarchal ghosts give to life is a mission to destroy it, as Polonius and old Fortinbras and old Hamlet gave to their sons, as parents give to children in so many different codes and times and places. The world is still full of Cold Warriors and Holy Warriors, armies propelled at each other in bloody vengeance by ghosts of their fathers in armor. The ghost's words threaten Hamlet's ear with effects strikingly similar to those of Claudius's poison (compare 1.5.15–22 with 1.5.68–73); rumors "infect [Laertes'] ear / With pestilent speeches of his father's death" (4.5.90–91). Is there anything worse that could be poured in human ears than these legacies of blame and hatred? *Hamlet* converts John's admonition in the New Testament—"Beloved, do not believe every spirit, but test the spirits to see whether they are of God"[38]—into a parable urgently applicable to a modern secular world. Whether or not Prosser is correct in diagnosing a recognizable Elizabethan demon, this kind of ghost seems dangerously unholy, bringing malediction. Again, revenge entails not just a violation but a parody of Christian orthodoxy. To identify the ghost as the incarnation of Hamlet's feelings[39] is to get things backwards: Hamlet is martyred as an incarnation of his father's desires, desires not for mercy but for punishment.

Recognizing the arbitrariness of the ghost's dictates and of Hamlet's obedience, recognizing both as desperate responses to a situation that permits no reasonable response, may liberate us to obey neither God the Father nor the fathers' ghosts when they tell us to kill each other for the sake of our immortality. If the world is a prison, as Hamlet suggests, then we should at least understand our sentence and recognize our fellow prisoners. Denmark has gone from Eden to prison to killing-field to graveyard. If we follow ghosts to a deadly brink or commanders to pointless battles, if we blindly trust some paternal deity to shape our deadly ends, it will be all too easy to take our world along the same tragic path.

To interpret *Hamlet* in this polemical manner is to give up the ghost as a real justification or consolation, isolating it instead within the fictive form as a projection of the various mythologies by which conscious mortals sustain a sense of purpose. But exorcism is itself a risky process, and not a simple one. "Man giveth up the ghost, and where is he?"[40] Claudius convinces Laertes that abjuring revenge for our lost kin would mean abjuring love for them as well. Hamlet fears the same equation, and fears more deeply that giving up such ghosts might mean giving up entirely. If Ophelia must refuse Hamlet's love because it is "A violet in the youth of primy nature, / Forward, not permanent, sweet, not lasting, / The perfume and suppliance of a minute, No more" (1.3.8–10), then any human love—even the love of life—is too risky to accept, since Hamlet's affections are here belittled with the same terms commonly used to describe mortal existence in the *contemptus mundi* and *carpe diem* traditions. As Hamlet is "subject to his birth" in this regard (1.3.18), so are we all subject to our death, and to the deaths of those around us. Ophelia complains that the "violets . . . withered all when my father died" (4.5.182). The image of my lapsed-preacher father, some twenty years deceased, returns to ask (paradoxically) whether I really want to join him in believing that the dead are simply dead. In some ways the compelling ghost of a father is a nightmare devoutly to be wished, but it will not tell the secrets of its house, and at the crowing of the cock, it is gone again:

HAMLET: Do you see nothing there?

GERTRUDE: Nothing at all; yet all that is I see.

HAMLET: Nor did you nothing hear?

GERTRUDE: No, nothing but ourselves.

(3.4.132–35)

Since we assume that artists convey deep truth, and that our own beliefs are deeply true, we tend to deduce (by the fallacy of the undifferentiated middle term) that artists endorse our beliefs. This false deduction unites many ironizing feminist and Marxist critics with the old-fashioned moralizers they scoff at. My preacherly (if atheistical) speculations on *Hamlet* can hardly evade the same accusation merely by hovering between an old humanist correctness (advocating peace as a universal good) and a newer radical version (advocating a revolutionary skepticism). For better or worse, my moralizing differs primarily in being less programmatic: it challenges the institutions generated by one human reflex without positing that some contrary institution would renew the earthly paradise. In that sense, I try not to deny *Hamlet* its identity as a tragedy.

Yet I did propose a seemingly impracticable alternative to these denial-driven cycles of revenge: "somehow making common cause against mortality." Though advances in medical care may delay slightly the death of the body, and advances in artificial intelligence may allow some aspects of an individual mind to continue functioning beyond that death, those are hardly satisfactory answers. As Marlowe's Faustus complains in his opening soliloquy, even curing the Black Plague does little to cure the plague of his individual mortality:

Yet art thou still but *Faustus*, and a man.
Couldst thou make men to live eternally,
Or being dead, raise them to life againe,
Then this profession were to be esteem'd.
Physicke farewell.

(B-text, 1.1.50–54)[41]

The first thirty-one lines of *All's Well* stress the same limitation. The most plausible and time-honored secular tactic in the human struggle against mortality is procreation. If tragedy insists we may not return to the Garden of Eden, comedy accepts its figuration in the Garden of Adonis, where (according to Spenser) creatures are "eterne in mutabilitie," and mortal transience is a necessary component of the machinery of life. In Shakespearean comedies such as *All's Well, Twelfth Night, Love's Labor's Lost*, and even *The Winter's Tale*, the procreative answer to mortality must overcome the rituals of mourning—not only the threat of death—as time passes. This is the alternative Hamlet overlooks in giving his father's deadly demands priority over his mother's hopes for his eventual marriage to Ophelia.

The gendering of these responses fits some familiar patterns. Hamlet accepts a predominantly male legacy of warlike vengeance; the worship of the father entails obedience to what are now commonly known (and condemned) in the academy as patriarchal values, which seek a violent closure. Gertrude is characteristically willing to let new people replace the old ones, even in her bed, always seeking to join the community together; the obvious matriarchal investment in nurturing a generational chain to resist death corresponds to a model of deferral commonly associated with female sexuality. On the brink of retirement from the fame and competition of play-writing in London to the domesticity of Stratford, Shakespeare showed Prospero, every third thought on his grave, turning from a campaign of vengeance against his brother to a campaign for progeny through his daughter.

Yet Shakespeare's *Measure for Measure* demonstrates that this procreative answer to death is finally as questionable as the vengeful responses explored in *Hamlet*. As the hope of Christian afterlife became inadequate to assuage the terror of mortality in Shakespeare's increasingly narcissistic culture, the pressure was redistributed onto other supporting mythologies such as honor and lineage. Shakespeare evidently recognized that these secular solutions would not bear the new load, because—despite the culture's efforts to portray them as products of personal desire—principles of honor and processes of procreation ultimately serve the survival of group structure rather than of individual subjectivity. Renaissance Stoicism would have warned that obeying the instincts of the body destroys the only real freedom, the only durable defense against fortune, mortality, and the state. In *Measure for Measure* the body is in command, and the only law it respects is that of biological process. From one perspective, Shakespeare's Vienna is largely a society of Rosencrantzes and Guildensterns, interchangeable parts only too pleased to live and die as functions of the national status quo.

Dying for the ancestral causes, for tribal honor, as Hamlet does, is arguably a sounder answer to mortality than blindly replicating those ancestors for tribal survival. Despite their obvious affinity for death, the symbolic and absolutist qualities of sacrifice are better suited to the psychic needs of a transient creature confronted by the infinite than are the messy compromises of procreation, so emphatically physical and so perpetually in need of renewal. Hamlet experiments with deferral, but feels more corruption than satisfaction as a result, calling himself "a very drab, / A scullion!" (2.2.582–83), until he can rejoin the fatal chain of honorable male violence. *Measure for Measure* expands this revulsion into a queasy comedy in which sexual reproduction takes priority over honor. If we refuse to follow the specter of Hamlet when it threatens to draw us over the edge into a suicidal madness (1.4.69–74), then we surrender meekly to our animal natures, to our mortality. Either way, death has a square meal, and the last laugh.

3

Comic Means, Tragic Ends

False Immortality in *Measure for Measure*

All tragedies are finished by a death,
All comedies are ended by a marriage;
The future states of both are left to faith,
For authors fear description might disparage
The worlds to come of both. . . .

—Byron, *Don Juan*[1]

Ending with marriage emphasizes the survival of the type through procreation; ending with death emphasizes the extinction of the individual creature. In *Measure for Measure*, Shakespeare stops short of explicitly disparaging both worlds to come, but the abrupt and formulaic comic ending encourages a suspicion that marriage and death alike eventuate in a merely biological process that shows no regard for human consciousness. To expand on Horace Walpole's aphoristic version of the genre distinction, "the world is a comedy to those that think" about the persistent traits of their species, "a tragedy to those that feel" their own mortality and that of the individual things they love. *Measure for Measure* is, from this perspective, a tragicomedy.[2] The play certainly portrays and extols the orderly perpetuation of human life, human society, and human virtue. Yet it also takes the three figurations of immortality to which people most commonly cling—genetic heirs, undying fame, and divine salvation—and undermines our faith in each of them, even as it undermines our faith in the comic formula as a whole by the unsatisfying impositions of marriage that conclude this death-filled play. Which is the means, and which the end, between the perpetuation of the species and the experience of individual life? The first part of this chapter delineates a comedy of family and state extolling the systematic reproduction of the human race; the second part turns to the tragic perspective of the individual, which subverts the comic promises of generational immortality; and the third part evokes from the play a satiric suspicion that we are each betrayed by the supposedly benevolent biological and political systems to which God has abandoned His human offspring.

A MORAL COMEDY

Measure for Measure comes closer than any other Shakespeare play to having a schematic, articulable moral. Its primary topic is sexuality, and its primary argument is that neither individuals nor societies can thrive unless license and repression keep each other in balance. Naturally critics are reluctant to admit that sexual morality is what the play is about, because that is what it *seems* to be about.[3] But in this case it may pay to surrender our ingenuity in the face of the obvious. The polar outposts of this play are brothels and convents, prudery and lechery are what chiefly characterize its characters, and its two crucial actions are bouts of sexual intercourse, one a premarital impregnation, the other a form of attempted rape. From beginning to end, the dominant motive is the need to convert lustful fornication into marital fecundity. Vienna's Sigmund Freud defines as perversion any sexual activity not primarily directed toward heterosexual genital intercourse;[4] Shakespeare's Vienna defines as treason any such intercourse not directed toward legitimate procreation. For the individual, marriage becomes—as in the patristic commonplaces—a way of reconciling unruly sexual desire with necessary sexual restraint; for the state, it becomes a way of maintaining the substance and order of the social fabric. Though *Measure for Measure* is notorious for its strayings from comic sentiment, it thus builds toward the typical comic conclusion far more forcefully and logically than most comedies: by the end, marriage becomes an overdetermined resolution.

The premise of the play is that the Duke of Vienna—by preferring fornication, which creates life, however unlawfully, to execution, which destroys life, however lawfully—has allowed sexual license to corrupt his city. This is an understandable error in a humane ruler, all the more understandable in a theater that had been closed by epidemic plague the previous year (1603), in a city that had lost close to a quarter of its population to the plague over the preceding decade. Despite some bad harvests in the 1590s and some complaints about the tendency of young people to procreate before they were ready to support a family,[5] population explosion was hardly to be feared; on the contrary, a common measure of a state's health was the growth of its population. Moreover, as the opening of the second scene reminds us, city-states such as Vienna were perpetually on the brink of war, with its voracious appetite for what Falstaff calls "food for powder, mortal men." So there would have been some sociological force to Lucio's warning that Angelo's more severe policy might "unpeople the province," an inverted reminder of the Biblical injunction so often emphasized by Renaissance preachers: "Be fruitful and multiply." Even Puritanical figures such as Phillip Stubbes—who laments that "untill every one hath two or three Bastardes a peece, they esteeme him no man," and furiously condemns anyone who argues that "Otherwyse the World wold become barren"— stress the obligation to multiply *within* marriage. Like Duke Vincentio, Stubbes concludes, "let all men that have put away their honest wyves be forced to take them again, and abandon all whores, or els to taste of the law."[6]

The Duke's problem is that, though his former course may have been understandable, it has not been understood. Lucio remarks that before the Duke "would have hanged a man for getting a hundred bastards, he would have paid for the nursing a thousand. He had some feeling of the sport; he knew the service; and that instructed him to mercy" (3.2.113– 17). This is intolerable for the Duke, for both the motives and the numbers it claims to reveal. One pious Jacobean tract argued that "it is more Prince-like to save then to destroy, and more difficult to revive one dead man, then to kill a thousand living,"[7] but Lucio's analysis presents the problem as a disease spreading outward from the Duke's unruly body to his entire body-politic, rather than as an enlightened choice for mercy and healthy growth. It also suggests the exponential growth of the problem, in a world where even one bastard child is one too many:

the villains of Jacobean tragedy are often illegitimate children who necessarily attack the social order that excludes them. So the Duke stages for his city, as Shakespeare does for his, an averted tragedy that characterizes all aberrations from married procreation as collaborations with death.

Angelo applies a simplistic system of accounting to this political commodity, the legitimate son; the Duke's calculations are more complex and seemingly humane, but perhaps ultimately more cynical as well. According to Angelo, the making of a counterfeit coin, the forging of that aspect of the state's wealth, is a theft equivalent to the stealing of a real coin:[8]

> It were as good
> To pardon him that hath from nature stolen
> A man already made, as to remit
> Their saucy sweetness that do coin heaven's image
> In stamps that are forbid. 'Tis all as easy
> Falsely to take away a life true-made,
> As to put mettle in restrained means
> To make a false one.
>
> (2.4.42–49)

The comparison is typical of Angelo in being too cold and abstract to be wholly convincing, but given the trends Lucio's speech reveals (however slanderously and hyperbolically), the exchange rate in Vienna has shifted disastrously, devaluing legitimacy against desire. The Duke is thus obliged to intervene with a temporary didactic choice of order over passion, a morally instructive bit of tragicomic theater. The laxity of his reign leads directly to the excessive restraint promised by Angelo. When Lucio asks the manacled Claudio, "Whence comes this restraint," Claudio replies, "From too much liberty, my Lucio. Liberty, / As surfeit, is the father of much fast; / So every scope by the immoderate use / Turns to restraint" (1.2.116–20). The prisoner's individual experience is significantly parallel to that of the state, not just the result of it.

Angelo argues that Isabella should be willing to commit fornication with him in order to save Claudio's life, since she has implied that Claudio's fornication was not enough of an evil to merit death: measure for measure. This conundrum allows Shakespeare to offer further proof that unlimited fornication is not the right cure for mortality, because this supposed antidote for Claudio's fate turns out to be a swifter poison: when Angelo believes he has enjoyed Isabella's body, he orders that the execution be expedited by a few hours. In terms of the moral argument of the play, her supposed yielding only replicates Claudio's crime and therefore can only accelerate his punishment. The real cure, the Duke and his creator seem to suggest, is marriage, and the substitution of Mariana in the bed allows the Duke to achieve the maximum possible number of living and legitimate Viennese.

Sex and death were conventionally associated in the Renaissance, but (as in its emphasis on venereal disease) *Measure for Measure* uses that association in a particularly tendentious way. Lucio's final words— "Marrying a punk, my lord, is pressing to death, / Whipping, and hanging" (5.1.520–21)—echo a theme pervading the play. The covert and unholy alliance between these supposed mighty opposites—fornication and repression, conception and execution—surfaces again when the Duke assigns Pompey the bawd to work for Abhorson the executioner. Both men object to the partnership, but Pompey soon concedes, "I have been an unlawful bawd time out of mind, but yet I will be content to be a lawful hangman. I would be glad to receive some instruction from my fellow-partner" (4.2.14–17). The Provost insists that they "weigh equally" in any ethical scale, they promise mutual professional courtesy, and Pompey eventually discovers that "many of [his] old customers" from the brothel require his new services at the jail (4.3.1–4). The pun lurking in Abhorson's elided name neatly encapsulates the pattern: the executioner is evidently an abhorred whoreson. Promiscuity again appears to generate its own punishment; the executioner has been created by the fornicator.

If excessive liberty leads to excessive restraint, as the appointment of Angelo demonstrates, then excessive restraint leads to excessive liberty, as the corruption of Angelo demonstrates. Behind the closing down of whorehouses in Vienna lurks the relatively recent memory of closing down monasteries in England. The case of Isabella reinforces the same ideas more subtly: that discipline can lead to perversion, that severe rectitude reflects a battle against dangerously powerful appetites, and provokes repressed sensuality into a guerilla war against outward propriety. Angelo insists that Isabella's virgin modesty is what paradoxically inspires his lust; again, extraordinary self-restraint—hers as well as his own—becomes the provocation to an extraordinary self-indulgence. The erotics of Isabella's renunciation could hardly be more lurid:

> were I under the terms of death,
> Th'impression of keen whips I'd wear as rubies,
> And strip myself to death as to a bed
> That longing have been sick for, ere I'd yield
> My body up to shame.[9]

(2.4.100–104)

Furthermore, she extends her death-wish (as does Angelo) to all the fallen creatures around her. On hearing the tale of Mariana's star-crossed love for Angelo, Isabella exclaims, "What a merit were it in death to take this poor maid from the world! What corruption in this life, that it will let this man live!" (3.1.231–33). Her advice to the lovelorn is invariably execution, Robespierre ghostwriting for Ann Landers. The moral rectitude of Angelo and Isabella becomes nearly indistinguishable from their masochistic appetites.

While Isabella faces genetic extinction through her implied sexual repression, her brother faces execution for a manifest sexual liberty. The ascetic and libertine tendencies (though each is rather sympathetically represented in this pair) appear as a double-edged sword cutting down a family tree. *Measure for Measure* is a tragicomedy not only because a convincing threat of barrenness or death appears before sexual desire resolves itself into marriage, but also because the play exposes the potentially deadly attributes of sexuality itself. Both fornication and its extreme repression are wastrel expenditures of the bodies natural and politic. If a society suspects that the monastic life breeds perversion rather than immortality, then the only remaining answer to death—the answer of Protestant society—is fruitful marriage.

A TRAGEDY OF STATE

Within this relatively standard moral admonition about physical, social, and psychological decadence, Shakespeare develops a potentially heretical, even blasphemous, meditation about the fate of the human individual. *Measure for Measure* evokes a tragic resistance to comic solutions, not only by emphasizing the destructive potential of sexuality, but also by widening our perspective on its creative potential. Valuing procreation as a demographic contribution rather than as individual assertion and gratification may not sound especially sinister. But the anti-Malthusian conclusion that all is well as long as the population of Vienna keeps growing does not really answer the fears roused by the various threats of execution, and particularly by Claudio's confused but eloquent terror of death. The man whose first fear is that his body is doomed "To lie in cold obstruction, and to rot," then that his spirit may "be imprison'd in the viewless winds / And blown with restless violence round about / The pendent world," hardly encourages the happy surrender of the worldly self to dispersal:

The weariest and most loathed worldly life
That age, ache, penury and imprisonment
Can lay on nature, is a paradise
To what we fear of death.

(3.1.117–31)

So it is not surprising that Claudio finds no consolation in the disguised Duke's argument that, from the standpoint of atomistic philosophy, he really has no self to lose (3.1.19–21); nor is he reconciled to his fate by the idea that he has fathered a child to take his place, which should be thoroughly consoling if genetic survival were truly felt to be an adequate compensation for individual death.

On the contrary, Claudio endures a literalist version of the principle that haunts parents such as Prospero, and perhaps sons such as Hamlet as well: he is condemned to death precisely by the visible evidence of his biological replacement. When the disguised Duke speaks to Juliet about this fetus, he calls it "the sin you carry"; and for Claudio this is precisely the sin whose wages are death.[10] Sir Thomas Browne's warning about the inadequacies of generational love seems painfully germane: "Thus I perceive a man may bee buried alive, and behold his grave in his owne issue" (p. 160). As the more vivid instance of Macbeth will confirm, the lineal succession that is satisfactory for the purposes of the state may not eradicate our terrifying vision of individual will and consciousness obliterated by nature and mortality.

Tragicomedy commonly abets the comfortable illusion that procreative love is the opposite of death. What makes *Measure for Measure* so disturbing is its subversion of that binarism. As Becker argues (p. 163),

Animals who procreate, die. Their relatively short life span is somehow connected with their procreation. . . . If sex is a fulfillment of [man's] role as an animal in the species, it reminds him that he is nothing himself but a link in the chain of being, exchangeable with any other and completely expendable in himself. . . . This point is crucial because it explains why sexual taboos have been at the heart of human society since the very beginning. They affirm the triumph of human personality over animal sameness.

While the plot of the play appears dismissive toward the asceticism of Angelo and Isabella, a thematic counter-movement endorses their intuition that sexual intercourse is a surrender to mortality, not a cure for it. The comic triumph in *Measure for Measure* belongs not to love or to the hero, but instead to a version of what Michel Foucault calls "biopower": specifically, the need of the state, under the guise of personalized benevolence, simply to keep the procreative machine running. Indeed, *Measure for Measure* refutes Foucault's claim that this concern was an invention of the eighteenth century, since the ending of this Jacobean play could be trenchantly described in exactly the terms Foucault uses to describe this supposedly post-Enlightenment mode of government: "It is no longer a matter of bringing death into play in the field of sovereignty, but of distributing the living in the domain of value and utility."[11]

In *Measure for Measure* domestic bliss is exposed as a euphemism for the domestication of the human animal; it is not only bawds (as Elbow supposes) who "buy and sell men and women like beasts" until "all the world drink brown and white bastard" (3.2.2–3). That is the leading industry of the state, and all other industries depend on the successful management of that breeding-farm. Elbow's complaint immediately follows the Duke's scheme to trick Angelo into impregnating Mariana with a legitimate fetus. Again, human bodies are the fungible coins— and the indifferent food—of the state. Fifty lines later, we learn that the "dear morsel" Mistress Overdone—worn out in the "service" of nine husbands—"hath eaten up all the beef, and is herself in the tub" (3.2.54–57).

Men have commonly blamed women for such Circean transformations, but that is hardly surprising, since (through the figure of Eve) men have long blamed women (who issue mortal bodies and rouse decadent lusts) for death itself.[12] But even Angelo recognizes that Isabella is not really a "tempter" culpable for his own descent into "carrion"; such decay is merely the dark side of biology (2.1.162–68). The comic dance of marriage is, measure for measure, also a Dance of Death, and the disguised ruler in the dark cowl may carry a sickle as well as a pardon. The state has reached an accommodation with the jealous god Death, and as we play out our biological roles, each of us becomes a propitiary sacrifice. No wonder statecraft is so oddly associated with pregnancy in Vienna (e.g., 1.1.11, 4.4.18). Against the ongoing decimations of the Grim Reaper, *Measure for Measure* pits a Duke who might be called the Grim Breeder, hardly more appealing in his ways of creating people than the Reaper is in destroying them. Vienna is left without eternals, with only maternals and paternals to take their place.

The Reformation encouraged people to find some version of immortality in their legitimate progeny, yet was obliged to acknowledge that this was not really immortality at all. The idea that resurrection occurs "dayly" through "generation" was heretical,[13] and the process "whereby the *Parents* were said . . . to *live again* in their *Posterity*" was utterly inadequate to replace the promise of full bodily resurrection of each individual at Last Judgment.[14] Nor could this form of immortality escape the painful paradox still haunting the modern cult of sexuality, which encourages people to seek their transcendence and the highest affirmation of their individual value in precisely the activities that enlist them in the common creaturely project.[15] The way the Duke retrieves his citizens both from convents and from brothels to enlist them in the work of orderly social replication may remind us that the normal social compromise fails to satisfy either our spiritual or our narcissistic cravings.

While thus questioning the adequacy of procreation as a response to human mortality, *Measure for Measure* also subjects honor and piety to similarly cynical psychological and political inspection. These virtues, and the hopes commonly attached to them, stand exposed (from Freudian and Machiavellian perspectives) as merely illusory forms of personal redemption. This devastating interrogation of the principal modes in which individuals attempt to perpetuate their individuality brings me to my main topic: false immortality. *Measure for Measure* resists its genre by undermining the three modes in which comedy usually promises immortality—fame, salvation, and procreation—and replacing them with an emphasis on the destruction of the individual, an emphasis that is typical of tragedy. Whether or not we accept the pseudo-biographical impression that Shakespeare here vandalizes his own comic form in deference to the great tragedies he had recently begun to write, we can hardly deny the inadequacies of the comic resolution of *Measure for Measure*, the darkness it fails to dispel. It is tragicomic not only because death is strongly present prior to the resolution, but more crucially because mortality remains imperfectly refuted at the center of that resolution.

Neither progeny nor Christianity, neither self-indulgence nor self-denial, provides an adequate response. The ailments of the Duke's city take the classic alternative forms—libertine and ascetic—of a psyche confronting the terror of mortality.[16] As Freud warned that psychoanalysis could at best convert neurotic dysfunction into normal human unhappiness,[17] so the Duke aspires only to limit social dysfunction so that death can resume its normal functions. There is finally domesticity again in the slaughterhouse, and good and evil make undifferentiated contributions to a system whose only absolute law is supply and demand.

"One can see *Measure for Measure* as a play that opens with the law being invoked to punish fornication by death and that closes with the law being utilized to punish fornication by marriage."[18] This witty observation cuts deep: it opens for inspection the common discomfort with the "comic resolution" of *Measure for Measure*: two marriages tainted by unwilling and undesirable bridegrooms, the other two compromised by their peculiar brides, one arguably reluctant and still in a nun's habit, the other newly out of jail and barely back on her feet after childbirth. Given the fact that even the most promising marriages in Shakespeare's plays often teeter on the brink of tragic collapse, we can hardly foresee great good coming of all these awkward alliances, except perhaps in tidying up the bookkeeping of the Viennese bureaucracy.

And yet it is not so cynical or unreasonable for a government to treat marriage as merely another, preferable instrument for controlling desire—which is one plausible definition of punishment. From the normal perspective of the romantic individual or of romantic comedy, the absence of choice and love in this matchmaking may be disturbing, but from the perspective of the state, choice and love are subordinate values. The state cannot finally concern itself with the motivation behind marriage any more than it can condemn citizens for unacted evil desires: "Thoughts are no subjects," Isabella tells the Duke, "Intents, but merely thoughts" (5.1.451–52). The opening lines of the play invite us to recognize what follows as a dramatized treatise on the properties of government, and that is largely what we get. But by presenting that treatise in the form of an impassioned human story, Shakespeare creates a peculiar disturbance in our fantasies of personal significance. Amid the threats of death to characters in this play, which fit it to most definitions of tragicomedy, lurks a threat to the spectators' strategies for immortality, a threat to expose supposedly transcendent values as mere instruments of state and to expose the hope for individual survival as a hollow fantasy subserving the survival instincts of the body-politic. As in the heraldic structure of aristocratic Jacobean funerals, which insisted on including indifferent technical heirs to the exclusion of genuine mourners, the demand for an assurance of social continuity far outweighs the demands of personal emotion.[19]

The cure for mortality offered in *Measure for Measure* thus works far better sociologically than psychologically. The resurrection of Claudio and the pardons for Angelo and Barnardine are political tricks that only defer the question of mortality. Claudio was told that Angelo's ill-won pardon would gain him merely "six or seven feverous winters"; will the Duke's nobler pardon gain him so much more? The one gesture toward a truly eternal solution—Isabella's religious vocation—apparently yields to the demands of dynastic survival, and the play does not audibly mourn for it. The essence of the Duke's final triumph (and Shakespeare's comic solution) is marriage—not as individual fulfillment, but as a practical, worldly, even legalistic solution to the problem of maintaining the size and structure of the Viennese population, and to the no more romantic problem of controlling illegitimacy and venereal disease among the city's many wayward citizens. The question of personal annihilation might thus be neatly avoided—except that the play raises it, indirectly but repeatedly. The focus on government appears to offer some respite from the question of individual death, but the question haunts the play nonetheless.

Measure for Measure opens with the Duke fashioning Angelo into a son and heir to the throne:

> I say, bid come before us Angelo.
> What figure of us, think you, he will bear?
> For you must know, we have with special soul
> Elected him our absence to supply;
> Lent him our terror, drest him with our love,
> And given his deputation all the organs
> Of our own power.

(1.1.15–21)

The Duke intends thus to make Angelo "at full ourself." Angelo responds to the suggestion that he is to bear a figure of his predecessor when, later in the scene, he expresses his anxiety about having "so great a figure . . . stamp'd upon" him (1.1.48–49); in the next act he will use the same coining metaphor to refer to procreation (2.4.45). The Duke's implicit fantasy of parthenogenesis is common in the struggle of Shakespeare's tragically misguided men (such as Coriolanus and Leontes) against their own mortality.[20] For them to acknowledge either the means or the need to procreate would be to confess the mortally fallen nature of their bodies. Only when he sees, mirrored back by Angelo, the life-defeating implications of this death-denying narcissism can the Duke accept his own place in the procreative economy of the state.

To be mere coins in some usurious biological economy can hardly satisfy the desire for personal significance, whether the usurer is perceived as an earthly monarch or a heavenly one. The Duke's introductory remarks make the practices of heaven in this regard seem suspiciously congruent with those of nature:

Heaven doth with us as we with torches do,
Not light them for themselves; for if our virtues
Did not go forth of us, 'twere all alike
As if we had them not. Spirits are not finely touch'd
But to fine issues; nor nature never lends
The smallest scruple of her excellence
But, like a thrifty goddess, she determines
Herself the glory of a creditor,
Both thanks and use.

(1.1.32–40)

"Thanks, but no thanks," might be the reply of the heroic actor cast as a mere torchbearer. Great creating nature demands back ashes for ashes and dust for dust, and a few pounds more than we were given at the start. Ben Jonson's epitaph "On My First Son" demonstrates that this loan-shark aspect of God could elicit bitterness, despite all the standard gestures of submission to divine will. When Gertrude remarries so hastily, Hamlet remarks no less bitterly on the way "thrift" has been valued over grief for his dead father. Death tenaciously shadows the procreative process, and the efficiency of the biological economy is an insult to the human spirit, especially when a Ben Jonson is asked to accept the loss of a Ben Jonson, or a Hamlet the loss of a Hamlet.[21]

By staging his own miraculous return, in the manner of the disguised-ruler plot so popular on the early Jacobean stage, the Duke fulfills another fantasy familiar from Elizabethan drama: namely, the return of a father from death (or at least from a great distance or great poverty) to remedy the wrongs of the prodigal heir who has forgotten him and his ways. King Hamlet and King Lear are grim variations on this theme. The immediate provocation of such stories may have been anxieties about royal succession in England, but their persistent appeal probably resides in their implicit denial of death, in the fantastic defeat of the implacable process whereby children replace rather than reproduce their parents. In the case of *Measure for Measure*, the Duke's purpose in this arrangement is twofold, and will be served only to the extent that Angelo stumbles in the footsteps of his patron. First, the Duke must show his citizens the dangers of provoking excessive restraint by their false equation of life with sensual indulgence. Second, he must prove that even an apparently pure embodiment of his moral law makes a very poor substitute for his own wit and kindness, for the individual humanity that shines redeemingly through his disguise. The Duke thus entangles himself in a contradiction much like the one that troubled Jacobean society as a whole: trying to prove to his citizens that replacing oneself procreatively is more important than indulging selfish desires, yet aspiring to do so in a way that would prove himself irreplaceable.[22] Furthermore, the Duke's effort to end illegitimacy in Vienna involves making Angelo, in one sense, the Duke's own bastard son. Angelo's failure as a dynastic heir, precisely by the way it bolsters the Duke's claim to lasting political glory, ruins the Duke's figurative version of procreative survival.

His lack of a true heir is what the Duke must therefore repair at the end by marrying Isabella. He has evidently viewed his entire citizenry as his figurative children, himself as "the father of their idle dream" (4.1.64)—a complaint about the vulnerability of his fame that links it suggestively to his other immortalizing ploys as a figurative father, a kind of playwright, and a feigned holy "father" (as he is repeatedly called in his disguise). The ending of the play suggests, however, that neither this paternalistic stratagem with Angelo, nor the growth of Vienna's population, nor even his fame-winning masterstrokes in the theatricalized arts of state can adequately substitute for a fruitful marriage. In steering his subjects toward matrimony, the Duke discovers, not only a worthy spouse, but also the fact of his own mortality that obliges him, too, to marry. If there is any validity to the argument that *Measure for Measure* was written partly in tribute to the accession of King James, it would make sense for the play to contain some endorsement of a monarch who could offer a lineal successor (such as Prince Henry) rather than merely an appointive one, some transformation of the literary legacy that had worshipped a Virgin Queen—though of course it might have been awkward for Shakespeare to suggest that James's rather indirect accession resembled Angelo's. Power was intimately bound up with paternity for James,[23] and his voluntary legacy to his son Henry was the *Basilikon Doron*, a text on the proper management of a kingdom. From its very first lines, the Duke's obsessively paternalistic play presents itself as this sort of mixed representation of authority; but power, fatherhood, and authorship all fall short of assuring personal immortality.

The Duke follows another well-worn path in his quest for fame, including the putative immortalities of honor and of art. He spreads news of his death (4.2.200) and slips back into town (like Tom Sawyer) to study the reactions, but Lucio's gossip spoils the anticipated canonization. Of course, the Duke claims to be indifferent to fame, even to dislike it:

I'll privily away. I love the people,
But do not like to stage me to their eyes:
Though it do well, I do not relish well
Their loud applause and Aves vehement;
Nor do I think the man of safe discretion
That does affect it.

(1.1.67–72)

He doth protest too much, methinks; his nagging resentment of Lucio's casual slanders suggests that he cares very much about his audience and his reviews.[24] Vainly determined to convince Lucio that the Duke is a paragon, he soliloquizes bitterly about the injuries that await even the most carefully built public reputation, and promptly begins fishing shamelessly for compliments from Escalus (3.2.137–45, 179–82, 254–75, 224–31). Though it might be something King James would be pleased to hear,[25] the Duke's assertion that "slandering a prince" deserves "pressing to death, / Whipping, and hanging" (5.1.520–21) seems revealingly severe. When he reappears as himself at the start of the fifth act, the Duke seems to mock his own quest for a glorious place in future Mirrors for Magistrates. He extols Angelo's reign, which he intends soon to expose as mortally corrupt, with the same equivocal puns on "character" and uneasy suggestions of coining used earlier to conflate the immortalities of honor, art, and progeny: Angelo's conduct in office "deserves with characters of brass, / A forted residence 'gainst the tooth of time / And razure of oblivion" (5.1.12–14). The Duke's irony presses uncomfortably on Shakespeare's earlier explorations of the quest for immortality, in *Love's Labor's Lost* and the sonnets. The facts of fallen flesh and blood have already overthrown this project, before time and nature could even begin to erode gilded monuments.

Escalus's authoritative announcement to his disguised and unrecognized sovereign that "The Duke's in us" (5.1.293) would have summoned the doctrine of the monarch's two bodies in the minds of the audience. In a play so concerned with the paradoxical quest for personal immortality, this doctrinal echo (like Hamlet's "the body is with the King" at 4.2.26–29) invites our attention but finally offers no reassurance. After Angelo's corruption of the law renders him instant "carrion" (2.2.167), the Duke can hardly rely on his official role to preserve him in any meaningful way. The royal self is no longer that metal stamp of divine justice; it becomes indistinguishable from the sinful flesh. Angelo describes Isabella as "deflower'd . . . by an eminent body that enforc'd / The law against it!" (4.4.19–21). This phallic body-politic becomes a source of corruption and death, rather than symbolic immortality, to its citizens.

The Duke's immortal longings also lead him to experiment with piety, with the abjuration of the things of this world in hope of a place in the next. One highly popular Jacobean tract asserted that "It is *Piety* that *enbalmes* a *Prince his* good name,"[26] and *Measure for Measure* offers various hints that the Duke desires that sort of embalming, ranging from his claim to have always "lov'd the life remov'd" (1.3.8), to his request for reassurance of his reputation for preferring contemplation over pleasure (3.2.224–31), and the peculiar evidence that he has long served as a holy confessor to Mariana. But he uses these roles to effect the civil education and earthly salvation of Claudio, and to lure Isabella away from her own pious choice—away from her betrothal to Christ and into his own earthly marital embrace. Furthermore, the essentially hollow tone and ulterior motivation of his monkish lessons to Claudio serve to undermine the entire belief-system—both on stage and off—that views death as a blessing. Within the play's world, these religious postures all prove to be ploys of state, designed to foster stability in the form of dynamic equilibrium.

A PARODY OF PIETY

The Duke's speech to Claudio at the start of the third act is essentially a compilation of *contemptus mundi* and *ars moriendi* commonplaces. These are marked as clichés by their role in a theatrical performance (Duke as monk) that aims at civic reform through pietistic deception, rather than at any pious conversion that would mitigate the state's punitive power. The Duke's overall project clearly demonstrates that he is not actually scornful of this world and this life, and here he sedulously avoids any mention of the afterlife that might lead Claudio to value it above his imminent fatherhood.[27] It is also clear that Claudio accepts these formulaic assurances only formally, only superficially. Such pragmatic, even hypocritical, uses of the consolation ritual—making Last Things the means to a worldly end—place the audience in a similarly skeptical position toward the standard assurances of immortality offered by the church, and not only by the church.[28] The pious function of the Last Confessor becomes merely one more strategic role in a game of practical survival, reminiscent of the pious fraud Edgar perpetrates on Gloucester at the cliffs of Dover. Hearing it done so well

by these dissemblers only heightens our awareness that the most compelling consolatory arguments might prove to be fraudulent if we could
see the real faces and motives behind them. *Measure for Measure* thus
accords with the views reportedly held by the boldest of Renaissance
blasphemers: centuries before Karl Marx criticized religion as the opiate
of an oppressed populace, these radicals suggested that priest and
preacher were merely dummies for the Machiavellian ventriloquists who
held material power.[29]

In comforting Isabella for the supposed death of her brother, the
unveiled Duke reverts to some of his monkish formulas, in a form that
again suggests their hollowness:

> That life is better life, past fearing death,
> Than that which lives to fear. Make it your comfort,
> So happy is your brother.
>
> (5.1.395–97)

Editors struggle vainly to find more in this statement than double-talk.
If Claudio has overcome his fear of dying, it is only by no longer having
any life to lose; he has become (supposedly) an indifferent corpse, not a
laughing philosopher. The Duke's remark can be taken as a simple
endorsement of the afterlife, but (absurdly) the sole virtue it identifies in
that afterlife is that it lacks the fear of death; immortality consists only of
non-mortality. In its brittle piety, the Duke's consolation for Claudio's
supposed death echoes the pregnant Juliet's bitter complaint about
Claudio's scheduled execution:

> Must die to-morrow! O injurious love,
> That respites me a life, whose very comfort
> Is still a dying horror!
>
> (2.3.40–42)

" 'Tis pity of him," the Provost replies, but it is also pity of all consciously
mortal beings enlisted in the Sisyphean struggle of procreation to defeat
death. The soon-to-be-born child will likely someday voice the same
complaint, even if it is not so soon to be fatherless.

Arguably the Duke is mimicking good Christian practice by encouraging penance through mortification in Claudio, his sister, and his
fiancée; and one reward of pious daily dying is the seeming daily
demonstration of resurrection. But the theater of God's judgments
begins to look like an ordinary stage fiction. Claudio's supposed demise
is acceptable to the tragicomic form because we learn that the death, no

less than the consolation, is merely a piece of play-acting. But that evasion prepares us very poorly for instances where the death of those we love is real and the offered consolations sound all too similar, where (like Lear over the body of Cordelia) we wait bewildered for a comic resurrection that never arrives.

The standard complaints against the marriages of *Measure for Measure* apply to the threatened deaths as well. Death is not refuted any more wholeheartedly than marriage is affirmed. Furthermore, death is assigned rather arbitrarily (in Claudio's condemnation and Ragozine's illness) and avoided the same way (in the pardons of Barnardine and Angelo); we are given no compelling justification for the choice of corpses, any more than for the choice of spouses, beyond the mechanisms of biology and statecraft.[30] Perhaps it is not merely marriage that is undermined as a comic resolution in this play: all the fantasies of resurrection (by miracle or art or progeny), all the ordinary lines of comic consolation for the central and implacably tragic fact of individual annihilation, lie mortally wounded amid the formulaic resurrections of the final scene.

Terrible deaths have been averted, but in a way that provokes a modern suspicion that ordinary deaths are the most terrible of all. As Phoebe Spinrad writes, "Death, far from being the glorious martyrdom of Isabella's dreams, the comfortable sleep of the Duke's dreams, the nuisance of Barnardine's, the punishment of Angelo's, or the horror of Claudio's, is in fact simply a part of life, to be accepted on its own terms, and neither fled from nor sought after."[31] Not everyone will agree that this is good news; otherwise we would all agree that *Measure for Measure* is an exemplary comedy and would never turn from it to revenge-tragedies, detective novels, war stories, or religious texts for assurances that death is an unnatural event and an ideal occasion for heroism.

Faced with an increasingly infamous, impious, and sexually diseased city, Duke Vincentio experimentally revives the three main modes of secular immortality, using his disguise to increase his worldly fame, to appropriate the redemptive mysteries of the clergy, and to establish himself in the genetic future. But at the end the Duke's fame is under attack from Lucio's slanders, those nagging interruptions from the lower stratum of body and body-politic that mar Shakespeare's artistic resolution as well as the Duke's conclusive statecraft. If the raising of Claudio from the dead is a consoling spectacle, it also threatens to shift our perspective on the more fundamentally consoling story of Christ raising Lazarus: *Measure for Measure* transforms that Gospel truth into a markedly theatrical fantasy, perhaps even a fraud. If the Duke's glorious return from supposed death echoes the story of Christ's own Resurrection, it seems at times a travesty designed to endorse the most cynical reading of that Resurrection: as a trick engineered by a fake holy-man for his own aggrandizement.

Moreover, this reappearance compromises the principal Christian arguments (which the Duke stressed to Claudio) for the willing surrender of earthly life: that death is certain, and that true happiness and justice exist only beyond it. The play alludes to the conventional idea that the entire world is a prison from which death is the only true escape,[32] yet several characters are eventually released from Death Row into worldly pleasures. The pardons constitute a happy ending, but one which (precisely because it *is* happy) subverts a metaphor frequently employed in the Renaissance, within and beyond this play, to reconcile human beings to mortality. Furthermore, the two pleas we hear for bail from prison are hardly reassuring models of redemptive prayer: Claudio's becomes a solicitation of his sister to fornication—a striking perversion of the prayer to the Virgin for salvation that resonates throughout the play—and Pompey's is met only by diabolical jeering (3.2.40). We cannot know whether such veiled but persistent blasphemies were the reason—the monastic aspects of the story would naturally have drawn attention—but it is interesting to note that, when an English Jesuit censored Shakespeare's works for the Inquisition in the 1640s, *Measure for Measure* was the only play he removed entirely. Occasional words and passages are blotted out in other plays, but *Measure for Measure* was amputated like a cancer, the stubs of the pages cut back almost to the binding.[33]

The skeptical potential of the play threatens the vital organs of the Christian body-politic, compromising functions and mythologies essential from Shakespeare's time to our own. Procreation is exposed as essentially a mechanism of biology manipulated by the state, which (aided by the church) strives to harness, rationalize, even sentimentalize the relentless directionless march of nature. With Isabella apparently about to surrender her virginity, Mariana (by the convention of such stories) probably newly impregnated, Juliet newly delivered, and Lucio's whore the mother of his young child, *Measure for Measure* presents a kind of time-lapse photograph, showing the self-perpetuating natural system to be far more in control than the vagaries of individual human will. Angelo presses Isabella to show that she is a woman "By putting on the destin'd livery" (2.4.137); this equation of her identity as a woman with sexual submission earns Angelo the jeers of even the most mildly feminist audience, yet the very play that thus makes him the villain suggests that the procreative sheets—and the swaddling cloths, and the burial shroud—are indeed the destined livery of each human being, for all our protestations of free will. One critic interprets Angelo's line as an effort to force Isabella back into "the taint of sexuality" that she "had hoped to escape by putting on the livery of a nun";[34] my suggestion is that Isabella's flight from the limitations of a female identity based in sexuality is only part of a more general flight from the limitations of a human identity based in reproductive biology. Another critic understandably complains about the lack in *Measure for Measure* "of women's personal autonomy—her right to control her body,"[35] but men hardly seem to fare better in that category, whether in bed or in prison. It is not only social hierarchy, as some political critics assume, that the state must mystify to sustain itself: the bodily cycle of birth and death seems to demand and receive a similar disguise.

Isabella is determined to abjure physical pleasure, public life, and procreation, yet she is repeatedly pulled back from the pursuit of salvation to the businesses of body, family, and state. The condemnation of Claudio forces Isabella to confront the conflict between (on the one hand) the instincts that resist physical death and (on the other) the daily death at the heart of her religious vocation, with its strident rejection of this world and its confident anticipation of another. In her first confrontation with Angelo, Isabella interprets her brother's threatened execution as a sacrificial preparation for heaven. The proprieties of slaughter seem quite clear to her: as other animals become merely food after death, so human beings become purely souls (2.2.85–88). The fact that she can offer so comfortably this grotesque analogy demonstrates her facile confidence in the scheme of salvation (it may also remind us how deeply Western culture depends, for its spiritual complacency as well as its food supply, on the same absolute distinction). Death to her is merely the tiny unpleasant fraction of human experience shared with a crushed beetle; she cannot imagine sacrificing "a perpetual honor" for "six or seven winters" of "feverous life" (3.1.73–80).[36] Spectators may wince at this reminder of the corrupt bargains they have made with fallen angels for a few extra years of survival. But is honor necessarily any more perpetual than bodies are, or than souls might be?

When Isabella tells Angelo that she would "rather give my body than my soul" to save her brother, Angelo is curtly amenable: "I talk not of your soul" (2.4.56–57). Throughout the play, Isabella is thus steadily drawn into the marketplace of the physical, into a mentality that thinks more about desire than about religion; more about the threat of death than about the hope of immortality; more about bodily confinement (a jail or a grave) than about a spiritual injury (disgrace or damnation) that would be a "restraint / Though all the world's vastidity you had" (3.1.67–68). Both siblings worry about the "pollution" of their bodies, but they have virtually opposite definitions of the term, Isabella associating it with sexual reproduction and Claudio with mortal decay. When Claudio thinks the alternative to instant death is "perpetual durance," he means imprisonment of his body for the duration of its life—a characteristic misreading of the word "perpetual" as Isabella understands it. By disallowing her orthodox reference to eternals that would easily resolve the dilemma, the play disables the same simplifying reflex in the audience. No wonder critics alternately condemn her declaration that "More than our brother is our chastity" (2.4.184) as mean-spirited hysteria and defend it as correct Renaissance theology. This stubbornly socio-biological play is as subversive to more recent humanistic pietisms as it is to medieval Christian ones, and there seems to be no defensible middle ground.

Claudio finally tells his sister that "If I must die, / I will encounter darkness as a bride, and hug it in my arms" (3.1.83–85). This is an otherworldly resolution with some symptoms of weakness. He makes the afterworld into an image of his earthly desires and deeds—this death sounds like another imperfect marriage prematurely embraced—even while equating that afterworld with pure darkness, a plausible symptom of annihilationism. Isabella nonetheless congratulates him for this perspective—not surprisingly, if we remember that she herself had conceived of death as an erotic spouse (2.4.102). The peculiar terms of her congratulation show how the various approaches to immortality mingle together in the desperately denying minds of these characters. To salvation and honor Isabella now adds a ghost of procreation: "There spake my brother: there my father's grave / Did utter forth a voice. Yes, thou must die" (3.1.85–86). Presumably Isabella means the last four words to be in her own voice rather than her father's: otherwise, as a standard and starkly unconsoling message from the grave, they would undo the subtle implication of the preceding sentence that by dying properly (and in defense of his sister's procreative purity), Claudio will become eligible for this kind of procreative, not to say paganish, resurrection.[37] Claudio thus receives a version of the offer Hamlet cannot refuse, a manipulative reminder that the likeness of a son means that the father does not really die into a rest of silence. When Claudio weakens again some fifty lines later, she turns the same set of assumptions against him. "Is't not a kind of incest, to take life / From thine own sister's shame" (3.1.138–39), she asks accusingly, as if the life he would save by escaping execution were virtually indistinguishable from the life he would make by procreating within his own genetic field.

For Isabella, there is no way out of the human prison, no way to avoid the compromises and corruptions of her place in the human family. From the very start, her dedication as a spiritual Bride of Christ is subverted and even parodied by her conversion into a procreative bride for the body-politic. Isabella's name proclaims her devoted to God, but Vienna, through an ingenious translation of that devotion, enforces its claim on her womb. Her name also matches that of a harried virgin whose mournful struggle against a series of wooers in *Orlando Furioso*, culminating in a mistaken beheading, "parodies the chastity sacred to the female saint's life."[38] For her first fifteen lines, Shakespeare's Isabella is allowed to profess asceticism; then Lucio rings the bell at the convent and says, "Hail virgin, if you be" (1.4.1–16). This might be an unremarkable greeting under the circumstances, except that it awakens some truly remarkable echoes. Lucio's salutation translates the beginning of the basic prayer to the Virgin Mary, and then questions whether Isabella is actually suited to the role.[39] Furthermore, that hailing of the Virgin (in a Roman Catholic society such as the play depicts) immediately followed the ringing of a bell, a bell that (even under Elizabethan Protestantism) was known as the Angelus bell.

Lucio arrives to lure Isabella out of the convent as an agent of both Angelo (who wants to turn her into a sexual object) and the Duke (who then wants to turn her into a procreative agent). Furthermore, *Ave virgo* marks the opening of the Annunciation, as reported by Luke (whose name recalls Lucio)—precisely the event the Angelus prayer celebrates, the summoning of the Virgin to the task of redeeming human immortality by bearing the son of the Lord. Theologians of course stressed that the Annunciation was by no means an angelic rape but instead the occasion of the Virgin's free consent to the patriarchal Lord of whom the angel was merely a deputy (and Angelo is called Vincentio's "deputy" a dozen times in the play). The process of Isabella's seduction reduces the decorum of the Annunciation to a "good cop, bad cop" tactic employed by the interrogating figures of Angelo and the Duke. Indeed, it looks oddly similar to a bawdy story in the *Decameron*, in which a friar disguises himself as the Angel Gabriel in order to seduce a reluctant woman;[40] and Marlowe's supposed assertion that "the Angell Gabriell was baud to the holy ghost, because he brought the salutation to Mary"[41] further demonstrates that this satiric idea was available in Shakespeare's cultural milieu.

The setting Angelo chooses for his tryst with Isabella is heavily marked as a version of the *hortus conclusus* that is the iconographic home of the Virgin Mary. Isabella reports that Angelo

> hath a garden circummur'd with brick,
> Whose western side is with a vineyard back'd;
> And to that vineyard is a planched gate,
> That makes his opening with this bigger key.
> This other doth command a little door
> Which from the vineyard to the garden leads;
> There have I made my promise
> Upon the heavy middle of the night
> To call upon him.
>
> (4.1.28–36)

Medieval depictions of the Annunciation often place Mary in front of a garden surrounded by walls and vineyards; sometimes, as in the accompanying illustration (see fig. 1), the descending angel holds the key to its portal.[42]

That this woodcut illustrates the erotic and even incestuous Song of Songs is clear from its built-in caption, which translates as "a locked garden is my sister, my bride." Given Isabella's recent complaint that agreeing to this tryst would be like committing incest with her brother (3.1.138–39), the echoes seem too systematically perverse to be accidental. Combining a philological insight with a psychological one, Shakespeare undoes the sublimation that produces a purely spiritual reading of Canticles. Iconographically, this strangely chaste assignation between Angelo and Isabella is at once an image of absolute virginity and an allusion to extreme sexual corruption. Angelo's markedly virginal garden is also strikingly similar to the trysting-places of the Elizabethan fornicators whom Phillip Stubbes reviles:

> . . . they have gardens, either polled or walled round about very high, with their harbers and bowers fit for the purpose. . . . And for their gates are locked, some of them have three or four keyes a peece, whereof one they keepe for themselves, the other their paramours have to goe in before them . . . to receive the guerdon of their paines.[43]

1. From *Canticum Canticorum* (Netherlands, c. 1465), p. 4 (lower right)
Reproduced by permission of The Pierpont Morgan Library, New York.
PML 21990.

Isabella is positioned as a holy virgin only to be displaced into an object
of sexual and reproductive desire, her symbols degradingly recon-
textualized.

The impressment of Isabella into the reproductive economy is
marked from the beginning as a queasy burlesque of her religious
mission. In the initial conversation, Lucio tells Isabella, "I hold you as a
thing enskied and sainted / By your renouncement, an immortal spirit";
she answers, "You do blaspheme the good, in mocking me" (1.4.34–
38). It is not clear whether Lucio is indeed mocking Isabella as he here
calls her back to the earthly business of the body; but it does seem clear
that Shakespeare is making a mockery of the pious notion that virginity
is a plausible or even socially permissible way to pursue immortality.
Isabella turns the immediate task of bearing Angelo's burden over to
Mariana—another refraction of the Mary, with a moated grange for her
hortus conclusus and an Angelo for the agent of her paradoxical chastity—but soon enough the bells will ring for Isabella as well. Presumably
she surrenders her quest for immortalizing chastity by taking the Duke's
hand in the final silence of the play, much as Coriolanus surrenders his

own heroic immortality-strategy by silently taking his mother's hand in the generational panorama. In silence, and by the body, our shared mortal natures reassert themselves.

When the revenant Duke suggests that Isabella accuses Angelo "in th'infirmity of sense," she replies,

> O Prince, I conjure thee, as thou believ'st
> There is another comfort than this world,
> That thou neglect me not with that opinion
> That I am touch'd with madness.

(5.1.51–54)

This conjuration makes it all the more interesting that her sanity—and thereby, implicitly, all faith in that otherworldly comfort—is repeatedly called into question as the scene continues, not only by Angelo but by the Duke as well: her complaint against Angelo is "somewhat madly spoken" (5.1.92), and her plea to spare his worldly life runs "against all sense" (5.1.431). Given the memorable evocations of sexual repression, the audience may already suspect a connection between Isabella's faith and her possible psychological infirmities; and her oath of affirmation here directs that suspicion against belief in the afterlife. It reminds us that this belief can be interrogated precisely because it is so necessary a comfort, just as romantic sentiment and the institution of marriage can be analyzed as by-products of biological and political imperatives.

As soon as one begins to look behind these necessities, to doubt these comforts—as *Measure for Measure* subtly but persistently invites us to do—the transcendent aspirations of Isabella and the others may indeed appear insane. But remaining stubbornly irrational about one's biological doom may be the only alternative to becoming insane from confronting it. A culture of religious faith (such as the Renaissance) commonly diagnoses atheism as a form of insanity;[44] an atheistic culture will tend to follow Freud in interpreting faith as a neurotic symptom. The perspective of modern science threatens to expose culture and religion as cover-stories designed to keep our excessively contemplative species from rebelling against either the earthly or the heavenly lords who tell us to be fruitful and fill out the census. *Measure for Measure* hovers uneasily between an old faithful world and a new skeptical one, leaving Isabella to make a bewildering shift from a religious to a procreative model of immortality. From another perspective, like so many of Shakespeare's audience, she must find a way from the old theology to a Reformed theology that argues, more than our chastity is our progeny.

Angelo is in many ways Isabella's dark shadow, and like her, he studiously rejects the allure of procreation (1.4.57–61) in favor of fame, honor, and purity. The willingness to die for these things—all linked in Renaissance notions of immortality[45]—by war, duel, or suicide is no less rational a response to mortal transience than our modern determination to delay death briefly by health care; but if the denial of death is indeed fundamental to the psychic viability of a society, we will necessarily again diagnose as a kind of insanity any conflicting version. As Rosencrantz and Guildenstern belong in the comic world of substitutions, so Angelo belongs in a tragic world of divided selfhood and failed transcendence. To unify himself, he must either mortify the flesh of Claudio, as a symbol of his own, or else corrupt the soul of Isabella, with the same projective purpose.

Shakespeare seems determined to reduce Angelo's motives, as well as Isabella's, to psychopathological symptoms. Lucio claims that "Angelo was not made by man and woman, after this downright way of creation," and is therefore "a motion ungenerative" (3.2.100–108). In his sensual restraint and his reluctance to consummate the marriage to Mariana, even in his suicidal impulses in the final scene, Angelo refuses to become merely another link in the long chain of corrupt and corruptible human flesh, which transmitted Original Sin (and therefore mortality) through the concupiscence of the generative act.[46] He seeks to be otherworldly here on earth; the coining metaphors may reflect the mercenary tendencies that led him away from Mariana, but they also suggest that he is ready to be stamped into the other kind of "angel," a suggestion that again conflates his official stature with holy transcendence. Yet—like Coriolanus in search of a similar transcendence[47]—Angelo cannot finally retrieve the coining metaphor from its conventional reference to procreation; the Duke converts him back into a marker of the fleshly aspect of the state's usuriously breeding wealth.

At the start of the play Escalus describes Angelo as worthy of the "ample grace" for which he has been "elected" (1.1.18–24); the vocabulary makes public reputation (what Cassio calls "the immortal part of myself" in *Othello*, 2.3.263) an alternative model of eternal salvation. But when the truth about his fleshly failings becomes public as well as private knowledge, Angelo tells the Duke that "your Grace, like power Divine / Hath look'd upon my trespasses . . . and sequent death / Is all the grace I beg" (5.1.367–72). Equating earthly judges with divine ones, he imagines that oblivion is all that this visitation of grace can offer. He sounds rather like Donne in the Holy Sonnet "If Poysonous Mineralls": "That thou remember them, some claime as debt, / I thinke it mercy, if thou wilt forget." As Angelo's brittle pride leads him to despair, so his fragile narcissism leads toward self-obliteration.

Angelo is fooled by the substitution of Mariana's maidenhead for Isabella's, and again by the substitution of Ragozine's head for Claudio's. The Duke is doubtless right that "death's a great disguiser" (4.2.174) and that the head of Barnardine might be thereby mistaken for Claudio's. But what reassures the Provost must disturb the audience: however indirectly, it invokes the *transi* figure of Medieval tomb-sculpture, the stark reminder that in decay all human bodies reveal their horrible sameness. This is the dirty secret that *Measure for Measure* half-reveals in half-concealing it: just as these two women's bodies (even at the moment they are supposedly expressing their most intimate quali-ties) may be virtually indistinguishable, so are all the rest of us when we fall into the clutches of the omnivorous Angel of Death. Shakespeare links the Ovidian comic proverb that all women look alike in the dark with the darker preacherly proverb that all bodies are food for worms.

More subtly disturbing is the renewed recognition that, from the perspective of nature or the state, in the functions of biology or politics, indifference makes perfect sense. Any body will do. The widespread critical discomfort with these two substitutions—the bed-trick as im-moral, the head-trick as implausible—may cover a symptomatic reluc-tance to recognize this indifference. Comedies often encourage that recognition, but in a far more pleasant manner, on behalf of communal life; tragedies often exhort us to protest against it, but they do so by offering a glimmer of heroic transcendence that *Measure for Measure* stubbornly refuses to endorse. The eagerness of commentators to dismiss these juxtaposed substitutions as merely two proximate mo-ments of inferior dramaturgy may partly reflect an unwillingness to see the play's darker purpose—its tragicomic thrust—which is to challenge the sentimental notion of our individual significance.

While humiliating the transcendent strategies of honor and piety that characterize Angelo and Isabella, the play seems, perversely, to reward and endorse the utter negligence of immortality that characterizes Barnardine. He is a kind of reverse synecdoche, a whole man symboliz-ing an autonomic nervous system, sleeping too soundly for his execution to be acceptably meaningful (4.2.61–66). Pompey urges that the slum-bering Barnardine "awake till you are executed, and sleep afterwards," and that "he that drinks all night and is hanged betimes in the morning may sleep the sounder all the next day" (4.3.31–46).[48] The simultaneous absurdity and propriety of these suggestions exposes the weakness of the conventional assurance that death is merely another sleep. Barnardine is a representative man in an unattractive disguise; despite superficial differences, he could stand in for almost anyone, as the Duke insists (4.2.169–74). He aptly represents all of us who wander through this mortal world with an unaccountable complacency, apprehending death "no more dreadfully but as a drunken sleep . . . insensible of mortality, and desperately mortal." As long as we have "the liberty of the prison," we remain bizarrely impervious to the death-sentence hanging over our heads, even on the occasions when a priest appears to remind us (4.2.142–45; cf. Claudio's "restraint / Though all the world's vastidity you had" under Angelo's sentence at 3.1.69). The fact that, until Angelo's reign, Vienna lacked "undoubtful proof" confirming Barnardine's death-sentence (4.2.136–37) mirrors the fact that, until Angelo's fall, it lacked confirmation that all human beings are mortally flawed.

Barnardine will finally be pardoned because the state can much better tolerate an unregenerate soul than an unregenerating body, but again the Duke feels obliged to obscure the distinction with his rhetoric:

> Sirrah, thou art said to have a stubborn soul
> That apprehends no further than this world,
> And squar'st thy life according. Thou'rt condemn'd;
> But, for those earthly faults, I quit them all,
> And pray thee take this mercy to provide
> For better times to come.

(5.1.478–83)

Barnardine is spared on earth because there is so little hope for him beyond. Perhaps the same worldly assumption underlies, and therefore undermines, the "resurrection" of Claudio and the pardon of Angelo that follow so quickly. Again, as with Gloucester on Dover Beach, providence seems to be an illusion manipulated by earthly leaders in vague imitation of a myth of grace, to conceal the possibility that human civilization is really only a confused crowd huddled together against an overwhelming and uncaring ocean—that is, an indifferent God indistinguishable from the flux of nature. Matthew Arnold's famous poem attempts to set romantic love on the same beach to take the place of the absent God; but Shakespeare had centuries earlier seen through that ploy, watching the waves make toward the pebbled shore, and our minutes hasten to their end (Sonnet 60).

The Duke's timely performance of a Last Judgment at the gates of his city, rather than the gates of heaven, is a culminating instance of the way

Measure for Measure parodies pious archetypes in asserting the priority of earthly order and human survival. The critics who assert that (for example) "The Duke's ethical attitude is exactly correspondent with Jesus'"[49] fall victim to the same manipulation of pious reflexes by which the Duke controls his citizens. They overlook the fact that the Duke prepares his redemptive intervention by its opposite: this Lord turns judgment over to a bad son who insists on the punitive letter of the law rather than the established principle of mercy. The Duke strategically regresses Vienna from the New Testament to the Old so that he can claim credit, as head of state, for reinventing Christian forgiveness. It may be true, as one Jacobean tract asserts, that "a Prince, that is slow to punish, [and] sory, when hee is constrained to be severe . . . doth most resemble the Prince of Princes."[50] Resemblances, however, are not identities—that is the problem with procreative immortality—and this version of redemption serves to defend, not faith or moral purity, but the public procreative order of Vienna. For all its gestures toward divine comedy, *Measure for Measure* generates a tragic and parodic attack on our fundamental hopes for individual survival: tragic in challenging the sufficiency of procreation as an answer to mortality, parodic in mocking the conventional fantasies of an existence above and beyond the bodies that make us slaves to the state and to our biological mortality. If providence and eternal life are nothing more than consoling metaphors, then the human body is a machine-like organism seeking automatically to reproduce itself, and so is the body-politic. This understanding does to individual human bodies what Averroes did to individual human minds, marking them as brief deformations of a unitary substance to which they will all eventually return. It matches a belief attributed to the radical wing of the Reformation that "the Divin essence in those persons shall be reduced into God again, but the persons shall be annihilated, for the soul is mortall and the body shall never rise from the dead, but was annihilated; the world shall ever endure by way of generation from time to time without end."[51]

Perhaps *Measure for Measure* is a product of the plague year 1603 not only in its emphasis on the replenishment of the population, but also in its Puritanical portrayal of a city abandoned by its benevolent but exasperated Lord to an agency of deadly retribution. Like some reactionary analyses of the AIDS epidemic, the sermons and literature of 1603 predominantly characterize the plague as God's scourge visited on an increasingly immoral nation. At times, the Vienna of *Measure for Measure* must seem to its citizens much as the world seems to those who

feel—as Reformation theology led many to feel—that God has mysteri-
ously absconded and left his children in an inscrutable universe, and in
the cold hands of Death:

> The Duke is very strangely gone from hence;
> Bore many gentlemen—myself being one—
> In hand, and hope of action: but we do learn
> By those that know the very nerves of state,
> His giving out were of an infinite distance
> From his true-meant design. Upon his place,
> And with full line of his authority,
> Governs Lord Angelo; a man whose blood
> Is very snow-broth; one who never feels
> The wanton stings and motions of the sense;
> . . . .
>   All hope is gone,
> Unless you have the grace by your fair prayer
> To soften Angelo.

>   (1.4.50–70)

The resemblance to the Epilogue of *The Tempest*—"And my ending is
despair / Unless I be reliev'd by prayer"—indicates how strongly this
speech partakes of more eschatological pleas for forgiveness, for relief
from the condemnation common to fallen flesh. Lucio is hardly a Job or
a Christ, but in this speech he might as well be asking why He has
forsaken us, why He has surrendered us to the dark fallen angel?

Isabella's warning to Angelo about the Last Judgment (2.2.73–79)
sounds plausibly like a warning about the promised Death of Death after
its temporary merciless reign of terror over humankind. When Claudio
complains that a seemingly capricious authority, armed with a deadly
blade, makes a few pay for a widely shared sin, he sounds as if he might
be talking as much about mortality punishing Original Sin as about
execution punishing fornication. Indeed, from the perspective of biological theory that describes death as a necessary by-product of the
invention of reproduction, each of us endures Claudio's sentence; by
linking the onset of mortality with the onset of sexuality, the story of the
Fall mythologizes this aspect of biology. Angelo tells Isabella that
though Claudio must die under his sentence, "Yet may he live a while;
and, it may be, / As long as you or I" (2.4.35–36). At the end of the play
Claudio is out of his manacles, but he is still in the food chain. Nor is this
Existential perspective on human freedom anachronistic in reference to
earlier seventeenth-century England. A parable proposed as a consola-

tion for bereaved parents carries the same implications: "A Cart full of Prisoners are brought to execution; what skills it which is first, or third, or sixt, or tenth, or sixteenth? All must dye. What gets hee that is delayed till the afternoone, above him that was executed in the morning?"[52]

Let me therefore propose one more imperfect but evocative allegory lurking in a play that has perhaps already been allegorized too often and too ingeniously:[53] the Duke, not simply as *imitatio dei*,[54] but as *imitatio dei absconditi*, Angelo as the Angel of Death, Claudio as Everyman, and Isabella as Faith. In this system, Barnardine may represent the body—the stupid force of heartbeat, survival instinct, and physical appetite—that is unwilling to die in the condemned Everyman, and is (here) finally spared. Lucio, finally, embodies doubt, baffling every path to immortality in mocking Isabella's pious virginity, the Duke's reputation, and the entire procreative process. The state can order that nagging cynical voice to be pressed to death, whipped, hanged, and married to shame, but it cannot be silenced. Even in the triumphant final scene it persists, ruining any hopes—the Duke's, Shakespeare's, ours—that the tragic facts of life can be dispelled (not just disguised) by the warm glow and consoling figurations of comedy. If life goes on, then so does death. "This news is old enough, yet it is every day's news" (3.2.223–24).

4

Another Day, "Another Golgotha"
Macbeth and the Tyranny of Nature

And first [Satan's] endeavours have ever been, and they cease not yet to instill a belief in the minde of man, There is no God at all . . . . that the necessity of his entity dependeth upon ours, and is but a Politicall Chymera. . . . Where he succeeds not thus high, he labours to introduce a secondary and deductive Atheisme; that although, men concede there is a God, yet . . . that he intendeth only the care of the species or common natures, but letteth loose the guard of individuals, and single existencies therein: That he looks not below the Moon, but hath designed the regiment of sublunary affairs unto inferiour deputations. To promote which apprehensions or empuzzell their due conceptions, he casteth in the notions of fate, destiny, fortune, chance and necessity. . . . Whereby extinguishing in mindes the compensation of vertue and vice, the hope and fear of heaven or hell; they comply in their actions unto the drift of his delusions. . . .

—Sir Thomas Browne,
Pseudodoxia Epidemica (1650)[1]

If Browne is right, then *Macbeth* does the devil's work. Admittedly, Shakespeare marks as sinister the creatures who first plant these doubts in the protagonist, puzzling him with paradoxes of fate and necessity until he forgets the significance of virtue and vice. But even the virtuous characters express only a token belief in Christian afterlife, and the idea of a divine presence in nature provides a suspiciously convenient endorsement for the established political hierarchies. Indeed, as in *The Spanish Tragedy*, monarchical power becomes guiltily associated with the implacable power of time and nature over human aspirations.

Furthermore, *Macbeth* nurtures what Browne calls "secondary Atheisme" by emphasizing the tragic implications of the generational answer to mortality. As in *Measure for Measure*, the surface celebration of procreative order fails to dispel an underlying anxiety that this order is adequate only to the subsistence needs of the group, not to the narcissistic needs of the individual: "common natures" survive, to the neglect of "single existencies." For an egoist such as Macbeth, the only meaningful system is one that gives each different animal "Particular addition from the bill / That writes them all alike. And so of men" (3.1.94–100). On this point *Macbeth* is less discursive than *Measure for Measure*, but imagistically more compelling. I have argued elsewhere that *Macbeth* offers a plaintive allegory about the doomed struggle of the aspiring human individual,[2] and so I will cover the ground quickly here, as an expressionistic coda to my argument about *Measure for Measure*.

In many ways, *Macbeth* presents itself as a story of positive moral order with strong Christian markings. The protagonist systematically violates all the cycles of regenerative nature in killing King Duncan, and is then fittingly punished by exclusion from the benefits of those same cycles: night and day, sleeping and waking, autumn and spring, parent and child. Close reading reveals an integrated symbolic system, reflecting the "Chain of Being" in its full extension. Yet the play finally slips free from that moralistic chain, and the overdetermined containment of political rebellion sets the stage for a much wider subversion. While *Macbeth* certainly echoes standard Elizabethan propaganda that defended the political status quo under the guise of defending the natural order, it makes that order appear smotheringly totalitarian. Hypocritical and even tyrannical abuses of the conventional analogy between natural and political order have been well documented in recent cultural criticism, and *Macbeth* alerts us to the dangers underlying even the most benevolent version of those orders. Behind the play's overt defense of legitimate royal succession lies a sympathetic parable about the fate of the politically dispossessed—in fact, about the fate of everyone betrayed by an Elizabethan culture that at once fervently provoked and fervently repressed grand ambitions.

And behind the political parable lies a sympathetic Existential parable about the fate of all human aspirations in a natural world that simultaneously demands and punishes artifice. Pico della Mirandola's "Oration" demonstrates that self-fashioning was not merely a social event in the Renaissance. It was viewed as a fundamental fact of spiritual existence, legible in the fundamental facts of bodily existence: the clothing and shelter human beings need in order to survive. Clothes and castles dominate the imagery of *Macbeth*, and the paradoxes of free will haunt its philosophy. Latent in the story of providence punishing evil is a disturbing portrayal of the forces of mutability obliterating all assertions of individual life. The flux of nature consumes all efforts to make the world conform to our desires and reflect our consciousness, as Birnam Wood swallows up Dunsinane castle—the central focus of ambition in the play. While Janet Adelman argues forcefully that Malcolm's arboreal stratagem is part of a persistent effort to "obscure the operations of male power, disguising them as a natural force," it could be argued, conversely, that nature appropriates Malcolm's campaign in order to accelerate, and to obscure under the disguise of legitimate male power, its own amoral triumph over the markers of human will.[3] Becker argues that human beings typically earn and defend a feeling of "cosmic specialness" and "unshakable meaning" by "carving out a place in nature, by building an edifice that reflects human value: a temple, a cathedral, a totem pole, a skyscraper, a family that spans three generations" (p. 5). In the fall of Macbeth and his castle, many common stratagems of denial collapse as well. Our susceptibility to the elusive promises of the supernatural derives from the recognition that mortality permeates the realm of nature. Freud associated his own superstitiousness with an aspiration toward immortality, and Norman O. Brown asserts that Hegel's category of human labor "is a transformation of the negativity or nothingness of death into the extroverted action of negating or changing nature."[4] In this sense, Macbeth's struggle to defend his exalted personal status, by magic spells and castle walls, against the orders of natural succession reflects a basic human struggle; Shakespeare costumes the struggle as villainy, but also invites our sympathetic recognition of humanity in the creature doomed to play this scene.

The camouflaged advance of a new generation, led by "Siward's son / And many unrough youths that even now / Protest their first of manhood" (5.2.9–11), represents springtime in the eternal forest of the world. In *Measure for Measure* a similar device allowed us to follow all the stages of human reproduction; in *Macbeth* it threatens to expose the way all generations chase and follow each other into death, which swallows up into its indifference all the aspirations we invest in life, all the physical structures by which we defend life, and all the narrative structures by which we try to imbue it with meaning. The destined enemy of each of our lives hides behind those branches, and creeps at a petty but relentless pace until we run out of tomorrows. When Macbeth boasts that his "castle's strength / Will laugh a siege to scorn" (5.5.2–3), he is not figuring on a millenium of weeds coming up through the cracks in the pavement. But, on one symbolic level, that subtle, gradual, implacable invasion—as much as Malcolm or vengeful cherubs or his own conscience—is what conquers Macbeth. The obsession with time that critics have often noticed in this play[5] reflects a central concern with mortality, with the way time inexorably propels us into timelessness.

Macbeth thus partly arises from, and nicely epitomizes, the mortality-crisis of its surrounding culture, which gazed deep into time and sometimes saw not God but annihilation:

All that the hand of man can uprear, is either overturned by the hand of man, or at length by standing and continuing consumed: as if there were a secret opposition in Fate (the unevitable decree of the Eternal) to control our industry, and countercheck all our devices and proposing. Possessions are not enduring, children lose their names. . . . (Drummond, pp. 47–48)

A suspicion that erasure rather than salvation awaits at the end of time would surely provoke the psyche to construe the supernatural as a sinister conspiracy—and perhaps as a conspiracy of women as well, of *wyrd* sisters who make us, but also make us temporary. The three witches begin to look like the three Fates, and (in an essay that bears richly on several of Shakespeare's works) Freud argues that these Morae who shape mortal destiny in humans arose from an increasingly uneasy reading of the Hours who shape seasonal time in nature.[6] The neat patterns of action and imagery in *Macbeth* prove only that nature has powerful reflexes, not that it has a sympathetic consciousness. It appears to reward standard morality, but there is no proof that it is operated by any providential wisdom, nor that it makes allowance for any human essence. Mother Nature is an admirably efficient housekeeper, but we crave love from her also, and in *Macbeth* she ignores our narcissistic desires and smothers us with the imprint of her own identity. This may be more than a casual analogy. Freud maintains "that the fear of death should be regarded as analogous to the fear of castration and that the situation to which the ego is reacting is one of being abandoned by the protecting superego—the powers of destiny—so that it has no longer any safeguard against all the dangers that surround it."[7] In *Macbeth* it is not the paternal superego but its maternal bodily counterparts that perform this betrayal; the protagonist loses not only his generative powers, but also the assurance of continued existence and omnipotence normally conferred by the mother's attentive gaze. Lady Macbeth, always threatening to abandon violently her nurturant role if Macbeth strays from her program, partly represents an unreliable Mother Nature who always gives too little and turns away from us too soon.

The play thus shares psychological roots with countless folk-tales about men led astray by temptresses who promise perfect love. The fundamental narcissism such promises reflect and generate make it hard to accept subordination, whether to a lawful king or to the laws of nature; the oedipal crisis is thus replayed and abreacted in the political and theological arenas.[8] *Macbeth* conflates the two forms of subjugation through Duncan's decision to make his throne hereditary; Macbeth's unwillingness to be a subject to Duncan's progeny becomes a synecdoche for his more general unwillingness to be subject to the usual laws of cyclical nature.

It is especially hard to accept these kinds of subjugation at glorious moments of triumph like the one Macbeth enjoys at the start of the play, moments when a voice that seems to come simultaneously from the supernatural and from the unconscious foretells some greater destiny. The speakers are weird sisters partly because they are displaced mothers. That these creatures and Lady Macbeth reflect some sinister distortion of motherhood has become virtually a critical commonplace, and an oedipal reading of that distorted mirroring is hardly less common. But the pattern has implications far beyond the predictable syndromes of sexual desire; it bears on the desire—arguably even more primal, and more frustrating—for lasting personal significance. Adelman perceptively identifies escape from women as a thematic fantasy in *Macbeth*, but perhaps this is fundamentally a fantasy of escaping the bodily vulnerability and bodily determinism women represent for men (as in Becker's revisionist reading of castration-anxiety). The Bible repeatedly insists that man born of woman is condemned to death; to survive in this scenario, Macduff must be "unnatural" in precisely that category. In the face of mortality, we must be all or we are nothing, and any obstruction of our majestic will evokes a murderous response.[9] Like Macbeth himself, we are each constantly losing an all-important battle against nature, losing even while spring and offspring burgeon within and around us—perhaps *because* of those burgeonings.[10] The terror of that recognition is constantly threatening to break through the reassuring surface of the play's moral argument. The apparently benevolent powers of natural order finally enforce the same doom that the apparently malevolent weird sisters do. It hardly requires a supernatural seer to predict that nature will briefly exalt and then permanently consume us, but it may take an extraordinary artist to trick us into confronting that possibility.

We are much more willing to believe in our immortality than our mortality; Christianity makes use of that willingness, and so do the witches. The repeated "hail" with which they first greet Macbeth should be counted as the first of the treacherous equivocations that provoke Macbeth to place too optimistic a reading on their promises. Addressed to Banquo, the word echoes the Annunciation (as in *Measure for Measure*), promising that his son will rise to glory, and that "of his kingdome shalbe no end" (Luke 1:33, Geneva Bible). Addressed to Macbeth, it may echo instead the fatal betrayal of Jesus by Judas (as in *3 Henry VI* and *Richard II*).[11] Since these supernatural agents hail him with "grace" (1.3.55), announce that he is in special favor with the Lord, promise him a kingship, and half-answer his puzzlement about how that could possibly occur, Macbeth can hardly be blamed for misleading his wife into associating the "tidings" of "great news" he brings her with the Biblical "tidings of great joye" (1.5.28, 36; Luke 2:10).[12]

Surely Macbeth is mistaken to believe the whole of the witches' prophecy merely because part of it comes true, yet that is precisely how Jacobean Christians were supposed to derive their faith in God's eternal providence: "Who can doubt of the performance of all, that sees the greatest part of a Prophesie performed?" (*Sermons*, VII, 62, translating Augustine). Macbeth lives out a dark shadow of the Christian story, and his *via dolorosa* proves a dead end. The blood-soaked sergeant of the opening scenes reports that Macbeth and Banquo fought as if they "meant to . . . memorize another Golgotha" (1.2.40). Shakespeare does the same: he reminds us of "the place of dead mens skulles" where even the dearest of God's children are betrayed to death by their mortal bodies, and where all our differentiations melt into our common heritage.[13] In *Richard II*, Carlisle warns that, if Bullingbrook is permitted to usurp Richard's throne, "The blood of English shall manure the ground . . . and this land be call'd / The field of Golgotha and dead men's skulls" (4.1.137–44). Civil war is surely terrible, but would the ground we walk on now hold the residue of any fewer corpses if Richard had held the crown in peace? Again violence and violation serve as the disguises, and the scapegoats, for the depredations of natural mortality over time—an epidemic cultural reaction-formation analyzed (I have argued earlier) in *The Spanish Tragedy* and *Hamlet*.

Macduff blames Macbeth's usurpation for the fact that in the "downfall birthdom" of Scotland, "each new morn, / New widows howl, new orphans cry" (4.3.4–5); but is any nation spared these cries? It may be true, as Macduff argues sixty lines later, that "Boundless intemperance / In nature is a tyranny," but the normative temporal bounds imposed by nature function like a tyranny as well, ruthlessly subjugating the primal will to immortality. As Montaigne reports, "To the men who told Socrates, 'The thirty tyrants have condemned you to death,' he replied, 'And nature, them.'"[14] If truth is indeed the daughter of time, then human life is an abortive birth, as so many are in this play's imagery. "One Church-yard in *Paris*," observed a 1630 Scottish tract, "hath moe sculls, then there are living heads in *Scotland*."[15] In truth—that is, in time—Macbeth's country is "another Golgotha," a heap of skulls. So was Shakespeare's London, and so are our own cities, for all our desperate denials:

> Alas, poor country,
> Almost afraid to know itself. It cannot
> Be called our mother, but our grave, where nothing
> But who knows nothing is once seen to smile.
>
> (4.3.166–69)

The time-lapse photography that promises renewal in the form of Birnam Wood and Malcolm's young cohort also threatens to reveal the world as a graveyard; like Renaissance *respice te finem* practices, it threatens to make us know ourselves as merely skulls. Donne insists that "all the ground is made of the bodies of Christians," and we each confront the bitter fatedness that Donne condoles in Christ, who "found a *Golgotha* (where he was crucified) even in Bethlem, where he was born" (*Sermons*, VI, 362, VII, 279).

Macbeth is a *memento mori* as well as a bloody melodrama, because it presents "strange images of death" less gory, but finally no less disturbing, than the play's actual killings (1.3.95). For Macbeth himself, bloodshed soon becomes merely tedious; what remains truly horrible is lifelessness, and that can be found almost anywhere once the bonds of denial have been broken. "Absence" becomes his synonym for "death" (3.1.135), and the principal terror of this terrifying play becomes less the process of dying than the stasis of death itself. When "the common enemy of man" (3.1.70)—whether that is Satan or death—takes away his wife, and with her his last hope for a procreative future, Macbeth's response is memorable mostly for its colorlessness. It is saturated, not with blood, as is the visual aspect of the play, nor with hell-fire, as most Christian-moralist readings would predict, but with the mortality-crisis that is the play's most compelling philosophical motive.

What is especially horrible about Macbeth's disillusioned soliloquy is that it makes life very much what death would be in a universe without salvation or damnation. As a sermon later in the century would warn, "if *Christ had not risen*, Death had been a meer *Destruction*, and not a *Sleep*: A perpetual *Banishment* from the Territories of *Nature*."[16] Surely that kind of banishment—from sleep, from procreation, from all the regenerative cycles of nature—is what steadily destroys these villains. Macbeth's speech describes a condition that is vivid and terrifying in its very blankness and banality: benighted days creep by one after another till the end of time, as we turn to dust, never hearing or speaking, returning at last to nothingness. Macbeth's complaints about his hollow life as king of Scotland comport a more expansive warning about our empty afterlives as subjects of nature:

> She should have died hereafter;
> There would have been a time for such a word.
> Tomorrow, and tomorrow, and tomorrow
> Creeps in this petty pace from day to day
> To the last syllable of recorded time;
> And all our yesterdays have lighted fools
> The way to dusty death. Out, out, brief candle,
> Life's but a walking shadow, a poor player
> That struts and frets his hour upon the stage
> And then is heard no more. It is a tale
> Told by an idiot, full of sound and fury
> Signifying nothing.
>
> (5.5.16–27)

Macbeth sounds remarkably like the antagonist in John Dove's *A Confutation of Atheism*—published the year before *Macbeth* probably appeared—who blows out a candle and announces scoffingly, "your soule is no more than the flame of that candle."[17] To a materialist, time and mortality expose the meaninglessness of life.

It may be possible to salvage the appearance of a conventional Christian moral by arguing that Macbeth experiences human existence as a series of walking shadows and insignificant tomorrows only because his peculiar sinfulness has drained his own life of meaning.[18] But no alternative view of life is asserted nearly so compellingly. Instead, Shakespeare shows us a wide variety of poor players whose strutting and fretting gives way to rehearsals for death—again, not for the act of dying, but for the non-act of being dead. Sleep and blindness are the main stage-business in this rehearsal, and together they adumbrate annihilation. Lady Macbeth's vow to kill Duncan takes the form of a vow that light will never see the dawn of his safe departure (1.5.59–60). When the sun refuses to rise the next day, as Ross reports (2.4.5–10), the living world is given a frightening moment of empathy with the man who died yesterday, with all the dead who have not awakened, who see merely darkness. Only in this radically negative way is the physical universe responsive to human events; only by abandoning us when we misbehave does Mother Nature give a hint of the character and concern we are so eager to register.

It is remarkable how frequently, and how uneasily, the commonplace consolatory comparison between sleep and death appears in the haunted nights of *Macbeth*. As in the cluster of references in 2.2, the comparison becomes another way of asking whether death is part of a redemptive cycle, or merely one last loss of consciousness. The voice in the murder chamber makes Macbeth think of sleep as "the death of each day's life" (2.2.41). Lady Macbeth compares the sleep of Duncan's drugged grooms to death, and tells her husband that "the sleeping, and the dead, / Are but as pictures" (2.2.56–57). She then smears the grooms with blood in their sleep, and has Macbeth kill them before they can fully awaken. Macduff urges Duncan's loyalists, "Shake off this downy sleep, death's counterfeit, / And look on death itself . . . As from your graves rise up" (2.3.70–73). What distinguishes death from sleep, it seems, is that awakening from death is impossible. Perhaps the horror of this recognition combines with the obvious regrets in Macbeth's response to the knocking at the gate: "Wake Duncan with thy knocking: I would thou couldst" (2.2.77). Later Macbeth complains,

> Duncan is in his grave.
> After life's fitful fever, he sleeps well;

Treason has done his worst: nor steel nor poison,
Malice domestic, foreign levy, nothing
Can touch him further.

(3.2.22–26)

Not even a judging God, it seems; nothing will come of nothingness. When "a hideous trumpet calls to parley / The sleepers of the house" (2.3.75–76), Duncan fails to resurrect, despite extensive hints that his death should be associated with the crucifixion.[19] Macbeth may imagine, with Hamlet, that dreams could infiltrate this sleep of death, but his remark as he approaches Duncan's bedchamber—"wicked dreams abuse / The curtained sleep" (2.1.50–51)—suggests merely another projective effort to moralize his own actions.

As in *Hamlet*, ghosts are also such guilty projections; they show us a path into the future, but at the end of that path lurk our darkest suspicions about life after death. Confronted by the ghost of Banquo, Macbeth talks about graves spitting out their half-digested food, like birds of prey (3.4.70–72). This is not a nice view of the general resurrection, because—like the vision of regicidal times conjured by Horatio in the first scene of *Hamlet*—it is not resurrection in any Christian sense, but a brutal parody. At Golgotha, the skulls are empty: "The time has been / That when the brains were out, the man would die, / And there an end" (3.4.78–80). The specter forces Macbeth, and us, to attribute to a dead body the full emptiness of its experience; we confront a demonic inversion of the promised afterlife: form without content, animation without anima. To be unseeing, and to be unseen, are alike tokens of death; the dead beckon us from beyond with their terrible passivity. "Thou hast no speculation in those eyes / Which thou dost glare with," Macbeth tells Banquo's ghost; "This is more strange than such a murder is" (3.4.82–83, 95–96). To be stared at by those blind eyes forces Macbeth to confront not only his peculiar guilt, but also his typical mortality, and nothing could be stranger than that. Throughout the play there is a terror of that oblivion, of the extinguished consciousness that has eyes but cannot see.

Lady Macbeth's petty pacing from night to night traps her in a timeless series of yesterdays. Though "her eyes are open . . . their sense is shut" (5.1.21–22); this zombie-like sleepwalking mirrors Banquo's nightmarish deathwalking. She insists that "Banquo's buried; he cannot come out on's grave" (5.1.53–54), but at that very moment she is living proof that the dead still walk, with their terrifyingly sightless eyes. These "strange images of death" culminate in Macbeth's head on a pole: a head that has been seeing and saying things for us all through the play now stares down at us blankly, unchangingly. This is death, and, all too clearly, it is not sleep.

More explicit and conventional comments about afterlife in the play ring remarkably hollow, as if the prospect of eternal reward or punishment were a token gesture toward stabilizing the definitions of earthly goods and evils. Macduff, for example, frantically summons his comrades to look at Duncan's murdered body and "see / The great doom's image": the Last Judgment (2.3.71–72). But this hyperbolic expression of his horror—like the similar one at the end of *King Lear*—may evoke in the audience a different kind of horror: what if the great doom's true image *is* merely a motionless corpse? Later Ross equivocates uncomfortably on the idea that Macduff's murdered family are "well at peace." When Macduff learns the truth, his diction strongly associates death with negation: "Naught that I am, / Not for their own demerits but for mine, / Fell slaughter on their souls. Heaven rest them now" (4.3.228–30). Their souls have apparently been slaughtered with their bodies, after being judged by the earthly king rather than any divine one. All heaven can offer is rest—and the rest is silence. Macduff says later that if Macbeth is "slain, and with no stroke of mine, / My wife and children's ghosts will haunt me still" (5.7.16–17). He no longer seems to suppose them in heaven; if they survive at all, they survive as a vengeful residue in his conscience, one that can be exorcised only through the symbolic transactions of revenge-tragedy.

Banquo speaks about "heaven's breath" only as a metaphor for the pleasant air in regenerative places on earth; and the troubled "heavens" Ross refers to during the dark morning after Duncan's murder belong to astronomy, not theology. The Porter jokes about being "porter of hell-gate," but concludes that "this place is too cold for hell. I'll devil-porter it no further" (2.3.1–13). The world is an ordinary physical place that resists the grand morality-dramas we sometimes project onto it. This Porter does admit people to a sort of hell, but it is only Macbeth's castle, where the torments of conscience and a seemingly predestined earthly doom take the place of any actual devil.

Macbeth hears the bell as "a knell / That summons [Duncan] to heaven or to hell" (2.1.63–64); but Duncan apparently sleeps quietly.[20] The Porter then promptly parodies the idea of answering that kind of eschatological summons. When Macbeth considers "the deep damnation" of murdering Duncan in 1.7, he is worried about "Heaven's cherubins" testifying to the mortal world. What concerns him is that "we still have judgment here," not any Day of Judgment hereafter. He mentions "the life to come" only as something he would gladly forfeit if he could count on reigning unopposed for a few decades. He worries that Duncan's "virtues will plead like angels" against the usurpation, not that angels themselves might punish the sin; religion retreats to the level of simile, and damnation to the level of political inconvenience. Indeed, Macbeth sounds something like the Renaissance annihilationists whose radical Protestantism coalesced with radical politics—"a companye aboute this towne that saye, that hell is noe other but povertie & penurye in this worlde; and heaven is noe other but to be ritch, and enjoye pleasures; and that we dye like beastes, and when we ar gonne there is noe remembrance of us. . . . "[21] All that remains is animal competition for material and evolutionary advantage.

The witches know "all mortal consequence," and that seems to be enough for Macbeth, who seems comforted to learn that he

> Shall live the lease of Nature, pay his breath
> To time and mortal custom. Yet my heart
> Throbs to know one thing. Tell me, if your art
> Can tell so much, shall Banquo's issue ever
> Reign in this kingdom?

> (4.1.98–102)

Surely this question about earthly political succession, though prominent in the plot of the play, is a let-down after the supernatural build-up. In Macbeth as in Prospero, the extraordinary obsession with controlling future generations looks like a desperate compensation for mortality, the deferral of an unanswerable question about human purpose. And if we seize too eagerly on this dynastic mode of consolation—as the play encourages us to do by offering Malcolm's and Fleance's eventual success in compensation for Duncan's and Banquo's unjust and premature deaths—then we find ourselves implicated in Macbeth's futile struggle to give his life meaning and justification. Macbeth's bloody campaign to control the Scottish succession thus appears as the tragic playing-out of a fundamental comic formula, the logical (if pathological) extension of a common tendency to submerge fears of personal mortality in fantasies of progeny.

Macbeth insists that if he can win the battle against Malcolm's forces, it will "cheer me ever"; he gives no thought to a time beyond his earthly reign. All that troubles him, as he had predicted, is a hollowing of his mortal life, not any harrowing thereafter:

> I have lived long enough. My way of life
> Is fall'n into the sere, the yellow leaf,
> And that which should accompany old age,
> As honour, love, obedience, troops of friends,
> I must not look to have.

(5.3.22–26)

The only palliative to the demise awaiting all natural entities is a cultural construct, the company misery loves, not any prospect of perpetual bliss. Macbeth does complain that he has given his "eternal jewel . . . to the common enemy of man" (3.1.69–70); but since that metaphor for the soul is (if conventional) so materialistic, and since it appears only as the fourth item in Macbeth's second listing of the good things he surrenders by murdering Duncan, it can hardly claim a prominent place in his concerns. Faustus seems quite otherworldly by comparison.

We last see Macbeth, not as a tormented soul, but as an indifferent head. He is not dragged down into any literal hell-mouth at his death, like Faustus; his damnation is his isolation from things human and divine during the brief remainder of his earthly existence.[22] That punishment may represent a rough translation of the Augustinian commonplace that hell is alienation from God, but it also contributes to the impression that there may be neither a hell nor a heaven waiting for Macbeth, that *Everyman* is being rewritten as *Waiting for Godot*. The same isolation reinforces the idea that Macbeth's crime and punishment alike are bound up with his individuality—the individuality that he fights so fiercely to affirm because it is so transient, that (like the dagger) becomes more transient the harder he tries to grasp it, and that leads him only toward death.

Macbeth's final visible punishment fits the crime—a quest for unnatural distinction and elevation—but his extraordinary fate may also be a dramatically heightened version of the fate awaiting many aspiring minds of the Renaissance. Like them, Macbeth is given a compelling belief in the transcendent potential of his interior self, a belief that becomes a torment when that self is doomed to eradication, and can never be made "perfect; / Whole as the marble, founded as the rock"— except perhaps in the form of tomb statuary (3.4.21–22). As long as the future belongs to someone else, Macbeth remains "cabined, cribbed, confined"; the real self is the one miserably trapped inside that tomb, where a constriction in space replaces the mortal constriction in time (3.4.24). The human awareness of mortality—as Freud argues—can make the evolving beauties of nature into an agonizing spectacle.[23] Preachers may have promised that "our Bodies, lying in the Grave, do not *perish*, but *lye Dormant*, like *Trees* in *Winter*, and like *Trees* do *take root* too";[24] but Birnam Wood advances to eradicate Macbeth, not to renew him. He is only a "yellow leaf" and, finally, a lifeless head on a lifeless stick. With his defeat, "The time is free" (5.9.22), but only because humanity—its doomed slave revolt at an end—has again agreed to accept time as its master.

In Bellini's "Assassination of St. Peter Martyr" (1507) the army hewing down the forest commits the martyrdom with the same weapons. To the extent that he embodies the human will to survive, and enacts all the rebellious violations it compels us half-inadvertently to commit, Macbeth dies for our sins, and we can read in his demise what Dostoyevsky perceived in Holbein's 1521–22 depiction of the dead Christ:

> Looking at that picture, you get the impression of nature as some enormous, implacable, and dumb beast, or . . . as some huge engine of the latest design, which has senselessly seized, cut to pieces, and swallowed up—impassively and unfeelingly—a great and priceless Being, a Being worth the whole of nature and its laws. . . . The picture seems to give the impression of a dark, insolent, and senselessly eternal power, to which everything is subordinated, and this idea is suggested to you unconsciously.[25]

So the image of Macbeth's bloody remains mocked on a pole may suggest a failed version of the Crucifixion and Resurrection that were supposed to cure human mortality forever. "Behold the King of the Jews" becomes "Behold where stands / Th'usurper's cursèd head" (5.9.21–22); Macbeth is hoisted on a stick of wood to be jeered at, with the inscription "'Here may you see the tyrant'" (5.8.27). Behind both monstrous inscriptions lies *Ecce Homo*: "Behold man," with all the potential ironies of that phrase brought to the foreground.

Another, more successful story of crucifixion and resurrection emerges in the play, as Malcolm redeems his father's people from the "Devilish Macbeth" (4.3.117). When Malcolm adds that "our country sinks beneath the yoke; / It weeps, it bleeds, and each new day a gash / Is added to her wounds," and promises that he therefore, as the son and heir, "shall tread upon the tyrant's head" (4.3.39–41), the Christian resonances become overwhelming. This may help to explain Malcolm's hyperbolic self-accusations that have so troubled readers of this scene:

Shakespeare again portrays the mechanisms of Christian redemption in a painfully earth-bound version, allowing a lord to absorb all the sins of his people, but not to cancel them, only to pass them on to a successor at the moment of death. At the start of the scene Malcolm suggests that Macduff surrender him to Macbeth, since it would be "wisdom / To offer up a weak, poor, innocent lamb / T'appease an angry god" (4.3.15–17). But later in the scene Malcolm warns that, if allowed to inherit the kingdom, he will embody

> All the particulars of vice so grafted
> That when they shall be opened, black Macbeth
> Will seem as pure as snow, and the poor state
> Esteem him as a lamb, being compared
> With my confineless harms.
>
> (4.3.51–55)

This atonement oddly replicates the way Macbeth "meant to bathe in reeking wounds" at his new Golgotha (1.2.39–40), and then assumed the regicidal sins of the previous Thane of Cawdor, allowing that rebel to die in a condition of remarkable grace (1.4.1–11). Redemption is trapped in a cycle that functions very much like Original Sin, a fatal burden passed to each new generation.

The idea of a supernatural soul offered by Christianity may function like the portents conjured by the weird sisters. The world that tempts us with dreams of the transmundane finally betrays us back to the facts of physical nature: bloody newborns, young men carrying branches, and the lifeless heads of an older generation that drop away like yellowed leaves. Like Hieronimo and Hamlet, we may join Malcolm in hoping to "make us med'cines of our great revenge / To cure this deadly grief" (4.3.216–17).[26] We may alternatively join the "crew of wretched souls" who wait patiently for the touch of a royal idol to cure the fleshly decay that is simply "call'd the evil" (4.3.141, 147). But (as Marlowe's Faustus complains in his opening soliloquy) there is no evidence that any sort of medicine actually cures mortality, and in our doubting hearts we may share Macbeth's scorn for such temporary symptomatic cures:

> Canst thou not minister to a mind diseased,
> Pluck from the memory a rooted sorrow,
> Raze out the written troubles of the brain,
> And with some sweet oblivious antidote
> Cleanse the stuffed bosom of that perilous stuff
> Which weighs upon the heart?

DOCTOR: Therein the patient
Must minister to himself.

MACBETH: Throw physic to the dogs, I'll none of it.
Come, put mine armor on; give me my staff.

(5.3.41–49)

Though the ostensible topic is the guilt of murder, Shakespeare takes advantage of Macbeth's necessary vagueness about what is troubling his wife to make a statement applicable to the psychological burdens of mortality itself.

What is left for Macbeth but to identify with the oppressor? When mortality hits close to home, Macbeth—like many tyrants, including Marlowe's Tamburlaine—responds by usurping death's power, by killing relentlessly as a way of reclaiming volitional control over death. When he declares, "Rebellious dead, rise never till the wood / Of Birnam rise" (4.1.96–97), Macbeth sounds like a deity who is frightened of staging the Last Judgment, lest the countless resurrected bodies stage a tyrannicide to avenge their measureless sufferings. This identification would have pleased the audience: as in figures from the traditional Grim Reaper to the mass-murderers of modern American movies and headlines, the indiscriminate killer becomes a figure of death itself—for all its horror, a consolingly localized and humanized one, embedded in narrative and susceptible to punishment.

Shakespeare's Duke of Vienna would have been pleased, too, if he read the news from Shakespeare's Scotland: having resigned in protest from the generational future, Macbeth discovers how resilient an organization it can be. Though Banquo has "twenty trenchèd gashes on his head, / The least a death to nature" (3.4.27–28), his scion survives and takes up the resistance. The power of those bonds of life does not, however, preclude the suspicion that the "great bond / Which keeps [us] pale" (3.2.49–50) also keeps us blind; perhaps only by doing it violence instead of homage can we achieve a final disillusionment. Macbeth's eyes are seldom watching God; except for that fleeting vision of heaven's cherubs, he lets nothing distract him from his fixation on human children and the war against the future that fixation reflects. Even that cautionary vision of heavenly horror may represent a deliberate inflation of his violation, so it will seem adequate to break him free from the ordinary bonds of mortality;[27] like a Raskolnikov, he wants nothing to "take the present horror from the time" (2.1.59), for fear of resubmitting himself to a future horror that is all the worse for its banality. The paranoid position—"God and nature are (now) out to get me"—is often merely the dark shadow of narcissism, a way of retaining grandiose self-importance in a universe that has proven uncooperative. Perhaps the spiritual masochism of Calvinist theology reflects the same kind of desperation.

For all its providential overtones, *Macbeth* subliminally evokes a universe without ultimate meaning. A play full of morals becomes swallowed up by the demoralizing vision of death, and the guilt of blood gradually washes away into the blackness or blankness of mortality. Those who have behaved better than Macbeth, and retain the honor and the troops of friends that he imagines might console old age, do not seem to escape into some preferable eternity. They may have a greater probability of passing life on to a new generation, but the notion that procreation somehow mitigates individual death is particularly problematic in the linear and inward-looking world of tragedy. Here, the blood of Duncan and his sound sleep, the gory Banquo and his haunting return, have a vividness, and a blankness, hardly altered by the political prospects of their sons.

Admittedly, Macbeth makes a very poor endorsement for atheistic morality—indeed, he seems designed to confirm some of the warnings discussed in my Introduction. His soliloquies do, however, prove that in Jacobean England it was already possible for one man to perceive an evolutionist earth, red in tooth and claw; and his actions suggest why it may have seemed imperative for most people to suppress that perception. To the extent that Macbeth's vivid perspective overwhelms the pallor of the moralists around him, Shakespeare seems to have been of the atheists' party, even if he did not partake of the entire ghostless banquet. And to the extent that those moralistic characters seem perfunctory in their religious references, the play demonstrates that an entire society could profess religious values it did not hold very deeply. As Claudius discovers in the prayer scene of Hamlet, pious words may briefly outlive pious convictions, but they cannot climb to any real heaven. All they can do is keep us momentarily clear of a psychological hell.

The fierce conjunction of sexuality and violence in *Macbeth*'s verbal texture suggests a proto-Darwinian perspective on the fundamental struggles of life. The emphasis on generation in the play anticipates the recognition of evolutionary biology—a recognition with parallels in traditional Christian moralizations of the Fall—that death is part of the same invention as sexuality. Aside from gradually inventing what we call consciousness, sexual reproduction invented individuality, the unique genetic heritage that a creature will strive to protect and extend. This is of course a very long reach from Shakespeare, but to the extent that there is an evolutionary parable available in *Macbeth* (and I think there is, with the protagonist as the original bad patriarch of early Freudian myth), it recites a tragedy dictated by our chromosomes. Distantly audible in the story of Macbeth is the endless cry of fear and pain that this system of individuality and mortality, with its endless violent competition, has evoked from our world.

The thematic heroes of the play—renewed life and renewed order—have feet of clay, and velvet fists. As Schopenhauer suggests, "to desire that individuality should be immortal really means to wish to perpetuate an error infinitely . . . something which it is the real end of life to bring us back from," but "this will not satisfy the claims which are wont to be made upon proofs of our continued existence after death, nor insure the consolation which is expected from such proofs" by human individuals.[28] This egoistic error is the sin that dooms Macbeth—and the rest of us—to the fear of death. Nor is it entirely anachronistic to perceive such concerns in Jacobean literature, because Macbeth also resembles the diabolically misguided man portrayed by the great mystic Jacob Boehme, a contemporary of Shakespeare whose writings inspired the Quakers on the radical wing of the Reformation.

Boehme records the tragedy of individual selfhood—of the man who "wanted to be his own Lord" but found that the "ego-centric will cannot inherit divine childhood"[29]—with less romantic sympathy than Shakespeare does. As soon as this typical diseased human creature "considers itself greater than it is . . . the fawning Devil comes to him," making him "intoxicated with his own selfhood," diabolically misguided into a greedy misreading of the universe as a prophecy of his own sovereignty.[30] After a brief career of strutting and fretting, the individual life discovers that this grand temptation was a treacherous illusion, and its brief candle is extinguished:

since it does not immediately feel its punishment, it thinks that it is no longer a serious matter, not knowing that the more it fashions itself into foolishness the greater a source of eternal pain it receives within itself, so that, when the light of external nature—in which for a time it had strutted its I-ness—breaks up within it, then it stands within its own eternal darkness and pain, so that its false, ego-centric desire is a vain, stinging, hard incisiveness and counter-will.

During this time it hopes for external aid, leading itself into lasciviousness of will, considering this its heavenly kingdom. But when the external light is put out in death, then it remains in eternal remorse, seeing no redeemer within or about it.[31]

The only escape from this tragic pattern, according to Boehme, is a mystical self-effacement that seems designed less to escape the sins of pride in a conventional Christian sense than to escape the agonies of competition necessarily involved in defending individual identity against a world of mutability. When Macbeth tears to pieces his great bond with the human and natural orders, he behaves like Boehme's misguided soul:

the Devil persuaded it that it might be useful and good to break off the emanation of the senses from [the divine harmony of being] and bring itself into its own image, according to the characteristics of manifoldness, to probe dissimilarity, i.e., to apprehend and experience evil and good.

Thus . . . it brought itself into ego-centric desire, impressing and fashioning itself into selfhood.

Immediately when the knowledge of the life of individualities became manifest, then nature held life caught in dissimilarity, and established her rule. This is why life became painful . . . striving against the unity, against the eternal rest and the one good.[32]

This amounts to a mystical prophecy of evolution, and Boehme's vision seems to anticipate not only Macbeth's restless suffering, but also the godless existence described by Hobbes. Boehme's archetypal individual "by its own desire made itself dark, painful, gruff, hard and rough. It became sheer restlessness, and it now lives in earthly power in an earthly ground . . . ruling the mortal energy of stars and elements like a special god of nature. By such dominion it has become foolish and crazy. . . ."[33] Boehme's heaven therefore has less to do with triumphant aerial cherubim than with a Nirvana-like surrender to undifferentiated being, which the egoistic modern psyche is bound to resist.

Much in the play's equivocal universe therefore depends on whether we are on Malcolm's side (and Boehme's), seeing the advancing Birnam Wood as nature serving a benevolent intelligence, or on Macbeth's, seeing in that wood a crushing reminder of the betrayal of human aspiration by an inscrutable creation. The new generations of vegetation and humanity that rise up against Macbeth are killers as well as saviors. The first two acts of the play feverishly insinuate that murder is sex, especially procreative sex;[34] the subsequent action implies conversely that sex, especially procreative sex, is murder. The cycle of life is harsh for those who have to die. Though we may seek in that cycle the consolation of generational immortality, the play repeatedly reminds us that the next generation is no less mortal. When parents are forced to confront that fact, they may collapse in despair (as Macduff does), or transfer their denial into a fiery vengefulness (as Malcolm recommends).

Or they may hide behind an icy stoicism, as does Old Siward—"a better soldier none / That Christendom gives out" (4.3.193–94)—when he must sacrifice his son to redeem Scotland from its diabolical tyrant. In a peculiar exchange, Ross says that the loss of this son "must not be measured by his worth, for then / It hath no end" (5.9.11–12). But what end would it have, we may wonder, if it were measured by time instead? Siward insists that, since his son died honorably,

> God's soldier be he;
> Had I as many sons as I have hairs,
> I would not wish them to a fairer death.
> And so his knell is knolled.
>
> MALCOLM: He's worth more sorrow,
> And that I'll spend for him.
>
> SIWARD: He's worth no more;
> They say he parted well and paid his score,
> And so God be with him. Here comes newer comfort.
>
> (5.9.14–20)

The stage direction then reads, "*Enter MACDUFF, with Macbeth's head.*" All one can do is harden one's heart, apply the decorations of social art to the facts of physical nature, pass things unquestioningly on to God, and look around quickly for distractions and compensations, even when the "comfort" proves to be merely another dead man's head. As earlier in the play (e.g., 1.2.27 and 3.2.39), the meaning of "comfort" is the death of an enemy.

One may die with honor; one may die with children; one may die with a task of revenge complete. But in the absence of absolute faith—and it seems to me stubbornly absent from this play—is there really any consolation for death, any honest way not to cower in the face of nature, in the long shadow of eternity? The prospect of a conscious afterlife is yet another topic on which this endlessly equivocal play equivocates, keeping the word of promise to our ear, and breaking it to our hope. *Macbeth* performs subliminally some of the same dangerous cultural work that *King Lear* performs explicitly, exploring and exposing the human need to believe in a providence behind the overwhelming processes of the physical universe, the womb and tomb called nature. If we care about consciousness and the idea of the self, then we are bound to have some reservations about celebrating the triumph of natural order represented in *Macbeth*. If "There is nor flying hence nor tarrying here" (5.5.47), then all that remains is a brief meaningless struggle against a doom seeded in our birth.

I hold this truth to be self-evident. Though often eclipsed by denial, it remains visible in stories of grim human destiny, from Sophocles' *Oedipus Rex* and the Book of Job in about the fifth century B.C. to the absurdist and Existentialist texts of the twentieth century A.D.—in other words, through all the recorded syllables of Western culture. Clearly the legacy of the Oedipus story in *Macbeth* goes beyond any psychosexual syndromes attributable to the protagonist. On a broader philosophical level, the role of prophecy in both stories reminds us of the many ways we find our way only to our doom, a doom latent in us from the moment of our creation, for all our proud denials and clever evasions. At the core of that story is a riddle about the creature who goes on four legs, then two, then three. Human beings resist recognizing themselves as the answer to that riddle, as Oedipus resists recognizing himself as the cause of the Theban plague, but we are biologically fated to rise from our infancy to full stature, and then shrivel into decay. Job confronts a similar conundrum: "What is man, that thou doest magnifie him?" (7:17), he asks, and finds his answer in a recognition that these sinful creatures "are exalted for a little, but thei are gone, and are broght lowe as all others: thei are destroyed, and cut as the top of an eare of corne" (24:24). A comparably bleak catechism lies near the heart of *Macbeth*, as the witches' riddling prophecies shrivel into the dark facts of natural reality. If the profound anxieties represented by these riddles about human nature—and the reflexive denial that disastrously delays the answering of the riddles—are not quite universal, they are at least remarkably transhistorical.

The allusions to Job in *Macbeth* run wide and deep, reinforcing the play's annihilationist undertones with their persistent imagery of extinguished candles, fleeting shadows, seasonal cycles, and the enslavement of humankind to a mortal destiny at once inscrutable and only too obvious.[35] "Beware Macduff" is as much as to say, "beware mortality":

Man that is borne of woman, is of short continuance, and ful of trouble. He shooteth forthe as a flowre, and is cut downe: he vanisheth also as a shadow, & continueth not. . . . For there is hope of a tre, if it be cut downe, that it wil yet sproute, and the branches therof wil not cease. . . . But man is sicke, and dyeth, & man perisheth, and where is he? (Job, 14:1–10)

When Bildad then insists that the wicked man shall be uprooted, plunged into darkness, and left without progeny (18:14–19), Job's reply sounds like a plaintive epilogue spoken by the ghost of Macbeth. Conceding his own failings, Job nonetheless protests that God

hath spoiled me of mine honour, & taken the crowne away from mine head. He hath destroied me on everie side & I am gone: & he hath removed mine hope like a tre. And he hath kindled his wrath against me, and counteth me as one of his enemies.

His armies came together, and made their way upon me, & camped about mine tabernacle. (19:8–12)

Deserted by his familiars as well as his family, Job now foresees nothing but a death tainted by supernatural betrayal. Like Macbeth, he is a representative man, capable of reminding us that our fundamental sinfulness does not necessarily make our mortal sufferings into a narrative of divine justice. The start of this chapter suggested that *Macbeth* performs the devil's work, as Thomas Browne defines it. To the extent that *Macbeth* provokes some guilty identification with its protagonist, the play puts us on the side of Job's complaints, and therefore, once again, on the side of the Satanic argument against God.

Among contemporary artworks, Akira Kurosawa's superb film adaptation of *Macbeth* provides the most compelling reading of the play as this sort of parable. *Throne of Blood* (1957) is framed, start and finish, with long shots of a barren plateau where wind and dust have erased everything but a memorial tombstone, accompanied by a chorus of Solomonic pessimism: "Behold, within this now desolated place, / There once stood a mighty fortress, / There once lived a proud warrior."[36] That Macbeth-figure encounters his prophetic witch while trapped in the "natural labyrinth" of the forest. She is a corpse-like figure bathed in white light, crouching in a loose bamboo hut, blankly spinning a wheel, and singing:

All men are mortal, all men are vain,
And pride dies first within the grave;
For hair and nails are growing still,

When face and fame are gone.
Nothing in this world will save
Or measure up men's actions here;
Nor in the next, for there is none.
This life must end in fear.
Only evil may maintain
An after-life [for] those who will,
Who love this world, who have no son,
To whom ambition calls.
Even so, this false fame falls;
Death will reign, man dies in vain.

At these words the Macbeth and Banquo figures furiously rush the hut and demand answers—as if they had not already heard a sufficient prophecy. Incredulous at human folly, the spirit provides essentially the same information Shakespeare's witches provide, then disappears on the wind. The warriors charge through the hut in pursuit, but when they turn back, instead of the hut they see mounds of human skulls and bones molded randomly together with mud. Embedded in these mounds are helmets and weapons that look like they might belong to medieval samurai, but might also belong to the armies of Hirohito. Again, from the perspective of deep time, the forest of the world is a place of skulls. At first glance one might suppose that human violence has caused these human ruins; but perhaps it is the other way around. *Throne of Blood* may seem to be a simple anti-war parable, a reverberation from Hiroshima and Nagasaki, but it is also the kind of complex anti-war parable I have been tracing throughout Renaissance drama: a warning that our vain struggle to deny the fatedness and the anonymity represented by these heaps of human remains constantly provokes us toward the pointless murders we call revenge and war and sacrifice. This place of skulls may be called Golgotha, if we want to put the blame on fundamental human wickedness and the demands of divine justice, but all the world's a grave, and what it finally signifies is ours to decide.

5

Duelling Death in the Lyrics of Love
John Donne's Poetics of Immortality

> Salomon, *whose disposition was amorous, and excessive in the love of women, when he turn'd to God, he departed not utterly from his old phrase and language, but having put a new, and a spiritual tincture, and form and habit into all his thoughts, and words, he conveyes all his loving approaches to God, and all God's answers to his amorous soul, into Songs, and Epithalamions.*
>
> (*Sermons*, I, 237)

Donne argues that the holy Song of Songs retains a superficial residue of Solomon's sensualist youth; this chapter argues that Donne's erotic *Songs and Sonets* deeply anticipate the immortal longings of his pious maturity. Donne's secular lyrics construct an elaborate mythology of personal immortality. When Donne talks about love (especially sexual love), he is also talking about death. When he yearns for enduring spiritual love, he is dreaming, at one remove, about immortality. When he laments an imminent separation from a lover, he is also lamenting the separation of his soul from his body at death; so when he imagines a reunion, he is consolingly imagining resurrection, and when he fears forgetfulness or betrayal, he is afraid that death will annihilate the desiring experiential self to which he is so devoted. Throughout his richly varied writings, Donne consistently expresses anxiety about the prospective fragmentation or nullification of his oneness—his uniqueness, his unity. His intense brittle egotism can never quite replace the infantile narcissism that protects most people from recognizing their individual ephemerality. In searching for a perfectly reciprocating lover, Donne searches for his own immortality: his misogyny reflects disgust at the idea that his body will die, and terror that body will take soul with it, into oblivion. His writings embody a hope that his consciousness can be perpetually reborn.

Donne's fundamental concern about Last Judgment is not whether God will forgive our sins, but instead whether He will restore our existence:

First *Erimus, We shall Bee*, we shall have a Beeing. There is nothing more contrary to God, and his proceedings, then annihilation, to Bee nothing, Do Nothing, Think nothing. . . . Whatsoever God hath made thee since, yet his greatest work upon thee, was, that he made thee; and howsoever he extend his bounty in preferring thee, yet his greatest largenesse, is, in preserving thee in thy Beeing. (*Sermons*, IV, 85; cf. III, 97)

For Donne, the important hierarchy is not political or even moral, but ontological: "If we bee compar'd with *God*, our *Being* with his *Being*, we have no *Being* at all, wee are *Nothing*. For *Being* is the *peculiar* and *proper* name of *God*" (*Sermons*, VIII, 76; cf. VI, 227). If we fail of "future glory," we would "sinke into nothing" (*Sermons*, VII, 54), not into some more vivid damnation. This resembles the Existentialist adage that hell is other people: for Donne, hell is the absence of the self.

Even when he strives toward a more orthodox view, Donne cannot quite relinquish his equation of damnation with negation: "aske this *sinner* to *morrow*, and he hath sold *himselfe* for *nothing*; for *debility* in his limnes, for *darknesse* in his understanding, for *emptinesse* in his purse, for *absence* of *grace* in his Soule," an absence resulting in a forfeiture of "the *Face* of *God* hereafter; a *privation* so much worse than *nothing*, as that they upon whom it falls, would faine be *nothing*, and cannot."[1] The great incentive to Christian devotion in Donne's preachings is the possibility of seizing the Day of Judgment, returning to a full pleasurable experience of the individual body. No wonder the dying Donne had himself depicted in his shroud, not supine as he would be buried, but upright, as he would emerge at the final trumpet. The distant sound of that trumpet, playing somewhere beyond the deafness of the grave, is the Muse enticing Donne throughout his poetry.[2]

Donne occasionally acknowledged the orthodox position that death is divine justice, and that escape from this fallen world through death is actually desirable.[3] Yet his sermons undergo remarkable contortions to justify theologically his emotional sense that "Death is . . . the worst enemy"; "We have other Enemies; Satan about us, sin within us . . . but when they are destroyed, [death] shall retaine a hostile, and triumphant dominion over us."[4] Donne's theological prose exhibits the distinct residue of a *carpe diem* assumption that the greatest evil is neither worldly dishonor nor mortal sin, but death itself, as the thief of memory and sensation. He wonders why anyone would want the use of eyes in the grave, "where there is nothing to be seen but loathsomnesse; or a nose there, where there is nothing to be smelt, but putrefaction; or an ear, where in the grave they doe not praise God?" (*Sermons*, III, 105). Presumably the question is rhetorical, but we still may wonder what compels him to ask it.

Donne's secular lyrics persistently and vividly fantasize about returning from death, or achieving perpetual life. Ghosts, relics, and posthumous initiatives are everywhere, pointing back to his Roman Catholic upbringing, and ahead to the fascination with resurrection that would dominate his thinking as an Anglican. What Donne hates about his sickbed is not only the ominous occlusion of sensation it imposes, but also that he "must practice my lying in the *grave*, by lying still, and not practise my *Resurrection*, by rising any more" (*Devotions*, pp. 11, 16). So in "The Canonization" he reconceives the consumption of the body in the bedroom as a joyful rebirth within the cycle of sexual desire:

> The Phoenix ridle hath more wit
> By us, we two being one, are it.
> So, to one neutrall thing both sexes fit.
> Wee dye and rise the same, and prove
> Mysterious by this love.
>
> (lines 23–27)

The poem ends by envisioning a posthumous summons back to this world as a teacher of love. In other poems, such as "The Apparition" and "The Dampe," the speaker returns with less positive messages about love—but he always returns, reborn precisely because he died for love. What he seeks from the love of women thus resembles what he seeks from the love of God; and both are introjected in Donne's remarkable narcissism, where the desirous body and the subjective intellect unite, where the female validates the perfect identity of the male, and the primary desire (as in Hobbes) is to desire anew.

This chapter seeks to articulate a broadly consistent mythology Donne assembled in order to reassure himself that the embrace of his body and mind was unbreakable. It also attempts to explain what may have necessitated and shaped this mythology. From the standpoint of object-relations psychology, the shared characteristics of Donne's amorous and pious personae suggest a psyche that, in its earliest formative moments, lacked the careful handling and the reassuring gaze of recognition that assures the infantile self of its acceptance and its coherence. All the most prominent characteristics of Donne's subsequent biography—his agonizing religious apostasy, his dangerous sexual choices, and his resulting career frustrations—build on this infantile anxiety, so that his lifelong terror of preterition and annihilation becomes overdetermined. Though Arthur Marotti is surely correct that Donne suffered from "the pain of being a sociopolitical nonentity," surely that anguish should not be separated from the fears of non-being that tormented Donne in less pragmatic categories.[5] The helplessness of infancy and the terror of annihilation frame the frustration of mid-life ambition; the uncertain favors of an omnipotent and inscrutable mother or Calvinist God magnify the uncertainties of courtiership into more than a practical problem.

Many of the peculiarities of Donne's writing thus become overdetermined as well: the chronic fragile egoism, the compulsion to reconceive the world from its foundations, and the compulsion to reconcile material and spiritual realms. Though inevitably speculative in both its foundations and its superstructure, this theory offers a generative coherence to Donne's life-work. "Character-traits are secret psyochoses," declared Sandor Ferenczi, a visionary among Freud's early disciples (Becker, p. 27). So are literary styles. In its determination to fuse the mental with the tangible, Donne's Metaphysical art bespeaks an obsession with keeping soul and body together. And in its fundamental reconception of the given universe, Donne's Metaphysical wit provides a defense against the extreme forms of self-alienation and hyperreceptivity now known as schizophrenia: "Thinking patterns in these patients are far from normal. There are dramatic leaps of logic, and absurd, unrealistic beliefs are common."[6] From the corrosive early satires, through the uneasy dependency on erotic exchange, to the anguished religious verse, Donne struggles with precisely the tendencies another of Freud's great early disciples, Alfred Adler, identifies with the classic schizoid personality:

> He mistrusts not only himself but also the knowledge and ability of others; nothing seems to him to be able to overcome the inevitable horrors of life and death—except perhaps the fantastic ideational system that he fabricates for his own salvation. His feelings of magical omnipotence and immortality are a reaction to the terror of death by a person who is totally incapable of opposing this terror with his own secure powers.[7]

Poetry represents Donne's auxiliary power, enabling his mind to define and defend itself. Within that magic circle, he can toy with his demons.

My readers may be forgiven for feeling their hearts sink at the prospect of watching yet another canonical author mapped onto yet another psychoanalytic model. The only reassurance I can offer immediately is that my goal is neither a clinical diagnosis of Donne as schizophrenic, nor a claim that his art and faith can be thoroughly explained by such a diagnosis. But it does seem worthwhile to notice how closely Donne's anxieties fit D. W. Winnicott's developmental categories, and how helpful a bridge those categories provide between infant psychology and Reformation theology:

> Unthinkable anxiety has only a few varieties, each being the clue to one aspect of normal growth.
> 1. Going to pieces.
> 2. Falling forever.
> 3. Having no relation to the body.
> 4. Having no orientation.
>
> It will be recognized that [these fears] belong, clinically, to schizophrenia, or to the emergence of a schizoid element in an otherwise non-psychotic personality.

The point is not that Donne is psychotic, but that his writing comprises a release of schizoid pressures through the channels available at the time. "Commonly," Winnicott argues, there is "a schizoid element hidden in a personality that is otherwise sane," and this element—often found in those who "show brilliance of intellect"—"can hide in a pattern of schizoid disorder that is accepted in a person's local culture."[8]

Reading Donne from psychoanalytic and Existential perspectives may seem hopelessly anachronistic, and yet in another sense it is both biographically and historically valid. The peculiarities of Donne's inner life may have sensitized him to the nascent cultural crisis that psycho-analysis and Existentialism eventually rose to answer. Perhaps Donne's writing embodies an intense early confrontation with a contradiction at the heart of modern Western culture, between the narcissistic attach-ment to individual human interiority and the perception of a merely material universe infinite in time and space. If Donne expresses the first sharp pang of a mortally wounded culture, then it is not surprising that he re-emerged as an important figure amid the more explicit and systematic disillusionments of Modernism.

Donne provides an unusually clear glimpse of modern mortality, perhaps because no cultural tactics adequate to disguise it (from so needy and penetrating a gaze) had yet been invented:

We can say that the schizophrenic is deprived precisely of this neurological-cultural security against death and of programming into life. He relies instead on a hypermagnification of mental processes to try to secure his death-tran-scendence; he has to try to be a hero almost entirely ideationally, from within a bad body-seating, and in a very personal way. Hence the contrived nature of his efforts. (Becker, p. 219)

John Dryden's and Samuel Johnson's famous critiques of Metaphysical poetic contrivance anticipate this analysis of schizophrenia. The eccen-tricities of Donne's art suggest a compelling anxiety barely under control. "The schizophrenic . . . cannot marshal an ego response, a directive control of his experiences. His own erupting meanings cannot be given any creative form" (Becker, p. 221). Art is Donne's way out of this psychological trap; but it is not an entirely comfortable way, because speech moves always toward silence, and in silence, chaos is come again, and so is oblivion.

To escape the pressure that closure commonly exerts on dreams of immortality, Donne explicitly identified death as merely a "parenthesis" in the unbroken syntax of the soul.[9] He fears annihilation so intensely that he cannot quite conceive it except in subordination to some continuous inscription of the ego. That—not a wholehearted desire for death itself—is why he could enjoy an exaggerated rumor of his demise: "A man would almost be content to dye, (if there were no other benefit in death) to hear of so much sorrow, and so much good testimony from good men, as I, (God be blessed for it) did upon the report of my death" (*Letters*, p. 209; cf. Drummond, p. 50). He would almost be glad to get death over with—if he could still preserve his narcissistic self, the loving attention that affirms it, and its ability to partake of language. So he preaches *Death's Duell* as "his own funeral sermon," arranges to die while gazing on a statue of his own corpse, and in several poems imagines people studying that corpse. As Freud argues, "It is indeed impossible to imagine our own death, and whenever we attempt to do so we can perceive that we are in fact still present as spectators."[10]

From the beginning of his poetic career, Donne used his Metaphysical imagination as a weapon against the closural force of death. When he undertakes to "sing the progresse of a deathlesse soule" in the early "Metempsychosis," he is certainly being playful, but play is often a means of approaching problems too serious to confront directly. "Metempsychosis" suggests that Donne would rather be a pagan, a believer in the transmigration of souls, than a mortalist, a Christian who believes that souls are susceptible to death.[11] Donne's strategies of perpetuation are no less ingenious than his strategies of renewal. Most of his canonical love-verse seeks immortality through a perfect reciprocity with his beloved. When that reciprocity fails, Donne reflexively turns to a version of the misogynistic commonplace that locates the source of human mortality in the female body. He insults the woman who has proved insufficient so that he can justify seeking in another woman the ideal she has compromised; he acknowledges the body's mortal frailty only so that he can isolate it in the female agent. In this sense, his misogynist outbursts have less to do with a judgment against living women than with projected bitterness at the failure of a formula for immortality. Perhaps the compulsive pursuit of new seductions suggested by Donne's love-lyrics reflects an effort to confirm that corrupt objects, not an inevitably decaying subject, explain all the previous failures of that formula. His notorious abstractions of love would then reflect less a neglect of the female Other who shares his bed than an evasion of the mortal Self destined for a grave. This is not to deny that Donne's lyrics are often clever exercises for casual occasions, written in persona; but (as psychoanalysis has demonstrated) the self can express itself most deeply outside of direct discourse, and (as Renaissance meditative practices emphasized) the dark business of mortality finds ways to manifest itself in even the lightest instances of life.[12]

Nor is it to deny that Donne was fundamentally a Christian believer, though there are grounds for supposing him susceptible to profound doubts. R. C. Bald's biography contains considerable (if circumstantial) evidence for Donne's flirtations with atheism, but swerves from acknowledging it as such. For example, Bald speculates that Donne probably gained his acquaintance with his chief patron, Sir Robert

Drury, through the recommendation of William Lyly, who already enjoyed Drury's patronage. The most substantial surviving report about Lyly suggests that Donne was hardly entering a hermetically sealed atmosphere of Christian confidence; indeed, it seems questionable whether a fervent Christian could have gained access to Drury through these channels. Joseph Hall reports that, upon taking office as rector at Hawstead,

I found there a dangerous Opposite to the Success of my Ministry, a witty and bold Atheist, one Mr. *Lilly*, who by reason of his Travails, and Abilities of Discourse and Behaviour, had so deeply insinuated himself into my Patron, Sir *Robert Drury*, that there was small hopes (during his entireness) for me to work any good upon that Noble Patron of mine. . . . [13]

Bald finds several reasons to believe that, in his thirties, Donne had substantial contact with Thomas Hariot; then professes surprise that "in spite of" such intellectual companionship, Donne became "deeply despondent at the lack of direction in his life." [14] If we recall contemporary testimony "that one Herryott of Sr Walter Rawleigh his howse hath brought the godhedd in question," [15] we may suspect that these contacts instead nurtured Donne's despondency at the direction of his life toward oblivion.

. If Donne's violently conflicted early religious experience brought him to "a period of unsettlement during which neither Catholicism nor Protestantism could wholly satisfy him," we should recall Bacon's warning that "discordant and contrary opinions in religion" nurture atheism—particularly since Donne's satires also register Bacon's other main culprits: scandalous priests, intellectual idleness, and a custom of scoffing.[16] Donne himself would preach that "the conniving at severall *Religions*, (as dangerous as it is) is not so *dishonourable* to *God*, as the suffering of *Iesters* at *Religion*: That may induce *heresie*; but this doe's establish *Atheisme*" (*Sermons*, VIII, 65). Unlike many of his contemporaries, Donne recognized the specific threat of atheism as distinct from, and indeed worse than, mere heresy within the Christian faith. For what it is worth, we might also note that Donne's only surviving sister married the aforementioned "bold Atheist" Lyly, and Donne's eldest son and namesake was eventually accused of being "an atheistical buffoon, a banterer, and a person of over free thoughts." [17] What ran in this family was hardly an untroubled stream of Christian piety.

Donne's literary critics, like his biographers, have generally been too quick to isolate the supposed sexual adventurism of Donne's cynical young manhood from his adult religiosity.[18] From my perspective, both forms of passion radiate from Donne's frantic quest for personal immortality; so do his melancholy, his egoism, and his passion for writing. Particularly Metaphysical writing: as the work of Soren Kierkegaard and Otto Rank suggests, "sin and neurosis are two ways of talking about the same thing—the complete isolation of the individual, his disharmony with the rest of nature, his hyperindividualism, his attempt to create his own world from within himself."[19] My goal in pointing out the correspondences is not to belittle the importance of religion in Donne; on the contrary, I am arguing that many of the impulses underlying his secular lyrics find more direct expression in his explicitly religious writing. My argument relies on the work of Winnicott, who argues that "there is no id before ego" and that life "is more nearly about BEING than about sex."[20] It therefore diametrically opposes the many critics who—noting the correspondences between secular lyrics that construe seduction as religion, and sacred poems that construe religion as seduction—have attempted to characterize Donne's adult zeal as largely a sublimation of his adolescent eroticism, the distorted return of repressed erotic drives.[21] Such critics resemble the bad companions Donne warns his congregation against, those who

think thy present fear of God, but a childishness and pusilanimity, and thy present zeal to his service but an infatuation and a melancholy, and thy present application of thy self to God in prayer, but an argument of thy Court-despaire, and of thy falling from former hopes there. (*Sermons*, VIII, 182)

Donne thus seems to have anticipated not only psychoanalytic commentaries, but New Historicist ones as well. John Carey's biography may be correct in asserting that Donne's unsatisfied ambition for "worldly success," along with the work-ethic of his Protestant culture, explains the sermons' horror at inactivity, typified by an insistence that idle persons "should be sent to the colonies and forced to work."[22] But the same horror may reflect Donne's characteristic fear of falling utterly and endlessly passive at death, as if insisting on physical activity in the New World could assure it in the next world.

Placing annihilationist anxiety at the psychological core of Donne's writings effectively inverts many of the commonplaces of Donne criticism. Julia J. Smith proposes that Donne's need for instant fulfillment of his sexual desires, as a stay against worldly inconstancy, "lie[s] behind his desire to possess heaven for the soul even at the moment of death."[23] Perhaps, conversely, his need to believe in an infallible Savior underlies his need for a perfectly responsive lover. My inclination is similarly to reverse Smith's claim that Donne "was perhaps attracted to mortalism because it enabled him to stress the unique drama of the General Resurrection, by which, as we shall see, he was much fascinated."[24] I suspect Donne persistently staged versions of that resurrection because it enabled him to disarm the mortalism—the prospect of soul dying with body—by which he was much terrified. Experimenting with losing and recovering his essential being, Donne plays a version of Freud's "fort-da" game, in which a child masters the experience of abandonment, throwing away and then retrieving an object symbolizing the mother.[25]

Donne's appetite for martyrdom is easily misread as a desire to die, whereas it may instead reflect a willingness to suffer even the most extreme agonies in order to make death somehow meaningful. Donald Ramsay Roberts asserts that "there is no utterance in the whole canon of [Donne's] works that can legitimately be interpreted as evidence of a personal fear of or aversion to death."[26] I would not quite venture to the opposite extreme (and one may suspect exaggeration from a critic who declares that Donne "never became anti-Catholic"), but it is important to notice the distinction between Roberts's large claim and the wording of his subsequent analyses: when in "the last months of Donne's life . . . he was clearly determined to see [his demise] as a '*mortem raptus*, a death of rapture and ecstasy' . . . do we not clearly discern the actions of a man playing out a drama to signalize to the world that death holds no terrors for him . . . ?"[27] If Donne was "determined" to perceive his death this way and to signal it theatrically to the world, then one can hardly call it an unalloyed, instinctive response. Surely this self-presentation could indicate a struggle to resist and disguise a fearsome aversion, to project orthodox comforts that he found difficult to take to heart.

D. W. Harding sees in Donne's writings on death a "constant effort . . . to convert the fear to longing."[28] But, like the pious commentators cited in my Introduction, Donne can only assert this longing in the evasive form of a rhetorical question: "if thou now feare death inordinately, I shoulde feare that thine eyes have not seen thy salvation to day; who can feare the darknesse of death, that hath the light of this world, and of the next too?" (*Sermons*, VII, 298). The conventional preacherly question—"shall I be loath to come to that?"—refuses to remain merely rhetorical (*Sermons*, V, 210; cf. *Devotions*, p. 78). A perpetual interrogative contemplation of death indicates a struggle with the associated fears, not an easy mastery. Donne lies in the dark thinking pious thoughts, but he does so primarily to scare away the demons of annihilationism hiding under the bed: "There is nothing so neare Immortality, as to die daily; for not to feele death, is Immortality; and onely hee shall never feele death, that is exercised in the continuall Meditation thereof; Continuall Mortification is Immortality" (*Sermons*, VIII, 168).

Critics such as John Stachniewski who find hints of despair in Donne's religious verse commonly attribute that despair to a Calvinist theology (reinforced by a lack of reliable patronage) that emphasized "the helplessness of man and the uselessness of human effort before vastly powerful, indiscriminate, and often merciless forces. . . . "[29] The same feelings would of course be evoked by a latent atheism informed by "new Philosophy," with its materialist reading of a Copernican universe.[30] In 1613 Thomas Fitzherbert, answering the *Pseudo-Martyr*, interpreted Donne's "malignity towards Catholickes" in much the same way I am portraying Donne's malignity toward female frailty: as "a Simptome to discover another more malignant, and dangerous disease bred in his hart, from whence he hath belched out so many Lucianicall, impious, blasphemous, and Atheisticall jests against Gods Saints and Servants, that he may well be thought to be one of those [who have] *set theyr mouth against heaven.*"[31] Donne himself reports that, in his efforts to disperse his fits of melancholy, "I am like an exorcist, which had long laboured about one, which at last appears to have the Mother, that I still mistake my disease" (*Letters*, p. 62). Perhaps the comparison is more than casual; perhaps, like that exorcist, Donne could deal more easily with the invigorating threat of damnation than with the melancholy possibility that there are no authentic supernatural manifestations in his personal universe, only the facts of mortal decay. Perhaps critics and biographers, too, have long mistaken (as lust and, later, zeal) the disease of annihilationist doubt that ate away at Donne's heart, and spoke at one remove through his secular lyrics. If Donne himself could declare that "our mortality, and our immortality . . . are the two reall Texts, and subjects of all our Sermons" (*Sermons*, II, 361), then perhaps those are the real subjects of the poems as well.

LOVE AS DEATH:
EXERCISES IN SUBSTITUTION

The warning of George Herbert's "Jordan (I)" against "Catching the sense at two removes" is bracing for the ingenious modern critic. I hope my search for the referred pain of mortality in Donne's erotic lyrics can be justified by noting his obsession with personal immortality, which often seems to be their only unifying characteristic. Such inferences will always be uncertain, if only because the degree of Donne's serious personal investment in his lyric speakers is uncertain. But imperfect evidence is not worthless evidence, and—as a disturbed wave pattern may delineate a submerged wreck—consistent and peculiar characteristics of poetic speech may help to reveal characteristics of the poet's mind.

The love-lyrics pursue immortality by an inventive system of substitution: not a scapegoat villain replacing the dead person in the transaction of revenge, or a child replacing a parent in the mortal cycle, or Christ replacing humankind in the economy of condemnation, but instead love replacing death in the manageable universe of poetic creation. Long before the *Death's Duell* sermon, where Walton acknowledges the morbid tendency, Donne's writings served "to discharge his memory of his preconceived meditations, which were of dying."[32] Like standard mortification exercises, Donne's poetic practice requires recognizing the figured presence of death in all the businesses of life. Donne's idiosyncracy is his insistence that his passion and his poetry can reverse the transaction, vivifying mortality by containing and transmuting it within his omnipresent experience of sexual love. It is not surprising that Donne would write that he and his wife lie "in two beds, or graves" during an illness (*Letters*, p. 145); but even the heartily sexual undressing in the "Elegy: Going to Bed" echoes common Reformation metaphors for dying.[33]

Love and death make a familiar pairing, and a simple code of substitution or inversion is a familiar mode of psychological evasion. Undoing this reaction-formation, replacing the references to love in Donne's poems with parallel references to death, often does surprisingly little violence to their colloquialism, their internal coherence, or their continuity with Donne's other writings. In "Loves Growth," for instance, a series of conventional proverbs about death are transformed into—or thinly disguised as—Metaphysical pronouncements about love.[34] If these delicate lyric entities can survive so crudely performed a transplant, then the theory underlying the operation will be partly vindicated. The fact that the poems accommodate *thanatos* precisely where they manifest *eros* does not preempt more straightforward readings, but it does indicate the psychological associations subliminally active in their creator.

In "The Sunne Rising," the lovers bear some odd resemblances to corpses. If they were dead rather than impassioned, it would indeed be irrelevant for the sun to intrude announcing morning, and absurd to imagine them undertaking any of the tasks of life—study, work, harvest. Death, as least as much as love, "all alike, no season knowes, nor clyme, / Nor houres, dayes, moneths, which are the rags of time" (9–10). In the oblivion of death, climate is changeless, and time a seamless shroud. The timelessness that love grants him is precisely what he elsewhere fears death will impose on him. Indeed, Donne eventually revives these same words to emphasize the supreme imperative of salvation: one sermon declares that there are "no seasons, no monaths, no yeares, no dayes" in the eternal hereafter,[35] and another asserts that "first and last are but the ragges of time, and his mercy hath no relation to time."[36] The only cure for eternal death is Resurrection: a Son rising, the limitless love of a personal savior. Donne's mate is indeed "all States, and all Princes, I" (21), if his terror of death is leading him (here as in lines 17–18 of "The Relique") into a characteristically megalomaniacal identification with that King of Kings. But, of course, not even that exalted identity confers a full immunity from death.

Donne's boast in the second stanza that he can eliminate the light of the sun merely "with a winke" (13) is the egotistical facet of solipsism; to assert that eclipsing one's own perception of the sun is indistinguishable from eliminating the sun itself is to risk recognizing that an entire universe disappears with the extinction of any individual consciousness. Donne was not alone in trying to handle this dangerously two-edged sword, which the Reformation emphasis on interiority would surely have sharpened. Thomas Traherne argues that "The sun in your eye is as much to you as the sun in the heavens. For by this the other is enjoyed. It would shine on all rivers, trees, and beasts in vain to you could you not think upon it."[37] And Thomas Browne characteristically puts the sword of ratiocination back into the sheath of faith: "Nor need we fear this term 'annihilation'. . . . For the eyes of God, and perhaps also of our glorified selves, shall as really behold and contemplate the world in its Epitome of contracted essence, as now it doth at large and in its dilated substance" (p. 124).

"Nothing else is," Donne announces. Perhaps—but all else is therefore nothing. Donne's religious prose again provides an analogue that reveals not only the theological implications of this poetic bravado, but also the specific fear—of closing his eyes into a perpetual darkness of death—that the poem displaces: "Only be thou present to me, O my God, and this bedchamber shall be all one room, and the closing of these bodily eyes here, and the opening of the eyes of my soul there, all one act" (*Devotions*, p. 70; *Sermons*, II, 182, seeks the same kind of instant transfer for his hearing). He cannot look away from the beloved object because their exchange of gazes seems to verify his fantasy of immortal and omnipotent consciousness:

the incapacity of the ego to accept separation results in . . . a mental force which separates the ego from reality, denies reality, represses reality. And the effect is to burden the narcissistic project of loving union with the world with the unreal project of becoming oneself one's whole world (the solipsism to which the philosophers regress).[38]

Taken together, Donne's Metaphysical conceitedness and his erotic fixations constitute predictable responses to annihilationist terror.

The ending of the second stanza echoes proverbial wisdom about the levelling functions of the house of death: "Aske for those Kings whom thou saw'st yesterday, / And thou shalt heare, All here in one bed lay" (19–20). Donne himself would preach that "All lie alike" in the earth, because the grave holds no special place for "dust Royall" (*Sermons*, IX, 64; cf. X, 238). Again what profess to be statements about the joys of unique love seem equally germane to the terrors of indifferent death. "Everything In One Place" is the current advertising slogan of the famous Forest Lawn cemetery. The fixing of the sun is a *carpe diem* motif designed to forestall the *ubi sunt* motif. A man who would later warn in a sermon "that yesterday is dead" (*Sermons*, IV, 52) must be perpetually afraid of allowing tomorrow to occur. The patronizing address to the aging sun arouses our common-sense awareness that the sun ages us long before we can weary it. Donne is not merely the aubade lover who refuses to accept that the rising sun must part him from his beloved; he also refuses to accept the parting of soul from body that time imposes on all mortals. In resisting, on behalf of his sexual relationship, social pressures toward ordinary daytime duties, Donne also resists, on behalf of his grandiose self-love, a standard Jacobean argument for accepting mortality: "Shall the heavens stay their ever-rolling wheels . . . and hold still Time, to prolong thy miserable days, as if the highest of their working were to do homage unto thee? Thy death is a piece of the order of this *All*" (Drummond, pp. 24–25). This is precisely the "all" that Donne tries to appropriate five times in lines 20–24.

"The Sunne Rising" does of course describe lovers defying the universe, rather than corpses submitting to it. But if Murray Roston is right, the poem is also an act of defiance against the Copernican universe that subordinates anthrocentrism to heliocentrism.[39] "The Sunne Rising" enlists the richness of insular experience and the egoistical potential of subjectivity as a defense against a bewilderingly unsympathetic cosmos. Donne's deep attachment to this mistress, and his unrealistic worship of her, serve much the same function that Rank and Becker perceive in psychoanalytic transference:

> Realistically the universe contains overwhelming power. Beyond ourselves we sense chaos. We can't really do much about this unbelievable power, except for one thing: we can endow certain persons with it. The child takes natural awe and terror and focusses them on individual beings, which allows him to find the power and the horror all in one place instead of diffused throughout a chaotic universe. *Mirabile!* The transference object, being endowed with the transcendent powers of the universe, now has in himself the power to control, order, and combat them.[40]

"The Sunne Rising" asserts the power of human love, but in that assertion we can see the outlines of the threat love must serve to neutralize. The poem presents one side—ostentatiously, one side only—in the human argument with the universe, an argument over which one can effectively declare the other irrelevant.

When Donne needs to retreat from hints of his cosmic insignificance, he uses an idealized lover and a significant setting to re-enslave the sun to human purposes. This battle against the implications of Copernicanism continues—this time in the depressive rather than the grandiose mode of narcissistic crisis—when he courts Lucy, Countess of Bedford, in Twickenham garden, part of which was laid out as a detailed model of the Ptolemaic universe.[41] "Twicknam Garden" ostensibly describes a pastoral retreat in which Donne's speaker laments an erotic rejection. Yet the diction of the poem suggests an unsuccessful struggle to retreat to a self-centered universe, and what he most laments is his own mortality. The speaker explains that he cannot appreciate the beauty of this refuge because he has become infected with an unlawful and unrequited sexual desire. But in Donne's lyrics, sexual desire for a woman is often a displacement of the narcissistic desire for an immortal self. Beneath the conventional sexual moral of "Twicknam Garden" lies a moral like that of Herbert's "The Flower": that the craving for individual immortality prevents us from accepting our place in a providential flow of nature.[42]

   Throughout Renaissance literature, gardens are both womb and tomb, reflecting both the Edenic immortality we have forfeited and the figurative, cyclical immortality we must learn to accept in its place. In mourning the passing seasons, as Gerard Manley Hopkins suggests in "Spring and Fall," we mourn ourselves. In the opening lines of "Twicknam Garden," the speaker accuses himself of converting the winds and rains of the season into expressions of his personal sadness:

> Blasted with sighs, and surrounded with teares,
>   Hither I come to seeke the spring,
>   And at mine eyes, and at mine eares,
> Receive such balmes, as else cure every thing. . . .

The prescription is conventional: some fresh air in the garden on an April day to purge the heart of sadness. But, as the weather indicates (and as his amorousness may too), the calendar spring has already arrived; the problem is accepting it as itself, rather than through an egoistical literary convention.

The medicine of seeing life renewed around him will surely fail if he is interested only in finding a cure for his entrapment in the cycle of life. The lovelorn Donne in Twickenham garden is like the childless Macbeth in Dunsinane castle, a "yellow leaf" who feels "aweary of the sun" as young trees spring up around him; the women who seemed to promise transcendence have betrayed him back into his mortal destiny. The poem has been characterized as a broad satire on the complaining Petrarchan lover,[43] but one of his letters shows Donne responding to a spring garden in very much the manner of the "Twicknam Garden" persona: "Because I am in a place and season where I see everything bud forth, I must do so too," he wrote to Goodyer in 1608, yet "the pleasantnesse of the season displeases me. Every thing refreshes, and I wither, and I grow older, and not better, my strength diminishes, and my load growes" (*Letters*, p. 68). And on his sickbed he would remark, "what a Minute is Mans life in respect of the Sunnes, or of a tree" (*Devotions*, p. 72).

The second stanza begins with a wish (like the rash wish of an angry child in a fairy tale) "that winter did / Benight the glory of this place, / And that a grave frost did forbid / These trees to laugh and mocke mee to my face" (10–13). In other words, he wishes for some reflex in nature to help conceal the fact that he creates his own misplaced misery. The emphases on winter, night, and that "grave frost" suggest death itself much more emphatically than they do sexual mortification. Clearly this speaker is haunted not only by a failure of transcendence, but also—like the speaker of Marvell's "Mower" poems, where again the grim reaper is thinly disguised as an unrequiting mistress—by a failure of the pathetic fallacy. The stubborn infantile conviction that the entire world is a harmonious extension of one's desiring faculty is gradually compromised by the good mother, briefly renewed by an ideal lover, and finally shattered by the specter of death.

Freud's famous meditation on "The Theme of the Three Caskets" ends by speculating about "the three inevitable relations that a man has with a woman—the woman who bears him, the woman who is his mate and the woman who destroys him . . . they are the three forms taken by the figure of the mother in the course of a man's life—the mother herself, the beloved one who is chosen after her pattern, and lastly the Mother Earth who receives him once more."[44] Bassanio's choice of the beautiful silent third casket in *The Merchant of Venice*, and Lear's reconciliation with the beautiful silent third daughter in *King Lear*, reflect men's efforts to reconceive their inevitable mortality as a chosen fulfillment. The device of this denial "in which the Goddess of Death was replaced by the Goddess of Love"—and the mother by wife and daughter—clearly resembles the code of substitution by which Donne seeks to control mortality.

But rituals can save only those who believe in their efficacy, and the infant learns resentfully that the nurturing entity is not really an eternal extension of the self. Spring may be like a priest administering extreme unction in "Twicknam Garden," as one critic has suggested,[45] but it cannot redeem the creature to whom mortality tastes as bitter as ashes, whose "spider love . . . transubstantiates all, / And can convert Manna to gall," a Host into a corpse, pure food into wormwood (6–7). Unable to imitate the self-sacrificing Christ, he instead replicates Satan's destructive egoism: "And that this place may thoroughly be thought / True Paradise, I have the serpent brought" (8–9). This is precisely the version of the Fall that the Renaissance mystic Jacob Boehme warned against: "This was that true paradise in which Thou didst place our first parents," warning them "not to becloud this holy Sabbath of Thy indwelling Vitality with ego-centric desire, and not to lead the serpent's cunning and falsity therein. . . ."[46] In Lucy's garden as in Adam's, the sin of pride and the craving for personal immortality are the most dangerous temptations.

The speaker then begs to be transformed into "Some senslesse peece of this place" (16); but (as the author of *Biathanatos* was well aware)[47] oblivion is always within the reach of those who truly want it. This ostensible request for extinction is really a quest for immortality: "Make me a mandrake, so I may groane [or "grow"] here, / Or a stone fountaine weeping out my yeare" (17–18). These are imitations of life, extensions of the very passive and mournful aspects of life he supposedly wishes to escape. The mandrake (as "Song: Goe, and catche a falling starre" indicates) was a plant superstitiously supposed to hold a human soul. What the speaker of "Twicknam Garden" seeks is a local habitation for his soul that will continue to express his emotional experience beyond the extinction of consciousness. The weeping stone fountain— again, tears to match the sighs—would serve that purpose; like Herbert's "Altar," it is a defense-mechanism against terminal silence. Further-more, the fountain is "weeping out its yeare" rather than bewailing the unkindness of a mistress. The emotion that the speaker projects onto the fountain—presumably the one he is evading in himself—is this sorrow at the transience of his own subjective existence.

As he weeps and drinks the beloved's tears, he must fight the recognition that the creature he desires to love eternally is himself. Burial, mourning, and immortality are all more vivid and prominent in "Twicknam Garden" than is the woman who supposedly inspires the poem. So when the speaker reaches the standard Petrarchan conclusion that his mistress's rejection "kills mee" (27), the literary convention makes explicit the psychological agenda. Exclusion from the bed of a woman he desires is merely one manifestation of a more profound fear that haunts Donne's lyrics, both sacred and profane: the fear of exclusion from the immortality that might be conferred by the absolute devotion of an omnipotent Other. When nature will not violate her principles to save him, then his death is precisely "her truth" (27).

In "The Sunne Rising," reciprocated love offers immortality; in "Twicknam Garden," unreciprocated love imposes death. "The Extasie" defines what Donne desires from love, and thereby hints what he fears from death. Without the full sensual experience of the body, love and immortality alike become meaningless abstractions. "The Extasie" begins with the lovers seemingly lying atop their own graves, resembling the spousal monuments that remained common throughout late Medieval Europe: "Wee like sepulchrall statues lay; / All day, the same our postures were, / And wee said nothing, all the day" (18–20). Even before this explicit comparison, the suggestion of corpses perme-ates what is ostensibly a scene of pastoral love. Where the swelling of the ground pushes up violets (which were commonly supposed to spring from graves, cf. *Hamlet*, 5.1.240), this motionless couple lie with their hands "cimented" and their eyes fixed, while their "soules . . . to advance their state, / Were gone out" (5, 15–16). Though their bodies remain separate, they meet on a higher plane, following a geometric model of enduring love that "Aire and Angels" and "A Valediction: Forbidding Mourning" will spell out more clearly.

Because it prepares souls and bodies to retie "That subtile knot, which makes us man" (64), this model looks ahead to resurrection. To attain the immediate goal of earthly seduction, as to attain the eventual goal of heavenly salvation, the speaker of "The Extasie" must temporarily abjure his body. Then he must recover it, because unless the loving soul involves the body in its joys, this passion resembles only a failed resurrection: "A man is not saved, a sinner is not redeemed, I am not received into heaven, if my body be left out; The soule and the body concurred to the making of a sinner, and body and soule must concur to the making of a Saint" (*Sermons*, VII, 103). In another sermon Donne insists,

I must have this body with me to heaven, or else salvation it self is not perfect; And yet I cannot have this body thither, except as S. *Paul* did his, *I beat down this body*, attenuate this body by mortification; *Wretched man that I am, who shall deliver me from this body of death?* (*Sermons*, II, 63; cf. IV, 47)

In the sermons the answer will be Christ; in the erotic verse the answer is a woman, the same kind of creature who delivered him into that body. Donne's craving to unify the divided self permeates his writings, and he uses sexual conjunction much as Browne used experiments on flowers: to provide "not only an ocular demonstration of our resurrection, but a notable illustration of that Psychopanny" which we endure in the grave.[48]

Donne's experiment appears to be no less successful. By refusing to admit a distinction between the two lovers (even in the pronouns), "The Extasie" constructs a mirror that captures their souls,

> And makes both one, each this and that.
>
> A single violet transplant,
>   The strength, the colour, and the size,
> (All which before was poore, and scant,)
>   Redoubles still, and multiplies.
>
> When love, with one another so
>   Interinanimates two soules,
> That abler soule, which thence doth flow,
>   Defects of lonelinesse controules.
>
>   (36–44)

This is a narcissistic transcription of the usual promises of procreation. By rescuing each of their essences from the vulnerability of residing in a single transient being, this dual soul is able to control the human defect known as mortality. Their physical and spiritual mating allows them to revivify, like violets, in the very face of death. By the peculiar way he advocates and articulates this embrace, Donne manages to make ecstasy—the going of the soul out of the self, as in death—compatible with the interiority he cherishes.

It would be misleading to read this seduction poem as pure philosophical speculation; its first reference, as well as its last resort, is to desiring bodies. Yet in seizing the body, Donne seizes the only form of timelessness he can stand to imagine. What Donne has really discovered is a new way into the old motifs of *carpe diem* poetry: instead of warning that death will end physical love, Donne presents spiritual love as a foreshadowing of death which can be dispelled by letting the moribund bodies rise to the occasion. This is sexual extortion of an unusually sophisticated sort. The ambiguity of the closing assurance—that any enlightened spectator "shall see / Small change, when we'are to bodies gone" (74–75)—effectively conflates two assurances: that physical lovemaking will simply fulfill their spiritual love, and that the love will persist even when its physical vehicles have expired. The resorting *to* bodies, and the escape *from* bodies, are intertwined defenses against the threat of "sepulchrall" mortality that haunts the early lines of the poem. Death will prove to be nothing other than love; bodies and souls will somehow eventually converge in unlimited delight. Those are the Christian rumors that Donne repeatedly seeks to confirm in his secular lyrics by making the conjugal bed a flattering mirror of the tomb.

RECIPROCITY AS IMMORTALITY: "LOVERS HOURES BE FULL ETERNITY"

From a Freudian perspective, sexual desire and religious belief share a foundation in a child's hopes and fears concerning its parents.[49] The vacillation in Christian theology between the traditional notion that damnation consists of punishment by God, and the Augustinian notion that damnation consists of isolation from God, corresponds to a basic dilemma of early childhood: demanding attention and remaining silent each carry dangers. As the Father's bad children, we may sometimes imagine that even annihilation is preferable to judgment. That is the reluctant conclusion of one Holy Sonnet: "That thou remember them, some claime as debt, / I thinke it mercy, if thou wilt forget" ("If Poysonous Mineralls," 13–14; cf. *Sermons*, III, 97, IX, 64). And at moments, like many Christians, Donne wonders whether it is fair that "I had a *Punishment*, before I had a *being*" (*Sermons*, VII, 78).

More often, however, Donne craves the punishment that will demonstrate divine attentiveness, as in "Batter my Heart" and "Goodfriday, 1613. Riding Westward." In his sermons he asserts that all the vivid tortures of hell are far easier to bear than "the privation of the sight of God, the banishment from the presence of God" (*Sermons*, IV, 86; see similarly I, 186, II, 129, and III, 51). He describes God as "like us, that he takes it worse to be slighted, to be neglected, to be left out, then to be actually injur'd" (*Sermons*, I, 195). That is the miserable story of abused children, and Donne the desperate sinner always retains traces of Donne the sick child, badly in need of a relational meaning for his body, badly in need of his creator's attentive handling:

I am abundantly rich in this, that I lie here possest with that feare, which is *thy feare*, both that this sicknesse is thy immediate correction, and not meerely a *naturall accident* . . . and that this feare preserves me from all inordinate feare, arising out of the infirmitie of Nature, because thy hand being upon me, thou wilt never let me fall out of thy hand. (*Devotions*, p. 33)

As my Introduction has argued, even a terrifying God is preferable to a universe that provides no limits, no narrative or cognitive structures to regulate experience.

An infant lives in terror of being carelessly dropped, into the abyss. So does Donne the preacher, whose desire for divine punishment again comports the infant's craving for maternal care:

. . . when Gods hand is bent to strike, *it is a fearefull thing, to fall into the hands of the living God*; but to fall out of the hands of the living God, is a horror beyond our expression, beyond imagination . . . that that God, who looked upon me, when I was nothing, and called me when I was not, as though I had been, out of the womb and depth of darknesse, will not looke upon me now . . . that that God, who hath often looked upon me in my foulest uncleannesse, and when I had shut out the eye of the day, the Sunne . . . with curtaines and windowes and doores, did yet see me, and see me in mercy, by making me see that he saw me. . . . (*Sermons*, V, 266; cf. III, 98 and VI, 124)

I were miserable . . . if before I had done well or ill actually in this world, God had not wrapped me up, in his *good purpose* upon me. And I were miserable againe, if . . . after my sinne had cast me into the grave, there were not . . . a gracious countenance to looke upon me, when I were risen. (*Sermons*, III, 107)

In these rhapsodies about God, Donne anticipates object-relations theories about the role of maternal responses in the formation of the infant self.[50] Donne's reciprocating mistresses are (among other things) a sublimation of this ancestry. The "Busie old foole" whose gaze invades Donne's bedroom "Through windowes, and through curtaines" in "The Sunne Rising" is a residue of the same parental figure, and the speaker resembles an adolescent boy establishing sexual independence by barring his mother from his room (1–3). But Donne's long terrifying evocations of abandonment make that gesture look like psychological bravado. His compulsive fear of isolation from the face and the care of the Almighty[51] culminates a lifelong fear of separation from the gaze of the beloved Other, who will not come in response to crying (*Sermons*, IX, 389). His terror of the dark resembles the "nameless dread" that "overwhelms an infant whose mother fails to contain his terrors and make them meaningful: 'The patient feels surrounded not so much by real objects, things-in-themselves, but by bizarre objects that are real only in that they are the residue of thoughts and conceptions. . . . '"[52] There is a cognitive as well as an emotive component to the need for the attentive consciousness of a caretaker—a *matrix*—and Donne cannot sustain perpetually his ostentatious intellectual control of the universe. Who will watch over his special reality while he sleeps?

A careless nursing mother, an indifferent Mother Nature, and the *deus absconditus* all coalesce in the ailing Donne's perplexity

that our *Nourse* should overlay us, and *Ayre*, that nourishes us, should destroy us, but that it is a halfe *Atheisme* to murmure against *Nature*, who is *Gods immediate Commissioner*, who would not think himselfe miserable to bee put into the hands of *Nature*, who . . . delights her selfe to blow him up like a *glasse*, till shee see him breake, even with her owne breath? (*Devotions*, p. 62)

It has become a psychoanalytic commonplace that "The child who has good maternal experiences will develop a sense of basic security and will not be subject to morbid fears of losing support, of being annihilated, or the like" (Becker, p. 13). Winnicott suggests that a compulsive interest in death reflects an early death of the self that was not acknowledged as such, leaving the adult to search continuously for some objective correlative to that repressed experience of personal erasure: "Death, looked at in this way as something that happened to the patient but which the patient was not mature enough to experience, has the

meaning of annihilation."[53] However conjectural any specific application may be, this modern formula is probably applicable to an Elizabethan psyche. As a distinguished anthropologist observes, across a wide
variety of cultures, "The threatening event of object loss suffered by the
infant in a series of separation traumas from the mother forms the basis
of our fears regarding the final farewell."[54]

The fact that Donne appears markedly less trustful than Herbert of
both women and providence may be more than a casual coincidence: it
suggests that Donne's experience of his mother (or perhaps his wet-
nurse) was much less reliably successful than Herbert's, that her attentions were perceived as less consistently benign. This difference would
also help to explain the contrast between Donne's egoistical erotic
aggression and Herbert's pleasure in submitting the self quietly to a
providential power. It is certainly difficult to imagine Herbert preaching, as Donne preaches, that "in the tendernesse of our childhood, we
suffer, and yet are whipt if we cry" (*Sermons*, VII, 54).[55]

Since we lack extensive testimony about the privy-training techniques
of Donne's mother, Elizabeth, it would be easy to credit the vague praise
of her tender care offered by Walton and Gosse.[56] But Donne's sense of
his mother's stability, purity and self-sacrificing protectiveness cannot
have been helped by the fact that she remarried twice before he left his
teens; nor indeed by the fact that five of the six siblings he knew died
before he was twenty-one (Elizabeth outlived even that one survivor,
and nearly outlived Donne himself). The point is certainly not that she
was to blame for these losses, only that her child might easily have
blamed her, however subliminally and irrationally. Her failures would
surely have offered a contrast with the woman this chapter will propose
as Donne's idealized mother-figure: Magdalen Herbert, whom he
described as excellent in "*ministring to the sicke*" (*Sermons*, VIII, 89),
who gave him shelter from the plague that had killed so many in
Elizabeth's family, and whose ten children (including the poet George)
all lived to adulthood. Nor would it have been entirely unreasonable for
Donne to blame some of his family's losses—including the death of his
close brother Henry, in prison for recusancy—on his mother's insistence
on loyalty to the forbidden Roman church.

Donne's sole extant letter to his mother promises "to look to you,
and provide for your relief," and concludes with a plea that she "for
God's sake, pardon those negligences which I have heretofore used
towards you." This may be merely conventional filial apologetic, yet it is
also possible to read, in the implied role reversal, the traces of an

unhappy family history, in which Donne himself endured (and perhaps reciprocated) the negligences of the woman who ought to have looked to him and provided relief. The evidence of this strain must admittedly remain highly speculative; but if Donne experienced some primal disappointment in his mother's nurturance (beyond what Heinz Kohut calls the "optimal frustration" that allows the child individuation without any sacrifice of maternal empathy), that would help to explain his seeming overreactions to the subsequent failures of women, and perhaps of God, to give him absolute assurance of his worthiness and their devotion.[57] To a system sensitized by a comparable early trauma, such renewed disappointments would have provoked the psychological equivalent of anaphylactic shock.

The displacement of these infant terrors into worship of God, predictable enough by the Freudian model of religion, makes all the more sense in the case of Donne, who wrenched himself so violently away from the Roman church that continued to command his mother's full devotion. In one sermon, Donne promises to spare his congregation what Catholicism imposes on its spiritual children: either "*dry breasts*" or milk so impure that they will "cast it up" (VI, 92; cf. 96). In another, Donne warns of "a withdrawing of *Gods* spirit from that *Church*, to whose breasts hee hath applied you," and later in the same sermon describes the breasts of the Roman church as swollen "into tumors, and ulcers, and blisters" (VII, 75, 83; cf. VI, 184). Heresy thus becomes figured as mastitis. One of his letters similarly describes that church, along with its Puritan counterpart, as "sister teats of [God's] graces, yet both diseased and infected" (*Letters*, p. 88)—a striking contrast to the sustaining purity of the "deare Mother" Herbert finds in "The British Church." Evidently Donne was not breast-fed by his mother: he reports (suggestively, in his funeral sermon for Magdalen Herbert) that he "suck'd *Christian* bloud, in my Mothers wombe, and *Christian* milke at my Nurses breast" (*Sermons*, VIII, 77; cf. VI, 96). George Herbert was more likely to have had the same woman play both roles: Magdalen Herbert was clearly a devoted mother, and upper-class Protestant women were often instructed to undertake this "duty."[58] In any case, where Herbert seems to have acquired his positive religious assurance directly from his mother, Donne reported acquiring his much later, primarily through his wife—and partly through Magdalen Herbert as a spiritual foster-mother.

As a child first achieves the status of individual person by its reflections in the mother's responsive face, as a lover feels discovered and fulfilled in the exchange with a romantic partner, so the soul (according to Reformation theology) can achieve its fulfillment and salvation only in intimate dialogue with God. In a midnight colloquy with the soul of the late Lord Harrington, Donne claims to

> discerne by favour of this light,
> My selfe, the hardest object of the sight.
> God is the glasse; as thou when thou dost see
> Him who sees all, seest all concerning thee. . . . [59]

These mirrorings are indispensable to the conclusion (itself seemingly indispensable in modern Western culture) that we are each uniquely valuable. The punishment Cain cannot endure, Donne argues, "is not that GOD would not looke graciously upon him, but that GOD would not looke at all upon him. Infinite, and infinitely desperate, are the effects. . . . " (*Sermons*, VII, 83).

Donne's search for a perpetually affirming confrontation with a lover, an ideal exchange of gazes, therefore takes on the obsessiveness and piety of a grail quest. If, as Debora Shuger argues, "The language of spiritual politics in Donne is . . . suffused by an erotic and infantile affectivity,"[60] then it is not surprising that the erotic diction conflates infantile and religious forms of worship. If, as a young man, Donne lost confidence in religion, and instead "sought distraction in activity of other kinds,"[61] then it is valid to look for the displaced religious function of those other activities. The devout preacher himself, at about age fifty, would look back and condemn "those false waies, in which we sought our comforts in our looser daies" (*Letters*, p. 116). According to a contemporary observer, Donne was then "a great visiter of Ladies" and "great writer of conceited Verses"[62]—corresponding to the erotic and artistic evasions of mortality that (Becker argues) are the chief alternatives to religious consolation in modern Western culture. His youthful devotion to sexual conquest and poetic creation are, from this perspective, foreshocks of his eventual Christian zeal. During his adolescence, John Donne began to play Don Juan, an apostate to chastity as well as to Catholicism; perhaps—having surrendered his faith in Virgin Mothers—he felt compelled to construct a perverse and radically willful myth of sexual salvation to sustain him until his Protestant faith solidified. Perhaps, too, any Arminian reflexes dormant in the aftermath of Donne's conversion to Protestantism found expression in a mythology suggesting that immortality—"Canonization"—was achievable through the works of earthly love and art.

Donne's letters reflect this effort to remove his immortality from dependence on an inscrutable Calvinist God, and reinvest it in a scheme that depends on the manipulable loving attention of a woman:

Madam,
I am not come out of *England*, if I remain in the Noblest part of it, your minde. . . . No Prince would be loth to die, that were assured of so faire a tombe to preserve his memory: but I have a greater vantage then so; for since there is a Religion in friendship, and a death in absence, to make up an intire frame there must be a heaven too: and there can be no heaven so proportionall to that Religion, and that death, as your favour. (*Letters*, p. 211)

Donne's lyrics, too, participate in a Platonic myth that is a major incentive to romantic love: the hope of remaining ageless in the heart, eyes, mind, and soul of the beloved.[63] He is on the side of Humpty Dumpty who, when Alice insists that "one can't help growing older," replies, "*One* can't perhaps, but *two* can."

In "The Primrose," for example, Donne suggests that his mysterious numerical balance with a beloved woman will allow him to tame the overwhelming universe. She must be neither too spiritual nor too physical ("a sixe, or foure," [12]) to draw him entirely into the loving exchange; she must instead be the "five" (22) that provides men with their other half, the number that Ben Jonson's "Masque of Hymen" cites as "The binding force of unity" in married love.[64] According to the early manuscript titles, the setting of "The Primrose" is Montgomery Castle, where in 1613 Donne was a guest of the Herbert family. Like Twickenham garden—where Donne similarly played both lover and dependent—this second home allows Donne to fantasize a second Eden. The terrifying "infinitie" of the Copernican universe is safely reduced to a "terrestriall Galaxie" of flowers through which he can stroll in search of a second Eve (5–6). By devoting themselves fully and faithfully to their bond of absolute spiritual and physical faithfulness this pair can—like the lovers in "The Extasie"—convert the infinite grave-yard back into a garden of life.

If the only reality is the beloved's perception, then achieving a privileged status within that perception precludes death. If lovers are truly "one anothers All," as in the last line of "Loves Infinitenesse," then they have nothing else to lose. Becker's model of psychoanalytic trans-ference illuminates Donne's model of romantic intimacy:

How wonderful and how facile to be able to take our whole immortality-striving and make it part of a dialogue with a single human being . . . to take this unspeakable mystery and dispel it straightaway by addressing our performance of heroics to another human being, knowing thus daily whether this performance is good enough to earn us eternity. (pp. 155–56)

The redemptive "dialogue of one" Donne seeks in "The Extasie" makes possible what Rankian psychology describes as the "cosmology of two" that confers the illusion of immortality in romantic love.[65] The ideal of romantic marriage proposes that an individual becomes irreplaceable, and a lifetime together becomes a sufficient eternity: the fact that mortality is shared effectively undoes it.[66]

"The Good-Morrow" provides a canonical example of the perfect romantic exchange through which Donne pursues immortality, as "The Sunne Rising" exemplified the encoding of death in love. "The Good-Morrow" traces a progression from oblivious biological existence toward a timeless mystical yoking of the spiritual and the physical. In the opening stanza the speaker compares his former self to a suckling infant in an undifferentiated merger with its universe, and compares his previous condition to a prodigious sleep from which love has awakened him, as Christianity did the seven sleepers of Ephesus, into the fulfillment of his best dreams. Romantic love thus takes the place of both infantile megalomania and Christian redemption simultaneously: instead of being pre- or post-mortal, the truly beloved lover can be immortal within a fully conscious condition of life. The allusion to the sleepers makes theological salvation and erotic transcendence alike dependent on an awakening. As the Ephesians would have slept forever if not for the Incarnation, so would we all remain dead forever if not for the Second Coming; this spiritualized love-affair saves the speaker from a comparable stupor.[67]

In the second stanza the soul reawakens, as if this were a psychopannychist Last Judgement. The infant's ability to control the universe by focusing on the nurse's sustaining breast gives way to the lover's version of that pleasure—a superior version, Donne suggests, and one which sustains life on a more meaningful and lasting level than nursing. The solipsistic shrinking of "every where" into the "one little roome" the lovers share not only disarms the fear that entombment entails surrender of the world; it also prepares us for a radically intellectual solution to mortality. Consciousness may exist only in life, but life exists only in consciousness. Deciding that the only existence that matters is the one shared with the beloved shrinks the devastating scope of eternity to the manageable scale of a human lifetime; finding the whole world in the beloved offers the infinite in the present. Donne preached that the "best help" against the vertiginous expanse of eternal time "is, to use well *Aeternum vestrum*, your owne Eternity; as *S. Gregory* calls our whole course of this life, *Aeternum nostrum*, our eternity."[68] He also asserted that "if there were any one minute in a mans life, in which he were safe from death, a man might in some sort be said to be immortal, for that minute; but Man is never so" (*Sermons*, V, 210). The last clause belongs to Dr. Donne; Jack Donne clung to the hope of achieving such a moment through earthly passion, as "The Good-Morrow" clearly demonstrates.

When Petrarchan lovers warn that rejection will prove fatal, they are practicing literary convention on one level, sexual blackmail on another. But on a third level the warning can serve to verify this imagined correspondence between consummated love and immortality. It is an indirect way of claiming the contrapositive: that fulfillment will preclude death. Tragic playwrights and pastoral poets of the Renaissance were often willing to kill off their protagonists in defense of this binaristic scheme. The death-impulse of bereaved lovers (in life as well as in literature) results partly from the need to sustain this myth of symmetry and synchronicity.[69] The third and final stanza of "The Good-Morrow" translates into an instantaneous metaphysical tableau the common sentimental vision of lovers whose lasting fondness and memories preserve each other's value: "My face in thine eye, thine in mine appeares" (15), joining two "hemispheres" into a traditional figure of immortal perfection (as mythologized, for example, in Plato's *Symposium*).[70] It not only recalls the reflexive maternal gaze that creates the self, it also anticipates the reflexive divine regard that immortalizes the self: "he will make thee see, that he is with thee; and never goe out of thy sight, till he have brought thee, where thou canst never goe out of his" (*Sermons*, VI, 185).

The poem concludes, not with pleasure in the loving or praise of the beloved, but with an abstract recipe for immortality:

> What ever dyes, was not mixt equally;
> If our two loves be one, or, thou and I
> Love so alike, that none doe slacken, none can die.
>
> (19–21)

A poem about rebirth has become a poem about stasis. The aubade that emphatically rejects parting becomes an elegy that provisionally rejects dying. In this tug-of-love, a tie is a victory for both sides. The tension produces and preserves a redemptive sympathetic reflex in the economy of consciousness, as pathetic fallacy does in the economy of biological nature.

When these reflexes fail—as "Twicknam Garden" acknowledges—the consequences are mortal. In stanza 21 of his "Metempsychosis," Donne warns that men died young in the primal horde because free love "slackneth so the soules, and bodies knot." This warning anticipates the closing line of "The Good-Morrow," and makes post-coital depression an anticipation of deadness itself. But as long as man and woman, soul and body, can sustain their enlivening embrace, they are immortal, never collapsing back into the stupor that preceded this fulfilled life. One need not ignore the technical references to alchemical health here to notice also a psychoanalytic model of mental health, in which the infantile oral desire (for the breast before sleep) has been reconstructed into adult genital sexuality. Nor need one focus on Renaissance theories of deferred orgasm to recognize something odd about this unslackening embrace, which resists both the figurative death of sexual climax and the actual death that sexual climax was supposed to accelerate.[71] This Tantric suspension is the logical heaven of Donne's scenario of erotic salvation. What he wants is omnipresent desire, not eventual progeny; he wants to perpetuate his unique bodily experience, not to participate in the common cycle of human life.[72]

What makes "Aire and Angels" so delightful, as well as so difficult, is the combination of theoretical abstraction and human tenderness in its exploration of the saving power of mutual love. The texture thus matches the argument, which seeks a truly metaphysical status for love, somewhere between the spiritual idea and the physical object. In the metaphysicality of his verse, Donne generally seeks to invent a new category of reality that rescues the inner will from its enslavement to the material universe, and returns abstraction to its home in sensual experience. In "Aire and Angels," he attempts to rescue love, and thereby mortal human experience, the same way: he exempts physical experience from the decay that normally follows its alienation from the soul, and exempts the soul from the threat of evaporation at the extinction of its physical vessel.

"Twice or thrice had I loved thee, / Before I knew thy face or name." From the collapse of time and identity in these opening lines to the closing assertion about what men and women "will ever bee," the poem is an escape from the time-boundedness of human bodies and the individual identities they carry, as much as from the limiting physical aspects of love-making. When the speaker allows his instinctive worship of angels to "fixe it selfe in thy lip, eye, and brow" (14), he performs an action resembling the romantic denial of death described by Rank and Becker: "Spirituality, which once referred to another dimension of things, is now brought down to this earth and given form in another individual human being."[73] At the same time he implicitly proposes to his lover that they perform for each other a version of the Incarnation by which Christ (according to the New Testament) purchased our redemption.[74] If they are willing to "die" (in either sense) for each other—to mingle their immortal souls with mortal bodies—then (and only then) will they be able to save each other. Their passion reproduces the central paradox of Christ's Passion. Each must submit the ethereal impulses of love to the taint of mortal flesh, so that the other will have a viable place to love eternally.

The poem's double-sonnet form reinforces the notion that expressions of love must be exchanged to achieve a better kind of closure. Its ending evokes not coy misogyny (as commonly supposed),[75] but a miraculous reciprocity. The lovers each offer and each receive a platform halfway between earth and heaven on which to stage their love—and thereby to stage, for an indefinite run, their mixed status as human beings. Neither one could offer it without receiving; otherwise they would either sink like corpses or fly away like the souls of the dead. Outside of love, there is only preterition—that is, mortality.[76] As in Donne's fiery sermons, the poise above the abyss of eternal darkness is a precarious one indeed, like the suspension of cartoon characters who can remain in the air only so long as they have faith that the ground is still solidly beneath them. As in many aspects of Reformation theology, emotional conviction functions as fact.

The peculiarity of "Aire and Angels" is that each lover can sustain the suspension as long as the *other* believes in it. There is something teasingly Lacanian in the idea that the only valid desire is to be desired, but there is something very Donnean as well. The only valid object of love is somewhere between the two poles of the human dualism, body and spirit; so the self who is loved is generated by the self who loves that way, at the crossing point of the "X" drawn by two spirits looking to each other's bodies, and two bodies looking to each other's spirits. In that sense, these ideal lovers are without differentiation. They know difference of sex no more than angels do, and the seemingly misogynistic distinction between "womens love, and mens" (28) merely reflects the speaker's perspective as a heterosexual man: it is finally only the distinction between the beloved and the lover. The separation of soul from body is for Donne the essential fact of death; the separation of male from female is his usual emblem for it. In "Aire and Angels" he posits a kind of mixed mutual desire that permits a pair of lovers to forestall any such separations. In seeking to love as angels love, the speaker seeks to live as angels do: forever.

Donne can admit only the slightest taint of mortal flesh, lest it sink rather than ballast his love. The beloved's illness in "A Feaver" threatens Donne's theory that lovers exempt each other from mortal frailty, and so he struggles to find a new position of comfort:

> To leave this world behinde, is death,
> But when thou from this world wilt goe,
>   The whole world vapors with thy breath.
> Or if, when thou, the worlds soule, goest,
>   It stay, tis but thy carkasse then,
> The fairest woman, but thy ghost,
>   But corrupt wormes, the worthyest men.
>
>   (6–12)

This attempted subversion of death's kingdom finally serves only to reinscribe its sovereignty. The conceit evokes, in the effort to invert them, some of the harshest adages of the *memento mori* tradition, which portray the world as a delusive vapor and all men as already corrupted by the worms that will eventually consume their bodies entirely. Indeed, if his love has so badly failed to protect her from decay, then he must reconceive men's sexual penetration of women as a preliminary vermiculation of corpses rather than a premonition of spiritual immortality.

The speaker must therefore identify with the illness instead of the cure; if he cannot feed on her immortality forever, he will (like the fever in stanzas five and six) feed on her mortal frailties until they are consumed:

> Yet t'was of my minde, seising thee,
>   Though it in thee cannot persever.
> For I had rather owner bee
>   Of thee one houre, then all else ever.
>
>   (25–28)

In this final stanza, the get-well card turns into a seductive love letter, by turning the life-destroying fever back into a precious heat of sexual intercourse. The temporal, temporary fulfillment of romantic love may resemble and provoke death, but if pursued with sufficient passion, it becomes an adequate prepayment for an eternal loss. Donne has thus moved from the admonitory image of Marvell's "To His Coy Mistress" in which "worms will try / That long-preserved virginity," to that poem's exhortatory conclusion: "Though we cannot make our sun / Stand still, yet we will make him run." If he cannot transcend time and fleshly frailty through his lover, Donne will plunge into the flesh so devoutly that eternity will seem irrelevant.[77]

Donne brings the conventions of Petrarchan love-poetry to life by bringing them to death. A failure of reciprocity is fatal, deflating the metaphors of love until they reveal the grim facts of the body; losing one's heart without receiving another in exchange means the end of life as well as of love. "The Legacie" begins as a morbid compliment:

> When I dyed last, and, Deare, I dye
>   As often as from thee I goe,
>   Though it be but an houre agoe,
> And Lovers houres be full eternity,
> I can remember yet, that I
>   Something did say, and something did bestow;
> Though I be dead, which sent mee, I should be
> Mine owne executor and Legacie.
>
>   (1–8)

Donne's love-affairs always involve subliminal negotiations with death, and parting from this beloved arouses classic annihilationist anxieties: the concern that the Hour of Death will become eternity, that it will eventuate in mere forgetfulness, and that the world will uncannily continue without his consciousness of it.

The second stanza describes a near-death, out-of-body experience:

> I heard mee say, Tell her anon,
>   That my selfe, that is you, not I,
>   Did kill me,'and when I felt mee dye,
> I bid mee send my heart, when I was gone,
> But I alas could there finde none. . . .
>
>   (9–13)

Like a prospective organ donor seeking the consolation of partial survival, he had hoped to retain some posthumous life by placing his heart within her. The loss of heart and even of life did not seem too great a price to pay for proving that love could mitigate the ordinary harsh rules of mortality. In the third and final stanza, however, he discovers what has actually killed him: she has given him only a faulty, incomplete heart in exchange for his own. This conceit literalizes, as a medical fact, the fear that haunts so many of Donne's love-lyrics: that imperfect requital will expose him to mortality.

Donne typically fears that parting from his lover will mean parting from an essential part of himself forever. "Song: Sweetest love, I do not goe" therefore changes very quickly (in the first stanza) into a meditation on death: "But since that I / Must dye at last, 'tis best, / To use my selfe in jest / Thus by fain'd deaths to dye" (5–8). The speaker proposes this deliberate rehearsal for death because, on this stage, he has the power to enact his own resurrection. His imminent sea voyage, and the love he carries through it, will demonstrate the possibility of keeping his interiority alive through the journey to Hamlet's undiscovered country of death, from which this traveller hopes to return with his selfhood intact: "the best of mee" (32), which he locates in his love of her. As (in the second stanza) he uses the diurnal solar cycle to reassure her that he will return from his sea voyage to resume their love, so he uses the sea voyage to reassure himself that he can return from death with an uninterrupted consciousness.

If she mourns his temporary absence, she will hasten or even cause his death, presumably by compromising the strategy of mutual denial, the assertion of total faith against total annihilation. The song concludes by suggesting that she "thinke that wee / Are but turn'd aside to sleepe; / They who one another keepe / Alive, ne'r parted bee" (37–40). This is a reciprocal of the formula of reciprocity: since they have not died, they must not actually have broken the bond of mutual affection that (in Donne's scheme) prevents death. By introducing the idea of sleep as a model of separation, Donne evokes the commonest Renaissance comparison for death. Clearly more is at issue here than a few days of earthly loneliness. Though the argument to his lover is playful and occasional, it continues the argument with death that runs all through his lyrics.

Walton's biography of Donne associates both "Sweetest Love" and "A Valediction: Forbidding Mourning" with Donne's efforts to console his wife about his departure to France with the Drury family. I believe they are further connected by an underlying allegory in which this separation represents the separation of soul from body at death. It seems only natural that the man who frequently compared the union of soul and body to a marriage (e.g., *Devotions*, p. 109; *Sermons*, VII, 257) would have been inclined to compare his marriage to that union. The "divorce" of body and soul appears to be the very essence of death for Donne, throughout his sermons, as their reunion is the essence of resurrection (e.g., VI, 71, 291; VII, 103, 108, 258). His terror of this estrangement may be intimately linked to a separation-anxiety rooted in his earliest experiences, and it may have helped to produce a poetic style in which "The most heterogeneous ideas are yoked by violence together," in Samuel Johnson's famous phrase.[78] Donne seeks to create an unbreakable bond, not only between male lover and female lover, but also between the spiritual and the physical. Perhaps Donne's characteristic fusing of intellectual and emotional events comes less from his situation prior to the seventeenth-century "dissociation of sensibility" (as T. S. Eliot suggests, in the second most famous phrase about the Metaphysicals) than from a personal psychology that craved an indissoluble union of soul and body, and that feared schizophrenic tendencies whereby "the relationship between thought and feeling is gradually disrupted."[79] The "direct sensual apprehension of thought" Eliot perceived in Donne may be the work of a man unwilling to allow even the ordinary gaps to open between his living senses and his abstracted consciousness. Destructively divided selves, according to current psychoanalytic theory, are often produced by parents who either ignore the fact that the child has a psychic identity or express disgust toward it as a physical entity. The fear of personal disintegration, Winnicott argues, is usually founded in this kind of partial or transient acceptance of the infant's formative self; and "Little alteration is needed to transfer the general thesis of fear of breakdown to a specific fear of death."[80] What Donne anticipates most eagerly about the general resurrection is the unity of self that eludes him in life: "I cannot say, you cannot say, so entirely now, as at the Resurrection, *Ego*, I am here; I, body and soul" (*Sermons*, III, 110).

Perhaps what Donne failed to receive from his mother, he sought from his mistresses—a starkly Freudian hypothesis, except that what Donne craved was less sexual gratification for its own sake than the implied affirmation of his whole self. The redemptive geometry of "Aire and Angels" requires the lovers not only to see the other as simultaneously body and soul, but also to love the miraculously mixed selfhood thereby reflected back to them. Donne pursued immortality through his deepest human relationships—the psychic and alimentary absorption of the woman who nurses him, the sexual absorption of his lovers through *coitus*, the intellectual absorption of his friends through letters—and when those connections prove physically variable and vulnerable, he immediately thinks of his own dissolution: "And though thou divide man and wife, mother and child, friend and friend, by the hand of *Death*, yet stay them that stay, and send them away that goe, with this consolation, that though we part at divers daies, and by divers waies, here, yet wee shall all meet at one place, and at one day, a day that no night shall determine, the day of the glorious *Resurrection*" (*Sermons*, VIII, 62). Donne yearned above all for a permanent reunion with his own body, and he used separation from the bodies of beloved women to prepare himself to endure the radical separation of self in the grave.

DEATH AS SEPARATION: VALEDICTIONS FOR THE SOUL'S VOYAGE OUT

Donne's search for a perfect bond with a mistress often reflects his desire for a permanent union of soul with body—in other words, for immortality. His devotion to heterosexual love gains supplementary energy from the way it can be mapped onto the dialectic of soul and body in Christian eschatology. Donne told his congregation, "Death is the Divorce of body and soule; Resurrection is the Re-union of body and soule"; he wrote to the bereaved Lady Kingsmel that "those things, which he takes in pieces, as he doth man, and wife, in these divorces by death, and in single persons, by the divorce of body and soul, God hath another purpose to make them up again."[81] Donne's valediction poems confirm the power, the purpose, and the persistence of this association between erotic and eschatological reunions. The fear in "A Valediction: Of Weeping" that both lovers will be obliterated by their parting—"thou and I are nothing then, when on a divers shore" (9)—seems hyperbolic, unless one recognizes that the situation taps Donne's fear that death will extinguish body and soul alike, simply by dividing them, that (as one Holy Sonnet expresses it) "black sinne hath betraid to endlesse night / My worlds both parts, and (oh) both parts must die" ("I Am a Little World Made Cunningly," 3–4). My intention is not to deny that the poems were written about actual partings from actual lovers, but instead to demonstrate that Donne consistently converted those sentimental occasions into opportunities to practice the dreaded farewell between his spiritual and physical aspects.

Donne looks at the English Channel he is about to cross, and seems
to see the River Styx.[82] Commentators have been mystified that Donne
would portray these crossings as so threatening, especially after surviving
considerably more dangerous sea voyages, such as the Cadiz and Azores
expeditions.[83] Perhaps, however, those earlier expeditions provided
Donne with less metaphoric provocation to ponder his mortal dissolution, since he was not then leaving behind a wife, with whom he was one
flesh—merely a metaphor, of course, but Donne's imagination is always
remarkably eager to construe latent metaphors as if they were material
facts. Abetted by his pregnant wife's anxieties, he may thus have
cathected his mortality-anxiety onto these relatively safe voyages, much
as Freud projected his mortality-anxiety onto rail travel.[84] Donne wrote
to his best friend Henry Goodyer, "I am near the execution of that
purpose for *France.* . . . I speake to you at this time of departing, as I
should do at my last upon my death-bed; and I desire to deliver into your
hands a heart and affections, as innocent towards you, as I shall to deliver
my soul into Gods hands then" (*Letters*, p. 81).

The evidence runs through all the forms of Donne's writing. "He that
sees every Church-yard swells with the waves and billows of graves,"
writes Donne in a sermon, "can think it no extraordinary thing to dye,
when he knows he set out in a storm" (I, 266). In the *Devotions* Donne
compares the prospect of a cure as "a discovering of *land* from *Sea,* after
a long, and a tempestuous *voyage*," and in the final paragraph begs God
to preserve him (like St. Paul) from shipwreck, "Though the *rockes*, and
the *sands*, the *heights* and the *shallowes* . . . do diversly threaten mee,
though mine own *leakes* endanger mee" (pp. 100, 127). Donne's letters
show him imagining death as a "shipwrack"—an image made particularly ominous by his tendency elsewhere to describe heaven as a safe
harbor.[85]

The letters also help to reveal what precious cargo Donne feared this
shipwreck might spill: "Out of this variety of mindes it proceeds, that
though all our souls would goe to one end, Heaven, and all our bodies
must goe to one end, the earth: yet our third part the minde, which is our
naturall guide here, chooses to every man a severall way" (*Letters*, p. 63).
The uniqueness of Donne's individual mind provides his only possible
exemption from the binary determinism of his destiny, and therefore the
essential redundancy of his identity—in other words, his only exemption
from the anonymity of death that his narcissism resists so bitterly.
Finally, the letters confirm Donne's tendency to make erotic separation
a test case for the mortal separation he hoped the general resurrection

would cure, even when the extended metaphor threatens to turn his flirtation with a young woman into a flirtation with blasphemy:

Madame,
I could make some guesse whether souls that go to heaven, retain any memory of us that stay behinde, if I knew whether you ever thought of us, since you enjoyed your heaven, which is your self, at home. Your going away hath made *London* a dead carkasse. A Tearm and a Court do a little spice and embalme it, and keep it from putrefaction, but the soul went away in you. . . . When you have a desire to work a miracle, you will return hither, and raise the place from the dead. . . . (*Letters*, pp. 1–2)

The hope that reciprocity is immortality has its dark converse in the suspicion that separation is death itself. Throughout the valediction poems, Donne rehearses for the interval between death and Last Judgment—rehearsals in which he must overcome the terror of forgetting all his lines, of losing the expressive power of his unique consciousness.[86]

The sibilant evaporation of a final breath, which marks death itself in the opening lines of "A Valediction: Forbidding Mourning," refers to the lovers' parting embrace in "A Valediction: the Expiration":

> So, so, breake off this last lamenting kisse,
>   Which sucks two soules, and vapors Both away,
> Turne thou ghost that way, and let mee turne this,
>   And let our selves benight our happiest day.
>
> (1–4)

Death is a breathless night that leaves no prospect for a happier day to follow.[87] If any redemption can be achieved under these circumstances, it will have to be done with mirrors. If their perfect love enforces a simultaneous annihilation, each will have remained eternally present within the span of the other's consciousness:

> Goe; and if that word have not quite kil'd thee,
>   Ease mee with death, by bidding mee goe too.
> Oh, if it have, let my word worke on mee,
>   And a just office on a murderer doe.
> Except it be too late, to kill me so,
>   Being double dead, going, and bidding, goe.
>
> (7–12)

Donne rarely surrenders to death without simultaneously plotting to subvert its power, and this suicide pact is a good example. A double-negative becomes a positive: two deaths—as in the mytheme of revenge-tragedy—cancel each other out. They each kill the self that killed the other, and the other that killed the self.

Donne's tender mission in "A Valediction: Forbidding Mourning" is to redefine the separation between lovers so that it will not seem a mournable separation at all. In doing so, he allows himself to experiment with different strategies for imagining the survival of his unitary selfhood through the voyage of death.[88] Once again Donne seems to be anticipating an admonition from his sermons: "Murmur not to admit the dissolution of body, and soul, upon your death-beds . . . till God be pleased to repair all, in a full consummation, and reuniting of body and soule in a blessed Resurrection" (*Sermons*, V, 212–13). Certainly it seems remarkable that a love poem—particularly one intended to suppress the mourning response—begins with a simile to a deathbed scene. This would be less remarkable if the lovers were compared to those whose mourning is mitigated by the recognition that the dying man's virtues foretell his salvation. But the lovers are compared to the dying man himself, and all they can aspire to is his silence:

> As virtuous men passe mildly'away,
>   And whisper to their soules, to goe,
> Whilst some of their sad friends doe say,
>   The breath goes now, and some say, no.
>
> So let us melt, and make no noise,
>   No teare-floods, nor sigh-tempests move,
> T'were prophanation of our joyes
>   To tell the layetie our love.
>
>   (1–8)

This is a love song in a Calvinist key: no deathbed ablutions or conversions can overrule their faith in determining their prospects for eternity.

Fortunately, they are not among the preterite:

> Dull sublunary lovers love
>   (Whose soule is sense) cannot admit
> Absence, because it doth remove
>   Those things which elemented it.
>
>   (13–16)

This prepares a conventional boast about the nobility of a more-than-sexual devotion, but it also echoes a conventional argument about the immortality of the soul. Renaissance attacks on the annihilationist heresy regularly and fiercely reject the idea that the soul is in any way physical, since that implies it would evaporate upon departure from its bodily habitation. Donne's boast of Platonic love allows him to distance himself from the fear that his soul might die when its sensory vehicle does.[89] The persistence of perfectly reciprocated love relieves the symptoms of physical mortality as well as of physical separation:

> But we by'a love, so much refin'd,
>   That our selves know not what it is,
> Inter-assured of the mind,
>   Care lesse, eyes, lips, and hands to misse.
>
>   (17–20)

Even while oblivious to the nature of their bond, they can somehow survive an interval of obliterated senses by relying on a higher consciousness that knows they belong together; romantic love is their provident God.[90] To the extent that this is a love poem, he is talking about missing each other's bodies; to the extent that it is a theological allegory, he is talking about missing his own.

In the fourth stanza the speaker assures his beloved that, like the confident dying man, they have already established a connection at the incorruptible super-lunary level.[91] But, either because his audience seems unconvinced by the goldsmith comparison, or because his own faith seems threatened by its atomistic implications,[92] the speaker of "Forbidding Mourning" next resorts to the notoriously hyperintellectual compass comparison. This comparison implies that while the earthly bodies appear to be isolated (from the other they love, or from their own souls), they remain connected at a higher level, like continents linked by a communication satellite. To legitimize sexual love in "The Extasie," Donne sketches for the woman a "V" shape, the souls descending to meet as bodies; to legitimize spiritual love in "Forbidding Mourning," Donne inverts that model (the combination generates the "X" I described in "Aire and Angels"). The simile helps him imagine that his buried body will somehow remain connected to its fugitive soul:

> And though it in the center sit,
>   Yet when the other far doth rome,
> It leanes, and hearkens after it,
>   And growes erect, as that comes home.
>
>   (29–32)

This is the Day of Judgment reconceived as second honeymoon.[93]

In the final stanza Donne completes the metaphor by addressing the beloved in terms that might well appear in a standard Renaissance dialogue of Soul and Body:

> Such wilt thou be to mee, who must
>   Like th'other foot, obliquely runne.
> Thy firmnes makes my circle just,
>   And makes me end, where I begunne.
>
>   (33–36)

At this moment the poem itself comes to an end, with its anti-closural mission complete: in consoling his lover about separation, Donne has consoled himself about mortality.[94] In fact, the compass metaphor suits the latter consolation better than the former. He can hardly perfect the circle by returning to his wife if she is the fixed foot. But if she comes to represent, through her unwavering love, the God of resurrection, then the metaphor has a fairly precise explication in Donne's sermons:

> Christ establishes a Resurrection, *A Resurrection there shall be*, for, that makes up *Gods circle*. The *Body* of Man was the first point that the foot of Gods Compasse was upon: First, he created the body of *Adam*: and then he carries his Compasse round, and shuts up where he began, he ends with the *Body of man* againe in the glorification thereof in the Resurrection.[95]

If he doubts the resurrection, if he doubts that love can perpetuate his existence, if he cannot recover the immortal intimations of pre-oedipal omnipotence, then the arc of his life will sketch only a zero. If we "consider man's life aright to be a Circle. . . . In this, the circle, the two points meet, the womb and the grave are but one point."[96] Donne's dual consolatory metaphors come together in the alchemical symbol for gold, the ultimate earthly desideratum and the key element in any serum of immortality: O.[97] But without God (whose center is everywhere and whose circumference is nowhere) to assure a reunification of the self, to assure a central meaning to the circles and cycles of biology, there would be, precisely, no point.

The correspondence I have been eliciting from these poems—between the husband on a sea voyage from his wife, and the soul on its expedition from the body between death and Last Judgment—would have been available to Donne in the works of Saint Ambrose, and was probably decipherable to his original readers. This is Zacharie Boyd, a

Jacobean preacher, speaking in the voice of a soul addressing its dying body:

As thy love is great toward mee, so is mine also great toward thee, my Bodie. But seeing it is the will of him who married us together, that now wee bee put asunder, wee must submit ourselves unto his good pleasure.

This separation shall be but for a little space, and that for *the well of us both*. The husband will *saile the seas* and goe farre from home, in hope to returne with advantage. The same hope encourageth his wife to live like a *widow* for a space. At last the husband's returne with expected profite, is welcomed with greater joyes than was his former presence.

It shall be so with us, my dear Bodie. At my returne in the day of the Resurrection there shall enter such a joye into thee, as eye never saw, ear never heard, yea, and which never could enter into the heart of man. As the long dark night maketh the morning seeme sweete to the wearied watch, who hath long looked for it, so shall our little absence bee a certaine commendation of that presence, which after the great day shall bee forever.[98]

It would be an exaggeration to call Boyd's rhapsody a perfect paraphrase of "Forbidding Mourning," but to read the poem without sensing this resonance is surely inadequate.

This same extended metaphor resurfaces in the religious hymns Donne wrote when he thought his body might indeed be on the brink of giving up the ghost. "A Hymne to Christ, at the Author's Last Going into Germany" begins by making his departure from England in a "torne ship" an "embleme" (1, 2) for his departure from this earthly life:

> Seale then this bill of my Divorce to All,
> On whom those fainter beames of love did fall;
> Marry those loves, which in youth scattered bee
> On Fame, Wit, Hopes (false mistresses) to thee.
> Churches are best for Prayer, that have least light:
> To see God only, I goe out of sight:
>   And to scape stormy dayes, I chuse an Everlasting night.
>
> (22–28)

The poem thus concludes by acknowledging that Donne's earlier obsessions had been misguided quests for the immortality, the "All," he now seeks through Reformation Christianity. Faith in the vision of a loving God now allows him to confront and overcome the terror of an uncertain voyage—that is, the terror of the annihilationist grave and its perpetual darkness.

The third stanza of the "Hymne to God My God, in My Sicknesse" conceives death as a voyage into the sunset and away from his dying body:

> I joy, that in these straits, I see my West;
>   For, though theire currants yeeld returne to none,
> What shall my West hurt me? As West and East
>   In all flatt Maps (and I am one) are one,
>   So death doth touch the Resurrection.
>
>   (11–15)

If the promise of resurrection answers Donne's fear of sailing, then he must have been anxiously associating such voyages with the separation of soul from body.[99]

Most editions of Donne's poetry place the "Hymne to God the Father" alongside the "Hymne to God My God, in My Sicknesse" as products of the same dire illness, but they have imagistic connections as well. The "Hymne to God the Father" figures salvation as rescue from a shipwreck, and (through the familiar pun on "sun" and "Son") represents immortality as a persistence of sunlight against the darkness of death that jeopardizes his continuous consciousness:

> I have a sinne of feare, that when I'have spunne
>   My last thred, I shall perish on the shore;
> Sweare by thy selfe, that at my death thy Sunne
>   Shall shine as it shines now, and heretofore;
>   And having done that, Thou haste done,
>   I have no more.
>
>   (13–18)

The word "more" works here as a pun on *mort*, so that (as the endings of the previous stanzas warn) Donne cannot fully trust God until it is clear that God will keep "Donne" safe from death.

Such a reading might seem overly ingenious, except that Donne often puts great weight on his name as a *locus* of lasting individual identity. The aspiration to an immortal name, in the common classical sense of fame, yields gradually during the Renaissance to the idea that a personal name conveys, contains, and protects the inward uniqueness of each human being.[100] Personal names became increasingly prominent on tombstones, apparently reflecting a heightened concern with defending the individual against obliteration by death—a vain effort, in one sense

or another.[101] What's in a name is an assertion of selfhood, and Donne—
contrary to recent claims that Renaissance minds could not think in
terms of continuous selfhood—asserted his individuality as brilliantly
and passionately as any voice recorded in our history.[102]

In "A Valediction: Of My Name in the Window," Donne characteristically strives to make a romantic connection immortal, and then to
reconfigure that connection as immortality itself. The speaker begins by
imagining that his name "engrav'd" on the glass has rendered that
seemingly fragile sheet immortal, and that his gravure in the woman's
heart will make him immortal there: "So shall all times finde mee the
same" (16). His beloved resembles a tomb holding his bodily remains,
while some essence of himself roams far away. Donne's dual fears—that
the engraved glass might shatter and that his lover might embrace
another body—correspond to his peculiar fascination in the prose works
with the problems God might confront in resurrecting bodies that have
been either scattered in pieces around the globe, or consumed into the
bodies of other people who will also need resurrecting.[103]

   In the third stanza the stability of this inscribed name is adduced,
ostensibly as proof of Donne's fidelity, but it is primarily a fidelity to
himself. In this monarchy of wit, the doctrine of the king's two bodies
is active: the written self can survive despite the transience of its fleshly
manifestations. In modern terms, the name serves as a kind of chromo-
some schematic by which his body can be cloned back into existence if
necessary.[104] Donne would propose a strikingly similar technique for
rebirth as an immortal child of God: "*Jehovah* is his *essentiall name*; and
in communicating . . . any letter of that Name, we become *semen Dei*, the
seed of God; and *filii Dei*, the Sonnes of God" (*Sermons*, VI, 194; cf. III,
128). Again Donne's quest for erotic fidelity partakes of a quest for
personal immortality.

   This renewal of the body will systematically reverse the annihilationist
ravages of silence, oblivion, decay, and blindness, by restoring speech,
understanding, growth, and sight:[105]

> It, as a given deaths head keepe,
>   Lovers mortalitie to preach,
> Or thinke this ragged bony name to bee
>   My ruinous Anatomie.
>
>   Then, as all my soules bee,
> Emparadis'd in you, (in whom alone

I understand, and grow and see,)
        The rafters of my body, bone
Being still with you, the Muscle, Sinew,'and Veine,
                Which tile this house, will come againe.

                    (21–30)

The general resurrection serves as a metaphor for the prospect of a physical reunion with his lover, but that metaphor flows in the other direction as well, until we feel that he desires the reunion as proof that resurrection is feasible, more than for love's own sake. Indeed, Donne's tactic for defending against erotic neglect looks remarkably like a common late Medieval tactic for defending the individual soul from neglect after death:

A simple way to link the perpetual memory of one's own name with the worship of the community was to give to the church . . . a chalice with one's name on lip or foot, so that as the priest raised it at the sacring he would read it. . . . A wider audience would be achieved with altar frontals and even Mass vestments 'with a scriptur on the back'. . . . the magnificent *Missale* . . . had a printed inscription asking for prayers for Morton, turning every church where the book was used into an informal chantry.[106]

In this poem as in revenge-tragedy, English Renaissance literature displays the imprint of a Protestant struggle to find equivalents of the forfeited Catholic means for assuring personal immortality.

Donne relies on the name in the window, the magic word of this immortalizing spell, to keep this woman's love, and also to keep some essence of his individuality alive until the resurrection of the body restores it to a viable autonomous environment:

            Till my returne, repaire
And recompact my scatter'd body so.
        As all the vertuous powers which are
        Fix'd in the starres, are said to flow
Into such characters, as graved bee
            When these starres have supremacie:

            So since this name was cut
When love and griefe their exaltation had,
        No doore 'gainst this names influence shut,
        As much more loving, as more sad,
'Twill make thee; and thou shouldst, till I returne,
            Since I die daily, daily mourne.

                    (31–42)

The speaker of "My Name in the Window" (like the speaker of "The Apparition") is an ineradicable ghostly presence, jealous of any life that goes on without him. His name shines down effacing that of any new lover (stanzas 9 and 10), as if indeed he were a demonic as well as a romantic possessor. But perhaps it is his own body that he finally aims to possess, or repossess.

Writing the self may be a futile tactic against mortality; certainly Donne's peers considered it inadequate to the task. Drummond (p. 26) warns that "This earth is as a table-book, and men are the notes; the first are washen out, that new may be written in." Browne (p. 309) is even more directly relevant to Donne's plan, and no more optimistic: "To be read by bare Inscriptions like many in *Gruter*, to hope for Eternity by Aenigmaticall Epithetes, or first letters of our names, to be studied by Antiquaries, who we were . . . are cold consolations unto the Students of perpetuity, even by everlasting Languages." Donne is too advanced a student of perpetuity to overlook the problem, and at the end the speaker of "My Name in the Window" throws wearily aside his collection of witty strategies for perpetuating himself in her heart, dismissing them as merely symptoms of encroaching physical mortality. Neither the etched lines nor the verse lines can preserve his love, or himself:

> But glasse, and lines must bee,
> No meanes our firme substantiall love to keepe;
> Neere death inflicts this lethargie,
> And this I murmure in my sleepe;
> Impute this idle talke, to that I goe,
> For dying men talke often so.

(61–66)

Many editors suppose this statement pertains to an actual illness; and during a convalescence Donne once wrote to Goodyer, "I may die yet, if talking idly be an ill sign" (*Letters*, p. 50; cf. "Obsequies," line 138). If Donne indeed wrote this "Valediction" from a sickbed, then its closing has a bitter autobiographical twist. Even if Donne was merely continuing to play on the idea of his departure as a death, however, the concession about the inadequacy of these reflections and writings remains the same: "As Man has an eternall not beeing before the Creation; so he would have another eternall not-being after his dissolution by death, in soule, as well as in body, if God did not preserve that beeing, which he hath imprinted in both, in both" (*Sermons*, VIII, 144–45). This printing of his name in the window is Donne's stay, not only against romantic betrayal, but also against the annihilation that accompanies decomposition.

"A Valediction: Of the Book" begins by announcing another plan for resisting the forces determined to dissolve a departing young man and his love in the seas of time. Though it repeats the twist that "Of My Name in the Window" puts on St. Paul's formula—these letters give eternal life—this new plan has as much in common with "The Canonization" as with the other valedictions: through their exchange of letters, these lovers will become immortal, even sacred, as a pattern of love. Donne asserts that this kind of bookish immortality will prove "as long-liv'd as the elements, / Or as the worlds forme, this all-graved tome" (19–20). The puns on "grave" as inscription and as burial surely provoke recognition of the word "tomb" behind "tome."[107] Once again Donne seeks a form of burial that both ensures resurrection and guards his aspiringly immortal words against death. The volume of love letters that Donne extols as a repository for civilization against barbarity (24–27) is also a repository for his own language against the silence of the grave. And to the considerable extent that Donne's language can truly represent passionate personal experience, that experience will survive fully in his writings, at least until some version of physical reunion or resurrection renders it superfluous. If "The Extasie" taught that "the body is [the soul's] booke" (72), this "Valediction" indulges the suspicion that a book can be the body, can lend the displaced soul a local habitation and a name. Donne becomes immortal as a man of letters. Writing—which Jacques Derrida claims is always an epitaph—here becomes an alternative form of personal afterlife, a prosthesis for Donne's prospectively crippled consciousness.

Donne's letters repeatedly claim this status, and this function: "I know what dead carkasses things written are, in respect of things spoken. But in things of this kinde, that soul that inanimates them, never departs from them" (*Letters*, p. 22). Another letter makes clear how much this kind of correspondence has in common with the exalted and redemptive correspondences of parted souls in "Forbidding Mourning":

I make account that this writing of letters, when it is with any seriousness, is a kind of exstasie, and a departure and secession of the soul, wch doth then communicate itself to two bodies: And, as I would every day provide for my souls last convoy, though I know not when I shall die, and perhaps I shall never die, so for these exstasies in letters, I oftentimes deliver my self over in writing when I know not when those letters shall be sent. . . . (*Letters*, p. 10; cf. p. 207)

Much virtue—and much denial—in "perhaps." With a pen in his hands, Donne feels emboldened to answer the annihilationist question he raises in the *Devotions* (p. 21): "what's become of [man's] soaring thoughts, his compassing thoughts, when himself brings himself to the ignorance, to the thoughtlessness, of the grave?" Within the limits of his technology, Donne is proposing an answer much like that of futurists who now propose to render their consciousness infinite by broadcasting digital schematics of their complete brain-structures out into space.[108]

The idea that an author's selfhood could be fully and permanently present in his book is suggested in Erasmus's *Ciceronianus*, stated in Bacon's *Advancement of Learning*, and fully articulated in Milton's *Areopagitica*.[109] Erasmus's spokesman particularly values literature that allows the reader "to discover from the language the feelings, the characteristics . . . of the writer as well as if one had known him for years." Bacon asserts that "the images of men's wits and knowledges remain in books, exempted from the wrong of time and capable of perpetual renovation." Milton claims that

books are not absolutely dead things, but do contain a potency of life in them to be as active as that soul was whose progeny they are; nay, they do preserve as in a vial the purest efficacy and extraction of that living intellect that bred them. . . . a good book is the precious lifeblood of a master spirit, embalmed and treasured up on purpose to a life beyond life. . . . We should be wary therefore . . . how we spill that seasoned life of man preserved and stored up in books.

Surely this notion of an immortality of wit would have caught the attention of Donne, who felt so sharply his lack of immortality, and had so clearly a surplus of wit.[110]

The second and fourth stanzas of "Of the Book" characterize this epistolary love as a new and better religion, one not susceptible to the "schismatiques" who compromised Donne's society's confidence in a single true path to immortality. But it is markedly a Reformation scripture, at once a public testament of love and a private conversation with his savior. Through a volume of their letters, "Love this grace to us affords, / To make, to keep, to use, to be these his Records" (17–18): the savior is the flesh made words, enabling him to endure "the darke eclipses" (63) without compromising his passion.[111]

The roots of Donne's anxious association of sea voyages with the separation of body and soul are traceable in the early autobiographical verse-narratives "The Storme" and "The Calme," which look ahead uneasily to death and afterlife. "The Storme," like Donne's sickness poems, was apparently composed under the threat of imminent death; Donne therefore promptly casts one of his defensive spells, establishing his addressee, in the first line, as an alter ego for the self that hovers on the brink of utter negation: "Thou which art I, ('tis nothing to be soe)." Like an engineer designing redundancy into a critical system, Donne pairs his unitary consciousness with another that is isolated from his immediate dangers.

The fear of personal destruction Donne presumably felt during the storm permeates his description of the ship in crisis, controlling the metaphors of the poem as if the storm were a metaphor for fatal illness, and not vice versa:

> Some coffin'd in their cabbins lye,'equally
> Griev'd that they are not dead, and yet must dye.
> And as sin-burd'ned soules from graves will creepe,
> At the last day, some forth their cabbins peepe:
> And tremblingly'aske what newes, and doe heare so,
> Like jealous husbands, what they would not know.
> Some sitting on the hatches, would seeme there,
> With hideous gazing to feare away feare.
> Then note they the ships sicknesses, the Mast
> Shak'd with this ague, and the Hold and Wast
> With a salt dropsie clog'd, and all our tacklings
> Snapping, like too-high-stretched treble strings.
> And from our totterd sailes, ragges drop downe so,
> As from one hang'd in chaines, a yeare agoe.
>
> (45–58)

The only part of this symptomology that strays from human disease is the over-taut strings, and even that recalls the opening of Donne's "Hymne to God My God, in My Sicknesse," in which he "tune[s] the Instrument here at the dore" of death (4). The desperate work of the sailors sounds like the death-throes of a cardio-pulmonary system in congestive failure: "Pumping hath tir'd our men, and what's the gaine? / Seas into seas throwne, we suck in againe" (61–62). The result is deafness and blindness, annihilationist symptoms that so often insinuate Donne's confrontations with mortality.[112]

Renaissance homilists commonly assuaged the fear of death by comparing death to a recuperative sleep; the nightmare, here as in *Macbeth*, is the impossibility of awakening. In "Obsequies to the Lord Harrington" Donne speaks of "the condemned man, / (Who when hee opes his eyes, must shut them than / Againe by death,) although sad watch hee keepe, / Doth practice dying by a little sleep" (21–24). In "The Storme" he endures a similar sentence, rising on a dark morning to confront the terror of mere oblivion in an undifferentiated universe:

> Sleepe is paines easiest salve, and doth fulfill
> All offices of death, except to kill.
> But when I wakt, I saw, that I saw not.
> I, and the Sunne, which should teach mee'had forgot
> East, West, day, night, and I could onely say,
> If the world had lasted, now it had beene day.
>
> (35–40)

This may remind modern readers of "I Heard a Fly Buzz," Emily Dickinson's terrifying narration of a death "Between the heaves of storm" when "the windows failed, and then / I could not see to see." In "The Storme," as in the "Hymne to God My God in My Sicknesse," death renders all earthly maps obsolete. The solipsistic bravado that allowed Donne to overcome geography in "The Sunne Rising" and the valediction poems comes back to haunt him. With the failure of the perceiving mind, all of creation returns to its indistinct primal condition, or might as well. So the poem ends with a vision of the loss of vision, an indistinction that is finally nullification, and a grand mythological allusion suggesting that resurrection would require rebuilding the entire universe:

> Darknesse, lights elder brother, his birth-right
> Claims o'r this world, and to heaven hath chas'd light.
> All things are one, and that one none can be,
> Since all formes, uniforme deformity
> Doth cover, so that wee, except God say
> Another *Fiat*, shall have no more day.
> So violent, yet long these furies bee,
> That though thine absence sterve me,'I wish not thee.
>
> (67–74)

This final line of the poem matches the first in emphasizing Donne's reliance on his correspondent for survival. No wonder he inverts the usual formula of a shipboard postcard by celebrating the fact that the missed friend is not along for this dark journey.

Critically surveying "The Calme" that follows this "Storme," the reader may wonder whether Donne has been saved or been killed. If "The Storme" explores the violent terror of dying, "The Calme" explores the eerier terror of being dead, the terrible stillness of the annihilationist grave; divine indifference, as in Donne's sermons, proves even more terrifying than divine anger. The biographical context provides some plausible explanations for the submerged metaphor. An ambitious young man, newly reminded of death, finds his aggressive voyage toward glory stalled indefinitely by the indifferent forces of nature. No wonder the ruined ship looks like a courtier gone threadbare.[113] Donne would surely have remembered the voice of Despaire that lured Spenser's exhausted gallant toward death:

> Is not short paine well borne, that brings long ease,
> And layes the soule to sleepe in quiet grave?
> Sleepe after toyle, port after stormie seas,
> Ease after warre, death after life does greatly please.
>
> (*Faerie Queene*, I, ix, 40)

As the reference to Aesop that opens "The Calme" suggests, the commonplace Christian desire to rest in peace fits the foolish-wish motif of folklore. Having eloquently wished (in the companion poem) for a storm to calm, Donne must have felt this irony keenly. The aftermath is a cruel joke on human desires: "Heaven laughs to see us languish thus" (6).

Donne's characteristic system of inter-reflective minds now adumbrates lifelessness instead of promising immortality. As life drains out (compare lines 5–8 of the "Nocturnall upon St. Lucies Day"), as faith melts away (in the form of a burning church), all that remains is blankness, passivity, pointlessness, and breathlessness:

> Smooth as thy mistresse glasse, or what shines there,
> The sea is now. And, as the Iles which wee
> Seeke, when wee can move, our ships rooted bee.
> As water did in stormes, now pitch runs out
> As lead, when a fir'd Church becomes one spout.
> And all our beauty, and our trimme, decayes,
> Like courts removing, or like ended playes.
> The fighting place now seamens ragges supply;
> And all the tackling is a frippery.

No use of lanthornes; and in one place lay
Feathers and dust, to day and yesterday.
Earths hollownesses, which the worlds lungs are,
Have no more winde then the'upper valt of aire.

(8–20)

Death seems to have retaken precisely the territory Donne liberated in
"The Sunne Rising" on behalf of love, which "all alike, no season
knowes, nor clyme, / Nor houres, dayes, moneths, which are the rags of
time" (9–10). His scheme to suspend the sun motionless where "All . . . in
one bed lay" is exposed as yet another foolish wish, now that it is a bed
of dust and not of lust (20).

Donne is gazing ahead into his grave, and indeed he sounds like the
soul pitifully regarding its decaying body in several homiletic Renaissance dialogues.[114] But this soul seems trapped in limbo. In a grim twist
on the extended metaphor established by the valediction poems, the sea-
voyager sits timelessly becalmed, helpless to revive the deteriorating
body by any return voyage. Nor, for all the inviting illusions, can it
escape that body anywhere but into death:

We can nor lost friends, nor sought foes recover,
But meteorlike, save that wee move not, hover.
Onely the Calenture together drawes
Deare friends, which meet dead in great fishes jawes:
And on the hatches as on Altars lyes
Each one, his owne Priest, and owne sacrifice.

(21–26)

The Jonah allusion of "The Storme" (33) here plays itself out without a
matching promise of redemption. Religious sacrifice (in fire) and deliri-
ous suicide (in water) have the same ultimate outcome; whether one dies
in high ritual or in primitive predation, one cannot escape stagnation
and reconsumption by a carelessly enveloping biological nature.

At the end of the poem the dead calm causes Donne to live out his
worst masochistic fantasy about death, imagining non-being as experienced by his vivid and yearning sensibility:

What are wee then? How little more alas
Is man now, then before he was? he was
Nothing; for us, wee are for nothing fit;
Chance, or our selves still disproportion it.
Wee have no power, no will, no sense; I lye,
I should not then thus feele this miserie.

(51–56)

This is the annihilationist irony: the only thing worse than oblivion is an awareness of oblivion.

WOMAN AS MORTALITY: "WHO WILL REDEEM ME FROM THIS BODY OF DEATH?"

Donne's fear of separation from a beloved woman is a phenomenon far beyond my ability to reconstruct reliably; but his anxiety about the stability of his love-affairs seems to link the problems of constructing the self at the beginning of life with the problems of relinquishing it at the end. Donne resorts frequently to the maxim (evoked in the gravedigger scene of *Hamlet*) that we begin dying at the moment of our birth: "I was *borne dead*, and from the first laying of these *mud-walls* in my *conception*, they have *moldred* away" (*Devotions*, p. 96). Perhaps (as in Oedipus's struggle against destiny) a desire to undo his mortality thus lends an additional incentive to his yearning to return to a woman's body through sexual intercourse. Perhaps that fierce yearning reflects, also, Donne's obsession with the prospect of returning at the general resurrection to his own body, which he so often casts as a beloved woman. Resurrection enacts theologically the psychological roots of regression, as well as of narcissism.

Donne's characteristic problem in engaging the world around him resembles the typical problem of the infant ego: how to accept a continuous connection with the nurturing forces that keep the self alive without erasing that self as an independent entity. Instead of outgrowing his original conflict between separation and individuation, Donne seems to have expanded it to the scale of his adult experience. The likeliest solution is a grandiose assertion of his masculinity to differentiate himself from the mother, whom he can identify with the vulnerable body, leaving his own spiritual interiority independent and immortal. This is castration-anxiety on a grander scale, but also perhaps in a more plausible form: what is at stake in the genital difference may be an imaginary exemption from bodily mortality.[115]

The persistent connections between Donne's misogyny and his annihilationism demand interrogation, for reasons of sexual politics as well as literary interpretation. From a feminist perspective there is no appealing choice between the Donne who sees women as objects of sexual appetite and the Donne who sees women as incubators of his personal immortality. If he has any defense against the familiar charges of misogyny, it may lie in his extraordinary egoism, which means that his representations of Man and Woman are largely metaphors for Soul and Body, and Self and Other. Unless his body clings to his soul, unless his beloved reciprocates his love, the result is annihilation, for which body and beloved must bear the blame. In "The Dreame," Donne insists that, if the beloved were truly herself, she would consummate his sexual dream about her; body must obey the desiring imagination. Donne's poetic will to power over reality thus reveals its connection with his erotic will to power over women. Even at Donne's most harmonious moments, the anxiety remains that everything around the self—everything confining it, everything apart from it—is necessarily irrelevant or even inimical to his immortality, which resides in a gorgeous, fragile narcissism. It was only too easy for him to conflate the patristic commonplace that the body is the corrupting prison of the soul with the patristic commonplace that women are the source of human mortality. The sexual mistrust thereby generated is aggravated by Donne's symbolic and egoistical reading of his universe: woman is the Other, and the Other is the death of the Self.

Freud identifies the narcissist as "a person who treats his own body in the same way in which the body of a sexual object is ordinarily treated."[116] Certainly Donne's tendency to imagine the world enchanted by his corpse long after his death (as in "The Dampe" and "The Relique") suggests a projection of his needy fascination with the promise of bodily resurrection. And from a Freudian viewpoint, Donne's narcissism might indicate a homosexual inversion that his valediction poems disguise as heterosexual love by displacing his body into the bodies of women, to the extent that he can perceive them as mirrors of his own. But any crisis of sexual orientation in Donne is secondary to a mortality-crisis. The nature of Donne's masculinist investment in the extended metaphor of the valediction poems becomes clear when he is forced to invert it, and allow the beloved woman rather than himself to represent the soul on its temporary journey away from the body.

The premise of "The Dissolution" is the death of the speaker's mistress; he is now the one left behind with the body, and his scramble to assert that body's continuing masculinity suggests how closely Donne associates his virility with his immortality. The transience of the sexual act closely parallels the transience of human life: "For though we have the Spirit of life in us, we have a body of death upon us. How loving soever the Spirit of life be, it will not stay in a diseased soul" (*Sermons*, IX, 349). At the end of "The Good-Morrow," Donne's speaker sought to overcome this aspect of mortality by perpetually deferring his orgasm. Though "The Dissolution" again presents the mistress as part of an immortalizing alchemical formula, her role here is to elicit the seminal excess, the elemental selfhood, that otherwise threatens to smother him from within:

> Shee'is dead; And all which die
> To their first Elements resolve;
> And wee were mutuall Elements to us,
> And made of one another.
> My body then doth hers involve,
> And those things whereof I consist, hereby
> In me abundant grow, and burdenous,
> And nourish not, but smother.
>
> (1–8)

Clearly this is a man less concerned about the woman's lost interiority than about his own lost outlet; indeed, he attributes to her no qualities whatsoever but her absorption of his.

My intention is not to score feminist points against Donne, but instead to highlight the way his craving for symbolic affirmations of his immortality constantly disrupts any authentic contact he might other- wise achieve with the women he desires; I read this pattern more in sorrow than in anger. Beneath the mourning of the poem and its extended alchemical metaphor is an extraordinarily petty kind of sexual selfishness; beneath that pettiness, however, is selfishness on a truly magnificent scale. Most men who believe that their wives hold the key to their immortality are thinking in terms of progeny, but Donne is interested only in the endless reproduction of himself. "The Dissolu- tion" is yet another refraction of Donne's fundamental myth of secular salvation, in which women are the agents of grace, the saviors who take into their own bodies the burden of his mortality.

Since his beloved has died before him, has fled like a fugitive soul, Donne's persona in "The Dissolution" finds himself awkwardly cast in the role of the body, which his private mythology, as well as Christian orthodoxy, has generally construed as female: "the body . . . should be a wife to the soule."[117] The possibility "That women might not be objects but subjects, not the other but the self" was, according to Stephen Orgel, the "greatest anxiety" of this period. By dying, Donne's mistress appropriates the role of psyche, leaving him to confront that anxiety in an intense symbolic form. As Stanley Fish notes in his reading of Donne's elegies, "The fear is not of one woman, or even of women in general, but of the condition that women seem particularly to embody, the condition of being open to interpretation, and therefore to change." Using terms that evoke a boy's struggle to establish his masculinity in differentiation from his mother, Fish describes Donne's fear that his phallic authorial power might "turn back and claim him for its own by revealing itself to be the very source of *his* identity (which would then no longer be his) . . . he would be like a woman and become the object rather than the origin of his own performance, worked on, ploughed, appropriated, violated."[118]

"The Dissolution" thus unites two kinds of castration-anxiety: the Freudian threat to the genitals and the existential threat to male independence from the creaturely identity the mother represents. Even its complex rhyme scheme reflects a heightened struggle with intertwining and separation. The fear of a phallic woman—evident in Donne's complaint about "Woamen in Menns *Apparrell*" in his "Essay of Valour"[119]—haunts "The Dissolution." Donne's masculine pride keeps him focused on his burgeoning seminal supplies rather than on her depleted personal qualities. He therefore refuses to undertake precisely the task he assigned to the beloved woman in "Of My Name in the Window": the task of preserving inside oneself (by a loyal celibacy) some schematic memory of the beloved's essential identity, whether for reproduction or resurrection. The obligation he bemoans—to "nourish" and "grow abundant" with the "burdenous" surrogate life of his sexual partner—is certainly suggestive of pregnancy (a fetus was commonly called a "burthen," as at 4.4.264 of *The Winter's Tale*). Everything he has resisted by locating it in the female Other, he now becomes: the body subject to biological process, the identity subjugated to the making of another identity, the passive object offering a locus of immortality in which it retains no share.

Against this threat Donne pits not only his obsession with his own accruing virility, but also the image of its eventual release in a massive orgasm, a violent "dying" that will allow him to reclaim the role as the (sexually validated male) soul who has left the (beloved female) body behind:

> This death, hath with my store
>   My use encreas'd.
> And so my soule more earnestly releas'd,

Will outstrip hers; As bullets flowen before
A latter bullet may o'rtake, the pouder being more.

(20–24)

In context, the grandiose ejaculatory character of this closing metaphor is surely significant; if "the distribution of libido in a life not at war with death is polymorphous perversity,"[120] then Donne's phallic obsession reflects instead ferocious combat. "The Dissolution" displays a necrophilia occluding mourning. Like those who earnestly, selfishly hope to die before their spouses, Donne would much rather she were the one left with the body; but again the surface selfishness covers a deeper one. As the "Anniversaries" demonstrate on a much grander scale, Donne will appropriate everything about a woman, even her death, to protect his position as the immortal masculine soul in the extended metaphor the valediction poems develop.

If Donne locates his prospective immortality in women, then it is hardly surprising that he hates them when their infidelities shatter the saving reciprocity—or when reminders of his undiminished mortality compel him to find a scapegoat. He needs to blame the failure of his formula on the insufficiencies of his love-objects, to discredit the variable rather than the function itself.[121] Donne's misogynistic tirades thus draw some of their fervor from the same mechanism as his vitriolic attacks from the pulpit of St. Paul's on his former co-religionists, the Jesuits. If you are not part of the solution to death, then you are part of the problem. When Donne feels obliged to choose a different path to salvation, he will typically conclude that you were leading him direly astray, whether that means calling you a whore of London or of Babylon.

Furthermore, if Donne believed that "the sexual union of man and woman on earth is the temporal and secular image which prefigures . . . the hypostatical union in body and soul of man and the Godhead in heaven,"[122] then the transience of that sexual union would have undermined his greatest hope. Conflating these two types of union would have focused Donne's attention on the common belief that Original Sin attaches to the human soul at the moment of conception, generated by the concupiscence of the proximate sexual act: "In the generation of *our parents*, we were *conceiv'd in sin*; that is, they sinn'd in that action . . . the *union* of this soul and body is so accompanied with Gods *malediction* . . ." (*Sermons*, II, 58). Spirit and flesh conjoin at the moment man and

woman do, and the transient conjunctions instantly summon up the
primal and permanent curse of mortality.

Exegeses of the Book of Genesis often identified the primal crime as
sexuality, with Eve as evil temptress—a tradition with strong resonances
of oedipal anxiety and important ramifications for sexual politics. Death
becomes a punishment for sexuality, both in the individual and in the
species. Donne's marriage would likely have confirmed this idea, since
his desire for Ann More led to dire exclusionary punishment by patriarchal authorities (her powerful father and uncle), a punishment Donne
repeatedly described as a death: "I dyed at a blow then when my courses
were diverted, yet it wil please me a little to have had a long funerall, and
to have kept my self so long above ground without putrefaction"
(*Letters*, p. 105). Donne's echoes of the Renaissance belief that orgasm
accelerates mortality may therefore express a truth symbolically present
across the range of his beliefs and experiences.

To Donne the seducer, sexual consummation is indispensable; to
Donne the preacher, physical resurrection is equally so. But while he
insists on being in the body, he refuses to be of it, since his essential
selfhood would then be at the mercy of biological death. So he must
isolate the weaknesses of the body in women, and the ecstasy of sexual
intercourse allows him a supreme occasion to do so, to experience his
own body through another's experience of it. As the inconsistent
compass metaphor in "Forbidding Mourning" suggests, his mistress is
partly a navigational device in a quest for reunion with his own redeemed
corpse. He will love women, die in them, then withdraw from them to
contemplate the experience, having in effect returned to them the
contagion of mortality they bequeathed him. But when he finds himself
back in his own body, still subject to his own mortality, post-coital
depression quickly turns into misogyny. Instead of affirming his transcendent interior self, women have pushed him further into an animal
identity, and closer to the hour of death.

The body's sexuality and its transience are inextricably linked. Sexual
consummation may offer a glimpse of freedom and immortality, but one
so fleeting as to provoke more bitterness at what we lack than joy in what
we have had. As *Measure for Measure* makes only too clear, erotic desire
is an equivocal assertion of individuality. The moment of greatest liberty
is also the greatest voluntary surrender to our creaturely determinism:
"Sex is an inevitable component of man's confusion over the meaning of

his life, a meaning split hopelessly into two realms—symbols (freedom) and body (fate). . . . We try to get metaphysical answers out of the body that the body—as a material thing—cannot possibly give. . . . This is why the mystique of sex is so widely practiced . . . and at the same time is so disillusioning" (Becker, pp. 44–45). Any hope for transcendence of the physical level, whether through erotic love or spiritual redemption, remains something of a metaphysical conceit, perpetually in need of sustaining metaphors to forestall a collapse into mere biology. The reductionist fallacy—that the least elaborate or exalted explanation is necessarily the truest one—thus leads directly to the annihilationist heresy. The skepticism of "Loves Alchymie" centers on the fear that the obvious physical facts are the only true facts—which would be as discouraging a notion about death as it is about love.

The speaker begins the poem digging for love, and through love, for meaning; he ends possessing, and possessed by, the bitterness of "*Mummy.*" The first line compares love to a mine, which can be taken as a brutally reductive figuration of sexual intercourse, since the comparison of a woman's body to a rich landscape was conventional in Jacobean erotic verse. This collapse of metaphor to a dispiriting literal level is not surprising,[123] because what worries the persona is precisely the possibility that the act of love will prove to be no more significant than its physical motion, resulting in some incidental fetishistic pleasures and perhaps a pregnancy along the way, but nothing centrally or transcendently meaningful:

> Some that have deeper digg'd loves Myne then I,
> Say, where his centrique happinesse doth lie:
>   I'have lov'd, and got, and told,
> But should I love, get, tell, till I were old,
> I should not finde that hidden mysterie;
>   Oh, 'tis imposture all:
> And as no chymique yet th'Elixar got,
>   But glorifies his pregnant pot,
>   If by the way to him befall
> Some odoriferous thing, or medicinall,
>   So, lovers dreame a rich and long delight,
>   But get a winter-seeming summers night.
>   (1–12)

This mining expedition fails to harrow his erotic hell; the epic voyage to the underworld yields no testimonials to afterglow, or afterlife. The search for the gold-based "Elixir" was more commonly a search for an immortality serum than for an aphrodisiac (even for Jonson's Epicure Mammon), and here it meets a dead end. The rich and long delight promised in heaven threatens to become a winter night to us after all, cold and (to the annihilated consciousness) seemingly an instantaneous passage.[124]

Women are "*Mummy*, possest" (24) because they finally preserve death, not life.[125] Donne's misogynistic flailing reflects a common male tendency to blame women not only for the failures of love (as in Petrarchan complaint) but also for the loss of immortality (as in the Genesis story). As "Aire and Angels" demonstrates, only a *meta*physical connection can overcome death; when mistresses fail in their spiritual responses, when men may not "Hope . . . for minde in women," sexual intercourse loses its ability to reinforce the union of mind and body that is life itself for Donne (23). Women are—their very wombs are—a treasure-mine of fool's gold in which men bury themselves with no real hope of rebirth.

"Farewell to Love" may be the most difficult lyric in Donne's entire knotty canon, but some sense can be made of it by recognizing its kinship with "Loves Alchymie." Both poems express doubts about spiritual immortality by questioning the ability of love to transcend the physical act. Post-coital depression again casts an uneasy eye on the promises of afterlife, the afterglow of a more literal kind of "dying." Donne links orgasm with actual death by observing parenthetically that "each such Act, they say, / Diminisheth the length of life a day" (24–25). The religious implications of this analogy are clear from the opening lines. His concern about disillusionment in romantic love immediately (and characteristically) focuses on religious uncertainty about death:

> Whilst yet to prove,
> I thought there was some Deitie in love
>   So did I reverence, and gave
> Worship, as Atheists at their dying houre
> Call, what they cannot name, an unknowne power,
>   As ignorantly did I crave.
>
> (1–6)

So Donne's youthful impulse to believe in the transcendent power of erotic desire (a belief doomed to disappointment) resembles a dying atheist's desperate need to believe in some transcendent Being. Perhaps the analogy to death, as at the start of "Forbidding Mourning," is more than an analogy; perhaps Donne the seducer is an atheist seeking an alternative path beyond time- and body-boundedness.

Furthermore, the analogy suggests that the atheist was right the first time: it is natural to wish for a deity, but mistaken to believe that one is truly present behind the uncaring machinery of biological nature. Indeed, this speaker's suspicion about sexual intercourse closely resembles the suspicion Donne attributes to atheists about intercourse with God.[126] Religious faith is thus associated with ignorance, however blissful. Wishful thinking can carry a person from atheism to agnosticism; but revelation and incarnation destroy rather than fulfill such hopes (lines 7–10). From all its living and appetizing glory, the erotic object decays (like a gingerbread man)[127] into a silly and disgusting construction:

> But, from late faire
> His highnesse sitting in a golden Chaire,
>   Is not lesse cared for after three dayes
> By children, then the thing which lovers so
> Blindly admire, and with such worship wooe;
>   Being had, enjoying it decayes:
>   And thence,
> What before pleas'd them all, takes but one sense,
>   And that so lamely, as it leaves behinde
> A kinde of sorrowing dulnesse to the minde.
>   (11–20)

Fearing mere stupor, Donne sounds rather like Keats in the "Ode on Melancholy," where "shade to shade will come too drowsily, / And drown the wakeful anguish of the soul."

But Donne's subsequent lines do not imply (as do Keats's Odes) that love and life are all the more fervently desirable because they are fleeting. The most difficult crux in this most difficult poem makes the most sense as a proto-Darwinian assertion that biology encourages intercourse frequent enough to preserve the species, but not so frequent as to exhaust individuals prematurely:

> Nature decreed (since each such Act, they say,
> Diminisheth the length of life a day)
>   This; as shee would man should despise
>   The sport,
> Because that other curse of being short,
>   And onely for a minute made to be
> Eager, desires to raise posterity.
>   (24–30)

The point becomes clearer if one accepts H. J. C. Grierson's emendation, in his 1912 edition, to "Eagers desire." The curse of brevity imposed on human love also haunts human life, and (as in *Measure for Measure*) one cannot renew love-making without aggravating mortality—unless one associates sexual renewal with procreative renewal, and neglects the fate of the individual. We could mate as often as cocks, or as seldom as lions (22), but we would still suffer the post-coital depression that corresponds to an exclusively human awareness of the oblivion that follows our little exertions of life. We may generously choose to perceive some high purpose in the making of progeny, but (from this viewpoint) the act itself proves depressing, disgusting, a bad joke we play on ourselves and each other.

If Donne is indeed comparing love-objects to gingerbread kings, his comparison implies a bitter religious parody that further undermines the hope for any immortality other than genetic approximation. The image suggests Christ on his golden throne, aptly transformed into an edible body of bread; the fact that, after three days, this Incarnation does not rise miraculously, but rots in the most ordinary way, offers a skeptical and even disgusted perspective on the Resurrection.[128] Even if Donne is referring to some other kind of toy king, the implications are scarcely less corrosive. As children with trinkets, as adolescents with erotic desire, so older people impose ridiculously high value on religious ideas; whereas in fact all these things are merely distractions designed to get us through the brief business of life without reproductive inefficiencies—including the disruptive recognition that we are mundane instruments of biology.

From virginal youth, a man falls into experience; from sexual pleasure, he falls into torpor. In both instances the movement is from good, warm, immediate desire to dull regret. Provoked by the religious references throughout the poem, we may extrapolate a third analogous transaction, in which our cursedly short lives lead only to an anticlimactic death. Donne's speaker therefore vows,

> I'll no more dote and runne
> To pursue things which had indammag'd me.
> And when I come where moving beauties be,
>   As men doe when the summers Sunne
>   Growes great,
> Though I admire their greatnesse, shun their heat.
>
>   (33–38)

As in many instances of Petrarchan misogyny, the speaker subliminally associates the damage done to his heart by women who fail to requite his desires with the damage done to all mankind by Eve. In a cynical version of Gnostic withdrawal from the corrupt world of procreation, he concludes by abjuring the allure of these radiant natural beauties: "Each place can afford shadowes. If all faile, / 'Tis but applying worme-seed to the Taile" (39–40). If he cannot hide from this provocative female radiance, he can resort to anaphrodisiacs, and if those measures fail, he can recognize his seduction as mere biology, not a transcendent disaster like the Fall.[129] There is neither salvation nor damnation, and conception is close kin to vermiculation: from sperm our bodies come, to worms they return, with a horrifying indifference. The ultimate cure for lust, as many Renaissance moralists suggested, is a contemplation of the *transi* figure, the flesh in its final decay. The morbid and sexually cynical voice behind Donne's shadowy "Farewell to Love" may therefore be Shakespeare's Hamlet, who also gives his frailty the name of woman.[130] Both the play and the poem are tales that end in wormwood.

"The Funerall" appears to reflect more respect for the rites of love and of death than does "Farewell to Love." Even here, however, the funeral baked meats make an uneasy accompaniment to an ostensibly romantic occasion. Donne begins with a characteristically elaborate and morbid revision of the Petrarchan convention that unrequited love will cause the speaker's demise:

> Who ever comes to shroud me, do not harme
> > Nor question much
> That subtile wreath of haire, which crowns my arme;
> The mystery, the signe you must not touch,
> > For 'tis my outward Soule,
> Viceroy to that, which then to heaven being gone,
> > Will leave this to controule,
> And keepe these limbes, her Provinces, from dissolution.
> > (1–8)

The uncertain methods for surviving abandonment by a beloved here become equivalent to the body's uncertain prospects for surviving its abandonment by the soul at death. This "subtile wreath" recalls "That subtile knot, which makes us man" in "The Extasie" (64), but the comparison of the autonomic spinal nexus to a bracelet of dead hair is ominous:[131]

> For if the sinewie thread my braine lets fall
> > Through every part,
> Can tye those parts, and make mee one of all;

> These haires which upward grew, and strength and art
>   Have from a better braine,
> Can better do'it; Except she meant that I
>   By this should know my pain,
> As prisoners then are manacled, when they'are condemn'd to die.

(9–16)

This penitentiary love is death row rather than protective custody for the speaker.

The fact that the original affectionate intent of this gift no longer accompanies the material token is both cause and metaphor for the speaker's demise. The physical component means nothing without its spiritual counterpart. The speaker justifies his determination to bury this bracelet by warning that "it might breed idolatrie, / If into others hands these Reliques came" (19–20). Taking what seems to be a solid Protestant perspective, Donne dismisses as heretical the supposition that any spiritual power persists in bodily remains. But precisely that idolatrous supposition—surrendered along with the childhood religion his mother inculcated—seems necessary to sustain Donne's narcissistic fantasies of complete personal immortality. With their transient gifts of body and love, women—as mothers, as lovers, as Otherness—have robbed him of any secure belief in the permanence and exaltation of his own body.

The same transaction emerges if we switch from a theological to a psychological vocabulary, and call the "wreath of haire" a fetish rather than an idol. In Freudian theory, the fetish-object serves to displace (in subsequent sexual situations) an early sexual attachment to an unreliably responsive mother. In Becker's revision of that theory, the fetish-object serves to disguise the mortal physicality of the mother and subsequent lovers. In Kohut's version, the fetish-object is an externalized *locus* for a dangerously unstable selfhood. All three functions are profoundly relevant to Donne, in his uneasy quest for a perfectly responsive lover to mirror and thereby affirm his personal immortality. When the beloved woman fails to do so, he can punish her only by subjecting the fetish-object to the same mortality he is now suffering: "since you would save none of mee, I bury some of you" (24). He can reject the object's power over him only by draining away its imputed meaning, making the fetish back into a mere physical artifact, even at the cost of confirming that he is merely physical as well.

The speaker's relationship to this wreath of hair bespeaks a classic psychological strategy for coping with an overwhelming universe. A child needs to contain, within limited transference objects, the whole problem of terror and power, making them the center of it in order to cut down and naturalize the world around them. Now we see why the transference object poses so many problems. The child does partly control his larger fate by it, but it becomes his new fate. He binds himself to one person to automatically control terror, to mediate wonder, and to defeat death by that person's strength. But then he experiences "transference terror"; the terror of losing the object, of displeasing it, of not being able to live without it. (Becker, p. 146)

This is very much how love-relationships function throughout Donne's lyrics. He invests women with such grandiose value in the defense of his own immortality that he is necessarily enslaved to them, and terrified and embittered by the prospect of separation or infidelity.[132]

It would hardly be surprising if the women in Donne's life—at least, in his verse—generally failed to meet this extraordinary standard, or declined to assume this gigantic task. Adequate explanations or compensations for mortality are hard to provide, in the absence of strong religious faith. Married couples may settle into blaming each other for the disappointments of life, and for the ordinary injuries to secondary narcissism, which romantic love is assigned to protect. Adventurers may attempt to minimize the sense of human mortality by gestures of courageous denial, and to minimize the costs of human transience by seizing each day and packing it with as broad or intense an experience of this world as possible. Blaming the Other for our mortal losses and limitations—the mytheme of revenge-tragedy—is usually an act of bad faith in real life. Expanding the Self is more heroic, but therefore also more poignant: when the multiplied experiential self is divided by an infinite oblivion, the quotient still looks pitifully small. Becker observes that "basic narcissism is increased when one's childhood experiences have been securely life-supporting and warmly enhancing to the sense of self, to the feeling of being really special, truly Number One in creation" (Becker, p. 22). But if that fantasy is disrupted, the self must choose between an unstable multiplicity and an implacable nullification.

"The Computation," like "The Primrose," shows Donne attempting to employ mathematics against mortality. Carey argues that this lyric seeks "to show how inadequate quantity is to love's intensities,"[133] but as the ostensible topic of love gives way to the submerged topic of death, the numbers Donne uses to regulate the experience of separation from a beloved necessarily give way to anxieties about infinity:

> For the first twenty yeares, since yesterday,
>   I scarce beleev'd, thou could'st be gone away,

For forty more, I fed on favours past,
    And forty'on hopes, that thou would'st, they might last.
Teares drown'd one hundred, and sighes blew out two,
    A thousand, I did neither thinke, nor doe,
    Or not divide, all being one thought of you;
    Or in a thousand more, forgot that too.
Yet call not this long life; But thinke that I
Am, by being dead, Immortall; Can ghosts die?

The complaint that hours of separation seem remarkably long is standard in Renaissance love-poetry—echoed passionately by Shakespeare's
Juliet and ironically by his Rosalind. Donne, with a typically Metaphysical desire to expand violently (and thereby defamiliarize) the object of
analysis, multiplies each hour into a hundred years. But no multiple of
his emotional desires can match the power of his religious terror, as the
sermons make clear: "if 60. if 80. yeeres, yet, *few and evill have his daies
beene.* . . . if every minute of [humankind's] 6000. yeeres, were multipli'd
by so many millions of *Ages,* all would amount to nothing, meerly
nothing, in respect of that *Eternity,* which hee is to dwell in" (*Sermons,*
VIII, 76; cf. VI, 331). Marvell uses this sort of exaggeration parodically
(in "To His Coy Mistress") to warn that death delimits the time for
earthly praises and pleasures; Donne uses it subliminally to warn that
death extends time immeasurably for the separated soul and body
hereafter. This allegorical aspect of "The Computation"—like the
"winter-seeming summers night" of "Loves Alchymie"—anticipates
Emily Dickinson's "Because I Could Not Stop for Death," which
concludes,

Since then—'tis Centuries—and yet
Feels shorter than the Day
I first surmised the Horses' Heads
Were toward Eternity—

In Donne as in Dickinson, behind the distortions of time lies a terror of
eternity, and the homely familiarity of the metaphor only intensifies the
incomparable estrangement of oblivion.

Numbers are futile weapons in the battle against mortality. Donne tries
to answer death with the oneness of his solipsism, the twoness of his
passionate exchanges with women, and with a variety of schemes of
multiplication. If a mortal being is not somehow made infinite, however,
its value approaches zero in the functions of eternity.[134] In his funeral
sermon for Magdalen Herbert, Donne feels compelled to promise an

afterlife lasting "for *ever*, and *ever*, and *ever*, and *infinite*, and *super-infinite evers*" (*Sermons*, VIII, 92). Clearly Donne's rhetoric and imagination are here straining their limits, yet anything less feels inadequate. For Donne to defy death with numbers is an act of bravado. For him as for Hamlet, just beyond the consolation of measurable human time is the terror of eternity, and just ahead of the one—the self—is the nothing: "that which was not made of Nothing is not threatened with this annihilation. All other things are, even Angels, even our *soules* . . . and if they were not made immortall by *preservation*, their *Nature* could not keepe them from sinking to this *center, Annihilation*" (*Devotions*, p. 51). *Ex nihilo* we come, as conscious living beings, and to nothing we may return.

DEATH AS NEGATION: LEVELLING THE MONARCHY OF WIT

Paradox serves to disturb the linear quality of the reality we ordinarily represent to ourselves; it is a crystallized form of deconstruction. The appetite of Metaphysical poetry for paradox reflects a malcontented resistance toward the commonly accepted hierarchies and ethos of the Renaissance universe, just as the formalities of Cavalier poetry reflect complacency. By isolating language from "common sense," by authorizing it to reshape the material universe, Donne can begin to challenge aspects of cultural consensus otherwise unavailable to interrogation. This is one of the significant correspondences between two radical movements in Jacobean culture: Puritan theology and Metaphysical poetry. Though Donne was certainly not a Puritan,[135] he radically empowered the word, enabling it to overthrow convention by exposing as corrupt illusions the familiar figurations and decorations of the physical universe. His iconoclasm was directed toward customary poetic forms and images as well as idolatrous churches; he resisted the mediation of poetic as well as patristic traditions; and though he did not participate in turning the world upside down, he certainly turned it inside out.

The human situation—as articulated in Hamlet's "What a piece of work is a man" speech (2.2.295–308)—is a painful paradox. Struggling to reconcile his narcissistic self-valuation with his future as a quintessence of dust, Donne responds with some paradoxes of his own—a homeopathic cure for the absurdity of human life. Donne's eroticism and the poetry it generates become tools for negating the huge negation known as death. The difficult lyric "Negative Love" dismisses sublunary lovers who feed on some particular attribute of their mistresses as little better than coffin-worms:

> I never stoop'd so low, as they
> Which on an eye, cheeke, lip, can prey,
>   Seldome to them, which soare no higher
>   Then vertue or the minde to'admire,
> For sense, and understanding may
>   Know, what gives fuell to their fire.
>
> (1–6)

If love is comprehensible in mind, it might be comprehensible in time as well, and therefore subordinate to eternity. The *blason* burns itself out far too quickly for this speaker's comfort. He must avoid not only attachment to the body, but even attachment to consciousness and self-consciousness, which are urgently at risk in their mortal vessel. To prevent the deadly disillusionments of "Loves Alchymie," he must avoid resolving either his beloved or his poem into a definable object.

Indeterminacy is thus a step toward immortality. The faculty of desire must be kept alive by keeping it aloof from any commodity that might die or be denied him. The reiterated determination of "The Sunne Rising" to make the beloved "all" is here retracted:

> To All, which all love, I say no.
> If any who deciphers best,
>   What we know not, our selves, can know,
> Let him teach mee that nothing; This
> As yet my ease, and comfort is,
> Though I speed not, I cannot misse.
>
> (13–18)

Instead of the urgent and focused desire that characterizes most *carpe diem* lyrics, Donne's speaker proposes a philosophy of love that resembles the theology of Eastern Christianity, which claims superiority over positive Western models because its negative descriptions avoid limiting the illimitable. By relinquishing object-desire, he deprives death of its most feared power. By embracing, exalting, and identifying with this negation, by immersing himself in the destructive element, he renders himself figuratively immune to its dissolving effects.

In Donne's highly paradoxical "The Will," failed love is a god overseeing death, and death becomes an overdetermined act of undoing. The superficial hope for partial survival as an organ donor yields to a deeper hope of perpetuating individual consciousness through the residue that is the poem itself. "The Will" presents itself as a last testament in which the speaker ironically bequeaths various aspects of himself to heirs. At first he stresses the superfluousness of what he leaves behind: Argus does not need his eyes, Fame his tongue, women or the sea his tears. These gestures toward survival are swallowed up by the pointless reduplications in the universe. Characteristically, Donne associates this notion that his mortal senses could prove superfluous with the possibility that he is similarly dispensable as a lover: "Thou, Love, hast taught mee heretofore / By making mee serve her who'had twenty more, / That I should give to none, but such, as had too much before" (7–9). Again Donne makes infidelity a cause of death in his plot so that he can manipulate it as a figure of death in his symbolism.

After several more stanzas of self-undoing, Donne's speaker concludes with a typically solipsistic threat to nullify the entire world as love (or death) has nullified him:

> But I'll undoe
> The world by dying; because love dies too.
> Then all your beauties will bee no more worth
> Than gold in Mines, where none doth draw it forth;
> And all your graces no more use shall have
> Then a Sun dyall in a grave.
> Thou Love taughtst mee, by making mee
> Love her, who doth neglect both mee and thee,
> To'invent, and practise this one way, to'annihilate all three.
>
> (46–54)

Underlying his parting threat is a threat of unredeemed burial (unmined gold) and a timeless oblivion: in the symbol of the buried sundial, darkness, irrelevance, and eternity eerily coincide. "I have no houreglasse in my grave to see how my time passes," Donne once declared (*Sermons*, III, 110; cf. *Devotions*, p. 9).

Yet, after all this undoing, something remains Donne. By unburdening and dispossessing himself in these Metaphysical paradoxes, he paradoxically immortalizes his indelible poetic signature. In this sense, "The Will" is a playful extension of the *Biathanatos*, a symbolic suicide that restores the mastery of individual will over mortal dissolution. In mourning as in heartbreak, "Griefe brought to numbers cannot be so fierce, / For, he tames it, that fetters it in verse" ("The Triple Foole," 10–11). Where no other numbers provide an insulation against infinity, poetic meter lends a meaningful shape to Donne's interior universe.

An abstract solution that satisfies the poetic mind may not, however, answer the needs of the deteriorating body, any more than abstract love could satisfy the desiring body in "The Extasie." When someone he cares about actually dies, Donne—like most clever theorists of death—finds no easy solution to the problems of the mourner. The geometrical and mathematical formulas by which Donne elsewhere evades mortal decay here become either terrifying or irrelevant, because geometry cannot plot a course out of the abyss, nor can numbers contain an infinite negation: "How barren a thing is Arithmetique . . . to expresse this Eternity?" (*Sermons*, IV, 87). When Donne attempts to measure what the actual eternal death of his beloved does to his formula of immortality, his instruments stubbornly read zero, and lead him nowhere.

In his "Elegie on Mris. *Boulstred*" Donne sounds like the Cowardly Lion of Oz; instead of the lion's propitiary "I *do* believe in ghosts," Donne insists that he does believe in death, now that he has seen such a frightening demonstration. The apostate Donne—not a person to play carelessly with the idea of recantation—begins,

> Death I recant, and say, unsaid by mee
> > What ere hath slip'd, that might diminish thee.
> Spirituall treason, atheisme 'tis, to say
> > That any can thy Summons disobey.
> Th'earths face is but thy Table; there are set
> > Plants, cattell, men, dishes for Death to eate.
>
> > > (1–6)

This anticipates the disturbingly dismissive list in Yeats's "Sailing to Byzantium": "Fish, flesh, and fowl." Human beings become merely another entree on the menu, and Death the Devourer becomes the one true God. "How could I think thee nothing," Donne asks death twenty lines later, "that see now / In all this All, nothing else is, but thou." The "Nothing else is" bravado of "The Sunne Rising" (22) echoes in the abyss, and the answer proves even more disturbing than the question. He could never have allowed Death to be that proud without in turn judging human life to be worthless.

In this elegy Donne climbs back out of that abyss by clinging to standard Christian consolations and his own valedictory formula:

> Death gets 'twixt soules and bodies such a place
>   As sinne insinuates 'twixt just men and grace,
> Both worke a separation, no divorce.
>   Her Soule is gone to usher up her corse.
>
> (43–46)

But the demeaning facts of material existence are always in pursuit, threatening to impose a literal reading of death itself.

The grandiose and depressive tendencies of the unstable narcissist are opposing manifestations of a single problem:

> Sin and neurosis have another side: not only their unreal self-inflation in the refusal to admit creatureliness but also a penalty for intensified self-conscious-ness: the failure to be consoled by shared illusions. The result is that the sinner (neurotic) is hyperconscious of the very thing he tries to deny: his creatureli-ness, his miserableness and unworthiness. . . . He tried to build a glorified private inner world because of his deeper anxieties, but life takes its revenge. The more he separates and inflates himself, the more anxious he becomes. The more he artificially idealizes himself, the more exaggeratedly he criticizes himself. He alternates between the extremes of "I am everything" and "I am nothing." (Becker, p. 197)

These polar conclusions match Donne's two opposite uses of the declaration that "nothing else is" in "The Sunne Rising" and the Boulstred elegy. Donne the Petrarchan lover again proves almost indis-tinguishable from Donne the penitent Calvinist. In the "Nocturnall upon St. Lucies Day," the two become one, and together they stare into nothingness. The "Nocturnall" systematically recants the love lyrics, as the death of his beloved (probably his wife) fulfills the bitter syllogism Donne reportedly composed when the exposure of their secret marriage badly damaged his courtly career: "*John Donne, Anne Donne, Un-done.*"[136] The mutuality that was supposed to ensure his immortality now causes his death. Indeed, the only way he could reaffirm that reciprocity was by dying himself; and Walton reports the widespread fear that "sadness for his wives death, would, as *Jacob* said, *make his days few* . . . and of this there were many visible signs."[137]

The fact that he attempts to nullify himself completely to permit a communion with St. Lucy—and thus with his deceased wife—suggests a suspicion that death is merely the absence of life. Though his wife may have died on the anniversary of the Virgin's Assumption, he betrays no hope that she is anything but annihilated, and this anniversary of the patron saint of light brings him only darkness. The grim opening lines closely echo one of Donne's flattering verse-letters,[138] but what was there the foil to a compliment, here has nothing to set against the blackness. The year and the day are at their lowest point, and at this moment the entire world seems to be a corpse sinking toward burial:

> The worlds whole sap is sunke:
> The generall balme th'hydroptique earth hath drunk,
> Whither, as to the beds-feet, life is shrunke,
> Dead and enterr'd; yet all these seeme to laugh,
> Compar'd with mee, who am their Epitaph.
>
> (5–9)

The bed, once a place of apotheosis—as in the contrary solar example of "The Sunne Rising"—serves here as a drain for the life that ceases to flow through its vital pathways, seeping instead into the ground. When the beloved woman dies before him, Donne is trapped in the blindness and passivity of the abandoned corpse. It is only appropriate, therefore, that he sounds like the plaintive Body in Vaughan's "Death: A Dialogue."[139] Imitation is the sincerest form of mourning, and Donne does his best to identify with the corpse sharing his darkness.

Whereas "The Canonization" proposes the impolitic lovers as saints on whom future lovers may model their own immortalizing exchanges, the "Nocturnall" dismisses rebirth through love as a transient effect, and urges lovers to recognize themselves in his destruction rather than his preservation:

> Study me then, you who shall lovers bee
> At the next world, that is, at the next Spring:
>   For I am every dead thing,
>   In whom love wrought new Alchimie.
>   For his art did expresse
> A quintessence even from nothingnesse,
> From dull privations, and leane emptinesse:
> He ruin'd mee, and I am re-begot
> Of absence, darknesse, death; things which are not.
>
> (10–18)

The "next world," a phrase commonly associated with the eternal afterlife, is here subjugated to the biological cycle of the seasons, as if there were no heaven beyond the renewal of earthly life. Again there is a clear transposition from Donne's theology: "God found me nothing, and of that nothing made me; *Adam* left me worse then God found me, worse then nothing . . . corrupted with the leaven of Originall sin" (*Sermons*, VII, 136). His love for her had been his redemptive God, their marriage his Eden; but now he has fallen into mortality.

Once he had felt that life was not truly life unless love provided an intimation of immortality. Now, with that intimation discredited, his continued existence is merely a premonition of death, a regression toward non-being. According to Thomas Browne (p. 307), "The most tedious being is that which can unwish it self, content to be nothing"; and the speaker of the "Nocturnall" describes himself as a distillation of emptiness, "the grave / Of all, that's nothing" (21–22). In this darkness of his lover's lost sight, the window that held Donne's name has become a mere transparency. According to Donne the preacher, "The name of the Creator is, I am, but of every other creature rather I am not, I am nothing" (*Sermons* VIII, 144). From a comfortable distance, as for example in a flattering comparison of a lord's favor to divine providence, Donne can perceive the creation *ex nihilo* as a promise of resurrection, rather than a threat of annihilation.[140] But in the "Nocturnall"—as in *King Lear*—the wonderful Christian faith in the creation *ex nihilo* recoils in horror, as the world of human meaning is systematically undone. Universal ontology recapitulates mortal ontogeny.

Like a dying tragic hero, Donne reverts briefly to the solipsistic hyperboles of his great earlier works, which suggested that the struggles of love pushed the world backward to the start of creation and anticipated the emptiness of death:

> Oft a flood
> Have wee two wept, and so
> Drownd the whole world, us two; oft did we grow
> To be two Chaosses when we did show
> Care to ought else; and often absences
> Withdrew our soules, and made us carcasses.
> (22–27; cf. *Sermons*, VII, 104)

But he evokes these old formulas only to dismiss them as now empty themselves, because the simple implacable fact of his beloved's death admits of no metaphorical conversion: mourning cannot now be forbidden. He cannot find any language adequate to euphemize her death, nor any analogy to describe his own consequent condition:

But I am by her death, (which word wrongs her)
Of the first nothing, the Elixer grown;
    Were I a man, that I were one,
    I needs must know; I should preferre,
        If I were any beast,
Some ends, some means; Yea plants, yea stones detest,
And love; all, all some properties invest;
    If I an ordinary nothing were,
    As shadow,'a light, and body must be here.

(28–36)

Donne thus anticipates the Cartesian *cogito*: if he were truly an existent soul, he would have some consciousness of himself. Instead, he is conscious only of lacking even the appetitive desires of a beast, even the motivation that will make a plant reach toward the sun or an iron stone reach toward a magnet.[141] None of his three souls survive. This sounds like acute clinical depression, the loss of any basis for outward desire and hence movement; if she is truly, purely, eternally annihilated, then no direction is toward her. He cannot even be the shadow he plays at becoming in earlier poems, since that would require a direction of light and a body to block it—a hopeless project for a nobody at midnight (cf. *Devotions*, p. 76). There is no signifier available to mitigate his utter insignificance in the face of death, no language adequate to the situation, no vindicating representation to be made.

Any reader waiting for a redemptive morning, now faces a rebuff. The "Nothing else is" of "The Sunne Rising" becomes: "But I am None; nor will my sun renew" (37). The speaker has lost his faith in the immortalizing power of metaphor (which, analogous to a shadow, would have required a partly occluded meaning to leave its residue). Left alone with the most intractable of mortal facts, he cannot assure relief at daybreak simply by associating his depression figuratively with the night. In the sermons and "The Second Anniversarie," Donne repeatedly deploys the hope of an eternal morning against the fear of a terminal darkness.[142] This is a standard corollary to the common Jacobean comparison of death to sleep: "for the night comes and goes, and comes againe: the Sunne doth set and rise againe: but when our life is gone, when our death is come, we returne no more to a life with men on earth: our night endes not, our Sunne riseth not, until that determined time of the Resurrection."[143] The long night of the "Nocturnall" never arrives at that "until." Donne's usual faith in the rising of a son or sun or Son, in the erotic or Christian solutions to mortality, is markedly absent.

Moreover, any reader waiting for "the next Spring" (11), the longer-term cyclical renewal of life, to renew the speaker's spirits, will again be rebuffed: "Enjoy your summer all" (41). This is spoken enviously, but also dismissively, because the speaker associates that season and its loves only with goatish lust (37, 41). Eroticism appears in its darker aspect, as an erasure rather than an affirmation of the human soul. In the "Nocturnall" as in "Twicknam Garden," the spectacle of cyclical nature is at best an irrelevancy to the speaker's depression, which is founded in the tragic fate of individuals, not the comic project of the species. From the pulpit, Donne may comfortably ask, "will the earth, that gives a new life to all Creatures, faile in us, and hold us in an everlasting winter, without a spring, and a Resurrection?" (*Sermons*, V, 215; cf. III, 97). Coming from a bereaved lover, however, the question is less clearly rhetorical. For Donne as for Macbeth, the loss of his wife makes life resemble annihilationist death: an absence of light, and an endless winter. So the "Nocturnall" ends precisely, explicitly, where it began, in stasis, despite the remarkable determination of critics (as with *King Lear*) to read redemption into this exhausted closure.[144] The words and thoughts of the poem have passed, but (as in death) we are still and always at the center of a dark night; the speaker is to us, as his beloved is to him, an endless absence in an endless presence, "since this / Both the yeares, and the dayes deep midnight is." That is the last word. In a mortal world, being is a property of time, and nothingness is what time bequeaths to us.

POEM AS SAVIOR: IMMORTAL LINES AND MORTAL LINEAGE

For a Renaissance poet—particularly one dependent on flattering powerful families and assuaging his own anxieties about death—Donne displays remarkably little interest in the traditional notion that procreation offers a version of immortality. Even in an epithalamion for a royal family—almost always an occasion for celebrating fecundity—Donne refuses to let the biological hope of progeny overshadow the symbolic miracle of romantic pair-bonding.[145] He compares King James's daughter Elizabeth and her husband Frederick to

> Two Phoenixes, whose joyned breasts
> Are unto one another mutuall nests,

Where motion kindles such fires, as shall give
Yong Phoenixes, and yet the old shall live.
Whose love and courage never shall decline,
But make the whole year through, thy day, O Valentine.

("An Epithalamion . . . on the Lady Elizabeth," 23–28)

Only by suspending or compressing time (on behalf of the patron saint
of love) can the intensely inward experience of love be reconciled with
its role in the perpetuation of the species. Children are merely the happy
by-product precipitated from a mutually affirming, mutually preserving
embrace:

To an unseparable union growe,
    Since separation
Falls not on such things as are infinite,
Nor things which are but one, can disunite.

(46–49)

Unity is infinity, and copulation is immortality: Iago's "beast with two
backs" functions almost like a two-personed God.

In fact, Donne usually portrays offspring as worse than an irrelevance.
Procreation proves dangerous to the parents' survival, and not only in
instances of malicious children like those depicted by *King Lear*.
"Farewell to Love" shows Donne's sensitivity to the Renaissance warning that orgasms shorten a man's life in creating a new one, and the
death of his wife in childbirth would have confirmed that procreation
was at least as dangerous for the mother as for the father. Even in life, the
children proved as much a burden as a consolation. During the Mitcham
years, Donne's letters complain vividly about the burdens of sharing his
small house and income with so many children and their dangerous
illnesses.[146]

Donne is by no means untender toward his children, and these
complaints should not be adduced in support of claims that, because of
high mortality rates, parents did not much care about their children until
adolescence or the nineteenth century, whichever came first.[147] After
barely surviving an illness that struck his household, Donne feels
compelled to express his grief, even in a letter to a powerful man by no
means his intimate, for even such a supposedly unworthy commodity as
a baby daughter: "I am fallen from fair hopes of ending all; yet I have
scaped no better cheap, then that I have paid death one of my Children
for my Ransome. Because I loved it well, I make account that I dignifie
the memory of it, by mentioning of it to you, else I should not be so

homely."[148] These wincing remarks suggest, however indirectly, that he values his children nearly as much as he values himself. But this attachment does not depend on the consoling myth—familiar from Shakespearean sonnets, Jacobean tragicomedy, and funeral sermons— that generations can redeem each other from death. Donne's ransom metaphor suggests rather the contrary: that one must die to spare the other.

Donne's "Elegie on the L. C." implies that a parent's mortality may in turn be contagious to the children:

> His children are his pictures, Oh they bee
> Pictures of him dead, senselesse, cold as he.
> Here needs no marble Tombe, since hee is gone,
> He, and about him, his, are turn'd to stone.
>
> (23–26)

The poem thus ends with an image reminiscent of the penultimate moments of Shakespeare's *The Winter's Tale*, when Hermione's statue appears lifeless, and threatens to draw her offspring ("more stone than it . . . standing like stone with thee") into the lifelessness of art or death as well. The same danger is writ large in the plot of *Hamlet*.

It is interesting, in this regard, that one of Donne's repeated arguments against the adequacy of classical religion is that the gods had genealogies, and therefore lacked the property of eternity necessary in a savior (*Sermons*, II, 201; VIII, 57–58; and X, 53). Reproduction again comports mortality. On a more particular level of Christian doctrine, Donne's resistance to the procreative solution to mortality may reflect his belief that the soul arises independent of the act of generation, since to acknowledge it the product of a physical act would render it susceptible to "dissolution with the body" at death. Donne wrote to Thomas Lucey that, in the dispute over whether new souls are made by parents or infused by God, "whosoever will adhere to the way of propagation can never evict necessarily and certainly a naturall immortality in the soul, if the soul result out of matter."[149] As Donne argues in "The Second Anniversarie," it is illogical to expect a "permanent effect / Of transitory causes" (388–89).

On a more personal, earthly level, Donne's intense subjectivity may help to explain his neglect of the consoling idea that our offspring undo our mortality. He was fiercely devoted to his unique consciousness and its experiential history—precisely what (short of some Lamarckian model of psychological evolution) no genetic simulation could reasonably hope to reproduce. Indeed, his role as a father only interferes with his reading, his writing, his inwardness:

Sir,

I write not to you out of my poor Library, where to cast mine eye upon good Authors kindles or refreshes sometimes meditation . . . nor from the high way, where I am contracted, and inverted into my self; which are my two ordinary forges of Letters to you. But I write from the fire side in my Parler, and in the noise of three gamesome children; and by the side of her, whom because I have transplanted into a wretched fortune, I must labor to disguise that from her by all such honest devices, as giving her my company, and discourse, therefore I steal from her, all the time which I give this Letter. (*Letters*, pp. 118–19)

Biological and intellectual life are competitors. As the valedictions "Of the Book" and "Of My Name in the Window" demonstrate, when Donne needs to invest himself beyond the entropic economy of the flesh, he invests himself in written language. Lines of verse take the place of family lineage in plotting a course into the future. When he announces, "I am thy Creator, thou my Saviour" ("To Mr. T. W.," *Complete Poetry*, no. 115, line 6), Donne is not addressing his children; in this case he is not even addressing a lover or the Christian God. He is speaking to his own poetry; that one talent which is death to hide. So while he may slight the idea that offspring will remain to immortalize the progenitor, Donne makes extensive and ingenious use of its usual counterpart, the idea that the author will survive through his writings; in terms of the classical pun, *libri* take precedence over *liberi*, and perhaps even appropriate some of their functions.

Admittedly, Donne showed more concern with the theory of such salvation than with the practice: he seems to have made little effort to preserve the poems that profess to preserve him. Yet his discussions of this issue are thick with displaced anxieties about his own prospects for procreative survival or irredeemable erasure:

In a Latin letter to Goodyer written in 1611 before his departure for the Continent, Donne indicated that some works existed in "copies . . . the originals having been destroyed by fire . . . condemned by me to Hell." Others . . . were kept to himself, "so unhappily sterile that no copies of them have been begotten." These last he foresaw as destined for "utter annihilation (a fate with which God does not threaten even the wickedest of sinners)."[150]

His ambivalence about the literary solution to mortality surfaces again, fittingly, concerning *Biathanatos*, which describes and justifies the suicidal tendency to which he never quite surrendered. He writes to Robert Carre that he has "always gone so near suppressing" this book "that it is onely not burnt." But Donne cannot bear to let go of himself, either as consciousness or as the transcription of that consciousness. On his departure for Germany—another apt occasion for mortality-anxiety—Donne sends the manuscript to Carre with the fervent but perplexing insistence that it "is a Book written by *Jack Donne*, and not by D[r]. *Donne*: Reserve it for me, if I live, and if I die, I only forbid it the Presse, and the Fire: publish it not, but yet burn it not; and betweene those, do what you will with it" (*Letters*, p. 19). These binarisms may be set roughly in parallel: as worldly life contrasts with death, body with soul, and the sensualist Donne with the pious Donne, so the unacceptably visible and vulnerable printed text contrasts with the unacceptably ephemeral burnt one. The work must neither accept a violent and premature death, nor participate fully in physical and social being.

This seemingly paradoxical request is actually quite consistent with Donne's other tactics in the battle for permanence. He is again seeking to put his intellectual legacy into the hands of an Other for safekeeping; and it is up to Carre, as it had been up to Donne's mistresses, somehow to lift him beyond the merely physical without quite causing him to go up in smoke. In preserving only manuscript versions of his writing, Donne reinscribes their essential personality; and in clinging to the middle ground of coterie publication, Donne seeks for his written legacy the paradoxical status that makes love immortal in works such as "Aire and Angels." Metaphysical poems must sustain some form of material being beyond what Donne's sermons call "*processio Metaphysica*, when thoughts proceed out of the minde; but those thoughts remain still in the mind within, and have no separate subsistence in themselves" (*Sermons*, V, 64).

Donne had earlier sent Carre "the Poems, of which you took a promise" (*Letters*, p. 18). Presumably this cache included lyrics—such as "The Canonization"—that, in unconventional ways, echo the conventional prediction that sonnets will both preserve and transcend the mortal lives of their subjects and authors. Such prophecies have a self-fulfilling quality, since the very act of reading them revives some trace of the poet's voice and mind (and those that have failed are never known to have failed). And even if they were to fail, Donne's dramatically occasional poems—by professing to care only about their immediate audience—may claim the same kind of *relative* immortality he hoped to share with his mistresses; as Freud argues in "On Transience," works of art may "crumble to dust, or a race of men may follow us who no longer understand the works of our poets . . . but since the value of all this beauty and perfection is determined only by its significance for our own emotional lives, it has no need to survive us and is therefore independent of absolute duration."[151]

"The Canonization" may be Donne's best-known tribute to true love; yet what the poem primarily attributes to love is its power to overcome death, a power that works only to the extent that love can be converted into poetry. The first stanza lists the various dangers more serious than love awaiting the speaker: why rescue me from love, he asks, when illness, age, or penury are likely to kill me sooner (2–3)? The second stanza compares love to the fatalities awaiting others: drowning, freezing, plague, and war (11–16). The third stanza turns from what might kill him to what might save him, relying on the *topos* of the phoenix (here a strategically exalted metaphor for sexual consummation) to suggest that love may be a demonstrable, palpable form of resurrection ("Wee dye and rise the same," 26).

And even if this love is death of a sort—the phoenix replaced by an urn, the fire by ashes[152]—the fourth stanza declares this kind of death gloriously "unfit for tombes and hearse" (29). It fits instead in the "pretty roomes" of "sonnets" (32). Love becomes a path to the immortality conventionally offered by art, the neat closure of which may serve to exclude rather than evoke death (28–34). As in "The Sunne Rising," the strategic self-deprecation of the opening becomes by the end a grandiose boast, as if to prove that his poetic conceits could transform the most extreme forms of subjugation and time-boundedness into the most lasting forms of triumph. The canonized lovers become not merely irrelevant to death; they become saints who receive and dispense immortality. God will preserve them as a model for lovers; the poem will preserve them as a self-sufficient work of romantic art that may be read outside of time (40–43). That atemporal reading—another exchange of love and meaning suspended between heaven and earth—will save author and reader alike. The "Canonization" becomes a reliquary designed to hold the self that exists in love, perpetually exempting it from putrefaction.

Donne's poetry takes on a more extensive reliquary function in his memorials to Elizabeth Drury, where he seeks to renew his own immortality as well as hers. His quest for short-term survival, by thus wooing Robert Drury as a patron, elides into a symbolic conquest of death. This quest encounters two obstacles familiar from Shakespeare's uneasy exploration of immortality *topoi* in his sonnets.[153] One is the suspicion that verse will prove an inadequate container for the full human being that death threatens to obliterate. The other is the recognition that eternity is as much the enemy of this mode of immortality as it is friend of Christian immortality. Poems, the paper they are written on, the language they are written in, are in constant danger of falling away into the same vasts of time that supposedly bring the general resurrection ever closer:[154]

> Can these memorials, ragges of paper, give
> > Life to that name, by which name they must live?
> Sickly, alas, short-liv'd, aborted bee
> > Those Carkas verses, whose soule is not shee.
> And can shee, who no longer would be shee,
> > Being such a Tabernacle, stoope to bee
> In paper wrap't; Or, when she would not lie
> > In such a house, dwell in an Elegie?
>
> ("A Funerall Elegie," 11–18)

In this first response to Elizabeth Drury's death, Donne turns the obstacles to advantage by displacing all the aspects of mortality from the eulogized corpse to the eulogy itself.

This elegy disguises the disastrous closure of her life story at age fourteen as a failure of closure in the narration of that story. Instead of conceding that Elizabeth Drury has fallen into oblivion, Donne can attribute the blank space to a *lacuna* in the narration of her potential biography:

> He which not knowing her sad History,
> > Should come to reade the booke of destiny,
> How faire, and chast, humble, and high shee'ad beene,
> > Much promis'd, much perform'd, at not fifteene,
> And measuring future things, by things before,
> > Should turne the leafe to reade, and reade no more,
> Would thinke that eyther destiny mistooke,
> > Or that some leafes were torne out of the booke.
>
> (83–90)[155]

"Future things," however, are measureless. As in "The Will" and the Harrington "Obsequies" (131–54), a disabled clock insinuates Donne's pious meditations on death, threatening to dissolve human chronology in endless waves of time:

> But must we say shee's dead? May't not be said
>   That as a sundred Clocke is peece-meale laid,
> Not to be lost, but by the makers hand
>   Repolish'd, without error then to stand. . . .
>
>   (37–40)

The resurrection will be a reassembly, and it will allow human measure to recapture the terrifying prospect of eternity: "for how so long a *day* soever thou make that *day* in the *grave*, yet there is no *day* between that, and the *Resurrection*" (*Devotions*, p. 76; cf. *Sermons*, VI, 273). But how can this disabled temporal creature know when its moment will come? Even if the Christian promise is fulfilled, how can the expired consciousness endure an interim that it will experience as identical to eternal annihilation? The question continues to haunt eschatology: Nietzsche writes that "Between your last moment of consciousness and the first ray of the dawn of your new life no time will elapse—as a flash of lightning will space go by, even though living creatures think it a billion of years and are not even able to reckon it."[156]

In "The First Anniversarie," Donne tries to escape this vertiginous temporal perspective by swerving to a safely general topic: the historical decay of human longevity. Despite this swerve, however, and despite the conventional moralizing it permits, Donne quickly becomes disoriented by the infinitesimal scope of an individual life in the incalculable span of eternity:

> Alas, we scarse live long enough to trie
> Whether a new made clocke runne right, or lie.
> Old Grandsires talke of yesterday with sorrow,
> And for our children we reserve to morrow.
>
>   ("First Anniversarie," 129–32)

Any single stroke in the cycle is—like a phoneme—meaningless. Except for the evanescent present moment, nothing but vague sorrow for the past and vague hope for the future gives us any temporal hold—a depressed version of Augustinian chronology. No wonder Donne is so eager for poetry to make an instant's passion an eternity, to stop the sun in the sky.[157]

"The First Anniversarie" concludes by making itself a model of the redemptive grave, one that will save Donne as well as Elizabeth Drury from oblivion:

Nor could incomprehensiblenesse deterre
Me, from thus trying to emprison her.
Which when I saw that a strict grave could do,
I saw not why verse might not doe so too.
Verse hath a middle nature: heaven keepes soules,
The grave keeps bodies, verse the fame enroules.

(469–74)

So Donne's poems are not merely *about* the desire to keep soul and body together; they are the only way to keep that "subtile knot" neatly tied. His Metaphysical mode strives to sustain a perpetual metaphysical suspension—above the fate toward which gravity steadily pulls the physical body, but below the ethereal abstractions of heaven. Only in that middle region is the individual meaningfully preserved.

"The Second Anniversarie," as the title indicates, reflects Donne's continuing need to control the overwhelming fact of death by parcelling time into installments.[158] Again Donne proposes that Elizabeth Drury and his memorial verse immortalize each other, and this time he explicitly subordinates the generational model of salvation to the authorial one:

my life shalbe,
To bee hereafter prais'd, for praysing thee,
Immortal Mayd, who though thou wouldst refuse
The name of Mother, be unto my Muse,
A Father since her chast Ambition is,
Yearely to bring forth such a child as this.
These Hymes may worke on future wits, and so
May great Grand-children of thy praises grow.
And so, though not Revive, embalme, and spice
The world, which else would putrify with vice.

(31–40)

This matches the conclusion of "The Canonization," except that the prospect of literary progeny replaces Donne's personal erotic investment. The closing couplet of "The Second Anniversarie" associates itself with the trumpet of First Corinthians, promising to raise the dead from corruption through the dictation of the risen Elizabeth Drury: "Thou art the Proclamation; and I ame / The Trumpet, at whose voice the people came."

Since she is clearly presented as the soul of the world, a female soul that has fled at death and left Donne trapped in the entropic realm of the physical, the death of Elizabeth Drury would seem to present Donne with the same problems as "The Dissolution." Yet the hyperbole and reiteration with which Donne endorses this metaphor suggests the release of massive psychological tensions, perhaps because he can now envision an escape from the trap of his sexual identity. Donne lavished on this virgin daughter a kind of worship that (Ben Jonson complained) seems apt only for the Virgin Mother. As Freud has demonstrated, the extreme admiration parents lavish on their children's attributes and achievements is largely a displacement of their own long-suppressed narcissistic needs, now safely disguised and socially endorsed as parental love. Among the many things going on in the Anniversaries, one is surely this kind of displacement; in paternally worshiping this "idea of a woman" (as Donne called it in response to criticisms like Jonson's),[159] Donne recovers his anima, a version of his soul prior to its corruption by apostasy, sexuality, and their accompanying cynicisms. The poems carry clear markings of Donne's characteristic efforts to preserve his unique inner self, only slightly displaced.[160] His praise of the dead girl's virginity may constitute a form of penitence for his own youthful indulgences, as if she were a patron saint of sexual purity who could bequeath a cure for his submissions to the frail flesh and the mortal consequences they comport.

In this sense, Jonson was right: Elizabeth Drury fills the place of the Virgin whose faith Donne abandoned along with his birth-mother. The morbid embrace of a magical daughter[161] brings this chapter back to the Freudian "Theme of the Three Caskets." While the prospects of patronage doubtless drew Donne to this example of mortality, that allure would have been augmented by the opportunity to elegize a human female who seemed as yet innocent of precisely the categories that linked women to death for him: physical mother, impure lover, the body in inevitable decay. Lacan and Kristeva postulate that language, particularly written language, serves as an escape from these same categories. In preserving Elizabeth Drury—whom he never met in body—as an incorruptible soul, in bringing her elaborately back to life in the annual rhythm of these anniversary poems, Donne could sublimate into piety all the self-(pre)serving functions of his erotic verse. This new symbolic way of investing his immortality in women—where formerly he projected his mortality—permitted Donne at last to cease repressing the recognition that his adult male self was trapped in a world of decay. Donne thus composed his own funeral elegies, as he would later compose (according to Walton) "his own funeral sermon."

MAGDALEN AS MOTHER: "PERCHANCE HER CABINET MAY HARBOUR THEE"

For Donne to make any meaningful progress against his own mortality, he must confront the "body of death" bequeathed to him by his mother, and by Eve, the mother of us all. He does so by finding alternative maternal figures who—precisely by their protectiveness, their Reformation theology, and their interest in poetry—represent a saving alternative to his birth-mother. These women provide a kind of appeals court in which he can challenge the conviction of mortal sin derived from his biological origins, by allowing him to live in the word, not merely in the flesh. Long before Freud offered his tripartite division of biological mother, chosen spouse, and the earth of burial, Donne's religion encouraged him to believe that he had "three births; one . . . we are borne of our naturall mother; one . . . we are borne of our spirituall Mother . . . and a third . . . we are borne of the generall Mother . . . in the Resurrection" (*Sermons*, VI, 135).

Lucy Harrington (Countess of Bedford) and Magdalen Herbert (mother of George Herbert) were powerful women, both firmly anti-Catholic, who fed Donne and took him into their houses. They evidently praised his accomplishments and used their disfavor to steer him back into good behavior when he began to stray. "Twicknam Garden" certainly suggests some oedipal tensions in his attraction toward Lucy, and his poems to Magdalen balance uneasily on the border between respectful filial admiration and courtly erotic desire. Of course these were metaphorical rather than literal mothers to Donne, but he seems to have preferred metaphorical to literal parentage; he desires to live as the sum of his interior being, not as the slave of his external form. Thomas Browne concedes that "in the midst of all my endeavours there is but one thought that dejects me, that my acquired parts must perish with my selfe, nor can bee Legacyed among my honoured Friends" (p. 138). Donne evidently feels the same regret, and therefore transmutes the procreative solution to mortality into a kind of apostolic succession, in which some aspect of the dead person's inward being, rather than merely the outward form, may be passed on.[162] Donne's verse letters appear to give this sort of moral re-incarnation—with poetry mediating the metempsychosis—more weight than the promises of Christ, the Incarnated Savior.

When Lucy's brother died, Donne composed an elegy that flirts with a cannibal theology in order to insist that this moral transmigration can overcome Heraclitan mutability:

> As bodies change, and as I do not weare
> Those Spirits, humors, blood I did last yeare,
> And, as if on a streame I fixe mine eye,
> That drop, which I looked on, is presently
> Pusht with more waters from my sight, and gone,
> So in this sea of vertues, can no one
> Bee'insisted on; vertues, as rivers, passe,
> Yet still remaines that vertuous man there was;
> And as if man feed on mans flesh, and so
> Part of his body to another owe,
> Yet at the last two perfect bodies rise,
> Because God knowes where every Atome lyes.
>
>   ("Obsequies to the Lord Harrington," 45–56)

The macabre vehicle of this comparison seems more important than its ostensible tenor, and it seems clear that Donne is more concerned with vindicating his own hopes of perfect resurrection than with soothing the sensibilities of a bereaved sister.

Donne's "Elegie to the Lady Bedford" associates her separation from her recently deceased friend Lady Markham with the separation between soul and body preceding the general resurrection: "She like the Soule is gone, and you here stay / Not a live friend; but th'other halfe of clay" (13–14). In suggesting that the material which "elemented" this unity becomes "spread in infinite" and then redeemed by the completion of a perfect circle (24–25), the poem is close kin to "Forbidding Mourning." In suggesting that their conjunction put "both rich Indies" of "spices" and "metalls" in one place (34, 33), it echoes "The Sunne Rising," which located "both the'India's of spice and Myne" (17) in the bedroom Donne shares with his perfectly beloved lover. The way the friends are "Pair'd like two eyes" (9) recalls "The Good-morrow." By deploying these metaphors against the losses of death, this "Elegie" makes explicit what I read as implicit in the poems ostensibly concerned with earthly heterosexual love. As Donne hopes his personal virtues will somehow transcend death in the consciousness of his lover, so he promises that Markham's virtues will survive undiminished in Bedford:

> So, to your selfe you may additions take,
>   But nothing can you lesse, or changed make,
> Seeke not in seeking new, to seeme to doubt,
>   That you can match her, or not be without;
> But let some faithfull booke in her roome be,
>   Yet but of *Judith* no such booke as shee.
>
> (39–44)

An immortal book takes the place of the dead friend, preserving her unique merits, and perhaps her name as well. Donne's own scripture seems to be the permanent residence of that immortal being.

In the closing lines of Donne's "Epitaph on Himselfe," he proposes to Lucy yet another complicated contract whereby his reciprocity with a woman will allow some essence of his character to survive:

> Heare this, and mend thy selfe, and thou mendst me,
> By making me being dead, doe good to thee,
>   And thinke me well compos'd, that I could now
>   A last-sicke houre to syllables allow.
>
> (21–24)

The pun on "compos'd" suggests that this immortal aspect of Donne's virtue is reflected in his verse as well as his character. By achieving a neat closure in the poem, he can preclude too definitive a closure of his mortal existence.

The speaker of "The Relique" imagines that a very personal kind of artifact—"A bracelet of bright haire about the bone" (6)—will mark him for affectionate recognition after death, sparing him the cruel anonymity that the *transi* figure threatens. Despite the decay of the corpse, something generated within mortal life still speaks eloquently of the self and its relationships; the poem, like the bracelet, preserves him from mortality. Literary history has uncannily endorsed this project: critics such as T. S. Eliot (in his seminal essay on "The Metaphysical Poets") have seized on this image of a skeleton still embraced by still-bright hair to characterize Donne's indelible individuality.[163] Such poetic conceits and images have kept the soul of his wit and the body of his work together.

"The Relique" begins with the dead rising, but it is a false alarm:

> When my grave is broke up againe
> Some second ghest to entertaine,
> (For graves have learn'd that woman-head
> To be to more than one a Bed). . . .
>
> (1–4)

This cynical parenthesis may suggest reciprocally that women, when they break the bonds of loving mutuality by infidelity, become the graves that swallow men into mortality. Again, what appears to be a gratuitous interjection of misogyny or morbidity in a Donne love-lyric proves deeply integral: it reflects his perpetual anxiety that, instead of assisting his immortality, women will prove the agency of his decay and annihilation. And if lines 17–18 imply that he will resemble Jesus, at whose tomb Mary Magdalen lingered ardently, then the fact that he is still rotting in his grave becomes (like the moldering gingerbread king of the "Farewell to Love") a very ominous bulletin about the prospects for resurrection:[164]

> If this fall in a time, or land,
> Where mis-devotion doth command,
> Then, he that digges us up, will bring
> Us, to the Bishop, and the King,
>   To make us Reliques; then
> Thou shalt be'a Mary Magdalen, and I
>   A something else thereby.
>
> (12–18)

In this self-aggrandizing way, Donne lends her his own consoling notion that "in the Grave we are bedded with" Christ (*Sermons*, VI, 358).

To avoid tainting his hopes for full immortality with the idolatrous Roman worship of relics practiced by his mother, however, Donne must exalt this relationship as spiritual rather than physical.[165] Though "A bracelet of bright haire about the bone" is sexually suggestive, it clings to its innocence as a symbol. The key revelation is that he has kept her at an erotic distance, as Jesus (unlike other men) did Mary Magdalen: "Difference of sex no more wee knew, / Then our Guardian Angells doe" (25–26). This resembles not only the relationship Donne claimed to have had with Magdalen Herbert, but also a suggestive passage in another sermon, in which God "is expressed in both sexes, man and woman; and all that can be ill in the love of either sex, is purged away, for the man is no other man then Christ Jesus, and the woman no other woman, then wisdom her self" (I, 239). Ordinarily a chaste relationship would seem an inadequate avatar of immortality for Donne, who is so concerned with bodily resurrection. But through his own Magdalen, Donne can be his own savior, because he has reconceived his immortality within the intelligence she admired in him, and the scripture she inspired in him.

Donne repeatedly converts Magdalen Herbert into a sort of maternal muse who carries both his verse and his soul toward eternal salvation. When he lauds her posthumously as *"best wife,"* *"best mother"* and *"best Friend"* (*Sermons*, VIII, 85), we may recall that he variously addressed her as a Platonic lover (in "The Relique"), a womb nurturing his poetry (in the verse letters), and a pious exemplar of the friendship that was his "second religion" (in a sermon). Donne could participate in the matrimonial and filial relationships only figuratively, but he often treated his figurations as a superior reality. At the close of this hagiographic sermon on her death, having described the way she transmitted her pious virtues to her actual children, Donne urges his congregation to inherit her virtues by the sort of re-incarnation I have been describing: "But if you wil wake her, wake her, and keepe her awake with an active imitation, of her *Morall*, and her *Holy vertues*" (*Sermons*, VIII, 93).

Read in retrospect from this sermon, Donne's earlier writings reflect various efforts to make himself Magdalen Herbert's spiritual offspring. What may have been an ongoing dialogue with this alternative mother, a plea for adoption, is still at moments legible as a sort of palimpsest of her morals on the pages of Donne's own writings. The sermon portrays her as the sworn enemy of exactly the sort of *"scoffers, jesters* in divine things" (*Sermons*, VIII, 86) that (we have seen) he himself had notoriously been prior to her influence. He describes her as "loving facetiousness, and sharpnesse of wit," but asks, "who ever heard her countenance a *prophane speech*, how sharpe soever, or take part with *wit*, to the prejudice of *Godlinesse*?" (*Sermons*, VIII, 86). When Donne writes of his poetry to his best friend, Henry Goodyer, he applies much the same standard: "I doe not condemn in my self, that I have given my wit such evaporations, as those, if they be free from prophaneness, or obscene provocations" (*Letters*, pp. 31–32).

244 DUELLING DEATH IN THE LYRICS OF LOVE

The poet whose "Of the Book" had concluded with his depressive
fear of "the darke eclipses" of mortality becomes the preacher who
remarks that Magdalen Herbert's "Occasionall *Melancholy* . . . never
Ecclipst, never interrupted her cheerfull confidence, and assurance in
God" (*Sermons*, VIII, 87). The poet whose "Extasie" compares the soul
uniting him with his lover to "A single violet transplant" that "Re-
doubles still, and multiplies" (37, 40), becomes a preacher comparing
her, in marriage, to "a flower that doubles and multiplies by transplantation." He even praises this older woman for marrying a younger man,
because the couple are somehow "twins of one hour" (*Sermons*, VIII,
88); in other words, he insists on discovering in her December-May
marriage a version of the miraculous mirroring he insisted on finding in
his own love-affairs.

In that same sermon, Donne lauds Magdalen Herbert for being so
attentive to her children, "proposing to her selfe, as her principall care,
the education of her *children*, to advance that, shee came with them, and
dwelt with them, in the *Universitie*; and recompenc't to them, the losse
of a *Father*, in giving them *two mothers*; her owne personall care, and the
advantage of that place" (*Sermons*, VIII, 87). Here again, Donne finds
an indirect way to claim her as his own mother, at least as the mother of
his intellectual being, by construing her as part of the alma mater that he
shared with her offspring.[166] Unable to pursue his full potential at
Oxford because of the recusancy inculcated by his biological mother, the
ambitious young man submitted himself to a powerful woman who was
a pillar of the proto-Anglican establishment. Probably the clearest
evidence that Magdalen Herbert might have served as this sort of
symbolic foster mother comes not from Donne's lyrics or sermons, but
from George Herbert's Greek poems commemorating her death:

> I mourn my mother, as well as other men
> Who do not make her now my clan's
> Especial guardian, but, since she was virtuous,
> Want her for their own mother.[167]

This from a poet who had watched his mother take John Donne under
her wing, and eventually into their household.

Donne's adoption of this other, Reformed mother may have been
eased by her association with a religion that believed in spiritual rebirth,
that favored revelations of the Word over legacies of the flesh. "In
Reformed theology [the Catholic] preference for the body over the text

is reversed," and the Reformed woman was typically pictured carrying a book.[168] Whatever nostalgia Donne felt for a more palpable connection evidently found expression in several safe forms, such as the painting of Mary Magdalen that apparently hung in his room, and the figuration of Magdalen Herbert as a version of the English Church, which Donne imagined as a mother who gives body to the words of Scripture, and breast-feeds its children when they are baptized in its faith.[169] In eulogizing Magdalen Herbert, Donne cannot resist contrasting her solid Anglicanism with the errors of those (such as his own mother) who "diverted towards the *Papist*, in undervaluing the *Scripture*" (*Sermons*, VIII, 89; see similarly VII, 120). Because Donne's verse letters to Magdalen Herbert thank her especially for valuing his writings, and depict her as their surrogate mother, that remark acquires some powerful resonances. Magdalen's valuing of his manuscript poetry seems intimately bound up with the Reformation valorization of the Scripture which his natural mother presumably opposed.[170] He once wrote to Magdalen that "I to my letters am rigid as a Puritan" (*Letters*, pp. 291–92), and she helped him reconceive himself as at once a man of letters and a man of the Word.

A painting of Mary Magdalene may have been "unusual decor . . . for a Protestant minister,"[171] but it makes perfect psycho-biographical sense if she was the figure authorizing his otherwise guilt-ridden shift from Catholicism to Protestantism. She provides a sort of maternal bridge between two incarnations, one as the bodily child of the Catholic Elizabeth Donne, the other as the piously born-again progeny of a Reformed Magdalene. Having left his own sins of the flesh behind, he could nonetheless continue loving the sight of this beautiful woman, if only as an image of the sublimation he had achieved: "For in the Book of Life, the name of *Mary Magdalen* was as soon recorded, for all her incontinency, as the name of the blessed Virgin, for all her integrity" (*Sermons*, VII, 153). A patron of Leonardo da Vinci's was obliged to evict a painting because he could neither overcome his erotic attraction to the figure it portrayed nor bring himself to erase her religious markings;[172] perhaps Donne retained his painting for the same reason. Unlike the women who had betrayed him in the past, her gaze offered a divine constancy; "As a well made, and well plac'd picture, lookes alwayes upon him that looks upon it; so shall thy God look upon thee. . . . " (*Sermons*, II, 237). Through this figure—the creature of words as Martha was of works, the creature whose passionate love mattered more than her failings of faith—he could construct a unified narrative of the self. Under her watchful, loving eyes, he could write himself at last into immortality.

Mary Magdalene was the only female saint to survive the first Anglican purge of Catholic idolatry, probably because her transition from loving Christ in the flesh to loving him in the Word supported a Protestant reading of theological progress.[173] As Donne himself asserts, physical contact is "that which Christ diverted *Mary* from, when after his Resurrection manifesting himself to her . . . Christ said to her, *Touch mee not* . . . that is, Dwell not upon this passionate consideration of my bodily, and personall presence, but send thy thoughts [to heaven] and contemplate mee there" (*Sermons*, VII, 267). Her miserable longing for the body of her beloved made the Magdalene a perfect figure for a sensual religion of transubstantiation and penance. But her conversion from this misguided search for the lost body of Jesus (like those in Protestant search-narratives such as Herbert's "Redemption" and Milton's "Lycidas")—conveniently parallel to her conversion from prostitution—made her an apt heroine for Reformation propaganda. It also would have made her an apt counterpart for Donne, who so often in the poems imagines eager autopsies and exhumations of his corpse, and so often in the sermons laments the prospective loss of his own body, and yearns for its return. Through the Magdalene figure he can subli-mate and exalt his narcissistic impulses. "The Relique" safely displaces his fixation on his own erotic body, his need to be loved beyond reason and beyond death, onto the timeless pious embrace of Magdalen Herbert, or at least of her hair; and, in fact, Mary Magdalene was sometimes depicted as wrapping the deposed body of Christ "gently in her hair, which was of surpassing beauty."[174]

Donne's sermon suggests that the reason Magdalen Herbert "contin-ued *twelve yeeres*" as a widow before remarrying was her determination to devote herself fully to her growing sons (*Sermons*, VIII, 88). The contrast to the alacrity with which Donne's mother twice remarried during his youth is unhappily suggestive; having extra fathers was probably poor recompense for the resulting distraction of his mother. Walton's report that Donne solemnly promised his children "never to bring them under the subjection of a step-mother"[175] suggests that Donne's own experience of step-parents was an unhappy one. Donne's poetic tribute to Magdalen Herbert when she eventually did prepare to remarry begins with fierce, oedipally-tinged ambivalence. The poem must choose between cremation and deterioration in a grave, as if the diversion of Magdalen's attention threatened Donne's poetic self—the "sonnes" she helped him make—with death:

> Mad paper stay, and grudge not here to burne
> > With all those sonnes whom my braine did create,
> At lest lye hid with mee, till thou returne
> > To rags againe, which is thy native state.
>
> ("To Mrs. M. H.," 1–4)

Anxiety about returning to his former state of social disadvantage resounds strongly in that last line.

A few lines later, the poem resounds with another regressive anxiety, seeking the maternal gaze that redeems life from the senseless oblivion of death:[176]

> But when thou com'st to that perplexing eye
> > Which equally claims *love* and *reverence*,
> Thou wilt not long dispute it, thou wilt die;
> > And, having little now, have then no sense.
>
> (13–16)

The pun on "sense" (as either meaning or sensation) links a loss of intellectual significance to a loss of phenomenological experience. Writing again becomes a surrogate for Donne's soul in its confrontation with mortality, and a woman's love—her receptivity to the visits of his extended soul—determines the prospects for eternal salvation. That Donne sounds more like George Herbert as the poem continues than in any other sustained piece of his verse is far from a mere coincidence:

> Yet when her warme redeeming hand, which is
> > A miracle; and made such to worke more,
> Doth touch thee (saples leafe) thou grow'st by this
> > Her creature; glorify'd more then before.
>
> Then as a mother which delights to heare
> > Her early child mis-speake halfe utter'd words,
> Or, because majesty doth never feare
> > Ill or bold speech, she Audience affords.
>
> (17–24)

In an indulgent Last Judgment, this maternal audience will afford his poems a kind of resurrection, figured here as nurturance in her private space: "Who knowes thy destiny? when thou hast done, / Perchance her Cabinet may harbour thee" (33–34).[177]

From such womb-like enclosures, an immortalized self can emerge. His poems to her may read like ordinary epistles of praise, but they take on the functions of Annunciation. As in "Of My Name in the Window," the woman's role is to make the words into human flesh; the "saples leafe" that was merely a written page must flow with life again. As Donne writes elsewhere, "Rhymes which never had / Mother, want matter" ("To Mr. B. B.," 23–24). The man who imagined that God "puts all the graines of thy dust into his Cabinet" to prepare for the general resurrection,[178] awaits a potentially eternal rebirth in the harboring "cabinet" of the woman who was (the next chapter will argue) both mother and God to George Herbert. In the love-lyrics, Donne construes women as body and himself as soul; in the sermons, he describes the body as "the Cabinet of thy soule" (*Sermons*, VII, 322). In another sermon Donne focuses on the promise that

where mans buried flesh hath brought forth grasse, and that grasse fed beasts, and those beasts fed men, and those men fed other men, God that knowes in which Boxe of his Cabinet all this seed Pearle lies . . . shall recollect that dust, and then recompact that body, and then re-inanimate that man, and that is the accomplishment of all. (*Sermons*, VII, 115)

The fact that Magdalen Herbert's attentions can cure precisely the fears of atomized selfhood Winnicott attributes to inattentive motherhood helps to confirm the psychoanalytic conjectures of this chapter, including the proposed link between Donne's experience of mother-love and his fears of divine judgment.

In his other verse letter to Magdalen Herbert, Donne again makes her into an agency of "The *Resurrection*," a creature who will (among the other goodness "Deliver'd of her") nurture his poetic immortality inside herself: "That they did harbour *Christ* himselfe, a Guest, / Harbour these *Hymns*, to his dear name addrest" (5–6, 13–14). Is Donne also, here as in "The Relique," addressing the implications of Magdalen's "dear name," and the miracles she supposedly worked against mortality? In the absence of such a good second mother, a symbolic rather than material mother, the self appears impossible to resurrect, and chaos is come again:

such a *Mother in Law* is the *Earth*, in respect of our *naturall Mother*; in her *wombe* we grew; and when she was delivered of us, wee were planted in some *place*, in some *calling* in the *world*; In the wombe of the Earth, wee *diminish*, and when shee is *delivered* of us, our *grave* opened for another, wee are not *transplanted* but *transported*, our *dust* blowne away with prophane dust, with every wind. (*Devotions*, p. 93)

As in the classic Freudian "family romance," a child fantasizes a more exalted legacy and dismisses its biological parents as mere step-parents.

Grierson has proposed that "La Corona," as well as "The Relique," was directed in tribute to Magdalen Herbert, and the close of the "Annunciation" sonnet of that sequence echoes Donne's hopes that he and this ideal woman can grant each other apotheosis:

> Ere by the spheares time was created, thou
> Wast in his minde, who is thy Sonne, and Brother,
> Whom thou conceiv'st, conceiv'd; yea thou art now
> Thy Makers maker, and thy Fathers mother,
> Thou'hast light in darke; and shutts in little roome,
> *Immensity cloysterd in thy deare wombe.*
>
> (23–28)

Magdalen becomes both Marys here, and in her cabinet—her casket, her womb—Donne again breeds some Metaphysical version of his immortal self immune to the vasts of time and space. Donne's earlier search for an immortalizing exchange of identities with his beloved subsumes the classic formula that closes Shakespeare's sonnet 18: "So long as men can breathe or eyes can see, / So long lives this, and this gives life to thee" (13–14). Now that promise outlasts earthly life: the Resurrection sonnet in "La Corona" boasts that "Feare of first or last death" shall not "bring miserie, / If in thy little booke my name thou'enroule, / Flesh in that long sleep is not putrified . . . " (77–79). Donne's "Of My Name in the Window" thus receives its explicit Christian translation.

Donne's salvational theology becomes more comfortable, and his erotic demands more benign, precisely when he manages to conflate the agency of immortality with a maternal love-object.[179] This conflation might also help to explain the uncharacteristic acceptance of aging and mortal time in Donne's "The Autumnall," which Walton (among others) plausibly associates with Magdalen Herbert. The sequence of italicized words in each stanza promises an escape from death and burial and decay, into the pious rebirth of resurrection. The poem is devoted less to praising a woman than to envisioning a process of bodily decay that does not finally kill the ability of the soul to love.

Donne's craving for romantic love—and he may not be alone in this—can be read as an effort to invent, confer, sustain, some metaphor of immortality within the span of human life. In seduction, he seeks not only physical pleasure, but also an object he can desire as limitlessly as he wishes to be desired, a consciousness that he can deem perfect so that its perception of his perfection can be trusted. When familiarity breeds contempt for a lover, when sexual boredom exposes the limits of the physical connection, Donne has little choice but to seek a new object, even though the change itself seems to invalidate his claim against mutability. Perhaps that is why the lyrics addressed to extraordinary women to whom Donne's attachment was probably not primarily or actively sexual are spared the manic-depressive swings between bravado and embitterment that mark the other love-poems. Donne's Metaphysical style reshapes the world, and in the process it invents for him an acceptable self, one with access to the experience of the body, but immune to its entropic destiny. A patroness such as Magdalen Herbert can help him create and inhabit that better universe without threatening its delicate narcissism, as erotic lovers threatened the fragile solipsism he paradoxically asked them to confirm. To live fully within the deathless metaphors he made, he needed someone to nurture them patiently into a fleshly form, and the Reformation provided metaphors that allowed him to imagine that possible; he could feed on "the milke of the word" (*Sermons*, II, 152).

Donne's changing strategies for combatting mortality follow the arc most biographers describe in his spiritual career as a whole. The changes also follow the course of oedipal development sketched by Freud, in which paternal prohibitions become internalized as guilt. In replacing his erotic fixation with a religious one, Donne ceases to seek immortality from the mutual affirmations of seduction, and turns instead to a merger with women's creative power. But in the process he submits himself to a judgmental patriarchal deity who threatens to nullify his powers of life. Donne's vengefulness, directed in the misogynistic lyrics against the women whose failures of reciprocity mirrored his fallible mortality, turns against heretics and his own sinfulness in the sermons and Holy Sonnets. Whatever anger he felt at whatever abandonment he had experienced, he turned first against women and against the men who guarded them; finally he turned it inward, identifying with the punitive godhead to whom his surrogate mother had already pledged her love.

In his love-lyrics, Donne battles the recognition I discern in Shakespeare's *Measure for Measure*, where sexuality, so commonly

sublimated and mystified, is exposed as itself a sublimation and mystification of an even more brutal evolutionary fact. Donne needs sexuality
to represent transcendence (of common mortality) rather than degrada-
tion (of the individual spirit); defiance, rather than capitulation, to
mortality. In his holy profession and holy writings, Donne battles the
suggestion I discern in Shakespeare's *Hamlet*, where fatal illusions fill
the human need to believe that life has ulterior meaning and a destination beyond the grave. By sublimating the ghostly father one level
deeper than Hamlet does, into a purely religious category, Donne can
imagine that following such a figure worshipfully into death is an
affirmation, not a cancellation, of his innermost being.

Christianity still offered the best hope for personal salvation—if
people could still be thoroughly faithful Christians, and if they could
imagine some prelapsarian version of themselves (as Donne perhaps
imagined in Elizabeth Drury) that God might choose to retrieve. But, if
I am correct, and if literature is any indicator of cultural pressures, then
Londoners at the turn of the seventeenth century were feeling increasingly obliged to fall back on secular methods of denying death, and
becoming increasingly dissatisfied with those methods—perhaps because revenge and procreation are essentially systems of substitution that
neglect the inwardness of individuals, a commodity of growing value in
that society.

Donne typically tells others how to feel and behave, primarily so he
can regulate his own unacknowledged anxieties. George Herbert typically does the opposite, wrestling with his own soul so that he can
console and reform his readers. Herbert recognized that part of his duty
as a Christian evangelist and apologist would be to trick the half-
materialized genie of Jacobean annihilationism back into its bottle.
With an air of effortlessness—perhaps enabled by a mother who successfully nurtured both his mortal body and his immortal soul—Herbert
wove the frayed strands of denial back into good cable. What poets such
as Donne admired and desired in their mistresses, Herbert could find in
his God: not only the beauty, but also the power of salvation. The
representation of God and sinner primarily as good parent and wayward
child in Herbert offers an alternative to Donne's supposition that
dialogue must be symmetrical and gendered to be redemptive. The
patriarchal heroics and erotics described in *Hamlet* and the *Songs and
Sonets* give way, in Herbert, to what might be called a matriarchal
alternative of nurturance. Refusing to exalt violent closure over continuation, either in form or in content, Herbert also refuses the tendency of

Hamlet and Donne to consider self-abnegating worship a last resort in a world otherwise terrifyingly empty of meaning. In *The Temple*, such worship is instead a first home that perpetually welcomes our return from the fallen world of mortality.

6

Word Without End
The Comforts of George Herbert's *Temple*

*And in this enumeration of [Donne's] friends, though
many must be omitted, yet that man of primitive piety,
Mr.* George Herbert *may not; I mean . . . the Author of
the* Temple *. . . in which by declaring his own spiritual
Conflicts, he hath Comforted and raised many a dejected
and discomposed Soul, and charmed them into sweet and
quiet thoughts.*

—Izaak Walton[1]

*Day and night I was upon the rack, lying down in
horrors and rising in despair. I presently lost all relish to
those studies I had been closely attached to, [but] with
Herbert's poems, gothic and uncouth as they were, I yet
found . . . my malady . . . never seemed so much alleviated as while I was reading him.*

—William Cowper[2]

*I find more substantial comfort, now, in pious George
Herbert's "Temple," which I used to read to amuse myself
with his quaintness—in short, only to laugh at—than in
all the poetry since the poems of Milton.*

—Samuel Taylor Coleridge[3]

These epigraphs all portray *The Temple* as a kind of euphoric tranquilizer relieving some severe but unspecified cause of depression. Modern Western culture has been in large measure shaped by our need to deny collectively our individual mortality—that is, to deny its inevitability, or its finality, or both. This need has been skillfully exploited, consciously and unconsciously, to enlist us in a variety of basic social projects, including war, worship, and procreation. The seductively pious lyrics of "The Church"—the lyric section of *The Temple*—boldly acknowledge that death is inevitable, in order to express the author's confidence that, for the faithful Christian, it will not be final. Herbert works ingeniously and relentlessly to dispel the anxieties attaching to closure. These poetic exertions indicate that such anxieties were indeed an epidemic threat among Herbert's Christian audience, in much the way that antibodies indicate exposure to a disease. Herbert offers a sort of Paracelsian cure: the reader absorbs poems that yield to, and then overcome, their own mortality. The terminal silence that becomes an occasion for heightened anxiety about annihilation in most Jacobean authors becomes in Herbert an occasion to celebrate, even demonstrate, the promise of Christian salvation, the redemptive renewal that faith or extrapolation allows us to perceive in the apparent blankness, the white space, that follows a physical ending. In the ending is a beginning, because the last human words—as if they were a human soul—are savingly assumed into the Word of God.

Herbert's lyric form thus recapitulates a standard Renaissance reply to a common Renaissance anxiety: "Let them feare death, who live without *Christ*," one Jacobean preacher proclaimed: "Christians dye not, but when they *please GOD* they are like Enoch translated unto *GOD*."[4] Another promised that "God then shall be our *Sanctuarie*, in whom we shall have joye and gladnesse without feare of ending."[5] The poems of "The Church" are these translations, these endless sanctuaries; and they offer incentives to Christian belief, because what looks like a concluding sequence proves to be part of an ongoing presence, what looks like a cessation proves to be a transfer of power to a comforting and everlasting Being who will allow our voices to blend into His. The closing couplet—associated in Renaissance drama with dying words[6]—becomes in Herbert's lyrics a marker of perfect reunion with God.

Herbert's persistence in this pattern suggests a strategic response to a specific anxiety in his culture. He offers heaven as an alternative, not to hell, but to mere termination. The eminent critic Joseph Summers echoes an assumption familiar from early commentators such as Walton and Coleridge through the latest historicist scholarship: namely, that Herbert's poetry can be properly read "only within the light of the ideas, beliefs, and conventions of early seventeenth-century England," and that primary among these cultural facts is the "wholeness of an earlier age's Christianity" which might be overlooked by our modern "secular culture."[7] While the importance of cultural context is beyond dispute, Summers's reading of that context is not. In any case, no absolute belief exists without the systematic exclusion of conflicting perceptions, and no culture can claim a "wholeness" of belief without leaving traces of its repressive strategies within that very claim. Those traces, in which the heterodoxy awaits recuperation, become increasingly visible as the repressive struggle becomes more urgent (as it did during Herbert's brief lifetime), and become increasingly legible as the culture reading them shifts to other systems of belief and consolation (as ours has partly done). What follows is an effort to define the dark shadow of Herbert's trustful Christianity by tracing the types of comfort he feels compelled to offer his audience.

DONNE AND HERBERT: REDEEMING RELATIONSHIPS

Donne once preached that death resembles poetic closure:

the force of the whole piece, is for the most part left to the shutting up; the whole frame of the Poem is a beating out of a piece of gold, but the last clause is as the impression of the stamp, and that is it that makes it currant.[8]

In the Christian model (as opposed to many Eastern religions, where escaping the cyclical business of life is itself the desideratum), the goal is not a stamping out but a stamping on, a judgment that marks the soul for renewed currency in heaven. Herbert follows out the logic of Donne's statement into an anti-closural poetic: his poems formally endorse the Christian idea that mortal endings are immortal beginnings.

Donne rehearses for death by parting from his beloved; Herbert does it by ending his lyrics. The parting shot of Herbert's "Artillerie" is typical: "I am but finite, yet thine infinitely" (32). The identical line could easily pass for the ending of a typical Donne love-lyric, a metaphysical plea for erotic fulfillment. What Donne seeks through intercourse with his mistress, Herbert seeks through an exchange with his deity, an exchange of Herbert's adoration for God's forgiveness. Where

Donne runs a thread horizontally between his eyes and those of his beloved, Herbert describes the uneven trade of his gratuitous words for God's efficacious ones as a vertical "Pulley." Donne's amorous "dialogue of one" ("The Extasie," 74) becomes "a supplemental society of two," as one critic describes "The Church"; Donne's sensual reciprocity becomes in Herbert what another critic calls a "reciprocity" of speech that metaphorically enacts "the redeeming bond of grace, in which sentience moves continuously in both directions between God and man."[9] The cure for mortal isolation that Donne seeks through the physical penetration of his mistress and the intellectual penetration of his reader, Herbert achieves more chastely through an inward catechistic exchange with God, reproduced as dialogue with the responding reader. Stanley Fish perceives this catechistic strategy as the very essence of *The Temple*, and formulates it as a logical analogy: "Reader : Herbert : : Herbert : God."[10] My point is that these relationships pertain to the defeat of closure as well as of ignorance: Herbert spares the reader from mere ending, as God spares Herbert.

Herbert repeatedly recasts the conventions of love-complaint into poems of spiritual frustration addressed to an elusive God. In Herbert's versions, however, the courtship and its narrative both end in a kind of redeeming capitulation that is neither conquest nor defeat. Stereotypical categories of male sexual aggression inform most Renaissance discussions of death: one must conquer it boastfully, or else suffer a mortifying negation. *The Temple* argues that this phallocentric approach, this linear and binary focus on final goals, tends to taint life with mortality-anxiety ("Death"), sexuality with performance-anxiety ("Love [III]")—and creativity with writer's block (the "Jordan" poems). Herbert obliges his lyric speaker to abandon misguided efforts to "pierce" God's ears with his will and his virtues (as in "Deniall"), proposing instead what might be described as a gynocentric model, replacing the desire for a single decisive ending with the satisfactions of an ongoing surrender to benevolence.[11]

Donne's compulsion to seek reassurance about his personal immortality in the transactions of sexual love appears to reflect a failure of the caretaker's gaze by which most children acquire their narcissistic faith. In the case of Herbert, usually so confident of the personal attention of a nurturant deity, the psychoanalytic critic can build on direct evidence of the poet's powerful attachment to his mother. Even for an early hagiographer such as Walton, that is where the story begins: "*George Herbert* spent much of his Childhood in a sweet content under the eye

and care of his prudent mother. . . . "[12] Magdalen Herbert's demeanor
toward her eldest son, Edward, after sending him to Oxford, sounds
remarkably like God's demeanor toward His human creatures throughout George Herbert's *The Temple*: "she continued there with him, and
still kept him in a moderate awe of her self: and so much under her own
eye, as to see and converse with him daily; but she managed this power
over him without any such rigid sournesse, as might make her company
a torment to her Child. . . . "[13] When Donne preached her funeral
sermon, he described her as particularly expert in dispelling the fear of
death:

> So her selfe, with her whole family . . . did, every Sabbath, shut up the day, at
> night, with a generall, with a cheerfull *singing of Psalmes*; This *Act of
> cheerfulnesse*, was still the last *Act* of that family, united in it selfe, and with
> *God*. . . . Truly, he that can close his eyes, in a holy cheerfulnesse, every night,
> shall meet no distemper'd, no inordinate, no irregular sadnesse, then, when
> *God*, by the hand of *Death*, shall close his eyes, at last. (*Sermons*, VIII, 86)

Aided by poetry and a cyclical ritual of renewal, the corporate family
could override the annihilationist anxieties surrounding closure and
darkness. Donne's sermon suggests that he watches that achievement—
the consoling spiritual unity of a family—with a predictable amalgam of
admiration and envy, like Milton's Satan gazing into a potentially
immortal Eden.

The Temple is proof that George Herbert learned from his mother's
example. In "Mattens," for example, he passes on to the reader this
maternally imbued faith that a provident God will follow every night
with a nurturant morning. The great mystery in the Protestant experience of God resembles the infant's no less wonderful and terrifying
mystery concerning the mother: as Herbert expresses it in "Mattens,"
what is this poor little mortal creature, "That thou shouldst it so eye, and
wooe, / Powring upon it all thy art, / As if that thou hadst nothing els
to do?" (10–12). This is the maternal godhead familiar from the writings
of Julian of Norwich, "a kind nurse that hath naught else to do but to
attend to the well-being of her child," a Jesus who feeds us from "his
blessed breast," and to whom we can say,

> "my most dear Mother, have mercy on me. I have made myself foul and unlike
> to thee; and I cannot or may not amend it but with thine help and grace." . . .
> For the flood of mercy that is his most dear blood and precious water is
> plenteous to make us fair and clean. . . . The sweet gracious hands of our
> Mother are ready and diligent about us.[14]

The God who is "ready there to catch / My morning-soul" in "Mattens" (2–3) reappears in Herbert's "The Glance" as a nearly transparent recollection of the caretaker who comes in the night to clean, feed, and comfort an infant needing all those services:

> When first thy sweet and gracious eye
> Vouchsaf'd ev'n in the midst of youth and night
> To look upon me, who before did lie
> Weltring in sinne;
> I felt a sugred strange delight,
> Passing all cordials made by any art,
> Bedew, embalme, and overrunne my heart,
> And take it in.
>
> Since that time many a bitter storm
> My soul hath felt, ev'n able to destroy,
> Had the malicious and ill-meaning harm
> His swing and sway:
> But still thy sweet originall joy
> Sprung from thine eye, did work within my soul,
> And surging griefs, when they grew bold, controll,
> And got the day.

(1–16)

As psychoanalytic theory would predict, the ability to weather the mid-life depressions stirred by mortality depends on the narcissism generated by that "originall" gaze of the provident caretaker. The similarity to Donne's God "who hath often looked upon me in my foulest uncleanesse" (*Sermons*, V, 266) is clear enough, but so is the contrast: what Donne primarily remembers about this gaze is his abysmal misery when it turns away, a misery he associates with unredeemed death. To win the love of God and "the grace of his lips," according to Donne, you must never "lock up your door till you have carried out your dust; never to shut your eyes at night, till you have swept your conscience, and cast your foulness into that infinite sea of the blood of Christ Jesus" (*Sermons*, I, 205). Though critics who make absolute and contradictory assertions about Herbert's political and doctrinal inclinations may accord in condemning as hopelessly speculative my attention to these far less contingent aspects of his experience, the conjecture still seems worth offering: perhaps the same infant bodily needs that made Herbert feel unreservedly forgiven left Donne tainted with a guilt that he translated into a harsher deity.

As E. Pearlman has forcefully argued,[15] Herbert grew up in a family characterized by an extreme polarity of conventionally masculine and feminine traits and occupations. The masculine stereotypes were claimed by his brothers, apparently following their father, who had "a manly or somewhat stern look" and a tendency to battle with mobs.[16] The brothers' lives reportedly comprised an astonishing catalogue of duels, single combats, and general martial fortitude. These stories appear in the rather fanciful and egotistical autobiography of Edward Herbert, who was not only a Metaphysical poet in the mode of Donne, but also a founding father of the deism that bred Enlightenment-style atheism. Voltaire identified Edward Herbert as "one of the first . . . who had the daring to stand up, not only against the Roman Church, but also against the Christian Church."[17] This may be an exaggeration, but there can be little doubt that George Herbert built his pious submissiveness against a variety of contrary pressures. Opting out of the emulative rivalry among his brothers, George chose to identify instead with conventionally feminine virtues: neatness, humility, frailty, piety, domesticity, artistry.[18]

From the ages of three to fifteen, Herbert had no father; then his mother—Magdalen Herbert, by all accounts a person of extraordinary strength, charm, and maternal attentiveness—married a man much closer to her son's age than her own, a man named John Danvers. Herbert himself remained single until his late thirties; then, two years after his mother's death, he married a relative of his step-father, a woman named Jane Danvers. The poet could hardly have overlooked the virtual homonym. Jane had no children during her marriage to Herbert, but did with her subsequent husband. In other words, Herbert fits the pattern of a man whose primary attachment to his mother—involving identification and a deeply conflicted eroticism—impairs some of the functions of conventional masculinity.

To discern this pattern in the biographical fragments is not to reduce Herbert's poetry, his religion, or even his sexuality to a single psychopathological reflex (nor is it to imply that conventional masculinity is necessarily better than some other kind). But these suggestive facts do lend extra weight to Herbert's remarkable emphasis on breast-feeding as a metaphor in his early writings, and cast new light onto works such as "The British Church," which anxiously describes religion as a mother who sometimes mistakenly presents herself either as a meretricious (Roman) Whore of Babylon or a naked (Puritan) ingenue.[19] Herbert sees his mother through a glass darkly, and recognizes his deity. The Christian God allowed Herbert to displace an oedipally dangerous mixture of filial and erotic feelings.

It is hardly surprising, then, that Herbert's poetic mission should feature so prominently an urgent and explicit determination to sublimate expressions of sexual desire into expressions of Christian piety: *eros* into *agape*. Nor, from this perspective, is it surprising that Herbert concludes a poem commemorating Magdalen Herbert's death by describing her as the source of both his mortal physical birth and his eventual rebirth into Christian immortality: "By you I was born into this world; by your example I am born into the other. You are twice a mother to me."[20] Here is a man who indeed believes that he ends at his beginning, that the savior who renews him at death is indistinguishable from the woman who bore him into mortality.

In the Holy Sonnet "Since She Whom I Lovd," Donne says that he was led to God by his wife;[21] Herbert was no less clearly led by his mother. Donne's model of divine love manifests all the heat and instability of adolescent sexuality; Herbert's God is nurturant, and his Magdalen is an erotic object miraculously transformed into an avatar of the Virgin Mother, who comforts him in a primal scene that seems to conflate a pietà with breast-feeding, a death scene with the renewal of earthly comforts. In another Latin poem, Herbert imagines competing for "access to [Christ's] breast, I claim the milk mingled with the blood."[22] In Communion, a sacrament which drew Herbert's special approbation, transubstantiation becomes a safely imperfect decoding of his sublimation.

At times this association—between the mother who first fed him and the God he hopes will finally save him—may have become too explicit for Herbert's own comfort. In "Longing" he strives to re-establish the orthodox priorities:

> Mothers are kinde, because thou art,
>   And dost dispose
>   To them a part:
> Their infants, them; and they suck thee
>   More free.
>
>   (14–18)

The mother nurses on God, the son on God in her. In constructing the final version of *The Temple*, moreover, Herbert omitted a poem called "Perseverence" which (after the speaker worries that his sins may forbid him to "wedd" his savior) depicts the penitent sinner as something very like that savior's suckling infant:

Onely my soule hangs on thy promisses
With face and hands clinging unto thy brest,
Clinging and crying, crying without cease
    Thou art my rock, thou art my rest.

(13–16)

The hand that rocks the cradle truly rules this world.[23]

"Love (III)," the final poem in "The Church," provides a culminating instance of Herbert's gynocentric eroticism, the ongoing surrender to benevolence I have contrasted to Donne's erotic *agon*. Perhaps the argument among critics over whether to read sexuality into the penetrations and tastings of this poem can best be resolved by recognizing that Herbert's own ambivalences toward the maternal body suspend the poem between the two alternatives. The sexual aspect of desire is necessarily both present and unacknowledged as he imagines yielding to the limitless kindness of this nurturant creature who made him ("Who made the eyes but I?" 12), consenting finally to taste her flesh.[24]

It might be objected that such modern psychoanalytic categories are inapplicable to a Jacobean family, but surely a nursing infant's experience is so primal that the burden of proof falls on those who would claim both that culture intervenes powerfully in that transaction, and that its mode of intervention in a behavior older than the species has shifted radically in the past few centuries. Herbert's persistent association of salvation with breast-feeding is strong evidence, instead, of a continuity with the patterns explicated by Melanie Klein and contemporary object-relations analysts. The preceding chapter offered some historical reasons to suppose that Herbert would have been nursed by his mother, and more direct and compelling evidence appears in his poems on his mother's death: "Your breasts, composed of air, untrue to me your child with an open mouth—are these what I possess? Cursed be the cloud weighed down with rain, not milk. . . . Begone, you ghost."[25] But the use of a wet-nurse would not eliminate the profound link between the infant's early feeding experiences and its sense of its place in the universe. Nor would changing social conventions likely alter the regressive character of Herbert's desire for a pre-linguistic—literally, "infant"—harmony with his creator. On behalf of this harmony, Herbert often surrenders the verbal form of his poem in order to replace it with a musical form that forestalls any ominous terminal silence— again, replicating a bonding ritual he evidently shared with his mother.[26]

In a sense, Herbert was as determined as Donne to expand, represent, and preserve the ego; he merely had a less boastful, less idiosyncratic way of making the universe a part of his own consciousness. As Summers observes, "For Herbert, Christianity provided the means of giving order and universal significance to his personal experience."[27] The fact that Herbert experimented with self-consuming verse forms does not necessarily demonstrate the self-annihilating impulse Stanley Fish deduces.[28] Instead, Herbert was able to find in the doctrines and rituals of his church, and the anti-closural devices of the poems that reflect them, a safe context for relaxing his grip on the mortal self. Even when Herbert is reluctant to save himself by eating, a voice coaxes him, as at the end of "Love (III)." When he is afraid to yield to regenerative sleep, he feels loving eyes watching him until he trusts their protection, as at the end of "Even-Song" and "Death."[29] When, in exhaustion and petulance, Herbert despairs of reaching an important destination, he can rely on being carried, as at the end of "The Pilgrimage." When he rebels in an escalating tantrum against the constraints on his desires, a call of "Childe" brings him safely back into obedience, as at the end of "The Collar."[30] If all these instances evoke the image of a boy testing the vigilance and resourcefulness of parental protection, the correlation may not be merely coincidental. Herbert's primary faith is in a provident maternal deity, and he repeatedly lets go of the living ego to prove that he will not be allowed to die, that "thou art ready there to catch / My morning-soul" ("Mattens," 2–3).[31] The Fall of Man can be rendered as harmless as the stumble of a loved child.

As Donne approaches closure, he usually finds himself alone on the brink of death; as Herbert approaches closure, he finds himself back in his mother's embrace. Donne struggles to tame death by focusing on it intently; Herbert instead brushes death aside by construing it as a milder echo of birth, as a transitional moment surrounded by life. In contrast to the fierce morbidity of Donne's preacherly role, Herbert's long treatise, *A Priest to the Temple, or, The Country Parson*, makes virtually no mention of either the funerals that must surely have engaged a large share of a parson's energies, or the *memento mori* themes that dominated the preaching of most of his contemporaries.[32]

Nor does Herbert seem eager here to confront the forces of disbelief; he comments parenthetically that "disputation is no Cure for Atheisme."[33] But, as the first stanza of the first part of *The Temple* asserts, "A verse may finde him, who a sermon flies" ("The Church Porch," 5). That principle may apply to Herbert's own confrontation with annihilationism: the role of poet permits him an advantageous release of the anxious energies accumulated in his role as priest. The dynamics of his lyric sequence systematically refute death and atheism, allowing him to confront boldly the very issues he evades in his clerical office.

My study of Donne's poems began with "The Good-Morrow." My study of Herbert's begins with the implicit revision of "The Good-Morrow" contained in "The Temper (I)." At the core of Donne's poem—indeed, in its central line—is the assertion that the presence of the beloved "makes one little room an everywhere" (11). The resolution of Herbert's poem—in its final line—is the recognition that his loving trust and God's powerful love together "Make one place ev'ry where" (28). What Donne seeks in the middle of his life (and poem) from a sexual counterpart, Herbert seeks at the end of his life (and poem) from a divine complement. Donne concludes that, if he and his mistress "Love so alike that none do slacken, none can die" (21); Herbert denies that such constancy can be achieved even in relation to God. Herbert thus characteristically confronts the fear that Donne's erotic megalomania evades, namely, that mortal endeavors may be swallowed up by an infinite universe:

> Although there were some fourtie heav'ns, or more,
>   Sometimes I peere above them all;
>   Sometimes I hardly reach a score,
>   Sometimes to hell I fall.
>
> O rack me not to such a vast extent;
>   Those distances belong to thee:
>   The world's too little for thy tent,
>   A grave too big for me.
>
> ("The Temper [I]," 5–12)

Both poets thus confront a basic problem, perhaps the basic problem that culture and human intimacy help us resolve on this side of insanity (by resolving it on this side of infinity). Lacking an Other who gives the Self a measure of worth, a sense of place, and a moment in (or out of) time, a human being would be utterly overwhelmed by the universe. Though the new "tuning of my breast" (23) Herbert requests is performed by faith rather than science, these poems emerge from the same Renaissance crisis that made astrology important "because it offered the reassurance of identifying with a circular destiny, solidary of a solid and visible cosmos whose eternal movements were known"; the same crisis produced a "vogue of astronomical clocks" by which the passage of time could be "transformed into spatial perspective," a perspective that was linked in turn to musical forms in which "duration or succession is replaced by simultaneity."[34]

"The Temper (I)" exposes the bravado of Donne's romantic solution to this cosmic agoraphobia. The distances are now immeasurably greater than those covered by Donne's "sea-discoverers," and the time-span dwarfs even Donne's hyperbolic comparison to "the seaven sleepers'" long repose (12, 4). Where Donne boasts of sustaining endlessly an ideal state of physical union with a mortal beloved, Herbert prays for a perpetual spiritual union with God. Donne's resolution had been to make his mistress the center of a sufficient—indeed, paradisal—universe; Herbert's solution is to hope that God, the being whose center is everywhere and whose circumference is nowhere, will become his lover and beloved.[35] The shrinking of the lines within each stanza reflects submission to the divine embrace.

PROTECTIVE CUSTODY: "A DAINTIE LODGING"

The theme of enclosure in Herbert's poetry has generally been thought to express an orthodox belief that the soul must escape the sinful body and gain the paradoxical freedom of pious restraint.[36] But what is consoling as theology—nothing can harm him "While the inclosure is thine ARM," Herbert asserts in "Paradise" (6)—proves equivocal as psychology. The agoraphobia of an infinite universe can quickly give way to the no less terrifying claustrophobia of a grave. As Herbert writes in "Mortification," a person's house is a "dumbe inclosure" that "maketh love / Unto the coffin, that attends his death" (23–24). The grave may prove to be a "dungeon" rather than a "house," as in "Grace" (6); a quarry of mere residual dregs, as in "Nature"; a "poore cabinet of bone," as in "Ungratefulnesse" (28); or a mere sin-filled box, like the heart in "Good Friday." Sometimes, as in "Confession," the nightmarish regress of boxes within boxes separating the speaker from God seems to demand a Houdini. As death and closure converge on his mortal body and his poetic voice, Herbert becomes an escape-artist, while the spectators squirm empathetically in their seats.

Yet, as the first great modern editor of *The Temple* comments, and as "The Temper (I)" confirms, "Herbert often shows a fear of unlimited space and loves the shelter of an enclosure."[37] If he is no longer oppressed by the constraints of the body and its burial, what is Herbert so afraid of? The answer is, everything. If the "Collar" of pious restraint constricts his visual aperture as well as his moral conduct ("While thou didst wink and wouldst not see," 26), then to rebel recklessly against it threatens not only his piety but his sanity as well, by offering him a glimpse of the infinite. Is there any sustainable middle setting between accepting the tunnel-vision of our mundane enterprises and confronting the devastating face of God? A person may go on "schooling his eyes" ("Mortification," 22), hiding from the universe in a nutshell, but we all have (as Hamlet says) bad dreams. Human beings need psychological enclosure for protection from the dizzying and demoralizing scope of the universe we inhabit, no less desperately than we need physical enclosure from the harsh forces of nature; we can be destroyed by exposure. Our cognitive development necessarily involves a deliberate ignorance of imponderable or unmasterable realities, and a narrowing of the spectrum of sensual input so that we can establish the categories without which we could not truly perceive at all, only dazzle—the glorious danger that propels Thomas Traherne's descriptions of childhood wonderment in his "Centuries," and lends Baldwin's *Beware the Cat* its sinister fascination.[38]

Avoiding such overload is the psychological aspect of the imperative which critics such as Robert Higbie have generally read theologically, as the promise that "if man accepts the limits God sets him, the contents of his mind will have value." Higbie observes that Herbert, though not exactly "hostile to the power of reason . . . seems to feel the need to limit it, to create some sort of wall in his mind, to keep it under lock and key."[39] Higbie attributes this reaction to an orthodox Christian mistrust of fallen, prideful intellection, but perhaps it reflects a blasphemous suspicion that any truly open-minded evaluation of the human situation would breed madness. To climb the Tower of Babel and not find a heaven would induce both vertigo and despair; it is a long way down, and there is nowhere else to go. A loss of boundaries—even if they were only arbitrary ones—makes Herbert "A wonder tortur'd in the space / Betwixt this world and that of grace" ("Affliction (IV)," 5–6), just as the morbid Hamlet finds himself miserably "crawling between earth and heaven" (3.1.128–29), and the morbid Donne tortures language into yielding him a metaphysical middle ground.

The constraint of an eternal tomb and the boundlessness of a godless universe are equally horrifying. So the poems themselves must both refute and restore closure.[40] Heaven—its confines and its hierarchy—offers the only alternative to an infinite scattering of the bodily dust and a permanent dissolution of the individual soul. The catacomb becomes a honeycomb: the nurturant "hive" of Herbert's "Home" (20) or "cupboard" of his "Providence" (49). The "chest of sweets" that became "winding sheets" in "Mortification" (2, 5) are neatly folded back into sweetness.

Human beings can imitate and anticipate that redeeming kind of containment through pious artistic structure. The music in church provides in itself a "daintie lodging" that leads to "heaven's doore" ("Church Musick," 4, 12); and the "closes" of Herbert's own poetic music ("Vertue," 11) can similarly offer the "stay against confusion" that Robert Frost (among others) has defined as poetry's essential gift to human morale in an age of deteriorating religious belief. If it is true that "Herbert makes poetry an enclosed epitome of the world and an incarnation of paradise,"[41] it may be because the lyric form generates an object enclosed and yet infinite, empowered and enlivened by its very constraints. When Herbert's immortal longings take on earthly forms, they enact the salvational process they celebrate.[42] If the structure of *The Temple* as a whole "may be called LEITOURGIA, a pattern of worship" divisible "into the liturgy of time and the liturgy of space,"[43] we must also notice that the individual poems are often *technopaignia*, with their implied worship of pattern as it tames time and space. These tightly designed, seemingly playful lyrics provide extreme examples of an essential function of the lyric: to sit on the page as an example of how linear human experience can overcome temporal sequence, if it achieves the virtue required to capture the eye and ear of an ideal reader. These poetic games are presumably what Coleridge initially found laughable about Herbert's verse; but, as the aging Coleridge discovered, they help to control a serious anxiety.

The first thing one encounters upon entering Herbert's "Church" is his "Altar," a sort of spiritual prosthesis Herbert trusts will speak for him if he should lose his capacity for prayer: "if I chance to hold my peace, / These stones to praise thee may not cease" (13–14). The poem thus acknowledges its function as a defense against terminal silences. Having his prayer carved into a sacred shape redeems it from the linear aspect of human utterances that doom them to ending, even as God's reshaping—"altaring"—of his heart will redeem the speaker from the fatally linear aspect of human life. Unlike the ordinary forms of verbal art, sculpture has no end-point; it achieves wholeness rather than extinction at the point of completion. By abjuring pride of creation, Herbert can further evade the pressures of closure.[44] The poem seeks, not to be flawed (like certain Asian artworks whose makers maim them as a gesture of pious humility) but to be temporarily incomplete. It reaches beyond its apparent boundaries, both for renewal (since the word "Sacrifice" in the penultimate line anticipates the following poem's title), and for a timeless fulfillment (since it looks forward to the communion table of "Love (III)," which will end the lyric sequence). The building of this "Altar" serves as a model for the defense Herbert constructs in assembling "The Church" as a whole, a sanctuary against the sentence of annihilation that haunts temporal human existence.[45]

A slightly different carving trick dictates the shape of "Paradise": within each tercet, the rhyme-word keeps losing its first letter. Clearly there is a suggestion of Adam and Eve pruning their own Paradise, but the final stanza makes this pattern of diminishment a model for the benevolent pruning performed on all Christians to prepare them for salvation, for finishing their lives in a new beginning, however decisively it may look like an END:

> Such sharpnes shows the sweetest FREND:
> Such cuttings rather heal than   REND:
> And such beginnings touch their   END.
>
> (13–15)

We arrive at this overdetermined closure only to discover—to our relief—that it is already compromised, both by its association with beginnings, and by the suggestion that it was there all along, present outside of time and waiting to be discovered. This subversion of the poem's apparent sequence assures us that the Divine presence transcends chronological events and the losses they appear to cause. Donne's unstable religious poetry suggests that any assurance about salvation must be repeatedly hard-won through the speaker's anguish and hard-sold to us through the voice of a preacher. Herbert's poetic constructions gradually reveal their solid foundation: the speaker's delight both in God and His gift of poetry become more manifest as extraneous conceits and letters are snipped away, and we approach the END.

"Coloss. 3.3" links its own poetical progression to a pilgrim soul's progress. By fusing poetic gimmickry and scriptural glossary, the poem

formally enacts the timeless grace overseeing the speaker's migration
through time toward death:

Our life is hid with Christ in God

My words & thoughts do both expresse this notion,
That *Life* hath with the sun a double motion.
The first *Is* straight, and our diurnall friend,
The other *Hid* and doth obliquely bend.
One life is wrapt *In* flesh, and tends to earth.
The other winds towards *Him*, whose happie birth
Taught me to live here so,   *That* still one eye
Should aim and shoot at that which *Is*   on high:
Quitting with daily labour all   *My* pleasure,
To gain at harvest an eternall   *Treasure.*

The divine Word—the excerpt from Scripture stretched at an angle
across Herbert's words—thus accompanies the speaker throughout his
lifetime, finally manifesting its ultimate bounty. The same Word also
saves the poem, giving the last word (after a minimal white-space) to a
Testamentary speaker who can sustain it forever. The poem, like "Life"
itself, has "a double motion," and in provoking its own retrospective
rereading, it refutes a tragically linear view of life. Playing off Augustinian notions of double time,[46] Herbert juxtaposes mortal sequence with
perpetual presence. Artistically, biographically, and theologically, death
becomes salvation. What is buried at the bottom of the poem, what
finally rises to view, is not a corpse but a living and "eternall *Treasure.*"

HIS MASTER'S VOICE:
"GOD DOTH SUPPLIE THE WANT"

In many other, less markedly contrived poems, Herbert's
last words belong to God. Herbert thus obeys his own recommendation
in *The Country Parson* that the preacher make "many Apostrophes to
God, as, Oh Lord blesse my people, and teach them this point; or, Oh
my Master, on whose errand I come, let me hold my peace, and doe thou
speak thy selfe."[47] Instead of seeking static integrity, as the pattern
poems sometimes do, these poems accept the self-effacement necessary
for admission to the divine sanctuary. As the soul (according to
Herbert's "The Flower") must overcome its narcissistic craving for
personal immortality, so must the poetic voice. The ability—and humility—to "copie out" the simplest word from God's book redeems both

the poet and his poem from the ending that is annihilation; the *imitatio Christi* becomes a redemptive act of plagiarism.[48] Copying becomes the ultimate achievement and explicit goal of the poem—I say "goal," because it is usually the opposite of a conclusion. To elicit a saving intervention, the voice of "The Church" must always acknowledge its own inadequacy, just as the speakers must avoid Pelagian impulses and, in a mortified Protestant spirit, let a divinity shape their rough-hewn ends. Anything else is not "a crown of praise" (the last words of "A Wreath") but a Tower of Babel.

"A True Hymne" argues that poetic success can be measured only by the piety it expresses and inspires. Technical skill may have its place, the poem asserts in its final lines, but

> if th' heart be moved,
> Although the verse be somewhat scant,
> God doth supplie the want.
> As when th' heart sayes (sighing to be approved)
> *O, could I love!* and stops: God writeth, *Loved.*
>
> (16–20)

This amendment validates the assertion in the moment of making it. Nothing more needs to be said, because the brief intervention of divine authorship both endorses and perfects a poetic effort whose voice has become, in several senses, passive. If "the soul unto the lines accords" (9–10), then the speaker's soul meets its end in a state of grace.

Herbert's "The Sacrifice" ends with Christ meeting His end:

> But now I die; now all is finished.
> My wo, mans weal: and now I bow my head.
> Onely let others say, when I am dead,
>   Never was grief like mine.
>
> (249–52)

One editor assures us that "the speaker throughout is Christ,"[49] but in this closing line, the poet's own words plausibly unite across time with Christ's endless ones, which have all along been in a continuing present tense. The line is invisibly double-struck on the page, to the extent that the grieving Herbert is among those "others." By recording this timely and timeless answer to the rhetorical question that ends the previous stanzas—"Was ever grief like mine?"—Herbert promptly responds to Christ's request. By rendering prophecy and fulfillment simultaneous, the poem evokes the atonement of the soul with its Savior at the (literally) crucial moment of ending. The speaker's words, like his salvation, come from the body of Christ, and will be repeated forever by the body of Christian believers.

"The Sacrifice" appears to reverse Herbert's usual pattern: most of the poem is spoken by the Savior, and the human persona shares only in the closing words. But which voice the poem chooses to track in the perpetual dialogue of humanity and divinity is less important than the ultimate union of those two voices, which dispels the closural anxiety of death enough to allow the poet to finish his lyric.[50] Herbert's penitent grief remains perpetually present to Christ's perpetual suffering. By providing this last reflexive sympathetic response, Herbert's speaker precludes the available vengeful reading of these last words; if Christ's killers are already sorry, then he need not tell them that they will be. The burden of guilt imposed by Christ's sacrifice becomes the refrain of a song the sinner shares with his savior—as Herbert shared pious songs with his mother—to dispel the terrors of their shared mortality.

The anticipation of a saving divine voice applies equally to the poem and the speaker in "The Method," which chronicles a struggle for reconciliation with God—a reconciliation joyfully achieved (where it is most badly needed) in the poem's final line. As in Herbert's other complaint poems, the speaker must move beyond his accusation that "God refuseth still" (2) and blame instead his own failure to "look" toward or "heare" the divine good (13, 27); God will cure blindness and silence—in other words, oblivion—if humanity will let Him. The conscientious readiness to read creates a blank page on which God Himself writes, just as the readiness to listen in the final lines of "Deniall" creates a silence in which God Himself speaks. The poem's speaker reminds himself: "Seek pardon first, and God will say, / *Glad heart rejoyce.*" And so it has been said. We cannot tell whether those italicized words come directly from God (their first cause) or through the speaker's hopeful voice (as an efficient cause), and really we need not choose: the distinction is, happily, without difference. In this sense, "The Method" is the same story as "The Sacrifice," told from the human side. The benevolent divine voice has always been present, needing only the subsiding of the speaker's cacophonous self-will to become audible. As the mystic Jacob Boehme wrote at about the same time Herbert composed *The Temple,* if a man can "remain quiet for an hour or less in his inner self-will and

speaking, then the divine Will might speak into him."⁵¹ The loss of that
will and its worldly values is life rather than death.

Even when God does not appear to speak for himself, he lends the
poet a redeemed voice in which to complete his verse, a tonic note that
gives health and fulfillment to both the soul of the speaker and the form
of the poem. The human voice can be made an echo of God's voice, as
our bodies are made in His image. The only price of this blessing, as a
citizen says to Shakespeare's Coriolanus, is to ask it kindly: a small price,
perhaps, but one with large implications for the doctrine of irresistible
grace. As Herbert himself writes in *The Country Parson*, "The thrusting
away of his arme makes us onely not embraced."⁵²

In the last stanza of "Nature" the struggling speaker asks God to write
a saving ending directly onto his wayward spirit, to edit his spiritual
tombstone into a tablet of commandments:

> O smooth my rugged heart, and there
> Engrave thy rev'rend law and fear;
> Or make a new one, since the old
>   Is saplesse grown,
>   And a much fitter stone
> To hide my dust, then thee to hold.
>
> (13–18)

The echoes of "The Altar" (as well as of the Bible) are clear enough, but
this time the speaker wants his heart to be reshaped into something *less*
concrete, to reassure him that new life will sprout from his desiccated
inward grave. Otherwise his soul might "turn to bubbles straight, / And
thence by kinde / Vanish into a winde" (9–11). God's engraving will be
an ungraving: the words will change the lifeless structure back into flesh.
What lies in unredeemed closure at the end of this poem corresponds
only to the speaker's body. What is beyond nature remains beyond
"Nature," gratifyingly outside the limits of both the tomb and the
poem. God will hold Herbert, if Herbert can be made worthy to hold
God.

The saving relationship proves even more dialogic than might appear
from this description: to save the speaker and the poem, God must
undergo the same kind of change they request for themselves. The
death-bound physical aspect of human existence, and the mortal flaws
reflected in the uncorrected verse, correspond to the Old Testament
covenant. Herbert and his words can escape closure only because the

Incarnation spared God's Word from the same fate. The antecedent of "new" and "old" in line fifteen is strategically ambiguous: God will make a smoother new heart in Herbert only by making a less fearsome new law for judging that heart. Until it is revised, the letter kills.

Noting in himself the signs of advancing age, the speaker of "The Forerunners" recurs repeatedly to some words from the Psalms—"*Thou art still my God*"—as a spell to ward off the threat of annihilation, of blankness, that might otherwise envelop both his poem and his consciousness:

> The harbingers are come. See, see their mark;
> White is their colour, and behold my head.
> But must they have my brain? must they dispark
> Those sparkling notions, which therein were bred?
>   Must dulnesse turn me to a clod?
> Yet have they left me, *Thou art still my God.*
>
> Good men ye be, to leave me my best room,
> Ev'n all my heart, and what is lodged there:
> I passe not, I, what of the rest become,
> So *Thou art still my God*, be out of fear.
>   He will be pleased with that dittie;
> And if I please him, I write fine and wittie.

(1–12)

The standard assumption that Herbert is worried about senility rather than death in this poem overlooks the use (by Herbert and his contemporaries) of "dulnesse" as a symptom of preterition rather than stupidity, and of "clod" as a synecdoche for the unredeemed corpse.[53] Relatedly, commentators have generally assumed that "I passe not" in lines 9 and 31 means "I do not care." But, given Herbert's distinct appetite for double meanings, the phrase is also likely to mean, "I myself do not pass away."[54] From this perspective, the speaker of "The Forerunners" derives full personal immortality, not merely an indifference to senility, from the magic psalmic phrase and the providential love it comports. Whatever other aspects of his poetic voice expire, he lives in that phrase as much as Donne does in his name inscribed in the window.

In "The Forerunners," Herbert multiplies his standard defense against the isolation of his mortal voice. To express and preserve what is truly essential about himself, paradoxically, Herbert must efface himself, quoting the psalmist who is quoting himself in a prayer God himself quotes and binds (as Psalm 31) into his eternal Bible. When death silences the poetic nightingale, that unembellished phrase will preserve the core of the poem, and the meaning of the phrase will preserve the core of the poet:[55]

> Yet if you go, I passe not; take your way:
> For, *Thou art still my God*, is all that ye
> Perhaps with more embellishment can say,
> Go birds of spring: let winter have his fee,
>   Let a bleak palenesse chalk the doore,
> So all within be livelier then before.
>
> (31–36)

That an imperious monarch threatens to seize the rooms which constitute the speaker's identity is the fundamental metaphor of the poem. That this monarch will fulfill the speaker's piety and poetry (as a provident God) rather than erase them (as a blankly indifferent Death) is the fundamental consolatory assertion. Like its pale writer, "The Forerunners" subsides into white space, as those undergoing near-death experiences report travelling into a white light, fully expecting to be met and affirmed there. Just as "*Thou art still my God*" escapes both the historical composition and the sequential development of the poem—remains, in both senses, immutable—the poet's soul may hope (if his God is still his God) to persist when the eye, like the page, goes blank. He has been marked, but marked for new life through a divine visitation.

Psalm 38 evokes and then dissipates annihilationist anxieties:

> But I am like a deaf man, I do not hear,
> like a dumb man who does not open his mouth.
> Yea, I am like a man who does not hear,
> and in whose mouth are no rebukes.
>
> But for thee, O LORD, do I wait;
> It is thou, O LORD my God, who wilt answer.
>
> (Psalm 38:13–15)

In "The Quip," this last line becomes Herbert's defensive spell, not only against worldly taunters and tempters, but also against the fears of voiceless oblivion. The speaker is a virtuous spirit withstanding the assaults and allures of Beauty, Money, Glory, Wit, and Conversation by allowing his silence to bespeak his faith in another world: each of the four middle stanzas ends with the Psalmist's, "But thou shalt answer,

Lord, for me." In the sixth and final stanza, however, the speaker looks forward to the day of final Judgment, when God will indeed answer for him simply by claiming his soul:

> Yet when the houre of thy designe
> To answer these fine things shall come;
> Speak not at large, say, I am thine:
> And then they have their answer home.
>
> (21–24)

The ambiguity of the pronouns in the penultimate line—since the saying may be either quotation or indirect discourse—is precisely the point. God belongs to the speaker, because the speaker belongs to God, because he has spoken in His voice. "The Quip" here goes a step beyond the poems that triumphantly escape closure by ending in God's voice. Here, God's simple powerful words promise to intervene in some indeterminate future, the mere anticipation of which spares Herbert the obligation to make any temporal argument or to close any temporal dialogue. The ending confidently awaits an ending, as the speaker's humble human silence confidently awaits God's home thrust, the word of divine judgment. "The Quip" thus becomes a triumph of wit in which Herbert settles for the role of straight man. To win the argument against worldly enemies with silence is to win, prospectively, the argument against annihilation.

The key to salvation in *The Temple* is a conjunction of divine grace with humble human faith—hardly a surprising doctrine in the writings of a moderate English cleric such as George Herbert. His "Faith" shows how, when plea replaces pride and complaint, "grace fills up eneven nature" (32); it also fills up uneven lines of verse. God is a faith-healer, and he works on poetic feet as well as human ones, allowing them to continue their spiritual pilgrimage beyond their physical limits: "That apprehension cur'd so well my foot, / That I can walk to heav'n well neare" (11–12). Herbert thus offers his anxious readers special incentives for their receptivity to grace, most notably the same equanimity the speaker expresses about his mortal end, and that the poem evinces in the face of its own demise:

> What though my bodie runne to dust?
> Faith cleaves unto it, counting evr'y grain
> With an exact and most particular trust,
>   Reserving all for flesh again.
>
> (41–44)

Herbert evokes the conventional association of closure with death for the sake of subverting it; the last words point to the Christian promise of a new beginning at the general resurrection.

"Deniall" begins with the poetic prayer threatened by silence, as the poet is by despair:

> When my devotions could not pierce
>   Thy silent eares;
> Then was my heart broken, as was my verse:
>   My breast was full of fears
>   And disorder:
>
> (1–5)

Here as in the other stanzas, the typography reflects this disorder, and the truncated and unrhymed final line echoes the discontented silence that God seems unwilling to complete with a (saving) reply. Eventually the poem obliges us to recognize, in retrospect, that the problem is not God's "denial" of the speaker's requests, but the speaker's profound denial of God in the spirit of those requests; "silent eares" is not a solecism, but a hint that the speaker has actually neither managed to pray, nor listened for a response—which for Herbert are indistinguishable failings. As a prominent contemporary of Herbert's, John Everard, preached, "All the Artillery in the World, were they all dischardged together at one clap, could not more deaf the ears of our bodies than the clamorings of desires in the soul deaf its ears, so you see a man must go into silence or else he cannot hear God speak."[56]

When Herbert's speaker turns from complaint to humble entreaty in the final stanza, God mends the terminal rhyme—"making a chiming of a passing-bell," as Herbert writes in "The Flower." In the final syllable "Deniall" achieves an affirmative closure: an imbalanced but harmonious couplet marking his recoupling with God. This poetic redemption grants the speaker a renewed confidence that salvation will arrive in his hour of need, when his heartbeat gives way to the tolls of a death-knell:

> O cheer and tune my heartlesse breast,
>   Deferre no time;
> That so thy favours granting my request,
>   They and my minde may chime,
>   And mend my ryme.
>
> (26–30)

Once denial is mercifully over, "Deniall" can end no less happily.[57] The disguised import of the title—that the speaker has been denying God, not vice versa—reminds us that we, too, were in danger of misperceiving and undervaluing God's generosity.

Herbert's punning titles in "The Church" (such as "The Collar" and "Redemption") are particularly remarkable because the names of lyrics commanded very little attention in the Jacobean period; most poems had no consistent title except for their opening words, and the few that did rarely assigned the title any real hermeneutic function.[58] Herbert, however, makes his titles surrogates of divine presence, seated on high as wise judges and teachers of the responding reader. The titles "Drop from above," as divine blessing does in Herbert's rendering of "Grace," once we are prepared to receive them piously. They demand an eschatological reading: backwards from the revelation of Last Things. Moreover, because they exist outside of a poem's narrative sequence, applying equally to each utterance within that sequence, they become reflections of the idea that God is perpetually present, making linear time—which seems to doom us to mortality—an illusion which can be cured by reference to an authority above. As Nicolas Cusanus writes, "I can only read one letter in turn after another. . . . But Thou, lord, dost see and read the whole page together, in an instant."[59]

A particularly revealing example of this divine function concludes Herbert's "Home." As in "Deniall," the speaker at first misunderstands the obstacle between himself and God as temporal rather than spiritual, and as God's fault rather than his own:

> Come Lord, my head doth burn, my heart is sick,
>   While thou dost ever, ever stay:
> Thy long deferrings wound me to the quick.
>
> (1–3)

Actually, God has not deserted, or even deferred, a good soul here; He is "staying" patiently by the sickbed of a sinner whose brain has contracted a hellish fever, whose heart has gone bad, and whose eyes have failed so severely that he pleads repeatedly for the Savior who is close by him to appear: "O shew thy self to me, / Or take me up to thee!" The speaker's yearning for home is here a yearning for death, which promises a reunion with God, schematized by the rhyme of "me" and "thee" in each refrain. The real self is waiting in death, not lost there:

> What have I left, that I should stay and grone?
>   The most of me to heav'n is fled:

My thoughts and joyes are all packt up and gone,
    And for their old acquaintance plead.
        O show thy, & c.

Come dearest Lord, passe not this holy season,
    My flesh and bones and joynts do pray:
And ev'n my verse, when by the ryme and reason
    The word is, *Stay*, sayes ever, *Come*.
        O show thy, &c.

          (67–71)

A poem conventionally seeks the closure of rhyme; a living body conventionally flees the closure of death. The strength of this speaker's pious yearning, however, overrides both conventions: the homing device in his soul overrides ordinary worldly navigation, and he chooses the word that expresses his feelings over the word that fulfills his rhyme-scheme. In "Deniall," God's merciful intervention provides the rhyme missing in the previous stanzas; here the craving for divine mercy removes the rhyme present in the previous stanzas.

But perhaps the rhyme is relocated rather than eradicated. "*Come*" establishes at least an eye-rhyme with the title of the poem, "Home," the thing to which the speaker wants to reconcile himself, the place of his only true completion.[60] This again implies a triumph over the dangerous worldly illusions of place and time: instead of responding to the local-ized demands of its own stanza, the final rhyme-word attunes itself to the word that is perpetually present overseeing the poem, as God oversees the world. "Home"—the word as well as the place—is the locale of a perpetual reunion, and so there is nothing to be feared from an apparent ending of the worldly and poetic journeys.

If the word "Home" seems more applicable to a point of origin than a destination, it is worth remembering that Herbert probably wrote this poem in the five years between his mother's death and his own.[61] After the primary source of his being, his feeding, his love, and his faith is consumed by death, the "meat and drink" and the "woman-kinde" of "this weary world" become disgusting to him (37, 39). Escaping to heaven would mean returning to the womb and the breast that first gave him life; death is, to that extent, a regressive fantasy for Herbert. When humanity was doomed to mortality, he reminds God, "The help did in thy bosome lie . . . / There lay thy sonne; and must he leave that nest, / That hive of sweetnesse?" (16–20). Herbert's complacency in the face of death reflects a deep-seated trust that his mother will (again) pick him up, and give him life, in a moment of need.

TIME OUT OF JOINT:
"OUR DISORDER'D CLOCKS"

The orderly measures and enclosures of poetry have always been a precious commodity in the economy of human morale. As an exponential function of language itself, poetry provides a structure that can preserve the impression of meaning, and can record (along with other great human conquests) the conquest of time. Verse has often been assigned to hold the myths that make our existence comprehensible and therefore bearable. From this perspective, deconstruction is a dirty business, next to godlessness; an indeterminate universe is profoundly unsatisfying to the terminal cases inhabiting it. To vanquish death, a religion must tame linear chronology. Whereas several Eastern religions reconceive time as purely irrelevant or illusory, Christianity subjugates it to eschatology: salvation is a timeless condition produced through time, which is both our reality and God's illusion.

Herbert's poems offer and then correct the illusion of sequence, to glorify the time-transcending power of the God they praise. Because "all time is *present* with God,"[62] we need not die in the verb tenses we live by. God's omnipresence remedies our isolation in endless space, and his "omni-present" tense remedies our isolation in endless time. As eternal salvation is produced through mortal chronology, so Herbert's lyrics could hardly exist as their triumphant final simplicities and silences alone; without the preparatory process, no one would value a poem that said only, "*My God, My King*" ("Jordan [I]"). But with that preparatory process, these lyrics can imply that oblivion is not the only escape from the temporal.

Little wonder that Christian authors strove so heartily to associate immeasurable time with a benevolent ordering consciousness. The apparent timelessness of death—its endlessness in the experience of mourners, its oblivion projected into the experience of the dead—has proven extremely threatening in modern chronometric Western culture. Death reminds us that, whatever our clocks might seem to say, "the time [is] neither wrong nor right," as Robert Frost reports in the poem "Acquainted with the Night,"[63] and as Ingmar Bergman vividly depicts in the nightmare sequence of his movie *Wild Strawberries*. These mortally terrifying modern evocations of the clock without hands recall Donne's broken clocks and buried sundials, but also Eliot's "Little Gidding," a modernist meditation on the paradoxes of time under a

Christian eschaton. The "Little Gidding" to which Eliot refers was a small religious community, led by Nicholas Ferrar, where Herbert probably wrote much of *The Temple*. There Herbert would have been exposed daily to Ferrar's "Harmonies," which cross-correlated Biblical passages in ways that undermined all conventional notions of chronological sequence.[64] Herbert's pious poetic denial of mortal chronology thus has a history all its own, a history at once synchronic and diachronic.

The history of Herbert's death suggests how heavily he relied on this denial of linear time as a means of denying death. According to Walton's biography:

The *Sunday* before his death, he rose suddenly from his Bed or Couch, call'd for one of his Instruments . . . and having tun'd it, he play'd and sung:

>   The Sundays of Mans life,
> Thredded together on times string,
> Make Bracelets, to adorn the Wife
> Of the eternal glorious King:
> On Sundays, Heavens dore stands ope;
> Blessings are plentiful and rife,
>   More plentiful than hope.

Thus he sung on Earth such Hymns and Anthems, as the Angels and he, and Mr *Farrer*, now sing in Heaven.[65]

Horatio-like, Walton feels compelled to deny the silencing of his hero's voice. But the lyric Herbert chose was itself an insistent refutation of mortal closure. "Sunday" begins:

>   O day most calm, most bright,
> The fruit of this, the next worlds bud,
> Th' indorsement of supreme delight,
> Writ by a friend, and with his bloud;
> The couch of time; cares balm and bay:
> The week were dark but for thy light:
>   Thy torch doth show the way.
>
>   (1–7)

Christ leads us from this world to the next, from darkness to light; otherwise "Man had straight forward gone / To endlesse death: but thou dost pull / And turn us round" (15–17). By making the human body an analogue to time itself (8–14), and playing on the Renaissance association of that body with the number seven, Herbert gives it a place in the Christian rhythm of renewal, which his prayers allow him to join "from sev'n to sev'n, / Till that we both, being toss'd from earth, / Flie hand in hand to heav'n!" (61–63). It is hard to imagine a more joyously assured choice of last words; on the seventh day, he will rest with God.

The joys of heaven and the defeat of time alike were purchased with Christ's agony and death. The first stanza of "Affliction (II)" urges God to recognize that killing the speaker daily with afflictions will prove both inadequate and superfluous, "since thy one death for me / Is more then all my deaths can be, / Though I in broken pay / Die over each houre of Methusalems stay" (2–5). The business of death, which includes making measurements (of time) absurd, has come under new management; God has reorganized it into a charity. The second stanza suggests that all men's tears, like their hours, are lost in an immeasurable sea; but since Christ has already absorbed more death and suffering than any mortal could experience, he has also perhaps absorbed the meaninglessness.

If "The Altar" is a poem prospectively replaced by its own configuration, "Affliction (II)" is a poem superseded by a symbolic form it cannot presume to imitate, a burden Christ must bear on its behalf. It is ultimately *His* "Affliction." The symbol of the cross—the symbol of death turned to life at the heart of Christianity—has prepaid and thus precluded "all my future mone" (15). And that is where the poem ends, not with its life or voice ended, but instead with its prospective sorrows retracted in favor of a silent joy, swallowed up into a redemptively agonized past rather than a meaningless future. The poet can afford to fall silent here because all his hopes and fears have already been spoken for. All that is really silenced is a cry of pain that he will never be compelled to emit. The apparent termination of the poem in the sequential experience of a reader is refuted by the recognition that Christ's sacrificial miracle has changed, not just the valence of suffering, but also the directionality of time. Affliction, time, even death, have become the agencies of joyous endless life.

The same point is made more starkly by "Mortification"—another title that changes in meaning to reflect a (perpetually available) Christian recognition. What seems to refer to the steady passage through and toward mortality finally refers to the Christian humility that defeats mortality. The poem asserts the smothering presence of death, its vermicular insinuation of all our seemingly lively and life-affirming activities. Each six-line stanza moves from a third line ending in "breath" to a sixth that ends in "death," and in sequence they tell a compressed Five Ages of Man story:

> How soon doth man decay!
> When clothes are taken from a chest of sweets
>   To swaddle infants, whose young breath
>   Scarce knows the way;
>   Those clouts are little winding sheets,
> Which do consigne and send them unto death.
>
> (1–6)

Like Marvell in "To His Coy Mistress," Herbert sedulously provokes claustrophobia in his audience, to augment the appeal of the release he finally offers from the linear path toward death. So when the poem expires—literally, runs out of the "breath" it has emphasized throughout—it does so with a plea for renewal: "Yet Lord, instruct us so to die, / That all these dyings may be life in death" (35–36). By the time the word "death" makes its closing appearance, it has already been neutralized by a new form of "life." If the process is full of endings, then the ending may be caught up in process; again, the retrospective activity of the responding reader corresponds to a reversal of the seemingly implacable movement through time and change toward death.

"Time" also describes a triumph over the conventional forces of chronological mortality, but its victory is equivocal. We come to the end of "Time," and yet the clock is still ticking. The speaker narrates an encounter with a Reaper whose grimness has been transformed by Christianity: if death is merely the passage to a better life, then this supposed "executioner" is actually "a gard'ner" (15–16). As in "Paradise" and "The Flower," even the harsher sort of agricultural metaphor can be adduced to offer a model for renewal after seeming annihilation; immortality manifests itself in perennials. But the Reaper becomes exasperated with—perhaps even suspicious of—the speaker's gloating, concluding that while the speaker claims to be eager to exchange his temporal existence for a blessed afterlife, "He doth not crave lesse time, but more" (30). This is deeply ambiguous: is the speaker proudly seeking eternity in place of earthly transience, or covertly seeking more time on earth through pious expostulations? Is this a prayer, or a filibuster? The former is the more orthodox reading, yet the poem certainly highlights the long-windedness of the speaker. Resisting vocal closure becomes a version of, and a symbol of, resistance to death—as in children who protract disputes to defer the terrors of bedtime, or critics who seem unable to end lengthy books. In his letters, Donne jokes about "the dilatory ceremonies" Catholics indulged in before execution.[66] The common Christian desire to prepare properly for death may sometimes mask a fearful tactic of deferral.

So while this ending may describe Time's perplexity in front of a man confidently yearning for his perpetual reward, it seems alternatively to diagnose the speaker's volubility as a symptom of doubt, an effort to forestall the very death he claims to crave. If so, it would nicely exemplify the pattern—fearful resistance disguised as Christian confidence—that this book seeks to excavate from Jacobean culture. Herbert himself apparently has enough distance from this tendency to criticize it, but who then does this speaker represent? How many other Renaissance proclamations about the irrelevance of earthly time, how many texts ostensibly expressing a Christian *contemptus mundi*, may prove to be evasions of temporal extinction—quests for fame or for divine favor— rather than wholehearted affirmations of eternal providence?

FAMOUS LAST WORDS: "MORE" AND *MORT*

Ars poetica and *ars moriendi* alike put considerable weight on last words.[67] Herbert's lyrics challenge poetic closure with the same riddle that Christian theology poses to death: when is an ending not an ending? He diligently marks closure as merely a "relief," or a "stay" awaiting ultimate Redemption. In the nothingness of death one may find "all" (as at the end of "Trinity Sunday," "The Quidditie" and "The Invitation"). Consider the last two poems discussed above. "Time" ends with the word "more," because the fundamental conflict between temporal life and Christian eternity generates an equivocation about what truly constitutes "more time." "Mortification" ends with the word "death," largely for the sake of proving that death can be defeated even in its native corner of the poetic landscape. Herbert's vocabulary of ending is largely divisible into these two words: "more," which promises to extend both life and poem into an indescribable Beyond; and "death," which is usually ingeniously transformed from a gravestone that marks termination into a stepping-stone toward a higher existence.

The great antecedent for Herbert's confidence in a closural "more" is Donne's "Hymne to God the Father," written (according to Walton) during Donne's dangerous illness of 1623.[68] Donne's first two stanzas end with the assertion that though God has forgiven him much, "When thou hast done, thou hast not done, / For, I have more" (5–6). The poem, too, has more to come at those moments, but since it will not always, the poet's mortality-crisis can accrete around the poem's closural crisis. This tangle of gratitude and fear activates a series of puns, "done" with Donne, and "more," not only with Ann More, but with *mort*, death, the seeming opposite of more.[69] The first two refrains mean what they say, but they also warn God that he does not really "have Donne" yet, has not securely captured him for salvation, because he is still susceptible to new sin, which is both cause and effect of his fears of mortality. So his essential selfhood (located characteristically in his name) remains susceptible to mere annihilation. God has not done/ Donne, because Donne has not God, because God has not Donne/ done. Donne's Christian faith is unsettled, because *mort* may not be more, because he lacks conviction that it will be.

The vindication of this reading lies in the anxious concluding stanza, which extends the punning to express Donne's fear that he will not have the sun, because the Son will not have him. Donne is not expressing confidence here that he will be spared hell by divine payment of his sins; instead, he is offering to reward God for assurances against dark and destinationless annihilation, conceived in a pagan mode (13–18). God can win him by assuring him that death will not be (deservedly) the onset of an ultimate darkness. "No more" carries an emphatic threat of closure, yet here it implies (like "Death, Be Not Proud") that death itself will be extinguished. As in Colin's punning emblem in Spenser's "November" eclogue, "*La Mort n'y Mord*": death has lost its sting.

The pun across languages serves to span the anxious gap between death and afterlife, and Herbert may have had Donne's word-play in mind when he ended "A Dialogue-Antheme" with "Christian" warning "Death" that, after the Last Judgment, Death itself "shalt be no more" (10). These last words announce that there will be no *mort*, that the ultimate closure will inaugurate eternal life. By allowing Death no reply, "A Dialogue-Antheme" displaces the burden of terminal silence, and employs the leverage of closure against the usual closural anxieties. "Praise (III)" ends each stanza of praise with the word "more," implying that neither version of the word marks a final enclosure:

> O that I might some hearts convert,
>   And so take up at use good store:
> That to thy chests there might be coming in
>   Both all my praise, and more!
>
> (39–42)

This time Herbert surrenders his poetic voice, not in order to merge with the Word of God, but in order to elicit the pious response of other Christians. "Praise (III)" is thus less a self-contained lyric than a verbal catalyst designed to rouse a louder song at the very moment its own voice falls silent, as if joining a heavenly chorus at the moment of death.[70]

Herbert's characteristic alternatives to this terminal assertion of a "more" that undoes *mort* are the no less comfortable suggestions that a good Christian ends at "heavens doore" ("Church Musick"), "in heav'n above" ("The Glance"), at God's "breast" ("The Pulley"), with "salvation" ("An Offering"), or in "eternall blisse" ("Holy Scriptures [II]"). The poem "Sunday," which (we have seen) Herbert chose as a poetic last word on his deathbed, ends at "heav'n." In Herbert's two "Even-Song" poems, the terminal words are "for ever" and "rest," each of which elicits a fundamental annihilationist concern in a context that allows Christianity to dispel that concern.

   The Williams manuscript version of "Even-Song" provides a stark example of Herbert's reliance on Christian faith and poetic form as allies against the fear of death. The occasion of Evensong—nightfall—is predictably an occasion for mortality-anxiety,[71] here manifest as a fear of endless repose in a dreamless darkness. Rather than permit the occasion of poetic closure to reinforce that anxiety, Herbert ends with a plea for new beginning, as evening services were understood as the beginning of the next liturgical day. Translated into Christian eschatology, the simple model of the daily solar cycle endorses the hope for renewal, as the seasonal cycle of vegetation in "The Flower" endorses that poem's warning that accepted endings are the only acceptable means to endlessness.

   Yet the mysterious darkness at the end of a day or a life is still so threatening that Herbert must confuse dark and light through a series of strenuous paradoxes, finally construing night or death as the time when the soul has internalized the eternal radiance of God:

> O lett my Soule, whose keyes I must deliver
>   Into the hands of senceles Dreames
>   Which know not thee; suck in thy beames
>   And wake with thee for ever.

The speaker, who at first sounded rather like the despondent Donne of the "Nocturnall upon St. Lucies Day," has found a "Good-Morrow"; the despairing entropy of the opening stanza, dusk to dust, has found its way to an endless sunlit morning, curing the horribly senseless dreams of the annihilationist grave. "Night, earths gloomy shade / fouling her nest," threatening to trap him in the cycles of natural decay (9–12), gives way to the sweet morning breast of Herbert's maternal God, who feeds with light instead of milk.

The poem that appears as "Even-Song" in "The Church" seems to run in the opposite direction: it begins with the blessing of "the God of love," and ends in simple "rest." But the struggle for light at the end of a dark tunnel remains prominent. The speaker must again confront the fear that the loss of the sun through time and of the Son through sin will turn his life into a brief, meaningless exhalation of the earth:

> Thy diet, care, and cost
> Do end in bubbles, balls of winde;
> Of winde to thee whom I have crost,
> But balls of wilde-fire to my troubled minde.
>
> Yet still thou goest on.
> And now with darknesse closest wearie eyes,
> Saying to man, *It doth suffice:*
> *Henceforth repose; your work is done.*
>
> Thus in thy Ebony box
> Thou dost inclose us, till the day
> Put our amendment in our way,
> And give new wheels to our disorder'd clocks.
>
> I muse, which shows more love,
> The day or night: that is the gale, this th' harbour;
> That is the walk, and this the arbour;
> Or that the garden, this the grove.
>
> My God, thou art all love.
> Not one poore minute scapes thy breast,
> But brings a favour from above;
> And in this love, more then in bed, I rest.
>
> (13–32)

The defense—the psychic defense that denies death—here "rests" too; the imminent condemnation has been skillfully deflected by testimony that the poetry itself serves to corroborate. The metaphors of the penultimate stanza all serve to blur the conventional distinctions between life and death, to alter its harsh binary arithmetic of one and zero; their redundancy suggests the overdetermination of this essential denial. Night entails more enclosure than day, but only inasmuch as ports are more enclosed than oceans, porches than paths, orchards than flower-beds. Life goes on, and it retains the imprint of human consciousness.

As in most of the poems discussed earlier in this chapter, God's vocal intervention corresponds to the moment of death. But by placing that italicized divine interjection in the middle of "Even-Song" rather than at the end, Herbert demonstrates that spiritual existence continues beyond death. Death becomes merely a "rest" before a new task, making nightfall and sleep into assurances about mortality rather than occasions to fear it. Herbert transforms the coffin-like "Ebony box" of stanza six into the fruitful protected landscapes of stanza seven, answering both the physical claustrophobia and the spiritual agoraphobia of annihilationism. In the same way, he offers an eternity that is not terrifyingly beyond measurable time. Herbert's God—an intervention-ist version of the watchmaker God his brother would bequeath to the Enlightenment—will simply make some repairs, and we will emerge from the timeless nightmare. God is a night-light, and an alarm clock. Assured that the Son or Sun of God will rise for him in love, whether on the cross or on the horizon, the speaker can dare to go to bed. As in "The Pulley," the word "rest" can promise "the rest," a residual benefit that matures beyond earthly limits (14–16). So as the final strains of "Even-Song" subside, the rest is not silence, but a sort of musical rest, a pause that emphasizes the beauty that follows. We may "rest" in peace without disappearing into eternity: in "the grave, the body lies still," Donne told his congregation, "but it is not a Rest, because it is not sensible of that lying still; in heaven the body shall rest, rest in the sense of that glory" (*Sermons*, V, 213). Herbert has again characteristically found a last word that allows him to elide fears into consolations.[72]

As a last word, "relief" is a viable alternative to the sabbatic "rest," particularly because "relief" suggests assistance and (as for the sentries in *Hamlet*) the beginning of a new cycle.[73] After a series of symmetrically enclosed stanzas, "Sighs and Grones" ends with a stanza expressly concerned with the fear of death as mere ending:

> But O reprieve me!
> For thou hast *life* and *death* at thy command;
> Thou art both *Judge* and *Saviour*, *feast* and *rod*,

Cordiall and *Corrosive*: put not thy hand
Into the bitter box; but O my God,
        My God, relieve me!

The prayers for reprieve or relief that bracket the stanza reflect an imperfectly voiced prayer for retrieval from the ending that is merely a box of wormwood. The poem threatens to forfeit its metaphoricity, revealing a man afraid he will be strewn with quicklime rather than any revivifying holy water. In this sense, "Sighs and Grones" treats death in much the way Donne's "Loves Alchymie" treats sex, hiding in plain sight a disgusting materialist perspective on the human body. Herbert's theological discussion of Last Judgment edges uneasily close to the fears of sheer physical decay, damnation reconceived as the corrosion of the grave, where the worm never dies.

All the standard symptoms of Renaissance mortality-anxiety haunt the brief lyric "Complaining": the fear of becoming mere "clay" and "dust" in stanza one, of resembling a pointlessly redundant and imminently mortal "flie" in stanza two, of forfeiting the ordinary functions of "throat or eye" in stanza three, and, in the fourth and final stanza, of amounting to a mere "houre" or "inch" in an infinite universe. When it ceases complaining, "Complaining" ceases, but does not die: "let thy gracious power / Contract my houre, / That I may climbe and finde relief" (18–20). There the poem willingly subsides, as if the turn from complaint to humble plea had itself been enough to earn the speaker, and the poem, an ending that is "relief."

Much of the appeal of "Redemption" lies in the shock value of its abrupt and enigmatic ending. The poem concludes with a paramount example of famous last words and a stark assertion of death: the Lord "straight, *Your suit is granted*, said, and died" (14). God's last word is, characteristically, "granted"; but the poem's last word is "died," marking the distance remaining between Christ's gift and the human recognition of that gift. The glorious paradox of Christianity (here radically defamiliarized) is that these are essentially the same word. Christ's real last word is His voluntary expiration, which renegotiates the speaker's stringent lease with God. Only by choosing to endure a mortal end does Christ enable us to escape our finitude. The speaker's stunned suspension between relief and sorrow at the end of the poem is a necessary suspension for any Christian contemplating the Passion. The abrupt poetic ending provokes us to continue intellectually beyond the end of the poem—or (which is essentially the same thing) to retreat back into the poem in review. As we review, absorb, and extend the poetic movement, we receive the poetic moral. Christ's physical dying redeems us from linear time, as well as from spiritual bankruptcy.

What looks literally and figuratively like a death-sentence at the end of "Vanitie (I)" is successfully appealed to the divine life-source. Herbert's usual tactics for opening his readers' hearts to God are all manifest here. The Christian God is a Lord of love, not merely of power, if we will accept His infinite tenderness; God is not hidden, He is everywhere obvious, if we will cease averting our eyes in petty pride and despair. The ostensible topic of "Vanitie (I)" is Renaissance discovery, the scientific and colonial explorations that (my Introduction argues) threatened to reveal a cold and overwhelming universe. To Herbert, these exertions of his imperialist culture are symptoms, as well as provocations, of doubt. The progress of the poem appears to ally itself with the progress of these technologies, before finally rejecting progress altogether in favor of presence, and technology in favor of theology. A divine revelation has been gloriously available all around us every day (stanza four), while men eke out the petty revelations of worldly analysis from top (astronomy, stanza one) to bottom (pearl-diving, stanza two) and everywhere in-between and within (chemistry, stanza three). The poem thus depicts an illusion of progress in the Renaissance, which by itself might appear to constitute a progression toward deeper and deeper truths, but (to the spiritual eye) produces only rape, decay, and destruction.

Against that scientific version of the Renaissance, God offers the miracle of spiritual rebirth. The end of "Vanitie (I)" insists that the saving truths are not found by accretive or corrosive process, but by immediate appreciation. To overlook life so badly in pursuit of it seems finally even stranger than the Christian paradox of finding life by seeking death. The dizzying heights of the sky and depths of the ocean become consolingly irrelevant, since blessedness is in the soil of every backyard and the soul of every willing Christian. As in our own bewilderingly large and technological world, a stubborn domesticity seems the nearest way to immortality. By abjuring progress, in either sense, the poem reinforces its assurance that one can escape the linear model of time and the facts of biological science that together steer us toward individual annihilation, and steer our cultures toward atomistic annihilationism.

Instead, the final line of "Vanitie (I)" (like those of "Mortification" and "Vertue") simply replaces the word "*death*" with "*life*"; as so often in Herbert's lyrics, God does His work in italics.

WAITING AT THE TERMINAL: "AS IF THY LOVE COULD FAIL"

Clearly Herbert was determined to demonstrate that death could be confronted at an ending, as an ending, without precluding hope for a redeemed afterlife. To prove his confidence, he plays at a kind of brinkmanship with the terrors of annihilationism. His "Longing" seems actually to expire in despair, with "dyes" as its last word. In theme and form, "Longing" is highly reminiscent of "Deniall," but this time there is evidently no response from God (or perhaps no room for Him in the desperate heart and the closed rhyme-scheme). By being closed in itself, in its own voice, the poem must merely end, as must the longing soul unless God graciously intervenes. What mitigates this threat is (aptly) Herbert's "Church," which rescues the individual poem from its damning isolation, as Herbert's church rescues souls whose individual communion with God might falter: the poem following "The Longing" begins, "Away, despair; my gracious Lord doth heare."[74] So this note of despair yields to a footnote of redemption, another ending transformed into a new beginning. But the danger of terminal failure apparently persists even within Herbert's "Church." It remains at least conceivable that the governor's pardoning call might never come—not audibly, at least—before the death-sentence is carried out as an irreversible closure.

Herbert's chief poetic effort to respond to the Passion, "The Thanksgiving," appears to fall short of any conventionally satisfactory ending. Yet what looks like final defeat may lead to final victory. The speaker finds apt ways to repay (often through writing) several of the blessings that Christ so painfully won for him, but each response falls two syllables short of repaying its metrical debt; and in the end the speaker must be simultaneously saved and defeated by the Passionate sacrifice which no mortal can reciprocate, since we have no immortality to abjure. This human incapacity breaks the balance and the flow of the poem, leaving no recourse for the poet or the poem other than meek surrender—which is the silence, the awed death of the will, that qualifies the unworthy soul for salvation.

The art of this poetry, like the art of Christian dying, lies in the terrible beauty born of failure. Only by welcoming its own demise can the human voice appropriately respond to the astonishing fact for which thanks are here given—most truly given by finally giving no thanks *except* astonishment. The failure of poetic closure, however guilt-ridden, celebrates the defeat of closure in individual human experience. The poem finishes its term with a deficit, but Christian salvation depends on an acknowledged debt; and in Reformation Christianity any expectation of closing out one's own accounts successfully would itself be damnable. In content as in form, neat closure would be an empty triumph indeed; but by defining death as debt (a familiar Renaissance pun), Christianity renders it susceptible to restitution from different sources. As so often in "The Church," when the poetic heartbeat falters, when the EKGs of meter and refrain suddenly read flat, that is precisely where true salvation can intervene; Christ's sacrifice is the heroic measure taken to save both poem and poet, at their moment of seemingly tragic failure.

Sometimes, however, the defaults of Herbert's spiritual repayment, marked by failed endings, threaten to foreclose his bond with God in a way that precludes redemption. Avoiding closure is consoling only if the continuation is marked as salvation. In "Grief," poetry is defeated—rather than enhanced, as Herbert usually implies—by theological concern. Trapped in the "narrow cupboard" of earth, the speaker's grief "excludes both measure, tune, and time." The poem overflows its sonnet form, but with an expression of despair rather than renewal: "Alas, my God!"[75]

Since Herbert's God responds to faith rather than to grievances, complaining about spiritual frustration initiates a vicious cycle; like the cycle of human generations, it is profoundly futile unless grace interrupts and augments it. Without any compass, without any point of celestial reference by which to navigate, the wayward soul can wander in circles indefinitely. "Sinnes Round" might be compared to another cyclical work such as "JESU," but this time the closing repetition of the opening line becomes an index of futility rather than redemption, since by the end it means nothing more to either the reader or the speaker than it did the first time.[76] The joyless carousel of "Sinnes Round" ends as it begins, with "Sorrie I am, my God, sorrie I am," itself a repetitive statement in which apology never breaks free from desperate self-denigration. In between, the final line of each stanza serves—or rather, imposes itself— as the opening line of the next one. The speaker is left repeating his apology like an actor desperately repeating a cue into the wings, waiting for the entrance of the divine voice that so often resolves both the religious and the prosodic perplexities of other poems; but his words never become Word.

Linear time can be even less consoling than cyclical time, because the body is bound to deteriorate regardless of the condition of the soul, and its endings are rarely happy. "Church-Monuments" is Herbert's most direct confrontation with the stubbornly physical aspect of human mortality. In form as in content, the poem studies death as decay: the lines and sentences about the crumbling of corpses and tombstones themselves collapse in enjambment and shifting syntax, and meaning disperses in the dust.[77] Nor does the message finally seem to escape this medium. "While" and "Here," the anchors of the first two lines, the anchors of human sanity as well, yield to infinities of time and space:

> While that my soul repairs to her devotion,
> Here I intombe my flesh, that it betimes
> May take acquaintance of this heap of dust;
> To which the blast of deaths incessant motion,
> Fed with the exhalation of our crimes,
> Drives all at last. Therefore I gladly trust
>
> My bodie to this school, that it may learn
> To spell his elements, and finde his birth
> Written in dustie heraldrie and lines;
> Which dissolution sure doth best discern,
> Comparing dust with dust, and earth with earth.
> These laugh at Jeat, and Marble put for signes,
>
> To sever the good fellowship of dust,
> And spoil the meeting. What shall point out them,
> When they shall bow, and kneel, and fall down flat
> To kisse those heaps, which now they have in trust?
>
> (1–16)

Signs here lose their reference in a kind of infinite regress, pulling each other into the abyss. What geologists call "deep time" atomizes even the tombstones meant to prolong our identities and forestall the scattering of our bodies. The love these stones supposedly express diminishes to a transient optical illusion, and our trust in them becomes an utterly futile defense against the implications of eternity for individual mortal beings. As in "JESU" and "The Flower," Herbert reverts to the metaphor of spelling, but this time, instead of discovering God's providential Word written everywhere in His world, the speaker finds his own body broken down into a kind of periodic table of elements. How can one adequately fit oneself against the "fall" that is the end of "Church-Monuments"? The poem contains an admonition against sin, but no assurance at all of salvation; philosophy, but no spirituality. The poem is moralized, but also demoralized; a *memento mori* is superfluous in an entropic vision of the universe. Deprecating the value of monumental tombs, Thomas Browne comments that a Christian "cannot excusably decline the consideration of that duration, which maketh Pyramids pillars of snow;"[78] but neither can a person who believes in eternal annihilation rather than eternal afterlife.

"Employment (II)" is arguably the blackest hole in the starry night of *The Temple*. In its darkness and futility, it comes even nearer to Donne's "Nocturnall upon St. Lucies Day" than does the Williams-manuscript "Even-Song." Though little noted and innocuously titled, "Employment (II)" expresses vividly the dangerous doubts that are generally visible only as resistance elsewhere in the volume.[79] Human life becomes a voyage to nowhere, a running in unenlightened circles until we drop straight into ultimate darkness. The moral of Herbert's poem sounds surprisingly like Drummond's wistful warning (written at about the same time) that "Every day we rise and lie down, apparel our bodies and disapparel them, make them sepulchres of dead creatures, weary them and refresh them; which is a circle of idle travails and labours, like Penelope's task, unprofitably renewed" (p. 31).

As Ernest Becker observes, employment is often a function of denial: "The defeat of despair is not mainly an intellectual problem for an active organism, but a problem of self-stimulation via movement. Beyond a given point man is not helped by more 'knowing,' but only by living and doing in a partly self-forgetful way" (p. 199). The speaker of "Employment (II)" never pauses to receive God's message, apparently for fear there will be none; what might pass for high aspiration is here exposed as a defensive compulsion. He will undertake the silly businesses of worldly life for lack of any better otherworldly offers, in a futile flight from death:

He that is weary, let him sit.
　　　　My soul would stirre
And trade in courtesies and wit,
　　　　Quitting the furre
To cold complexions needing it.

Man is no starre, but a quick coal
　　　　Of mortall fire:
Who blows it not, nor doth controll
　　　　A faint desire,
Lets his own ashes choke his soul.

　　　　　　(1–10)

Determined to remain in motion, the speaker becomes increasingly aware that his efforts are unproductive in themselves and impossible to sustain. Survival depends on remaining busily distracted from the pointlessness of survival. Employment seems justifiable only because a human being, like an ember, must move through the air to sustain its heat for a while.

No transcendence lends significance to these essentially physical efforts. The glowing coal might evoke symbolically the Hermetic spark, the Gnostic *pneuma*, except that it here seems doomed to die in a body of ashes and earth.

But we are still too young or old;
　　　　The man is gone,
Before we do our wares unfold:
　　　　So we freeze on,
Untill the grave increase our cold.

　　　　　　(26–30)

With this chilling last word, Herbert's characteristic wait for divine intervention has become Waiting for Godot.[80] The final chill corresponds to the silence of closure, both pointing toward the annihilationist grave. The man, the poet, is buried with his talents. The impossibility of properly serving God—the subject of many Herbert lyrics, and the titular subject of this one—transmutes into the possibility that there is no God to serve. If life seems a fool's errand, it may be because, as the Biblical fool says in his heart, there is no God, at least none offering a timely answer to these nihilistic anxieties. As idle hands are proverbially the devil's workshop, and out-of-work workers the arms of rebellion, so are unemployed spiritual yearnings the eyes of a terrible atheistic vision.

The corrosive function of my larger argument might be strengthened by ending on this despondent note, but that would misrepresent the consolatory thrust of Herbert's poetry as a whole, which must admit the possibility of suffering and despair to show the miraculous ease with which God can repair the body spiritual of the patient human. The Reformation both reflected and encouraged an increased emphasis on the individual in Renaissance society, and it is not surprising that (as Debora Shuger observes) "the locus of the sacred shrinks to the private spaces of the psyche" in *The Temple*.[81] This narrowing made heaven a cozier place, but also a smaller target; it became more difficult to tell faith from pride, and a paradise within from a solipsistic fantasy. Herbert had to demonstrate that, even in imposing the punishment of death, God remained a constant friend to our varying interiorities. Through his remarkable flair for parable and innocence of tone, Herbert maintains a voice that at once reflects the intimate subjectivity of Reformation piety, and remains open to a wide range of readers as an affirmation of their common experience of God. His speakers tell their individual stories of search and inward discovery in a way that allows us to travel along, sometimes even further than the speakers themselves.

The trip is not always a pleasant one, but it can lead to salvation, without ever moving toward it. At any place in the world, and at any moment in time, the blessed soul can step off the train of "Employment," off the unmerry-go-round of "Sinnes Round," and into the sweet chariot that carries weary pilgrims to a timeless "Home." Death is not an end, for Herbert, but a means to an end. "The Search," for example, ends with the finding of God, but it begins as if it were in the elegiac genre of "Lycidas," a futile search for some meaningful remainder of a beloved lost to death:

> Whither, O, whither art thou fled,
>   My Lord, my Love?
> My searches are my daily bread;
>   Yet never prove.
>
> My knees pierce th' earth, mine eies the skie;
>   And yet the sphere
> And centre both to me denie
>   That thou art there.
>
> (1–8)

As in the other complaint poems, God may seem to "denie" His presence, even if He has actually been present from the beginning, as in the "daily bread."[82] But what if it is God Himself—the sphere whose center is everywhere and whose circumference is nowhere—who has died? The notion of God's death is not merely glib modern skepticism or Nietzschean self-assertion; it is the most fundamental premise of Christianity. Herbert here assumes a voice much like that of the conventional Mary Magdalen figure who understands her beloved Christ as a bodily creature now gone forever. A terror that the Crucifixion had taken away the only God accessible to humanity seems to permeate "The Search":

> Where is my God? what hidden place
> > Conceals thee still?
> What covert dare eclipse thy face?
> > Is it thy will?
>
> > (29–32)

What if God's will now exists only as that other kind of testament, bequeathing to us a universe we cannot profitably manage on our own? If divine omnipresence makes one place everywhere, then this divine absence collapses anyplace into nowhere: "East and West touch, the poles do kiss" (43). We can only hope that (as in "Antiphon [II]") the countdown from two to one in the final line bespeaks an at-one-ment of the speaker with God, assuring eternal being, rather than a descent toward nullification.[83]

By refusing to narrate a satisfactory ending, "The Pilgrimage" instructs its readers in the Protestant answer to despair. The first words from Herbert's pilgrim, as from Dante's, suggest that he is in the middle of wandering through life, but the paradisal ending of the journey is far less explicit in Herbert's Reformed version than in Dante's more traditional one.

At some point in his hopeful expedition, the pilgrim confronts the prospect of mortality, which (as in the mid-life crisis depicted by modern social psychology) throws all his purposes into doubt at the height of achievement, leaving him (like the speaker of "Employment [II]") alternately frantic with denial and new enterprises, and passive with morbid depression:

> At length I got unto the gladsome hill,
> > Where lay my hope,
> > Where lay my heart; and climbing still,
> > When I had gain'd the brow and top,
> A lake of brackish waters on the ground
> > Was all I found.
>
> > (19–24)

Those final two lines describe and evoke a desperate letdown. The disappointment is worse than any defeat, because it arouses a terror that the world, which had seemed so richly populated with allegorical sigificances (4–6), might be merely a physical place in which our actions have no meaning beyond the schemes of desire we generate to keep ourselves in motion—as if *Don Quixote* were being rewritten as a theological tragedy. This pilgrim's anguish resembles the anguish of Donne's "Loves Alchymie" and "Farewell to Love," which expose his scheme of romantic transcendence as a shallow projection onto what is merely another all-too-temporal, all-too-physical event.

What if the human pilgrimage is merely employment rather than progress? What if the sufferings of this life are not a preparation for some eternal reward, and the envisioned mountaintop is merely a saltwater swamp, aswarm with stinging insects, to which we all contribute our tears:

> With that abash'd and struck with many a sting
> > Of swarming fears,
> > I fell, and cry'd, Alas my King;
> > Can both the way and end be tears?
> Yet taking heart I rose, and then perceiv'd
> > I was deceiv'd:
>
> My hill was further: so I flung away,
> > Yet heard a crie
> > Just as I went, *None goes that way*
> > *And lives:* If that be all, said I,
> After so foul a journey death is fair,
> > And but a chair.
>
> ("The Pilgrimage," 25–36)

This ending is hardly a satisfying closure; it seems, in both senses, graceless. The narrative and the poet seem to have given themselves over to mere exhaustion, just as the speaker has.

Yet by provoking our dissatisfaction, Herbert compels us to look beyond the end of the poem, and beyond the consciousness of the speaker. The paradox of Christian heroism makes the apparent anti-climax of "The Pilgrimage" into a perfect fulfillment. What the speaker (and very likely the reader) at first takes to be the voice of the standard way-blocker of chivalric romance—the troll at the bridge—can be reinterpreted, by thinking in a new genre, as the misunderstood voice of a benevolent God who says, "None sees my face and lives" (Exodus 33:20, King James version). Herbert characteristically provokes a generic misprision that exposes a theological error. At about the time Herbert apparently began writing *The Temple*, Zacharie Boyd attacked precisely this error with yet another rhetorical question: "What is this, that men should so feare death, which is the end of the foule and cumbersome way of our pilgrimage. Hath not God made death like a chariote to a wearied man, for to carie him to his everlasting rest?"[84]

By surrendering to death at the end, the speaker becomes eligible for the exaltation he sought all along. A train leaves from this terminal. In "Mortification," "A chair or litter shows the biere, / Which shall convey him to the house of death" (29–30); in "The Pilgrimage," the sedan-chair that the speaker sardonically imagines coming for him in the guise of death at the end may be a Charon for the penniless, a sweet chariot of Christian salvation.[85] Even if one finds traces of absolute meaning in the temporal world—rocks of Pride to sidestep, wilds of Passion to traverse, good Angels to embrace—one still cannot navigate to heaven. This, then, is a Reformed pilgrimage: a story of rescue rather than achievement. The ending of the poem and the ending of the speaker are again redeemed together, in a way that answers the darkest human fears.

LAST THINGS: FROM "DEATH" TO "LOVE"

"The Church" ends with a consolatory eschatology, a poetic sequence that resists closure by telling a story of salvation. Aptly, the sequence begins with "Death" and ends with the ultimate version of "Love,"[86] moving from a literalist view of the corpse to an allegory of eternal redemption. Herbert thus offers a perspective on mortality much like that of Thomas Browne (p. 116), who thinks

the way to be immortall is to die daily, nor can I thinke I have the true Theory of death, when I contemplate a skull, or behold a Skeleton with those vulgar imaginations it casts upon us; I have therefore enlarged that common *Memento mori*, into a more Christian memorandum, *Memento quatuor novissima*, those foure inevitable points of us all, Death, Judgement, Heaven, and Hell.

Herbert's "Death" begins by equivocating on the distinction between death as a realistic physical condition of humanity, and death as an allegorically externalized enemy of humanity:

> Death, thou wast once an uncouth hideous thing,
>   Nothing but bones,
>   The sad effect of sadder grones:
> Thy mouth was open, but thou couldst not sing.

(1–4)

This is the emblematic figure of the skeleton, but one deprived of articulation, deprived of even the prospective music by which Herbert repeatedly dispels the fear of mere oblivion.

Again Herbert arouses this annihilationist anxiety for the purpose of attributing it to a narrow, materialist conception of (last) things, the kind preceding centuries had expressed through the macabre:

> For we consider'd thee as at some six
>> Or ten yeares hence,
>> After the loss of life and sense,
> Flesh being turn'd to dust, and bones to sticks.
>
> We lookt on this side of thee, shooting short;
>> Where we did finde
>> The shells of fledge souls left behinde,
> Dry dust, which sheds no tears, but may extort.
>
>> (5–12)

The speaker thus reproaches us for imposing our worldly perspective—or, more precisely, our worldly horizon—on the fate of the soul. He hints, further, that while we do so under the guise of pity for the dead, we are actually seeking reassurance for ourselves. The dead feel no sorrow, and crave no commiseration, but extort our tears by holding hostage our narcissistic valuation of ourselves, displaced into the future. These stanzas discourage some of the commonplace strategies of denial, such as hiding behind time to avoid confronting timelessness, and mourning the residual body to avoid contemplating the evanescent soul. Herbert does not empower the macabre here (his decay is dry where Donne's is soggy), any more than he evokes hellfire in other poems, despite the immense popularity of disgusting *transi* figures and horrifying portraits of damnation in the art and sermons of the period.

In this sense, "Death" endorses my claim that such images became popular precisely by helping to hide the repressed fear of annihilation behind a bold acknowledgment of the fear of death; they are denial conveniently disguised as confrontation. In this reading of the denial of death, as in New Historicist readings of political hierarchy, the cultural conspiracy defends itself by permitting an apparent subversion that ultimately enables containment. The vivid residue of the body, even the vivid torments of hell, commonly serve to solve the unrepresentability of death, and thereby to mitigate the fear of purely annihilated consciousness. Morbidity appears as a sort of hysterical symptom, a limiting illness tolerated precisely because it helps limit a terrible thought cathected to it; in "Death," Herbert plays the role of psychotherapist, showing that we do not really need to hide from the eternal by fixating on the macabre. By showing himself unafraid to confront the transience and ultimate insignificance of the body, Herbert can more effectively project his confidence in the soul as a permanent bearer of meaning.

Against the nightmares born of repression, Herbert offers a dream-vision of death itself gloriously resurrected. Everyone is welcome at the doomsday celebration, because spiritual grace will assure physical grace:

> But since our Saviours death did put some bloud
>   Into thy face;
>   Thou art grown fair and full of grace,
> Much in request, much sought for, as a good.
>
> For we do now behold thee gay and glad,
>   As at dooms-day;
>   When souls shall wear their new aray,
> And all thy bones with beautie shall be clad.
>
> Therefore we can go die as sleep, and trust
>   Half that we have
>   Unto an honest faithfull grave;
> Making our pillows either down, or dust.
>
>   (13–24)

The poem reasserts its confidence by willingly ending in "dust." This speaker is neither afraid of the physical nor much impressed by it, and his confidence that the grave will prove a "faithfull" bed contrasts significantly with Donne's anxiety about that very topic in "The Relique."

What follows "Death"—after an indeterminate white-space—is "Dooms-day." In a characteristic swerve of genre, Herbert rewrites *carpe diem* motifs into a mild *Dies Irae* lyric.[87] The lover called upon is Christ, who, instead of initiating the experience of bodily love, will renew the experience of bodily life. Resurrection cures an ailment that is at once terrible physical pain and a complete lack of physical sensation, as if the agonies of dying had remained imprinted in these corpses through an oblivious interim:

>   Come away,
>   Make this the day.
> Dust, alas, no musick feels,
> But thy trumpet: then it kneels,
> As peculiar notes and strains
> Cure Tarantulaes raging pains.
>
>   (7–12)

The movement of the poem is backward toward the beginning (of the line) as well as onward toward the end (of the page); typography recapitulates Christian eschatology, in yet another formal defense against the notion of a linear path through time toward oblivion.

Herbert suggests that there is nothing to fear but this fear itself:

> Come away,
>   O make no stay!
> Let the graves make their confession,
> Lest at length they plead possession:
> Fleshes stubbornnesse may have
> Read that lesson to the grave.
>
> Come away,
>   Thy flock doth stray.
> Some to windes their bodie lend,
> And in them may drown a friend:
> Some in noisome vapours grow
> To a plague and publick wo.
>
>   (13–24)

Corpses threaten us with a spiritual as well as a physical contagion. Christ must hurry, because the longer the dead remain in their graves, the more people will begin to suspect and rumor that no resurrection is forthcoming—a loss of faith that might indeed doom us to eternal death.

Bodily decay is important only to the extent that it provokes a decay of belief. The chaotic scattering of human dust—the problem that worries Donne about the logistics of Judgment Day (*Sermons*, III, 97, 109)—reflects the threat of annihilation, and the decentering of the human project, in the Jacobean period:

> Come away,
>   Help our decay.
> Man is out of order hurl'd,
> Parcel'd out to all the world.
> Lord, thy broken consort raise,
> And the musick shall be praise.
>
>   (25–31)

The answer to this fatal disease called death in the individual, or death-consciousness in the culture as a whole, lies in poetic music or Christian mythology, things that (especially as Herbert combines them) restore shape and scope to our existence by promising to restore the integrity and viability of our bodies.

After this "Dooms-day" summons comes "Judgement," which emphasizes the consoling side of Reformation doctrines that allow God to
choose his own society of souls. Since no human being can testify on his
own behalf without thereby incriminating himself (of the deadly sin of
pride), the speaker invokes the New Testament as a defendant might
invoke the Fifth Amendment. Scanning his Book of Life for "some
leaves therein / So void of sinne" as to preclude damnation (8–9) would
be futile; as Donne observes, "if we will stand *mute*, and have nothing to
say to God, we are condemned already, condemned in our silence; and
if we do plead, we have no plea, but *guilty*" (*Sermons*, III, 203). This was
the paradox troubling Marlowe's Faustus in his opening soliloquy:

If we say that we have no sinne
We deceive our selves, and there is no truth in us.
Why then belike we must sinne,
And so consequently die,
I, we must die, an everlasting death.
(B-text, 1.1.69–73)[88]

Instead of turning to books of magic, Herbert's speaker replaces the
chronicle of his sinful life with "a Testament" of God's own words, with
Christ's testamentary will:

But I resolve, when thou shalt call for mine,
    That to decline,
And thrust a Testament into thy hand:
    Let that be scann'd.
There thou shalt finde my faults are thine.
(11–15)

This ending wittily converts Christ's voluntary assumption of the burden of human sinfulness into a version of the *Measure for Measure*
defense, in which a man cannot be condemned for a crime of which the
judge is no less guilty.

The result is evidently an acquittal, because the next poem is "Heaven."
The Echo device Herbert employs here crystallizes a central paradox of
Herbert's catechistic theology: that God can be omnipresent yet also
responsive, dialogic. God takes over the ending of every line in
"Heaven," as elsewhere in "The Church" He takes over the endings of
individual lyrics and, it is thereby implied, of individual lives. A close
look at any pious ending will find in it a signal of a redemption from

302 WORD WITHOUT END

beyond, harmonizing from heaven with the earthly voice. Poetic wit thus becomes a metaphor for divine benevolence, from the opening to the closing lines:

> O who will show me those delights on high?
> *Echo: I*
> Thou Echo, thou art mortall, all men know
> *Echo: No*
>
> (1–4)
>
> Light, joy, and leisure; but shall they persever?
> *Echo: Ever.*
>
> (19–20)

Like the Williams-manuscript "Even-Song," "Heaven" disavows its closure by ending with "Ever." The end of the line is not, so to speak, the end of the line; it is the site of a reunion with God. What is written on these pious "leaves" is indeed "the echo then of blisse" (5–12). As in *Paradise Lost*, the reader must learn to recognize the pagan deity as an inferior or misperceived type—indeed, a mere echo—of the redeeming Christian godhead.

To misread that typology is to court despair through skepticism. Echo is notorious for her attachment to Narcissus, and we might easily mistake divine responses for the projected residue of our egoistical desires. Many of Herbert's happy endings—which double as renewals of the divine voice—could be depreciated on precisely that basis. Correctly read, "Heaven" is a consoling exhibition, both in form and in content, because it suggests that what might seem merely a reverberation of our desires is truly an affirmation from beyond, however well hidden (like the "chime" in "Deniall") inside the words of human plea. That plea itself, as Reformation theology would insist, proves ultimately to be part of a redemptive plan for atonement with the divine Word.

We thus arrive in Heaven and meet a final incarnation of Love, "Love (III)." The house of death becomes a cozy inn, perhaps even the body of a beloved offering a desirable mutual consummation. The movement out of life proves finally to be a movement into love, and it becomes difficult even to know the difference. Like the scene encountered by the astronaut at the end of the film *2001*, this is, oddly, an interlude of ordinary earthly domesticity, somehow lifted out of time. Herbert ends "The Church" sequence not with a whisper, but a banquet, not with a muting finality, but with an extension of worldly sensual life. Part of the appeal of rituals, including Communion, is their existence outside of time, their ability to create their own stable and manageable chronology, as well as their ability to assert the local and sensible presence of the transcendent. The anti-closural poetic of the lyrics within *The Temple* culminates in the anti-eschatological theology of this closing scene.

"The Church" then ends with a coda of new beginnings. It announces its official "FINIS" with a quotation from the Book of Luke in the New Testament. Before disappearing back into heaven, the heavenly host spoke these same hopeful words, promising new birth, to the shepherds watching their flocks by night: *"Glorie be to God on high, and on earth peace, good will towards men."* These are the opening words of the Gloria in Excelsis that the Book of Common Prayer designated as the end of the Holy Communion service.[89] So this ending begins another ending that promises a new beginning and "world witthout end."[90]

Even this highly equivocal conclusion only prepares *The Temple* to begin again with "The Church-Militant," which is itself a kind of anti-closural device.[91] "The Church-Militant" begins by praising God for controlling the extremes of space and time—"The smallest ant or atome knows thy power, / Known also to each minute of an houre"—then closes with an "Envoy" that begs Christ to silence annihilationism:

> Let not Sinne devoure thy fold,
> Bragging that thy bloud is cold,
> That thy death is also dead,
> While his conquests dayly spread;
> That thy flesh hath lost his food,
> And thy Crosse is common wood.
> Choke him, let him say no more,
> But reserve his breath in store,
> Till thy conquests and his fall
> Make his sighs to use it all,
> And then bargain with the winde
> To discharge what is behinde.
>
> > *Blessed be God alone,*
> > *Thrice blessed Three in One.*
> > *FINIS.*
>
> (5–19)

Once the evil voice has expired, Herbert himself can speak Christian doctrine in the italics formerly reserved for Christ himself. In this odd closing piece (including what seems a strangely scatological joke),[92] the gentle Herbert turns harsh against an enemy which he calls Sin, but which seems to consist primarily of a materialist reading of mortality that would dismiss Christian resurrection as a fantasy.

Before silently resting my own case, therefore, I want to look back to my own beginning: Coleridge's response to Herbert's *Temple*. Coleridge insisted that "To appreciate this volume . . . the reader . . . must be an affectionate and dutiful child of the Church, and . . . find her forms and ordinances aids of religion, not sources of formality; for religion is the element in which he lives, and the region in which he moves."[93] But what is the threatening vacuum outside those formal structures and the pious atmosphere one breathes there? The reader of *The Temple*—an analytic if also appreciative reader—can legitimately infer repressed anxieties about annihilation from the redundant assurances Herbert arrays against them. All of Herbert's most characteristic maneuvers—the ingenious evasions of chronological sequence and ending, the word-play that disarms last words such as *mort* and rest, the personal demands on divine attention through a projection of maternal care, and the strategic transference of the confessional poetic voice to the validating divine Word—bespeak an elaborate psychological denial of death, performed on behalf of his culture as well as himself. W. B. Yeats was right to identify Herbert's poetry as a "form of propaganda."[94] *The Temple* is indeed supremely consoling, but only until we ask what it is consoling us about.

Epilogue
The Deaths of Two Women

Two years before Queen Elizabeth died, Katherine Brettargh died. Three years before King James died, Mary Gunter died. Brettargh and Gunter were obscure figures, but their crises of faith were notable enough to merit preservation in funeral publications, and together they may help to prove that the battle between Protestantism and Catholicism in this period bred atheistic doubts that focused most intensely on the prospect of death. The case of Brettargh shows how the deathbed terror of an individual provoked the society at large to reveal, in the form of argument between Protestants and Catholics, its annihilationist anxieties. The case of Gunter is more explicit, showing how an individual internalized that doctrinal schism as personal terror. In both cases the emotional needs of the women were repressed on behalf of the endangered Christian hegemony; the consolations failed, but the appearances had to be saved. The blankness of death had to be concealed, even if that required disguising it as the devil.

Like many of the Metaphysical lyrics I have been discussing, like conversion narratives in general, these women's stories were made to affirm, within the span of life, the promise of spiritual redemption after death—a promise that, especially for Calvinists, was disturbingly difficult to verify. Narratives of Puritan deaths as well as lives had to rehearse a pattern of desperate fall and joyous recovery, even when that required distorting the data. I hope these cases will add a meaningful emotional note to the conclusion of my long analytic argument. Ending with these biographies rather than with any further anatomies of imaginative literature reflects a recognition that human life-stories matter to me in ways the more abstruse functions of language and criticism do not, and a belief that literary analysis has an ultimate obligation to nurture human sympathy.

KATHERINE BRETTARGH

My sympathetic encounter with Katherine Brettargh began with the frontispiece of her funeral sermon: the Puritan hat and ruff look like millstones about to crush a haunted young face. My search for her legacy reached a dead end in a massive old chronicle of the region, which made the destiny of her only child a blank on the genealogical chart, and showed her entire family line ending more than two centuries ago, surrendering their name and their small ancestral manor a few miles from the city of Chester.[1] In between, her life story emerged mostly in subordination to that of her eldest brother, John Bruen, of the village of Bruen Stapleford. According to an 1848 commentator on a 1617 journal, John Bruen became a small-town hero of early Puritanism: "In the year 1587 he lost his father, and the care of twelve brothers and sisters, their education and fortunes, devolved upon him," and he "regulated his household according to the strict rules of religion. His self-denial and energy of character, were worthy of primitive times, although it must be admitted that some of his proceedings were singularly fanatical, and are calculated rather to excite a smile than to admit of imitation."[2]

What exactly are we being invited to smile at? According to a worshipful 1641 biography, in response to a pious recognition that hunting was cruel and immoral, Bruen "presently killed up the game, and disparked the Parke"—a paradoxical kindness, familiar perhaps from Spenser's Guyon in the Bower of Bliss. Since "Papists will have Images to bee lay mens bookes, yet they teach no other lessons but of lyes," and since the elaborate stained glass windows in the local chapel at Tarvin served to "obscure the brightnesse of the Gospell, [Bruen] presently tooke order, to pull downe all these painted puppets, and popish idols, in a warrantable and peaceable manner." This same impulse replicated itself in the domestic sphere: "finding over the Mantletree a paire of new cards, no body being there, I opened them, and tooke out the foure knaves, and burnt them." Other amusements fared no better: Bruen also reports that he took "the Dice, and all the Cards I found, and put them

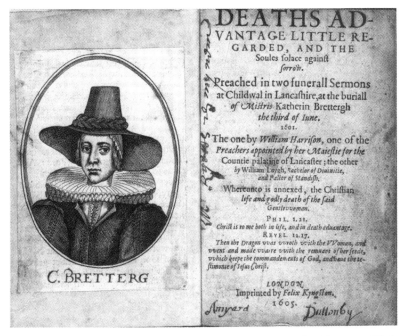

2. Frontispiece and title page from William Harrison, *Deaths Advantage Little Regarded* (London, 1605). Reproduced by permission of The Huntington Library, San Marino, California. RB230048.

into a burning Oven, which was then heating to bake Pies," because he considered them "grosse offenders, and such as could not have their faults (otherwise than by fire, or fornace) purged from them."[3]

As eccentric as these actions may seem, they are logical extensions of a basic Christian consolation for death: the belief (which Calvinism magnified) that things must be utterly destroyed in order to be eternally saved. The closing joke about "grosse offenders" makes it clear that this fiery zeal applied fully to Bruen's fellow humans. Indeed, his piety is described as arising directly from sharp punishments by his earthly father; and, passing on the favor, he "did not spare to use the rod of correction as Gods healing medicine to cure the corruptions of his children." When this zeal would cause him to "deale too violently with his hands," Bruen would then "have recourse unto his heavenly Father by humble and hearty prayer."[4]

After the death of his first wife, John Bruen married a daughter of John Foxe, and may then have made minor domestic martyrs of his family: "On his return to Bruen Stapleford he continued his eccentric though unaffected career of piety, ruling his house well, and rendering it a pattern of Christian morality." Somewhere in that pattern was "his saint-like sister, Mrs. Katherine Bretturgh or Brettargh"; but neither of these rather lengthy accounts of John's life manages to remark on what was, at the time, considered Katherine's very remarkable death.[5]

Doubtless some allowance should be made for the hagiographic tendencies of the occasion, but William Harrison's funeral sermon on Katherine Brettargh convincingly portrays her as an extraordinarily pious Puritan, in conduct as well as in sensibility:

She was by nature very humble and lowly, not disdaining any: very loving and kind, shewing courtesie to all: very meeke, and milde, in forbearing every one; so as they which daily did converse with her, could never see her angrie: and hereby she got the love of all. . . . so did she accustome her selfe to reade every day eight Chapters in the bible [and on the Sabbath] was greatly grieved, if she might not heare one or two Sermons. . . . She had a very tender conscience, and would often weepe not only for her owne sins, but also for the sins of others; especially if she espied a fault in those which were neere unto her, & whom she loved dearely.

She had evidently learned this last lesson from her brother, and duly applied it to her husband, through provocations great and small:

It is not unknowne to *Lancashire*, what horses and cattell of her husbands were killed upon his grounds in the night, most barbarously at two severall times by Seminarie Priests (no question) and Recusants that lurked thereabouts. And what a losse and hinderance it was unto him, being all the stocke hee had on his grounds to any purpose. This fell out not long after shee was married to him; yet . . . turning it into matter of praising God . . . Many times shee would pray that God would forgive them, which had done them this hurt, and send them repentance: and she would call upon her husband, that he would doe the like . . . without either desire of revenge, or satisfying his owne affections.

On a time, as her husband and shee were riding toward the Church, hee was angry with his man: *Alas husband* (quoth she) *I feare your heart is not right towards God, that can be thus angry for a trifle.* . . . Another time, a tenant of her husbands, being behinde with his rent, she desired him to beare yet with him a quarter of a yeare, which he did: and when the man brought his money, with teares she said to her husband: *I feare you doe not well to take it of him, though it bee your right, for I doubt he is not well able to pay it, and then you oppresse the poore.*[6]

This saintliness (perhaps easier for a husband to appreciate after her death) makes her deathbed crisis at once more explicable and more poignantly unjust. It was all too easy for her to blame her own venial moral failings for her deathbed agonies—a perverse consolation fundamental to Christian theodicy. The idea that these agonies foretold her damnation would of course have been unbearable, but no more so than the idea that they meant nothing, and that her lifelong forebearances would never be rewarded. She might have cried, like Herbert's pilgrim, "Alas, my king; / Can both the way and end be tears?"

These aspects of Katherine Brettargh's story are legible in a rather polemical narrative of her embattled life and death appended (in several editions) to the two sermons preached at her funeral in Childwall church on the third of June, 1601. The first sermon, by the Puritan preacher William Harrison, took its text from Isaiah 57:1 in the Geneva Bible: "The righteous perisheth, and no man considereth it in heart." Harrison's treatment first caught my attention because it seemed to be struggling to exclude an annihilationist suspicion, insisting that the word *"perisheth* . . . must not so be understood, as if he were quite destroyed, brought to nothing, and had no more being: as it befalleth bruite beasts at their death, whose soules being traduced with their bodies are mortall, and perish with their bodies: the righteous hath a being even after death." Harrison avoids even mentioning the possibility that people might understand death as a mere and universal fact of nature. Instead he insists that people see in it the mysteries of divine providence: "This carelesse contemning of their death, doth shew that ye harts of the comon people were possessed with great securitie, to make so small reckoning of such a strange worke of God." But how strange is it, in the common mind, that righteous people die like everyone else? Harrison adduces a standard sacred binarism to redeem death from its terrifyingly apparent indifference: "The godly are taken out of the world, because *the world was not worthie of them,"* Harrison asserts, "but the wicked are taken away, because they are unworthie to live in the world."[7] To relinquish the absolute Calvinist dyad of elect and preterite would be to admit that some people die because all people die. Moralizing death replaces an ontological mystery with a familiar transaction of punishment and reward.

The resulting compulsion to find portents of the afterlife in the scene of the deathbed places Harrison in the peculiar position of first insisting through most of his sermon that "an evill death can never follow a good life," and then having to close the same sermon by lauding a woman renowned for her miserable death as well as her pious life.[8] Harrison was not present during the worst of Brettargh's crisis, but those who had observed her raging against her pain and "want of feeling Gods mercie," accusing herself of unbelief and terrible sins, and throwing her Bible repeatedly to the floor, must have listened uneasily to the core of Harrison's funeral sermon:

> The wicked . . . dye impatiently, who doe not willingly beare the Lords correction, deserved by their sinnes; but rage, fret, and murmure, as if God dealt too rigorously with them. . . . Others die desperatly, their consciences accusing them most terribly for their sins. . . . The consciences of many wicked men lye quietly, and never trouble them all their life time, but are stirred up at their death, and then rage and torment them like a mad dog which is lately awaked out of sleep. But the righteous die most comfortably. . . .

Eventually Harrison evades the implications of this doctrine for Katherine Brettargh by at once externalizing her troubles into Satan and dismissing them as mere physiological manifestations of her bodily illness:

> if the righteous a little before death be dangerouslie tempted by Sathan, and shew their infirmitie by uttering some speeches which tend to doubting or desperation (though afterward they get victory, and triumph over the divell) carnall people think there is no peace of conscience, and therefore no salvation to bee had, by that religion: and so speake evill of it.

> Lastlie, others beholding them which were reputed righteous, to die very stranglie, to rave, to blaspheme, to utter many idle and impious speeches, to be unrulie and behave themselves verie foolishlie, they begin to suspect their profession: but let them know, that these things may arise from the extremitie of their disease. . . . it is not they which doe it, but the disease which is upon them.[9]

A Catholic who dies in anguish is being punished by God for sin and confessing hypocrisy; a Puritan who dies in anguish is being assaulted by the devil for virtue, and displaying the distortions naturally accompanying a high fever.

Yet there is more at risk here than factional propaganda; in defending Puritan Christianity, Harrison risks compromising Christianity as a whole. The parallel between demonic possession and biological disease in these passages threatens to expose the entire Christian scheme as an evasive allegorization of the hard facts of nature. Nor was this the only time this family had encountered that threat. Confronted with a case of supposed demonic possession that bears strong resemblances to his sister's deathbed crisis ("If one came neare him with a Bible," the possessed boy tried "to rend it in peeces"), John Bruen fought to preserve the supernatural moral drama: though "some ascribed all to naturall causes, few did endevour to see and acknowledge (as this Gentleman did) that though Satan might have a finger, yet the Lord had a chiefe hand in this Judgment."[10]

Harrison's sermon strives to contain a threat that goes far beyond Katherine Brettargh's personal reputation: "I have heard that some speake very uncharitably of her, by reason of her temptation, and thereupon mutter much against religion it selfe: but such should remember that which I have spoken before, that the Devill most assaulteth them which be most godly, thinking to hinder all religion, if he may prevaile with such."[11] Christianity thus anticipates the self-verifying device of the modern belief-system called psychoanalysis, in which every lapse in the supporting evidence can be attributed to the repression of that evidence; in the case of Harrison's sermon, every visitation of atheistic doubt confirms the workings of Satan, and hence the existence of God. If Katherine Brettargh had been tormented simply by a fear that Christian damnation rather than Christian salvation was imminent, or if her torment had been merely an occasion for Catholics to condemn Protestantism, why should it have provoked mutterings "against religion it selfe"; how could it "hinder all religion" as Harrison charges?

Harrison's larger anxieties suggest that Katherine Brettargh's death-bed crisis had annihilationist overtones. Pain and fever produced delirium, doubt, and resentment. Lacking an alternative discourse of Existential heroism, the pious observers in the sickroom—including Brettargh herself—were obliged to perceive these symptoms as diabolical temptation in order to avoid perceiving them as mere biology. Restored to the orthodox categories, her sufferings became commodities accessible to the competing claims of Catholicism and Protestantism. The Devil is placed in the sick-room to block a window into non-religious death, and the unnamed complainants against religion per se may have been—anticipating radicals such as Winstanley[12]—condemning the way pressures toward religious orthodoxy demanded that the dying woman generate spiritual misery to match her physical condition, a sort of theological inversion of pathetic fallacy. Without that subjective correlative, death is ruined as a work of divine art and divine justice.

The other sermon delivered at Katherine Brettargh's funeral, by William Leigh (who elsewhere declares that there can be "no blessed life without a blessed death")[13] manifests similar symptoms of resistance to some lurking annihilationist initiative. Leigh chooses a text concerning the sleep of the righteous, which he describes as

an Antidote to prevent a poyson much infecting all flesh: who without all comfort of future blessednes, do, to the hazard of their soules, stand doubtfull of the resurrection, as also of the rest of their soules, after they be departed. The one sort are the *Atheists*, the other are the *Papists* of these dayes & times: but the text is powerfull to put backe both *Jordans*, that the *Israel* of God may enter *Canaan* without crosse or feare. For if the Lords elect shal rest in their beds, they shal rise from their beds. Rest implyeth a resurrection, when the time of *refreshing* shall come. It is an improper speech to say, hee resteth, who never riseth. It may bee some go to bed who never rise, strooken with a deadly sleepe or lethargie, but none to the grave, but out he must, at the generall sommons. . . .

The obvious speciousness of such an argument is less important in itself than as a symptom of the compulsion to make an argument. After a series of anxious references to lost sight and hearing, Leigh concedes that when Brettargh fell ill, "The Lord hid his face from her, & she was troubled."[14] In the context of Brettargh's particular anxieties, this Scriptural formula begins to sound like a euphemism for the terrifying idea of a *deus absconditus*.

Two poems appended to these sermons also attempt to control the interpretation of Katherine Brettargh's far-from-tame death.[15] The first, under the guise of allowing the deceased to testify posthumously in her own behalf, personifies her disbelief as a safely conventional Christian adversary: "True it is I strove: But 'twas against mine enemie," declares the opening line. The other poem, a kind of antiphonic response, begins, "It's not unlike (Christ's deare) such conflict you endur'de." The parenthetical compliment—indeed, the entire invention of a posthumous dialogue—begs the fundamental question.

The terms of our responses having been thus prepared and circumscribed, the narrative of her life and death can begin. Still, when that narrative arrives at her final illness, the syntax becomes notably rich in defensive modifications and subordinate clauses, and notably determined to achieve a happy piety before yielding to its own closure:

Her sicknes tooke her in the manner of *a hot burning Ague*, which made her according to the nature of such diseases, now and then to talke somewhat idly, and through the tempters subtiltie, which abused the infirmitie of her bodie to that end, as he oftentimes useth to do in many, from idle words, to descend into a heavy conflict, with the infirmitie of her owne spirit; from the which, yet the Lord presently and wonderfully delivered her. . . .

But this delivery comes only after considerable labor pains: "she began to feele some little infirmitie and weaknes of faith. . . . shee thought shee had no faith, but was full of hypocrisie. . . . Sometime she would cast her Bible from her."[16] Particularly if one allows for the euphemizing tendency of the pious narrator, this sounds more like an abandonment of Christian religion than like a fear of Christian damnation.

A woman of such selfless piety might begin to mistrust the justice—and hence the existence—of the Christian God as she lay in mortal agony at age twenty-two. This is hardly an anachronistic speculation, because the narrator feels compelled to defend against it, as perhaps Brettargh did herself:

Many times shee accused her selfe of impatience, bewayling the want of feeling Gods spirit, and making doubt of her election, and such like infirmities. Shee wished, that she had never beene borne. . . . But every one saw that these things proceeded of weakenes, emptines of her head, and want of sleepe, which her disease would not affoord her.

These fits though they were for the time grievous to her selfe, and discomfortable to her friends: yet were they neither long nor continuall, but in the very middest of them, would she oftentimes give testimonie of her faith. . . . Once in the middest of her temptation, being demaunded by *Master William Fox: whether she did beleeve the promises of God, nor no? and whether she could pray?* she answered: *O that I could, I would willingly, but he will not let me. Lord I beleeve, helpe my unbeliefe.*[17]

However paradoxical, this last plea is a common enough quotation (from Mark 2:24) among struggling Christians. But it becomes increasingly clear that Brettargh resorts to quoting such Christian formulas because she cannot believe deeply or spontaneously in the promise of personal afterlife she so badly needs on this premature deathbed:

And when shee was moved to make confession of her fath, shee would doe it oftentimes, saying the Apostles *Creede*, and concluding the same with words of application to her selfe: I beleeve the remission of (*my*) sinnes, the resurrection of (*my*) bodie, and eternall life (*to mee*) Amen. And having done, she would pray God to confirme her in that faith. . . . But the difficulty shee had sometimes to apply these generals unto her owne soul in particular, made the case more full of anguish to her selfe, and fearefull and lamentable to the standers by.[18]

The poignance of this "difficulty" needs little pointing—except perhaps to Foucauldian critics and historians who would claim that only the alienated individualism of a twentieth-century *episteme* could produce this sort of *anomie*. When this woman found that she "could hardly

appropriate each thing to her selfe," she exposes the damage that
Reformation individualism (with its inward God and His inscrutable
election) had already done to conventional Christian consolations for
death.

At last, this narrator insists, came a happy ending: "being laide downe
againe in her bed, she confidently spake these words: *I am sure that my
redeemer liveth, and that I shall see him at the last day, whom I shall see,
and mine eyes shall behold: and though after my skin, wormes destroy this
bodie, yet shall I see God in my flesh with these eyes, and none other.*" Thus
finally the wild death of Katherine Brettargh was tamed by the promise
of afterlife, tapering off from the sufferings of Job to a pious silence, but
not without a Desdemona-like coda of loving forgiveness toward the
Lord who decreed her terrible death:

> her tongue failed her, and so she lay silent for a while, every one judging her
> then to be neere death, her strength and speech failing her: yet after a while
> lifting up her eyes with a sweete countenance and still voyce, said . . . *he is my
> God, and will guide me unto death: guide me O Lord my God, and suffer me not
> to faint, but keepe my soule in safetie.* And with that shee presently fell a sleepe
> in the Lord, passing away in peace, without any motion of body at all; and so
> yeelded up the Ghost, a sweete Sabboaths sacrifice about foure of the clocke
> in the afternoone, of *Whitsunday,* being the last of *May* 1601.[19]

The narrator thus seizes on the instant of tame death, and plants it firmly
back in a Christian frame of time.

The justification offered for appending this "Brief Discourse," with
its extensive and harrowing account of Katherine Brettargh's deathbed
suffering in body and soul, seems almost as perverse as the thematic
argument of Harrison's sermon. At the very least, this justification
resounds with denial:

> But sure her death was such, her behaviour in her sicknes so religious, her
> heart so possessed with comfort, her mouth so filled with praises of God, her
> spirit so strengthened against the feare of death, her conquest so happy over
> her infirmities, that such as loved her most have greatest cause to rejoyce in
> her death, and by seeing the wonderfull worke of God in her, to learne to
> renounce their owne affections. . . . I thought so great mercie of God shewed
> to one among us, ought not to be forgotten, but should remaine to us & our
> children an example, to teach how good God is to them that love him, and to
> assure us that he will never forsake us; but, in like manner as he did her, helpe
> and comfort us, when we shall by death be called unto him. I considered the
> ungodly and uncharitable tongues of the *Papists* abiding in our countrey, who,
> since her death, have not ceased to give it out that she died despairing, and by

her comfortles end, shewed that she professed a comfortles Religion. Wherein they bewray their malice & madnes. . . . [20]

Though this narrative does stress that Katherine Brettargh recovered her peace of mind in the final day of her illness, it is hard to believe her story to be such an extraordinary demonstration of God's gentleness and unfailing comfort that it demanded publication. More probably, it was sufficiently threatening that it demanded revisionistic commentary. If pious contemporary commentators could claim Katherine Brettargh as a fine example of comfortable Christian dying, then it is easy to see why modern commentators, taking the earlier ones at their word, have mistakenly supposed that all Renaissance Christians died confident of an afterlife.

Harrison claims that his purpose in publishing *Deaths Advantage* is "to cleere her from the slanderous reports of her popish neighbours, who will not suffer her to rest in her grave, but seeke to disgrace her after her death."[21] In fact, Katherine Brettargh's death has never been allowed to rest, in pain or in peace, as a simple fact of nature. Instead it became, in her conscious mind, a gigantic struggle between God and Satan for her soul. It became, in a skirmish of Jacobean pamphlets, a furious debate between Puritans and Romanists over which religion could promise the more merciful death. In an early example of spin-control in the popular press, the narrator of Brettargh's life story demands of the Catholic jeerers, "what can any man see that might give just occasion to report our religion comfortles, or [that] the Gentle-woman dyed despairing," and points out the prominent Catholics "which have dyed most fearefully indeede."[22] Nor can she yet rest in peace, to the extent that I am imposing yet another abstract binarism by interpreting the same feverous delirium as a subliminal struggle between Christian orthodoxy and repressed annihilationism.

From the age of eight, Katherine Brettargh was raised by a brother who (even according to his hagiographer) "sometimes made rather too small an allowance for the material part of man, and treated him, unwisely, as altogether a spiritual being."[23] In the grip of a bitterness she could not fully understand (indeed, was forbidden to understand), in the agony of a violent fatal illness, Brettargh was left no choice but to accuse herself of spiritual failure and to anticipate eternal torment in hell. It is not a very good brief for religion, but it does exemplify the pathos and pathology of the human individual trying to comprehend and endure mortality.[24]

MARY GUNTER

Mary Gunter's story survives in a "Profitable Memoriall" of "the life and death of this sweet Saint, as it was observed and now faithfully witnessed by her mournfull husband, who wisheth both his life and latter end like unto hers"—a sentiment more sweet than credible.[25] This memorial appeared in 1622, and was reprinted in 1633, both times appended to the Puritan sermon preached at her funeral. It is a form of conversion narrative, but the conversion is socially imposed:

This gracious Woman was for birth a Gentlewoman, but descended of Popish Parents, who dying in her infancy, shee was committed unto the tuition of an old Lady, honourable for her place, but a strong Papist, who nousled and misled this Orphan in Popery, till shee came about foureteene yeeres of age; at which time this Lady died. Upon which occasion, God (having a mercifull purpose towards her conversion) by his good Providence, brought her to the service of that Religious and truly honourable Lady, the Countesse of *Leicester*. . . . To this Honourable Countesse shee came a most zealous Papist, and resolute, as soone as possibly shee could apprehend a fit opportunity, to convey her selfe beyond the Seas, and become a Nunne. . . . But shee could not so closely carry her secret devotions and intentions, but that by the carefull eye of her Honourable Lady, they were soone discovered, and not sooner discovered then wisely prevented; for presently her Lady tooke from her all her Popish bookes, Beades and Images, and all such trumpery, and set a narrow watch over her, that shee might bee kept from her Popish Prayers, and not absent her selfe from the daily Prayers of the Family, which were religiously observed: further, requiring her to read those Prayers that her honour daily used to have in her private chamber with her women.

Her Ladiship also carefully prevented her from her Popish company and counsel by word or writing, for neither might shee write nor receive any letter without the view and consent of her Honour (pp. 159–62)

Despite the narrator's approbation, or perhaps because of it, modern readers may be reminded of the cruel benevolence by which Shakespeare's Shylock is converted, and perhaps also of the tactics employed by modern "deprogrammers" of religious cultists.

The young woman put up some strategic resistance: to cover her stubborn recusancy, "shee in short time obtayned great ability to communicate to others the substance of those Sermons" she had been forced to attend (p. 163). But mimicry soon became identity, and the concealed Self became the enemy Other. One Puritan preacher proved so compelling that "in short time, it pleased God that shee was won to beleeve the Truth, and renounce her former superstition and ignorance. And as it is the property of a true Convert, being converted her selfe, she endevoured the conversion of others" (p. 164). This might be a valuable instance for those claiming a radical malleability of selfhood in Renaissance England, except that this conversion proved agonizingly difficult: "Now presently Satan . . . begins to rage, and reach at her with strong and violent temptations," including "the dreadfull and foule suggestion of selfe murder" (pp. 165–66). In other words, she was nearly compelled to destroy her identity in order to save it—or in order to save the Kohutian self-object in which she had formerly invested her immortality.

Mary Gunter could maintain her selfhood, her sanity, even her life, only by making her Protestantism a fetishized shadow of her former Catholicism. Forbidden the ritual comforts of the Roman religion, she made a ritual out of the Bible study central to Protestantism: "shee tyed her selfe to a strict course of godlinesse, and a constant practice of Christian Duties, which she religiously observed even till her dying day. . . . shee would every yeare read over the whole Bible in an ordinary course, which course shee constantly observed for the space of fifteene yeares together, beginning her taske upon her birthday. . . . " (p. 171). The timing is psychologically revealing: she must be born-again in order to recover the stability of her original identity, which religious schism had subverted. By systematically internalizing the text the schismatics had in common, she reconstructs herself: "by her great industry in the Scriptures, shee had gotten by heart many select Chapters, and speciall *Psalmes*; and of every Booke of the Scripture one choyce verse: all which shee weekly repeated in an order which shee propounded to her selfe" (p. 173). But the entwining of Protestant autobiography with the reading of Scripture could easily have reinforced a suspicion that the Calvinist salvational scheme had no room for unique interiorities. Mary Gunter built prayer-system on prayer-system, fasted (a familiar tactic for reclaiming the autonomy of the self), and kept a moralistic vigil over herself, as if she might otherwise not only sin, but disappear: "for the space of five yeares before her death, she kept a Catalogue of her daily slips, and set down even the naughty thoughts which shee observed in her selfe. . . . " (pp. 174–77). The problem she confronts here is the same Donne confronts in "Goodfriday, 1613. Riding Westward" and the Holy Sonnets, and Herbert confronts in "Good Friday" and "Judgement": the zealous Protestant must construct a narrative of the self, yet that narrative is inevitably so deeply entwined with sin that God will, at best, erase it.

In her early Papist days, Mary Gunter had been led venially astray: "Whilest shee was a childe bred up in the chamber of that old Lady, shee was entised by lewd servants who fed her with figges, and other such toyes, fit to please children withall, to steale money out of the Ladies Cabinet." Now, as a Protestant, she paid that unsuspected debt back to the Catholic woman's heir, with generous interest, from her marriage portion (pp. 178–80). But the debt of her apostasy was not so easily appeased. Her Catholicism reasserted itself as something worse: now Satan

would confound and oppresse her with multitudes of blasphemous thoughts, and doubts. Now must shee beleeve there is no God: That the Scriptures are not his Word, but a Pollicie. . . . for, how could shee be sure that this was the truth which she now professed, seeing there are as many, or more learned men of the one opinion as of the other, and all of them maintaine their opinions by the Scriptures. Thus was shee vexed and exercised with Armies of roving and unsetled conceits for five or six yeares together. (pp. 168–69)

Unable to distract herself entirely with her systematic exertions of piety, she thus settled into the kind of rational doubts supposedly impossible in this period. In doing so, she confirmed Bacon's axiom that schism in religion breeds atheism. The image of Satan was again superimposed to keep that threat from appearing in its own guise. Identifying atheism as a Satanic temptation provides a fail-safe device for Christianity; unbelief is imprisoned in a labyrinth. But that labyrinth is only rhetorical: neither the need of pious public commentators to subjugate these women's doubts to the official system, nor even the eventual willingness of the women to accept that consoling formula, undoes the fact that they were able to conceive such doubts. Christianity was no longer—if it ever had been—a perfectly self-perpetuating response to death; instead, the hysterical conjuration of Satan suggests a kind of reaction-formation in defense of the culture's theological consensus.

Mary Gunter's spirit recovered from this crisis, but her flesh "was of weake and sickly constitution many yeares before her death," and her final illness allowed a recurrence of these agonizing religious doubts:

But thirty dayes before her departure, she finding her paines increasing, and growing very sharpe and tedious, she spent an houres talke with me concerning her desire for the things of this life; and having said what she purposed, shee thus concluded her speech: Now, sweet Heart, no more words betweene you and me of any worldly thing. . . . (pp. 183–84)

All she asked was her husband's help in praying for her soul, which proved needful, because "onely three dayes before her death, she began to be dejected in the sense of her owne dulnesse, and thereby began to call in question Gods love towards her, and the truth of Gods grace in her" (pp. 185–86). Again, Calvinist preterition seems difficult to distinguish from annihilationism.

Her husband is quick to assure us that this spiritual crisis only proves how merciful God is to Puritans, "for that he had now so chained Satan at this time of her great weaknesse, that having beene formerly molested, and daily vexed with his assaults, for the space of above six yeares together, now he would not suffer him to rest on her with his malice above six houres" (pp. 186–87). Exacerbated by the slippage in the male pronouns, the manifold sexual overtones of this claim about the Satanic possession of his wife suggest that he was almost willing to be cast as the devil who tempts her, if it would rescue her from an irreligious universe. In any case, the parallel to the earlier crisis clearly suggests that atheistic annihilationism was as much a part of Mary Gunter's deathbed crisis as it was of her midlife crisis. Doubtless her deathbed anxieties expressed themselves primarily as a fear of preterition, but preterition took many forms in Mary Gunter's experience. She would have been deeply sensitized to the threat of losing her interior and relational selves. Even at the end, even filtered through orthodox Christian interpreters, her words suggest less concern with Christian damnation than with the obliteration of the identity she has built, as if she were surrendering this-worldly domesticity ("the things of this life," the structures of house and family) with no otherworldly destination.

The Christian God had provided for Mary Gunter's interiority so unreliably in life that she could easily have doubted its preservation after death. Exclusion from God had already proven a lonely experience of privation for her; it had erased the core of her former Catholic identity, and the superimposed Protestant beliefs suggested that God's presence could be known only in the interiority that was now again at risk through death. As D. W. Winnicott has speculated, the fear of death is closely related to a fear of breakdown, and those who have experienced some unacknowledged psychic death at a formative stage are likely to recognize physical death as a sort of objective correlative to the earlier psychic loss. In Heinz Kohut's terminology, a "fulfilled parting" from this life is possible only for those whose personality has "no significant admixture of disintegration anxiety."[26] Given the severe mutability of Mary

Gunter's objects of immortality and idealization, it is hardly surprising that the fear of annihilated selfhood weighed so heavily on her deathbed. Nor is it surprising, given the importance (in Kohut's view) of a reliably empathetic observer to ease these fears,[27] that her husband's vigil by the deathbed was so crucial to her endurance.

It is a commonplace of seventeenth-century religious tracts that deathbeds cure atheism, but the case of Mary Gunter, like that of Katherine Brettargh, suggests that these final agonies may have evoked rather than erased atheistical doubts and annihilationist fears. Theological schism seems to have accentuated this tendency, and it certainly accentuated the compulsion to exempt one's own faction from the taint of mortal terror. As with Katherine Brettargh, a happy ending is hastily cobbled onto Mary Gunter's terminal illness (and the only modern commentary I have found strangely whitewashes Gunter's story);[28] but it scarcely conceals the evidence that the Reformation had dangerously unsettled the standard mythology of Christian afterlife. "Neither could so gracious a life be shut up but by an answerable, that is, an happy death," the husband insists (p. 182); and Mary Gunter herself is determined to uphold that mythology, asking God for a clear mind with which to enjoy her death, "for she said, If I through paine or want of sleepe (which she much wanted) should have any foolish or idle talke, I know what the speech of the world useth to be; This is the end of all your precise folke, they die mad, or not themselves, &c." (p. 189). But are atheism and annihilationism always madness, or only maddening? And who was Mary Gunter, when she was herself?

In early seventeenth-century England, the fear of lost selfhood began to eclipse the threat of hellfire; at least for Protestants, the fear of being unloved by any deity often replaced the fear of divine anger. Like John Donne, Mary Gunter was violently dislodged in adolescence from the identity she had built around her intense Catholic indoctrination; like Donne, she fell into a period of skepticism that left her forever vulnerable to the fear of both death and personal instability. But the annihilationist anxieties haunting these apostates are also legible in figures of stable familial Protestantism such as George Herbert and Katherine Brettargh. From her parents' "dying in her infancy," from the death of the Catholic woman who raised her "to about fourteene yeeres of age," and from the tactics of isolation then used to compel her conversion, Mary Gunter would have learned the annihilationist lesson: that abandonment can be even more terrifying than punishment. But even in the assured piety of Herbert's *The Temple*, God's abandonment is a more real and active threat than His punishment. When Satan torments Katherine Brettargh on her deathbed, he does so merely by forbidding her to apply the promise of salvation to herself. In a world of individuals, Satan is no longer the Seven Deadly Sins, in all their vivid allegorical guises. He is instead the figure who threatens to pull off his traditional mask; that is, to pull the mask off death, and show us its unspeakably blank face.

Retraction

This is a special way of being afraid
No trick dispels. Religion used to try;
That vast moth-eaten musical brocade
Created to pretend we never die,
And specious stuff that says No rational being
Can fear a thing it will not feel, *not seeing*
That this is what we fear—no sight, no sound. . . .
—Philip Larkin ("Aubade")[1]

Be not apt to call any opinion false, or hereticall, or
damnable, the contrary whereof cannot be evidently
proved.

(*Sermons*, IX, 139)

    The original intent of this project was to assert anni-hilationism as a transhistorical truth differently evaded in different periods. The ethical motive was a quasi-psychoanalytic supposition that the repression of this truth produced more suffering than a confrontation with it would produce. If Christianity was guilty of facilitating this unhealthy denial (by promising to make our individuality somehow compatible with infinitude), and perhaps even of magnifying the threat so that its consolations would become all the more saleable, then its claim on my cultural heroes had to be challenged.

    But annihilationism is the classic unprovable hypothesis. No one could return to confirm it without contradicting it, nor can anyone disprove the existence of an afterlife that is professedly inaccessible to mortal perception, particularly the perception of an unbeliever. "Annhilation" is a signifier that signifies nothing; no phenomenon can be produced to validate it. Thomas Browne is surely correct in classifying death as something "which no Man fears by Experience" (p. 405). Perhaps what annihilationists fear is less the intense silence of death than the cacophony they imagine swirling around it, like a hurricane around its eye. Resting in peace means neglecting to sort or manage the continuing roar of the noumenal world. As Jesus warns in the Book of Matthew (12:30), "he who does not gather with me scatters."

So, while my doubts about afterlife remain, my argument has evolved away from theology and toward psychology; and within psychology, it has moved away from Freud and toward Winnicott.[2] In the process, it has become more sympathetic toward the mythmaking impulse, recognizing that converting experience into comfortable narratives is a necessary function of human consciousness, not only to maintain our morale in the face of death, but also to maintain our sanity in the face of life. Human beliefs are susceptible to the same moral questions commonly applied to poetry in the Renaissance: are they lies, or merely preferable ways of organizing destructively chaotic experience? As all cognition is a construct consisting of exclusions and imprecise categorizations of a virtually infinite world of sense-phenomena, so the denial of death may be a narrative necessarily imposed on the unmanageably infinite concept of personal annihilation, a concept which prospectively removes precisely the consciousness necessary to manage it. Without some story of afterlife, a completely unorganized self travels into an eternal structureless future: even in anticipation, death threatens to swamp our powers of comprehension with the impossible calculation of infinity squared.

Little wonder that, as object-relations psychologists report, death anxiety runs highest in people whose weakly defined selfhood constantly reminds them that the life of the mind, as of the body, is a struggle to maintain the integrity of the system. Why would anyone worry about an insentient future after death, unless that prospect tapped a latent fear that surrendering control during life, ceasing to hold the self vigilantly together, would lead to a catastrophic collapse and dispersal? According to Donne, God must constantly prompt us "to recollect our selves, to recapitulate our selves, to assemble and muster our selves," which would otherwise be scattered "by reason of the various fluctuation of our corrupt nature, and the infinite multiplicity of Objects."[3] Not the absence of one's physical self from the world, but the loss of the

organizing consciousness by which we have held that world, may be
what makes annihilationist mortality so unsustainable a thought. We
dare not imagine the world without the self to make sense of it, and yet
we know the world will outlast the self, which is therefore superfluous,
and is all we have. Recognizing both the self and its mortality provokes
desperation. If we did not recognize all the work the mind does in
taming the world, we would not fear leaving that work undone; we
could not imagine it undone. Culture therefore promises to define the
world for us, beyond the scope of our individual minds; art and religion
promise to provide or discover a lasting order. Otherwise, around our
graves, Eden grows wild, as if it had never been tended.

Notes

1. Compare Imre Lakatos, *The Methodology of Scientific Research Programmes*, ed. John Worrall and Gregory Currie (Cambridge: Cambridge University Press, 1983), and Thomas Kuhn, *The Structure of Scientific Revolutions* (Chicago: University of Chicago Press, 1962), on the pattern of scientific revolutions. Checking these notes at a makeshift outdoor table less than two days after the largest earthquake in modern Los Angeles history, and less than two miles from its epicenter, I cannot resist offering the analogy to the steady movement of tectonic plates that manifests itself in sporadic violent shifts.

2. James L. Calderwood's characteristically fresh and insightful *Shakespeare and the Denial of Death* (Amherst: University of Massachusetts Press, 1987) builds directly on Becker, as does Kirby Farrell's thoughtful *Play, Death, and Heroism in Shakespeare* (Chapel Hill: University of North Carolina Press, 1989).

3. Andrew Marvell, "A Dialogue between Thyrsis and Dorinda," lines 1–4, in *The Complete Poems*, ed. Elizabeth Story Donno (London: Penguin, 1985), p. 21.

4. Thomas Heywood, A *True Discourse of the Two infamous upstart Prophets* (London, 1636), p. 7; cf. Richard Hooker, *Works*, ed. Jan Keble (New York: Burt Franklin, 1970), II, 21: "With our contentions their irreligious humour also is much strengthened." The case of Mary Gunter, which will be described in my Epilogue, grimly verifies that prediction and its applicability beyond the sphere of skeptical intellectuals.

5. Foucault himself acknowledges that the fifteenth-century "substitution of the theme of madness for that of death does not mark a break, but rather a

torsion within the same anxiety," and I would suggest that the anxiety may have focused primarily on personal disintegration rather than (as Foucault suggests) a cynical nihilism; see *Madness and Civilization*, trans. Richard Howard (New York: Vintage, 1973), p. 16.

Perhaps cultural critics have underestimated the continuity of human anxieties about death partly because they underestimate the continuity of selfhood assumed in earlier cultures. The fact that the invention of individuality always seems to occur during the period in which the investigator specializes should give some pause. Along with the familiar emphasis on heightened individualism in thirteenth- and fourteenth-century Europe (in the works of Burckhardt and his followers), the scholarly world has been treated to extensive claims (in the works of Colin Morris, Philippe Ariès, Joel Fineman, Catherine Belsey, and Francis Barker) for nascent individuality in each century from the eleventh through the seventeenth—none of which explain such powerful and various documents of continuous and interior selfhood, haunted by mortal frailty, as *Oedipus Rex*, the Book of Job, the *Meditations* of Marcus Aurelius, and the *Confessions* of Saint Augustine. Indeed, the doctrine of resurrection, as articulated by the church fathers and the scholastics, would have made little sense if individual identity had been as attenuated as is now sometimes claimed. On the patristic insistence that the same person is resurrected who lived, see Caroline Walker Bynum, "Material Continuity," *History of Religions*, 30 (1990), p. 70; on the investment in the continuity of bodily selfhood during the thirteenth century, see Bynum, p. 77.

For further instances of critics inclined to disallow modern notions of selfhood in Renaissance culture, see *Reconstructing Individualism*, ed. Thomas C. Heller et al. (Stanford: Stanford University Press, 1986). An article by David Aers, "Reflections on Current Histories of the Subject," *Literature & History* (1991), pp. 20–34, has strongly refuted these claims, as has Richard Levin's characteristically sharp-edged "Unthinkable Thoughts in the New Historicizing of English Renaissance Drama," *New Literary History*, 21 (1990), especially pp. 436–37 and 442–44, and David Quint's admirably measured introduction to *Literary Theory/Renaissance Texts* (Baltimore: Johns Hopkins University Press, 1986), especially pp. 1–5. This is not to deny that there are important fluctuations in the degree and configuration of psychological individualism, as domestic arrangements and religious practices change. But the fluctuations are subtle, and it is unlikely that they have ever completely erased the fear of personal extinction in Western culture from the Medieval period to the present. As Walter Ralegh ruefully reported, while the roles and the stages of our lives may change, "we die in earnest, that's no jest"—and we each die as ourselves. Nor would anyone have had it otherwise, even back then: "tho we may wish the prosperous Appurtenances of others, or to be an other in his happy Accidents; yet so intrinsical is every Man unto himself, that some doubt may be made, whether any would exchange his Being, or substantially become another Man" (Browne, "Letter to a Friend," p. 404).

6. Sigmund Freud, "Thoughts for the Times on War and Death," *Complete Psychological Works*, Standard ed., trans. James Strachey (London: Hogarth

Press, 1957), XIV, 296 and 294, which further speculates that this primal mourner "devised a compromise; he conceded the fact of his own death as well, but denied it the significance of annihilation." My theory is that this compromise is perpetually renegotiated, in a variety of cultural languages, throughout modern Western cultures. Throughout his works, D. W. Winnicott insists that basic human psychological crises remain similar in virtually any historical setting.

7. See, for example, Browne, *Religio Medici*, p. 116: "I say, every man hath a double Horoscope, one of his humanity, his birth; another of his Christianity, his baptisme, and from this doe I compute or calculate my Nativitie, not reckoning . . . my selfe any thing, before I was my Saviours, and inrolled in the Register of Christ."

8. Clare Gittings, *Death, Burial and the Individual in Early Modern England* (London: Croom Helm, 1984), p. 83.

9. Michael MacDonald and Terence R. Murphy, *Sleepless Souls: Suicide in Early Modern England* (Oxford: Clarendon, 1990), pp. 15–16. The current fetishizing of the boundary between life and death is evident in arguments and trials about doctor-assisted suicide.

10. Phillipe Ariès, *Western Attitudes toward Death: From the Middle Ages to the Present*, trans. Patricia Ranum (Baltimore: Johns Hopkins University Press, 1974), p. 138, discusses the emergence of autobiographical elements from the twelfth century onward. Gittings, p. 33, argues that "From the early fourteenth century . . . the name of the person commemorated was now displayed on the monument," and speculates that this change was "symptomatic of a growing emphasis on the individual." On p. 144 she cites evidence that, in seventeenth-century Kent, "ordinary people as well as their social superiors" increasingly sought tombstones; and on p. 148 she argues that "the type of remembrance of the deceased fostered by epitaphs underwent a striking change during the early modern period," placing less emphasis on genealogy and social role, and more on personal qualities. Peter Burke, "Death in the Renaissance, 1347–1656," in *Dies Illa: Death in the Middle Ages*, ed. Jane H. M. Taylor, Vinaver Studies in French (Liverpool: Francis Cairns, 1984), p. 60, sees in Burckhardt's Renaissance an emphasis on "the modern sense of fame," exemplified by the increasing emphasis on tombs. In the elegies collected by Anthony Stafford, *Honour and Vertue, Triumphing over the Grave* (London, 1640), a "Jo. Goad." writes, "For though here lyes the *Corps* of *Stafford* dead, / His *Name* and *Epitaph* can't be Buried" (sig. S4r); contrast Marcus Aurelius Antoninus, *Meditations*, trans. Meric Casaubon (London, 1634), VI, 42: "Nay they that have not so much as a Name remaining, what are they the worse for it?"

11. When John Donne finds himself suffering a sickness unto death, he wonders why God would forbid "those, that serve thee in *holy services*, to doe any *office* about the *dead*"; he then decides to "satisfie my selfe with this; that in those *times* . . . a great part of the *Idolatry* of the *Nations*, flowed from . . . an *over-zealous celebrating*, and *over-studious preserving* of the *memories*, and the *Pictures* of some *dead persons*." From this he manages to derive a needed assurance resisted by his own strict Protestant reading of the Bible: that God

"dost certainly allow that we should doe *offices* of *piety* to the *dead*" (*Devotions*, pp. 93–94). Theo Brown, *The Fate of the Dead: A Study in Folk-Eschatology in the West Country after the Reformation* (Ipswich: D.S. Brewer, 1979), p. 15ff., cites the Reformation rejection of "Popish superstitions" about the dead as the cause of various anxious folk-practices of this period. What Brown perceives leaking out into folk-culture, I believe is visible in canonical high-culture as well. On the impact a strict Reformation theology would have on our consoling rituals surrounding death, see Glen W. Davidson, "In Search of Paradigms: Death and Destiny in Seventeenth-Century North America," in *Religious Encounters with Death*, ed. Frank Reynolds and Earle Waugh (University Park: Penn State University Press, 1977), p. 229, describing the stark prayerless burials practiced by New World Puritans. Browne, p. 67, lists among his heresies one "which I did never positively maintaine or practice, but have often wished it had been consonant to Truth, and not offensive to my Religion, and that is the prayer for the dead."

12. Robert Pricke, *A Verie Godlie and Learned Sermon* (London, 1608), sig. F1r.

13. Pricke, sig. D1v.

14. Norman T. Burns, *Christian Mortalism from Tyndale to Milton* (Cambridge: Harvard University Press, 1972), pp. 39–89. Richard Greenham, *Workes*, ed. H. Holland, 3d ed. (London, 1601), p. 3, tells of a man taught by the Familists "that there was no God"; and several sects taught that this life held the only true heaven.

15. Burns, p. 59.

16. Giles Firmin, *Real Christian*; quoted in John Stachniewski, *The Persecutory Imagination* (Oxford: Clarendon Press, 1991), p. 58.

17. See, for example, Donne's Holy Sonnet "If Poysonous Mineralls"; Herbert's lyrics "Nature" and "Good Friday"; and Jacob Boehme's 1622 prayer: "Receive Thou me into Thy Death! Strike down my self-assumed I-ness so that no longer do I live, since sin is the only active [thing] within me!"; *The Way to Christ* (1622), trans. John J. Stoudt (Westport, CT: Greenwood Press, 1979), pp. 11–12 (*De Poenitentia Vera*, I, 19). The doubter in Richard Sault's *A Conference Betwixt a Modern Atheist and his Friend* (London, 1693) complains that the soul will lack individuality after death.

18. Theodore Spencer, *Death and Elizabethan Tragedy* (Cambridge: Harvard University Press, 1936), p. 138.

19. Browne, p. 111. In a 1627 wedding sermon Donne describes marriage as "a *second* and a *suppletory eternity*, in the continuation and propagation of Children," but only for the purpose of contrasting it with the condition of resurrected angels, who need no such supplement (VIII, 99). Stafford's eulogy remarks that humankind "is onely immortall here below by succession" (p. 84), and Jo. Castillian's elegy lamenting Stafford's dying without progeny expresses the failure of a similar hope: "Thy soule might still have liv'd, in others breath, / Whose single life, is now a numerous death" (sig. Q2v).

20. Browne, p. 61. Locke used travel literature to dispute Edward Herbert's argument that God was a universal and therefore innate and therefore true idea; see David Berman, "The repressive denials of atheism in Britain in the seven-

teenth and eighteenth centuries," in *Royal Irish Academy Proceedings*, vol. 82, sec. C, no. 9 (Dublin, 1982), p. 241.

21. William Leigh, *The Christians Watch* (London, 1605), sig. E4r, claims that "The beastely Epicures"—familiar villains in Jacobean anti-atheistical tracts—were "doubly damned in their thoughts for that they deem'd soules mortall, and worldes immortal."

22. Mary Beth Rose, *The Expense of Spirit: Love and Sexuality in English Renaissance Drama* (Ithaca: Cornell University Press, 1988), p. 175; see also Robert N. Watson, "Tragedy," in *The Cambridge Companion to English Renaissance Drama*, ed. A.R. Braunmuller and Michael Hattaway (Cambridge: Cambridge University Press, 1990), pp. 301–51. Spencer, pp. 15–16, links Renaissance tragedy to Renaissance realism.

23. Christopher Walter, "Death in Byzantine Iconography," *Eastern Churches Review*, 8 (1976), p. 144, argues that "The chief consolation which Antiquity could offer, faced with the fact of death, was that heroes also had to undergo this awful experience."

24. C. John Somerville, *The Secularization of Early Modern England* (New York: Oxford University Press, 1992), p. 179.

25. Roy W. Battenhouse, *Shakespearean Tragedy: Its Art and Christian Premises* (Bloomington: Indiana University Press, 1969), p. 133. For a recent example particularly relevant to my argument, see Arthur Kirsch's review of Calderwood's *Shakespeare and the Denial of Death* in *Shakespeare Quarterly*, 40 (1989), pp. 348–49.

26. T. Stocker, trans., *An excellent treatise of the Immortalytie of the Soule* by John Calvin (London, 1581), sig. A2r.

27. John Proctor, *The Fal of the late Arrian* (1549), sig. A8v.

28. John Calvin, *Institutes*, II.viii.9; quoted by Richard Strier, *Love Known* (Chicago: University of Chicago Press, 1983), p. 177.

29. Pricke, sig. Aa1v.

30. Thomas Jackson, *A Treatise* (London, 1625), p. 31; Jeremy Corderoy, *A Warning for Worldlings* (London, 1608), sig. A4v.

31. The contrast with several Asian cultures which devalue individuality and make annihilation the desideratum of their theology is instructive.

32. Freud, "Jokes and their Relation to the Unconscious," VIII, passim.

33. Pricke, sig. C1v.

34. This general idea of culture bears some resemblance to M.M. Bakhtin's "chronotope," a way of formulating space and time; see *The Dialogic Imagination*, trans. Michael Holquist and Caryl Emerson (Austin: University of Texas Press, 1981). It may be objected that the theocentric Renaissance world-view safely proscribed such dizzying infinities, but in fact Donne's sermons are rich in examples. See also Jean Pierre Camus, *A Draught of Eternitie*, trans. Miles Car (Douay, 1632), which suggests, in a morally conventional section-heading, "That all the evill in the world, comes from want of thinking of Eternity" (p. 8). Camus's closer analysis, however, suggests that this is a draught in which we might easily drown: "Now Eternitie being of this nature, who sees not, that no definition can comprehend or compasse that, which in it selfe hath no bound" (p. 47).

35. John Dove, *A Confutation of Atheism* (London, 1605), sig. B2r. The pun on *matrix* is suggestive: the mother is the primal source of order and harmony for most infant psyches.

36. This version of the social contract remains in force beyond the grave—perhaps especially there. According to Eamon Duffy, *The Stripping of the Altars* (New Haven: Yale University Press, 1992), p. 323, in return for the prayers intended to help the dying person navigate the beyond, that person "was expected to affirm the common framework of value and belief by manifesting orthodox faith and the approved signs of piety." Ariès, p. 604, approaches my viewpoint in asserting that "The ritualization of death is a special aspect of the total strategy of man against nature," but he understands nature primarily as the jungle that sometimes surrounds the individual and the sporadic unruly emotions within, overlooking the perpetual struggle to conquer the wilderness of a mental landscape overrun by unsorted data from the entire external world.

37. *The Works of Francis Bacon* (London: C. & J. Rivington, 1826), VIII, 7–78.

38. Ronald Levao, *Renaissance Minds and Their Fictions* (Berkeley: University of California Press, 1985), p. xvii.

39. Lynn White, "Death and the Devil," in *The Darker Vision of the Renaissance*, ed. Robert S. Kinsman (Berkeley: University of California Press, 1974), p. 26, argues that the Renaissance "was the most psychically disturbed era in European history," its only rival being "the late Hellenistic and Roman period, with its . . . rapid spread of the concept of an afterlife of either bliss or eternal torture."

40. Abraham Darcie, "The World's Contempt," in *Frances Duchesse Dowager of Richmond & Lenox her Funerall Teares* (London, 1624), sig. Bb4v.

41. Heinz Kohut, *How Does Analysis Cure?*, ed. Arnold Goldberg and Paul Stepansky (Chicago: University of Chicago Press, 1984), p. 3; his *Restoration of the Self* (New York: International Press, 1981), pp. 102–14; and D. W. Winnicott, "Disintegration Anxiety," in his *Psycho-Analytic Explorations*, ed. Clare Winnicott et al. (Cambridge: Harvard University Press, 1989).

42. Quoted by Berman, p. 226.

43. Quoted by Berman, p. 238. A century later Edmund Burke recognized that his warning against rebellion on behalf of some abstract principle of absolute liberty applied to the psychological as well as the political system: after "throwing off that Christian religion . . . we are apprehensive (being well aware that the mind will not endure a void) that some uncouth, pernicious, and degrading superstition might take the place of it"; quoted by Berman, p. 242.

44. Heywood, pp. 7–8.

45. Richard Bentley, *The Folly of Atheism* (London, 1691–92), pp. 34–35; and *A Confutation of Atheism from the Origin of Humane Bodies* (London, 1692), pp. 11–14.

46. King Utopus has "made the whole matter of religion an open question and left each one free to choose what he should believe. By way of exception, he conscientiously and strictly gave injunction that no one should fall so far below the dignity of human nature as to believe that souls likewise perish with the body." Thomas More, *Utopia*, ed. Edward Surtz (New Haven: Yale University

Press, 1964), p. 134; on the acceptance of communism, see pp. 53–55. This aversion to annihilationism may reflect More's own psychological fears. According to Richard Marius, *Thomas More: A Biography* (New York: Random House, 1984), p. 516, "The Catholic Church was his only assurance against hell, or worse—non-being."

47. On the argument that men became "Atheisticall naturalists" primarily to rationalize their sensual desires, see Richard Carpenter, *The Soules Sentinel* (London, 1616), p. 76; also Jean Paget, *Meditations of Death* (London, 1628), pp. 179, 416. Richard Sault, in *The Second Spira*, part II (London, 1693), sig. B3r, discusses "those two great Evils of Atheism and Debauchery (which usually produce one another)." Hamlet's "To be or not to be" soliloquy is an interesting variant which seems to conclude that annihilationism would lead, not to hedonism, but to mass suicide—though perhaps suicide is the hedonistic choice in the miserable world Hamlet perceives. J. Huizinga, *The Waning of the Middle Ages* (London: Edward Arnold, 1924), p. 179, suggests that "What the Church dreaded above all in the idea of the annihilation of the personality was the consequence, accepted by the extremist mystics of all religions, that the soul absorbed in God, and therefore having no will, can no longer sin, even in following its carnal appetites. How many poor ignorant people had been dragged by such doctrines into the most abominable license."

48. Farrell, p. 133, speculates that "the patriarch appropriated the role of death himself, subjecting it to human rules. By being perfectly obedient one could hope to placate if not control death." On Winnicott's view that monarchs still help to sustain the psychic health of the British, see Peter Rudnytsky, *The Psychoanalytic Vocation* (New Haven: Yale University Press, 1991), p. 107. Becker, pp. 133 and 149, associates the wild lamentations that generally follow the assassination of political leaders with their role as immortality-surrogates; if the leader can die, then the people realize that they can too. There is also, however, an aspect of celebration in the ritualized hysteria of these mournings. Death has been made into a remarkable, even an aberrant event—and one that inspires universal worship of the victim, who lives on in the name of government buildings, a palpable body-politic replacing the natural body.

49. John Dunton (?), *A Mourning-Ring in Memory of your Departed Friend* (London, 1692), p. 107. Compare the Monty Python skit which uses a rather one-sided interview of several distinguished corpses to conclude that there probably *isn't* life after death.

50. Clearly the divided legacy of old historicism and New Criticism presents contemporary critics with a dilemma that may help to explain the division of advanced literary study into the polar camps of Marxists, to whom literature is a window into the work-house, and post-structuralists, to whom it is yet another playing-field. This is not to deny that the extremes might temporarily cooperate in exposing the constructions of social or verbal reality as arbitrary and hence open to radical revision. But the progressive vision of dialectical materialism seems incompatible with deconstructionist disavowals of authentic dialogue and ultimate points of reference. Jacques Derrida's suggestion, in "Racism's Last Word," *Critical Inquiry*, 12 (1985), pp. 290–99, that his semiotic system somehow attacks "apartheid" more than it does other words reveals how anx-

ious deconstructionists can be to disguise this problem, and to claim some palpable verification for their abstract philosophical system by aligning it with an established ethical consensus.

51. Michel de Montaigne, *Essays*, ed. Donald Frame (Stanford: Stanford University Press, 1965), p. 64. Browne, *Hydriotaphia*, p. 314, translates this skeptical idea into his own ecstatic rhetoric: "Pious spirits . . . made little more of this world, then the world that was before it, while they lay obscure in the Chaos of pre-ordination"; Browne, p. 303, suggests that "A Dialogue between two Infants in the womb concerning the state of this world, might handsomely illustrate our ignorance of the next." For evidence that Montaigne's comments represent a twist on a standard consolatory metaphor, see Zacharie Boyd, *The Last Battle of the Soul in Death* (1629), ed. Gabriel Noel (Glasgow, 1831), who asserts that at death "My paines do not dismay mee, because I travaile to bring foorth eternall life," and that "The buried bodies of the Sainctes are in their grave like Babes lapped in swaddling cloathes in their cradles"; see also Marcus Aurelius Antoninus, IX, 3, comparing birth and death.

52. Compare Freud's argument that a stabilizing narcissism "would not be a perversion, but the libidinal complement to the egoism of the instinct of self-preservation, a measure of which may justifiably be attributed to every living creature" (XIV, 73–74).

53. This loss is potentially quite destructive to the benevolent cross-cultural political agenda generally associated with New Historicism and Cultural Materialism. Comparably, post-structuralist exaggeration of the role of verbal forms in constructing our reality has reinforced the patronizing alienation from other species that has led to so much careless cruelty; from an animal-rights perspective, the enlightened new boss in literary theory is even more tyrannical than the old boss. The complaint is germane to the argument of this book, because that disdainful neglect of other species (either on the ground that they lack verbal language, or on the ground that they lack souls) seems to me an extension of the narcissistic compulsion to invent reasons why we are somehow exempt from the plain biological death we see visited on so many of our fellow creatures.

54. Jean E. Howard, "The New Historicism in Renaissance Studies," *English Literary Renaissance*, 16 (1986), pp. 21–23.

55. *Los Angeles Times*, June 17, 1993, p. A6.

56. Stephen Greenblatt, "Invisible Bullets: Renaissance Authority and Its Subversion," in *Shakespeare's "Rough Magic,"* ed. Peter Erickson and Coppélia Kahn (Newark: University of Delaware Press, 1985), p. 279. Greenblatt's assertion is closely echoed in Stachniewski, p. 329: "Atheism may have been almost unthinkable."

57. Greenblatt, p. 277.

58. William Towers, *Atheismus Vapulans* (London, 1654), pp. 13–14. See also Robert Welcome, *The State of the Godly, both in this life, and in the life to come* (London, 1606), pp. 60–61—"What plainer for to stop the mouths of *Atheists* ye contradict ye immortality of the soul then ye saying of Christ our Lord in ye Gospel"—though he may mean Christian annihilationists rather than atheists, which would make a more logical argument. In any case, it is also clear that some defenders of faith recognized the problem with this approach: Corderoy's atheistic traveller warns his pious interlocutor that "in vaine you

shall heape testimonies out of the Scripture: for if I did beleeve there were a God, I would beleeve the Scripture" (p. 38). So stupidity should not be mistaken for an epistemic limit.

59. Deposition from the Cerne Abbas commission records, in Hadrian Dorrell (?), *Willobie His Avisa* (1594), ed. G. B. Harrison (Edinburgh: University Press, 1966), p. 269.

60. William Sclater, *A Funerall Sermon* (London, 1629), p. 14.

61. Thomas Morton, *A Treatise of the Nature of God* (London, 1599), p. 30.

62. Lucien Febvre, *The Problem of Unbelief in the Sixteenth Century*, trans. Beatrice Gottlieb (Cambridge: Harvard University Press, 1982), passim.

63. Martin Fotherby, *Atheomastix* (London, 1622), pp. 131–32. A 1685 defense of belief displays a similarly revealing circular quality, when the anonymous "Person of Honour" who presented *The Atheist Unmasked* claims to disprove atheism by proving that those who were not really atheists were not really atheists: "But this fear terrifies the Atheist most when he comes to dye not so much the fear of Death, as what shall become of him after Death"—by which this author means the fear of hellfire, not annihilation.

64. Samuel Ward, *The Life of Faith in Death* (London, 1622), p. 88.

65. *Sermons*, VI, 325, compares nature's abhorrence of a vacuum to the way "the devill will get into Gods roome, rather then the heart of man shall be without the opinion of God; There is no Atheist; They that oppose the true, do yet worship a false god; and hee that sayes there is no God, doth for all that, set up some God to himselfe."

66. Corderoy, p. 323, defends himself against posited readers "who thinke it not convenient, that any question should be made, whether there be any God or no, because . . . the very calling of it in question, breedeth scruples in the mindes of those, who made no question of it before." Don Cameron Allen, *Doubt's Boundless Sea* (Baltimore: Johns Hopkins University Press, 1964), p. 20, cites several other instances of this pattern. David R. Riggs, in a paper delivered to the 1991 Shakespeare Association of America Convention, suggests that Christopher Marlowe may have fallen victim to a similar transaction. Somerville, p. 163 argues that the common efforts to explain away atheists by naturalistic causes such as sensual comfort or mental illness inadvertently opened religious tendencies to skeptical scientific analysis.

67. Hooker, II, 19.

68. Henrie Smith, *Gods Arrowe against Atheists* (London, 1593), sig. B1r-v. Similarly moralistic readings of the atheistical psyche appear in Corderoy, p. 326, and Paget, pp. 179 and 416.

69. Pricke, sig. D4r-v.

70. William Hammon, *Answer to Priestly*, quoted by Berman, p. 244.

71. Michael Hunter, "The Problem of 'Atheism' in Early Modern England," *Transactions of the Royal Historical Society*, 5th Series (1985), p. 137, tries to dismiss the various assertions of atheism he finds in the period as "isolated cases of anti-religious talk," but the number and directness of the assertions make that claim difficult to sustain; and to say they are scattered is as much as to say they are widespread.

72. The historian David Wooten has theorized that Puritanism, since it identified its community only by a shared faith in God, necessarily defined

334   NOTES FOR PAGES 26-28

anyone outside the group as atheist (David R. Riggs, personal communication). Radford Mavericke, *Three treatises religiously handled* (London, 1603), sig. H3v, typifies this culture's anxiety about disbelief: "worst of all, are the Nullifidians, or Atheists of our time [who] care not what religion they be, but weigh not whether there bee any religion at all, far worse than the Turkes, that acknowledge there is a God, but allow none but *Mahomet* to bee his prophet." Hunter notes the severity of the resistance, citing Fuller, p. 383, who insists that "*Atheisme in England is more to be feared then Popery*"; Donne, *Sermons*, IX, 145, argues that "Idolatry is better then Atheisme"; Greenham, p. 3, describes a countryman who "feared rather Atheisme than Papisme in the Realme"; and Adam Hill, *The Crie of England* (London, 1595), p. 32, identifies atheism as "the sinne of all sinnes." Even the tolerant Hooker, II, 20–21, suggests that England has been "too patient" with its atheistical scoffers, and recommends "that decree of Nabuchodonosor" that made such blasphemies capital crimes.

73. Dove, sig. A3r.

74. William Perkins, *Treatise of Mans Imaginations* (Cambridge, 1607), pp. 50, 31, 34.

75. Fotherby, sig. B2r.

76. Thomas Adams, *Sermons*, ed. John Brown (Cambridge, 1909), pp. 35 and 146; Adams, *The White Devil* (London, 1613), p. 25.

77. Welcome, pp. 72–73.

78. Towers, pp. 3–4.

79. Sault, *A Conference*, sig. A2v.

80. William Birnie, *The Blame of Kirk-Buriall* (Edinburgh, 1606), sig. B1r. The Christian speaker in Sault's *Conference*, p. 30, suggests that "there are but few amongst such as are call'd Atheists, tha[t] can (if they dare think) doubt of his Existence," but that a much greater number doubt the immortality of the soul.

81. D.P. Walker, *The Decline of Hell* (London: Routledge, 1964), pp. 8–9, 80–81.

82. Leigh, sig. B3r.

83. Walker, pp. 40–41, discusses Bayle's futile efforts to disprove "the effectiveness of savage deterrants" such as the threat of hellfire.

84. Adams, *Workes* (London, 1629), p. 756. A few pages earlier Adams warns that "The day of judgement, when it comes, shall finde no Atheist. What those degenerate creatures would not believe, they shall see . . . " (p. 753; see similarly p. 412).

85. Smith, sig. B8r.

86. Hunter, XXXV, 140; see similarly, Sir George More, *A Demonstration of God in His Workes* (London, 1597), p. 20.

87. Samuel Gardiner, *The Scourge of Sacrilege* (London, 1611), sig. C3v; cf. Corderoy, sig. A4r. Sclater, p. 16, strives to exempt the man he is eulogizing from the evil of their society "wherein the doctrine of judgement is holden a fable, and nothing but a meere policy to keepe fooles in awe." Even during the Elizabethan period, this may have been a familiar perspective in some cynical academic circles (it appears in Lyly's *Euphues*), and a century later Hobbes brought it fully into the open, but even then it more often took the form of a

skeptical voice the author mimics for the purpose of attacking it: "*Heaven, Hell, Futurity*, and the *Immortality of the Soul*, all which are but politick Inventions of Priests and cunning Magistrates, to enrich themselves and keep the Vulgar in Awe, who are naturally Superstitious and Fearful" (Sault, *Second Spira*, part I, p. 5).

88. Thomas Taylor, "A Profitable Memoriall," appended to *The Pilgrims Profession* (1622); rpt. in his *Three Treatises* (London, 1633), p. 168.

89. Heinz Kohut, *The Restoration of the Self* (New York: International Press, 1981), p. 177, suggests that "during early psychic development a process takes place in which some archaic mental contents that had been experienced as belonging to the self become obliterated or are assigned to the area of the nonself while others are retained within the self or added to it. As a result of this process a core self . . . is established."

90. William Worship, *The Christians Mourning Garment*, 3d ed. (London, 1603), sig. C6r.

91. Smith, sig. B1r. Morton, p. 30, condemns true atheists as "not men but beasts in the likenesse of men."

92. Daniel Donne, *A Sub-Poena from the Star-Chamber of Heaven* (London, 1623), p. 54.

93. Alexander Grosse, *Deaths Deliverance* (London, 1632), p. 8.

94. Edward Coffin, *A True Relation of the Last Sicknes and Death of Cardinall Bellarmine* (1622), Epistle, pp. 3–4. A similar structure emerges in the assertion of Thomas Tuke, *A Discourse of Death* (London, 1613), p. 67, that "when a beast dies, his soul doth vanish, and is dissolved: but when a man dies, his soule still continues." See also Welcome, p. 56: "the soule (or life) of beasts proceeded from the same substance and matter whereof their bodies were made: but the soule of man is a spirituall and divine thing, which because it proceeded from god, must needes remaine for ever."

95. Hunter, p. 151, quotes this accusation of John Derpier in 1607.

96. Sault, *A Conference*, p. 2.

97. William Crompton, *A Lasting Jewell for Religious Woemen* (London, 1630), sig. C3r; see also Spencer, pp. 197–99, on the necrophiliac aspects of Renaissance tragedy.

98. It is interesting, in this regard, that in the later Middle Ages female saints were especially obliged to remain "incorrupt after burial"; see Bynum, p. 77.

99. *Non-Entity*, pp. 2–3. Donne, *Sermons*, IX, 405, strives to answer that "heavy charge" against Protestant theology.

100. *Non-Entity*, p. 154. Strikingly similar charges are levelled by Benjamin Carier, *Copy of a Letter* (1615), p. 41, against those who abused Catholics; they are reported to have stunk like half-rotted corpses from the moment of their death.

101. Carier, p. 3.

102. Towers, p. 108.

103. See, for example, Hunter, p. 144.

104. More, *Demonstration*, p. 20.

105. Quoted by Burns, p. 119, n. 42.

106. Tuke, pp. 2 and 13. Edward Grimeston's *History of Polybius* (London, 1633), on the other hand, mistranslates the classical original to conceal its Machiavellian reading of religion; I am indebted to Debora Shuger for this reference.

107. Casaubon, in his edition of Marcus Aurelius, pp. 8–9.

108. David Humphreys, in his edition of *The Apologetics of the Learned Athenian Philosopher Athenagoras* (London, 1714), p. 92. William Morray, *A Short Treatise of Death in Sixe Chapters* (Edinburgh, 1631), p. 24, similarly asserts that Solomon is "speaking in the person of the Atheist" in parts of Ecclesiastes.

109. Welcome, p. 54.

110. Samuel Gardiner, *Doomes-day Booke: Or, an Alarum for Atheistes* (London, 1606), p. 47.

111. Tuke, sig. A2v and p. 8.

112. Welcome, p. 56.

113. Abraham Holland, *Hollandi Post-Huma* (Cambridge, 1626), sig. L3r.

114. N. Campbell, *A Treatise upon Death* (Glasgow, 1630), sig. G6r; see also sigs. E7v and F1r.

115. Alexander Grosse, *Eliahs Fiery Charet* (London, 1632), p. 35.

116. Donne, *Sermons*, V, 210. Cf. VII, 298: "who can feare the darknesse of death, that hath had the light of this world, and of the next too?"; and X, 245: "To us that speake dayly of the *death* of *Christ* . . . can the memory or the mention of our owne *death* bee yrkesome or bitter?" See also the *Devotions*, pp. 30 and 78.

117. Francis Dillingham, *A Sermon Preached [for] Lady Elizabeth Luke* (1609), p. 21.

118. Nicholas Guy, *Pieties Pillar* (London, 1626), pp. 35–36. See also the Chorus to act 3 of the Countess of Pembroke's translation of Robert Garnier's *Marc Antonie*; Holland, sig. I2r; and John Milton, *Paradise Lost*, II, 92–98, in *Complete Poems and Major Prose*, ed. Merritt Y. Hughes (New York: Bobbs-Merrill, 1957), where it compromises Moloch's bravado about annihilation.

119. I Corinthians, 15:54, Geneva Bible; even Paul's rhetorical question earlier in verse 12—"Now if it be preached, that Christ is risen from the dead, how say some among you, that there is no resurrection of the dead?"—shows more willingness to acknowledge the possibility of real disbelief than the Jacobeans apparently could tolerate.

120. Grosse, p. 38. In an interesting variant, preachers could also demand of a father, "Would [David] have so bitterly lamented [Absalom's] death, if the soule and body dyed together?"; see Welcome, p. 62.

121. John Gaule, *A Defiance to Death* (London, 1629), p. 21, may declare that "death is a nothing, and are we afraid of we know not what?"; but when Montaigne, p. 64, asks his version of the same question—"why should we fear to lose a thing which once lost cannot be regretted?"—the rhetoric comports as much real perplexity as strategic dismissal.

122. Sclater, p. 7.

123. Camus, p. 149. According to Camus, pp. 21–22, whoever fails to consider eternity risks "loosing the eternall light of glorie," whoever "walkes in so palpable darknesse" will be "buried in the shadowes of so black an oblivion!"

124. Timothy Oldmayne, *Lifes Brevitie and Deaths Debility* (London, 1636), p. 51. According to E. B., *A Buckler against the fear of Death* (London, 1640), sig. B8r, only a Christian can say to Death, while walking in its shadow, "Though with thee in the dark I dwell a space, / Yet canst thou not eternally benight me," since a Christian can hope for "an everlasting day, / And an uneclipsed light." See similarly Stephen Denison, *Another Tombestone* (London, 1627), p. 39: "there will come a day, wherein [the Saints departed] shall lift up their heads out of the grave in shining brightnesse." See also Browne's plea, "Let not my sinnes, blacke as the night, / Eclipse the lustre of thy light" (p. 156); and the promise of Marvell's Thyrsis that "There always is a rising sun" in Elysium (35).

125. Adams, *Workes*, p. 14.

126. Boyd, I, 13; II, 400, 8, 424.

127. Stafford, pp. 88, 79. This imagery evidently proved so effective that it was still in use at the end of the seventeenth century: atheists are "blinded with so thick a mist of Night, / That they shall never more behold the light"; William Dawes, *An Anatomy of Atheism*, (London, 1694), p. 8.

128. Paget, pp. 66–69, 431–2.

129. *A Mourning-Ring*, "House of Weeping," p. 204; "Death-Bed Thoughts," p. 143. Dawes's *Anatomy of Atheism* falls back on the Cartesian "good bet" argument for belief in an afterlife, hoping that God exists, because "If not the worst event that we can have / Is to lye senslesse in the silent Grave."

130. Thomas Fuller, *The Holy State and the Profane State* (Cambridge, 1642), p. 382.

131. Arthur Gorges, *The Olympian Catastrophe*, lines 1027–32; quoted by Dennis Kay, *Melodious Tears: The English Funeral Elegy from Spenser to Milton* (Oxford: Clarendon Press, 1990), p. 147.

132. Thomas Newton, *Atropoion Delion* (London, 1603), sigs. A3v, B2r, B4v. The acronymic dedicatory verse begins by reporting that "E.Yes that before her death, did then behold her, / L.Amentes in flood of teares to loose their gazing." Though the Queen had once been a miraculous generator of vision, Newton reports that "At length to Church I brought my *Delia*'s Hearse, / Blindfolded (for my eyes were blinde with crying)," and in fact "all her Mourners eyes were vailde and blinde" (sig. B2r).

133. Darcie, sigs. A6r, Aa1r, Bb1r.

134. Coffin, pp. 3–4.

135. See Gillian Murray Kendall's insightful "Overkill in Shakespeare," *Shakespeare Quarterly*, 43 (1992), pp. 33–50.

136. Spencer, pp. 199–200, discusses the permutations of this motif.

137. Holland, "The Description of the last great Plague" (1625), in *Hollandi*, sig. E4r-v. Cf. Huizinga, p. 129: "Towards 1400 the conception of death in art and literature took a spectral and fantastic shape. The macabre vision arose from deep psychological strata of fear; religious thought at once reduced it to a means of moral exhortation. As such it was a great cultural idea, till in its turn it went out of fashion, lingering on in epitaphs and symbols in village cemeteries."

138. Holland, "The Plague a dreary Punishment," in *Hollandi*, sig. G1r. The fact that Holland died soon after writing this account of the plague, and

even sooner after vowing to undertake a religious life if spared, somehow makes his vivid narrative very poignant—perhaps because we are used to identifying with narrators who are the survivors. Norbert Elias, *The Loneliness of the Dying*, trans. Edmund Jephcott (Oxford: Blackwell, 1985), p. 11, argues that "It would certainly be possible to make dying easier for some people if repressed guilt-fantasies . . . could be alleviated or dispelled." My suspicion, on the contrary, is that we generate such fantasies precisely because a death meant as punishment is more tolerable than the alternative: a death without meaning.

139. Spencer, p. 71.

140. Huizinga, p. 134, observes that "The desire to invent a visible image of all that appertained to death entailed the neglecting of all those aspects of it which were not suited to direct representation." I suspect that was often precisely why such illustrations were performed, to conceal the impossibility of comprehending oblivion.

141. Duffy, p. 339.

142. Holland, "To His Friends," in *Hollandi*, sig. I2r.

143. Lewes Bayly, *The Practise of Pietie* (London, 1613), pp. 909, 101, 96.

144. Bayly, p. 125.

145. Camus, p. 101; he goes on to describe their sense of smell powerfully affronted by the stench of corpses and sulphurous brimstone, their bodily thirst and hunger not ended but intensified (pp. 108–10).

146. Camus, pp. 162–65. Humphrey Sydenham, *Natures Overthrow and Deaths Triumph* (London, 1626), p. 8, describes death as "a *privation* onely, having *name* (saith *Augustine*) but no essence."

147. Camus, pp. 90, 136.

148. Adams, *Workes*, p. 758. Adams himself warned elsewhere that atheists were worse than the devil (pp. 184–85).

149. Quoted by Walker, p. 81.

150. Tuke, p. 81.

151. On the exemption of funerary monuments in 1550 and again in 1643, see Joshua Scodel, *The English Poetic Epitaph* (Ithaca: Cornell University Press, 1991), p. 208; on the exemption of Last Judgment scenes, see Huston Diehl, "To Put Us in Remembrance," in *Homo, Memento Finis*, Early Drama, Art, and Music Monograph Series 6, ed. David Bevington (Kalamazoo, MI: Medieval Institute, 1985), pp. 179–80. This helps to explain the paradox noted by Farrell, p. 91, that "Calvin and Luther both insisted that what lies beyond death is ineffable," yet "they used traditional imagery to make the point."

152. Gardiner, *Doomes-day*, pp. 102–3.

153. *Paradise Lost*, II, 666–70; in Hughes.

154. For examples of scholarship that—though valuable—largely accepts these boundaries, see Arnold Stein, *The House of Death* (Baltimore: Johns Hopkins University Press, 1986); Harry Morris, *Last Things in Shakespeare* (Tallahassee: Florida State University Press, 1985); Michael C. Andrews, *This Action of Our Death* (Newark: University of Delaware Press, 1989); Nancy Lee Beaty, *The Craft of Dying* (New Haven: Yale University Press, 1970); and Robert F. Willson, Jr., *Shakespeare's Reflexive Endings* (Lewiston, NY: Edwin Mellen Press, 1990).

155. Freud, "On Hysteria," II, 305.

156. John Milton, "The Christian Doctrine," in Hughes, pp. 900–901.

157. Humphreys, trans., *Apologetics*, p. 89.

158. Jonathan Culler, *Framing the Sign* (Norman: University of Oklahoma Press, 1988), pp. 69–82. For a revealing parallel, see Gary Wills, *Under God: Religion and American Politics* (New York: Simon and Schuster, 1990), who speculates that ordinarily glib journalists, sensing the low "number of church-goers in the national press, as opposed to the general population . . . are oddly tongue-tied when the Bible is brought up. And editors seem to prefer inarticu-lacy on the subject" (p. 18).

159. See, for example, the superb scholarship of Debora Shuger, *Habits of Thought in the English Renaissance* (Berkeley: University of California Press, 1990), pp. 218–49, who argues that Christianity remained a haven of valuable subversions throughout the Renaissance; that models of justified rebellion, of economic redistribution, even of a nurturant patriarchy, were recuperated largely from Christian traditions. Wills, p. 384, points out similar progressive functions in modern American Christianity.

160. In that sense, multiculturalism is a contradiction in terms, and its advocates should not be too surprised (or too patronizing) when they meet deep-seated resistance. My point is not to endorse the hegemony (and accom-panying privileges) of white male Eurocentric culture in American universities, but to warn against complacency in the well-intended efforts to alter that hegemony. Universities—and literary studies in particular—may be one of the few settings in which such changes can be successfully negotiated, if only because nothing material is obviously and immediately at stake. But a prema-ture, insincere truce in the struggle between different beliefs at universities almost ensures an eventual war between differing believers in society at large. Instead, universities must strive toward providing diverse people and opinions with channels for meaningful mutual critiques as well as for consensus.

But how open and diverse can such discussions actually be, without collaps-ing into chaos? The sophisticated left wing as well as the fundamentalist right have begun to argue that the standard of rational debate reflects a (male and/or European) cultural bias and thus unfairly prejudices the key issues. I believe that the rational standard is deeply valid, and a necessary premise for any community of higher learning—but that may only prove that, as a rationalist, I am as devoted to my belief-system as anyone else to theirs, and similarly unable to conceive my universe without it.

161. For a prominent exception, see Stephen Greenblatt, *Renaissance Self-Fashioning* (Chicago: University of Chicago Press, 1980), p. 99; and Shuger, passim.

162. Wills, p. 16, cites recent statistics confirming that 80 percent of Ameri-cans "believe they will be called before God on Judgment Day," and that Americans give God more importance in their lives than any other nation surveyed except Malta.

163. *Times Literary Supplement*, June 7, 1974, p. 597. In fact, this phase of Empson's great career has been treated dismissively by most of the literary establishment.

164. Robert M. Adams, "Lucy and Lucifer," *New York Review of Books*, March 1, 1990, pp. 38–40.

165. C. S. Lewis, "What Christians Believe," in *Broadcast Talks* (London: G. Bles, 1943), pp. 41–43.

166. For the history of this obligation, see Susanne Klingenstein, *Jews in the American Academy, 1900–1940* (New Haven: Yale University Press, 1992), particularly concerning the careers of Lewisohn, Zeitlin, and Trilling.

167. Denis Donoghue, *New York Review of Books*, November 5, 1992, p. 50.

168. Shuger, pp. 17–90 and passim.

169. Nicholas Bownde, *The Unbelief of St Thomas the Apostle* (1608), (London, 1817), pp. 52–53, 33; see also p. 132, and Bownde's reminder on p. 113 that, in the matter of fearful doubts about death, "it is thus with the best, one time or other."

170. Perkins, p. 35.

171. Robert Burton, *The Anatomy of Melancholy*, ed. Holbrook Jackson (New York: E. P. Dutton, 1932), III, 417.

172. Compare the struggle of the great Victorian Catholic humanist John Henry Newman, who can bring himself to concede that England's cultural heritage is primarily "a Protestant literature" only by noting that it is therefore not "atheistical." Newman finds special cause for "thankfulness that the most illustrious amongst English writers has so little of a Protestant about him," and is further thankful that "there is in Shakespeare neither contempt of religion nor skepticism. . . . There is no mistaking in his works on which side lies the right; Satan is not made a hero, nor Cain a victim"; *The Idea of a University* (Oxford: Clarendon, 1976), p. 262. My chapters on Shakespeare will contest this pious portrait.

173. Worship, sig. C4v.

174. Marcus Aurelius Antoninus, IV, 39.

175. Montaigne, p. 60, recommends reversing the usual practice of denying death and instead conquering its terrors by diligent confrontation. No doubt Thomas Browne became the guiding Virgil of this Introduction because I reread him feverishly during a recent expedition (to another damned conference), after the plane lost an engine and careened around thunderstorms for an hour before landing in the hellish glare of arrayed fire-trucks—my version of Greenblatt's famous airplane anecdote at the end of *Renaissance Self-Fashioning*, and another clear example of the way criticism becomes suffused with autobiography.

176. Thomas Taylor, p. 143.

RELIGIO VINDICIS

1. Peter Sacks, "Where Words Prevail Not," *ELH*, 49 (1982), p. 579, offers a brilliant analysis of this transaction. He quotes Durkheim's observation in *The Elementary Forms of Religious Life* that "If every death is attributed to some

magic charm, and for this reason it is believed that the dead man ought to be avenged, it is because men must find a victim at any price, upon whom the collective pain and anger may be discharged." Sacks adds that "retribution is sought regardless of whether or not the deceased has been murdered. Thus seen, revenge is a crucial marshalling of anger, but more significantly, an action in which the survivor assumes *for himself* the power that has bereaved him. It is perhaps in this sense that Bacon wrote 'Revenge conquers Death'"; see "Of Unity in Religion," in *The Works of Francis Bacon* (London: C. & J. Rivington, 1826), II, 247. What I would further derive from Durkheim's observation, and add to Sacks's analysis of the drama, is that a valuable supplementary consolation arises from believing that, without murder, there would be no death. This, too, would explain the need for a scapegoat.

2. Cf. Samuel Daniel's 1603 *Panegyrike Congratulatory* on James I's memorial to his executed mother: "he lookes thereon / With th'eye of griefe, not wrath, t'avenge the same, / Since th' Authors are extinct that caus'd that shame" (stanza 31).

3. Helen Gardner, *The Business of Criticism* (Oxford: Clarendon Press, 1959), p. 41.

4. J. R. Mulryne, ed., *The Spanish Tragedy*, New Mermaids ed. (New York: W. W. Norton, 1987), p. xxiv.

5. Compare Browne, p. 141: "*Cain* was not therefore the first murtherer, but *Adam*, who brought in death; whereof hee beheld the practise and example in his owne sonne *Abel*, and saw that verified in the experience of another; which faith could not perswade him in the Theory of himselfe." Browne thus establishes himself as an early critic of the mechanisms of denial, both at the cultural level of mythmaking and at the individual level of narcissistic psychological evasion. Browne's Adam obeys the precept stated by Sigmund Freud in his "Thoughts for the Times on War and Death," *Complete Psychological Works*, Standard ed., trans. James Strachey (London: Hogarth Press), XIV, 289, that we never really believe ourselves to be mortal. Cf. Browne's *Pseudodoxia Epidemica*, p. 172, on Adam and Eve's disbelief in their own mortality.

6. Compare Browne's *Hydriotaphia*, p. 306:

If they dyed by violent hands, and were thrust into their Urnes, these bones become considerable, and some old Philosophers would honour them, whose souls they conceived most pure, which were thus snatched from their bodies; and to retain a stranger propension unto them: whereas they weariedly left a languishing corps, and with faint desires of reunion. If they fell by long and aged decay, yet wrapt up in the bundle of time, they fall into indistinction, and make but one blot with Infants.

7. Alexander Ross, *Mystagogus Poeticus* (London, 1648), p. 69, speculates that "Christ is truly *Ceres*, which having lost mankinde . . . went down to Hell, and rescued us from thence." He later speculates that Pluto became god of the underworld because he invented the custom of burial (p. 364). On etymological associations between "Proserpine" and "serpent," see Vincenzo Cartari, *The Fountaine of Ancient Fiction* (London, 1599).

8. See Philip Edwards, "Thrusting Elysium into Hell," in *Elizabethan Theatre XI*, ed. A. L. Magnuson and C. E. McGee (Ontario: P. D. Meaney, 1990),

which speculates incisively about this play's blasphemous undertones, and finds it "remarkable that Thomas Kyd should provide a pagan context for his story of a modern Christian Spain" (p. 117). As in Shakespeare's *King Lear* (though less subtly), this displacement is intermittently compromised to allow a subversive commentary on the Christian promise of salvation.

9. Freud, XIV, 290–1, notes our tendency "to lay stress on the fortuitous causation of the death," but also that, in war, "the accumulation of death puts an end to the impression of chance."

10. Eamon Duffy, *The Stripping of the Altars* (New Haven: Yale University Press, 1992), p. 350; Theodore Spencer, *Death and Elizabethan Tragedy* (Cambridge: Harvard University Press, 1936), p. 135.

11. When Ben Jonson wrote additions to the play, he characteristically emphasized the failure of art to replace a lost son. As Jonson attempts to identify with his buried son in that poetic epitaph, so Hieronimo attempts to mirror his son's fate of death by hanging—hardly the most efficient choice under the circumstances.

12. The Viceroy will make very much the same offer, claiming that his death in war would somehow have been more "natural" than his son's. When the Viceroy first supposes his son is dead, he also echoes the annihilationist model of death, attributing blindness and deafness to the agency of mortality (here, Fortune), and striving to sustain a connection to his son by plunging himself into essential darkness and silence: "Fortune is blind and sees not my deserts, / So is she deaf and hears not my laments" (1.2.23–24).

13. Michel de Montaigne, "That to philosophize is to learn to die," in *The Complete Essays of Montaigne*, trans. Donald M. Frame (Stanford: Stanford University Press, 1965), p. 65.

14. Balthazar's pride is injured, but so, more importantly, is his narcissism. When he confronts evidence that Bel-imperia is giving her love to Horatio instead, he pleads for all the correlative insensibilities of annihilationist death— sleep, blindness, deafness—to spare himself from recognizing the defeat of his ultimate immortality-strategy:

> O sleep mine eyes, see not my love profan'd;
> Be deaf my ears, hear not my discontent,
> Die heart, another joys what thou deserv'st.

Lorenzo offers the alternative solution to this problem, using revenge to undo all these little deaths, all these foreshocks of oblivion, including dishonor and failed love as well as sensory deprivation:

> Watch still mine eyes, to see this love disjoin'd;
> Hear still mine ears, to hear them both lament,
> Live, heart to joy at fond Horatio's fall.

> (2.2.18–23)

15. Later Lorenzo asks, "Thou art assur'd that thou sawest [Pedringano] dead?" and the Page replies, "Or else, my lord, I live not" (3.10.2–3).

16. *The Poetry of Robert Frost*, ed. E. C. Latham (New York: Holt Rinehart, 1969), p. 428.

17. I. C., *A Handkercher for Parents Wet Eyes* (London, 1630), p. 21—a remarkably Existentialist metaphor for a Renaissance writer.

18. John Foxe, *Fox's Book of Martyrs*, ed. William Forbush (Philadelphia: John C. Winston, 1926), pp. 214–15; on the martyrs' trust that their "salvation is already sealed in heaven," see p. 175.

19. Quoted in Arthur Freeman, *Thomas Kyd: Facts and Problems* (London: Oxford University Press, 1967), p. 26.

20. The Introduction to Edwards's edition of the play asserts that "Marlowe never wrote a less Christian play than *The Spanish Tragedy*" (p. lii).

21. Hieronimo does ascend to the lovers' branch of heaven, but that version of redemption only serves to identify his escape as a metaphor for the consolation of progeny he was so desperate to recover.

22. See Stephen Greenblatt's insightful explication of the compulsive repetitions by which Marlowe's characters metadramatically defend their identities; *Renaissance Self-Fashioning* (Chicago: University of Chicago Press, 1980), p. 200. For a comparable infernal metadramatic ending, see *Lust's Dominion* (1600), ed. J. Le Gay Brereton (Louvain: Uystpruyst, 1931), lines 3793–94, where the dying Eleazar promises to "out-act you all in perfect villany" when he arrives in hell.

23. Perhaps the blasphemous implication that Hieronimo is punishing God (in kind) for death helps to explain the fascination his story held for an Elizabethan culture haunted by circumambient death and unstable theology. After identifying with various lesser bereaved fathers, Hieronimo appears to identify with the paternal deity. In accusing the men who hung his son on a tree to die, he sounds strangely like an angry Calvinist God condemning Adam for corrupting the garden, leading to Cain's murder of his brother and humankind's killing of Christ as their ransom:

> They did what heaven unpunish'd would not leave.
> O false Lorenzo, are these thy flattering looks?
> Is this the honour that thou didst my son?
> And Balthazar, bane to thy soul and me,
> Was this the ransom he reserv'd thee for?
> Woe to the cause of these constrained wars,
> Woe to thy baseness and captivity,
> Woe to thy birth, thy body and thy soul,
> Thy cursed father, and thy conquered self!
> And bann'd with bitter execrations be
> The day and place where he did pity thee!
> But wherefore waste I mine unfruitful words,
> When naught but blood will satisfy my woes?
>
> (3.7.56–68)

From the erotic garden to the tree of martyrdom, from procreation to blood-revenge, we cannot seize life without soliciting death. Neither the father's law of talionic punishment nor the son's law of redemptive sacrifice provide reliable answers to the problem of mortality. William Empson may be wrong in defining Christianity as a religion of torture, but it certainly seems like a religion of revenge; see *Milton's God*, revised and expanded ed. (Cambridge: Cambridge

University Press, 1981), pp. 229–77. (René Girard would argue that Christianity is instead the sole cure for revenge.) Kyd invests his play with a remarkable level of dramatic tension by simultaneously destabilizing the revenge mytheme and the Christian story, threatening to expose them as merely defensive constructions, and to plunge the culture into the abyss of a renewed mortality-crisis. Partaking of that endless fall, that "endless tragedy," the audience may justly fear sharing Hieronimo's madness and despair, as well as his silent death.

GIVING UP THE GHOST

1. James Baldwin, *The Fire Next Time* (New York: Dell, 1962), p. 105. Norbert Elias, *The Loneliness of the Dying* (Oxford: Blackwell, 1985), p. 5, similarly ponders the injuries human beings "have done to each other in the name of a belief that death was not an end."

2. Eamon Duffy, *The Stripping of the Altars* (New Haven: Yale University Press, 1992), p. 353.

3. Alexander Welsh, "The Task of Hamlet," *Yale Review*, 69 (1979–80), keenly recognizes that "revenge is a function of mourning" but his sensible reminder that "two deaths do not make a life" may not seem as true to the subconscious as it does to the conscious mind (pp. 488, 496–97).

4. Sigmund Freud, "The Ego and the Id," *Complete Psychological Works*, Standard ed., trans. James Strachey (London: Hogarth Press), XIX, passim; Jacques Lacan, *The Language of the Self*, trans. Anthony Wilden (New York: Dell, 1975). Whether the male orientation of this symbolism is necessary—for Shakespeare, Freud, or Lacan—is certainly debatable, but for the purposes of this chapter I will adopt it. A feminist revaluation of such "chaos" as a generative multiplicity slandered by a defensive patriarchy would only reinforce the gendering of this idea of logical authority; it might also reinforce my general argument that this linear conception of the human legacy provokes violence against Others in defense of that legacy. Compare the way the Duke abandons his patriarchal authority in *Measure for Measure*, then reclaims it in order to supervise a less puritanical, more comic response to the works of the id.

5. Bridget Gellert Lyons, *Voices of Melancholy* (New York: Norton, 1971), p. 106, discusses this juxtaposition.

6. Welsh, p. 488.

7. W. W. Greg, "Hamlet's Hallucination." *Modern Language Review*, 12 (1917), pp. 393–421, is the classic instance of this argument. Marjorie Garber, *Shakespeare's Ghost Writers* (London: Methuen, 1989), discusses the way absent presences help to construct and deconstruct the meaning of works such as *Hamlet*.

8. Eleanor Prosser, *Hamlet and Revenge* (Stanford: Stanford University Press, 1967), argues that the ghost would have been clearly recognizable to an Elizabethan audience as a demonic tempter.

9. Avi Erlich, *Hamlet's Absent Father* (Princeton: Princeton University Press, 1977), pp. 38–39.

10. Harold F. Searles, "Schizophrenia and the Inevitability of Death, *Psychiatric Quarterly*, 1961 (35), pp. 633–34; quoted by Ernest Becker, *The Denial of Death* (New York: Free Press, 1973), p. 63. Becker, pp. 29–30, places the curing of denial among the highest moral projects: "If we had to offer the briefest explanation of all the evil that men have wreaked upon themselves and upon their world since the beginnings of time right up until tomorrow, it would be not in terms of man's animal heredity, his instincts and his evolution: it would be simply in *the toll that his pretense of sanity takes*, as he tries to deny his true condition." By calling these the "*costs of pretending not to be mad*," Becker inadvertently suggests the strong relevance of this problem to Hamlet, where the confrontation with death leads to a half-pretended madness that only completed vengeance (or death, or both) can cure.

11. Duffy, p. 328.

12. William Hazlitt, *Collected Works* (London, 1902), I, 232. The tendency of all sorts of people to identify deeply with Hamlet is notorious. There is obviously a critical pitfall in identifying too deeply with dramatic characters, and when I assert that a character thinks or wants something, I am using a familiar shorthand for the idea that the character is depicted in such a way that readers may infer those ideas or desires. Meta-critics who reflexively attack psychological readings for treating these verbal artifacts as if they were real people should, however, ask themselves whether their own readings could withstand a rigorous application of their principle, whether any meaningful response to drama is possible without somehow imagining that the words represent or constitute human beings.

13. G. Wilson Knight, *The Wheel of Fire*, 5th ed. (Cleveland: World Press, 1964), pp. 38–39.

14. Cf. Claude Lévi-Strauss, *Tristes Tropiques*, trans. John Russell (New York: Atheneum, 1972), p. 219: "To say . . . that death is either natural or unnatural is meaningless [in Bororos culture]. When a native dies, the village organizes a collective hunt . . . to make Nature pay her debt."

15. Once again Browne provides useful evidence that this reading is not an anachronistic imposition: "we are what we all abhorre, *Antropophagi* and Cannibals, devourers not onely of men, but of our selves; and that not in an allegory, but a positive truth" (p. 107). Montaigne's essay "Of Cannibals" discusses a captive's warning that, in eating him, the captors "will be eating at the same time their own fathers and grandfathers, who have served to feed and nourish his body"; *Complete Essays*, trans. Donald M. Frame (Stanford: Stanford University Press, 1965), p. 158. Clare Gittings, *Death, Burial and the Individual in Early Modern England* (London: Croom Helm, 1984), pp. 158, 162–63, shows that some Renaissance Englishmen found the idea of eating at funerals, or even at memorial services some weeks later, disturbing.

16. Hamlet mimics these symptoms when he visits Ophelia disguised as a sort of *memento amori*, "Pale as his shirt . . . As if he had been loosed out of hell / To speak of horrors," letting out an expiration that seems to "end his being," and finds his way out "without his eyes" (2.1.81–83, 96–98). If Hamlet is indeed playing dead here, perhaps it is to test whether his dead self will be as pathetically rejected by his beloved as his father's dead self has been.

17. Erlich, p. 203, points out that this ghost makes "night hideous" instead of "wholesome," bringing news of a corruption through sexuality (the medium of Original Sin and hence mortality) that inverts the glad tidings enabled by Christ's virgin birth. Erlich puts this observation in service of a psychoanalytic diagnosis of Hamlet's "highly complex search, partially unconscious, for a strong father" (260); I prefer to associate this search with the more general symbolic need for some mission in life that death does not simply cancel.

18. C. S. Lewis, "Hamlet: The Prince or the Poem." *Proceedings of the British Academy*, 28 (London: Oxford University Press, 1942), pp. 147–52.

19. Roy D. Waldman, *Humanistic Psychiatry* (New Brunswick, NJ: Rutgers University Press, 1971), pp. 123–24; quoted by Becker, p. 181. Hamlet would probably find a more graceful phrasing, but he could certainly say of the ghost what (according to Becker, p. 212) the analysand characteristically says of the analyst at the peak of transference: "'I am immortal by continuing to please this object who now may not be alive but continues to cast a shadow . . . and may even be working its powers from the invisible spirit world.'"

20. Clifford Geertz, "Religion as a Cultural System," in *Anthropological Approaches to the Study of Religion*, ed. M. Banton (New York: Praeger, 1966), p. 4.

21. Ernest Jones, *Hamlet and Oedipus* (New York: Doubleday, 1955), passim. Ronald Levao, *Renaissance Minds and Their Fictions* (Berkeley: University of California Press, 1985), p. 348, points out that Hamlet identifies extensively with "he that plays the king" in the play within *Hamlet*.

22. Thomas Adams, *Workes* (London, 1629), p. 555. For more specific verbal echoes of the play, see, for example, p. 928, where Adams asks, "who can say, which was the Client, which the Lawyer: which the borrower, which the lender: which the captive, which the Conqueror; when they all lie together in the blended *dust*?" The sentiment may have been conventional, but this array of instances was not. Two paragraphs later, Adams describes human beings as an impressive "piece of work," and on the following page describes God as sending "his Sergeant Death to arrest us," echoing the dying Hamlet's description of "this fell sergeant, Death" as "strict in his arrest" (5.2.341–42). What makes such echoes particularly surprising is Adams's affiliation with the virulently antitheatrical Puritans.

23. For a recent and typical example, the parents of murdered actress Rebecca Shaeffer have dedicated their lives to gun control: "We face death every morning," her father told a reporter; "You never cease missing the person. The gun issue lets us focus our anger" (*Los Angeles Times*, August 13, 1991, p. E1).

24. *Directory for the Public Worship of God* (1644); quoted by Joshua Scodel, *The English Poetic Epitaph* (Ithaca: Cornell University Press, 1991), p. 185. Cf. Freud, "Obsessive Actions and Religious Practices," IX, p. 118, on the way the neurotic cannot renounce formalities that may "seem quite meaningless to us . . . for any deviation from the ceremonial is visited by intolerable anxiety, which obliges him at once to make his omission good."

25. On the implication of a Black Mass in this poisoned chalice, see Roy W. Battenhouse, *Shakespearean Tragedy* (Bloomington: Indiana University Press, 1969), p. 250. The suggestion that Ophelia is damned by immersion in water, perverting the promise of baptism, reinforces this pattern of inversion. The idea

of cannibalism often raised anxieties in Renaissance minds about the feasibility of the general resurrection, since bodies would have to compete for their constitutive material.

26. Daniel E. Van Tassel, "Clarence, Claudio, and Hamlet." *Renaissance and Reformation*, New Series, 7 (1983), pp. 48–62.

27. Roland Mushat Frye, *The Renaissance "Hamlet"* (Princeton: Princeton University Press, 1984), pp. 82–102.

28. See for example *Death Repeal'd By a Thankfull Memoriall* (Oxford, 1638), which emphasizes in several places the immortalizing power of the monuments Lord Bayning of Sudbury has charitably helped to build.

29. Frye, p. 258, insists that Hamlet's remark is perfectly compatible with an expectation of Christian afterlife; but the contrast with the compelled speech of Hamlet's revenant father, and the correction ("flights of angels sing thee to thy rest") urgently offered by Horatio, suggest otherwise. Instead, the last words look ahead to Flamineo's farewell in Webster's *The White Devil*: "I have caught / An everlasting cold; I have lost my voice / Most irrecoverably . . . rest breeds rest . . . " (5.6.266–68).

30. René Girard, *A Theater of Envy* (New York: Oxford University Press, 1991), pp. 271–89, perceives many of the same concerns in *Hamlet* that I do, and explores them brilliantly, but finally deduces that Shakespeare is advocating Christianity as humanity's last best hope against the cycle of retributive violence. The evidence of plot runs against this recuperation of a devoutly Christian Shakespeare. Hamlet's supposed conversion only escalates the violence, violence that is clearly homologous with Christian stories about punishing a primal sin and sacrificing an innocent son.

31. Compare Becker, p. 90, summarizing Kierkegaard: "One goes through it all to arrive at faith, the faith that one's creatureliness has some meaning to a Creator; that despite one's true insignificance, weakness, death, one's existence has meaning in some ultimate sense because it exists within an eternal and infinite scheme of things brought about and maintained to some kind of design by some creative force." Levao, p. 354, perceives Hamlet "longing for the coherent force of fictions."

32. Richard Levin, *New Readings vs. Old Plays* (Chicago: University of Chicago Press, 1979).

33. Philippe de Mornay, *Discourse of Life and Death*, trans. Mary Herbert Pembroke (1592); ed. Diane Bornstein, Medieval and Renaissance Monograph Series, III (1983), 46.

34. Cf. Girard, pp. 286–89, on the moral admonition *Hamlet* offers a world of nuclear technology. This fear of fratricide further equates Hamlet's revenge with Claudius's primal crime.

35. Cf. Freud, "Thoughts for the Times on War and Death," XIV, 292: "the bewilderment and the paralysis of capacity from which we suffer, are essentially determined among other things by the circumstance that we are unable to maintain our former attitude towards death, and have not yet found a new one."

36. Maurice J. Quinlan, "Shakespeare and the Catholic Burial Services," *Shakespeare Quarterly*, 5 (1954), pp. 303–6.

37. Lucretius, *On the Nature of Things*, trans. William E. Leonard (New York: Dutton, 1957), I: 99–100. Bacon, "Of Unity in Religion," II, 236, quotes this passage. Shakespeare seems to have recognized this pattern from the first scene of what may have been his first play, where Exeter asks,

> We mourn in black, why mourn we not in blood?
> Henry is dead, and never shall revive.
> Upon a wooden coffin we attend,
> And death's dishonorable victory
> We with our stately presence glorify,
> Like captives bound to a triumphant car.

Exeter is evidently proposing to correct this situation by a war against "the subtile-witted French" who may "By magic verses have contrived his end" (*Henry VI, Part I*, 1.1.17–27). Kirby Farrell, *Play, Death, and Heroism in Shakespeare* (Chapel Hill, University of North Carolina Press, 1989), p. 57, notes that this speech "reduces death to a military humiliation that the survivors can undo by destroying the French and, through them, death itself."

38. First Letter, iv.1; see (Sister) Miriam Joseph, "Discerning the Ghost in *Hamlet*," *PMLA*, 76 (1961), pp. 493–94. See also Isaiah 8:19, "Should they consult the dead on behalf of the living?"

39. In addition to Greg, see Arthur Kirsch, "Hamlet's Grief," *ELH*, 48 (1981), pp. 17–36.

40. Job 14:10, quoted by John Dunton (?), "House of Weeping," in *A Mourning-Ring* (London, 1692), p. 44. Hamlet's father performs a role like that of the virtuous pagan Cyrus, who "forbids his sonnes to thinke . . . that he shall be *Nothing* any more after his death" (Tuke, p. 2), rather than the role suggested by Augustinian theology, in which dead fathers "are where they doe not see, nor hear what things are done or chaunceth in this life"; William Leigh, *The Soules Solace Against Sorrow* (London, 1602), p. 30, citing Augustine's *De Spiritu*, 2.9.

41. *Marlowe's Doctor Faustus 1604–1616: Parallel Texts*, ed. W. W. Greg (Oxford: Clarendon Press, 1950).

COMIC MEANS, TRAGIC ENDS

1. Canto III, stanza 9; ed. Leslie A. Marchand (Boston: Houghton Mifflin, 1958).

2. Darryl J. Gless, *"Measure for Measure," the Law, and the Convent* (Princeton: Princeton University Press, 1979), pp. 15–60, attempts to locate the genre of the play; see also Mary Lascelles, *Shakespeare's "Measure for Measure"* (London: Athlone, 1953), which classifies the play as tragicomic on a more traditional basis; Gregory W. Lanier, "Physic That's Bitter to Sweet End," *Essays in Literature*, 14 (1987), pp. 15–36; and Arthur C. Kirsch, "The Integrity of *Measure for Measure*," *Shakespeare Survey*, 28 (1975), pp. 89–105.

3. For example, Paul Hammond's "The Argument of *Measure for Measure*," *English Literary Renaissance*, 16 (1986), pp. 496–519, resists its own title by asserting that there is finally no moral argument discernible in the play.

4. Freud, "Three Essays on the Theory of Sexuality," *Complete Psychological Works*, Standard ed., trans. James Strachey (London: Hogarth Press), VII, 149–50.

5. See, for example, Phillip Stubbes, *The Anatomie of Abuses* (London, 1583), sig. H4r.

6. Stubbes, sigs. G8v–H8r. Jacques Rossiaud, *Medieval Prostitution*, trans. Lydia G. Cochrane (New York: Basil Blackwell, 1988), pp. 86–103, suggests that some medieval Europeans felt obliged to procreate in order "to save both city and Christendom before they were overwhelmed" by the decimations of war and plague, and that this obligation led to an increasing tolerance of brothels and a decreasing valuation of pious celibacy. These attitudes—reflected in Guillaume Saignet's fifteenth-century allegory that showed Nature under attack "by two frightful harpies, Pestilence and War, accompanied by a maiden of virtuous appearance but shameful behavior, Chastity"—offer an enlightening context for *Measure for Measure*. Duke Vincentio appears to share Saignet's belief that "Marriage is a good thing, for it permits the multiplication of men at the same time as it avoids fornication."

7. Thomas Tuke, *A Discourse of Death, Bodily, Ghostly, And Eternall* (London, 1613), p. 13.

8. Compare an observation in a Jacobean sermon by Thomas Adams: "There is law against coiners; and it is made treason justly, to stamp the king's figure in forbidden metals. But what is metal to a man, the image of God?"; *The Sermons of Thomas Adams, The Shakespeare of Puritan Theologians*, ed. John Brown (Cambridge, 1909), p. 99.

9. The erotic undertones of religious flagellation throughout *Measure for Measure*, the ways mortification of the flesh becomes gratification instead, have been well documented by Carolyn E. Brown, "Erotic Religious Flagellation and Shakespeare's *Measure for Measure*," *English Literary Renaissance*, 16 (1986), pp. 139–65.

10. Janet Adelman, *Suffocating Mothers* (New York: Routledge, 1992), p. 87, reads this ominous locution as marking the play's mistrust of sexuality and maternal origins. Here as elsewhere, I would amend her argument by reading this mistrust as part of a general mistrust of mortal bodies, linked in this instance by the doctrine that Original Sin is transmitted at the moment of conception.

11. Michel Foucault, *The History of Sexuality*, trans. Robert Hurley (New York: Pantheon, 1978), I, 144. Foucault maintains that

In the eighteenth century, sex became a "police" matter—in the full and strict sense given the term at the time: not the repression of disorder, but an ordered maximization of collective and individual forces. . . . One of the great innovations in the techniques of power in the eighteenth century was the emergence of "population" as an economic and political problem: population as wealth, population as manpower or labor capacity. . . . At the heart of this economic and political problem of population was sex: it was necessary to analyze the birthrate, the age of marriage, the legitimate and illegitimate births, the precocity and frequency of sexual relations, the ways of making them fertile or sterile, the effects of unmarried life or of the prohibitions. . . . this was the first time that a society had affirmed, in a constant way, that its future and its fortune were tied . . . to the manner in which each individual made use of his sex. (I, 25–26)

Surely this description fits the governmental work that propels *Measure for Measure*. Perhaps Shakespeare is once again being prescient—or perhaps Foucault is once again exaggerating the disjunctions in recent human history. On "bio-power" as an eighteenth-century invention, see I, 138–45; on its strained relation to the death-penalty—again anticipated by *Measure for Measure*—see I, 138.

12. In a difficult passage defending Claudio against Angelo's sentence, Isabella seems to raise the question of women's responsibility for the mortality inherited with Original Sin:

ANGELO: We are all frail.

ISABELLA: Else let my brother die,
           If not a feodary but only he
           Owe and succeed thy weakness.

ANGELO: Nay, women are frail too.

ISABELLA: Ay, as the glasses where they view themselves,
          Which are as easy broke as they make forms. (2.4.121–25)

The commonplace that women are as frail as mirrors thus gives way to an Augustinian warning that life is even more fragile (cited, for example, by Tuke, p. 55).

13. Nicholas Guy, *Pieties Pillar* (London, 1626), attributes this idea to "Helvetian Hereticks."

14. Thomas Pierce, *Death Consider'd as a Door to a Life of Glory* (London, 1690), p. 13, scoffs at this consolation as "all the Resurrection Those Hereticks would allow."

15. Becker, p. 42, argues that it is "difficult to have sex without guilt . . . because the body casts a shadow on the person's inner freedom, his 'real self' that—through the act of sex—is being forced into a standardized, mechanical, biological role." On p. 230, Becker quotes Otto Rank's contention that "in essence sexuality is a collective phenomenon which the individual at all stages of civilization wants to individualize, that is, control." This would help to explain the appeal of various perversions, particularly fetishism.

16. Gnosticism provides some intriguing parallels to this darker, blasphemous side of *Measure for Measure*. The Gnostics commonly protested that the individual spirit was trapped in a degradingly physical universe controlled by a demi-urge claiming to be the sole and benevolent deity, and their strategies for defying these limitations followed the ascetic and libertine paths. See Hans Jonas, *The Gnostic Religion* (Boston: Beacon Press, 1958).

17. Freud, "On Hysteria," II, 305.

18. Philip C. McGuire, *Speechless Dialect: Shakespeare's Open Silences* (Berkeley: University of California Press, 1985), p. 71. Victoria Hayne, in her forthcoming U.C.L.A. dissertation, will argue against this perspective by dem-

onstrating that the reluctant grooms are merely forced to honor the marital commitments they have already made by word or deed.

19. Clare Gittings, *Death, Burial and the Individual in Early Modern England* (London: Croom Helm, 1984), p. 175.

20. Robert N. Watson, *Shakespeare and the Hazards of Ambition* (Cambridge: Harvard University Press, 1984), passim. Becker, p. 118, associates a man's desire "to bypass the woman and the species role of his own body" with a determination "to procreate himself spiritually through a linkage with gifted young men, to create them in his own image," rather than "to be used as an instrument of procreation in the interests of the race."

21. The argument that Angelo's "virtues" (a word with seminal implications) must go forth in "issues" (1.1.27–43) echoes the standard arguments for procreation in Shakespeare's sonnets and in fact throughout Renaissance literature, exhortations not to waste nature's finest models by failing to reproduce them in a new generation. In the same passage, the Duke talks about Angelo's life-story as if it were a stable and legible text to be read, and such writing (again with a pun on "character") becomes another metaphor for procreation at 1.2.144. This word-play further interweaves the procreative and artistic aspects of the Duke's immortality-strategy—the same pair of projects linked so persistently in Jonson's epitaph and in Shakespeare's sonnets. Yet as those sonnets demonstrate, Shakespeare remains painfully aware that these modes of immortality are merely figurative and highly vulnerable; see Gillian M. Kendall, "Shakespeare's Romances and the Quest for Secular Immortality" (Ph.D. diss., Harvard University, 1986), which illuminates Shakespeare's highly equivocal endorsement of these answers to death.

22. Gittings, p. 175, describes the role-based funeral practices of the period, yet notes that "This view of society, in which no one was indispensable and everyone could simply be replaced by another person of similar rank, was greatly at odds with the growing feeling of individualism, with its emphasis on personal uniqueness."

23. Jonathan Goldberg argues that the paternal metaphor permeates James's assertions of authority; see "Fatherly Authority," in *Rewriting the Renaissance: The Discourses of Sexual Difference in Early Modern Europe*, ed. Margaret Ferguson, Maureen Quilligan, and Nancy Vickers (Chicago: University of Chicago Press, 1986), pp. 3–32.

24. The excellent BBC-TV "Shakespeare Plays" production emphasizes this trait when the Duke triumphantly stages himself to the people's eyes in the final scene.

25. Gless, pp. 161–62, compares the Duke's complaints about slander with those of King James; others, notably Josephine Bennett, *"Measure for Measure" as Royal Entertainment* (New York: Columbia University Press, 1966), pursue the connection more extensively. However, Richard Levin, *New Readings vs. Old Plays* (Chicago: University of Chicago Press, 1979), pp. 167–93, forcefully refutes this instance of "occasionalist" interpretation. Critics are now likely to depict the play as allegorically attacking James's leadership, not endorsing it. My contention, comparably, is that the play can be read as allegorical blasphemy

no less forcefully or coherently than as a positive Christian allegory. Perhaps the tragicomic mixture allows *Measure for Measure* to straddle questions of tyranny and theodicy more easily. In any case, these arguments and ambiguities are more likely to verify the notion of Shakespeare's elusiveness than to provide any defensible paraphrases of the play as political or theological assertion.

26. Lewes Bayly, *The Practise of Pietie* (London, 1613), Epistle Dedicatory, sig. A2r.

27. Brown, "Erotic Religious Flagellation," p. 151, summarizing an observation several critics have made, comments that the consolations the disguised Duke offers are "conspicuously devoid of the promise of a Christian afterlife." Lever, in the Introduction to the edition of *Measure for Measure* used in this chapter, p. lxxxvii, characterizes the Duke's argument as "essentially materialist." Julia Reinhard Lupton, "Afterlives of the Saints," *Exemplaria* (Fall, 1990), p. 379, notes perceptively "the play's systematic exclusion of references to heaven and resurrection."

28. Stephen Greenblatt, "Invisible Bullets," in *Shakespeare's "Rough Magic,"* ed. Peter Erickson and Coppélia Kahn (Newark: University of Delaware Press, 1985), pp. 276–302, skillfully explores the notion that, in improvising cynically on the belief systems of Native Americans, English colonists might have compromised their own Christian confidence.

29. This Marxist/Machiavellian perspective on religion is most obvious in the writings of the radical Reformers, though it insinuated humanist training, and traces of it may be found in canonical figures such as Marlowe, Lyly, Montaigne, and Hobbes, as well as in Mary Gunter, whose case will be discussed in my Epilogue.

30. Indeed, the use of Ragozine invites us to ask a question that our culture, abetted by its newscasts, fiercely resists: is death by disease any less arbitrary or important than death by accident or execution?

31. Phoebe S. Spinrad, *"Measure for Measure* and the Art of Not Dying," *Texas Studies in Literature and Language*, 26 (1), 1984, p. 91. She also (on p. 82) analyzes Claudio as an anticipation of the modern "quasi-solipsist who in his own demise sees the disappearance of the universe."

32. On the body as the soul's prison, see, for example, Zacharie Boyd, *The Last Battle of the Soul in Death* (1629), ed. Gabriel Noel (Glasgow, 1831), pp. 396 and 413; William Harrison, *Deaths Advantage* (London, 1602), p. 33, sees death as an escape "from a prison, to a place of libertie." On hell as the next prison, see Jean Pierre Camus, *A Draught of Eternitie*, trans. Miles Car (Douay, 1632), pp. 127 and 145.

33. Roland M. Frye, *Shakespeare and Christian Doctrine* (Princeton: Princeton University Press, 1963), pp. 291–92, records this censorship.

34. Adelman, p. 94.

35. Irene Dash, *Wooing, Wedding, and Power: Women in Shakespeare's Plays* (New York: Columbia University Press, 1981), p. 251.

36. This effort to turn the bodily discomforts of both wintry cold and feverous heat against Claudio's prospective nostalgia for the earthly life of the senses backfires when both extremes reappear less than fifty lines later as part of his terror of death.

37. Later the Duke similarly warns that Claudio's "ghost his paved bed would break, / And take her hence in horror" if Isabella were to forgive Angelo (5.1.433–34). Again the prospect of a posthumous voice is used to extort an earthly response, demanding sacrifices (as sociobiology would predict) in defense of close genetic kin.

38. Lupton, p. 377.

39. The discussion of the Virgin Mary in Donne's *Sermons*, VI, 180, suggests how threatening Lucio's question might be: "It is not enough for a virgin to bee a virgin in her owne knowledge. . . . She must appeare . . . as they that see her, may not question, nor dispute, whether she be a maid or no." Gless, p. 103, notes the echo by which Lucio's "salutation mocks Catholic devotion to the Blessed Virgin," but overlooks the further resonances of the Annunciation, which make it much harder to isolate the blasphemy as simple anti-monasticism in the mouth of a profane scoundrel. Virtually the entire Annunciation text, which the Book of Common Prayer takes directly from Luke, offers suggestive parallels to Isabella's experience, from the initial novitiate's unease at Lucio's apparently mocking greeting, and embarrassment at the sexual implications of his message, to the submission to shadowy powers that will make her the prospective mother of her Lord's son:

And the Angel went in unto her, & said, Haile . . . And when she sawe him, she was troubled at his saying, & thoght what maner of saltacion that shulde be. [Her child] shalbe great, & shalbe called the Sonne of the moste High. . . . Then said Marie unto the Angel, How shal this be, seing I know no man? And the Angel answered, and said unto her, The holie Gost shal come upon thee, & the power of the moste High shal overshadowe thee. (Luke 1:28–35, Geneva Bible)

An eerie futurist echo of Shakespeare's twist on the Annunciation story occurs in Margaret Atwood's recently filmed novel *The Handmaid's Tale* (New York: Random House, 1985), in which the few women still fertile are dressed in red nuns' habits and forced to bear the children of the patriarchs in order to perpetuate the society.

40. Lupton, p. 398n9, adduces this precedent, and also mentions the resemblance between Lucio's name and Luke's. Her very intriguing study of the hagiographic traditions reveals that Isabella's pursuit of a saintly martyrdom is "consistently perverted by the sexual dynamics of a contemporary Vienna," and that "Angelo's language reduced *agape* to *eros* by rewriting Christian charity as the granting of sexual favors and by deflating the holy sexuality of ancient martyrdom to the boiling corruption of modern Vienna" (p. 80). This argument seems clearly synergistic with my own, though I am more concerned with the fall from transcendence into biology than with the specific fall from saintliness into sin.

41. Quoted by John Bakeless, *The Tragicall History of Christopher Marlowe* (Cambridge: Harvard University Press, 1942), I, 111.

42. Stanley Stewart, *The Enclosed Garden* (Madison: University of Wisconsin Press, 1966), pp. 40–41. Other critics have noted some similarity between this setting and a Marian garden; see Roy W. Battenhouse, "*Measure for Measure* and Christian Doctrine of Atonement," *PMLA*, 61 (1946).

43. Stubbes, p. 87, in the version of the *Anatomie* edited by W. B. D. D. Turnbull (Edinburgh, 1836); this passage does not appear in the 1583 first edition, but was included well before the time of *Measure for Measure*.

44. See, for example, Martin Fotherby, *Atheomastix* (1622), pp. 150–51, construing even the most stable forms of atheism as madness. For a modern perspective on this tendency, see G. E. Aylmer, "Unbelief in Seventeenth-Century England," in *Puritans and Revolutionaries*, ed. Donald Pennington and Keith Thomas (Oxford: Clarendon Press, 1978), pp. 33–34.

45. Philippe Ariès, *The Hour of Our Death*, trans. Helen Weaver (New York: Random House, 1981), p. 215, discusses "The difficulty in separating the idea of supernatural survival from the idea of fame acquired during earthly life . . . After the sixteenth century, rational and scientific thought, like Protestant and Catholic religious reform, tried to dissociate the two forms of survival," but "did not immediately succeed." Between the Counter-Reformation defense of "the ancient communication across the barrier of death," and the way, "in Puritanism, worldly success remained attached to the idea of predestination," the neat distinction between worldly deeds and otherworldly destiny would have been under attack from all sides.

46. This resistance—predictable in a narcissistic age, according to Becker's theory—had parallels across Renaissance culture. See Browne, "Letter to a Friend," p. 402, praising Robert Loveday for his determination to leave "no Earnest behind him for Corruption or Aftergrave, having small content in that common satisfaction to survive or live in another, but amply satisfied that his Disease should dye with himself. . . . " Donald R. Howard, "Renaissance World-Alienation," in *The Darker Vision of the Renaissance*, ed. Robert S. Kinsman (Berkeley: University of California Press, 1974), pp. 59–60, discusses the Cathar belief that "the worst of crimes was procreation, because it imprisoned another good soul in another evil body." This seems to be a residue of Gnosticism.

47. Watson argues that Coriolanus's effort to extricate himself from the mortal flesh he shares with his fellow Romans obliges him to define his "coining" as a mechanical rather than a procreative process; see pp. 145–61, 169–70, 178, 183, 188.

48. Compare Angelo's assertion at 2.2.91 that "The law hath not been dead, though it hath slept." He is resurrecting, by a standard consolatory metaphor, the moral laws by which he defines his own immortality.

49. G. Wilson Knight, *The Wheel of Fire*, 5th Edition (Cleveland: World Press, 1964), p. 82. Huston Diehl, "To Put us in Remembrance," in *Homo, Memento Finis*, Early Drama, Art and Music Monograph Series 6, ed. David Bevington (Kalamazoo, MI: Medieval Institute, 1985), pp. 192–95, compares the Duke's return to the Last Judgment. Pamela Sheingorge and David Bevington, "Alle This Was Token Domysday," in the same volume, offers the same comparison (p. 122).

50. Tuke, p. 13.

51. Thomas Edwards, *Gangraena*, 2d ed. (London, 1646), I, 219; quoted by Norman T. Burns, *Christian Mortalism from Tyndale to Milton* (Cambridge: Harvard University Press, 1972), p. 79.

52. I. C., *A Handkercher for Parents Wet Eyes* (London, 1630), p. 21. John Donne, *Devotions*, p. 82, attempts to convert this Existential metaphor back into conventional terms of justice, and does so in a manner highly reminiscent of *Measure for Measure*, by discussing a fateful "*Bell* in a *Monastery*": "If these *Bells* that warn to a *Funerall* now, were appropriated to none, may not I, by the houre of the *funerall*, supply? How many men that stand at an *execution*, if they would aske, for what dies that Man, should heare their owne faults condemned, and see themselves executed, by *Atturney?*"

53. Lever, p. lvii, cites the various Christian allegories that have been applied. Gless, pp. 4–5, also comments on the oversupply of "personification allegory" concerning *Measure for Measure*; then, pp. 53–60, offers a different way of allegorizing the play. On pp. 247–50, Gless discusses the possibility of identifying the Duke with the Christian God. See also Knight, p. 74; Battenhouse, 1029–59; and Robert G. Hunter, *Shakespeare and the Comedy of Forgiveness* (New York: Columbia University Press, 1965), pp. 204–26.

54. Louise Schleiner, "Providential Improvisation in *Measure for Measure*," *PMLA*, 97 (1982), pp. 227–36, characterizes the Duke's actions as an *imitatio dei*.

ANOTHER DAY, "ANOTHER GOLGOTHA"

1. Browne, *Pseudodoxia Epidemica*, p. 193. On reports of a heretical belief in the Ralegh family that "there was a god in nature," see the deposition of William Arnolde during the Cerne Abbas commission hearings, in Hadrian Dorrell (?), *Willobie His Avisa* (1594), ed. G. B. Harrison (Edinburgh: Edinburgh University Press, 1966), p. 262.

2. Robert N. Watson, *Shakespeare and the Hazards of Ambition* (Cambridge: Harvard University Press, 1984), pp. 83–141.

3. Janet Adelman, *Suffocating Mothers* (New York: Routledge, 1992), p. 145, argues that the male character of the retributive force precludes reading it as truly natural. From my perspective, the exclusion of women (and hence human fertility) from this march shows how *Macbeth* raises the stakes: this is not merely (as in *Measure for Measure*) the triumph of a species-project over an individual one, but also the triumph of vegetative nature over the symbolic aspirations of the entire human race. And in *Macbeth* as in *Hamlet*, the men are too distracted by their internecine rivalries to notice that they are abetting the cause of the ultimate "common enemy of man" (3.1.70).

4. Freud, "Psychopathology of Everyday Life," *Complete Psychological Works*, Standard ed., trans. James Strachey (London: Hogarth Press), VI, 250; Brown, p. 102.

5. Donald Foster, "Macbeth's War on Time," *English Literary Renaissance*, 16 (1986), pp. 319–42, comes closest to my own perspective on this obsession; his p. 323n7 provides a list of other scholarship on time in *Macbeth*. Norman O. Brown, *Life against Death*, p. 102, argues that, "according to Hegel, time is what man makes out of death."

6. Freud, "The Theme of the Three Caskets," XII, 297–98. Cf. the dying speech of Chapman's Byron:

Summer succeeds the spring; autumn the summer;
The frosts of winter the fall'n leaves of autumn;
All these and all fruits in them yearly fade,
And every year return: but cursèd man
Shall never more renew his vanished face.

> (George Chapman, *The Conspiracy and Tragedy of Charles Duke of Byron*, Revels Plays, ed. John Margeson [Manchester: Manchester University Press, 1988], 5.4.249–53)

Byron's fervor in perceiving contrast rather than similarity between his transience and that of each leaf only confirms the crisis of human narcissism in Jacobean culture.

7. Freud, "Inhibitions, Symptoms and Anxiety," XX, 130; quoted by Becker, p. 53.

8. These infantile imprints can produce, conversely, a desire for subjugation to an external order, but only if we associate that order with the admired tyranny of a paternal figure, and stories about temptresses usually make the king-father a vulnerable and feminized figure, as *Macbeth* does.

9. Freud, "Thoughts for the Times on War and Death," XIV, 297, remarks that "every injury to our almighty and autocratic ego is at bottom a crime of *lèse-majesté*. And so, if we are to be judged by our unconscious wishful impulses, we ourselves are, like primaeval man, a gang of murderers. It is fortunate that all these wishes do not possess the potency that was attributed to them in primaeval times." Watson, pp. 83–96, argues that Macbeth is destroyed by precisely such a combination: persistent wishes to subdue nature to the individual will, and the nightmarish potency of those wishes to become a murderous reality.

10. Ninian Campbell, *A Treatise upon Death* (Glasgow, 1630), sig. C2r, observes that "one generation is the death of another."

11. Braunmuller's note to 1.3.46 observes that "Shakespeare elsewhere associates" the phrase "All hail" with this betrayal, and that the association plausibly derives from the York and Chester mystery-play cycles.

12. In a demonic inversion of Virgin Motherhood, however, Lady Macbeth prays for a sexuality devoid of fertility; I am indebted to Jennifer Bryan, "To the Last Syllable," unpublished essay, p. 11, for articulating these Annunciation patterns.

13. Mark 15:22, Geneva Bible; cf. Thomas Jackson, *Sinnelesse Sorrow for the Dead* (London, 1614), pp. 6–7: "in Golgotha no difference betwixt that skull which wore the Crowne, and that which bare the Tankard: all fellow-heires of the same inheritance; but one kingdome, yet all raigne."

14. Michel de Montaigne, *The Complete Essays*, trans. Donald M. Frame (Stanford: Stanford University Press, 1965), p. 64.

15. Campbell, sig. F8v.

16. Thomas Pierce, *Death Consider'd As a Door to a Life of Glory* (London, 1690), p. 8.

17. John Dove, *A Confutation of Atheism* (London, 1605), sig. I4v. An even clearer echo, in a more orthodox vein, occurs in John Gaule's *A Defiance to Death* (London, 1629), p. 9: "Man is a Candle, that either consumes himselfe upon the candlesticke of the world, or else swetes away under the bushell of his Mothers wombe. . . . Man is . . . moving dust. . . . our whole life is but the way to death." Perhaps Shakespeare is hinting that Macbeth is (like Faustus) characteristically a few fatal points off the true Christian line, which associated breath with the soul rather than the soul's extinction. Phillipe Ariès, *The Hour of Our Death*, trans. Helen Weaver (New York: Random House, 1981), p. 248, suggests that in Renaissance iconography the dying man's soul is generally "depicted as a naked child . . . being exhaled by the recumbent figure. . . . As the soul comes out of the mouth, it is caught by angels . . . and it is in this manner that it is conveyed to the heavenly Jerusalem." Perhaps, too, this misprision is already evident in Macbeth's odd picture of the aftermath of Duncan's murder: "Pity, like a naked newborn babe / Striding the blast, or heaven's cherubin horsed / Upon the sightless couriers of the air" (1.7.21–23).

18. See for example Kenneth Muir, in the introduction to the Arden *Macbeth* (London: Methuen, 1982), p. liii: "Macbeth, by his own actions, has robbed life of meaning. Shakespeare restores meaning to life by showing that Macbeth's nihilism results from his crimes."

19. These hints include darkness at noon and a rending of "The Lord's annointed temple" (2.4.6–10, 2.3.68), as well as Lady Macbeth's Pilate-like efforts to wash her hands of the business, unaware that water will not suffice to clear her of her primal violation; see Bryan, pp. 12–13.

20. Cf. Macbeth's assertion that Banquo's "soul's flight, / If it find Heaven, must find it out tonight" (3.1.140–41). Much villainy in "If." Again, Macbeth seems to mean heaven as opposed to hell, but we may think instead of a soul lost forever in the darkness of this unusually black night—and the horrible, hovering reappearance of Banquo as a ghost would only reinforce that impression.

21. Dorrell (?), p. 264. Burns, *Christian Mortalism* (Cambridge: Harvard University Press, 1972), p. 39, discusses the enthusiasts who believed that "The birth, Crucifixion, and Resurrection of Christ that took place inwardly in each regenerate man put him in a state that was not just *like* heaven, but one that was the *actual* heaven promised in the Gospel. Those who were in bondage to . . . the 'dead and killing Letter' of Scripture were in hell, in thrall to sin. . . . " For an apt, though considerably later, version of this attitude, see Stephen Crisp, *A Faithful Warning* (London, 1684), p. 16, quoted by Norman Burns, p. 87: "if he doth Evil, his Hell is only here in his own Conscience, but when he leaves the World all things will be as if they had not been, and the Soul shall dye with the Body, and suffer an Annihilation as well as the Body, or shall be swallowed up out of all particularity, as a drop of Water into the Sea, and so then what matter." A little water clears us of this selfhood, and with it the burden of guilt.

22. R. A. Foakes, "Images of Death: Ambition in *Macbeth*," in *Focus on Macbeth*, ed. J. R. Brown (London: Routledge, 1982), p. 8, discusses this distinction perceptively.

23. Freud, "On Transience," XIV, discusses the anticipatory mourning that makes the natural beauty a source of great sadness. Lady Macbeth's claim to feel "The future in the instant" (1.5.56) resembles her husband's symptoms of this-worldliness, since it means that she looks ahead to their worldly gains, not that she feels any concern about its consequences for their immortal souls. In that sense her remark is comparable to the "instant fires" Andrew Marvell promises his coy mistress, which might be worldly passion, but might also be an ironic anticipation of hellfire.

24. Pierce, p. 20.

25. Fyodor Dostoyevsky, *The Idiot*, trans. David Magarshack (London: Penguin, 1955), p. 419.

26. The function of this medical intervention is made unusually explicit in the report that the "Revenges" burning in Malcolm and his allies "Would to the bleeding and the grim alarm / Excite the mortified man" (5.2.3–5).

27. Foster, p. 330, comments insightfully on this possibility.

28. Arthur Schopenhauer, *The World as Will and Idea*, trans. T. Haldane and J. Kemp (London: Routledge, 1948), III, 286, 260; quoted by Jacques Choron, *Death and Western Thought* (New York: Collier, 1963), p. 184.

29. Jacob Boehme, *The Way to Christ* (1622), trans. John J. Stoudt (Westport, CT: Greenwood Press, 1979), p. 194 (*Theoscopia*, IV, 4).

30. Boehme, pp. 51–52 (*De Aequanimitate*, I, 9–14).

31. Boehme, p. 171 (*Theoscopia*, I, 39–40).

32. Boehme, p. 173 (*Theoscopia*, II, 4–6).

33. Boehme, p. 174 (*Theoscopia*, II, 9).

34. See, for example, James L. Calderwood, *If It Were Done: "Macbeth" and Tragic Action* (Amherst: University of Massachusetts Press, 1986), p. 47, who astutely evokes the hints that "'murder is coition'" in the play's opening acts.

35. Compare, for example, the peculiar retraction of Lady Macbeth's fertility, and the invocations of unnatural darkness by her husband (1.5.50–55, 2.4.6–10, 3.2.46), with Job's first words: "Let the daye perish, wherein I was borne, and the night when it was said, There is a manchilde conceived. Let ye day be darkenes, let not God regarde it from above, nether let the light shine upon it. But let darkenes, & the shadowe of death staine it: let the cloude remaine upon it, & let them make it fearefull as a bitter day" (3:3–6, Geneva Bible; similarly, 3:9). For if Job had not been born at that ill-starred moment, "so shulde I now have lyen and bene quiet, I should have slept then, and bene at rest, / With the Kings. . . . The wicked have there ceased from their tyrannie, and there they that laboured valiantly, are at rest" (3:13, partly echoed by *Macbeth*, 3.2.19–26). Lady Macbeth's handwashing clearly recalls Job's complaint that "If I wash my self with snowe water, and purge mine hands moste cleane, / Yet shalt thou plonge me in the pit, and mine owne clothes shal make me filthy" (9:30–31). See also the putting out of the candle (21:17) and the self as a brief shadow destined for darkness (7:2, 17:7).

36. These quotations are transcribed from the English-language subtitles.

DUELLING DEATH IN THE LYRICS OF LOVE

1. *Sermons*, VII, 79; cf. II, 99, 247; V, 80. Donne makes the point with obsessive insistence: "evill is nothing, sin is nothing; that is, it hath no reality, it is no created substance, it is but a privation, as a shadow is, as sickness is; so it is nothing" (VI, 239); "this state of their grave . . . is not an annihilation, no part of Gods Saints can come to nothing" (VI, 363). In his poetic compliment to Thomas Woodward, Donne claims that "'tis decreed our hell is but privation / Of him" (9–10); before Donne completes this nearly blasphemous compliment, the enjambment awakens the fear that the punishment waiting in death is merely oblivion and negation.

2. "The dead heare not Thunder . . . but yet there is a voyce, which the dead shall heare . . . *and they that heare shall live*. . . . They shall be then but such bodies, as they were when they were laid downe in the grave, when, though they were intire bodies, they could not heare the voice of the mourner. But the voyce of the Archangel shall enable them to heare" (*Sermons*, IV, 69–70). This voice becomes the ultimate performative utterance in the *Devotions*, p. 13: "Though I be dead, I shall heare the voice; the sounding of the voice, and the working of the voice shall be all one; and all shall rise there in a lesse *Minute*, then any one dies here."

3. See, for example, *Letters*, pp. 43–45; but even there he retreats from the fear that the condition of death will be mere oblivion, desiring instead some version of personalized, violent, perhaps sexual, conquest: "I would not that death should take me asleep. I would not have him meerly seise me, and onely declare me to be dead, but win me, and overcome me."

4. *Sermons*, IV, 55, 46. "But yet if God have naturalized death, taken death into the number of his servants, and made Death his Commissioner to punish sin, and he doe but that, how is Death an enemy? First, he was an enemy in invading Christ, who was not in his Commission, because he had no sin; and still he is an enemie, because still he adheres to the enemy. Death hangs upon the edge of every persecutors sword . . . " (IV, 54). The passage continues for some time insisting that, because bad people cause deaths, death itself must be evil; because it attacks at times of weakness, it is evil; and so on. The impression of a man scrambling to find logical and theological defenses for an essentially anti-Christian intuition seems to me unmistakable. See also I, 185: "*Christ Jesus*, had all our infirmities, and imperfections upon him, hunger, and weariness, and hearty sorrow to death, and that, which alone is All, Mortality, Death it self."

5. Arthur Marotti, *John Donne, Coterie Poet* (Madison: University of Wisconsin Press, 1986), p. 195. John Stachniewski, *The Persecutory Imagination* (Oxford: Clarendon Press, 1991), p. 291, speculates that Donne "felt his dependence on God to resemble his dependence on secular patronage, with its attendant frustration, humiliation, and despair." That Donne associated a lack of social status with a loss of life itself is clear from his sympathy in the *Devotions* for the diseased poor who "have no more hope of helpe, though they die, then

of preferment, though they live" and "doe no more expect to see a *Phisician* then, then to bee an *Officer* after" (p. 36). Sandor Lorand, "Psycho-Analytic Therapy of Religious Devotees," *International Journal of Psycho-Analysis*, 42 (1963), pp. 50–52, associates patients who "feel utterly unworthy, and are in continual fear of committing mortal sins, and at times fear death and hell-fire" with "severe trauma in adolescence or early childhood . . . and frustrations . . . intensified by the particular type of religious influence they were exposed to during the developmental years."

6. Dr. Keith Nuechterlein, quoted in *UCLA Medicine*, 14 (1993), p. 16.

7. Alfred Adler, *The Practice and Theory of Individual Psychology* (London: Kegan Paul, 1924), pp. 256–60, paraphrased by Becker, p. 218. On Donne's parallel use of prayer to defend the integrity of the self against a universe of mutability, see *Sermons*, IX, 175.

8. D. W. Winnicott, *The Maturational Processes and the Facilitating Environment* (New York: International University Press), pp. 58–59. Winnicott's work "enables us to join together the private psychological and the public cultural," because "parental loss, object loss, and doubts about reality, and the sustained existence of objects" are part of a continuum, and "That response to loss, which concerns the psychoanalyst, is that to which the philosopher gives the name 'skepticism'"; Richard Kuhns, "Loss and Creativity," *The Psychoanalytic Review*, 79 (1992), p. 202.

9. *Death's Duell*, ed. G. Keynes (Boston: Godine, 1973), p. 241. Cf. *Devotions*, p. 71: "*Eternity* is not an everlasting flux of *Tyme*; but *Tyme* is as a short *parenthesis* in a longe *period*." e e cummings appropriates this idea in a famous closing line: "and death i think is no parenthesis."

10. Freud, "Thoughts for the Times on War and Death," *Complete Psychological Works*, Standard ed., trans. James Strachey (London: Hogarth Press), XIV, 289. On this tendency in Donne, see also *Sermons*, II, 267: "when his hand that loves thee best hangs tremblingly over thee to close thine eyes . . . thy Saviours hand shall open thine eyes, and in his light thou . . . shalt see, that though in the eyes of men thou lye upon that bed, as a Statue on a Tomb, yet in the eyes of God, thou standest as a *Colossus*." Cf. also Heinz Kohut, *How Does Analysis Cure?*, ed. Arnold Goldberg and Paul Stepansky (Chicago: University of Chicago Press, 1984), pp. 18–19, arguing that the crucial deathbed consolation is a sense of being watched by an empathetic figure up to the moment of extinguished consciousness. On Freud's idea that we believe only in the deaths of others, cf. *Sermons*, VI, 354, where Donne (aided by his reflexive egoism) tries to overcome this tendency by imagining, "when I see him execute a judgment upon another . . . that that judgment belonged to me."

11. The fact that Donne leaves this poem unfinished may reflect an unwillingness to acknowledge any terminus to the earthly journey, for all its permutations: he would rather abjure closure altogether than have it apply directly to the experience of the soul. Freud, "Thoughts," XIV, 295, posits a primordial tendency in civilizations "to extend life backwards into the past, to form the notion of earlier existences, of the transmigrations of souls and of reincarnation, all with the purpose of depriving death of its meaning as the termination of life"; among Donne's contemporaries, Browne, p. 311, similarly observed that an-

cient cultures found consolation in the idea of "plurall successions" through a "variety of beings." Even the Jewish model of death and mourning evidently had some appeal to Donne, perhaps because it proposed a form of succession that did not subordinate the ideational to the biological, and a form of immortality that did not depend on resurrection and afterlife. In his travels he went out of his way to attend and admire the Jewish service at which an heir regularly "comes to the Altar, and there saith and doth some thing in the behalfe of his dead father, or grandfather respectively" (*Sermons*, VII, 169). The emphasis is less on lineal survival than on the periodic renewal of the self in sacred—but personal—language. Perhaps these visits were a displacement of the Catholic heritage, with its consoling prayers for the dead, that Donne had uneasily forsworn (*Devotions*, pp. 93–94); perhaps his poetry was, too.

12. On the functions of play as a strategy, often adopted by writers, for revising unacceptable realities, see Freud, "Creative Writers and Day-Dreaming," IX, 144.

13. Quoted by R. C. Bald, *John Donne: A Life* (London: Oxford University Press, 1970), p. 239.

14. Bald, pp. 228–30.

15. Hadrian Dorrell (?), *Willobie His Avisa* (1594), ed. G. B. Harrison (Edinburgh: University Press, 1966), p. 258. On Hariot's scandalous reputation see George T. Buckley, *Atheism in the English Renaissance* (Chicago: University of Chicago Press, 1932), pp. 130, 137–40; and Stephen Greenblatt, "Invisible Bullets," in *Shakespeare's "Rough Magic,"* ed. Peter Erickson and Coppélia Kahn (Newark: University of Delaware Press, 1985), pp. 276–302.

16. Bald, p. 72. On p. 63, Bald acknowledges that, as a law student, Donne's "restless intellectual curiosity" may have "brought him perilously close to complete cynicism in matters of religion, for he was not unreceptive to that Renaissance spirit of scepticism and free-thought which to many serious minds was more dangerous and deadly than heresy." Bacon's warning is found in his essay "Of Atheism," in *The Works of Francis Bacon* (London: C. & J. Rivington, 1826) II, 249.

17. Quoted in Bald, Appendix B, pp. 551–52.

18. An important exception is John Carey, *John Donne: Life, Mind and Art*, (London: Faber, 1981), p. 125, who sees that the two versions of Donne "give rein to identical passions"; but Carey here identifies those passions as an "impulse to reach beyond language and thought into wonder," and thereby to "think the unthinkable." My argument is that Donne used his mistresses, his God, and his poetry for precisely the opposite purpose: to contain threateningly limitless recognitions within verse forms and rational formulae, to unthink the only too thinkable idea of annihilation. Another important exception is Annabel Patterson, "All Donne," in *Soliciting Interpretation*, ed. Elizabeth D. Hardy and Katharine Eisaman Maus (Chicago: University of Chicago Press, 1990), p. 47: "the sharp break between the 'early' and the 'mature' work was a wishful critical construction."

19. Becker, p. 196. On p. 197 Becker attempts to delineate

the historical difference between the classical sinner and the modern neurotic: both of them experience the naturalness of human insufficiency, only today the neurotic is stripped of the symbolic world-view, the God-ideology that would make sense out of his unworthiness and would translate it into heroism. Traditional religion turned the consciousness of sin into a condition for salvation; but the tortured sense of nothingness of the neurotic qualifies him now only for miserable extinction. . . .

By exaggerating the disjunctions in cultural history, this passage conceals an important fact: the author of the *Songs and Sonets* already had one foot in Becker's uneasy "today," at least until some form of exhaustion or insight allowed him to resume a Christian pursuit of immortality.

20. Quoted by Peter Rudnytsky, *The Psychoanalytic Vocation* (New Haven: Yale University Press, 1991), p. 295. Cf. Norman O. Brown, *Life against Death* (Middletown, CT: Wesleyan University Press, 1959), p. 116: "the sexual organizations, pregenital as well as genital, appear to be constructed by anxiety, by the flight from death. . . . "

21. See, for a distinguished example, Arnold Stein, "Donne and the Satiric Spirit," *ELH*, 11 (1944), p. 272, who proposes that "One of the more important sources of Donne's melancholy is a disturbed interest in sex." My counterproposal is that Donne's melancholy and his disturbed and obsessive sexuality might both be symptoms of his mortality-anxiety, of his faltering Christian denial. Debora Shuger, "Saints and Lovers," in *Reconfiguring the Renaissance*, ed. Jonathan Crewe (Cranbury, NJ: Associated University Presses, 1992), p. 158, quotes the historian Nicholas Perella's observation that for medieval man, "The whole matter of yearning for the beloved, the restless longing for something superior to and beyond the grasp of mortality . . . is at the very heart of troubadour love poetry; but all this was first at the very heart of Christian spirituality." Becker would probably agree, and so laud Donne's return to Christianity as a triumph: "The religious geniuses of history have argued that to be really submissive means to be submissive to the highest power, the true infinity and absolute—and not to any human substitutes . . . " (p. 251).

22. Carey, p. 60; *Sermons*, IV, 272.

23. Julia J. Smith, "Moments of Being and Not-Being in Donne's Sermons," *Prose Studies*, 8 (3), (1985), p. 17.

24. Julia Smith, p. 15.

25. Freud, *Beyond the Pleasure Principle*, XVIII, 14–16.

26. Donald Ramsay Roberts, "The Death Wish of John Donne," *PMLA*, 62 (1947), p. 959.

27. Roberts, pp. 974 and 960. Cf. Becker, p. 15, citing the theory of "the noted psychoanalyst Gregory Zilboorg . . . that most people think death fear is absent because it rarely shows its true face; but he argues that underneath all appearances fear of death is universally present."

28. D. W. Harding, "Coherence of Theme in Donne's Poetry," *Kenyon Review*, 13 (1951), p. 439; Harding also observes that this fear seems to have more to do with annihilation than with hellfire. See also Evelyn Hardy, *Donne: A Spirit in Conflict* (London: Constable, 1942), p. 254: "At some time in childhood, or even in early manhood, perhaps at the loss of his brother, Donne had looked too closely into the face of death" and had developed an "attraction to the very thing which he feared. . . . " My object-relations perspective puts a slight twist on Hardy's observation: perhaps in childhood Donne looked in the

face of his mother—a figure of both attraction and fear—and saw only his own non-existence.

29. John Stachniewski, "John Donne: The Despair of the 'Holy Sonnets,'" *ELH*, 48 (1981), p. 702.

30. Many commentators have questioned whether the Jacobeans had yet registered the existential implications of this "new Philosophy," but in his melancholy musings on human mortality, Drummond, p. 35, echoes line 206 of "The First Anniversarie," word for word: "The element of fire is quite put out . . . the earth is found to move, and is no more the centre of the universe," discoveries which "leave the imagination in a thousand labyrinths."

31. Quoted by Bald, p. 225. Given the tension between Donne and his Catholic mother, some conjunction of these attitudes would not be surprising.

32. Izaak Walton, *Lives,* ed. George Saintsbury (London: Oxford University Press, 1950), p. 75.

33. Robert G. Collmer, "The Meditation on Death and Its Appearance in Metaphysical Poetry," *Neophilologus,* 45 (1961), p. 324. Cf. *Sermons,* III, 101: "Death is nothing else, but a devesting of those defects, which made us lesse fit for God," and the dead—"clothed in white"—"are not gone into any other wombe, then we shall follow them."

34. Drummond, p. 51, asks those seeking posthumous fame, "How is not glory temporal, if it increase with years and depend on time?"; Donne comparably begins "Loves Growth" by remarking that his love

> doth endure
> Vicissitude, and season, as the grasse;
> Me thinkes I lyed all winter, when I swore,
> My love was infinite, if spring make'it more.
> But if this medicine, love, which cures all sorrow
> With more, not onely bee no quintessence,
> But mixt of all stuffes, paining soule, or sense,
> And of the Sunne his working vigour borrow,
> Love's not so pure and abstract as they use
> To say. . . .
>
> (3–12)

The dead live all seasons and know none, travelling through incremental time to eternity. All flesh is grass. Death cures all sorrow—and should not be proud, though in its very nothingness it is the ultimate blow both to soul and to sense. But death is not entirely an abstraction, as Donne was always vividly aware: the sun breeds maggots in a corpse. The extrication of these proverbs from the text may not be neat enough to prove that Donne deliberately encoded them, but the cluster does suggest that death was at least subliminally on his mind. The exercise of substituting the word "death" for "love" yields interesting results in the apostrophe of "Loves Exchange," which most editors juxtapose with "Loves Growth."

35. *Sermons,* VI, 331; cited by G. F. Waller, "John Donne's Changing Attitudes to Time," *Studies in English Literature,* 14, p. 87. Compare Robert Welcome, *State of the godly* (London, 1606), pp. 46–47.

36. *Sermons,* VI, 170; cited by Helen Gardner, in her edition of Donne's *Elegies, Songs, and Sonnets* (Oxford: Clarendon Press, 1966), p. 201.

37. Thomas Traherne, "The Second Century," sec. 90, in *Centuries of Meditations,* ed. Bertram Dobell (London: Dobell, 1934), p. 139. This anxiety has primal roots. Geza Roheim, *The Origin and Function of Culture,* Nervous and Mental Disease Monographs 69 (New York: 1943), discusses the infantile and primitive versions of this fear that the dead will swallow the entire universe. A Jacobean tract quotes Cicero to similar effect: "Death is terrible unto them, with whose life al things be extinguished"; Samuel Garey, *Great Brittans little Calendar* (London, 1618), p. 172.

38. Brown, p. 117.

39. Murray Roston, *The Soul of Wit* (Oxford: Clarendon Press, 1974), p. 14; cf. Tilotama Rajan, "'Nothing Sooner Broke,'" *ELH,* 49 (1982), p. 810, which suggests that "the hyperbolical claim that the sun revolves around a pair of earthly lovers knows itself to be based on an exploded cosmological fiction."

40. Becker, *Denial of Death,* p. 145, citing Rank, *Beyond Psychology* (New York: Dover Books, 1958), pp. 130, 136. No wonder kings are found in bed with these lovers: this was precisely the kind of transcendent power attributed to royal couples in Donne's lifetime by poets such as Thomas Carew: "This royal pair, for whom Fate will / Make motion cease, and Time stand still, / Since Good is here so perfect, as no worth / Is left for after-ages to bring forth" (*Coelum Britannicum,* lines 1093–96); quoted by Graham Parry, *The Seventeenth Century* (London: Longman, 1989), p. 31.

41. Parry, p. 55.

42. Many of the poetic arguments for accepting death that are at the center of "The Flower" reappear a few years later in the closing stanza of E. Buckler's *A Buckler against the fear of Death* (London, 1640), sig. I8v:

My life's a flower: but when it withers here
It is transplanted into paradise,
Where all things planted flourish all the year,
Where Boreas never breaths a cake of ice.
With sweet air the place is blest;
There is an eternall spring:
Thither, Lord, thy servant bring.
Here my homely Muse doth rest.

As so often in Herbert's poems—and so rarely in Donne's—mortal ends and poetic closure reassuringly coincide. In the *Roxburghe Ballads* collection, R. C.'s "A Comparison of the Life of Man" compares it "unto a Flower / That grows and withers all within one hour" (I, 364). This echoes the "bringing down to hell / And up to heaven in an houre" of Herbert's "Flower" (16–17), and again the theme is the renewability of human life in heaven. Drummond, pp. 61–62, observes that death makes us wish

we could be transported (O happy colony!) to a place exempted from the laws and conditions of time, where neither change, motion, nor other affection of material and corruptible things were, but an immortal, unchangeable, impassible, all-sufficient, kind of life, it were the last of things wishable, the term and centre of all our desires. Death maketh this transplantation; for the last instant of corruption, or leaving-off of anything to be what it was, is the first of generation, or being of that which succeedeth.

It seems clear enough what *topoi* Donne's egoism is rebelling against in "Twicknam Garden," and it seems worth noting that Magdalen Herbert, the maternal figure on whom both Donne and Herbert evidently relied for pious consolation, was a dedicated gardener; see Herbert's "Memoriae Matris Sacrum" sequence, passim, in *The Latin Poetry of George Herbert*, trans. Mark McCloskey and Paul R. Murphy (Athens: University of Ohio Press, 1965).

43. Philip Martin, "Donne in Twicknam Garden," *Critical Survey*, 4 (1970), pp. 172–75.

44. Freud, XII, 301. He also associates the discovery of the subject-object dualism with the infant's frustrated efforts to find the nurse's breast; see Brown, p. 116.

45. Roston, p. 141.

46. Jacob Boehme, *The Way to Christ* (1622), trans. John J. Stoudt (Westport, CT: Greenwood Press, 1979), p. 235 (*Suspira Viatorum*, sec. 54).

47. See, for example, Donne's Preface: "whensoever any affliction assailes me, mee thinks I have the keyes of my prison in mine owne hand, and no remedy presents itselfe so soone to my heart, as mine own sword."

48. Quoted by Parry, p. 161. See also Browne, p. 121, on his belief that one "can from the ashes of a plant revive the plant, and from its cinders recall it into its stalk and leaves again. What the Art of man can doe in these inferiour pieces, what blasphemy is it to affirme the finger of God cannot doe in these more perfect and sensible structures?"

49. Julia Smith, p. 7, summarizes Donne's view of the human relation to God in terms that evoke an infant's experience of its earthly creators: "He seems to see in the creature's dependence a continual threat of annihilation, and obversely is fascinated by the security of God's self-existent being."

50. Rudnytsky, p. 79, demonstrates that Winnicott "summarily refutes Lacan's theory of the mirror stage with his dictum that '*the precursor of the mirror is the mother's face*.'" Kuhns, p. 207, quotes Winnicott's acknowledgment that the way a baby sees itself by watching the mother is virtually "unverbalizable except in poetry."

51. Bette Anne Doebler, *The Quickening Seed* (Salzburg: Institut für Englische Sprache und Literatur, 1974), pp. 245–46, examines this pattern.

52. A. Alvarez, quoting the psychoanalyst W. R. Bion, *The New Yorker*, March 8, 1993, p. 50.

53. D. W. Winnicott, "Fear of Breakdown," *International Review of Psychoanalysis*, 1 (1974), p. 106.

54. Roheim, p. 96.

55. John McDargh, *Psychoanalytic Object Relations Theory and the Study of Religion* (Lanham, MD: University Press of America, 1983), p. 140, cites studies validating Freud's hypothesis of a correlation between parental behavior and a child's idea of God, and specifically "that beliefs in the male violence of the supernatural world correlate positively with punitive infant and child rearing practices, while beliefs in the benevolence of the supernatural world will corre-

late with more nurturant practices. . . . " W. W. Meissner, "Religion as Transitional Conceptualization," *The Psychoanalytic Review*, 79 (1992), p. 194, observes that "guilt-ridden patients reflect a god of harsh judgment and punitive retribution—based on the model of the remote and punitive father figure. . . . "

56. Walton, p. 24; Edmund Gosse, *The Life and Letters of John Donne* (London: William Heinemann, 1899), I, 14.

57. Cf. Janet Adelman, *Suffocating Mothers* (New York: Routledge, 1992), p. 66, on the implied psychology of Othello: "Thus re-understood, abandonment becomes the burden of his tale, and helps to explain both his terrible hunger for Desdemona and the terrible speed with which he believes that she, too, has abandoned him."

58. See, for example, Nicholas Guy, *Pieties Pillar* (London, 1626), p. 45, which eulogizes a woman for fulfilling "this bounden dutie" to her own children despite the accompanying discomforts and inconveniences; also Elizabeth Clinton, *The Countesse of Lincolnes Nursurie* (1628), sig. B1r, on *"the duty of nursing due by mothers to their owne children"*; and Patricia Crawford, "The Construction and Experience of Maternity in Seventeenth-Century England," in *Women as Mothers in Pre-Industrial England* (London: Routledge, 1990), especially pp. 14–25. Magdalen Herbert was clearly dutiful enough, both as a mother and as a Protestant, to make it likely that she heeded such admonitions; see pp. 256–61 below.

59. "Obsequies to the Lord Harrington," lines 29–32. Cf. Zacharie Boyd, *The Last Battle of the Soul in Death* (1629), ed. Gabriel Noel (Glasgow, 1831), p. 320: "As for God, everie Soule shall love him *better than itselfe*, because it shall then perfectlie know, that *God hath loved it more than it was able to love itself.*"

60. Debora Shuger, *Habits of Thought in the English Renaissance* (Berkeley: University of California Press, 1990), p. 193. Compare Carey, p. 38, who finds Donne's "religious preoccupation" showing through in the word "Pilgrimage"—a word that also evokes the Roman religion of Donne's mother—in "Song: Goe, and Catche a Falling Starre."

61. Bald, p. 72.

62. Quoted by Bald, p. 72.

63. For an example (though perhaps an ironic one) of the Renaissance revival of this myth, see Sidney's quasi-Neoplatonic adaptation in Book One of *The Countess of Pembroke's Arcadia*, where Argalus sustains his love for the ruined beauty, Parthenia, because he "still held the first face in his memory"; ed. Maurice Evans (Harmondsworth: Penguin, 1977), pp. 90–91. From another perspective, Donne's lyrics hyperrationalize (by translating into mathematics or geometry) a troubadour convention that makes the mistress the only key to the only meaningful happiness.

64. Quoted by A. J. Smith, *The Complete English Poems* (London: Penguin, 1976), p. 395.

65. Otto Rank, *Will Therapy and Truth and Reality* (New York: Knopf, 1936; single-volume ed., 1945), p. 303; quoted by Becker, p. 161.

66. This notion of achieving immortality by conceiving time as relative is one resource of romantic love that Becker overlooks in dismissing it as an

inadequate response to mortality: "The lover does not dispense cosmic hero-ism. . . . The reason is that as a finite being he too is doomed . . . " (p. 167).

67. In *Sermons*, VI, 187, Donne describes childhood in terms that evoke annihilationist death: "to be *speechlesse*, to be *thoughtlesse*."

68. *Sermons*, IV, 87. Compare Waller's observation that "An urgent preoc-cupation that lies behind many of the love poems is a search for a fixed source of permanence within this flux to give ultimate meaning to the mutability of life . . . a search within concrete human experience for significant moments within the passing of time which, even though time passes, may capture a *stasis*, an eternal moment within time" (p. 81). Elsewhere in his *Sermons* (VIII, 59), Donne insists on the distinction between perpetuity, a property of the soul, and eternity, a property of God. The mythographer Joseph Campbell comments on the conquest of the eternal, in several religions, by full absorption in the beauty of the present.

69. These are the figurations mythologized in works such as *Romeo and Juliet* or *Antony and Cleopatra*, stories of immortality through love, through the very fatality of love. Donne himself, in "Obsequies to the Lord Harrington," complains that his society forbids "That testimonie of love, unto the dead, / To die with them, and in their graves be hid" (248–49). Abraham Darcie's "Funerall Complaints," in *Frances Duchesse Dowager of Richmond and Lenox her Funerall Teares* (London, 1624), sig. A5r, provides a real Jacobean widow with precisely this stance:

Alas! I had sworne by these amourous darts,
By which we have exchang'd each others hearts.
Thou in thy selfe not living but in me:
I in my selfe not living but in thee.
Thou couldst not die if that I did survive,
Nor I be dead whilst that thou wert alive.

The widow further wishes that, the better "our mutuall concorde to display, / Our loves and lifes had ended in a day." She can live on only by determining that "With this sole comfort shall my life be led, / The more I live, the lesse Thou shalt be dead" ("Funerall Teares," sig. B1r). This romantic attachment bears a strong resemblance to the religious devotion Donne would later extol in St. Paul, who pursued

this manner of a mutuall endearing, and a reciprocall embowelling of himselfe in the Congregation, and the Congregation in him, (as, certainly, if we consider all unions, (the naturall union of Parents and children, the matrimoniall union of Husband and Wife) no union is so spirituall, nor so neare to that, by which we are made *Idem spiritus cum Domino*, the same Spirit with the Lord, as when a good Pastor, and a good flock meete, and are united in holy affections to one another) to unite himselfe to his Ephesians inseparably, even after his separation, to be still present with them, in his everlasting absence, and to live with them even after death. . . . (*Sermons*, VIII, 169–70)

Donne's "Epithalamion Made at Lincolnes Inn" describes conjugal intercourse as this same kind of ritual: "The priest comes on his knees t'embowell her" (90). The idea that the energies Donne devoted to erotic pursuits in his youth were rechanneled into his later preacherly role is even more directly verified by the epigraph to this chapter.

70. R. E. Pritchard, "Dying in Donne's 'The Good-Morrow,'" *Essays in Criticism*, 35 (1985), p. 215, notes this possible allusion. See also the representations of Eden in globe form, and the description of mortal illness subsuming two-dimensional mortal maps in the "Hymne to God My God."

71. See Pritchard, pp. 213–22. For the medieval background of this anxiety about orgasm accelerating death, see M. McVaugh, "The 'Humidum Radicale' in Thirteenth-Century Medicine," *Traditio*, 30 (1974), pp. 259–83.

72. On the relation between orgasm and conception, see Thomas Laqueur, *Making Sex*, pp. 2–3. On Donne's resistance to the common procreative answer to mortality, see pp. 229–32 below.

73. Becker, p. 160. Janel Mueller, "Women among the Metaphysicals," *Modern Philology*, 87 (1989), p. 145, observes that "Women serve these males' psyches to . . . limit what is other than the self, what is otherwise finally the vastness of the world."

74. Peter De Sa Wiggins, "'Aire and Angels': Incarnations of Love," *English Literary Renaissance*, 12 (1982), p. 96, suggests that this embodiment "will be like Christ's assumption of a body for the purpose of redeeming fallen mankind, except that her act will be limited to redeeming him."

75. See for example Helen Gardner, *The Business of Criticism* (Oxford: Clarendon Press, 1959), p. 68.

76. Compare the way "Some old lovers ghost" reminds Donne's persona in "Loves Deitie" of a time when "Correspondencie / Only his subject was; It cannot bee / Love, till I love her, that loves mee" (12–14). The recognition that this time is past makes the speaker an "Atheist" to the "God of Love" (22, 18). Love is dead as a deity if it no longer sustains this version of immortality. For an intriguing variant of this idea that an imbalance between lovers threatens their survival, see "The Prohibition."

77. In realistic moments, when the recognition of decay impinges, Donne acknowledges that his ideal erotic solution to death works only on an imaginative level. In "The Anniversarie," as in "A Feaver," the more practical solution is to place as high a value as possible on the experience of love within a span of life. "The Anniversarie" begins with a claim reminiscent of "The Good-Morrow"—"Only our love hath no decay; / This, no to morrow hath, nor yesterday"—but then turns to a more orthodox promise of an even better love among souls once they have escaped their bodily "graves," which threaten a deadly "divorce" that will render "these eyes, and eares" useless (7–15). Once again, mutual love elides into salvation: "Who is so safe as wee? where none can doe / Treason to us, except one of us two" (25–26). If they can live in this mutual defense, then (like Macbeth willing, too late, to settle for living out "the lease of nature" in ordinary domesticity) they will be satisfied to live out "threescore" years in mutual love (30). The greatest tribute he can pay to his beloved is that he is willing to share time, and time-boundedness, with her.

78. "Life of Cowley," in Johnson's *Lives of the English Poets*, ed. George Birkbeck Hill (Oxford: Clarendon Press, 1905).

79. T. S. Eliot, "The Metaphysical Poets," in *Selected Essays: 1917–1932* (New York: Harcourt, Brace, 1932), pp. 246–47. The characterization of schizophrenia is by Dr. Arnold Scheibel, quoted in *UCLA Medicine*, 14 (1993), p. 13.

80. Winnicott, "Fear of Breakdown," p. 105. See also his "Physiotherapy and Human Relations," in *Psycho-Analytic Explorations*, ed. C. Winnicott et al. (Cambridge: Harvard University Press), pp. 561–68:

> One wants to be able to say that the psyche and the soma . . . do not start off as a unit. They form a unit *if all goes well in the development of that individual*; but this is an achievement. . . . the development cannot take place unless the person who is looking after the child is able to manage the baby and the baby's body as if the two form a unit. . . . When those who care for a baby or small child have this kind of a difficulty of their own, then the child they care for cannot become integrated into a unit.

Donne seems to fit this syndrome in important ways, and appears to work on his poems like a former abused child determined on one level to spare his own creations the specific trauma imposed by his creators, and compelled on another level to re-enact that traumatization.

81. *Sermons*, VI, 72; *Letters*, pp. 6–7. See, similarly, *Sermons*, VII, 103: "in naturall death, there is *Casus in separationem*, The man, the person falls into a separation, a divorce of body and soul; and the resurrection from this fall is by the Re-union, the soule and body are re-united at the last day." See also VII, 257; X, 176; and V, 117, where Donne observes that "God loves *Couples*; He suffers not our body to be alone, nor our soule alone, but he maries them together."

82. According to Nigel Llewellyn, *The Art of Death* (London: Reaktion Books, 1991), pp. 13–15, "the famous *Unton Memorial* picture of 1596" portrays Unton's life "as a journey which ends with his corpse crossing the sea, more like the Styx than the English Channel."

83. On Donne's disproportionate anxieties about his trip to Germany, see Bald, p. 343. Accepting Walton's assertion about "Forbidding Mourning," commentators often associate all these poems with Donne's departure from his wife to accompany the Drurys on a trip to France. My commentary builds on that association, but does not necessarily depend on it.

84. Walton, p. 39, reports that Donne's wife "profest an unwillingness to allow him any absence from her; saying, *her divining soul boded her some ill in his absence.*" On Freud's railway phobia, see Ernest Jones, *The Life and Work of Sigmund Freud*, abridged ed. (New York: Anchor, 1963), p. 198.

85. *Letters*, p. 44. *Sermons*, IV, 22–23, provides several instances in which Donne represents salvation as a voyage successfully concluded; see similarly *Sermons*, V, 77; VI, 76; VII, 100; and VIII, 64; and cf. also the Christian commonplaces which describe Christ and the Church as arks.

86. The Holy Sonnet "At the Round Earths Imagin'd Corners Blow" seems to defer the soul's elevation until the body's resurrection; see Kathryn R. Kremen, *The Imagination of the Resurrection* (Lewisburg, PA: Bucknell University Press, 1972), p. 113. For a brief survey of the different opinions available in Donne's world about the nature of this interval (if any), see Julia Smith, p. 14.

87. Contrast this ominous dispersion with the optimism Donne would later display in his sermons: "death is not a dissolution, but a redintegration; not a divorce of body and soule, but a sending of both divers wayes, (the soule upward to Heaven, the body downeward to the earth) to an indissoluble marriage to him, who, for the salvation of both, assumed both, our Lord and Saviour Christ Jesus" (*Sermons*, VIII, 168). "The Expiration" envisions only a bitter (if no-fault) divorce, with no prospect of reconciliation. The poem makes mortal destiny, not the tragicomedy of the sermon, which culminates in joyous family reunions and marriage to a forgiving Prince, but a tragedy in which a legalistic Solomon dooms the self to a fatal division between its soul-father and its body-mother.

88. J.D. Jahn, "The Eschatological Scene of Donne's 'A Valediction: Forbidding Mourning,'" *College Literature*, 5 (1978), p. 40, sees the poem united by similitudes that "originate from events in a resurrection scene," but interprets this as mere reinforcement of the promise of romantic reunion. My suspicion is the opposite, that these echoes reveal a profound yearning for resurrection after death underlying the surface yearning for reunion in life.

89. Donne experimented (in Paradox VI of his *Paradoxes and Problems*) with the possibility that the soul "is enabled by our body, not this by that."

90. In "The Second Anniversarie" Donne addressed the soul as similarly confident of its immortality while oblivious to the nature of that immortality: "Nor dost thou, (though thou knowst, that thou art so) / By what way thou art made immortall, know" (259–60).

91. Cf. *Sermons*, II, 248: "And so as your eyes that stay here, and mine that must be far of, for all that distance shall meet every morning, in looking upon that same Sun. . . . That if I never meet you again until we have all passed the gate of death, yet in the gates of heaven, I may meet you all. . . . "

92. The difference between a "breach" in the continuity of existence and "an expansion . . . to ayery thinnesse" (23–24) resembles the difference between mortalism (the temporary death of the soul) and psychopannychism (the temporary sleep of the soul).

93. On the sexual implications of this "erection," see A. B. Chambers, "Glorified Bodies and the 'Valediction: Forbidding Mourning,'" *John Donne Journal*, 1 (1982), p. 19, n. 46; and Jahn, p. 42. On its connection to earthly marriage, see *Sermons*, III, 247: "The husband helps as legges to her, she moves by his motion; The wife helps as a staffe to him, he moves the better by her assistance"; quoted by Jahn, p. 42.

94. The very practice of the lyric form—as my subsequent chapter on Herbert will argue—allows the poet to demonstrate that the rest of silence, the white space that marks the closure of any single poem, leads to a renewal rather than an annihilation of the consciousness the poem embodies. The rhythm of utterances provides a model that ought to dispel the fear of death as an ending, as Donne asserted in terms clearly reminiscent of "Forbidding Mourning": "death is in nature but *Expiratio*, a breathing out and we do that every minute" (*Sermons*, IV, 53, quoted by Jahn, p. 36).

95. Quoted by Chambers, pp. 16–17. Cf. *Sermons*, IV, 68; VIII, 335–36; and VII, 164, where the promise of a circle going from baptism to death at the

opposite pole is described as "words of a great extent, a great compasse." In the "Obsequies to the Lord Harrington," Donne asks, "O Soule, O circle, why so quickly bee / Thy ends, thy birth and death, clos'd up in thee?" (105–6). Elsewhere he challenges his congregation, "art thou loath to make up that Circle, with returning to the earth again?" (*Sermons*, VI, 52); one would be loath, if that perfect completion were ultimately termination and nullification. In Meditation 10 in the *Devotions*, Donne warns that all entities created out of nothing "bend to the same *Center*, and if they were not made immortall by *preservation*, their Nature could not keep them from sinking to this *center*, *Annihilation*." There must be some affirmation of his being at that center. Otherwise "Man hath no *center*, but *misery*; *there* and onely *there*, hee is *fixt*" (*Devotions*, p. 111).

96. *Sermons*, II, 199–200. As women thus place him in space, from birth-mother to mother-earth, God is a fixed foot guiding him through time: "Fixe upon God any where, and you shall finde him a Circle; He is with you now, when you fix upon him; he was with you before . . . and he will be with you hereafter" (*Sermons*, VII, 52; cf. VI, 175 and *Devotions*, p. 9).

97. W. A. Murray, "Donne's Gold-Leaf and his Compasses," *Modern Language Notes*, 73 (5), (1958), p. 329, discusses the possible relevance of this symbol.

98. Boyd, p. 426. Cf. Jean Pierre Camus, *A Draught of Eternitie* (Douay, 1632), p. 449, and William Harrison, *Deaths Advantage* (London, 1602), p. 43. Drummond, pp. 57–58, asks, "Why shouldst thou be fear-stricken and discomforted for thy parting from this mortal bride, thy body; sith it is but for a time, and such a time as she shall not care for, nor feel anything in, nor thou have much need of her; nay, sith thou shalt receive her again more goodly and beautiful . . . ?" See similarly his p. 22. When Richard Lovelace recast Donne's conceit a few years later in "To Lucasta, Going Beyond the Seas," he developed his own explicit version of the metaphor:

> Though Seas and Land betwixt us both,
>   Our Faith and Troth,
>   Like separated soules,
>   All time and space controules:
> Above the highest sphere wee meet
> Unseene, unknowne, and greet as Angels greet.
>
> So then we doe anticipate
>   Our after-fate,
>   And are alive i' th' skies,
>   If thus our lips and eyes
> Can speake like spirits unconfin'd
> In Heav'n, their earthy bodies left behind.
>
>   (13–24)

This lacks the gendering of soul and body underlying Donne's version, and (*pace* Chambers, p. 11) in that sense seems closer to "Aire and Angels" than to "Forbidding Mourning."

For St. Ambrose, see "Satyrus," Bk. II, 14–15, in *A Select Library of Nicene and Post-Nicene Fathers*, trans. H. De Romestin, X, 176; cited by Jahn, p. 45, n.

7. The idea of death as specifically a divorce of body and soul is extremely common in Jacobean funeral sermons.

99. He thus forces the world-explorations that endangered Christian confidence back into the service of that confidence (cf. *Sermons,* VI, 212). The conceit of circumnavigating the globe, like the connection at the compass-top in "Forbidding Mourning," allows Donne to add an extra dimension to his lifeline, one that supersedes the usual earthly measures of progression, and hence of decay. Heading into the sunset is heading toward the sunrise. On the brink of darkness, Donne once again derives comfort from the solar cycle. Phoebus becomes another avatar of Donne's phoenix, endlessly reborn from its own burning out. Browne, p. 211, interprets "the story of the Phoenix" as the way the ancients "induced the Resurrection from principles of their own."

100. This is the distinction Iago so effectively elides in telling Othello at 3.3.155 that "Good name in man and woman, dear my lord, / Is the immediate jewel of their souls." The idea of "reputation" may have been a mediating term in this shift from ceremonial fame to a personal name—a shift with Reformation overtones. There may also have been a high culture/low culture tension between the classical use of cognomens and the feudal use of names based on places and occupations.

101. Philippe Ariès, *The Hour of Our Death,* trans. Helen Weaver (New York: Random House, 1981), passim. In the *Devotions,* p. 36, Donne compares his own situation with the neglected poor who will be buried "in *oblivion.* . . . For they doe but fill up the number of the dead in the Bill, but we shall never heare their *Names,* till wee reade them in the Booke of life, with our owne."

102. Indeed, Donne envisioned a self continuous far beyond a lifetime: "I was built up scarce 50. years ago, in my Mothers womb, and I was cast down, almost 6000. years agoe, in *Adams* loynes; I was *borne* in the last Age of the world, and *dyed* in the first" (*Sermons,* VII, 78). In the *Sermons,* V, 71, Donne speaks of "the *Ego,* the particular, the individuall, I"; III, 109, displays a similar redundancy, stressing that at the general resurrection, "*Ego,* I, I the same body, and the same soul, shall be recompact again, and be identically, numerically, individually the same man." Janel Mueller, "Donne's Epic Venture in the *Metempsychosis,*" *Modern Philology* (1972), p. 137, asserts that Donne, like Augustine, "came to adopt an intensely subjective approach to experience, one which shifted emphasis from the metaphysics of the universe to the mortality and spirituality of the self." Efforts to refute the time-honored perception that Donne was intensely invested in his individual subjectivity—most extensively, Thomas Docherty, *John Donne, Undone* (London: Methuen, 1986), pp. 123–46—have thus far made few converts.

103. See, for example, *Sermons,* III, 97 and IV, 66, 69. Julia Smith, pp. 17–18, traces this concern elsewhere in the sermons.

104. See Becker, p. 149, on the ways people preserve the immortality-fantasy invested in their leaders when those leaders die: "Immediately men begin to rename city streets, squares, airports with the name of the dead man: it is as though to declare that he will be immortalized physically in the society"; see also Woody Allen's film *Sleeper,* which literalizes this tendency into a plan for cloning the dead leader.

105. Without the name-tag, the cherished identity and all its sensibilities might be unrecoverable. When portraying the mortal illness of the world after the death of Elizabeth Drury, Donne's "First Anniversarie" emphasizes that the direst symptoms are

> That thou hast lost thy sense and memory.
> T'was heavy then to heare thy voyce of mone,
> But this is worse, that thou art speechlesse growne.
> Thou hast forgot thy name. . . .
>
> (28–31)

Senselessness, unconsciousness, silence, and anonymity are again the essence of this death, but Drury's is a valediction without a name, a glance through a window that is therefore the merest transparency. Donne here displaces into the surviving world the losses of the dead. As a rhetorical trick, this kind of reversal is conventional enough, within and beyond the genre of funeral elegy. But it is remarkable that this displacement allows the symptomology of annihilation to surface, allows Donne to make explicit the mere blankness of death that his other works suggest more obliquely. The role of God is to cure precisely these annihilationist anxieties with "an universall eye, that pierceth into every darke corner," and an ear that "heares even the silent, and speechlesse man . . . " (*Sermons*, VI, 47).

106. Eamon Duffy, *The Stripping of the Altars* (New Haven: Yale University Press, 1992), p. 330.

107. The fact that "tomb" appears in a similar context in "The Canonization" helps highlight the connection. On the viability of this pun, see Doniphan Louthan, "The *Tome-Tomb* Pun in Renaissance England," *Philological Quarterly*, 29 (1950), pp. 375–80. On the utter mortality of "renown by papers, which is thought to make men immortal," see Drummond, p. 48.

108. Ed Regis, *Great Mambo Chicken and the Transhuman Condition: Science Slightly Over the Edge* (Reading, MA: Addison-Wesley, 1990).

109. Erasmus, *Ciceronianus*, trans. Izora Scott (New York: Teacher's College, 1908), p. 121; Bacon, *Advancement of Learning*, I, 64; Milton, *Areopagitica*, in *Complete Poems and Major Prose*, ed. Merritt Y. Hughes (New York: Bobbs-Merrill, 1957), p. 720. I am indebted to Hughes for the Bacon precedent, and to Debora Shuger for the Erasmus precedent. See also an elegy lamenting a childless death in Anthony Stafford, *Honour and Vertue, Triumphing over the Grave* (London, 1640), sig. Q3v: "But of *Stafford* w'have lost all / Both transcript, and originall, / Onely some margent notes are left / To tel's of what we are bereft."

110. On Donne's identification of a book with the experiential and potentially immortal self, see *Sermons*, VI, 286. His verse letters confirm their function as havens of individuality against the finality of death. He writes to Rowland Woodward (*Complete Poetry*, no. 122),

> my letter is like me, for it
> Hath my name, words, hand, feet, heart, minde and wit;
> It is my deed of gift of mee to thee,
> It is my Will, my selfe the Legacie.
>
> (5–8)

Indeed, an unresponding correspondent is therefore just as dangerous as an unloving beloved. In another verse letter (*Complete Poetry*, no. 128) Donne accuses Henry Wotton of being essentially dead for failing to answer a letter. Better the rest of him should die, Donne insists, "Then that your waking mind should bee a pray / To lethargies" (8–9) A collapse of the "Respective friendship," the mutual consciousness, carried by their "letters," is more dangerous than what the "shotts" of war can do to the body (3, 18, 9).

111. Cf. the way *A Buckler against the fear of Death* (London, 1640), sig. B8r, offers the Christian believer "an uneclipsed light"; and Humphrey Sydenham, *Natures Overthrow and Deaths Triumph* (London, 1626), p. 6, assures the faithful that "the soule as a Sunne that is eclips'd, or clouded, shall shine againe." Perhaps most deeply relevant is Thomas Jackson, *A Treatise* (London, 1625), p. 18: "Atheism is but a compleat or totall eclipse" of both the inner natural light of reason and the manifest divine light of God.

112. See for example *Death's Duell*, p. 4; "The Second Anniversarie," 297–300, 339–41; "Metempsychosis," 151; and (in an imaginative effort at reassuring reversal) the Holy Sonnet "What if This Present," 5–8.

113. Marotti, p. 115, compares this becalmed ship to a ruined gallant.

114. Marvell and Vaughan are among the canonical poets who work explicitly in this subgenre, but it was also widely used in popular works of moral admonition.

115. There could have been some specific historical resonance in this symbolic pattern for Donne, since castration followed by death was a common punishment for Catholics, and he would have been a Catholic had he not split violently away from his mother.

116. Freud, "On Narcissism," XIV, 73.

117. *Sermons*, VII, 104. On the gendering of body and soul in English attitudes toward death, see Erwin Panofsky's *Tomb Sculpture* (New York: Abrams, 1964), p. 82; also Debora Shuger, *The Renaissance Bible* (Berkeley: University of California Press, 1994), on the historical shifts in that gendering.

118. Stanley Fish, "Masculine Persuasive Force," in *Soliciting Interpretation*, pp. 228–29; Stephen Orgel's assertion is quoted from an unpublished conference paper. In my reading, Donne's fundamental anxiety is not so much that he would be a woman or a homosexual, as that he might cease to be at all.

119. On Donne's discomfort concerning these transvestites and "neat youths," see Marotti, p. 188. Carey, p. 30, observes that Donne tends to attack the "proneness of Roman Catholics to homosexuality," again conflating threats to his chosen theological immortality-strategy with threats to his chosen erotic immortality-strategy.

120. Brown, p. 116.

121. "If your partner is your 'All' then any shortcoming in him becomes a major threat to *you*," Becker warns (pp. 166–67); "The shadow of imperfection falls over our lives, and with it—death and the defeat of cosmic heroism. 'She lessens' = 'I die.' This is the reason for so much bitterness, shortness of temper and recrimination in our daily family lives." I would adjust Becker's formula only slightly. For the embittered Donne, "I am still dying" = "She must have lessened."

122. Kremen, pp. 92–93. For evidence of this conflation elsewhere in the culture, see Francis Quarles's emblem-poem, "Behold Thy Darling," which at first appears to be a warning to men to avoid corruption by the allurements of women, but proves finally to be a warning to souls to avoid a similar threat from the bodies they inhabit.

123. Though literal, it is of course magnified; it has that in common with the pornographer's attempt to capture the richness of sexuality and restore it to a jaded audience merely by depicting ever larger organs and orgies, or ever closer close-ups, as if hyperbole could restore meaning without moving beyond a purely physical level.

124. For evidence that this comparison may apply to mortal as well as sexual brevity, see *Sermons*, II, 199: "The Patriarchs in the old Testament had their Summer day, long lives; we are in the Winter, short lived."

125. On the understanding of *mummia* as a posthumous preservative in seventeenth-century medicine, see Theo Brown, *The Fate of the Dead* (Ipswich: D. S. Brewer, 1979), p. 59.

126. *Sermons*, VI, 217, complains that when God bestows his love and music on us, we mistake them for "naturall accidents, casuall occurencies, emergent contingencies, which as an Atheist might think, would fall out though there were no God, or no commerce, no dealing, no speaking between God and Man."

127. Shawcross, p. 151n, suggests the gingerbread man reference, though his paraphrase gives Donne's lines more of a romantic *carpe diem* emphasis than I think they will bear.

128. D. F. Rauber, "Donne's 'Farewell to Love': A Crux Revisited," *Concerning Poetry*, 3 (1970), pp. 51–63, explores the parodic aspects of the poem, reaching conclusions quite compatible with mine: "The gist of the parody is a denial of the doctrine of personal immortality, a denial of the craving for continuance of individual being which is the center of the poem. . . . The whole point of the discussion is the realization that nature performs her task with a single-minded concentration, completely indifferent to the fate of the individual, completely indifferent to the human world" (pp. 57, 60). This point is also quite compatible with my reading of *Measure for Measure*.

129. Shawcross offers two readings of this remark: "(1) that shunning these beauties is like applying an anaphrodisiac to his sexual organ, and ironically (2) that if he does nonetheless succumb to woman's 'heat,' it is only applying his generative seed to her (to beget children)." It seems to me that the two readings are valid in sequence, particularly if we recognize that "'Tis but" could have meant "It is only a matter of" (i.e., "all that is needed is"), as well as "All it amounts to is."

130. Hamlet also warns that "the sun breeds maggots in a dead dog, being a good kissing carrion" (181–82) and that Ophelia therefore must "not walk i'th' sun" (184) if she is to avoid a corrupting pregnancy. When "the King is a thing . . . Of nothing" (4.2.27–29), and love becomes merely another slave of the material universe, there is little encouragement to trust in the soul's transcendence.

131. See also Donne's "Metempsychosis," stanza 16, in which the wandering soul resides briefly in a mandrake, which has a human shape, but suffers

precisely the modes of silence, blindness, and oblivion feared by annihilationists: "A mouth, but dumbe, he hath; blinde eyes, deafe eares, / And to his shoulders dangle subtile haires" (151–52). See also *Sermons*, I, 192, and V, 212, which describes the resurrection—that is, the reunion of soul and body—as "the knot of all" for the Christian believer.

132. It is also reminiscent of the occasional malfunctions of Metaphysical conceit, when Donne becomes enslaved by the internal logic of the devices he created for controlling an otherwise unmanageable universe.

133. Carey, p. 126.

134. Cf. Browne, p. 307: "Our dayes become considerable like petty sums by minute accumulations; where numerous fractions make up but small round numbers; and our dayes of a span long make not one little finger."

135. But see *Sermons*, IX, 166, where Donne feels able to say that, to the extent that Puritans are fanatically pious, "I am a Puritan."

136. Walton, p. 29.

137. Walton, p. 54; on the connection of this poem with Ann, see Carey, p. 92, and the notes in the Shawcross and A. J. Smith editions. Walton, p. 51, describes Donne's wife as "the delight of his eyes."

138. "To the Countesse of Salisbury; August, 1614": "the Sunne / Growne stale, is to so low a value runne . . . all is wither'd, shrunke, and dri'd, / All Vertues ebb'd out to a dead low tyde" (3–4, 9–10). See similarly the opening of the "Obsequies to the Lord Harrington."

139. But if all sense wings not with thee,
And something still be left the dead,
I'll wish my curtains off to free
Me from so dark and sad a bed;

A nest of nights, a gloomy sphere,
Where shadows thicken, and the cloud
Sits on the sun's brow all the year,
And nothing moves without a shroud.

(7–14)

Quoted from *George Herbert and Henry Vaughan*, ed. Louis Martz, Oxford Authors series (Oxford: Oxford University Press, 1986), p. 252.

140. Donne writes to the Earl of Rochester that "good Divines have made this argument against deniers of the Resurrection, that it is easier for God to recollect the Principles, and Elements of our bodies, howsoever they be scattered, then it was at first to create them of nothing" (*Letters*, pp. 247–48).

141. Contrast this immobility with the conventions of elegiac pursuit exemplified by the early portions of Milton's "Lycidas," and Donne's effort to pursue his wife's soul in the Holy Sonnet "Since Shee Whome I Lovd." The death in nature in line two of the Holy Sonnet promptly becomes an assumption into heaven in line three, allowing the persona (though his "good is dead") a direction in which to aspire. The foremost concern of the sonnet as a whole is not that either he or she is now unreal, or that he lacks any purpose or direction, but instead that—misled by a residue of the body—he is going in the wrong direction to recapture her.

142. See, for example, *Sermons*, VIII, 79: "*Beloved*, the day of our *death* is the *Eve* of this *day* of the *Lord*. . . . the next day after my *death*, is the day of *Judgement*"; see also II, 267. "The Second Anniversarie" echoes these consolations by personifying death as "a Groome, / Which brings a Taper to the outward roome, / Whence thou spiest first a little glimmering light, / And after brings it nearer to thy sight: / For such approches doth Heaven make in death" (85–89). This hope, and the further promise of "The Second Anniversarie" that a funeral "Laies thee to sleepe but a saint Lucies night. / Thinke these things cheerefully" (120–21), are lost in the limitless darkness of the "Nocturnall." Donne may still believe that "the Sun does not set to any Nation, but withdrawe it selfe, and returne againe" (*Sermons*, VI, 173), but he is now in the position of a Claudio or a Macbeth, caring about the fate of individuals rather than nations.

143. Thomas Tuke, *A Discourse of Death* (London, 1613), p. 60; for the dark side of this, see Drummond's suggestion that, in death, "The sun perpetually setteth" (p. 22).

144. See, for example, Clarence H. Miller, "Donne's 'A Nocturnall upon S. Lucies Day' and the Nocturns of Matins," in *Essential Articles for the Study of John Donne's Poetry*, ed. John R. Roberts (Hamden, CT: Archon Books, 1975), p. 305.

145. Heather Dubrow, *A Happier Eden* (Ithaca: Cornell University Press, 1990), discusses Donne's aberration from the normal emphases of epithalamia. Mueller, "Women," p. 147, credits Donne for lending "no credence to essentialist views of sexual difference, for his poetry is unmarked by their major premise—that a woman's capacity to bear children defines her and her relation to a man." Perhaps this virtue is merely a by-product of Donne's determination not to be defined by procreative biology.

146. See Bald, p. 156, and *Letters*, pp. 118–19. *Letters*, p. 132, explains that one such illness "meets a fortune so ill provided for physique and such relief, that if God should ease us with burials, I know not well how to performe even that." Carey, pp. 73–74, comments that Donne expresses very little of the pride or pleasure in his offspring that one might expect from a young father.

147. Many such assertions derive from Lawrence Stone's valuable *The Family, Sex and Marriage in England, 1500–1800*, abridged ed. (New York: Harper, 1979), pp. 82–87.

148. *Letters*, p. 233; see also p. 154, and Bald, p. 279. In the sentence following the bitter quip about burials, Donne adds, "I flatter myself in this, that I am dying too: nor can I truly dye faster, by any waste, then by losse of children." It is interesting to ask, in the context, what provoked the apparitions of what can only be called paternal and conjugal guilt so common among the great English authors of this period. Donne's vision of his wife (whom he also had left behind as she neared childbirth) at exactly the time she (unbeknownst to him) gave birth to a stillborn child (Walton, p. 40), may be added to canonical examples such as Milton's "Methought I Saw My Late Espoused Saint" and Jonson's vision of his ascended first son at exactly the time the boy (whom he had left behind in plague-ridden London) was (unbeknownst to him) dying. Saying that such stories may have been improved for the telling does not explain away the compulsion to tell them.

149. *Letters*, p. 15. See also Julia Smith, pp. 8–9.

150. Marotti, p. 16; the book as a whole explores insightfully the practical implications of Donne's choice of manuscript circulation over full publication. See also Carey, pp. 70 and 93; and Dubrow and Patterson on the implications of Donne's Somerset eclogue.

151. Freud, "On Transience," XIV, 305.

152. Rajan, p. 812; contrast Kremen, p. 105, who sees "a progression 1) from the small, separate, and natural to the large, unified, and supernatural and 2) from what is consumed and dies to what is reborn the same and finally better."

153. On this uneasiness in Shakespeare's sonnets, see Gillian M. Kendall, "Shakespeare's Romances and the Quest for Secular Immortality" (Ph.D. diss., Harvard University, 1986), pp. 300–342.

154. Aside from the obvious dangers of fire and neglect, there was in Donne's society the active threat of government censorship, which—my study of revenge-tragedy has argued—corresponds to the annihilation threatened by the overwhelming and unsympathetic powers of the material universe against rebellious assertions of individual being. Donne relies on the radical personality of his poetry, as he relies on a radically personal salvation: "the intimation of mine owne soule," which is "more conspicuous then any Edition, any impression of any Author, for Editions may be called in, but who can call in the testimony of his owne soule?" (*Sermons*, V, 69).

155. Compare King Henry's bitter remarks in Shakespeare's *2 Henry IV*, 3.1.45–56.

156. Quoted by Jacques Choron, *Death and Western Thought* (New York: Macmillan, 1963), p. 204.

157. "How weak a thing is Poetry," he would declare in a sermon on the general resurrection; "How infirme, how impotent are all assistances, if they be put to expresse this Eternity?" (*Sermons*, IV, 87). In 1611, however, before his ordination, Donne was not quite ready to surrender the defense of poetry.

158. Donne's alternative titles for the First and Second Anniversaries also suggest their contribution to his denial of mortal closure. The "Anatomy of the World" is largely an autopsy proving that nothing can actually have killed Elizabeth Drury, and his "Of the Progress of the Soule" insists she has found a better life beyond this one. The author's repetition-compulsion, predictably, proves to be a defense against the oceanic, against the scope of an undifferentiated universe, the mutability of the body, the erasure of the ego.

159. See Jonson's "Conversations with Drummond," and the embarrassed defenses in Donne's letters. Harding, p. 431, observes that the young woman Donne describes as the "best, and first originall / Of all faire copies" seems to be "not merely a virgin but a virgin mother." In *Sermons*, VI, 183, Donne attacks a Puritan tendency to "ascribe too little, to the blessed Virgin."

160. For example, Donne insists that (in a Renaissance world increasingly conscious of subjectivity) role and progeny, body-politic and family legacy, are no longer adequate answers to the absolute mortality demonstrated by the irreparable loss of the incomparable Elizabeth Drury:

Prince, Subject, Father, Sonne, are things forgot,
For every man alone thinkes he hath got
To be a Phoenix, and that there can bee
None of that kinde, of which he is, but hee.

(215–18)

As the masculine references suggest, Donne is primarily pondering his own immortality here, his own determination (as in "The Canonization") to be a Phoenix whom the world must endlessly revive because it cannot adequately replace him.

161. Instead of taking the role of lover, he becomes a surrogate maker of her soul and protector of her honor. Elizabeth Drury was of course much younger than Donne (though, it is worth remembering, not so much younger than Ann Donne was when she began bearing his children), and his primary connection to her was through her father.

162. This tactic resembles Otto Rank's model of transference, as endorsed by Becker, p. 212: "to strive for immortality by fulfilling the moral code represented by the object . . . even after the death of the object." It also resembles Hamlet's fatal accession to the role his father bequeaths him. Dennis Kay, *Melodious Tears* (Oxford: Clarendon Press, 1990), p. 102, credits Donne with innovation "where the subject's example survives in the lives of virtuous people on earth. The shift from physical to spiritual memorials . . . epitomizes Donne's transformation of the genre. . . . "

163. Eliot, pp. 242–43.

164. *Sermons*, VI, 178, is insistent that Christ "was made my flesh . . . assumed my body." Perhaps, in "The Relique," the egoistical Donne returns the favor.

165. On Donne's mistrust of bodily relics, see *Sermons*, VI, 271.

166. Michael Schoenfeldt, *Prayer and Power* (Chicago: University of Chicago Press, 1991), p. 254, makes clear that "For Herbert, the University truly was an *alma mater*"; in his role as University Orator, Herbert describes the institution as "a matron holy" that must be kept free from erotic associations.

167. *Latin Poetry*, p. 153.

168. Debora K. Shuger, "Saints and Lovers," p. 156. John King, "The Godly Woman in Elizabethan Iconography," *Renaissance Quarterly*, 33 (1985), p. 41, reports that "godly women . . . throughout the literature of the English Renaissance and Reformation [c]haracteristically. . . . hold books in their hands." King, p. 55, reproduces an illustration from *The First Examinacyon of Anne Agnew* showing her defeating the mortal serpent with her book.

169. On the Magdalen painting, see Gosse, II, 360; on these maternal functions of the church, see *Sermons*, VI, 96–97, 282–84.

170. "The Canonization" appears to be an exception, perhaps a nostalgic fantasy in which Donne associates his poetry with the salvational power of Catholicism; see Carey, p. 43.

171. Shuger, *Renaissance,* p. 168.

172. Schoenfeldt, p. 230, quotes this anecdote from Leonardo's *Paragone*.

173. Shuger, *Renaissance*, p. 191, describes the way the figure of Mary Magdalene "passes from the cloistral devotions of the Middle Ages into early modern representations of a privatized, autonomous inwardness." John J. McDermott, (Ph.D. diss., U.C.L.A., 1964), pp. 116–17, 140–41, discusses the ways the Magdalen story was lent distinct Protestant undertones.

174. Quoted by Shuger, *Renaissance*, p. 168.

175. Walton, p. 51.

176. From the perspective of object-relations psychology, the mother's responsive gaze must help the child sort a good and manageable universe out of the overwhelming input of its senses and emotions, without eradicating any essential part of its body or ego in the process—in other words, she must dispose of the bathwater without dumping the baby as well.

177. In dedicating a sermon to the Countess of Montgomery, Donne again asks a woman to guard his "name in your memory, or in your Cabinet" when he fears he may be going "out of the world" (*Sermons*, VII, 179).

178. *Sermons*, IV, 66; cf. V, 73: "I am in my Cabinet at home, when I consider, what God hath done for me, and my soule." Donne writes to another woman that his "hope that I have a room in your favour keeps me alive, which you shall abundantly confirme to me, if by one letter you tell me that you have received my six" (*Letters*, p. 2).

179. For confirmation of this association, see Donne's letter of August 2, 1607, to Magdalen Herbert: "As we must dye before we can have full glory and happiness, so before I can have this degree of it, as to see you by a Letter, I must . . . come . . . to plaguy *London*, a place full of danger, and vanity, and vice. . . . And such it will be, till your return redeem it" (quoted by Walton, p. 336).

WORD WITHOUT END

1. Izaak Walton, *Lives*, ed. George Saintsbury (London: Oxford University Press, 1950), p. 63.

2. William Cowper, "Memoir of His Early Life" (c. 1752), in *George Herbert: The Critical Heritage*, ed. C. A. Patrides (London: Routledge, 1983), p. 164.

3. Samuel Taylor Coleridge, letter to William Collins, December, 1818, in *Critical Heritage*, p. 168.

4. Lewes Bayly, *The Practise of Pietie* (London, 1613), p. 934; this lengthy handbook went through many editions in the Jacobean period.

5. Zacharie Boyd, *The Last Battle of the Soul in Death* (1629), ed. Gabriel Noel (Glasgow, 1831), p. 4.

6. Theodore Spencer, *Death and Elizabethan Tragedy* (Cambridge: Harvard University Press, 1936), p. 206.

7. Joseph H. Summers, *George Herbert* (London: Chatto and Windus, 1954), pp. 185–86. Compare Yeats's (or at least Jane's) conclusion about religion and poetry: "For nothing can be sole or whole / That has not been rent" ("Crazy Jane Talks with the Bishop").

8. *Sermons*, VI, 41. See also VIII, 78: "The last words that *Christ* speakes in the *Bible* (and amongst us, last words make deepest impressions) are, *Surely I come quickly.*"

9. Debora K. Shuger, *Habits of Thought in the English Renaissance* (Berkeley: University of California Press, 1990), p. 105; Mark Taylor, *The Soul in Paraphrase* (The Hague: Mouton, 1974), p. 42.

10. Stanley Fish, *The Living Temple* (Berkeley, University of California Press, 1978), p. 167. This dialogic aspect of both Donne's and Herbert's verse may also support the common impression that Metaphysical poetry echoes some of the complex effects of English Renaissance drama.

11. On the strong hints of male sexuality in Herbert's poems, see Michael C. Schoenfeldt, *Prayer and Power* (Chicago: University of Chicago Press, 1991), pp. 230–70; Chana Bloch, *Spelling the Word* (Berkeley: University of California Press, 1985), p. 111n; Helen Vendler, *The Poetry of George Herbert* (Cambridge: Harvard University Press, 1975), p. 51, and Richard Strier, *Love Known* (Chicago: University of Chicago Press, 1983), pp. 252n63, 39n30, 48n45, and 89 with n16. Bloch's comments on the "inhibited" sexual responses of the speaker of "Love (III)" to "a gently loving, patient woman" (p. 111) are quite compatible with my reading of the oedipal tensions in Herbert's relationship to the nurturant figure who is at once his mother and his God. But it is important also to recognize, before putting too much weight on these figurations, that some of the phrases are conventional: the effort to pierce God's ears appears before Herbert in the Epilogue to Shakespeare's *The Tempest*, and a few years after in *Sermons, Meditations, and Prayers, upon the Plague* (London, 1637), sig. O4r: "that these prayers may ascend, and pierce thy Eares."

12. Walton, p. 262.

13. Walton, p. 264.

14. Julian of Norwich, *Revelations of Divine Love*, trans. James Walsh (New York: Harper, 1961), pp. 164–68 (Chapter 61).

15. E. Pearlman, "George Herbert's God," *English Literary Renaissance*, 13 (1983), 100–101. The entire argument (pp. 88–112) is compelling if predictably controversial, and several of my subsequent instances appear in Pearlman's discussion of Herbert's conflation of mother with God and breast-feeding with worship. See also Herbert's remark, quoted by Walton, p. 308, concerning "my Mother, the Church of England."

16. Edward Herbert, *Autobiography*, ed. Sidney L. Lee (London: John C. Nimmo, 1886), pp. 3–4, on his father, and pp. 21–27, on his brothers.

17. Voltaire, "Lettre sur les auteurs anglais," in *Oeuvres complètes de Voltaire* (Paris, 1879), XXVI, 482; cited and trans. by Eugene D. Hill, *Edward, Lord Herbert of Cherbury*, Twayne English Authors Series (Boston: G. K. Hall, 1987), Preface. D. P. Walker, *Ancient Theology* (London: Duckworth, 1972), pp. 164–93, argues for the revolutionary character of Edward Herbert's theology.

18. It is intriguing in this regard that Herbert's God seems to alternate between male and female gender, and between domineering violence and gentle nurturance (as in "The Flower"). It is also intriguing to compare Shuger's observation (p. 104) that Herbert "departs from contemporary Puri-

tan theology . . . precisely because he has no sense of 'the brethren.'" For
Shuger, this leaves Herbert lonely, except for God; I would add that he must
similarly have been lonely among his biological brethren. On Herbert's apparently closer bond with his frail sister, see Amy M. Charles, *A Life of George
Herbert* (Ithaca: Cornell University Press, 1977), p. 76. Charles, p. 86, describes "Affliction (I)" in terms that clearly suggest Herbert's struggle to define
his literary and religious achievements as a version of his brothers' military
achievements.

19. Leah Sinanoglou Marcus, *Childhood and Cultural Despair* (Pittsburgh:
University of Pittsburgh Press, 1978), p. 115, notes some interesting correspondences between Herbert's description of this institution and the characteristics of Magdalen Herbert's household. Herbert's tendency to assume a
childlike persona in his lyrics may help to justify my inquiry into the childhood
roots of those lyrics.

20. *The Latin Poetry of George Herbert*, trans. Mark McCloskey and Paul R.
Murphy (Athens: Ohio University Press, 1965), p. 130; my translation of "Per
te nascor in hunc globum / Exemplóque tuo nascor in alterum: / Bis tu mater
eras mihi." Compare the way Vaughan, who so often worshipfully echoes
Herbert, describes death as an interval during which the body "Shalt in thy
mother's bosom sleep" ("Death: A Dialogue," 28).

21. On Ann Donne's role in drawing her husband into Christian fervor, see
R. C. Bald, *John Donne: A Life* (London: Oxford, 1970), p. 328.

22. *Latin Poetry*, p. 119.

23. Cf. *Latin Poetry*, p. 145: "Root and staunchest rock you are to me, my
mother; I am as polyps, fixed by tentacles to rocks."

24. If this is regression, it is precisely the kind Becker perceives in love-based
sexuality, which "allows the collapse of the individual into the animal dimension
without fear or guilt, but instead with trust and assurance that his distinctive
inner freedom will not be negated by an animal surrender" (p. 42).

25. *Latin Poetry*, p. 137. On the historical likelihood that Magdalen
Herbert breast-fed her own children, see n. 58 to chapter 5.

26. For examples of this replacement, see "Sion," "Employment (I),"
"Deniall," and "Doomsday." For evidence that music was part of Magdalen
Herbert's comforting of her son, see *Latin Poetry*, p. 127, where this "sweet
moderating influence . . . seems as it were to be a tiny prelude of celestial
music," and p. 143, where he wonders, "how can there be laurels for me, how
nectar, unless with you I pass the day in song?"

27. Summers, p. 186.

28. Stanley Fish, *Self-Consuming Artifacts* (Berkeley: University of California, 1972), pp. 156–223.

29. Cf. Heinz Kohut, *How Does Analysis Cure?*, ed. Arnold Goldberg and
Paul Stepansky (Chicago: University of Chicago Press, 1984), pp. 18–19, on
the way Bismarck's terror of personal disintegration allowed him to go to sleep
only if he knew he was being constantly watched by a trusted aide.

30. Here again Herbert appears to be conflating his earthly caretaker with
his God; compare the complaints of "The Collar" with Walton's remark that
Magdalen Herbert "would by no means allow him to leave the University, or to

travel; and, though he inclin'd very much to both, yet he would by no means satisfie his own desires at so dear a rate . . . " (p. 275).

31. Again, Donne's long passage about the divine gaze is relevant because, to keep from falling into the abyss, he relies on the proven care of this Creator, "who hath so often said to my soule, *Quare morieris?* Why wilt thou die?" (*Sermons*, V, 267).

32. Death appears momentarily near the beginning of the treatise, but only in a subordinate clause sharply circumscribed by references to life. The only other references appear in the brief "Authour's Prayer before Sermon," when the direct discourse about his duties is over; Herbert speaks of death only to God, not to his readers or parishioners. Even in this relatively private meditation, death appears only in its negation through Christ, and the grave is mentioned only once, in the middle of a list of things Christ overcame. This omission and subordination looks more like strategic avoidance than like triumphant disdain.

Since no recent edition of *The Country Parson* seems to be both fully reliable and widely available, I will take the text from *The Works of George Herbert*, ed. F. E. Hutchinson (Oxford: Clarendon Press, 1941), but will also provide the corresponding page numbers from *The Country Parson; The Temple*, ed. John N. Wall, Jr. (London: SPCK, 1981), and from *The English Works of George Herbert*, ed. George Herbert Palmer (Boston: Houghton Mifflin, 1915). The reference to death occurs in Hutchinson on pp. 227–28, in Wall on p. 57, and in Palmer on p. 214. Christ overcoming the grave appears in Hutchinson, p. 288; Wall, p. 113; Palmer, pp. 325–26.

33. Hutchinson, p. 281; Wall, p. 106; Palmer, p. 312.

34. Marc Bensimon, "Modes of Perception of Reality in the Renaissance," in *The Darker Vision of the Renaissance*, ed. Robert S. Kinsman (Berkeley: University of California Press, 1974), pp. 260, 236.

35. Compare Browne's ecstatic use of Christianity to control and localize the extremes of time and space: "though my grave be *England*, my dying place was Paradise, and Eve miscarried of mee before she conceiv'd of *Cain*" (p. 132).

36. See for example Robert Higbie, "Images of Enclosure in George Herbert's *The Temple*," *Texas Studies in Literature and Language*, 15 (4), 1974, pp. 627–38, which interprets this emphasis on enclosure ("walls, locked doors, houses . . . boxes and cabinets," p. 627) as both a reminder of the limitations of our unsatisfactory earthly prison, and an evocation of the divine embrace that promises to protect us from all evil. But clearly I disagree with his assertion that these poems finally insist on their own "enclosed nature . . . their tight confinement within strict forms" (p. 628). For me, the crucial fact about these poems is the way they leak at the bottom, and thereby escape the tombs where they seemed doomed to lie still forever. John J. Pollock, "George Herbert's Enclosure Imagery," *Seventeenth Century News*, 31 (2), 1973, p. 55, links the emphasis on enclosure to the quest for unified poetic structure and to the "interenclosure" of the Eucharistic sacrament.

37. Hutchinson, p. 494. Higbie, p. 629, cites examples of this agoraphobia in lines 139, 144, 150, 204, and 418 of "The Church Porch," as well as in "The

Discharge," "Assurance," "Content," and "Holy Communion." Cf. William Bouwsma, *John Calvin* (New York: Oxford University Press, 1988), on the double fear of abyss and labyrinth.

38. William Baldwin, *Beware the Cat* and *The Funerals of King Edward the Sixth*, ed. William P. Holden (New London: Connecticut College, 1963), pp. 46–47 (the end of the second part of Maister Streamers Oration). Though it invites puns and speculation, the relationship between this necessary matrix and the mother seems to me less important in this regard than the struggle of the individual for a meaningful place in time and space. The infant's experience of the mother is doubtless connected, on the level of cognitive development, to this quest for universal orientation; but an effort to associate the desire for enclosure with a specifically oedipal desire for a return to the mother's womb, or (as Pearlman speculates on pp. 108–9) with "Herbert's identification with his mother as housekeeper," strikes me as less plausible and generative than the broader spiritual interpretation.

39. Higbie, pp. 629, 630.

40. This squares nicely with Higbie's observation, p. 633, that "as we move towards the poems of resolution at the end of 'The Church' . . . instead of asking God to let him out of his own imperfect enclosure, the poet is asking God to let him into God's perfect enclosure."

41. Harold E. Toliver, *Pastoral Forms and Attitudes* (Berkeley: University of California Press, 1973), p. 119.

42. Mark Taylor, p. 117, argues that "The notion of the incarnation, of the fleshly revelation of the Word, is in fact a promise of eternity, a signal that man will transcend the temporal limitations of mortality. Therefore, a poem about this transcendence, through its emphasis on a 'hieroglyphic' meaning that endures beyond the finite words in which it is couched, gains a life beyond itself." Herbert seems to find this paradox and this possibility extraordinarily compelling, and his "pattern poems" are the starkest examples of that compulsion.

43. Brewster S. Ford, "George Herbert and the Liturgies of Time and Space," *South Atlantic Review*, 49 (4), 1984, 19. Ford, p. 24, notes the way Herbert manages to encapsulate time within space, and space within our bodies, in "Church-Monuments": "The fleshe is but the glasse, which holds the dust / That measures all our time" (20–21).

44. Fish, *Temple*, p. 162. This theory strikes me as more applicable to "The Wreath" than to "The Altar," however.

45. For an interesting alternative example of concrete poetry as a defense against death, see the pyramid of words at the end of Niccols's *Monodia* (London, 1615). "Easter Wings," like "The Altar," goes outside the sequential (and hence terminal) flow of language, to become a whole object designed to outlast Herbert's death—to outlast even the death of the English language. Its graphic shape offers an objective correlative to its primary topic, namely, the idea that human beings can aspire to a redemptive flight even after (indeed, only because) a fall from grace threatened to crush them into earth. As the middle lines of each stanza shrink to two syllables, describing the decline of the species and the individual, the threat to biological survival and the threat to poetic continuity converge. The rest of those lines is silence. But by taking on the wings of praise

that the Christian model offers, the speaker and his poem escape together. Furthermore, the correlation of spiritual ontogeny (stanza one) with spiritual phylogeny (stanza two) allows Herbert to redeem his individual experience from annihilation, by "imping" himself onto the generational and eschatological identity of his species. This is the divine comedy that edges toward blasphemous parody in *Measure for Measure*. Herbert's individual life participates in the biological cycle that renews the human race toward its eventual redemption. The physical shape of the two stanzas asserts their blessedness beyond the transiency of language, and the congruency of the two stanzas recaptures the cycle of wing-beats into a static image of immortal animation.

46. Mark Taylor, pp. 59–62, suggests the relevance of Augustine's solar analogies. Compare the escape from linear time in "Affliction (II)."

47. Hutchinson, p. 233; Wall, p. 63; Palmer, p. 225.

48. Cf. "Jordan (I)." If the efficacious deathbed conversion of these poems recalls Catholic theology, perhaps its agency—a redemptive personal intervention of the Word—is Reformed enough to put Herbert back on his characteristic middle ground.

49. Mario A. Di Cesare, *George Herbert and the Seventeenth-Century Religious Poets* (New York: Norton, 1978), p. 4

50. An earlier closural gesture, in the fifty-fourth stanza, had failed because the act of faith, and therefore the poetic line, remained incomplete.

51. Jacob Boehme, *The Way to Christ* (1622), trans. John J. Stoudt (Westport, CT: Greenwood Press, 1979), p. 176 (*Theoscopia*, II, 17).

52. Hutchinson, p. 283; Wall, p. 108; Palmer, p. 315. Toliver, p. 132, argues that Reformation theology could not permit the human request to cause the divine response: "the poet's suit must be granted even before he asks, for the asking itself will not change God's mind." "Redemption" would seem to bear out that theory, but generally Herbert seems willing to sustain a principle of limited and paradoxical condignity, even if it is only a necessary illusion in human life and poetic form. On the importance of humility as a preparation for hearing God's word, see parts 1 and 4 of Augustine's *De Doctrina Christiana*.

53. See, for example, Herbert's "Dulnesse"; the deathbed complaint of Mary Gunter (in my Epilogue); Claudio's complaint about becoming "a kneaded clod" after death (in *Measure for Measure*, 3.1.120); and (to combine the two words) Herbert's "Divinitie," line 3.

54. As the "passing-bell" of Herbert's "The Flower" demonstrates, the verb "to pass" could mean "to die" or "to elapse" as easily as "to care." The only other place where Herbert could arguably be using the latter meaning—the reference in "Time" to people who "did passe" when visited by the Grim Reaper—connects plausibly to the former meanings as well. Cf. Mary Herbert Pembroke's 1592 translation of Philippe de Mornay's *Discourse of Life and Death*, ed. Diane Bornstein, Medieval and Renaissance Monograph Series, III, 1983, p. 66: "were it not of force we must passe, and that God in despite of us will doe us a good turne, hardly should we finde in all the world one, how unhappy or wretched soever, that would ever passe."

55. If Herbert is indeed concerned here with sustaining some expressive aspect of his identity against the approach of his mortality, then "The Forerunners" supports my general argument against a sea of troublesome historical

and methodological objections. The emphasis on the privileged "I" that Herbert is so anxious to preserve—its uncontested inwardness and the fear of its erasure by mortality—contradicts New Historicist claims that the idea of continuous selfhood was barely nascent during Herbert's lifetime, and that Renaissance identities were entirely based in social role rather than in Cartesian self-consciousness. The same evidence also contradicts old historicist claims that Renaissance Christianity effortlessly precluded any concern about personal annihilation.

56. Quoted by Norman T. Burns, *Christian Mortalism from Tyndale to Milton* (Cambridge: Harvard University Press, 1972), p. 86.

57. An analogue in modern American culture is the climax of the movie *Close Encounters of the Third Kind*, in which the descended spaceship at last magnificently chimes in with the final note of a signature melody played out to it repeatedly in apparently futile greeting. Rather less anachronistically, Thomas Taylor, in a sermon republished in the same year as *The Temple*, asserts that when "with an Aprill showre of mournfull teares for thy sinne . . . thou hast prevailed against Gods silence; thou shalt heare a sweete and comfortable Answere in due season"; *Three Treatises* (London, 1633), p. 101.

58. Alastair Fowler, *Kinds of Literature* (Cambridge: Harvard University Press, 1982), p. 96. For a different perspective on Herbert's use of titles, see Mary Ellen Rickey, *Utmost Art* (Lexington: University of Kentucky Press, 1966), pp. 92–102, 115–19.

59. Quoted by Gordon Braden and William Kerrigan, *The Idea of the Renaissance* (Baltimore: Johns Hopkins University Press, 1989), p. 99.

60. Mark Taylor, pp. 83–84, discusses the relationship between rhyme and homecoming in "Home." The same rhyme—"come" with "home"—concludes the rhyme-scheme of "The Quip."

61. It is also worth noting, in this regard, that the preacher Thomas Taylor provides a perfectly contemporary analogue in describing mortal man: "the neerer he is to death, he is so much neerer home" (p. 143).

62. George Wither—a poet-preacher contemporary with Herbert, though on the Puritan wing—also wrote that "although the mysteries of the Gospell, of which the *Psalmes* treat, were not then fulfilled in act, in respect to us to whom they were to be manifested in *Time*: yet in regard to God, with whom all *Times* are present, they might be properly enough mentioned as things alreadie effected"; quoted by Heather Asals, "The Voice of George Herbert's 'The Church,'" *ELH*, 36 (1969), p. 525.

63. *The Poetry of Robert Frost*, ed. E. C. Latham (New York: Holt Rinehart, 1969), p. 255.

64. Stanley Stewart, *George Herbert* (Boston: G. K. Hall, 1986), pp. 57–82, discusses the effect of Ferrar's "Harmonies" on Herbert's *Temple*. On Western chronometrics, see Donald Wilcox, *The Measure of Times Past*, (Chicago: University of Chicago Press, 1987).

65. Walton, pp. 316–17.

66. Donne, *Letters*, p. 106, jovially reports to Henry Wotton that the Paris executioner "swore he had rather execute forty Huguenots, then one

Catholique, because the Huguenot used so few words, and troubled him so little, in respect of the dilatory ceremonies of the others, in dying."

67. See, for example, Barbara Hernnstein Smith, *Poetic Closure* (Chicago: University of Chicago Press, 1968); Robert Pack, *Affirming Limits* (Amherst: University of Massachusetts Press, 1985); and Frank Kermode, *The Sense of an Ending* (London: Oxford University Press, 1968).

68. Walton, p. 61.

69. Jonathan F. S. Post, building on the work of E.K. Chambers, has been studying the implications of this pun.

70. "More" works similarly as the last word of Herbert's "Providence," another poem that avowedly overflows its ending with praise. A precursor of Gerard Manley Hopkins's "Pied Beauty," "Providence" culminates its admiration of the multiplicity of Creation by declaring that its own capacity for praise has been multiplied at the very moment it appears to be silenced.

71. Robert G. Collmer, "The Meditation on Death and its Appearance in Metaphysical Poetry," *Neophilologus*, 45 (4), (1961), p. 325, mentions "the theory that the best time to think on death was at the close of the day;" cf. "Repentance," lines 23–24, and the regenerative converse in "Mattens."

72. As at the end of "Perseverance" in the Williams manuscript, "rest" suggests an end that is a waiting, an interregnum more full of promise than of doubt. For Herbert as for Donne, "rest" is a word laden with its Old Testament significance, promising an end of earthly wandering. But it also carries the promise of an escape from earthly time, rather than an ultimate submission to that pharaonic tyrant. Augustine concludes his *Confessions* by contemplating God's rest after seven days of Creation:

And in your Book we read this as a presage that when our work in this life is done, we too shall rest in you in the Sabbath of eternal life. . . . The rest that we shall enjoy will be yours, just as the work that we now do is your work done through us. But you, O Lord, are eternally at work and eternally at rest. It is not in time that you see or in time that you rest: yet you make what we see in time; you make time itself and the repose which comes when time ceases.

(Augustine, *Confessions*, XIII, 36–37; quoted by Mark Taylor, p. 63)

Herbert's "Church" is designed to confirm that presage of heavenly repose. His book persistently subverts the illusion of chronological sequence running from title to last word of the lyrics, largely by abjuring his role in creating those words.

73. The speaker of Herbert's "A Parodie," afflicted and affrighted on a "stormie night" by his Savior's "eclipsed light" (14–16), thus escapes the burden of mortality in the final lines:

> O what a deadly cold
>   Doth me infold!
>   I half beleeve,
> That Sinne sayes true: but while I grieve,
>   Thou com'st and dost relieve.
>
> (26–30)

In the Williams manuscript, "The Knell" begins with a tolling bell and ends with a plea that Christ's sacrificed blood "may bee / Julips & Cordials when wee call on thee / ffor some relief."

74. "The Bag." Bloch, pp. 240 and 270, comments on this transition.

75. The human speaker of "Dialogue" becomes so anguished by his unworthiness of the sacrifice Christ made for him that he interrupts the reassuring divine voice, ending (similarly) with "Ah! no more: thou break'st my heart." Here, as in "Grief," ending the poem in the speaker's own limited exclamatory voice corresponds to a threat of physical death in a state of spiritual despair—unless, of course, the breaking of his heart is exactly what will save him, enabling a merger with Christ's own pitying and pitiful voice (as in the Latin epigraph of Vaughan's *Silex Scintillans*, a work full of contemporary clues to Herbert's meaning). Herbert's speakers must learn to find success in such failures, enabled by and modeled upon the triumph that Christ achieved by accepting humiliation and destruction.

76. This is the threat narrowly averted by the shift of a single letter from the first line to the last in "Justice (I)"; the Lord works in subtle ways. Schoenfeldt, pp. 242–43, demonstrates persistent allusions to masturbation in "Sinnes Round"; presumably these relate to the inadequacies of any love, including spiritual love, that fails to discover its ultimate relationship to an object outside the self.

77. Summers, pp. 129–35; Fish, *Self-Consuming Artifacts*, pp. 164–69.

78. Browne, p. 309; see also his p. 313. For a despondent materialist response to precisely the observation Herbert and Browne make piously, see Antonio's observation, in John Webster's *The Duchess of Malfi*, that in a ruined abbey,

>   naked to the injuries
> Of stormy weather, some men lie interr'd
> Lov'd the church so well, and gave so largely to't,
> They thought it should have canopi'd their bones
> Till doomsday. But all things have their end:
> Churches and cities, which have diseases like to men
> Must have like death that we have.
>
>   (New Mermaids edition, ed. Elizabeth M. Brennan, 2d ed.
>   [New York: Norton, 1983], 5.3.13–19)

79. It is worth noting however, that the poem called "Employment" earlier in *The Temple* is among those that fall ominously short of completing their form. "Employment (I)" opens with a *topos* of mortality, and with a stanza that seems "Nipt in the bud" by those very words, until it can expand again into the volume of divine praise:

>   If as a flowre doth spread and die,
>   Thou wouldst extend me to some good,
>   Before I were by frosts extremitie
>   Nipt in the bud;
>
>   The sweetnesse and the praise were thine;
>   But the extension and the room,

Which in thy garland I should fill, were mine
          At thy great doom.
                    (1–8)

The problem is what to do with the interims of silence—the wordless wait for poetic inspiration, the prayerless wait for spiritual renewal, the stuporous wait for the trumpet of final resurrection:

Let me not languish then, and spend
A life as barren to thy praise,
As is the dust, to which that life doth tend,
          But with delaies.
                    (13–16)

Life without worship resembles death without redemption; the unredeemed man consists inwardly of the barren dust that will soon become his outward form as well. The only hope is that death will draw him to heaven instead of leaving him to push up daisies:

I am no link of thy great chain,
But all my companie is a weed.
Lord place me in thy consort; give one strain
          To my poore reed.
                    (21–24)

If any song follows, it will have to be from God's own breath, playing through the speaker as wind through an Aeolian harp. Without divine inspiration, the rest is silence.

80. Beckett's title appears to be a parody of Simone Weil's *Waiting for God* (1950), a fact worth noting in this context because Weil was heavily influenced by Herbert. So Beckett's critique of Weil's writing entails an indirect critique of the consolations commonly derived from Herbert's verse.

81. Shuger, p. 118. See also Strier, p. 143, on "the extraordinarily strong stress on individual inner experience in Herbert's poetry," which allies that poetry with Lutheran theology.

82. Patrides, p. 168n.

83. The dangerously misguided search for a localized savior receives more comfortable treatment in "Peace." As in "Redemption," the explicit story doubles as a parable about Christ's life and legacy. Both levels are important, because the allegorical level reflects back consolingly on the literal, as supernatural imagery must palliate our vision of natural death. The parable of Christ's saving powers is told in images that vividly evoke our fears, and then our hopes, about death. The three opening stanzas search for Peace in a cave of mere emptiness and negativity, in bright colors that disintegrate with the clouds, and in a "gallant flower" that has a devouring worm rather than Peace at its root (14). The parable then portrays Christ as buried and reborn as a sweet grain that thrives, and is praised, "Through all the earth" (32). Though the primary reference is surely to Christ's disciples and Communion, this story also associates the theological promise of salvation with a dispersal of our fears about burial, darkness, and vermiculation. In place of those fears it offers a promise

that resembles Eastern as much as Western religion, Boehme as much as Luther: a promise of selfless participation in an ongoing natural world—the same emotional resource drawn upon by "The Flower." The search for peace can end satisfactorily only with the finding (and accepting) of the right sort of death.

84. Boyd, p. 4; cf. Drummond, p. 46: "Life is a journey in a dusty way, the furthest rest is death."

85. Marvin Morillo, "Herbert's Chairs: Notes to *The Temple*," *English Language Notes*, 11 (1974), p. 273, responds to the common assumption of a modern stationary chair by asserting that "The idea of the hearthside chair, the stationary resting place, seems directly contrary to Herbert's point that death is *not* a resting place but only a stage in the journey." My point is that the persona of the poem seems to share this error with most modern critics. "Chair" seems to have been a word in transition at the turn of the seventeenth century, and Herbert effectively exploits the ambiguity.

86. Stanley Stewart, "Time and the Temple," in *Essential Articles for the Study of George Herbert*, ed. John Roberts (Hamden, CT: Archon, 1979), p. 369, describes the correspondence between these final titles and Christian eschatology.

87. Patrides, p. 212, discusses the *carpe diem* legacy; Herbert's rewritings of such erotic conventions into Christian worship often resemble the process Harold Bloom describes in *The Anxiety of Influence* (New York: Oxford University Press, 1973), whereby a poet attempts to portray a prior work as a misconceived or incomplete effort to write his later version.

88. *Marlowe's Doctor Faustus 1604–1616: Parallel Texts*, ed. W. W. Greg (Oxford: Clarendon Press, 1950).

89. Wall, 316n.

90. Cf. Daniel Donne, *A Sub-Poena from the Star-Chamber of Heaven* (London, 1623), p. 120: "wee shall at length bee brought by him who is *Alpha* and *Omega* the *beginning* and the *ending*, unto the *beginning* of that unspeakable Happinesse which shall have *no ending*."

91. Fish, *Living Temple*, pp. 154–57, argues for the anti-closural properties of this long poem.

92. Schoenfeldt, p. 260, notes this "surprising recourse to 'the material bodily lower stratum'"; but it is less surprising if we recognize it as part of Herbert's response to his culture's need to associate bodily corruption with the devil, and thereby prevent a materialist reading of death.

93. Coleridge, in *George Herbert: The Critical Heritage*, p. 170.

94. Phase 25; quoted by Strier, p. xii.

EPILOGUE

1. George Ormerod, *History of the County Palatine and City of Cheshire* (London, 1819), p. 173, reports that "John Bruyn, son and heir of John, had a pardon under the great seal of England, 1st Mary. He died the 14th of May, 29 Eliz. . . . The township [of Bruen Stapleford] is about seven miles distant from Chester to the right of the road of Tarporley. The hall is destroyed. No court is

held or claimed for the manor." The genealogy on p. 175 lists: "KATHERINE, wife of Wm. Brettargh, of Brettargh Holt, esq. co. Lanc. bapt. Feb. 13, 1579, obiit ult. Maii 1601." "The Holie Life and Christian Death, of Mistris Katharin Brettergh" (anonymous), in William Harrison, *Deaths Advantage* (London, 1602), sig. O4v, reports that the text of Isaiah 40–43 was read to Brettargh as a kind of comforting last bedtime story. From a modern perspective that gives biology more credence than typology, its promise that God would reward her piety by spreading her progeny in glory all across the earth appears to have been little more than a fairy tale.

2. F. R. Raines, Introduction to *The Journal of Nicholas Assheton*, in *Remains Historical and Literary Connected with the Palatine Counties of Lancaster and Cheshire*, vol. 14 (Manchester: Chetham Society, 1848), p. xvi.

3. William Hinde, *A Faithfull Remonstrance* (London, 1641), pp. 47, 79, 116, 171–72.

4. Hinde, pp. 7–10, 54.

5. Raines, pp. xix and xxiii; Hinde, sig. B2r, quickly praises her piety and mentions the sermons about her without acknowledging the occasion of those sermons.

6. Harrison, sig. F8r-v; "Holie Life," sigs. N7r–N8r, O1r-v. Hinde, p. 187, attributes to John Bruen a similar charity toward his debtors.

7. Harrison, sigs. C5r, D4r, D2r-v.

8. Harrison, sig. E4r. Compare John Chadwich, *A Sermon Preached at Snarford in Lincolnshire at the Funerals of Sir George Sanct-Paule* (London, 1614), which similarly asserts that "a good life is graced and blessed with a happy death" (p. 16), before describing Sir George's troubled deathbed, where "he was divers times and wayes assaulted by the Tempter" and was compelled to call on God to "helpe my unbeleefe" (pp. 25–26). This instance also points to another interesting aspect of Jacobean funeral oratory: its shortage of gender distinctions. Naturally there are some differences of focus resulting from the different tasks commonly assigned to men and women in their lives, but the concerns and rhetoric are otherwise remarkably consistent.

9. "Holie Life," sig. O4r; Harrison, sigs. D8v–E1r, E4v, E6r-v. For Donne's denial that a wild death indicates damnation, see *Sermons*, X, 240–42.

10. Hinde, pp. 150, 148.

11. Harrison, sig. G1v.

12. Criticizing the way a preacher might respond to a suffering parishioner, Winstanley observed that "if the passions of sorrow predominate, then he is heavy and sad, crying out, *He is damned, God hath forsaken him, and he must go to Hell when he dye, he cannot make his calling and election sure*. . . . this divining Doctrine, which you call *spiritual and heavenly things*, torments people always when they are weak, sickly, and under any distemper"; quoted by John Stachniewski, *The Persecutory Imagination* (New York: Oxford University Press, 1991), p. 55, from *The Law of Freedom in a Platform*.

13. William Leigh, *The Christians Watch* (London, 1605), sig. A4v. Hinde, p. 108, discussing the sudden death of Bruen's first wife, asserts that "The life of the righteous findes never any worse end than the death of the righteous." He also spends dozens of pages extolling Bruen's own peaceful and holy demise. All

NOTES FOR PAGES 311–15

this—and the ascription of several faith-cures to Bruen at about the time of Katherine's death—make the omission of her death from this lengthy hagiography seem deliberately evasive.

14. William Leigh, *The Soules Solace Against Sorrow* (delivered at Childwall Church, Lancashire; published and bound with Harrison); sigs. H6v–H7r, M2r. According to Raines, Leigh (or Leygh) "was one of the county magistrates to whom the affair of the Saintesbury witches was referred in 1612, and appears to have suspected a seminary priest of instigating certain parties to accuse the supposed witches, but his suspicions were not confirmed" (p. 57n). This capsule biography discusses *The Soules Solace* and *A Brief Discourse of the Life and Death of Mrs. Katherine Brettargh*, again without any acknowledgment of the deathbed crisis that was their chief occasion and topic (p. 58n).

15. Harrison, sigs. N3v–N4r.

16. "Holie Life," sig. O2r-v.

17. "Holie Life," sig. O3r-v.

18. "Holie Life," sigs. O4r–O5r.

19. "Holie Life," sigs. P5v, P7v.

20. Harrison, sigs. M6v–M7v.

21. Harrison, sig. A3v.

22. "Holie Life," sigs. O6v–O7v. The efforts of Catholicism to refute this *tu quoque* defense are evident in Edward Coffin, *A True Relation of the Last Sicknes and Death of Cardinall Bellarmine*. This 1622 Jesuit tract mocks the Protestants who in 1614 "urged it, as a great argument for the truth of their Ghospell, seeing that God had punished the chiefe defendour of the Catholike Faith of our Age with such a disastrous and dreadfull death," when in fact Bellarmine was alive and well for another eight years (pp. 50–51). In place of these stories Coffin offers a description remarkably similar to the deathbed scene "The Holie Life" provides for Brettargh, with its delicate elision of mortal closure again matched by a reluctant syntactical closure:

with the end of the Creed he ended his speach, these being the last wordes that ever he spake cleerly and distinctly in this life: *Et vitam aeternam, Amen*: and life life everlasting *Amen*. After which his voice so fayled, that they could scant with all diligence used, heare him, yet he sayd very softly to himselfe in such manner as he was able Jesus, Jesus, Jesus, and continued still in the same till the last gaspe, which of such as beheld him was in a manner insensible, without any violent motion of his body or contracting of his countenance, any writhing of his mouth, any panges or gasps, in so still, quiet, and peaceable fashion as it seemed a sleep rather then death, rather a mylde and voluntary passage, then a matter of horrour or dread, rather a Saint-like repose then a finall departure out of this life. (p. 61)

23. Raines, intro. to Assheton, p. xxii.

24. Another Jacobean funeral sermon—Stephen Denison's *The Monument or Tombe-stone* (London, 1620), pp. 79–81—suggests that this pious attitude toward women's premature and agonizing deaths was common:

she was not full seven and twentie yeares old when God tooke her away. . . . her paines were very great, her triall was a fierie triall. . . . her sicknesse was not onely dolorous, but likewise it was long and tedious, continuing upon her with great extremitie for the space of a yeare and upwards. God did grinde her in the mortar of his fatherly correction like spice, that so she might be made the more fragrant sacrifice unto himselfe. . . . And let us not thinke it strange if she roared and cried with paine at some times. . . . It is the propertie of a good child to crie whilest he is a beating, as well as of a bad. But here is the difference; a good child, when the smart is gone, will kisse the rod, and love his parents, and be sory for his fault.

25. Thomas Taylor, *The Pilgrim's Profession* (1622); rpt. in his *Three Treatises* (London, 1633), pp. 190–91; further citations to this work will appear parenthetically in the text.

26. D. W. Winnicott, "Fear of Breakdown," pp. 103–7. Heinz Kohut, *How Does Analysis Cure?*, ed. Arnold Goldberg and Paul Stepansky (Chicago: University of Chicago Press, 1984), p. 18.

27. See Kohut's comments, pp. 18–19, on Bismarck's inability to permit himself the surrender of conscious selfhood into sleep unless Schweuinzer was watching him, and more generally "that in order to enable the dying person to retain a modicum of the cohesion, firmness, and harmony of the self, his surroundings must not withdraw their selfobject functions at the last moment of his conscious participation in the world."

28. Bettie Anne Doebler and Retha M. Warnicke, "Sex Discrimination After Death," *Omega*, 17 (1986–87), p. 316, passes over the entire story as a "somewhat simple biography" appended to a funeral sermon. Thoroughly eliding the anguish and coercion, the authors observe only that "the conversion of Mary to Puritanism as a girl is laid to the discipline and influence of her patron. The Countess apparently constructed a way of life that drew Mary into this faith."

RETRACTION

1. "Aubade," lines 21–27, in Philip Larkin, *Collected Poems*, ed. Anthony Thwaite (Farrar, Straus, and Giroux, 1989), p. 208.

2. W. W. Meissner, "Religion as Transitional Conceptualization," *The Psychoanalytic Review*, 79 (1992), p. 179, summarizes the distinction succinctly: "Freud believed that religious beliefs are little more than vain wish-fulfillments. For Winnicott, they are essential illusions answering to fundamental and ineradicable human needs." While I cannot quite follow Becker's concluding admonition to conjure a higher power and then give myself over to it, I can accept Winnicott's argument that a capacity for "belief-in" is an aspect of health rather than an invitation to fraud, an extension of the ordinary work of the psyche rather than a negative superimposition on that psyche.

3. *Sermons*, IX, 175; cf. III, 109–10. Cf. Stephen Greenblatt, "Psychoanalysis and Renaissance Culture," in *Literary Theory/Renaissance Texts*, ed. David Quint and Patricia Parker (Baltimore: Johns Hopkins University Press, 1986), p. 222: "But for Hobbes there is no person, no coherent enduring identity, beneath the mask; strip away the theatrical role and you reach either a chaos of unformed desire that must be tamed to ensure survival or a dangerous assembly of free thoughts. . . . " Perhaps Alzheimer's disease makes an especially disturbing last illness because it seems to confirm the association between death and dispersed consciousness.

Works Cited

The following bibliography omits works listed in the "Note on Texts" at the front of the book, as well as a few that are not directly relevant to the topic of the book as a whole and are cited only once in its notes.

Adams, Robert M. "Lucy and Lucifer." *The New York Review of Books* 37 (March 1, 1990): 38–40.

Adams, Thomas. *The Sermons of Thomas Adams, The Shakespeare of Puritan Theologians.* Edited by John Brown. Cambridge, 1909.

——— *The White Devil.* London, 1613.

——— *Workes.* London, 1629.

Adelman, Janet. *Suffocating Mothers: Fantasies of Maternal Origin in Shakespeare's Plays, "Hamlet" to "The Tempest."* New York: Routledge, 1992.

Adler, Alfred. *The Practice and Theory of Individual Psychology.* London: Kegan Paul, 1924.

Aers, David. "Reflections on Current Histories of the Subject." *Literature & History* (1991): 20–34.

Allen, Don Cameron. *Doubt's Boundless Sea: Skepticism and Faith in the Renaissance.* Baltimore: Johns Hopkins University Press, 1964.

Alvarez, A. "The Dark at the Top of the Stairs." *The New Yorker* (March 8, 1993): 44–55.

Andrews, Michael C. *This Action of Our Death: The Performance of Death in English Renaissance Drama.* Newark: University of Delaware Press, 1989.

Ariès, Philippe. *The Hour of Our Death.* Translated by Helen Weaver. New York: Random House, 1981.

——— *Western Attitudes toward Death: From the Middle Ages to the Present.* Translated by Patricia Ranum. Baltimore: Johns Hopkins University Press, 1974.

Asals, Heather. "The Voice of George Herbert's 'The Church.'" *ELH* 36 (1969): 511–28.

Assheton, Nicholas. *The Journal of Nicholas Assheton*. Edited by F. R. Raines. In *Remains Historical and Literary Connected with the Palatine Counties of Lancaster and Cheshire*. Vol. 14, Chetham Society, 1848.

The Atheist Unmasked. London, 1685.

Aurelius, Marcus [Antoninus]. *Meditations*. Translated by Meric Casaubon. London, 1634.

Aylmer, G. E. "Unbelief in Seventeenth-Century England." In *Puritans and Revolutionaries: Essays in Seventeenth-Century History Presented to Christopher Hill*. Edited by Donald Pennington and Keith Thomas. Oxford: Clarendon Press, 1978.

Bacon, Francis. *The Works of Francis Bacon*. New Edition. In 10 volumes. London: C. & J. Rivington, 1826.

Bakeless, John. *The Tragicall History of Christopher Marlowe*. Cambridge: Harvard University Press, 1942.

Bakhtin, M. M. *The Dialogic Imagination: Four Essays*. Translated by Michael Holquist and Caryl Emerson. Austin: University of Texas Press, 1981.

Bald, R. C. *John Donne: A Life*. London: Oxford University Press, 1970.

Battenhouse, Roy W. "*Measure for Measure* and Christian Doctrine of Atonement." *PMLA* 61 (1946): 1029–59.

——— *Shakespearean Tragedy: Its Art and Christian Premises*. Bloomington: Indiana University Press, 1969.

Bayly, Lewes. *The Practise of Pietie: Directing a Christian How to Walk that He may Please God*. London, 1613.

Beaty, Nancy Lee. *The Craft of Dying: A Study in the Literary Tradition of the Ars Moriendi in England*. Yale Studies in English 175. New Haven: Yale University Press, 1970.

Bennett, Josephine. *"Measure for Measure" as Royal Entertainment*. New York: Columbia University Press, 1966.

Bensimon, Marc. "Modes of Perception of Reality in the Renaissance." In *The Darker Vision of the Renaissance: Beyond the Fields of Reason*. Edited by Robert S. Kinsman. Berkeley: University of California Press, 1974.

Bentley, Richard. *A Confutation of Atheism from the Origin of Humane Bodies*. London, 1692.

——— *The Folly of Atheism*. London, 1691–92.

Berman, David. "The Repressive Denials of Atheism in Britain in the Seventeenth and Eighteenth Centuries." *Proceedings of the Royal Irish Academy*. Vol. 82, sec. C, no. 9 (1982): 211–46.

Birnie, William. *The Blame of Kirk-Buriall*. Edinburgh, 1606.

Bloch, Chana. *Spelling the Word: George Herbert and the Bible*. Berkeley: University of California Press, 1985.

Boehme, Jacob. *The Way to Christ*. 1622. Translated by John J. Stoudt. Westport, CT: Greenwood Press, 1979.

Bouwsma, William. *John Calvin: A Sixteenth-Century Portrait*. New York: Oxford University Press, 1988.

Bownde, Nicholas. *The Unbelief of St Thomas the Apostle.* 1608. Rpt. London, 1817.

Boyd, Zacharie. *The Last Battle of the Soul in Death.* 1629. Edited by Gabriel Noel. Rpt. Glasgow, 1831.

Braden, Gordon, and William Kerrigan. *The Idea of the Renaissance.* Baltimore: Johns Hopkins University Press, 1989.

Brown, Carolyn E. "Erotic Religious Flagellation and Shakespeare's *Measure for Measure.*" *English Literary Renaissance* 16 (1986): 139–65.

Brown, Norman O. *Life against Death.* Middletown, CT: Wesleyan University Press, 1959.

Brown, Theo. *The Fate of the Dead: A Study in Folk-Eschatology in the West Country after the Reformation.* Ipswich: D. S. Brewer, 1979.

Bryan, Jennifer. "To the Last Syllable." Unpublished essay, 1993.

Buckler, E. *A Buckler against the fear of Death.* London, 1640.

Buckley, George T. *Atheism in the English Renaissance.* Chicago: University of Chicago Press, 1932.

Burke, Peter. "Death in the Renaissance, 1347–1656." In *Dies Illa: Death in the Middle Ages.* Edited by Jane H. M. Taylor. Vinaver Studies in French. Liverpool: Francis Cairns, 1984.

Burns, Norman T. *Christian Mortalism from Tyndale to Milton.* Cambridge: Harvard University Press, 1972.

Burton, Robert. *The Anatomy of Melancholy.* Edited by Holbrook Jackson. In 3 volumes. New York: E. P. Dutton, 1932.

Bynum, Caroline Walker. "Material Continuity." *History of Religions* 30 (1990): 51–85.

C., I. *A Handkercher for Parents Wet Eyes.* London, 1630.

C., R. "A Comparison of the Life of Man." *Roxburghe Ballads.*

Calderwood, James L. *If It Were Done: "Macbeth" and Tragic Action.* Amherst: University of Massachusetts Press, 1986.

———— *Shakespeare and the Denial of Death.* Amherst: University of Massachusetts Press, 1987.

Campbell, Ninian. *A Treatise upon Death.* Glasgow, 1630.

Camus, Jean Pierre. *A Draught of Eternitie.* Translated by Miles Car. Douay, 1632.

Carey, John. *John Donne: Life, Mind and Art.* London: Faber, 1981.

Carier, Benjamin. *Copy of a Letter.* 1615.

Carpenter, Richard. *The Soules Sentinel.* London, 1616.

Cartari, Vincenzo. *The Fountaine of Ancient Fiction.* London, 1599.

Chadwich, John. *A Sermon Preached at Snarford in Lincolnshire at the Funerals of Sir George Sanct-Paule.* London, 1614.

Chambers, A. B. "Glorified Bodies and the 'Valediction: Forbidding Mourning.'" *John Donne Journal* 1 (1982): 19.

Charles, Amy M. *A Life of George Herbert.* Ithaca: Cornell University Press, 1977.

Choron, Jacques. *Death and Western Thought.* New York: Collier, 1963.

Clinton, Elizabeth. *The Countesse of Lincolnes Nursurie.* Oxford, 1628.

Coffin, Edward. *A True Relation of the Last Sicknes and Death of Cardinall Bellarmine.* 1622.

Collmer, Robert G. "The Meditation on Death and Its Appearance in Metaphysical Poetry." *Neophilologus* 45 (4) 1961: 323–33.

Corderoy, Jeremy. *A Warning for Worldlings.* London, 1608.

Crawford, Patricia. "The Construction and Experience of Maternity in Seventeenth-Century England." In *Women as Mothers in Pre-Industrial England.* Edited by Valerie Fildes and Dorothy McLaren. London: Routledge, 1990.

Crompton, William. *A Lasting Jewell for Religious Woemen.* London, 1630.

Culler, Jonathan. *Framing the Sign: Criticism and Its Institutions.* Norman: University of Oklahoma Press, 1988.

Daniel, Samuel. *A Panegyrike Congratulatory.* 1603.

Darcie, Abraham. *Frances Duchesse Dowager of Richmond and Lenox her Funerall Teares.* London, 1624.

Dash, Irene. *Wooing, Wedding, and Power: Women in Shakespeare's Plays.* New York: Columbia University Press, 1981.

Dawes, William. *An Anatomy of Atheism.* London, 1694.

Death Repeal'd By a Thankfull Memoriall. Oxford, 1638.

Denison, Stephen. *Another Tombestone.* London, 1627.

——— *The Monument or Tombe-stone.* London, 1620.

Di Cesare, Mario A. *George Herbert and the Seventeenth-Century Religious Poets.* New York: Norton, 1978.

Diehl, Huston. "To Put Us in Remembrance." In *Homo, Memento Finis: The Iconography of Just Judgement in Medieval Art and Drama.* Early Drama, Art and Music Monograph Series 6. Edited by David Bevington. Kalamazoo, MI: Medieval Institute, 1985.

Dillingham, Francis. *A Sermon Preached [for] Lady Elizabeth Luke.* 1609.

Directory for the Public Worship of God. London, 1644.

Docherty, Thomas. *John Donne, Undone.* London: Methuen, 1986.

Doebler, Bette Anne. *The Quickening Seed: Death in the Sermons of John Donne.* Salzburg: Institut für Englische Sprache und Literatur, 1974.

——— and Retha M. Warnicke. "Sex Discrimination After Death." *Omega* 17 (1986–87): 309–20.

Donne, Daniel. *A Sub-Poena from the Star-Chamber of Heaven.* London, 1623.

Donne, John. *Death's Duell.* Edited by G. Keynes. Boston: Godine, 1973.

——— *Elegies, Songs, and Sonnets.* Edited by Helen Gardner. Oxford: Clarendon Press, 1966.

Donoghue, Denis. "Book of Books Books." *New York Review of Books* (November 5, 1992): 46–50.

——— "Some Versions of Empson." *Times Literary Supplement* (June 7, 1994): 597–98.

Dorrell, Hadrian (?). *Willobie His Avisa.* 1594. Edited by G. B. Harrison. Edinburgh: University Press, 1966.

Dove, John. *A Confutation of Atheism.* London, 1605.

Dubrow, Heather. *A Happier Eden: The Politics of Marriage in the Stuart Epithalamium.* Ithaca: Cornell University Press, 1990.

Duffy, Eamon. *The Stripping of the Altars: Traditional Religion in England, 1400–1580.* New Haven: Yale University Press, 1992.

Dunton, John (?). *A Mourning-Ring in Memory of your Departed Friend.* London, 1692.

Edwards, Philip. "Thrusting Elysium into Hell: The Originality of *The Spanish Tragedy.*" In *Elizabethan Theatre XI.* Edited by A. L. Magnuson and C. E. McGee. Ontario: P. D. Meaney, 1990.

Edwards, Thomas. *Gangraena.* 2d Edition. London, 1646.

Elias, Norbert. *The Loneliness of the Dying.* Translated by Edmund Jephcott. Oxford: Blackwell, 1985.

Eliot, T. S. "The Metaphysical Poets." In his *Selected Essays: 1917–1932.* New York: Harcourt Brace, 1932.

Empson, William. *Milton's God.* Revised and Expanded Edition. Cambridge: Cambridge University Press, 1981.

Erasmus. *Ciceronianus; or, A Dialogue on the Best Style of Speaking.* Translated by Izora Scott. New York: Teachers College, 1908.

Erlich, Avi. *Hamlet's Absent Father.* Princeton: Princeton University Press, 1977.

Farrell, Kirby. *Play, Death, and Heroism in Shakespeare.* Chapel Hill: University of North Carolina Press, 1989.

Febvre, Lucien. *The Problem of Unbelief in the Sixteenth Century: The Religion of Rabelais.* Translated by Beatrice Gottlieb. Cambridge: Harvard University Press, 1982.

Fish, Stanley. *The Living Temple: George Herbert and Catechizing.* Berkeley: University of California Press, 1978.

——— "Masculine Persuasive Force: Donne and Verbal Power." In *Soliciting Interpretation.* Edited by Elizabeth D. Hardy and Katharine Eisaman Maus. Chicago: University of Chicago Press, 1990.

——— *Self-Consuming Artifacts: The Experience of Seventeenth-Century Literature.* Berkeley: University of California Press, 1972.

Foakes, R. A. "Images of Death: Ambition in *Macbeth.*" In *Focus on Macbeth.* Edited by J. R. Brown. London: Routledge, 1982.

Ford, Brewster S. "George Herbert and the Liturgies of Time and Space." *South Atlantic Review* 49 (4) 1984: 19–29.

Foster, Donald. "Macbeth's War on Time." *English Literary Renaissance* 16 (1986): 319–42.

Fotherby, Martin. *Atheomastix: Clearing Foure Truthes, Against Atheists and Infidels.* 1622.

Foucault, Michel. *The History of Sexuality.* Translated by Robert Hurley. New York: Pantheon, 1978.

——— *Madness and Civilization: A History of Insanity in the Age of Reason.* Translated by Richard Howard. New York: Vintage, 1973.

Fowler, Alastair. *Kinds of Literature: An Introduction to the Theory of Genres and Modes.* Cambridge: Harvard University Press, 1982.

Fox[e], John. *Fox's Book of Martyrs.* Edited by William Forbush. Philadelphia: John C. Winston, 1926.

Freeman, Arthur. *Thomas Kyd: Facts and Problems.* London: Oxford University Press, 1967.

Freud, Sigmund. *Complete Psychological Works.* Standard Edition. Translated by James Strachey. In 24 volumes. London: Hogarth Press, 1953–74.

Frye, Roland Mushat. *The Renaissance "Hamlet."* Princeton: Princeton University Press, 1984.

——— *Shakespeare and Christian Doctrine.* Princeton: Princeton University Press, 1963.

Fuller, Thomas. *The Holy State and the Profane State.* Cambridge, 1642.

Garber, Marjorie. *Shakespeare's Ghost Writers: Literature as Uncanny Causality.* London: Methuen, 1989.

Gardiner, Samuel. *Doomes-day Booke: Or, an Alarum for Atheistes.* London, 1606.

——— *The Scourge of Sacrilege.* London, 1611.

Gardner, Helen. *The Business of Criticism.* Oxford: Clarendon Press, 1959.

Garey, Samuel. *Great Brittans little Calendar.* London, 1618.

Garnier, Robert. *Marc Antonie.* Translated by Mary Herbert Pembroke. London, 1595.

Gaule, John. *A Defiance to Death.* London, 1629.

Geertz, Clifford. "Religion as a Cultural System." In *Anthropological Approaches to the Study of Religion.* Conferences on New Approaches in Social Anthropology. Edited by Michael Banton. New York: Praeger, 1966.

George Herbert and Henry Vaughan. Edited by Louis Martz. Oxford Authors Series. Oxford: Oxford University Press, 1986.

George Herbert: The Critical Heritage. Edited by C. A. Patrides. London: Routledge, 1983.

Girard, René. *A Theater of Envy: William Shakespeare.* New York: Oxford University Press, 1991.

——— *Violence and the Sacred.* Translated by Patrick Gregory. Baltimore: Johns Hopkins University Press, 1977.

Gittings, Clare. *Death, Burial and the Individual in Early Modern England.* London: Croom Helm, 1984.

Gless, Darryl J. *"Measure for Measure," the Law, and the Convent.* Princeton: Princeton University Press, 1979.

Goldberg, Jonathan. "Fatherly Authority: The Politics of Stuart Family Images." In *Rewriting the Renaissance: The Discourses of Sexual Difference in Early Modern Europe.* Edited by Margaret Ferguson, Maureen Quilligan, and Nancy Vickers. Chicago: University of Chicago Press, 1986.

Gosse, Edmund. *The Life and Letters of John Donne.* London: William Heinemann, 1899.

Greenblatt, Stephen. "Invisible Bullets: Renaissance Authority and Its Subversion." In *Shakespeare's "Rough Magic."* Edited by Peter Erickson and Coppélia Kahn. Newark: University of Delaware Press, 1985.

——— "Psychoanalysis and Renaissance Culture." In *Literary Theory/ Renaissance Texts.* Edited by David Quint and Patricia Parker. Baltimore: Johns Hopkins University Press, 1986.

——— *Renaissance Self-Fashioning: From More to Shakespeare.* Chicago: University of Chicago Press, 1980.

Greenham, Richard. *Workes*. Edited by H. Holland. 3d Edition. London, 1601.

Greg, W. W. "Hamlet's Hallucination." *Modern Language Review* 12 (1917): 393–421.

Grimeston, Edward. *History of Polybius*. London, 1633.

Grosse, Alexander. *Deaths Deliverance*. London, 1632.

——— *Eliahs Fiery Charet*. London, 1632.

Guy, Nicholas. *Pieties Pillar*. London, 1626.

Hammond, Paul. "The Argument of *Measure for Measure*." *English Literary Renaissance* 16 (1986): 496–519.

Harding, D. W. "Coherence of Theme in Donne's Poetry." *Kenyon Review* 13 (1951): 439.

Hardy, Evelyn. *Donne: A Spirit in Conflict*. London: Constable, 1942.

Harrison, William. *Deaths Advantage Little Regarded*. London, 1602.

Hayne, Victoria. Ph.D. Diss., U.C.L.A. (forthcoming).

Herbert, Edward. *Autobiography*. Edited by Sidney L. Lee. London: John C. Nimmo, 1886.

Herbert, George. *The Country Parson; The Temple*. Edited by John N. Wall, Jr. London: SPCK, 1981.

——— *The English Works of George Herbert*. Edited by George Herbert Palmer. Boston: Houghton Mifflin, 1915.

——— *The Latin Poetry of George Herbert*. Translated by Mark McCloskey and Paul R. Murphy. Athens: University of Ohio Press, 1965.

——— *The Works of George Herbert*. Edited by F. E. Hutchinson. Oxford: Clarendon Press, 1941.

Heywood, Thomas. *A True Discourse of the Two infamous upstart Prophets*. London, 1636.

Higbie, Robert. "Images of Enclosure in George Herbert's *The Temple*." *Texas Studies in Literature and Language* 15 (4) 1974: 627–38.

Hill, Adam. *The Crie of England*. London, 1595.

Hill, Eugene D. *Edward, Lord Herbert of Cherbury*. Preface. Twayne English Authors Series. Boston: G. K. Hall, 1987.

Hinde, William. *A Faithfull Remonstrance*. London, 1641.

Holland, Abraham. *Hollandi Post-Huma*. Cambridge, 1626.

Hooker, Richard. *Works*. Edited by Jan Keble. New York: Burt Franklin, 1970.

Howard, Donald R. "Renaissance World-Alienation." In *The Darker Vision of the Renaissance: Beyond the Fields of Reason*. Edited by Robert S. Kinsman. Berkeley: University of California Press, 1974.

Howard, Jean E. "The New Historicism in Renaissance Studies." *English Literary Renaissance* 16 (1986): 13–43.

Huizinga, Johan. *The Waning of the Middle Ages: A Study of the Forms of Life, Thought and Art in France and the Netherlands in the XIVth and XVth Centuries*. London: Edward Arnold, 1924.

Humphreys, David, ed. and trans. *The Apologetics of the Learned Athenian Philosopher Athenagoras*. London, 1714.

Hunter, Michael. "The Problem of 'Atheism' in Early Modern England." *Transactions of the Royal Historical Society*. Fifth Series, 1985, 135–57.

Hunter, Robert G. *Shakespeare and the Comedy of Forgiveness*. New York: Columbia University Press, 1965.

Jackson, Thomas. *A Treatise*. London, 1625.

——— *Sinnelesse Sorrow for the Dead*. London, 1614.

Jahn, J. D. "The Eschatological Scene of Donne's 'A Valediction: Forbidding Mourning'" *College Literature* 5 (1978): 34–47.

Johnson, Samuel. *Lives of the English Poets*. Edited by George Birkbeck Hill. Oxford: Clarendon Press, 1905.

Jonas, Hans. *The Gnostic Religion*. Boston: Beacon Press, 1958.

Jones, Ernest. *Hamlet and Oedipus*. New York: Doubleday, 1955.

——— *The Life and Work of Sigmund Freud*. Abridged Edition. New York: Anchor, 1963.

Jonson, Ben. *The Complete English Poems*. Edited by A. J. Smith. London: Penguin, 1976.

Joseph, Miriam. "Discerning the Ghost in Hamlet." *PMLA* 76 (1961): 493–502.

Julian of Norwich. *The Revelations of Divine Love of Julian of Norwich*. Translated by James Walsh. New York: Harper, 1961.

Kay, Dennis. *Melodious Tears: The English Funeral Elegy from Spenser to Milton*. Oxford: Clarendon Press, 1990.

Kendall, Gillian Murray. "Overkill in Shakespeare." *Shakespeare Quarterly* 43 (1992): 33–50.

——— "Shakespeare's Romances and the Quest for Secular Immortality." Ph.D. Diss., Harvard University, 1986.

Kermode, Frank. *The Sense of an Ending: Studies in the Theory of Fiction*. London: Oxford University Press, 1968.

King, John. "The Godly Woman in Elizabethan Iconography," *Renaissance Quarterly* 33 (1985), 41–84.

Kirsch, Arthur C. "Hamlet's Grief." *ELH* 48 (1981): 17–36.

——— "The Integrity of *Measure for Measure*," *Shakespeare Survey* 28 (1975): 89–105.

——— Review of Calderwood's *Shakespeare and the Denial of Death*. *Shakespeare Quarterly* 40 (1989): 348–49.

Klingenstein, Susanne. *Jews in the American Academy, 1900–1940: The Dynamics of Intellectual Assimilation*. New Haven: Yale University Press, 1992.

Knight, G. Wilson. *The Wheel of Fire*. 5th Edition. Cleveland: World Press, 1964.

Kohut, Heinz. *How Does Analysis Cure?* Edited by Arnold Goldberg and Paul Stepansky. Chicago: University of Chicago Press, 1984.

——— *The Restoration of the Self*. New York: International Press, 1981.

Kremen, Kathryn R. *The Imagination of the Resurrection*. Lewisburg, PA: Bucknell University Press, 1972.

Kuhns, Richard. "Loss and Creativity." *The Psychoanalytic Review* 79 (1992): 197–208.

Kyd, Thomas. *The Spanish Tragedy*. New Mermaids Edition. Edited by J. R. Mulryne. New York: W. W. Norton, 1987.

Lacan, Jacques. *The Language of the Self: The Function of Language in Psychoanalysis.* Translated by Anthony Wilden. New York: Dell Publishing, 1975.

Lanier, Gregory W. "Physic That's Bitter to Sweet End." *Essays in Literature* 14 (1987): 15–36.

Laqueur, Thomas. *Making Sex: Body and Gender from the Greeks to Freud.* Cambridge: Harvard University Press, 1990.

Lascelles, Mary. *Shakespeare's "Measure for Measure."* London: Athlone, 1953.

Leigh, William. *The Christians Watch: or, An Heavenly Instruction.* London, 1605.

———— *The Soules Solace Against Sorrow.* Published and bound with Harrison.

Levao, Ronald. *Renaissance Minds and Their Fictions.* Berkeley: University of California Press, 1985.

Levin, Richard. *New Readings vs. Old Plays: Recent Trends in the Reinterpretation of English Renaissance Drama.* Chicago: University of Chicago Press, 1979.

———— "Unthinkable Thoughts in the New Historicizing of English Renaissance Drama." *New Literary History* 21 (1990).

Lewis, C. S. "Hamlet: The Prince or the Poem." *Proceedings of the British Academy* 28. London: Oxford University Press, 1942.

———— "What Christians Believe." In *Broadcast Talks.* London: G. Bles, 1943.

Llewellyn, Nigel. *The Art of Death: Visual Culture in the English Death Ritual c. 1500–1800.* London: Reaktion Books, 1991.

Lorand, Sandor. "Psycho-Analytic Therapy of Religious Devotees." *International Journal of Psycho-Analysis* 42 (1963): 50–56.

Louthan, Doniphan. "The *Tome-Tomb* Pun in Renaissance England," *Philological Quarterly* 29 (1950), 375–80.

Lucretius. *On the Nature of Things.* Translated by William E. Leonard. New York: Dutton, 1957.

Lupton, Julia Reinhard. "Afterlives of the Saints." *Exemplaria* (Fall 1990): 375–401.

Lust's Dominion. 1600. Edited by J. Le Gay Brereton. Louvain: Uystpruyst, 1931.

Lyons, Bridget Gellert. *Voices of Melancholy.* New York: Norton, 1971.

MacDonald, Michael, and Terence R. Murphy. *Sleepless Souls: Suicide in Early Modern England.* Oxford: Clarendon, 1990.

Marcus, Leah Sinanoglou. *Childhood and Cultural Despair.* Pittsburgh: University of Pittsburgh Press, 1978.

Marius, Richard. *Thomas More: A Biography.* New York: Random House, 1984.

Marlowe, Christopher. *Marlowe's Doctor Faustus 1604–1616: Parallel Texts.* Edited by W. W. Greg. Oxford: Clarendon Press, 1950.

Marotti, Arthur. *John Donne, Coterie Poet.* Madison: University of Wisconsin Press, 1986.

Martin, Philip. "Donne in Twicknam Garden." *Critical Survey* 4 (1970): 172–75.

Marvell, Andrew. *The Complete Poems.* Edited by Elizabeth Story Donno. London: Penguin, 1985.

Mavericke, Radford. *Three treatises religiously handled.* London, 1603.

McDargh, John. *Psychoanalytic Object Relations Theory and the Study of Religion.* Lanham, MD: University Press of America, 1983.

McDermott, John J. *Mary Magdalene in English Literature from 1500–1650.* Ph.D. Diss., U.C.L.A., 1964.

McGuire, Philip C. *Speechless Dialect: Shakespeare's Open Silences.* Berkeley: University of California Press, 1985.

Meissner, W. W. "Religion as Transitional Conceptualization," *The Psychoanalytic Review* 79 (1992): 175–96.

Miller, Clarence H. "Donne's 'A Nocturnall upon S. Lucies Day' and the Nocturns of Matins." In *Essential Articles for the Study of John Donne's Poetry.* Edited by John R. Roberts. Hamden, CT: Archon Books, 1975.

Milton, John. *Complete Poems and Major Prose.* Edited by Merrit Y. Hughes. New York: Bobbs-Merrill, 1957.

Montaigne, Michel de. *The Complete Essays of Montaigne.* Edited and translated by Donald M. Frame. Stanford: Stanford University Press, 1965.

More, George. *A Demonstration of God in His Workes.* London, 1597.

More, Thomas. *Utopia.* Edited by Edward Surtz. New Haven: Yale University Press, 1964.

Morillo, Marvin. "Herbert's Chairs: Notes to *The Temple.*" *English Language Notes* 11 (1974): 271–75.

Mornay, Philippe de. *Discourse of Life and Death.* Edited by Diane Bornstein, and translated by Mary Herbert Pembroke (1592). Medieval and Renaissance Monograph Series, III. Detroit: Fifteenth-century Symposium, 1983.

Morray, William. *A Short Treatise of Death in Sixe Chapters.* Edinburgh, 1631.

Morris, Harry. *Last Things in Shakespeare.* Tallahassee: Florida State University Press, 1985.

Morton, Thomas. *A Treatise of the Nature of God.* London, 1599.

Mueller, Janel. "Donne's Epic Venture in the *Metempsychosis.*" *Modern Philology* (1972): 109–39.

——— "Women among the Metaphysicals: A Case, Mostly, of Being Donne For." *Modern Philology* (1989): 142–58.

Murray, W. A. "Donne's Gold-Leaf and his Compasses." *Modern Language Notes* 73 (5), 1958: 329.

Newton, Thomas. *Atropoion Delion.* London, 1603.

Niccols, Richard. *Monodia.* London, 1615.

Oldmayne, Timothy. *Lifes Brevitie and Deaths Debility.* London, 1636.

Ormerod, George. *History of the County Palatine and City of Cheshire.* London, 1819.

Pack, Robert. *Affirming Limits.* Amherst: University of Massachusetts Press, 1985.

Paget, Jean. *Meditations of Death.* London, 1628.

Panofsky, Erwin. *Tomb Sculpture: Four Lectures on Its Changing Aspects from Ancient Egypt to Bernini.* New York: Abrams, 1964.

Parry, Graham. *The Seventeenth Century: The Intellectual and Cultural Context of English Literature, 1603–1700.* New York: Longman, 1989.

Patterson, Annabel. "All Donne." In *Soliciting Intepretation.* Edited by Elizabeth D. Hardy and Katharine Eisaman Maus. Chicago: University of Chicago Press, 1990.

Pearlman, E. "George Herbert's God." *English Literary Renaissance* 13 (1983): 88–112.

Perkins, William. *Treatise of Mans Imaginations.* Cambridge, 1607.

Pierce, Thomas. *Death Consider'd as a Door to a Life of Glory.* London, 1690.

Playfere, Thomas. *The Meane in Mourning.* London, 1596.

Pollock, John J. "George Herbert's Enclosure Imagery," *Seventeenth Century News* 31 (2), 1973: 55.

Pricke, Robert. *A Verie Godlie and Learned Sermon.* London, 1608.

Pritchard, R. E. "Dying in Donne's 'The Good-Morrow.'" *Essays in Criticism* 35 (1985): 213–22.

Proctor, John. *The Fal of the late Arrian.* 1549.

Prosser, Eleanor. *Hamlet and Revenge.* Stanford: Stanford University Press, 1967.

Quinlan, Maurice J. "Shakespeare and the Catholic Burial Services," *Shakespeare Quarterly* 5 (1954): 303–06.

Quint, David. "Introduction." In *Literary Theory/Renaissance Texts.* Edited by David Quint and Patricia Parker. Baltimore: Johns Hopkins University Press, 1986: 1–19.

Rajan, Tilotama. "'Nothing Sooner Broke,'" *ELH* 49 (1982): 805–28.

Rank, Otto. *Beyond Psychology.* New York: Dover Books, 1958.

——— *Will Therapy* and *Truth and Reality.* New York: Knopf, 1936; Single-Volume Edition, 1945.

Rauber, D. F. "Donne's 'Farewell to Love': A Crux Revisited." *Concerning Poetry* 3 (1970): 51–63.

Reconstructing Individualism: Autonomy, Individuality, and the Self in Western Thought. Edited by Thomas C. Heller et al. Stanford: Stanford University Press, 1986.

Rickey, Mary Ellen. *Utmost Art.* Lexington: University of Kentucky Press, 1966.

Roberts, Donald Ramsay. "The Death Wish of John Donne," *PMLA* 62 (1947): 958–76.

Roheim, Geza. *The Origin and Function of Culture.* Nervous and Mental Disease Monographs 69. New York, 1943.

Rose, Mary Beth. *The Expense of Spirit: Love and Sexuality in English Renaissance Drama.* Ithaca: Cornell University Press, 1988.

Ross, Alexander. *Mystagogus Poeticus.* London, 1648.

Rossiaud, Jacques. *Medieval Prostitution.* Translated by Lydia G. Cochrane. New York: Basil Blackwell, 1988.

Roston, Murray. *The Soul of Wit: A Study of John Donne.* Oxford: Clarendon Press, 1974.

Rudnytsky, Peter. *The Psychoanalytic Vocation: Rank, Winnicott, and the Legacy of Freud.* New Haven: Yale University Press, 1991.

Sacks, Peter. "Where Words Prevail Not." *ELH* 49 (1982): 576–601.

Sault, Richard. *A Conference Betwixt a Modern Atheist and his Friend.* London, 1693.

——— *The Second Spira: Being a Fearful Example of F. N. An Atheist.* London, 1693.

Schleiner, Louise. "Providential Improvisation in *Measure for Measure.*" *PMLA* 97 (1982): 227–36.

Schoenfeldt, Michael C. *Prayer and Power: George Herbert and Renaissance Courtship.* Chicago: University of Chicago Press, 1991.

Sclater, William. *A Funerall Sermon.* London, 1629.

Scodel, Joshua. *The English Poetic Epitaph.* Ithaca: Cornell University Press, 1991.

Searles, Harold F. "Schizophrenia and the Inevitability of Death." *Psychiatric Quarterly* 35 (1961): 631–65.

Sermons, Meditations, and Prayers, upon the Plague. London, 1637.

Shakespeare, William. The Arden *Macbeth.* Introduction. Edited by Kenneth Muir. London: Methuen, 1982.

Sheingorge, Pamela, and David Bevington, "Alle This Was Token Domysday." In *Homo, Memento Finis,* Early Drama, Art and Music Monograph Series 6. Edited by David Bevington. Kalamazoo, MI: Medieval Institute, 1985.

Shuger, Debora K. *Habits of Thought in the English Renaissance: Religion, Politics, and the Dominant Culture.* Berkeley: University of California Press, 1990.

——— *The Renaissance Bible.* Berkeley: University of California Press, 1994.

——— "Saints and Lovers: Mary Magdalene and the Ovidian Evangel." In *Reconfiguring the Renaissance.* Edited by Jonathan Crewe. Cranbury, NJ: Associated University Presses, 1992: 150–71.

Sidney, Philip. *The Countess of Pembroke's Arcadia.* Edited by Maurice Evans. Harmondsworth: Penguin, 1977.

Smith, Barbara Hernnstein. *Poetic Closure: A Study of How Poems End.* Chicago: University of Chicago Press, 1968.

Smith, Henrie. *Gods Arrowe against Atheists.* London, 1593.

Smith, Julia J. "Moments of Being and Not-Being in Donne's Sermons." *Prose Studies* 8 (3), 1985: 17.

Somerville, C. John. *The Secularization of Early Modern England: From Religious Culture to Religious Faith.* New York: Oxford University Press, 1992.

Spencer, Theodore. *Death and Elizabethan Tragedy: A Study of Convention and Opinion in the Elizabethan Drama.* Cambridge: Harvard University Press, 1936.

Spinrad, Phoebe S. "*Measure for Measure* and the Art of Not Dying." *Texas Studies in Literature and Language* 26 (1), 1984: 74–93.

Stachniewski, John. "John Donne: The Despair of the 'Holy Sonnets.'" *ELH* 48 (1981): 677–705.

——— *The Persecutory Imagination: English Puritanism and the Literature of Religious Despair.* Oxford: Clarendon Press, 1991.

Stafford, Anthony. *Honour and Vertue, Triumphing over the Grave.* London, 1640.

Stein, Arnold. "Donne and the Satiric Spirit." *ELH* 11 (1944): 266–82.

———— *The House of Death: Messages from the English Renaissance.* Baltimore: Johns Hopkins University Press, 1986.

Stewart, Stanley. *The Enclosed Garden: The Tradition and the Image in Seventeenth-Century Poetry.* Madison: University of Wisconsin Press, 1966.

———— *George Herbert.* Boston: G. K. Hall, 1986.

———— "Time and the Temple." In *Essential Articles for the Study of George Herbert.* Edited by John Roberts. Hamden, CT: Archon, 1979.

Stocker, T., trans. *An excellent treatise of the Immortalytie of the Soule* by John Calvin. London, 1581.

Stone, Lawrence. *The Crisis of the Aristocracy, 1558–1641.* Oxford: Clarendon Press, 1965.

———— *The Family, Sex and Marriage in England, 1500–1800.* Abridged Edition. New York: Harper, 1979.

Strier, Richard. *Love Known: Theology and Experience in George Herbert's Poetry.* Chicago: University of Chicago Press, 1983.

Stubbes, Phillip. *The Anatomie of Abuses.* London, 1583.

Summers, Joseph H. *George Herbert: His Religion and Art.* London: Chatto and Windus, 1954.

Sydenham, Humphrey. *Natures Overthrow and Deaths Triumph.* London, 1626.

Taylor, Mark. *The Soul in Paraphrase: George Herbert's Poetics.* The Hague: Mouton, 1974.

Taylor, Thomas. *The Pilgrim's Profession.* 1622. Reprinted in his *Three Treatises.* London, 1633.

Toliver, Harold E. *Pastoral Forms and Attitudes.* Berkeley: University of California Press, 1973.

Towers, William. *Atheismus Vapulans.* London, 1654.

Traherne, Thomas. *Centuries of Meditations.* Edited by Bertram Dobell. London: P. J. & A. E. Dobell, 1934.

Tuke, Thomas. *A Discourse of Death, Bodily, Ghostly, And Eternall.* London, 1613.

Van Tassel, Daniel E. "Clarence, Claudio, and Hamlet." *Renaissance and Reformation.* New Series, 7 (1983): 48–62.

Vendler, Helen. *The Poetry of George Herbert.* Cambridge: Harvard University Press, 1975.

Waldman, Roy D. *Humanistic Psychiatry: From Oppression to Choice.* New Brunswick, NJ: Rutgers University Press, 1971.

Walker, D. P. *The Ancient Theology: Studies in Christian Platonism from the Fifteenth to the Eighteenth Century.* London: Duckworth, 1972.

———— *The Decline of Hell: Seventeenth-Century Discussions of Eternal Torment.* London: Routledge, 1964.

Waller, G. F. "John Donne's Changing Attitudes to Time." *Studies in English Literature* 14: 79–89.

Walter, Christopher. "Death in Byzantine Iconography." *Eastern Churches Review* 8 (1976): 144.

Walton, Izaak. *The Lives of John Donne, Sir Henry Wotton, Richard Hooker, George Herbert and Robert Sanderson.* Edited by George Saintsbury. London: Oxford University Press, 1950.

Ward, Samuel. *The Life of Faith in Death.* London, 1622.

Watson, Robert N. "Tragedy." In *The Cambridge Companion to English Renaissance Drama.* Edited by A. R. Braunmuller and Michael Hattaway. Cambridge: Cambridge University Press, 1990: 301–51.

——— *Shakespeare and the Hazards of Ambition.* Cambridge: Harvard University Press, 1984.

Webster, John. *The Duchess of Malfi.* Bristol: Bristol Classical, 1989.

Welcome, Robert. *The state of the godly both in this life, and in the life to come.* London, 1606.

Welsh, Alexander. "The Task of Hamlet." *Yale Review* 69 (1979–80): 481–502.

White, Lynn. "Death and the Devil." In *The Darker Vision of the Renaissance: Beyond the Fields of Reason.* Edited by Robert S. Kinsman. Berkeley: University of California Press, 1974.

Wiggins, Peter De Sa. "'Aire and Angels': Incarnations of Love," *English Literary Renaissance* 12 (1982): 87–101.

Wilcox, Donald. *The Measure of Times Past: Pre-Newtonian Chronologies and the Rhetoric of Relative Time.* Chicago: University of Chicago Press, 1987.

Wills, Gary. *Under God: Religion and American Politics.* New York: Simon and Schuster, 1990.

Willson, Robert F., Jr. *Shakespeare's Reflexive Endings.* Lewiston, NY: Edwin Mellen Press, 1990.

Winnicott, D. W. "Fear of Breakdown." *International Review of Psycho-analysis* 1 (1974): 103–7.

——— *The Maturational Processes and the Facilitating Environment.* New York: International University Press, 1965.

——— *Psycho-Analytic Explorations.* Edited by C. Winnicott et al. Cambridge: Harvard University Press, 1989.

Winstanley, Gerrard. *The Law of Freedom in a Platform; or, True magistracy restored.* Edited by Robert Kenny. New York, Schocken Books, 1973.

Worship, William. *The Christians Mourning Garment.* 3d Edition. London, 1603.

Index

Literary works are listed under their authors. Material in the notes is indexed only where it is substantive.

Protestantism. *See* Reformation
psychoanalytic criticism, 13–15, 21, 50,
    54, 86, 160–61, 164, 256, 258,
    345n. 12. *See also* Adelman, Adler,
    Becker, cognitive psychology,
    Ferenczi, Freud, infant psychology,
    Lacan, Klein, Kohut, Kristeva, Rank,
    schizophrenia, Winnicott
psychopannychism. *See* soul-sleeping
purgatory, 5, 6, 61, 62, 75, 84
Ptolemy. *See* astronomy
Puritanism, 33, 42, 87–88, 105, 130,
    179, 221, 259, 305, 306, 308, 310,
    315, 316, 320, 328n. 11, 346n. 22,
    354n. 45

Quakers, 6, 150
Quarles, Francis, 375n. 122

Ralegh, Walter, 43, 163, 326n. 5,
    355n. 1
Rank, Otto, 13, 164, 170, 182, 185,
    350n. 15
Ranters, 6
Rauber, D. F., 375n. 128
recusancy, 32–33, 75, 178, 244, 316–20
Reformation, 5–7, 9, 28, 32–33, 42, 48,
    50, 60, 61, 75, 88, 108, 110, 126,
    130–31, 160, 163, 168, 180, 185,
    199, 202, 218, 244–46, 250, 290,
    294, 295, 297, 301, 302, 305, 314,
    316–20, 327–28n. 11, 340n. 172,
    352n. 29, 354n. 45, 385n. 48,
    386n. 55
resurrection, general, 37, 84, 118, 228,
    299, 304, 312, 326n. 5, 388–89n. 79;
    compared to procreation, 110–11,
    122, 328n. 19; Donne's view of, 157,
    158, 165, 174, 188, 189–206, 207,
    208, 212, 234, 236, 240, 247–48,
    249, 370n. 88, 376n. 140; doubts
    about, 27, 52, 61, 347n. 25;
    parodied, 78–79, 89, 119, 142
Resurrection of Christ, 69, 78–79, 120,
    142, 146, 168, 216, 242
revenge-tragedy, 32, 44, 56–58, 62, 67,
    75, 85, 88, 90, 119, 143, 147, 167,
    193, 219
rhetorical questions, 34–36, 85, 158, 165
Roberts, Donald Ramsey, 165
Ross, Alexander, 341n. 7

Rossiaud, Jacques, 349n. 6
Roston, Murray, 169

Sacks, Peter, 340n. 1
Sadducees, 27, 34
Saignet, Guillaume, 349n. 6
schizophrenia, 13–15, 159–61, 189
Schopenhauer, Arthur
selfhood. *See* individualism
Seneca, 24, 27, 75
sensory deprivation, 3, 37–39, 40, 42,
    141, 142, 158, 168–69, 173, 196,
    198, 203, 270, 299, 322, 337n. 124,
    337n. 127, 129, 132, 338n. 145,
    342n. 12, 14, 359n. 2, 373n. 105,
    374nn. 111, 112, 375–76n. 131
Shakespeare, William, 54, 68; religion of,
    10, 75, 340n. 172; *All's Well*, 31,
    101; *Antony and Cleopatra*, 367n. 69;
    As You Like It, 220; *Coriolanus*, 113,
    125–26, 127, 271; *Hamlet*, 11, 12,
    39, 43, 44, 45, 64, 74–102, 109,
    114, 116, 122–23, 127, 139, 142,
    149, 173, 188, 207, 217, 221, 231,
    250, 265, 375n. 130; *2 Henry IV*,
    105, 378n. 155; *Henry V*, 54;
    1 Henry VI, 348n. 37; *3 Henry VI*,
    138; *King Lear*, 39–40, 45, 63, 114,
    117, 119, 129, 153, 172, 229, 230,
    342n. 8; *Love's Labor's Lost*, 101, 116;
    Macbeth, 43, 44–45, 58, 89, 109,
    133–55, 171, 204, 229; *Measure for
    Measure*, 43, 44–45, 101–32, 134,
    135, 138, 148, 212, 216, 250–51,
    301, 344n. 4, 375n. 128, 385n. 45;
    Merchant of Venice, 172, 316; *Othello*,
    39, 55, 127, 230, 314, 366n. 57,
    372n. 100; *Richard II*, 16, 138–39;
    Richard III, 71; *Romeo and Juliet*, 8,
    220, 367n. 69; *Sonnets*, 116, 129,
    235, 249, 351n. 21; *Tempest*, 19,
    101, 109, 131, 144; *Titus
    Andronicus*, 83; *Twelfth Night*, 101;
    Winter's Tale, 92, 101, 113, 231
Shawcross, John, 375n. 129
Shuger, Debora K., 180, 294, 339n. 159,
    381–82n. 18
Sidney, Philip, 13, 366n. 63
Smith, Henrie, 28, 30
Smith, Julia J., 164–65
Socinianism, 27, 42